# Eagle Rules?
## Foreign Policy and American Primacy in the Twenty-First Century

Edited by Robert J. Lieber
Georgetown University

Published in cooperation with the Woodrow Wilson
International Center for Scholars

Prentice
Hall

Upper Saddle River, New Jersey 07458

**Library of Congress Cataloging-in-Publication Data**

Eagle rules? : foreign policy and American primacy in the twenty-first century / edited
by Robert J. Lieber.
    p. cm.
    Includes bibliographical references and index.
    ISBN 0-13-090987-4
    1. United States—Foreign relations.    I. Lieber, Robert J.

JZ1480 .E16 2002
327.73—dc21

2001019903


VP, Editorial director: Laura Pearson
Senior acquisitions editor: Heather Shelstad
Assistant editor: Brian Prybella
Editorial assistant: Jessica Drew
Executive managing editor: Ann Marie McCarthy
Production liaison: Fran Russello
Editorial/production supervision: Bruce Hobart (Pine Tree Composition)
Prepress and manufacturing buyer: Ben Smith
Cover art director: Jayne Conte
Cover designer: Jayne Kelly
Cover image illustrator: Ruth Weisberg, 2001
AVP, Director of marketing: Beth Gillett Mejia

This book was set in 10/12 Times Roman by Pine Tree Composition, Inc.,
and was printed and bound by Courier Companies, Inc.
The cover was printed by Phoenix Color Corp.

© 2002 by Robert J. Lieber
Pearson Education, Inc.
Upper Saddle River, New Jersey 07458

Printed in the United States of America

10 9 8 7 6 5 4 3 2 1

ISBN 0-13-090987-4

Pearson Education LTD., London
Pearson Education Australia PTY, Limited, Sydney
Pearson Education Singapore, Pte. Ltd
Pearson Education North Asia Ltd, Hong Kong
Pearson Education Canada, Ltd., Toronto
Pearson Educación de Mexico, S.A. de C.V.
Pearson Education—Japan, Tokyo
Pearson Education Malaysia, Pte. Ltd
Pearson Education, Upper Saddle River, New Jersey

# Contents

# Part III: Security Issues

# Part IV: Globalization and Its Discontents

# Preface

*Eagle Rules?* embodies a double meaning. The words suggest both that the United States enjoys a remarkable degree of international primacy and that it possesses a unique ability to shape the terms by which international relations take place. Rarely has any country held such a position. Yet the question mark in the title of this book should not be overlooked, for it reflects a recognition that the exercise of this power can be inconsistent and cumbersome, and that power itself does not always translate into effective influence. How, then, can we account for American primacy? Is it likely to persist? How do domestic politics impact on America's world role? And what are the longer-term implications for foreign policy?

*Eagle Rules?* is an entirely new work that follows in the footsteps of five previous *Eagle* books, for which I have been the editor or coeditor. This book assesses what we now know about world politics and American foreign policy after more than a decade of the post–Cold War era and the wider implications of this experience both for the U.S. role in the twenty-first century and for international relations more broadly. In contrast to predictions of decline that were common less than fifteen years ago, America's international primacy has become remarkably robust. Other powerful states have yet to challenge its preeminence, and international institutions have for the most part failed to take on more decisive roles in "global governance." Although we differ to some extent among ourselves over, for example, specific regional problems, defense policy, and the balance between unilateral and multilateral strategies, we share a common purpose in making sense of the changed international landscape, the indispensability of America's role, and the problems in its exercise. The authors who have joined together for this inquiry thus approach their subjects in light of three broad tendencies. Though there are countervailing tendencies, each of these can be stated as a proposition. *First*, America's remarkable international primacy is likely to continue for some time. *Second*, American leadership remains the necessary catalyst for action on the most pressing international problems. *Third*, the absence of foreign threats on the scale of World War Two or the Cold War complicates the task of policy-makers in gaining international agreement as well as domestic support for key policies and collective action. As a result, a disparity between power and influence often emerges. That is, despite the extraordinary primacy that America now enjoys, this power by no means translates automatically into the kind of influence or outcomes that policy-makers seek.

Previous *Eagle* books have been widely cited in both policy and scholarly debates about American foreign policy. The contributors to this volume are once again leading authorities in their fields, and half of them have policy-making experience as well. Our inquiry is thus positioned at the intersection between the world of affairs and the world of ideas. We seek to assess the most important lessons from recent experience, consider the effects of American predominance, weigh the influence of domestic politics on foreign policy, and then set out the implications for the role of the United States in the twenty-first century.

The introductory chapter develops the framework for *Eagle Rules,* advances the theme of primacy, and elaborates upon the three propositions noted before. I find that although there is evidence of international resentment at America's power and wealth, the greater long-term peril is less likely to be America's over extension or of its galvanizing an international coalition against itself than of the consequences were the United States to opt for withdrawal and abdication. Though improbable, the latter course would be more likely to prove harmful not only to the development of a more benign international political and economic environment but also to the national interests of the United States.

The authors in Part I focus upon the domestic setting for foreign policy. Ole R. Holsti (Duke University), in his chapter on public opinion and foreign policy, provides compelling evidence that the American public continues to support an internationalist and even multilateralist foreign policy, even though its attention has become focused primarily on domestic issues. Andrew Bennett (Georgetown University), assesses the balance of foreign policy powers between the presidency and the congress since the end of the Cold War. In doing so, he analyzes the impact that these tensions have had on foreign trade, on confirmation of foreign policy officials, and on the use of force and treaty ratification, and he concludes with specific recommendations for the Bush administration so that this struggle between these branches of government does not derail American foreign policy.

Part II of *Eagle Rules* turns to the most important regional problems. Ivo H. Daalder (Brookings) argues that a partnership of genuine equality between the United States and Europe is ultimately both desirable and feasible. He provides a detailed case for why, over the longer term, this will be preferable to the unbalanced relationship that has continued to exist, as well as to a Europe divorced from the United States. Gail W. Lapidus (Stanford), reviews three competing arguments in an emerging "Who Lost Russia" debate and provides a reexamination of assumptions underlying American policy. She finds that most of these critiques exaggerate the impact of American policy and finds this trend to be a sobering illustration of the limits on America's ability to translate its political primacy and power into influence over the character and behavior of this former superpower.

Robert A. Pastor (Emory University) finds that U.S. primacy vis-à-vis Latin America does not by itself provide an answer in translating goals of democracy and freer trade into policies and agreements. The continuing problem for Washington revolves around whether these goals should be pursued unilaterally or collectively. The Latin American countries remain similarly ambivalent on seeking greater autonomy or more interdependence.

Harvey Sicherman (Foreign Policy Research Institute) weighs America's Middle East role as the single preponderant power in the region. He finds that this domination is not, however, sufficient to achieve Washington's objectives. Although the U.S. role remains unique, sole superpowerdom there does not convey omnipotence, and the problems that the Bush administration inherits from the Clinton administration present compelling long-term problems.

Robert S. Litwak (Woodrow Wilson International Center) focuses on the evolution of U.S. strategy from dual to differentiated containment in regard to Iraq and Iran. He argues that the key issues in dealing with Iran are those of dialogue and limited engagement. By contrast, there is a continuing need for containing and isolating Iraq.

Edward Friedman (University of Wisconsin, Madison) addresses both the uncertainties and potential confrontation with a rising China. He finds it crucial that the United States deter war in the medium term, avoid strictly unilateral responses, and act in concert with regional allies in East Asia, while remaining vigilant. The objective is to provide time for the rise of pragmatic and less antagonistic forces within China.

Donald Rothchild (University of California, Davis) examines the distance that exists in American relations with Africa. He identifies the gap between the executive branch, on the one hand, and Congress and the American public with its weak support for Africa's needs and aspirations, and he concludes that drift and detachment continue to mark U.S. policy toward the region.

In Part III of *Eagle Rules*, the contributors deal with compelling security issues that cut across regional boundaries.

Cindy Williams (Massachusetts Institute of Technology) believes that America's armed forces, though preponderant globally, have yet to be adapted for the post–Cold War world. She suggests innovative strategies for adjusting both priorities and force structures that would trim conventional forces and their costs while maintaining a strong and capable military.

Bruce W. Jentleson (Duke University) examines the crucial and controversial question of when, where, and how the United States uses force abroad. In doing so, he weighs normative and policy dilemmas and concludes that a more robust ethnic conflict deterrence posture and more effective humanitarian intervention strategy may be the worst alternative of the United States—except for all the others.

Michael Nacht (University of California, Berkeley) argues that weapons proliferation now requires new thinking and difficult policy choices. His approach echoes the theme of this volume: namely, that American power has never been greater, yet without U.S. leadership, international efforts against proliferation cannot be effective. Moreover, the supremacy of American military power does not readily translate into U.S. influence in shaping international policies. He concludes with an ominous warning about the future use of chemical, biological, and nuclear weapons.

Part IV of this book focuses on globalization and its discontents. Benjamin J. Cohen (University of California, Santa Barbara) examines what the American government can do to contain the threatened backlash against globalization. His fundamental premise is that in order for the world economy's strengths to be preserved, it will require determined leadership from the United States, but that this approach requires that the legitimate concerns of globalization's critics be directly addressed.

Robert Paarlberg (Wellesley College) writes that the United States can take little comfort from knowing that it is an "essential" country. This status is anything but a guarantee of policy success. Domestic politics have often proved difficult, and being the essential nation abroad does not help to solve political problems at home. In reviewing the Convention on Biodiversity and a subsequent Biosafety Protocol, he demonstrates that U.S. disengagement can ultimately result in real damage to practical U.S. interests.

In the concluding chapter of this volume, Stanley Hoffmann (Harvard University) writes of the perpetual tug of war between the United States, as a hegemonic power with a desire to push its vision of world order through the intricate mechanisms of regional and international organizations, and the impulse to act unilaterally whenever these institutions are deemed to be hindrances. He observes that between a government sure of America's power but unsure about the best uses of it, and international organizations that are increasingly important as sources of legitimacy and stability but that are often mismanaged and devoid of adequate means, there can be no easy fit.

The contributors to this book deserve thanks not only for the quality of their chapters, but for their engagement in the entire endeavor, thus making *Eagle Rules?* far more than the sum of its parts. The authors have contributed valuable insights about each other's essays as well as to the overall conception of this volume, and their esprit and sense of craft have made the writing and editing a particular pleasure. Though this work is now the sixth in the *Eagle* lineage, I again wish to acknowledge the admirable role of my former colleagues, Kenneth Oye and Donald Rothchild, in co-editing and conceptualizing our original *Eagle* volume and three of its successors. Colleagues in the Government Department and School of Foreign Service at Georgetown University have provided a stimulating environment in which I presented initial ideas for this book, and at various stages of this project I have also benefitted from the insights and/or critiques of Fouad Ajami, Louise Branson, Dieter Dettke, Dusko Doder, George Downs, Robert Hathaway, Robert Hunter, Aharon Klieman, Keir Lieber, Charles Lipson, Sir Michael Quinlan, Yossi

Shain, Ruth Weisberg, and William Wohlforth, as well as the research assistance of Jeff Pietka, Mira Sucharov and William Josiger

Finally, it is an enormous pleasure to acknowledge the support of the Woodrow Wilson International Center for Scholars in Washington, D.C., and its Director, Lee Hamilton; Deputy Director Michael Van Deusen; Associate Director Samuel Wells; and Director of International Studies Robert Litwak. In addition to making it possible for me to spend a rewarding year there as a Public Policy Scholar, the Center hosted a meeting of *Eagle* authors, so that we could present and debate our original chapter drafts. This interchange has contributed in no small way to the overall coherence and quality of our joint undertaking.

Robert J. Lieber
Washington, D.C.

# About the Editor

Robert J. Lieber is Professor of Government and Foreign Service at Georgetown University, where he served as Chair of the Government Department from 1990 to 1996 and as Interim Chair of Psychology from 1997 to 1999. He is an expert on American foreign policy and on U.S. relations with Europe and the Middle East. Lieber was born and raised in Chicago, and received his undergraduate education at the University of Wisconsin and his Ph.D. at Harvard. He has held fellowships from the Guggenheim, Rockefeller, and Ford Foundations, the Council on Foreign Relations, and the Woodrow Wilson International Center for Scholars. He also taught at Harvard, Oxford, and the University of California, Davis, and has been Visiting Fellow at St. Antony's College Oxford, the Harvard Center for International Affairs, the Atlantic Institute in Paris, the Brookings Institution and the Woodrow Wilson Center in Washington, and Fudan University in Shanghai.

Dr. Lieber is author or editor of twelve other books on international relations and U.S. foreign policy. His authored works include *No Common Power: Understanding International Relations, Fourth Edition* (Prentice-Hall, 2001), *The Oil Decade* (1986), *Oil and the Middle East War: Europe in the Energy Crisis* (1976), *Contemporary Politics: Europe* (coauthor, 1976), *Theory and World Politics* (1972), and *British Politics and European Unity* (1970). In addition, he is editor and contributing author of *Eagle Adrift: American Foreign Policy at the End of the Century* (1997). And with Kenneth Oye and Donald Rothchild, he is coeditor and contributing author of four previous volumes on American foreign policy: *Eagle in a New World: American Grand Strategy in the Post–Cold War Era* (1992); *Eagle Resurgent? The Reagan Era in American Foreign Policy* (1987); *Eagle Defiant: U.S. Foreign Policy in the 1980s* (1983); and *Eagle Entangled: U.S. Foreign Policy in a Complex World* (1979).

Dr. Lieber also has been a foreign policy advisor in several presidential campaigns, a frequent contributor to both scholarly journals and newspapers, and a participant in foreign affairs analysis on television and radio. Among his other credits are "killer" tennis and a walk-on part in the Alfred Hitchcock film classic *North by Northwest*.

# 1

# Foreign Policy and American Primacy

## ROBERT J. LIEBER
Georgetown University


*"Eagle Rules?"* embodies a double meaning. The words suggest both that the United States enjoys a remarkable degree of international primacy and that it possesses a unique ability to shape the terms by which international relations take place. With the start of the twenty-first century, and more than a decade after the end of the Cold War, other powerful states have yet effectively to challenge America's preeminence, and international institutions have for the most part been unable to take on more decisive roles in "global governance." Rarely has any country held such a position. Yet the question mark in the title of this book reflects a recognition that the exercise of this power can be inconsistent and cumbersome, and that power itself does not always translate into effective influence. How, then, can we account for American primacy? Is it likely to persist? And what are the implications for foreign policy?

Answering these questions has become a notoriously treacherous task, not least because generalizations about America's world role have often been unreliable. As recently as the late-1980s, shortly before the end of the Cold War and the collapse of the Soviet Union, it had become commonplace to describe the United States as facing the prospect of decline that previous world powers had experienced over the ages, whether in ancient times as in the case of the Roman Empire, or in the modern era as with Great Britain.[1] In part, these conclusions were the product of the 1970s, including American withdrawal from Vietnam, the oil crisis, revolution

---

[1]E.g., Paul Kennedy, *The Rise and Fall of the Great Powers: Economic Change and Military Conflict from 1500 to 2000* (New York: Random, 1987.) Though for a counterpoint published shortly after Kennedy's book, and which was both less pessimistic and more accurate, see Joseph S. Nye, *Bound to Lead: The Changing Nature of American Power* (New York: Basic Books, 1990.)

in Iran, the Soviet invasion of Afghanistan, and stiffening international economic competition. Propositions about decline rested on several assumptions: that the American economy had become stagnant and was failing to sustain the kind of growth required both for its international commitments and to remain ahead of potential challengers, that military competition was becoming more costly and dangerous, and that the country was becoming overextended as commitments came to exceed resources. For some observers, Japan loomed as the potential leading power ("Japan as Number One"), and not only its economy but also its society were held up as a model against which the United States was deemed to be lacking, whereas for others the scope of the USSR's military strength and its ambitious interventions in the developing world suggested a daunting great power challenge.

Within less than a decade, following the opening of the Berlin Wall in November 1989, the end of the Cold War, the successful American-led battle to oust Saddam Hussein's forces from Kuwait, and the dissolution of the Soviet Union at the end of 1991, predictions of decline receded. Yet, they also gave way to depictions of a new world order in which international and global institutions, especially the United Nations, would become increasingly central. At the same time, international economic issues were said to be dominating the global agenda, with traditional high politics concerns of military strength and great power rivalry a thing of the past, and even the role of states themselves fading in importance as the forces of globalization increased in scope.[2]

Economic globalization has become more pervasive, yet massive flows of trade and investment, the revolution in information technology and a widening agenda of global issues have not displaced the role of states[3] nor the ultimate importance of power and security issues. To be sure, institutions such as the World Trade Organization and the European Union have become increasingly significant, and others, such as the International Monetary Fund and United Nations, continue to play substantive roles. By themselves, however, international and regional organizations have often been incapable of coping effectively with the most urgent international problems such as humanitarian intervention (as in Rwanda, Bosnia, and Kosovo), conflict resolution (the Sudan, Angola, Liberia, Kashmir, Colombia), proliferation of weapons of mass destruction (Iraq, Iran, North Korea, Pakistan, India), and poverty and disease in parts of the developing world.

At the same time, and with the evidence of more than a decade of post–Cold War experience, it has become evident that the United States occupies a unique position in world affairs. In analyzing both the indispensability of America's role and

---

[2]Jessica T. Mathews, "Power Shift," *Foreign Affairs*, Vol. 76, No. 1 (January/February 1997): 50–66, at 50. In a more recent article, she has argued that "Nation-states will not disappear, but new channels of interaction will so proliferate that governments' preeminence will wane." Mathews, "The Information Revolution," *Foreign Policy*, No. 119 (Summer 2000): 63–65, at 64.

[3]Indeed, an effective state role is a prerequisite for effective participation in the globalized world economy. See especially Robert Pastor (ed.), *A Century's Journey: How the Great Powers Shape the World* (New York: Basic Books, August 1999); also, Thomas Friedman, *The Lexus and the Olive Tree* (New York: Farrar, Straus and Giroux, 1999).

the problems in its exercise, three broad tendencies seem increasingly evident. Though there are countervailing tendencies, each of these can be stated as a proposition. *First,* America's remarkable international primacy is likely to continue. *Second*, American leadership remains the necessary catalyst for action on the most pressing international problems. *Third,* the absence of foreign threats on the scale of World War Two or the Cold War complicates the task of policy-makers in gaining international agreement as well as domestic support for coherent policies and collective action. In the following pages, I set out these three propositions and their implications; consider whether the assumptions on which they—and U.S. primacy— are based may be reversible; and then assess the consequences for America's international role in the twenty-first century.

## THREE PROPOSITIONS ABOUT AMERICA'S WORLD ROLE

**1. American primacy has been sustained and even enhanced, and it is likely to continue.**[4] The dimensions of this primacy include, *inter alia,* military strength, the capacity to project power at great distance, technology, economic dynamism, and culture (broadly defined to include lifestyle and entertainment). These dimensions appear to be reinforced by the revolution in information technology, which is having an economic and a social impact comparable in many respects to the industrial revolutions of the late eighteenth and late nineteenth centuries.

Some have suggested that technological change will erode U.S. primacy and sovereignty by globalizing commerce and communications in ways that no state can control. However, a strong argument can be made that because of the advantages accruing to the United States through its early lead in information technologies, as well as economies of scale and the dynamism of American cultural, economic, political, and social structures in accommodating technological change, both U.S. preponderance and U.S. sovereignty are likely to endure.

Primacy is a relational concept, in the sense that it measures the power of one actor as compared with others. Thus, an additional reason for anticipating that American preeminence will not be of brief duration is the absence of a plausible challenger in the near to medium term. Consider the following alternatives.

*Japan*, for a host of reasons, has acquired neither the economic nor the military strength that once seemed to lie in its future. Its economy has stagnated for more than a decade, and the structural, governmental, and social reforms that could rejuvenate its performance are not yet evident. As one of Japan's leading statesmen,

[4]For an earlier assessment of U.S. primacy, see Robert J. Lieber, "Eagle Revisited: A Reconsideration of the Reagan Era in U.S. Foreign Policy," *The Washington Quarterly*, Vol. 12, No. 3 (Summer 1989): 115–126; also, "Eagle Without a Cause: Making Foreign Policy Without the Soviet Threat," in Lieber, *Eagle Adrift*, (N.Y.: Longman, 1997), pp. 3–25. For a recent, compelling treatment, see William Wohlforth, "The Stability of a Unipolar World," *International Security*, Vol. 24, No. 1 (Summer 1999): 5–41.

Yasuhiro Nakosone, has recently observed, "Politics, economics and society—we have three bubbles that burst on us. Yet blueprints for dealing with the 21st century . . . are sadly lacking."[5] Moreover, as the military power of China has grown, Japan has tended to balance against its regional rival by moving closer to the United States rather than away from it. Only if the United States were to withdraw from Asia would Japan be likely to build up its military power and possibly acquire nuclear weapons, in order to counter a rising China.

*China's* economic development during the past quarter century has been extraordinary, but it faces vast problems in coping with unemployment, huge but decrepit state industries, the potential insolvency of its banking system, corruption, and political demands from an increasingly educated and attentive public as well as from a rising professional and entrepreneurial class that is less inclined to tolerate the dictates of the Communist Party. China has begun to modernize and strengthen its military capacity; its leaders have been stoking nationalist sentiment in an effort to sustain their own rule; and as Edward Friedman argues in his contribution to this volume, the country ultimately could emerge as a major challenger to the United States. Nonetheless, China is unlikely to attain more than regional power status for at least a generation.

*Russia* remains deeply troubled in its economy, society, and demography, and the course of its democratic transition remains unpredictable. A viable market economy, a rational system of taxation, and even the rule of law have yet to be achieved, and the country faces regional fragmentation and potential political instability as well. The public health system is in chaos, and male life expectancy has dropped to levels more typical of the developing world.[6] These features do not preclude the consolidation of power by a hardline nationalist figure bent on reconstituting the country's status as a great power, but although remaining the one country in the world able to threaten the United States at the strategic nuclear level, its military remains in disarray, and Russia lacks the other attributes of great power status.

*Germany* after unification remains linked to the United States, and since the end of the Cold War, it has become even more deeply imbedded in Western institutions, including the European Union and NATO. While the strongest and most powerful of the European economies, it nonetheless continues to face major tasks in absorbing the former German Democratic Republic (GDR), dealing with high unemployment, and adapting its economy and social welfare system to an era of globalization and the information technology revolution. For historic reasons, including the continuing American security presence and a now deeply implanted set of social attitudes, Germany has not sought to acquire the kind of military or nuclear power that its wealth and technology would make possible, and despite frequent disagree-

---

[5]In the magazine *Chuo Koron*, as quoted in Frank B. Gibney, "Reinventing Japan . . . Again," *Foreign Policy*, No. 119 (Summer 2000): 74–88, at 85.

[6]See, e.g., Murray Feshbach et al., *Ecocide in the USSR: Health and Nature Under Siege* (New York: Basic Books, 1993); and Zbigniew Brzezinski, "Living With Russia," *The National Interest*, No. 61, Fall 2000: 11.

ments with the United States, its leaders remain committed to the Atlantic relationship. Moreover, not only does the American connection provide a hedge against future uncertainties in Russia, Southeastern Europe, and the Mediterranean, but it also eases the historical anxieties of Germany's neighbors.

*The European Union*, despite its expansion and deepening, the establishment of the Euro, and aspirations for a military identity, remains devoid of real integration in foreign, and especially security, policy.[7] The statistics for its total population, economic size, and even armed forces are misleading in any great power calculation because the EU continues to consist of fifteen separate states. As a result, the cumulative effect of its 375 million people and combined GDP greater than that of the United States is far less than if the EU were a real federation or a United States of Europe. In addition, enlargement of the EU will bring in Eastern European countries, such as Poland, Hungary, and the Czech Republic, whose histories provide strong motivation for embracing the American connection. Moreover, the EU countries' heavy reliance on the United States for both leadership and air power in Kosovo demonstrated a continuing need for American capabilities, both in its power projection and its ability to overcome problems of collective action in European security.

If major challengers to the United States have not emerged, there remains a question about the extent to which America can successfully use its primacy to exert influence. This touches on a long-standing issue in gauging power, that is, the extent to which a country can effectively determine outcomes.[8] The question became especially relevant when, despite its enormous military and economic strength, the United States encountered frustrating reversals in Vietnam and later in Iran. A generation later, and in a unipolar rather than a bipolar world, America faces a complicated task in translating its power into political influence.

**2.  American leadership is the necessary catalyst for most significant international collaboration if it is to be timely and effective.** In a sense, America really has become the "indispensable nation." This reality is evident in a series of post–Cold War cases. In responding to Iraq's August 1990 invasion of Kuwait, the United States organized the international response, gained legitimation from the UN Security Council, and led a 44-country coalition in Operation Desert Storm to oust Saddam's forces. Despite the UN authorization and the wide political backing, this undertaking would have been inconceivable without U.S. direction, not only in

---

[7]I develop this argument in "No Transatlantic Divorce in the Offing," *Orbis,* Vol. 44, No. 4 (Fall 2000): 571–584.

[8]For an earlier discussion of the gap between power and influence and of the limits of U.S. power to determine outcomes, see Jeffery Hart, "Three Approaches to the Measurement of Power," *International Organization,* Vol. 30, No. 2 (Spring 1976): 289–306. For definitions of power as the capacity to shift the probability of outcomes, see, e.g., Robert J. Lieber, *Theory and World Politics* (Cambridge, MA: Winthrop Publishers, 1972), pp. 89–98. Gil Merom finds that societal forces in liberal democracies, especially since World War Two, constrain their ability to fight small wars. Such constraints stem not only from a growing sensitivity to their own casualties but also because democracies are less able to use brutal means of coercion against their opponents. See *Why Democracies Lose Small Wars: France in Algeria and Israel in Lebanon* (New York: Cambridge University Press, forthcoming.)

providing the political and diplomatic impetus, but in supplying 550,000 troops (more than two-thirds of those taking part in the allied operation), the most advanced weaponry and military technology, as well as overall alliance leadership.

Much the same can be said for the American-led intervention in Bosnia in 1995 and in Kosovo in 1999. More broadly, the United States plays a unique role in underwriting security and stability not only in Europe but also in the Middle East and East Asia. Moreover, American involvement is often a prerequisite both for strategic stability and effective military or humanitarian intervention, as well as for economic and other issues. Responses to financial crises in Mexico, East Asia, Russia, and Brazil, although mostly organized through the International Monetary Fund, required active American leadership and involvement, as do most major initiatives dealing with trade, developing country debt, the environment, and other pressing issues.

The indispensability of the American role is at least as evident in cases when the United States chooses not to lead as when it has done so. In the case of Bosnia, from 1991 to early 1995, the Bush and the Clinton administrations preferred to avoid active involvement and deferred to the Europeans and the UN. The resulting ethnic cleansing and warfare took some 200,000 lives before the Clinton administration finally led the NATO countries in military efforts and launched the process leading to the Dayton Agreement.

Rwanda provides an even more deadly example. There, in early 1994, the Clinton administration was willing neither to act by itself nor to support UN Security Council measures that might have limited the massacres of Tutsis and moderate Hutus by Hutu extremists, and that ultimately claimed between 500,000 and 800,000 lives.[9] The administration had been burned by its debacle in Somalia, where American peacekeepers had been drawn into a civil conflict and became enmeshed in a nation-building effort that led to casualties; and as a result, it would not agree to UN intervention that might commit the U.S. in some unforeseen way. The Clinton administration did urge dozens of countries to provide peacekeeping forces in Rwanda, but in the absence of America's willingness to act, others were reluctant to step in.

Haphazard or ill-conceived American intervention can also be a serious problem. In the case of Sierra Leone during 1999–2000, the Clinton administration appeared to have shaped a May 1999 peace agreement between an embattled civilian government and a murderous and destructive rebel group, the Revolutionary United Front (RUF), whose hallmarks included forced recruitment of child soldiers and mutilation and murder of women and children. Brokered by Jesse Jackson as a presidential emissary, with discreet involvement by American diplomats, the accord handed important parts of governmental authority and control of Sierra Leone's rich diamond mines to the RUF. The deal collapsed a year later, with an RUF rampage

---

[9]Philip Gourevitch, *We Wish to Inform You That Tomorrow We Will Be Killed With Our Families: Stories From Rwanda* (New York: Farrar, Straus & Giroux, 1998.) See also the candid report commissioned by UN Secretary-General Kofi Annan, summarized in the *New York Times*, December 17, 1999, p. 1.

and seizure of 500 UN peacekeepers as hostages. A semblance of order in the capital city, Freetown, was restored only with the arrival of peacekeeping forces from Britain, the former colonial power.[10]

Occasionally, regional powers are in a position to act. For example, in the case of East Timor, Australia led the UN peacekeeping mission ("Interfet"), with logistical and airlift support from the United States. Nonetheless, the alternative to American international leadership is often inaction. In most circumstances, should the United States be unwilling to lead, other major powers or international or regional institutions have neither the will nor the capacity to act effectively and on a timely basis. This situation does not mean that action without the United States is impossible, nor does it mean that the United States should serve as the world's policeman. Often, if the United States takes the lead, others are willing to do their share, as in the Gulf War in which they provided $70 billion and 240,000 troops, and in Bosnia and Kosovo, where more than 80 percent of the peacekeeping forces are non-American. Nonetheless, the larger, more urgent, more costly, and more difficult the effort required, the more American participation and leadership becomes the *sine qua non*. Cases such as Bosnia and Kosovo do illustrate the problem of timeliness. In both instances, effective intervention by the international community would not have been possible without American leadership. Yet, because of difficulties in achieving agreement, as well as constraints within the United States, the action came belatedly, and the outcome in both places may have been less successful than if intervention had come earlier.[11]

Recognition of these realities does not, however, give rise to easy cooperation at the international level. Among the permanent members of the UN Security Council, Russia and France have continually exhibited deep-seated resentment at their diminished status. For the French, this manifests itself mostly at the rhetorical and symbolic levels (as, for example, when the French President announces in Beijing that he is seeking a partnership with China to counter American hegemony).[12] As Stanley Hoffmann has noted elsewhere, France has had two obsessions throughout the past century. One obsession has been with the power of Germany, the other, with the fear of decline,[13] and it is the latter that continues to manifest itself in response to American preeminence. For the Russians, coping with precipitous decline has stimulated resentment of the United States, and Moscow has frequently proved obstructive in the UN Security Council, where it (as well as China) can rely on the

---

[10]A detailed account appears in Ryan Lizza, "The Betrayal of Sierra Leone: How the Clinton Administration and the President of Liberia Ensured Violence and Chaos in Sierra Leone," *The New Republic*, July 24, 2000.

[11]Bruce W. Jentleson and others have raised the issue of conflict prevention; see Jentleson and Jane E. Holl, (eds.), *Opportunities Missed, Opportunities Seized: Preventive Diplomacy in the Post-Cold War World* (New York: Carnegie Commission on Preventing Deadly Conflict, and Rowman & Littlefield, 1999). See also Jentleson's chapter in this volume.

[12]See, e.g., Ron Laurenzo, "In House, Bipartisan Suspicions About European Defense Plan," *Defense Week*, February 22, 2000.

[13]Stanley Hoffmann, "France: Two Obsessions for One Century," in Robert Pastor (ed.), *A Century's Journey: How the Great Powers Shape the World* (New York: Basic Books, 1999), p. 63.

implicit threat of its veto to exact a political price. Russia's dealings with Iraq and Iran reflect a similar logic. In the case of Iraq, Moscow has repeatedly delayed or opposed U.S.-supported measures to maintain sanctions against the regime of Saddam Hussein and to deal with Iraqi violations. With respect to Iran, the Russians have continued to provide material and technology for nuclear and missile programs that run counter to nonproliferation agreements and that are of concern to the United States.

More broadly, international cooperation problems remain a reality, as does the trade-off between consultation and efficiency. The wider the group of countries involved, the harder it is to gain agreement on a timely basis. Yet, if the United States acts precipitously or unilaterally, this action can stimulate resentment or even opposition that undercuts the very purposes of the proposed action. Within the UN Security Council, even when the permanent members are able to reach agreement, there remains resentment among lesser states at not being included in the decision making. This has given rise to proposals to expand the Security Council, but even if agreement can be reached on which additional regional powers to include, a significantly larger body is likely to find itself even less able to act than can the current one. Cooperation problems in other international institutions are evident as well, for example, in the acrimonious disagreements that pitted the United States and a group of African and Middle Eastern states against the EU countries in choosing a new head for the International Monetary Fund,[14] and even in the previous arguments among the Europeans themselves in choosing a leader for the European Central Bank.

Legitimacy versus effectiveness poses another collective action dilemma. Reflecting on the debacles in Rwanda and Bosnia, and on the aftermath of Kosovo, UN Secretary General Kofi Annan addressed the issue of humanitarian intervention by the world community, arguing that sovereignty cannot be taken as an absolute when egregious human rights violations are occurring. In his words, "massive and systematic violations of human rights—wherever they may take place—should not be allowed to stand."[15] However, two serious obstacles obstruct wider application of this principle.

One of these obstacles concerns the lack of agreement within the Security Council. During the Kosovo crisis, Russia and China initially opposed UN intervention, and the Security Council thus could not act. Faced with the option of doing nothing while massive ethnic cleansing took place, the United States, Britain, and the NATO countries ultimately undertook air strikes in March 1999, even though they did so, according to some interpretations, without valid authorization under international law. As Kofi Annan later observed, "The inability of the international community in the case of Kosovo to reconcile these two equally compelling interests—universal legitimacy and human rights—can only be viewed as a tragedy."[16]

---

[14]Ivo Daalder describes the IMF dispute in his chapter for this volume.

[15]Address to 54th Meeting of UN General Assembly, September 20, 1999. See "Secretary-General Presents His Annual Report to General Assembly," United Nations Press Release SG/SM/7136, GA/9596. Http://www.un.org/NewsPress/docs/1999.

[16]Ibid.

In short, in the absence of agreement among the five permanent members of the Security Council, humanitarian intervention under UN auspices either may not be available on a timely basis, or its conduct may lack international legitimacy.

A second obstacle also exists. Despite increasing international support for humanitarian intervention, developing countries tend to remain wary of it because of their concern about sovereignty, and they have expressed misgivings about the implications of such intervention. In response to Annan's advocacy of more robust humanitarian intervention, foreign leaders have stated their concerns quite explicitly. India and Algeria were especially vocal, and China's foreign minister criticized the notion of "human rights taking precedence over sovereignty," insisting that respect for national sovereignty and noninterference in another country's affairs are "the basic principles governing international relations," adding that any new form of gunboat diplomacy would "wreak havoc," and stridently condemning the NATO intervention in Kosovo for taking place without approval by the UN Security Council (where China could have exercised its veto).[17]

Whether the issue involves the protection of America's vital interests or those of its allies, on the one hand, or broader matters of humanitarian intervention, on the other, there are few effective alternatives to the U.S. role. At the same time, significant international obstacles to the exercise of that role exist as well, including coordination, decision-making, and burden-sharing issues in dealing with allies; status resentments of Russia, China, and France; and problems of organization, authority, and legitimacy that limit the capacity of international institutions. In sum, the American role is often a necessary but not always sufficient condition for collective action.

**3. Without an external threat on the scale of World War Two or the Cold War, policy-makers find it more difficult to gain domestic support for foreign policy.** The end of the Cold War brought to a close a period of a half century in which the United States faced profound threats to its national security and its most vital interests, and in which there was a high priority for the making and conduct of foreign policy. During World War Two and the Cold War, even when deep differences existed over policy and when partisanship was often evident in debates about American purpose and action, there remained a shared sense of overarching threat. In the early 1980s, for example, the Reagan administration used the politically effective metaphor of a "bear in the woods" to make the point. In the twenty-first century, however, and without a relatively unambiguous perception of threat, the domestic consensus necessary for an effective foreign policy may be much more elusive. There are several dimensions to this problem.

First, although opinion data do not show that the public or elites have become isolationist and although data provided by Ole Holsti confirm that since 1943, public opinion has remained internationalist by margins of more than two to one,[18] the

---

[17]Quoted in Barbara Crossette, "China and Others Reject Pleas That the U.N. Halt Civil Wars," *New York Times*, September 23, 1999, p. A13. These issues are assessed at greater length in Lieber, *No Common Power* (New York: Prentice-Hall, 4th ed., 2001), chapter 12.

[18]See Figure 1 ("Should the United States Play an Active Role in World Affairs, or Should It Stay Out?") in Ole Holsti's chapter for this volume.

overall level of public and media attention to foreign affairs has declined. This trend can be measured in several ways: in the reduced coverage of the subject in the press and on national network news telecasts, in the lessened salience of foreign policy issues during presidential and congressional election campaigns, in the proportion of members of congress with experience abroad or in the armed services, and even in a drop in foreign travel by members of congress.

Second, the nation devotes a substantially smaller share of its economy and of its budget to foreign affairs and national security than it has in more than half a century. Federal outlays for national defense have dropped from 9.2 percent of GDP in 1962 and 6.2 percent of GDP in 1986 to just 3.0 percent at the start of the twenty-first century.[19] Those who are concerned about maintaining American military primacy point out that this is the lowest proportion of GDP devoted to defense since the Japanese attack on U.S. forces at Pearl Harbor thrust America into World War Two in December 1941. (In absolute terms, however, U.S. defense outlays are equal to more than two-and-a-half times the combined spending of potential enemies, including Russia, China, North Korea, Iran, and Iraq.[20])

In addition, appropriations for the international affairs budget (State Department, foreign aid, United Nations, information programs, etc.) have been sharply reduced, both in real terms and as a share of the economy and the federal budget. Outlays for international affairs declined by 20 percent in real terms between 1986 and 2000. As a share of GDP, they fell from 1.0 percent in 1962 and 0.4 percent in 1986 to a low of 0.2 percent by 2000. And by the turn of the century, international affairs outlays accounted for just 1.2 percent of federal spending, compared with 5.1 percent in 1962 and 1.8 percent in 1986.[21] In the early months of the George W. Bush administration, Secretary of State Colin Powell did gain approval for a modest spending increase, but the overall resource problem remained.

These cuts have a number of consequences, not the least of which is that reduced resources provide policy-makers with fewer sources of leverage in dealing with foreign actors, as well as a reduced capacity to make the case for American policies. The ability to shape multilateral negotiations or to bring participants in a

---

[19]Similarly, whereas national defense outlays accounted for 49 percent of total federal spending in 1962 and 28 percent in 1986, by 2000 they had dropped to just 16 percent of the federal budget. *The Budget of the United States Government, Fiscal Year 2001, Historical Tables* (Washington, DC: U.S. Government Printing Office, 2000), Table 6.1: "Composition of Outlays: 1940–2005."

[20]Calculations by Cindy Williams, based on spending figures from *The Military Balance, 1999–2000* (London: International Institute for Strategic Studies). Comparisons are for total defense-related outlays. The IISS currency conversion to dollars uses purchasing power parity for China, North Korea, and Russia. It uses 1998 exchange rates for other countries. Williams also finds that in absolute terms, U.S. total defense outlays in 2000 came to about 90 percent of their Cold War average in real terms. Calculations based on *The Budget of the United States Government, Fiscal Year 2001, Historical Tables*, Table 6.1, 1996 constant-dollar figures, using 1954 to 1989 as the Cold War period.

[21]*The Budget of the United States Government, Fiscal Year 2001, Historical Tables*, Table 8.2: "Outlays by Budget Enforcement Act Category in Constant (FY 1996) Dollars, 1962–2005," Table 8.3: "Percentage Distribution of Outlays by Budget Enforcement Act Category, 1962–2005"; and Table 6.1: "Composition of Outlays: 1940–2005." See also Lawrence Korb versus Condoleezza Rice and Robert Zoellick, in *Foreign Affairs*, Vol. 79, No. 2 (March–April 2000): 149–152.

conflict to the negotiating table rests not only on the size and power of the United States but also on its ability to contribute toward desired outcomes. To illustrate, the Israeli-Egyptian peace process was greatly enhanced by the ability of the United States to provide aid to both parties. Over two decades, this has amounted to some $100 billion. But it remains to be seen whether resources of this magnitude might be available to facilitate a future Israeli-Palestinian or Israeli-Syrian peace agreement.

Third, and accompanying these spending cuts, a shift in governmental authority and influence, and away from traditional defense and foreign policy priorities, has become much more pronounced. World War Two and the Cold War stimulated the growth of expanded presidential and executive powers, and a high level of attention by congress, the media, and the public to foreign policy issues.[22] The relative deference of congress to the executive was most marked during the 1950s and early 1960s.[23] This trend resulted from the build-up of the national security state and a large defense and foreign policy establishment in response to the challenge posed by the Soviet Union.

The experiences of Vietnam and Watergate triggered a reaction and then initial steps toward a reassertion of congressional prerogatives. With the end of the Cold War and the collapse of the Soviet Union, this congressional role has increased. Especially toward the latter part of the Clinton presidency, as Andrew Bennett observes in his chapter for this volume, foreign policy becomes increasingly contested in the relations between the administration and congress, and domestic constraints were often a significant limiting factor in Clinton foreign policy.[24]

Moreover, the balance of governmental authority has been affected. In noncrisis situations, and absent the galvanizing effects of a significant external threat, the American political system becomes unwieldy, and it is often difficult to undertake coherent policy initiatives. The absence of a security imperative reduces the priority and urgency of foreign affairs for most Americans and makes it significantly more onerous for an administration to gain agreement with congress and even within the executive branch itself. The problem is especially evident on issues with a strong domestic component. This tendency, in turn, can make it harder for the United States to exert the kind of international leadership that is in its national interest and that at the same time is conducive to a more stable international order. A president can still prevail in foreign policy, but to do so requires that the president be actively involved, as in the case of permanent normal trade relations (PNTR) with China. When the president fails to play an active domestic leadership role, however, policy failures are

---

[22]For elaboration on this point, see Lieber, "Domestic Political Consequences of the Cold War's End: The International Impact on America's Foreign Policy Capacity," in Miroslav Nincic and Joseph Lepgold (eds.), *Being Useful: Policy Relevance and International Relations Theory* (Ann Arbor: University of Michigan Press, forthcoming, 2000), pp. 153–173.

[23]James M. Lindsay, *Congress and the Politics of U.S. Foreign Policy* (Baltimore: Johns Hopkins University Press, 1994).

[24]James M. McCormick, "Clinton and Foreign Policy: Some Legacies for a New Century," in Steven E. Schier (ed.), *The Postmodern Presidency: Bill Clinton's Legacy in U.S. Politics* (Pittsburgh: University of Pittsburgh Press, 2000).

more common, as in the case of the Clinton administration's inability to secure "fast track" authority from Congress for a new round of international trade negotiations, and in the refusal of the Senate to ratify the Comprehensive Test Ban Treaty.

In essence, the end of the Cold War and the disappearance of the Soviet threat ended a period of more than half a century in which the United States faced critical foreign threats (fascism, World War Two, the Cold War) to its most vital interests and values. The disappearance of these relatively unambiguous threats has led to a degree of erosion of presidential power and some reassertion of the Madisonian features of the American political system. Those features (separation of powers, checks and balances, a reassertion of congressional power, divided government, federalism) are a product of the late-eighteenth-century origins of the American political system and its distrust of centralized executive power. From Alexis de Tocqueville to Seymour Martin Lipset, astute observers of America have pointed to fundamental factors shaping the American character, including the lack of a feudal past, a "nonconformist" religious tradition, and the manner in which, during the nineteenth century, the legacy of the American Revolution evolved into a liberalism that emphasized individualism and antistatism. As Lipset has observed, Americans prefer a competitive, individualist society with equality of opportunity and effective but weak government.[25] Taken together, these elements have served American democracy well over the centuries. However, in the absence of an external threat, they tend to make it relatively more difficult for any administration to develop and carry out a foreign policy that responds to the major tasks facing the United States.

## REVERSIBLE ASSUMPTIONS?

To the extent that the three assumptions set out above prove to be robust, this analysis of the United States and its role in foreign policy is likely to be more durable than the kinds of predictions prevalent in the early 1980s and early 1990s. Nonetheless, it is important to consider the circumstances in which these assumptions could be overturned.

First, could American primacy prove more short-lived than anticipated? In the economic realm, this result would require a severe economic crisis, perhaps coupled with social unrest; otherwise, it is difficult to foresee another major actor overtaking the United States during the short to medium term. Nor is it easy to envision the United States being outpaced in high technology. In the military arena, despite problems of readiness and recruitment, the American preponderance also seems likely to endure, except perhaps in the unlikely event that the country found itself mired in a bloody and an inconclusive land war.

Second, is American leadership likely to remain the *sine qua non* for effective international efforts at intervention and collaboration? Absent the kind of

[25]Seymour Martin Lipset, "Still the Exceptional Nation?" *The Wilson Quarterly*, Vol. XXIV, (Winter 2000): 31–45, at 45.

dramatic advance in developing a common European foreign and defense policy, which seems beyond the reach of the EU for the immediate future, it is hard to see an alternative. Sustained collaboration or alliance among rising or disgruntled powers such as China, India, Russia, and Iran seems implausible, even if two or more of them may cooperate at times. Nor, despite their increasing importance, are the UN or other international institutions suddenly likely to acquire the capacity to act decisively on their own. As a result, major alternatives to American leadership remain unlikely. On the other hand, as Peter Rodman has observed, "policy ineptitude" could make the country's preponderance less impressive. Here, factors such as political will, credibility, the willingness to take risks and bear burdens, and a reputation for competence all affect America's ability to influence events.[26]

An example of this problem was evident in diplomatic negotiations over the controversial treaty to create an International Criminal Court, which the Clinton administration signed only on the last possible date, December 31, 2000, and which neither the Clinton nor the following Bush administration sought to submit for Senate ratification. International environmental policy issues have provided yet another case in point. As Robert Paarlberg demonstrates in his chapter for this volume, these issues included diplomatic deadlock over the Kyoto Climate Change Agreement and the Bush administration's March 2001 rejection of the Treaty, as well as the Clinton administration's failure to ratify the Convention on Biodiversity. The latter event later proved damaging to American national interests when an accompanying Biosafety Protocol was established in the year 2000 under circumstances that left American representatives at a serious disadvantage in shaping the agreement. This Protocol frustrated the efforts of American agricultural exporters and biotechnology companies, while effectively favoring European competitors. Moreover, it even harmed poor farmers in developing countries who need biotechnology to boost farm productivity while using fewer pesticides and herbicides.

Third, is the United States likely to continue to experience the absence of major threats? In this regard, the picture may be less clear. If Russia or China were eventually to shift toward a more avowedly hostile stance and to acquire the relevant economic and military capabilities, then a great power threat could reemerge. Alternatively, there remains the contested "rogue state" issue. Some observers within the United States and especially among America's European allies have come to regard this potential danger as exaggerated, particularly as this affects the question of national missile defense. Robert Litwak has argued that the term should be discarded in favor of addressing each of the relevant countries individually.[27] On the other hand, the bipartisan Rumsfeld Commission did conclude in 1998 that the

---

[26]Peter W. Rodman, "The World's Resentment: Anti-Americanism as a Global Phenomenon," *The National Interest*, Summer 2000, p. 40. Also see Rodman's elaboration of these points in *Uneasy Giant: The Challenges to American Predominance* (Washington, D.C.: The Nixon Center, 2000).

[27]Robert S. Litwak, *Rogue States and U.S. Foreign Policy* (Baltimore: Johns Hopkins University Press, 2000).

rogue state threat was "broader, more mature and evolving more rapidly than has been reported . . . by the intelligence community." Within a year of that report, North Korea tested an ICBM, and in September 1999, the National Intelligence Council concluded that during the next fifteen years, the United States "will most likely face intercontinental ballistic-missile threats from Russia, China and North Korea, probably from Iran and possibly from Iraq."[28]

Such threats, especially if accompanied by the threat or use of biological, chemical, or nuclear weapons, could quickly cause a reassertion of foreign policy as a priority within the American political system, and the administration of George W. Bush has indicated the need for increased attention to such dangers. Moreover, there is always the possibility that the United States could be dragged into a major regional war, for example, if North Korea were to attack South Korea; if China were to attack Taiwan; or if Iran, Iraq, or Syria were to engage in an escalating conflict against Israel or Saudi Arabia.

Conversely, there could emerge an entirely different type of problem. If the United States fails to remain involved at a sufficiently active level, the global system in which it exists could become much more unstable in ways that are harmful not just to the countries and populations immediately involved but to the interests of the United States as well. The perils here include not only military escalation and the use of weapons of mass destruction but also a dire economic or trade crisis on a scale comparable to that of the 1930s, that overwhelms the countries directly involved and escalates to affect an entire region and even the world economy more broadly.

# IMPLICATIONS FOR FOREIGN POLICY

Kenneth Waltz and others have argued that friends as well as foes will seek to balance against the current international predominance of the United States.[29] However, at least for America's traditional allies, this assessment remains doubtful. More than a decade after the end of the Cold War, and despite sometimes acrimonious disagreements over beef, bananas, genetically modified foods, aircraft exports, the Kyoto Treaty and national missile defense, the Europeans continue to retain their tie with the United States as a hedge against future security uncertainties in the areas to their east and south. Notwithstanding recent calls for a common defense identity, Europe's continuing inability to achieve an effective foreign and security policy leaves it little choice. In addition, though Waltz dismisses the characterization of the United States as a benign hegemon, the reality

---

[28]Quotes from *The Economist*, February 19, 2000, p. 30.

[29]Kenneth Waltz, "Globalization and Governance," in *PS: Political Science and Politics*, Vol. 32, No. 4 (December 1999). For a rejoinder and an elaboration of the points made here, see Robert Lieber, "U.S. Global Hegemony: A Reality Unlikely to Fade," in *PS: Political Science and Politics*, Vol. 33, No. 2 (June 2000): 141–142. Also see Waltz, "Structural Realism After the Cold War," *International Security*, Vol. 25, No. 1 (Summer 2000).: 5–41.

of this role does help to explain the absence of balancing. Stephen Walt has previously argued that countries balance not against power per se but against threat.[30] But whatever the friction in relationships with its allies—and rhetorical flourishes by the French—the United States is not seen as a threat. Ironically, if the United States were to disengage from its security commitments in Europe, Asia, and the Middle East, the major European countries and Japan would be more likely to rebuild their own military power and to return to great power balancing against regional rivals.[31]

Waltz also implies that America's predominance is likely to be ephemeral and that in anticipation of this, the United States should be less assertive in its international leadership. However, in the absence of an alternative great power challenger, it is not evident that America's current military status will be threatened for at least the short to medium term. In the economic realm, though predictions are notoriously difficult (bringing to mind the economists' own tongue-in-cheek caution about never combining a specific prediction with a date), there is, again, no obvious claimant. In addition, America's lead in culture, in technology, and in the all-important information revolution shows no signs of diminishing and may actually be widening. Indeed, the extent of overall U.S. primacy and the gap between it and others tends to discourage potential challengers.[32]

As for the issue of leadership, in the absence of more effective international institutions, common problems such as humanitarian intervention, international financial stability, economic openness, and the global environment are more likely to be addressed effectively if the United States remains actively engaged, especially as a catalyst and in leading coalitions, than if it pulls back. Although there is evidence of international resentment at America's power and wealth, not only in Russia and China but also in parts of Asia and the Middle East and, to some extent, among allies, the more important consideration concerns the judgment and skill with which leadership is exercised. In essence, the greater long-term peril is less likely to be one of America's overextension or of its galvanizing an international coalition against itself than of the consequences were the United States to opt for withdrawal and abdication. Though improbable, the latter course would be more likely to prove harmful not only to the development of a more benign international political and economic environment but for the national interests of the United States as well.

---

[30]Stephen Walt, *Origins of Alliances* (Ithaca, NY: Cornell University Press, 1987). It should be noted, however, that Walt has argued for America to begin the process of disengagement from Europe. See "The Ties That Fray," *The National Interest*, No. 54 (Winter 1998/99): 3–11; and a rejoinder, Lieber, *National Interest*, No. 55 (Spring 1999): 114.

[31]See Josef Joffe, "Germany: The Continuities from Frederick the Great to the Federal Republic," in Robert A. Pastor (ed.), *A Century's Journey: How the Great Powers Shape the World* (New York: Basic Books, 1999), pp. 91–138.

[32]William Wohlforth makes this point and provides a compelling argument for the robustness of American primacy. See "The Stability of a Unipolar World," *International Security*, Vol. 24, No. 1 (Summer 1999): 5–41.

# 2

# Public Opinion and Foreign Policy

## OLE R. HOLSTI
### Duke University

A diverse group of pundits, politicians, and policy-makers has depicted public opinion as the proverbial 800-pound gorilla on the back of officials who seek to protect vital national interests in the post–Cold War international arena. One line of criticism, often associated with "realists," depicts an emotional but poorly informed public that, energized by television images of unspeakable suffering at the hands of local tyrants, has pushed the United States into well-intentioned but hopeless and often dangerous undertakings—for example, "nation-building" in Somalia or "restoring democracy" in Haiti. George Kennan, the dean of American realists, chided the Bush administration for its intervention in Somalia on precisely these grounds (Kennan, 1993, A25).

According to other critics, the end of the Cold War has had a retrogressive impact on public opinion, which, it is asserted, has reverted to its traditional stance, ranging between skepticism and outright hostility, toward an active American role in the world. Arthur M. Schlesinger, Jr., the distinguished historian and one-time adviser to President Kennedy, charged that after fifty years of commitment to the "magnificent dream of collective security," the general public and opinion leaders are pushing the country "back to the womb" by espousing isolationism and unilateralism (Schlesinger, 1995). Similar diagnoses have emerged from other quarters. According to these analyses, the euphoria engendered by the

Ole R. Holsti, George V. Allen Professor of International Affairs at Duke University, served as President of the International Studies Association in 1979–80. His publications include *Public Opinion and American Foreign Policy.* He has received lifetime achievement awards from the American Political Science Association and from the International Society of Political Psychology, and the Teacher-Scholar Award from the International Studies Association.

fall of the Berlin Wall, followed by the dramatic victory in the Persian Gulf War, has evaporated. After a half century encompassing the period between the attack on Pearl Harbor that brought the United States into World War Two and the disintegration of the Soviet Union, the public is allegedly eager to lay down the mantle of international leadership and to turn its attention and energies to domestic and private endeavors. Schlesinger and others have described contemporary public opinion as

- Lacking in enthusiasm for peacekeeping missions unless the areas in question have a direct link to such vital national interests as oil from the Middle East.
- Unwilling to undertake or persist in any foreign undertakings that might entail casualties.
- Suffering from "compassion fatigue," resulting in ever-diminishing support for assistance programs other than emergency relief for natural disasters.
- Withdrawing its long-standing support for international institutions, including but not limited to the United Nations and NATO, partly because of a belief that the United States contributes more than its fair share to their activities, partly because they are thought to have outlived whatever utility they had during the Cold War.
- Unwilling to accept multilateral missions abroad; if such undertakings are unavoidable, it is better to act unilaterally. The public is described as especially adamant in opposing any mission that could place American forces under the command of non-American officers.

Consequently, fearful of a public backlash against international undertakings that entail significant costs or risks, policy-makers have been seriously hamstrung in efforts to play an effective leadership role appropriate to the world's only superpower.

Is Schlesinger's obituary for internationalism valid? Has it been replaced by the spirit of isolationism and unilateralism? For five decades after Pearl Harbor, there was a widespread belief among both leaders and the general public that vital national interests require the United States to play a leadership role in world affairs; disagreements tended to focus not on the desirability of assuming the burdens—and enjoying the benefits—of international leadership but, rather, on the goals, strategies, and tactics to implement that role. Thus, if Schlesinger is correct, withdrawal of domestic support for internationalism would represent a sea change, comparable to the collapse of isolationism during World War Two.

In order to assess these depictions of public opinion and their relevance for the third theme identified by Robert Lieber in his introduction to this volume, this chapter examines evidence from general surveys conducted by Gallup, the National Opinion Research Center (NORC), and others, as well as more specialized surveys conducted by the Chicago Council on Foreign Relations (CCFR), the Foreign Policy Leadership Project (FPLP), the Program on International Policy Attitudes (PIPA), and the Pew Research Center for the People and the Press. Several of these projects have also surveyed opinion leaders, providing an opportunity to compare their opinions with those of the general public.[1] After a brief overview of public assessments of America's proper role in the world, the analysis examines attitudes on more specific international issues.

## INTERNATIONALISM OR ISOLATIONISM

The dawn of the "age of polling" coincided with bitter debates during the second Roosevelt administration on the proper American policy toward expansionist dictatorships in Europe and Asia. Gallup and other surveys revealed strong isolationist sentiments that contributed to Roosevelt's caution in confronting a congress intent upon passing various forms of "neutrality legislation" to ensure that the United States would not again be drawn into a world war.

Roosevelt and others who pointed to American isolationism during the interwar period as one of the causes of World War Two took an interest in gauging public attitudes toward active international engagement after the war. Since 1943, Gallup, NORC, CCFR, and other polling organizations have asked the public whether the United States should "play an active role in world affairs, or should it stay out." The first survey found that 76 percent favored the internationalist option, whereas only 14 percent preferred withdrawal. Subsequent surveys encompassed the end of World War Two; the onset of the Cold War; two long costly wars in Asia and a short victorious one in the Persian Gulf region; crises in the Caribbean, Taiwan Straits, Berlin, and the Middle East; several periods of warming relations between Moscow and Washington, followed by the end of the Cold War and disintegration of the USSR; and post–Cold War deployment of American armed forces abroad, both unilaterally and in conjunction with NATO and the United Nations.

Despite this period of almost unprecedented international turbulence and some variations in the precise wording used in the surveys, responses to these questions about the appropriate international stance of the United States have remained relatively stable (see Figure 1). Notwithstanding fears of a post-1945 public reversion to isolationism expressed periodically by distinguished analysts—Hadley Cantril (1967); Gabriel Almond (1950); Walter Lippmann (1955); and George F. Kennan (1951)—no survey has shown a ratio of less than three-to-two in favor of internationalism. By the late 1980s, a period marked by dramatically improving relations between Washington and Moscow, that margin had increased to more than two-to-one.

Fears about an American return to isolationism have recently resurfaced, but the end of the Cold War did not bring about a dramatic reorientation of public attitudes about the country's general stance toward the world. In the wake of the Persian Gulf War, a *Washington Post* survey revealed that more than three-fourths of the public favored an active American role in the world. Two years later, when the Gulf War euphoria had worn off and it had become clear that the end of the Cold War had not ended troubling conflicts into which the United States might be drawn,

---

[1]Responses to survey items are highly sensitive to their wording. Thus, identically worded questions posed repeatedly over an extended period by the CCFR (1974–1998) and FPLP (1976–1996) studies are especially useful for analyzing continuity and change in public opinion.

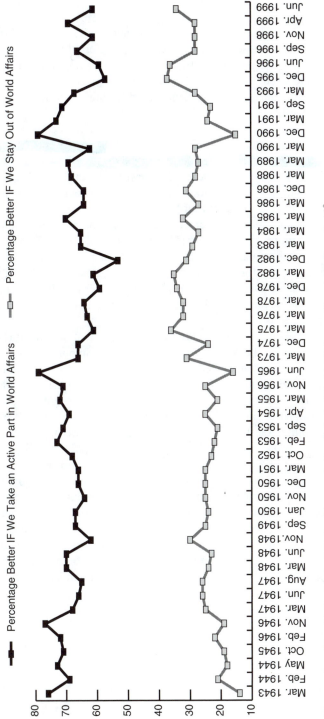

**Figure 1.** Should the United States Play an Active Role in World Affairs, or Should It Stay Out?*

Percentage Better IF We Take an Active Part in World Affairs

Percentage Better IF We Stay Out of World Affairs

support for an internationalist American role remained quite high, as 67 percent favored that position as against only 28 percent who preferred to "stay out of world affairs." Even controversies over the American role in peacekeeping operations had little impact on the strong majority (61 percent to 28 percent) favoring "an active part in world affairs" during the turbulent weeks leading up to the 1998 congressional elections (Rielly, 1999, 8).

Although comparable evidence about leaders' preferences is less extensive and it is heavily concentrated in the post-Vietnam era, most of it indicates that elites outstrip the general public in their support for active involvement in international affairs. The CCFR surveys, which posed the question directly to the general public and to a smaller sample of elites starting in 1978, have revealed strong and consistent differences. During the twenty-four-year period (1974–1998), the general public preferred an active American international role rather than withdrawal by margins ranging from 66 to 24 percent (1974) to a low of 53 to 35 percent (1982). In contrast, leaders taking part in the CCFR studies have been virtually unanimous in judging that it is better for the United States to "take an active part in world affairs"; that option never failed to gain the support of fewer than 96 percent of them. Indeed, it is hard to find any other significant question about foreign policy that has yielded such one-sided results.

These responses might seem to lay to rest charges that the public is leading a post–Cold War stampede back to isolationism, but it is important not to read too much into them. Because "an active part in world affairs" can encompass a wide array of international commitments and undertakings, the data should not be counted as decisive evidence of a broad foreign policy consensus or of sustained support for all manner of international activities, which can range from humanitarian assistance, multilateral trade agreements, and arms control negotiations to military interventions abroad. Nor do they reveal how the public might react when confronted with trade-offs or with the costs of active international involvement, especially when the price is paid in the coin of American casualties. Moreover, even those favoring an "active role" can differ on crucial questions of implementation. Unilateralists prefer that the United States go it alone, unbridled by the need to consult, coordinate, and cooperate with other countries. In contrast, multilateralists favor acting and sharing the burdens with others, even if doing so requires some compromises. Thus, we need to turn to appraisals of specific international threats, and then to preferences of both the general public and opinion leaders on more specific issues such as foreign policy goals, globalization, trade and protectionism, foreign aid, and deployment of troops abroad.

## THREATS TO VITAL U.S. INTERESTS

Although the disintegration of the USSR at the end of 1991 brought the Cold War to an end, most Americans continue to perceive a world that poses a plethora of threats to vital U.S. interests. The Chicago Council surveys asked both the general

**Table 1.** Threats to Vital U.S. Interests: Assessments by the General Public and Leaders in the Chicago Council on Foreign Relations Surveys, 1990–1998 (percentage of "critical" ratings)

| | 1990 | | 1994 | | 1998 | |
| --- | --- | --- | --- | --- | --- | --- |
| | *Public* | *Leaders* | *Public* | *Leaders* | *Public* | *Leaders* |
| International terrorism | — | — | 69 | 33 | 84 | 61 |
| Chemical and biological weapons | — | — | — | — | 76 | 64 |
| The possibility of unfriendly countries becoming nuclear powers | — | — | 72 | 61 | 75 | 67 |
| AIDS, Ebola virus, and other potential epidemics | — | — | — | — | 72 | 34 |
| The development of China as a world power | 40 | 16 | 57 | 46 | 57 | 56 |
| Large number of immigrants and refugees coming into the U.S. | — | — | 72 | 31 | 55 | 18 |
| Economic competition from Japan | 60 | 63 | 62 | 21 | 45 | 14 |
| Global warming | — | — | — | — | 43 | 27 |
| Economic competition from low-wage countries | — | — | 33 | 39 | 40 | 16 |
| Islamic fundamentalism | — | — | 32 | 16 | 38 | 31 |
| The military power of Russia* | 33 | 20 | — | — | 34 | 19 |
| Regional ethnic conflict | — | — | — | — | 34 | 26 |
| Economic competition from Europe | 30 | 41 | 27 | 11 | 24 | 16 |

*Soviet Union in 1990

*Source:* John E. Rielly, *American Public Opinion and U.S. Foreign Policy 1991*. Chicago: Chicago Council on Foreign Relations, 1991. Also, similar monographs edited by Rielly in 1995 and 1999.

public and leaders to assess such threats. The most recent survey presented respondents with a much broader menu than had been the case in 1990 and 1994 (see Table 1).

Compared with leaders, the public has been consistently more apprehensive about external threats; that was the case with all thirteen items presented in the 1998 survey. Solid majorities in both groups rated terrorism, chemical and biological weapons, nuclear proliferation, and China's ascendancy as "critical" threats. Increasing apprehension about China is especially evident among leaders, fewer than one in six of whom expressed such concerns as recently as 1990. (See also Chapter 9 concerning China.) In contrast to these areas of agreement, the public was far more inclined to assign a "critical" rating to threats arising from AIDS and other epidemics, immigration, and global warming. Similarly, although perceived economic threats stemming from competitors abroad have abated substantially among leaders, members of the general public are less persuaded on that score; gaps between the two groups are quite large with respect to competition from Japan (31 percent), low-wage countries (24 percent), and Europe (8 percent). Finally, even among the threats judged to be less critical—Islamic fundamentalism, Russian military power, and regional ethnic conflict—the gaps between leaders and the general public are quite wide.

## FOREIGN POLICY GOALS

Each of the CCFR surveys has included a cluster of items asking respondents to assess the importance of various foreign policy goals. The results, summarized in Table 2, reveal that in 1998, the general public gave very high priority to defending the country's economic interests. This finding does not, however, constitute a post–Cold War change of priorities. Protecting the jobs of American workers has ranked as the top goal in all but three of the surveys, and it just barely missed doing so in 1974 as well; in the most recent study (1998), it ranked second to stopping the flow of illegal drugs into the United States, as it had done four years earlier. Energy security has also consistently been accorded a "very important" rating by more than 60 percent of the public. Two surveys during the 1990s also saw an increase in the number of respondents who rated "protecting the interests of American business abroad" as a top priority.

In contrast to the urgency accorded to protecting economic interests—and despite occasional charges that the American public has been obsessed with Cold War concerns—such goals as "containing communism" and "matching Soviet military power" have ranked at the top of the foreign policy agenda in none of the CCFR surveys, not even in those conducted prior to the disintegration of the USSR. Indeed, the public has consistently been at least as concerned about arms control and preventing nuclear proliferation. A more general military/security goal, "maintaining superior military power world wide," ranked tenth among the sixteen goals rated by those taking part in the 1994 CCFR survey. Despite persistent Republican

**Table 2.**  The Importance of American Foreign Policy Goals: Assessments by the General Public in the Chicago Council on Foreign Relations Surveys, 1974–1998 (percentage of "very important" ratings)

"For each [foreign policy goal], please say whether you think that it should be a very important foreign policy goal of the United States, a somewhat important foreign policy goal, or not an important goal at all."

| | 1974 | 1978 | 1982 | 1986 | 1990 | 1994 | 1998 |
|---|---|---|---|---|---|---|---|
| *World order security issues* | | | | | | | |
| Preventing the spread of nuclear weapons | — | — | — | — | 59 | 82 | 82 |
| Combating international terrorism | — | — | — | — | — | — | 79 |
| Strengthening the United Nations | 46 | 47 | 48 | 46 | 44 | 51 | 45 |
| Protecting weaker nations against aggression | 28 | 34 | 34 | 32 | 57 | 24 | 32 |
| Worldwide arms control | 64 | 64 | 64 | 69 | 53 | — | — |
| *World order economic and environmental issues* | | | | | | | |
| Combating world hunger | 61 | 59 | 58 | 63 | — | 56 | 62 |
| Improving the global environment | — | — | — | — | 58 | 58 | 53 |
| Helping to improve the standard of living in less developed countries | 39 | 35 | 35 | 37 | 41 | 22 | 29 |
| *U.S. economic interest issues* | | | | | | | |
| Stopping the flow of illegal drugs into the U.S. | — | — | — | — | — | 89 | 81 |
| Protecting the jobs of American workers | 74 | 78 | 77 | 78 | 65 | 83 | 80 |
| Securing adequate supplies of energy | 75 | 78 | 70 | 69 | 61 | 62 | 64 |
| Controlling and reducing illegal immigration | — | — | — | — | — | 72 | 55 |
| Reducing the U.S. trade deficit with foreign countries | — | — | — | 62 | 56 | 59 | 50 |
| Protecting the interests of American business abroad | 39 | 45 | 44 | 43 | 63 | 52 | — |
| *U.S. values and institutions issues* | | | | | | | |
| Promoting and defending human rights in other countries | — | 39 | 43 | 42 | 58 | 34 | 39 |
| Promoting market economies abroad | — | — | — | — | — | — | 34 |
| Helping to bring a democratic form of government to other nations | 28 | 26 | 29 | 30 | 28 | 25 | 29 |
| *Cold War/Security issues* | | | | | | | |
| Maintaining superior military power worldwide | — | — | — | — | — | 50 | 59 |
| Defending our allies' security | 33 | 50 | 50 | 56 | 61 | 41 | 44 |
| Containing communism | 54 | 60 | 59 | 57 | 56 | — | — |
| Matching Soviet military power | — | — | 49 | 53 | 56 | — | — |

*Source:* John E. Rielly, editor, *American Public Opinion and U.S. Foreign Policy 1975.* Chicago: Chicago Council on Foreign Relations, 1975. Also, similar monographs edited by Rielly in 1979, 1983, 1987, 1991, 1995, and 1999.

charges that the Clinton Administration had permitted dangerous erosion of military capabilities, this goal moved up only three places four years later.

Another Cold War concern, "defending our allies' security," appeared among the top three goals only after the Cold War had ended. Its high ranking in 1990 reflected events surrounding the invasion of Kuwait by Iraq and, perhaps, the fact that the United States and the Soviet Union were on the same side rather than adversaries in that conflict, thereby eliminating the risk of a major confrontation between them. By 1994 and 1998, however, the goal of protecting allies received its lowest ratings since 1978. A more general and open-ended security concern, "protecting weaker nations against aggression," received a high rating only in 1990, when Iraqi forces still occupied Kuwait.

It is impossible to measure long-term trends on some issues because there are no Cold War baselines against which to compare responses to the two most recent CCFR surveys. Stopping the flow of illegal drugs ranked among the top three foreign policy goals in both studies, but concern with illegal immigration declined from its position as the fourth highest goal in 1994. Nevertheless, 55 percent of the public still rated stopping immigration as "very important" four years later; a similar number of respondents had judged that immigration poses a "critical" threat to the United States (Table 1).

Finally, the public has rarely expressed much enthusiasm for promoting American values and institutions abroad. Although the Bush and the Clinton administrations placed the expansion of democracy high on their foreign policy agendas, at least rhetorically, the public seems unpersuaded. With a single exception, efforts to promote human rights or democratic forms of government abroad have ranked among the least important foreign policy goals. The human rights goal was accorded an untypically high rating in 1990, probably reflecting widespread reports of human rights violations by Iraqi invasion forces in Kuwait.

The foreign policy goals questions were also posed to leaders by the CCFR, although there were variations in the specific items presented to the two groups. Many of the same questions also appeared in the six FPLP surveys. These two studies thus provide data on a wide range of foreign goals in thirteen surveys conducted during 1974 to 1998. Aside from a shared judgment that energy security and combating world hunger are very important, other goals accorded the highest rating by leaders revealed a somewhat broader set of priorities than those of the general public. Their top goals included such world order issues as arms control, "fostering international cooperation to solve common problems, such as food, inflation and energy," and the global environment. In contrast to the views of the general public, "defending our allies' security" was given a high priority by leaders in three earlier CCFR surveys (1978, 1982, 1986); after declining in importance in 1990, this goal rebounded in the judgment of leaders to rank as the third most important, behind only preventing nuclear proliferation and combating international terrorism, in both 1994 and 1998.

The CCFR surveys found that, compared with leaders, the general public generally rated "strengthening the United Nations" as more important. Despite

Schlesinger's lament that post–Cold war American isolationism often takes the form of unilateralism, ample evidence indicates that although the public is skeptical of some kinds of interventions abroad, it prefers that such operations be undertaken in conjunction with others (Kull and Destler, 1999, 77–80; Rielly, 1999, 5, 25). Thus, a stronger United Nations may be seen as a form of risk- and burden-sharing. Support for the UN among leaders increased sharply in the 1990 CCFR and 1992 FPLP surveys, reflecting Security Council activities in the wake of Iraq's invasion of Kuwait in August 1990, before dropping in 1994 and 1998, when only one-third of them rated strengthening that organization as a very important foreign policy goal. (See also Chapter 16 on international organizations.)

There are, finally, some broad similarities in the less highly rated goal priorities of the general public and leaders. Such Cold War goals as containment or "matching Soviet military power" dominated the rankings of neither group. Nor did either leaders or the general public exhibit a great deal of fervor for promoting U.S. values and institutions abroad. "Promoting and defending human rights in other countries" as a foreign policy goal only once received a "very important" rating from even half of either group. Even though many communist and other authoritarian regimes collapsed in the late 1980s and early 1990s, few respondents, whether among the opinion leaders or the general public, expressed much interest in "helping to bring a democratic form of government to other nations." Indeed, that goal consistently ranked among the lowest in the priorities of both groups. The difficulties of achieving success, especially in countries lacking any tradition of democratic institutions, probably contributed to these ratings. There is also compelling evidence that a "pretty prudent public" supports interventions abroad to cope with aggression but is much less enthusiastic about efforts to reform governments (Jentleson, 1992; Jentleson and Britton, 1998; see also Chapter 12 on Use of Force Dilemmas). Perhaps abuse of the term *democracy* by American officials when referring to friendly tyrants—for example, when President Reagan compared the Nicaraguan "contras" to the American founding fathers, or when other presidents toasted the Shah of Iran or Ferdinand Marcos of the Philippines in glowing terms as friends of democracy—has also made both opinion leaders and the general public somewhat cynical about America's ability to export democracy.

## GLOBALIZATION, TRADE, AND PROTECTIONISM

The final decade of the twentieth century witnessed important steps toward a globalized economy featuring lowered trade barriers, creation of such trade organizations as the North American Free Trade Association (NAFTA) and the World Trade Organization (WTO), vastly expanded international markets in currencies and securities, and movement of production facilities from high production cost to low-cost areas. The United States emerged from the Cold War as the predominant military power. America's position as the leading economic power is equally evident, in part because countries that earlier seemed poised to challenge the U.S. position—

notably Japan, Germany, and the Soviet Union—suffered serious economic set-backs during the 1990s, whereas the United States has enjoyed an extended period of high employment, low inflation, and rising stock markets—and a steadily widening gap between the most and the least affluent sectors of society.

When asked in the 1998 CCFR survey to assess globalization, "especially the increasing connection of our economy with others around the world," 54 percent of the public judged it to be "mostly good," whereas only 20 percent responded "mostly bad." (See also Chapter 14 on Globalization). Respondents with a favorable verdict on globalization also held internationalist views on other aspects of foreign affairs, including participation in U.N. peacekeeping forces, repaying its back dues to that organization, foreign aid, and membership in NATO (Rielly, 1999, 22). Support for globalization is even stronger among leaders who, by a margin of 87 to 12 percent, judged it favorably.

Broad support for globalization notwithstanding, there is also evidence of public disquiet. Recall that the public has not shared the view among leaders that threats arising from international economic competition have declined sharply, and it has consistently ranked "protecting the job of American workers" at or near the top of the foreign policy agenda. The six most recent CCFR surveys asked both the general public and leaders whether they "sympathize more with those who want to eliminate tariffs or those who think such tariffs are necessary" (see Table 3). The results reveal a wide gap between the two groups, with a steady majority of the general public supporting tariffs through the 1990 survey. Four years later, in the midst of energetic efforts by the White House and many congressional leaders in both political parties to gain approval of the treaty incorporating the Uruguay Round of GATT and creation of the WTO, support for tariffs fell below 50 percent; however, proponents of such trade barriers still outnumbered those who would eliminate them by 48 percent to 32 percent, and the margin in favor of tariffs was virtually identical in 1998. Contrary to the widespread belief that protectionism is largely confined to union members and blue-collar workers, retention of tariffs actually received slightly higher than average approval from the college-educated and those with incomes above $50,000 (Rielly, 1995, 29–30).

In contrast, although there had been some increase in support for protectionism among leaders during the dozen years ending in 1990, that position was espoused by no more than one-third of those taking part in any of the CCFR surveys. By 1994, only one leader in five wanted to retain tariffs, but that figure increased to 34 percent four years later. However, wording of the CCFR question may have affected the results, because respondents were not offered such options as "maintain tariffs at current levels" or "reduce but do not eliminate tariffs."

Opposition to protectionism also emerges from a question posed four times between 1984 and 1996 to larger samples of leaders in the FPLP surveys. Even though the question was phrased in a manner that explicitly incorporates the most widely used argument for protectionism—"erecting trade barriers against foreign goods to protect American industries and jobs"—fewer than one leader in four expressed either strong or moderate agreement with such a policy in any of the four

**Table 3.**   Opinions on Trade, Protectionism, and Trade Organizations:
The General Public and Leaders, 1978–1998

| | Date | Survey | Percentage Who Favor Tariffs | |
|---|---|---|---|---|
| | | | *General Public* | *Leaders* |
| "Generally, would you say you sympathize more with those who want to *eliminate* tariffs or those who think such tariffs are *necessary?*" | 1978 | CCFR | 57 | 23 |
| | 1982 | CCFR | 57 | 28 |
| | 1986 | CCFR | 53 | 29 |
| | 1990 | CCFR | 54 | 33 |
| | 1994 | CCFR | 48 | 20 |
| | 1998 | CCFR | 49 | 34 |
| | | | Percentage Who Agree Strongly or Somewhat | |
| Please indicate how strongly you agree or disagree with . . . | | | | |
| "Erecting trade barriers against foreign goods to protect American industries and jobs" | 1984 | FPLP | — | 24 |
| | 1988 | FPLP | — | 16 |
| | 1992 | FPLP | — | 21 |
| | 1996 | FPLP | — | 22 |
| "Opening negotiations for a free-trade zone with Mexico" | 1992 | FPLP | — | 84 |
| "Creating a free-trade zone with Canada" | 1992 | FPLP | — | 95 |
| | | | Percentage Who Favor NAFTA | |
| Favor or oppose the North American Free Trade Agreement | 1993 | T-M | 46 | 89 |
| | 1993 | Gallup* | 38 | — |
| | 1994 | CCFR** | 50 | 86 |
| | 1996 | FPLP | — | 80 |
| | 1997 | Pew | 47 | — |
| Signing the GATT trade agreement and joining the World Trade Organization (WTO) | 1996 | FPLP | — | 80 |

*Average of "favor" NAFTA responses in four surveys conducted in August, September, early November, and mid-November. The average "oppose" and "no opinion" responses in these surveys were 43 percent and 19 percent, respectively.
**Respondents who rated NAFTA as "mostly good" for the U.S. economy.
*Note:* CCFR = Chicago Council on Foreign Relations surveys; FPLP = Foreign Policy Leadership Project surveys; T-M = T*imes Mirror* survey, "America's Place in the World."

surveys, and by 1996, opponents of trade barriers outnumbered proponents by a margin of 77 to 22 percent.

Finally, assessments of NAFTA, a controversial pact bringing Mexico, Canada, and the United States into a free-trade zone that narrowly passed through the congress in December 1993, and the WTO provide further evidence of attitudes on trade. Leaders taking part in surveys conducted by three organizations across a three-year period expressed overwhelming support for NAFTA. The WTO received comparable support in the 1996 FPLP study. In contrast, the public was much more evenly divided on NAFTA, with opponents slightly outnumbering supporters until 1994, when the CCFR poll found that NAFTA was judged as "mostly a good thing for the U.S. economy." But the latter survey was undertaken just before the financial crisis triggered by devaluation of the Mexican peso. Thus, the wide gap between the general public and leaders on trade spans general attitudes toward tariffs as well as such specific undertakings as NAFTA.

## FOREIGN ECONOMIC ASSISTANCE

The general public favored such early post–World War Two foreign-aid undertakings as the Marshall Plan; a November 1948 Gallup survey found that the public supported it by an overwhelming 65 to 13 percent margin. During the past two decades, however, international economic and technical assistance programs have been far less popular, often ranking as the top candidates for budget cuts. Many members of congress point to public disfavor as a powerful reason for paring aid budgets. But there is also strong evidence that many survey questions do not fully plumb sentiments about foreign assistance; the public generally overestimates the amounts that the United States spends on foreign aid. Queries about the "appropriate" level for American foreign aid spending revealed that the median amount proposed is far higher than actual expenditures (Kull and Destler, 1999, 125).

The CCFR surveys again provide directly comparable evidence about opinions on foreign aid among leaders and the general public. When asked, "on the whole, do you favor or oppose our giving economic aid to other nations for purposes of economic development and technical assistance?" the general public has been quite evenly divided on the question, with support ranging between 45 percent (1990 and 1994) and 53 percent (1986). In 1998, supporters of foreign aid narrowly outnumbered opponents by 47 percent to 45 percent. A plurality of respondents favored keeping the same level of assistance to Africa, Russia, Poland, Israel, and Egypt, but it also preferred reducing rather than increasing aid to them. College graduates, liberals, travelers abroad, and those with higher incomes have been the strongest supports of foreign aid (Rielly, 1999).

A comparison of public attitudes with those of opinion leaders reveals a dramatic gap, as leaders have consistently expressed strong approval of economic assistance. In none of the CCFR surveys through 1990 did fewer than 90 percent of the leaders express support for foreign aid when asked the identical question. In 1998, the public-leader gap was more than 40 percent—88 percent approval by leaders compared with 47 percent by the general public. Among leaders, business executives and members of congress expressed the strongest opposition to foreign aid (Rielly, 1995, 31). A related question asked opinion leaders taking part in the FPLP surveys whether they would support economic aid to poorer countries "even if it means higher prices at home." Following an equal division between supporter and opponents on the issue in 1976, moderate majorities of opinion leaders in the subsequent five surveys favored such assistance.

## DEPLOYMENT OF U.S. TROOPS ABROAD

The deployment of troops abroad has often generated bitter debates. A public controversy was sparked during the War of 1812 when militia units refused to invade Canada on the grounds that fighting for "the common defense" could be done only on American soil. During the Mexican-American War, young Congressman Abraham Lincoln mercilessly hectored the Polk administration with "spot resolutions," demanding to know the exact location of the bloodshed that allegedly justified the American invasion of Mexico. Even before World War Two, there were also numerous deployments of U.S. troops abroad without declarations of war—for example, to quell the Philippine insurrection after the Spanish-American War and to pursue Pancho Villa in Mexico during the Wilson administration. The issue became even more visible with the expanded American international role after 1945. Symbolizing the controversies were contentious debates over the obligations entailed in the NATO Treaty; the constitutionality and wisdom of the War Powers Resolution of 1973, a congressional effort to restrict the president's ability to send troops into combat or into situations that might entail combat; and the extremely close vote in the congress on authorizing the use of force to expel Iraq from Kuwait.

Each of the CCFR surveys asked leaders and the general public to indicate whether they favored or opposed the use of the American troops in various hypothetical situations, including several that involved an invasion of such American friends or allies as Western Europe, South Korea, Israel, Saudi Arabia, Taiwan, and Poland. Similar questions were included in surveys conducted by the *Times-Mirror,* the Pew Center for the People & The Press, and the most recent FPLP study (see Table 4). The results have varied substantially by geographical area. The only case in which majorities among the general public consistently approved the use of American troops concerned a hypothetical Soviet or Russian invasion of Europe. Although Poland recently joined NATO, in 1998 less than one-third of the public expressed similar approval in support of the Warsaw government.[2]

In 1990, while American forces were being deployed in the Persian Gulf area after Iraq's invasion of Kuwait, a slight majority of the public approved using U.S. troops if Iraq invaded Saudi Arabia. This attitude remained little changed through 1997, long after the troops that had been engaged in Operations Desert Storm and Desert Shield had been withdrawn, but by 1998, that approval fell below 50 percent. Although Israel has never asked for aid in the form of American troops,

[2]According to Steven Kull, if the question about assistance to Poland includes the phrase "as part of a multilateral force," a clear majority favors U.S. action in support of Poland. *Private Communication*, October 2000.

**Table 4.**   Opinions on Use and Stationing of U.S. Troops Abroad: The General Public and Leaders, 1976–1998

"Would you favor or oppose the use of U.S. troops if . . . "

|  |  |  | Percentage Who Favor | |
|---|---|---|---|---|
|  | Date | Survey | General Public | Leaders |
| Soviet troops invaded Western Europe | 1978 | CCFR | 54 | 92 |
|  | 1982 | CCFR | 65 | 92 |
|  | 1986 | CCFR | 68 | 93 |
|  | 1990 | CCFR | 58 | 87 |
| Russia invaded Western Europe | 1994 | CCFR | 54 | 91 |
|  | 1996 | FPLP | — | 88 |
| Russia invaded Poland | 1998 | CCFR | 28 | 58 |
| North Korea invaded South Korea | 1978 | CCFR | 21 | 45 |
|  | 1982 | CCFR | 22 | 50 |
|  | 1986 | CCFR | 24 | 64 |
|  | 1990 | CCFR | 44 | 57 |
|  | 1993 | T-M | 31 | 69 |
|  | 1994 | CCFR | 39 | 82 |
|  | 1996 | FPLP | — | 63 |
|  | 1997 | Pew | 35 | 77 |
|  | 1998 | CCFR | 30 | 74 |
| Arab forces invaded Israel | 1978 | CCFR | 22 | 31 |
|  | 1982 | CCFR | 30 | 47 |
|  | 1986 | CCFR | 33 | 57 |
|  | 1990 | CCFR | 43 | 70 |
|  | 1993 | T-M | 45 | 67 |
|  | 1994 | CCFR | 42 | 72 |
|  | 1996 | FPLP | — | 61 |
|  | 1997 | Pew | 45 | 74 |
|  | 1998 | CCFR | 38 | 69 |
| Iran invaded Saudi Arabia | 1982 | CCFR | 25 | 54 |
|  | 1986 | CCFR | 26 | — |
| Iraq invaded Saudi Arabia | 1990 | CCFR | 52 | 89 |
|  | 1993 | T-M | 53 | 74 |
|  | 1994 | CCFR | 52 | 84 |
|  | 1996 | FPLP | — | 78 |
|  | 1997 | Pew | 54 | 86 |
|  | 1998 | CCFR | 46 | 79 |
| China invaded Taiwan | 1978 | CCFR | 20 | 18 |
|  | 1982 | CCFR | 18 | 15 |
|  | 1986 | CCFR | 19 | — |
|  | 1996 | FPLP | — | 40 |
|  | 1998 | CCFR | 27 | 51 |
| People in Cuba attempted to overthrow the Castro dictatorship | 1994 | CCFR | 44 | 18 |
|  | 1996 | FPLP | — | 15 |
|  | 1998 | CCFR | 38 | 18 |
| Serbian forces killed large numbers of ethnic Albanians in Kosovo | 1998 | CCFR | 36 | 54 |

(*continued*)

**Table 4.**  Opinions on Use and Stationing of U.S. Troops Abroad: The General Public and Leaders, 1976–1998 (*continued*)

| | Date | Survey | General Public | Leaders |
|---|---|---|---|---|
| "Please indicate how strongly you agree or disagree with " . . . " | | | Percentage Who Agree Strongly or Somewhat | |
| Stationing American troops abroad encourages other countries to let us do their fighting for them. | 1976 | FPLP | — | 60 |
| | 1980 | FPLP | — | 54 |
| | 1984 | FPLP | — | 63 |
| | 1988 | FPLP | — | 66 |
| | 1992 | FPLP | — | 65 |
| | 1996 | FPLP | — | 58 |

*Note:* CCFR = Chicago Council on Foreign Relations surveys; FPLP = Foreign Policy Leadership Project surveys; T-M = *Times-Mirror* survey; Pew = Pew Research Center for People & The Press.

Saddam Hussein's frequent and vocal threats, combined with Scud missile attacks against that country during the Persian Gulf crisis, also appear to have resulted in a sharp increase among those favoring assistance to Israel. That support persisted into 1997 but declined slightly a year later. (See also Chapter 7 on the Arab-Israeli conflict.)

Finally, the United States has had several security commitments in Asia, but the public generally has been less willing to use troops in that area. Although American armed forces have long been stationed in South Korea, at no time during the past quarter century has a majority expressed support for using U.S. troops to defend South Korea against another attack from North Korea. The use of American forces in response to an invasion of Taiwan by China gained even less approval. However, in the face of Chinese threats against Taiwan in recent years, public attitudes may be undergoing some changes. The 1998 CCFR study found that public support for using U.S. troops to aid Taiwan rose to 27 percent, and another survey in 1999 revealed that the general public was prepared to accept quite high American casualties if required to defend Taiwan (Feaver and Gelpi, 1999).

Compared with the general public, leaders have consistently been more willing to employ American armed forces in the hypothetical situations previously described, with one notable exception. Whereas fewer than one leader in five would support sending American troops to Cuba if people there attempted to overthrow the Castro regime, more than twice as many among the general public would approve such action. Differences between the two groups on the use of troops abroad are typically quite large, ranging from 9 percent to more than 40 percent. An FPLP survey item posed the issue of troops abroad in a somewhat more general manner. Instead of focusing on reactions to using U.S. armed forces in specific hypothetical conflicts, the survey item asked leaders to appraise the general critique that "Stationing American troops abroad encourages other countries to let us do their fighting for them." Consistent majorities of those taking part in these six leadership surveys, reaching a peak of 66 percent in 1998, expressed agreement. Thus, although leaders are generally predisposed to come to the aid of key friends and allies under siege, it appears that they are also wary of more general commitments, especially to countries that may be willing to turn the fighting over to the United States because they are unable or unwilling to make a full commitment to self-defense. These views are, at least in part, a lingering residue of the Vietnam War.

United Nations and NATO peacekeeping activities during the past decade have generated controversies centering on two points: under what circumstances should U.S. forces be included in peacekeeping forces, and under whose command should they be permitted to serve? Former Senator Robert Dole's proposed "Peace Powers Resolution" would have restricted the president's ability to deploy American forces in international peacekeeping efforts, and the Republican "Contract with America" would also have limited the circumstances under which U.S. forces might serve under foreign commanders. These controversies notwithstanding, a multitude of surveys during the 1990s revealed broad, if not unconditional, public support, ranging between 57 percent and 91 percent, for U.S. participation in peacekeeping activities, especially if the United States votes to take part (Kull and Destler, 1999, 98; Rielly, 1999, 25). It is, of course, inconceivable that the United States could be forced against its will to join any such undertaking. The PIPA, CCFR, and FPLP surveys also indicate that neither opinion leaders nor the general public would balk at having American peacekeeping forces serve under foreign commanders appointed by the UN or NATO (Kull and Destler, 1999, 109–111; Rielly, 1995, 8).

In that climate of controversy, proposals to send troops to Bosnia stimulated vigorous debates about the feasibility and desirability of American intervention, the proper role of public opinion in policy-making, and the meaning of survey data on the Bosnia issues (Kull, 1995–1996; Newport, 1995; Rosner, 1995–1996; Saad, 1995; Saad and Newport, 1995; Sobel, 1995, 2001). Proponents of intervention acknowledged the lack of public enthusiasm for deploying U.S. troops but asserted that it was imperative for the United States to assume a leadership role in maintaining a tolerable world order (Schlesinger, 1995). Emphasizing that American interests rather than values should govern foreign policy, opponents of intervention attacked President Clinton for "applying the standards of Mother Teresa to U.S. foreign policy" (Mandelbaum, 1996). Survey data revealed persisting and stable opinions on several points: a solid majority believed that solution of the Bosnia issue was a "very important" or "somewhat important" foreign policy goal; an equal proportion of the public asserted that Congress must approve any military involvement; and, although few Americans believed that unilateral intervention in Bosnia was either a moral obligation or a matter of the national interest, there was moderately strong support for deploying U.S. troops as part of a United Nations peacekeeping force. These opinions remained relatively stable after President Clinton's decisions to send American forces into Bosnia as part of a multinational effort to enforce the 1995 Dayton peace accord. Whether public support for the Bosnia or the later Kosovo peacekeeping undertakings would collapse were they to result in even moderate casualties—a proposition that, fortunately, had not yet been put to a test—remains uncertain. Survey evidence on this point depends on the manner in which the question is posed (Saad, 1995). More generally, the issue of casualties lies at the heart of controversies about post–Cold War undertakings.

Questions about the willingness of the public in democracies to accept combat deaths predate the end of the Cold War. Catastrophic losses during World War One are often linked to French and British unwillingness to confront Hitler's Germany through most of the 1930s, and some historians have faulted American military strategy during World War Two as excessively driven by casualty-aversion (Kennedy, 1999). A leading critic of U.S. policy in Vietnam, George Ball, warned in 1965 that the conflict could not be won because the public would not accept large casualties: "Producing a chart that correlated public opinion with American casualties in Korea, Ball predicted that the American public would not support a long and protracted war" (Clifford, 1991, 412). A study of the Korean and Vietnam Wars indeed revealed a strong inverse relationship between public support and combat deaths (Mueller, 1973). More broadly, Luttwak (1994) has argued that postindustrial societies, including the United States, are afflicted by casualty-aversion arising from the smallness of families, preventing them from effectively playing the role of great powers. The U.S. response to the 1993 ambush of eighteen Rangers in Mogadishu is often cited as proof that the U.S. public cannot accept the almost inevitable costs of military operations abroad. Indeed, Somali faction leader Mohamed Farah Aideed reportedly stated that his strategy for driving U.S. forces out of Somalia derived from a belief that Americans would not tolerate casualties.

These episodes seemingly provide a rich base of evidence supporting those who assert, whether with satisfaction or dismay, that a long history of public casualty-aversion has a powerful constraining grip on policy decisions. Most commentaries on the 1999 NATO air war against Yugoslavia asserted that public opinion had created a virtually insurmountable barrier against the introduction of ground troops to protect Kosovars from ethnic cleansing by the Milosevic regime in Belgrade because NATO troop deployments would surely entail costs—casualties—that Western publics were unwilling to tolerate. The strategy of flying beyond the reach of Serbian air defense systems, even if the less precise high altitude bombing campaign resulted in collateral deaths among civilians, was also linked to the public's alleged unwillingness to countenance the loss of pilots.

Yet some compelling evidence indicates that this depiction of public casualty-aversion is overdrawn. A study covering an extended period of American history reveals that the public will accept high casualties, as during World War Two, to achieve goals that are deemed to be important (Larson, 1996). Even controversial post–Cold War interventions have evoked public responses that cast some doubt on the conventional wisdom. The initial reaction to the Mogadishu ambush was to stay the course rather than withdraw. When confronted with a hypothetical scenario involving one hundred U.S. fatalities in Bosnia, a plurality of respondents (37 percent) wanted to "bring in reinforcement," another 26 percent preferred to "strike back," and 10 percent wanted to "stay the course" (Kull and Destler, 1999; see also

Logan, 1996). Finally, a 1999 survey of the general public, civilian leaders, and military elites revealed that the latter two groups were actually less willing than the general public to accept casualties in a series of six hypothetical scenarios, including "To prevent widespread 'ethnic cleansing' in Kosovo." According to Feaver and Gelpi (1999), "The public can distinguish between suffering defeat and suffering casualties." Although this evidence does not suggest that the public is indifferent to combat fatalities, especially in undertakings for which the administration is unable or unwilling to demonstrate that American intervention is desirable (because of a compelling link to vital national interests), and feasible (there is a reasonable prospect for success), it does raise questions about the alleged "iron law" of the post–Cold War policy: public insistence on casualty-free operations.

The data just summarized reveal a consistent pattern of substantially higher support by leaders for various aspects of internationalism, not only in the form of stronger approval for an "active part in world affairs" but also in greater support for liberal trade policies, economic assistance, and deployment of American troops abroad. The evidence indicates also that both leaders and the general public make distinctions between various types of international policies and undertakings, and these distinctions appear to reflect events and developments in the international arena.

## PARTISANSHIP: PERSISTENCE OR ABATEMENT?

During the middle 1980s, three perceptive analysts of American foreign policy, one of whom later served as National Security Adviser to President Clinton, asserted: "For two decades, the making of American foreign policy has been growing far more political—or more precisely, far more partisan and ideological" (Destler, Gelb, and Lake, 1984, 13). Although their observation was not specifically focused on public opinion, it brings up an interesting question: Has the end of the Cold War served to bridge partisan differences on foreign policy? Even if partisanship and ideology were the primary sources of cleavages during the early years of the Reagan administration, is that diagnosis still valid for the post–Cold War era? After all, Ronald Reagan, a highly partisan and ideological president, almost completely reversed his attitudes about the USSR during his presidency, as did the general public.

"Politics stops at the water's edge" has been a favorite political slogan, especially among administration officials debating critics of their foreign policies. Whether it is also a broadly accurate depiction of the foreign policy process is more questionable. Partisan differences colored debates on issues as diverse as responses to the wars arising from the French Revolution, the tariff issue at various times during the nineteenth and early twentieth centuries, and the question of American participation in the League of Nations. On the other hand, efforts by the Roosevelt administration to develop a bipartisan coalition in support of American membership in the United Nations were successful, and the agreement between Cordell Hull and John Foster Dulles assured that U.N. participation would not become a partisan issue in the 1944 election. During the early post–World War Two years, bipartisan cooperation between the White House and congress on many European issues made possible such initiatives as aid to Greece and Turkey (the Truman Doctrine), the Marshall Plan, and the North Atlantic Treaty Organization. Agreement among prominent leaders of the two major parties no doubt contributed to the fact that, among the general public, Democrats and Republicans differed little with respect to these and other major foreign policy undertakings. A 1946 Gallup survey revealed that 72 percent of respondents in both political parties favored an "active" international role for the United States, and the 1947 program of aid to Greece and Turkey also received identical levels of approval from Democrats and Republicans. Issues relating to the Far East tended to be more contentious and placed greater strains on bipartisan cooperation, especially after the Truman-MacArthur confrontation during the first year of the Korean War. But even on most Asian issues, survey data revealed limited partisan differences. The absence of strong partisan cleavages extended into the early years of the Vietnam War, as majorities within both parties expressed strong support for the policies of the Johnson administration.

For two decades spanning the Truman, Eisenhower, Kennedy, and early Johnson administrations, then, whatever differences divided the American public on foreign policy issues rarely fell along partisan lines. Barry Hughes (1978, 128) concluded that the "evidence points overwhelmingly to insignificant party differences in the general population" on most foreign policy issues. Indeed, during the pre-Vietnam period, the distribution of attitudes among supporters of the two major parties was sufficiently similar that the self-identified "independents" usually stood on one side or another of the Democrats and Republicans, rather than in between them.

The period since the Vietnam War has witnessed the emergence of striking partisan differences on a broad range of foreign and defense policy issues, and efforts by several administrations to create a foreign policy consensus fell short of enduring success. The Nixon-Kissinger campaign to create a post-Vietnam foreign policy consensus grounded in détente with the Soviet Union ultimately failed. Attempts by the Carter administration to achieve the same goal through an emphasis on human rights, and by the first Reagan administration to create a consensus around a more assertive stance toward the Soviet Union, were equally unavailing in the longer run. Surveys during the 1980s revealed sharp and persistent partisan differences on foreign and defense issues as varied as the intervention in Lebanon (25 percent), the appropriate size of the defense budget (31 percent), the trade embargo on Nicaragua (39 percent), aid to the contras in Nicaragua (15 percent), and the Strategic Defense Initiative (29 percent). Gallup polls since the end of the Cold War have shown little change in this respect, as most foreign policy issues continue to generate wide partisan gaps; these include the decision to lift economic sanctions against South Africa (21 percent), join NAFTA (12 percent), cut in defense spending (14 percent), deploy U.S. peacekeeping forces in Bosnia prior to (20 percent) and after (27 percent) the Dayton agreement, introduce U.S. ground troops into Kosovo (19 percent), and approve of the peace agreement ending the war against Yugoslavia (16 percent). The bifurcation among partisan lines has been sufficiently great that, unlike during the pre-Vietnam period, responses of political independents typically fell between those of Democrats and Republicans.[3]

The end of the Cold War has been marked by diminution of partisan differences on questions such as the perception of a diminished threat from Moscow, as well as on a few nonstrategic issues. Despite these areas of converging opinions, there is little evidence of a broad post–Cold War foreign policy consensus. Even the Persian Gulf War—a short, successful conflict against an adversary that almost everyone could "love to hate," that resulted in relatively light American casualties—revealed partisan differences before, during, and after the war (Holsti, 1996, 136–138). The fruits of the Persian Gulf conflict have not included a bipartisan consensus on such questions as when, how, against what adversaries, and for what purposes, force should be used.

The congressional votes in January 1991 on using military force against Iraq and the Republican "Contract with America," prepared for the 1994 congressional elections, are striking illustrations of the extent to which bipartisanship among leaders in foreign and defense policy is a relic of a bygone era.[4] (See also Chapter 3 on congress.) Surveys of opinion leaders also provide revealing evidence about the persistence or abatement of partisan differences. The Chicago Council "goals" question summarized in Table 2 was also included in the six FPLP surveys of opinion leaders that spanned a two-decade period through 1996. Table 5 provides the overall "very important ratings" for each goal, as well as the size of the partisan gap.

At first glance it appears that the data provide support for the thesis of declining importance attached to some important aspects of foreign affairs, especially when the 1992 and 1996 responses are compared. However, a longer-term perspective indicates that in several cases, the 1992 results may represent an anomaly. For example, the importance attached to strengthening the United Nations reached an exceptionally high level in that year, no doubt because the Gulf War was conducted under the formal authorization of several Security Council resolutions. Support for strengthening the UN declined quite sharply in 1996, but to a level that was quite typical of the four surveys conducted prior to the end of the Cold War. A similar pattern emerged on several other questions, including arms control and protecting weaker nations from aggression. The latter goal received higher than normal support in 1992 as a result of the successful liberation of Kuwait a year earlier.

The evidence in Table 5 also suggests a declining sense of urgency among leaders about other foreign policy goals, especially those clustered under the heading of "world order economic and environmental issues." The end of the Cold War has coincided with an especially sharp decline in the importance attributed to combating hunger, improving the standard of living in less developed countries, the global environment, and international economic cooperation. Moreover, the 1996

---

[3]These figures are drawn from various Gallup polls conducted between 1984 and 1999. With a few exceptions—aid to the Contras, NAFTA, and the peace agreement in Yugoslavia—majorities of Democrats supported one position, whereas majorities of Republicans favored the opposite position.

[4]The national security policy features of the Contract with America are discussed in *1994 CQ Almanac,* 46D–49D.

**Table 5.** The Importance of American Foreign Policy Goals Rated by Leaders in the Foreign Policy Leadership Surveys, 1976–1996: Assessments of Importance and Partisan Gaps

Here is a list of possible foreign policy goals that the United States might have. Please indicate how much importance should be attached to each goal.
Percentage of "Very important" ratings, entire leadership sample
(Partisan gaps: Percentage of Republican VI ratings minus Percentage of Democrat VI ratings)

| | 1976 | 1980 | 1984 | 1988 | 1992 | 1996 |
|---|---|---|---|---|---|---|
| *U.S. economic interest issues* | | | | | | |
| Stopping the flow of illegal drugs into the U.S. | — | — | — | — | — | 58 [18] |
| Protecting the jobs of American workers | 30 [3] | 30 [2] | — | 36 [4] | 32 [5] | 29 [-2] |
| Securing adequate supplies of energy | 72 [8] | 78 [8] | 85 [3] | 76 [2] | 68 [7] | 53 [15] |
| Controlling and reducing illegal immigration | — | — | — | — | — | 33 [26] |
| Reducing the U.S. trade deficit with foreign countries | — | — | — | 64 [0] | 49 [11] | — |
| Protecting the interests of American business abroad | 14 [11] | 20 [17] | 23 [19] | — | 24 [13] | 20 [14] |
| Keeping up the value of the dollar | — | 64 [8] | — | — | — | — |
| *U.S. values and institutions issues* | | | | | | |
| Promoting and defending human rights in other countries | — | 28 [-12] | 34 [-19] | 39 [-12] | 39 [-10] | 23 [-22] |
| Promoting market economies abroad | 6 [5] | 10 [12] | — | — | — | — |
| Helping to bring a democratic form of government to other nations | 7 [0] | 10 [-1] | 18 [1] | 25 [8] | 23 [0] | 15 [-8] |

| | 1 | 2 | 3 | 4 | 5 | 6 |
|---|---|---|---|---|---|---|
| *Cold War/Security issues* | | | | | | |
| Maintaining superior military power worldwide | — | — | — | — | — | 40 [34] |
| Defending our allies' security | 37 [8] | 44 [11] | 48 [13] | 51 [8] | 34 [13] | 36 [4] |
| Containing communism | 39 [34] | 42 [17] | 39 [30] | 36 [34] | 12 [12] | 15 [15] |
| Matching Soviet/Russian military power | — | — | 41 [23] | 33 [18] | 18 [14] | — |
| Promoting and defending our own security | 85 [9] | 90 [5] | 84 [14] | — | — | — |
| Strengthening countries who are friendly toward us | 23 [10] | 38 [8] | — | — | — | — |
| *World order security issues* | | | | | | |
| Preventing the spread of nuclear weapons | 25 [-11] | 32 [-13] | 27 [-13] | 27 [-8] | 87 [-1] | 83 [-5] |
| Strengthening the United Nations | 18 [0] | 24 [3] | — | — | 44 [-12] | 26 [-27] |
| Protecting weaker nations against aggression | 66 [-9] | 55 [-21] | 71 [-21] | — | 28 [3] | 18 [-8] |
| Worldwide arms control | 70 [-6] | 76 [-7] | — | 68 [-15] | 73 [-11] | 60 [-16] |
| Keeping peace in the world | 44 [-7] | 57 [3] | 44 [10] | — | — | — |
| Maintaining a balance of power among nations | — | — | — | — | — | — |
| *World order economic and environmental issues* | | | | | | |
| Combating world hunger | 50 [-13] | 51 [-18] | 56 [-16] | 57 [-16] | 55 [-14] | 36 [-28] |
| Improving the global environment | — | 48 [-19] | 54 [-20] | 69 [-19] | 66 [-19] | 46 [-37] |
| Helping to improve the standard of living in less developed countries | 38 [-12] | 43 [-11] | 59 [-17] | 51 [-19] | 43 [-17] | 28 [-19] |
| Worldwide population control | — | 47 [-9] | 55 [-8] | 55 [-12] | — | — |
| Fostering international cooperation to solve common problems such as food, inflation, and energy | 70 [-15] | 73 [-11] | 66 [-19] | 70 [-20] | 71 [-15] | 56 [-30] |
| Helping solve world inflation | 49 [-3] | — | 45 [-7] | 47 [-7] | — | — |
| Averting financial crises arising from Third World debts | — | — | — | — | — | — |

*Note*: Gaps exceeding 6 percent are significant at the .001 level.

responses to these goals are not merely a drop from abnormally high levels in 1992; they are part of a longer-term trend of "compassion fatigue."

Among goals encompassing U.S. economic interests, energy security continues to be regarded as very important by most respondents, but two others—protecting jobs and the interests of American business abroad—have been regarded as being of great urgency by only small numbers of respondents. Drug trafficking and illegal immigration did not appear in surveys prior to 1996, precluding any assessment of trends. Security goals that formed the core of American foreign policy during the Cold War did not evoke a great deal of urgency in 1996, but, with one exception, these results do not represent a sharp shift from earlier surveys. It is no surprise that, "containing communism" has ranked as the least important goal since the end of the Cold War. Nor have opinion leaders taking part in the FPLP surveys ascribed much importance to promoting such American values as human rights and democracy abroad. During the Cold War, efforts to support human rights and democracy other than at the rhetorical level risked alienating some allies—"friendly tyrants"—as well as escalating tensions with adversaries. Yet there is scant evidence that the end of the Cold War has been widely perceived as providing a low-risk environment for elevating human rights and democracy toward the top of America's foreign policy agenda.

The partisan gaps in Table 5 offer only modest evidence that the end of the Cold War has resurrected a foreign policy consensus among opinion leaders. Bipartisan agreement on the importance of preventing the spread of nuclear weapons is diluted somewhat by the substantial gap—16 percent—on the importance of "worldwide arms control." There are also rather muted differences between Republicans and Democrats on several of the less highly rated goals: defending allies, protecting weaker nations, protecting the jobs of American workers, and promoting democracy abroad.

In contrast, substantial partisan gaps emerged on many other issues. World order security issues gave rise to significant differences, with Democrats attributing considerably greater importance to these goals. A similar pattern, though with even greater partisan differences averaging almost 30 percent in 1996, characterizes responses to the world order economic and environmental issues. On the other hand, compared with Democratic leaders, Republicans typically attributed greater importance to American economic interests and security goals. Just as Republicans gave a higher priority to matching Soviet military power during the Cold War, in 1996 they were far more enthusiastic than Democrats about "maintaining superior military power worldwide." Finally, as noted earlier, promoting American values abroad has gained a great deal of support in none of the FPLP surveys, but as overall support for human rights has declined, reaching a new low in 1996, the gap between Republicans and Democrats actually widened.

Although partisan cleavages are evident on a great many issues, trade stands out as a notable exception. As demonstrated by protests at the 1999 World Trade Organization meeting in Seattle and by groups criticizing permanent normal trade status for China in 2000, trade issues have given rise to a bipartisan coalition of opponents—liberal Democrats who favor imposing stricter environmental and workplace regulation on America's trade partners have joined forces with conservative Republicans who demand that China be held accountable for its persecution of dissidents, Christians, and Tibetans, as well as its threats against Taiwan. The 2000 election is a good case in point. George W. Bush and Al Gore largely agreed on the virtues of trade liberalization, whereas staunch conservative Patrick Buchanan and ultraliberal Ralph Nader were of a mind in attacking free trade and globalization. The most recent FPLP survey of opinion leaders also found scant evidence of partisan cleavages. A majority of Democratic and Republican opinion leaders opposed erecting trade barriers; rated protecting jobs as a foreign policy goal of limited importance; and approved major steps toward trade liberalization, including NAFTA, GATT, and the WTO agreements. The grant of "most favored nation" trade status to China divided leaders almost evenly, but the cleavages cut across rather than along party lines. Finally, bipartisan agreement on trade liberalization was supported by the widespread belief—shared by Republicans, Democrats, and independents—that economic competition, whether from Europe or Japan, does not constitute a serious threat to the United States. It should be noted that the absence of partisan divisions on trade issues in 1996 represents continuity rather than change in the views of opinion leaders; earlier surveys also found that trade is among the few issues on which cleavages do not follow closely along party lines.

In summary, although the Destler-Gelb-Lake thesis about the growing partisan gaps on foreign affairs was articulated almost two decades ago, well before the disintegration of the Soviet Union, the data in Table 5 suggest that it continues to provide an insightful perspective on many foreign policy issues.

## CONCLUSION

The evidence indicates greater persistence than change in public attitudes toward foreign affairs since the end of the Cold War: Opinion leaders continue to be more internationalist than the general public on virtually all issues; the general public has shown little indication of a mindless retreat toward isolationism, and even less support for unilateralism in preference to action in cooperation with NATO or the United Nations; and most issues other than trade continue to give rise to partisan cleavages among both leaders and the general public. It is also hard to find persuasive evidence supporting either of the charges summarized at the beginning of this chapter. The public has shown neither much support for crusades to make the world over in the American image, nor for the agenda of those who would withdraw from most international organizations, eliminate foreign aid, withdraw American forces stationed abroad, and otherwise seek to cut the ties that have enmeshed the United States in the global system. One exception is immigration, which has been a major concern of the general public, and to a much lesser extent, of leaders.

Thus, although the data reveal declining support for some international endeavors and disquiet about the effects of economic globalization—a concern that predates the end of the Cold War—evidence of continuity in public opinion dominates signs of sharp change. Even with respect to the most controversial post–Cold War undertakings, military interventions abroad that may pose the risk of casualties, the public is selectively supportive rather than reflexively opposed. Support is most likely for interventions in such areas of traditional concern as Europe, when the purpose is to prevent or punish aggression rather than to promote American values or institutions, and when there is a reasonable prospect of success. Whether or not one agrees with these criteria, they bear considerably greater resemblance to traditional "realism" than to "isolationism." Indeed, they are less stringent than the so-called "Weinberger doctrine," a set of six preconditions for military interventions abroad proposed by the Secretary of Defense in 1984 and opposed by his cabinet colleague, George Shultz (*New York Times*, November 29, 1984; Shultz, 1993).

Domestic politics certainly have complicated and sometimes damaged Washington's ability to conduct foreign affairs and to demonstrate essential leadership in attempting to cope with the "buzzing, blooming confusion" of the post–Cold War international arena. This is not an unfamiliar pattern. Periods of crisis and conflict, when there is an accretion of power by the executive branch, are often followed by congressional efforts to restore its prerogatives and, more generally, by the intrusion of domestic political concerns into the conduct of foreign affairs. The years following the Civil War, World War One, and the Vietnam War illustrate this pattern, and the post–Cold War era appears to be no exception.

But where is the primary locus of the problem? Is it in a public that recently focused more attention to domestic issues than to international ones? Or in intensified partisanship in congress? Or in the willingness of some congressional leaders to engage in such damaging frivolities as withholding payments of legitimate dues to the United Nations or holding up ambassadorial and other appointments for reasons that are unrelated to the qualifications of the nominees? Or in the print and electronic media that have drastically reduced coverage of foreign affairs in recent years (Emery, 1989)? Or in parochial single-issue interest groups that find it easier to thrive in the absence of an overriding international threat? Many of these actors state that they are, in fact, accurately reflecting public preferences. Media leaders assert that, in focusing on domestic issues and entertainment, they are merely giving the public what it wants.[5] Many senators and representatives argue that, in their opposition to peacekeeping operations, foreign aid, or the United Nations and other international institutions, they are reflecting the views of an increasingly isolationist public that has lost patience with recalcitrant allies, inefficient international organizations, and Third World kleptocracies that look to America to bail them out of problems of their own making.

There is compelling evidence that foreign and defense policy have lost a good deal of their salience for the general public. Domestic issues seem to impinge more

[5]According to Allen Alter, foreign editor for *The CBS Evening News,* "We assumed during the Cold War that there was a secure market for international news. Now it's difficult to figure out who our clients are and what foreign stories they want, if any." Quoted in Hadar, 1994.

directly on the daily lives of most citizens, and the declining coverage of international affairs by the print and the electronic media reinforces and exacerbates the public tendency to focus on problems at home in the absence of wars, crises, and other dramatic events abroad. In virtually every post–Gulf War survey asking, "What are the major problems facing the country today?" the list is dominated by such issues as drugs, crime, education, poverty, immorality, the economy, Social Security, and similar concerns. The paucity of international issues near the top of these lists is not, however, necessarily an unambiguous or even especially valid indicator of isolationism. Indeed, public inattention to international problems during the closing years of the twentieth century derives at least in part from a general sense of satisfaction with the administration's conduct of foreign affairs. Not only did former President Clinton's overall approval ratings remain at a remarkably high level, but respondents to the 1998 CCFR survey, conducted during House impeachment proceedings against Clinton, gave him the highest percentage of "very successful" ratings for his foreign policies of any post–World War president. When "somewhat successful" responses are included, Clinton ranked second only to his immediate predecessor, George Bush (Rielly, 1999, 36–37; Lipset and Bowman, 2000; and Walt, 2000).

The 1998 CCFR survey revealed that, when asked to identify "the two or three biggest foreign policy problems facing the United States today," only 7 percent cited "getting involved in the affairs of other countries" or "excessive foreign aid," two points often emphasized by such proponents of isolationism as columnist, author, and perennial presidential candidate Patrick Buchanan; these expressions of disquiet were down sharply from the 1994 survey, when the comparable figures were 19 percent and 16 percent, respectively. In contrast, three times that many could not think of a single major international problem although, as shown in Table 1, many perceive a world posing multiple threats to vital U.S. interests. These responses seem to point to a public that is rather poorly informed about the world (as usual), inattentive, generally satisfied with the conduct of foreign affairs—but not necessarily leading a charge of "back to the womb." The public mood is perhaps most accurately described as "apathetic internationalism" (Lindsay, 2000).

American military and economic preponderance, the absence of an immediate and a credible threat to national security—"rogue states" such as Iran, Iraq, Afghanistan, North Korea, Sudan, and Cuba clearly cannot fill the boots worn by Nazi Germany, Imperial Japan, or the Soviet Union during the past six decades. Although a long period of economic growth and low unemployment has mitigated some domestic problems, the persistence of drug-related crime, urban decay, crumbling infrastructure, pockets of poverty, and educational deficiencies has, not unreasonably, focused public attention toward the domestic arena. That focus does not, however, necessarily constitute isolationism, or even indifference to everything that lies beyond America's shores. The evidence summarized before, as well as from other studies, indicates that leaders who claim to be surfing on powerful waves of isolationism and unilateralism among the American people are in fact "misreading the public" (Kull and Destler, 1999). Even the alleged casualty-aversion of the public may be an instance of elite misperception; indeed, leaders who underestimate the public's willingness to engage in peacekeeping and other undertakings that pose the risk of casualties may be seeking to legitimate their own reluctance to take part in such activities.[6]

The latter point raises an interesting question. Why, when leaders are consistently more internationalist than the general public, do they seem more reluctant to tolerate casualties? In the case of the Clinton administration, legitimating a reluctance to take actions by pointing to the alleged casualty-aversion of the public may have served to avoid confrontations with the military and congress. The military have generally expressed limited enthusiasm for the kinds of interventions that have characterized the past decade (the "Powell Doctrine"), and even less for former President Clinton. As Clinton learned from almost his first day in the Oval Office, when he attempted to implement his campaign pledge on gays in the military, there is little to be gained by arousing the wrath of senior military officers. Similarly, the Marine barracks bombing in Lebanon and the death of eighteen Rangers in Mogadishu revealed that, even though the initial public reactions may be to reinforce military units and/or seek to punish the culprits, congressional reactions to casualties are at least as likely to be directed against administration policies.

Where does that outcome leave a new administration that seeks to have the United States play an effective leadership role in world affairs? Although one should exercise great caution in attempting to draw historical parallels, it may be instructive to recall the half decade immediately following the end of World War Two. Some pioneering opinion analysts of that period feared that a fickle and poorly informed public, weary of the sacrifices imposed by four years of war, would resist any efforts to continue shouldering the burdens of world leadership. In a memo to President Roosevelt, just prior to his departure for the Yalta Conference in 1945, Hadley Cantril warned that "it is unrealistic to assume that Americans are international-minded . . . The present internationalism rests on rather unstable foundations: it is recent, it is not rooted in broad or long range conceptions of self-interest, it has little intellectual basis" (Cantril, 1967, 76). Gabriel Almond (1950) examined responses to questions about the "most important problems facing the country." Noting that wartime concerns with international issues had been replaced with domestic ones, he concluded that a volatile and inattentive public provided very shaky foundations upon which to sustain global leadership. Yet, during the 1945 to 1950 period, the public came to support a number of unprecedented undertakings that have been described as "the revolution in American foreign policy," suggesting that there is a significant difference between an inattentive and an isolationist public. Effective presidential leadership, often bridging partisan lines, was able to generate public support for innovative undertakings, some of which ran

---

[6]According to a study of post–Cold War public opinion in the Netherlands, "In this connection one is struck by the facile way in which the body bag argument is used by politicians and the media. There is a tendency to parrot one another and to anticipate on situations, which may indeed be caused by such talk. Frequent statements of politicians and observers about the expected body bag effects on public support may turn out to be self-fulfilling prophecies" (Everts, 2000).

counter to such deeply embedded axioms as George Washington's admonition "to steer clear of permanent alliances with any portion of the foreign world."

We should be wary of pushing too far the parallels between the 1945 to 1950 period and the present. The most striking difference is that Stalin's Soviet Union posed a threat to vital interests far greater than any that exists today. Nevertheless, the example suggests that because even a poorly informed and an inattentive public is not necessarily isolationist, it can be persuaded to support an American leadership role in a broad range of international undertakings if it can be shown that they are both desirable and feasible. A critical element is a presidential leadership that is capable of making an effective case for its foreign policy agenda; of avoiding the mendacity that all too often has marred efforts to use the "bully pulpit" to gain public support, with the consequence that public trust in government has declined precipitously during the past several decades; and of reading the public accurately rather than misreading it.

## ELECTION POSTSCRIPT

President George W. Bush began his term with some significant handicaps arising from the divisive 2000 election and its tumultuous aftermath. Persisting doubts about the validity of the crucial vote count in Florida would similarly have dogged Al Gore had he ultimately been declared the victor, but the election also created other difficulties for Bush. Although Congress remained very narrowly under Republican control, defeat in the popular presidential vote and GOP losses in the Senate and House races made it difficult for the administration to claim a strong mandate, especially on controversial domestic initiatives.

One domestic political strategy for a president who was elected by a very narrow margin is to forge a bipartisan coalition. John F. Kennedy did so four decades ago when he appointed prominent Republicans to two of the key foreign policy positions: Secretary of Defense Robert McNamara and Secretary of the Treasury Douglas Dillon.

President Bush has chosen a different strategy. Despite pre- and post-election pledges to unite Americans, the administration's initial domestic and foreign policies are clearly aimed at placating the most conservative elements within the Republican Party and the largest donors to his presidential campaign. Domestically, this strategy has manifested itself in a highly controversial $1.6 trillion tax cut plan that runs counter to strong public preferences for using the current budget surplus to buttress Social Security and to reduce the $5.8 trillion national debt. Other examples include reversing regulations on workplace safety, environmental protection of national forests and monuments, and opposing proposals to reduce permissible levels of arsenic in public water supplies.

The Bush administration's foreign and defense policies are also marked by unilateralist proclivities that appeal to the Jesse Helms wing of the GOP rather than to moderates. Although Secretary of State Colin Powell is highly respected by the public and in Congress, he has already been overruled publicly on two issues. Powell's nominee for the Population, Refugees and Migration Bureau was rejected, as was his statement that the United States would continue negotiations with North Korea on weapons of mass destruction and the means of their delivery. By reversing Powell on the latter issue, the Bush administration also headed off the possibility, admittedly a long shot, that a verifiable arms control agreement with North Korea would call into question a key argument for another project dear to the hearts of conservative unilateralists—a national missile defense system. Other manifestation of policies that appeal to the most conservative elements in the Republican Party include undercutting the Kyoto Protocol on Climate Change; appointing an outspoken opponent of the United Nations and arms control (John R. Bolton) to a key State Department position on arms control; and reducing spending on aid programs to Russia to stop the spread of weapons of mass destruction. China presents a more difficult problem for the Bush administration, as its business supporters are strong proponents for engagement through expanded trade, whereas its unilateralist supporters advocate a much harder line toward Beijing and greater military assistance for Taiwan. The defection in May 2001 from the GOP of Senator James Jeffords, who found himself increasingly at odds with Republican policies, resulted in Democratic control of the Senate. Whether that will moderate Bush administration policies is not yet clear.

The evidence summarized in this chapter offers only modest support for the Schlesinger diagnosis of a rush toward unilateralism. However, should the Bush administration continue along that path, it is unlikely to provoke powerful resistance from a public whose foreign policy preferences are generally internationalist and multilateralist, but whose attention is focused primarily on domestic issues. It may thus ultimately turn out that Schlesinger's concerns were premature rather than invalid.

## REFERENCES

Almond, Gabriel. *The American People and Foreign Policy.* New York: Harcourt Brace, 1950.
Cantril, Hadley. *The Human Dimension: Experiences in Policy Research.* New Brunswick, NJ: Rutgers University Press, 1967.
Clifford, Clark, with Richard Holbrooke. *Counsel to the President: A Memoir.* New York: Random House, 1991.
Congressional Quarterly. *1994 CQ Almanac.*
Destler, I. M., Leslie H. Gelb, and Anthony Lake. *Our Own Worst Enemy.* New York: Simon and Schuster, 1984.
Emery, Michael. "An Endangered Species: The International News Hole." *Gannett Center Journal,* 3 (Fall 1989): 151–164.
Everts, Philip. "Public Opinion After the Cold War: The Case of the Netherlands in Comparative Perspective." In Brigitte L. Nacos, Robert Y. Shapiro, and Pierangelo Isernia, editors, *Decisionmaking in a Glass House: Mass Media, Public Opinion, and American and European Foreign Policy in the 21st Century.* Lanham, MD: Rowman and Littlefield, 2000.
Feaver, Peter D. and Christopher Gelpi. "How Many Deaths Are Acceptable? A Surprising Answer." *Washington Post.* November 7, 1999, B3.
Hadar, Leon. "Covering the New World Disorder: The Press Rushes in Where Clinton Fears to Tread." *Columbia Journalism Review* 33 (July 1994): 26–29.

Holsti, Ole R. *Public Opinion and American Foreign Policy.* Ann Arbor: University of Michigan Press, 1996.

Hughes, Barry B. *The Domestic Context of American Foreign Policy.* San Francisco: Freeman, 1978.

Jentleson, Bruce W. "The Pretty Prudent Public: Post-Vietnam American Opinion on the Use of Military Force." *International Studies Quarterly* 36 (1992): 49–73.

Jentleson, Bruce W. and Rebecca L. Britton. "Still Pretty Prudent: Post–Cold War American Public Opinion on the Use of Military Force." *Journal of Conflict Resolution* 42 (August 1998): 395–417.

Kennan, George F. *American Diplomacy, 1900–1950.* New York: Mentor Books, 1951.

———"Somalia, Through a Glass Darkly." *New York Times,* September 30, 1993: A25.

Kennedy, David. *Freedom From Fear: The American People in Depression and War, 1929–1945.* New York: Oxford University Press, 1999.

Kohut, Andrew. *America's Place in the World, Part II.* Washington, DC: Pew Research Center for the People and Press, 1997.

Kohut, Andrew and Robert C. Toth. "Arms and the People." *Foreign Affairs* 73 (November/December 1994): 47–61.

Kull, Steven. "What the Public Knows That Washington Doesn't." *Foreign Policy,* no. 101 (1995–1996): 102–115.

Kull, Steven and I. M. Destler. *Misreading the Public: The Myth of a New Isolationism.* Washington, DC: Brookings Institution Press, 1999.

Larson, Eric V. *Casualties and Consensus: The Historical Role of Casualties in Domestic Support for U.S. Military Operations.* Santa Monica, CA: RAND Corporation, 1996.

Lindsay, James M. "The New Apathy: How an Uninterested Public Is Reshaping Foreign Policy." *Foreign Affairs* 79 (September/October 2000): 2–8.

Lippmann, Walter. *Essays in the Public Philosophy.* Boston: Little, Brown, 1955.

Lipset, Seymour Martin, and Karlyn H. Bowman. "Clinton: Assessing the 42nd President." *Public Perspective* 11 (January–February 2000): 5–13.

Logan, Carolyn J. "U.S. Public Opinion and the Intervention in Somalia: Lessons for the Future of Military-Humanitarian Interventions." *The Fletcher Forum of World Affairs* 20 (Summer/Fall 1996): 155–180.

Luttwak, Edward N. "Where Are the Great Powers? At Home with the Kids." *Foreign Affairs* 73 (July/August 1994): 23–29.

Mandelbaum, Michael. "Foreign Policy as Social Work." *Foreign Affairs* 75 (January–February 1996): 16–32.

Mueller, John E. *War, Presidents, and Public Opinion.* New York: John Wiley, 1973.

*New York Times.* November 29, 1984, A5:1.

Newport, Frank. "Presidential Address on Bosnia Changed Few Minds." Princeton, NJ: Gallup Organization. November 30, 1995.

Rielly, John E., editor. *American Public Opinion and U.S. Foreign Policy, 1975.* Chicago: Chicago Council on Foreign Relations, 1975. Also, similarly titled monographs in 1979, 1983, 1987, 1991, 1995, and 1999.

Rosner, Jeremy D. "The Know-Nothings Know Something." *Foreign Policy,* no. 101 (1995–1996): 116–129.

Saad, Lydia. "Americans Back Clinton's Plan to Keep the Peace in Bosnia." Princeton, NJ: Gallup Organization. October 27, 1995.

Saad, Lydia and Frank Newport. "Americans Want to Keep at Arms Length from Bosnian Conflict." *The Gallup Monthly,* no. 358 (July 1995): 16–18.

Schlesinger, Arthur, Jr. "Back to the Womb?" *Foreign Affairs* 74 (July–August 1995): 16–18.

Shultz, George. *Turmoil and Triumph: My Years as Secretary of State.* New York: Charles Scribner's, 1993.

Sobel, Richard. "What People Really Say About Bosnia." *New York Times,* November 22, 1995: A23.

———*Public Opinion and American Foreign Policy: From Vietnam, to the Nineties.* New York: Oxford University Press, 2001.

Walt, Stephen. "Two Cheers for Clinton's Legacy." *Foreign Affairs* 79 (March–April 2000): 63–79.

# 3

# Who Rules the Roost?
## Congressional-Executive Relations on Foreign Policy After the Cold War

## ANDREW BENNETT
### Georgetown University

## INTRODUCTION

Three historic developments over the last decade—the end of the Cold War, the globalization of markets and media, and a prolonged period of U.S. economic growth—have raised new questions on how America's political culture and institutions are adapting to new demands and opportunities for international leadership. The end of the Cold War and the absence of any new global competitor mean that for the first time in fifty years, there is no single overarching threat to American security and economic interests. At the same time, the globalization of markets and media has presented new opportunities for reshaping the rules of international politics. The U.S. economic boom, coupled with America's lead in information technologies as well as its military power, underscores that the United States is better positioned than any other country to make use of this opportunity to change international rules and institutions, even to the point of being a "necessary catalyst" for effective multilateral action.[1] This state of affairs is proving more durable and far-reaching than many expected, but it will not last forever. This consideration suggests that the United States should use the present window of opportunity to shape

Andrew Bennett is Associate Professor of Government at Georgetown University. He is the author of *Condemned to Repetition? The Rise, Fall, and Reprise of Soviet-Russian Military Interventionism 1973–1996* (1999), and he coedited and contributed to *Friends in Need: Burden Sharing in the Gulf War* (1997). He has also written on foreign policy in the 2000 presidential campaign, on peacekeeping, and on research methods. From 1994–1995, he was Special Assistant to the Assistant Secretary of Defense for International Security Affairs, Joseph S. Nye, Jr.

[1]Robert J. Lieber, "Eagle Rules: Foreign Policy and American Primacy in the 21st Century," in Robert J. Lieber, ed., *Eagle Rules? Foreign Policy and American Primacy in the 21st Century.*

international institutions in ways that will allow it to promote its interests and values far into the future, whether or not the United States continues to be relatively free from threats and preeminently powerful vis-à-vis other states at that future time.

The central conundrum of contemporary U.S. foreign policy, however, is that in the absence of compelling threats, America's political culture and institutions can interact in ways that make it hard to mobilize support for a far-sighted policy of active international leadership and institution building. The danger is not that the United States will retreat to unabashed isolationism and protectionism as it did in the 1930s, the last time that many in the United States thought they did not face compelling international threats. The hard-won lessons of that period persist, and as Ole Holsti's chapter in this volume documents, roughly two-thirds of the U.S. public and virtually all foreign policy elites continue to agree that after the Cold War's end, the United States should remain actively engaged in world affairs. The real danger is that if the president and congressional leaders fail to rouse the public out of what Holsti terms its "apathetic internationalism,"[2] foreign policy interest groups and narrow partisan political factions will dominate the policy process and create a policy that is not as internationalist, multilateralist, and focused on the public good as the public desires or international circumstances require.

This particular danger is more acute with regard to the Congress because members of Congress represent discrete geographic districts and face frequent elections, making them more vulnerable to transient populist sentiments and interest group pressures. The president and vice president are the only nationally elected public officials, and regardless of their party, they tend to be more internationalist and more likely to focus on public goods like national security and an open trading system. Thus, a post–Cold War shift toward greater congressional assertiveness in the foreign policy process would make it more difficult for the United States to take the initiative in building international institutions.

In late 1997, for example, the Congress withheld U.S. dues owed to the United Nations at a time when the United States needed the UN's help in crises in the Balkans and the Middle East, delayed additional funding for the International Monetary Fund (IMF) when the United States needed the IMF to address the Asian economic crisis, and failed to renew the president's "fast-track" trade negotiating authority when U.S. leadership was needed to maintain progress toward an open trading system. The congress, recognizing its vulnerability to partisan and parochial interests, has at times "depoliticized" its foreign policy processes and partially insulated them from interest group pressures. For example, by creating the fast-track trade process, which required the Congress to vote on trade agreements without amendment and within 90 days after transmittal by the president, the Congress insulated its individual members from interest group pressures to introduce amendments favorable to specific economic groups. The failure to renew fast-track negotiating

[2]Ole Holsti, "Public Opinion and Foreign Policy," in Lieber, ed., *Eagle Rules?*

authority in 1997 symbolizes not only a missed opportunity for building international institutions but also a "repoliticization" of the foreign policy process.[3]

The United States does not face an all-or-nothing choice, however, between executive or congressional dominance of the foreign policy process, or between an effective foreign policy or a democratic one. Effectiveness and democracy can go hand in hand, as they did in allowing the United States to prevail in the Cold War without becoming a "garrison state."[4] Each branch has unique comparative advantages that it can bring to bear to save the other branch from its particular form of excess. The presidency offers the possibility of a foreign policy that is decisive, proactive, and when necessary, secret, and the Congress offers diversity of opinion, deliberation, democracy, openness wherever possible, and consensus building.[5] The question is whether we can achieve "a balance between Congress and the president—a clearer identification of the areas where each has a comparative advantage over the other."[6]

In this light, this chapter assesses the balance of foreign policy powers between the presidency and the Congress since the end of the Cold War. It first identifies the differences in the two institutions' foreign policy perspectives and the domestic and international changes that have traditionally caused one branch or the other to become more assertive in the making of foreign policy. It then looks at the domestic and international changes accompanying the end of the Cold War that have affected each branch's foreign policy roles. Next, the chapter examines the two institutions' roles over the last decade on the key issues of international trade, the confirmation of top foreign policy officials, the use of force, and the ratification of treaties.

The chapter reaches three central conclusions. *First,* the Congress has become more assertive on the "intermestic" issues—international issues with a large domestic component—that matter the most to voters, such as international trade. It has been less assertive in using its war powers authority, although even here it has been more activist than during the Cold War. *Second,* these changes in the relative foreign policy roles of the Congress and the executive reflect not only factors that could prove short-lived, such as the predominance of divided governments since 1980 and the sharp personal antipathy toward President Clinton among many in

[3]Another example of repoliticization is the breakdown of the Base Realignment and Closure (BRAC) process. The Congress developed the BRAC process to put the public good ahead of factional interests by establishing a commission to decide upon a list of military bases deserving closure or reduction. The Congress would then vote on closing the resulting list of bases as a group, since voting on each base closure separately would generate fierce opposition from each relevant congressional district. The BRAC process was at first enormously successful in clearing out a backlog of unneeded bases after the Cold War, but the process ground to a halt when the Clinton administration repoliticized it by protecting bases in California and Texas in anticipation of the 1996 elections. See James Kitfield, "The Battle of the Depots," *The National Journal,* April 4, 1998, pp. 746–750.

[4]Aaron Friedberg, *In the Shadow of the Garrison State: America's Anti-Statism and Its Cold War Strategy* (Princeton, NJ: Princeton University Press, 2000).

[5]Thomas E. Mann, "Making Foreign Policy: President and Congress," in Mann, ed., *A Question of Balance: The President, the Congress, and Foreign Policy* (Washington, DC: Brookings, 1990), p. 2.

[6]Ibid, p. 4.

Congress, but also long-lasting international and domestic changes that will challenge the Bush administration and its successors regardless of whether divided government returns. *Third,* the presidency and Congress have not consistently used their comparative advantages as well as they might have to promote American interests. Sometimes, the two have constituted a de facto good-cop-bad-cop team, winning concessions from other states, but at other times their conflicting signals have been self-defeating. The chapter ends with recommendations for reforming the foreign policy process to make better use of the comparative advantages of each branch of government in an era of U.S. international leadership and institution-building.

## PRESIDENTIAL VERSUS CONGRESSIONAL PERSPECTIVES ON FOREIGN POLICY

The U.S. Constitution has been described as an "invitation to struggle for the privilege of directing American foreign policy."[7] This is so not only because there is ambiguity regarding the foreign policy powers shared by the presidency and the Congress but also because the institutions have different constituencies and different political timetables. The president is elected every four years by the entire nation, whereas members of the House serve congressional districts and are elected every two years, and senators serve the states and are elected every six years. This arrangement makes the House the body most responsive to public opinion, and the framers of the Constitution insulated foreign policy somewhat from public opinion by giving power over the ratification of treaties and confirmation of appointments to the Senate. Yet the House still has considerable power over the budget, trade policy, and other aspects of foreign policy of great concern to interest groups, and House members' frequent elections increase their reliance on campaign contributions from these groups. Senators and presidents are not immune to interest group pressures despite their less frequent elections, but their larger geographic constituencies provide greater assurance that they will feel the weight of groups on several sides of an issue.

House members are thus the most subject to populist and interest group pressures, presidents are the least so, and senators fall somewhere in between. For most of American history prior to World War Two, the public's isolationism consequently made the House the least internationalist body and the presidency the most internationalist. This generalization is a more consistent guide to the foreign policy orientations of American leaders than these leaders' party affiliations, and the parties have changed the mantle of internationalism as they have won or lost the White House, particularly when the opposition party has a majority in the congress. President George Bush senior, for example, lost his campaign for reelection in 1992 in

[7]Edward Corwin, *The President: Office and Powers, 1787–1957,* 4th rev. ed. (New York: New York University Press, 1957), p. 44.

part because the public felt that he focused too much of his attention on foreign policy, where he was an active internationalist, whereas William Clinton ran and won on a platform that emphasized the importance of the U.S. economy. Once Clinton became president and the Republican Party gained a majority in the congress, however, Clinton became more internationalist than the Republican Congress on issues ranging from the use of force to paying U.S. dues owed to the UN. Meanwhile, the Republican party's 1994 "contract with America" campaign platform devoted little attention to foreign policy. There are already indications that these interbranch differences will persist under President George W. Bush who, during the 2000 campaign, criticized an effort by some Republicans in Congress to put a time limit on the deployment of U.S. troops in Kosovo.

There are two additional reasons that the executive branch tends to be more internationalist than the legislative branch, both of which are evident in many other democracies as well. First, presidents and their cabinet officers meet with foreign leaders and officials far more frequently than their legislative counterparts and in smaller and less public settings, so that they feel international pressures and assess international realities more quickly, directly, and personally. The Congress tends to be more skeptical of international alliances and institutions, and more unilateralist in its policies.[8] Second, Presidents have to worry about both policy risk, or the risk that a foreign policy will fail to achieve its objectives, and political risk, or the risk of being blamed by voters for failures in foreign policy.[9] Legislators, especially those in the opposition party, are more populist and parochial because they know that voters are more likely to blame the executive for failures in foreign policy. Members of Congress can therefore advocate foreign policies that are unrealistic in the international arena but popular with voters at home, safe in the knowledge that presidents will either oppose these policies or suffer the political blame for policy failure if they adopt them. The Congress is thus sometimes tempted to "free-ride" by allowing internationalist presidents to do the right thing while they do the popular thing. This situation is true of policies that appeal to interest groups as well as those that appeal to the public at large. Thus, perennial favorite themes of opposition members of Congress and candidates for president include "getting tough" with unpopular countries, over whom the United States may have little leverage, and insisting on more burden sharing from allies, who may already be shouldering considerable burdens. The 2000 presidential campaign was no exception, with the nonincumbent candidate George W. Bush hinting at tougher policies toward Iraq, China, Russia, and North Korea, and suggesting that the United States was bearing too much of the peacekeeping burden in the Balkans even though other states have supplied the majority of the troops to peace operations in the region.

---

[8]Lee Hamilton, remarks to a meeting of the Trilateral Commission in Washington in 1999, *http://www.trilateral.org/annmtgs/trialog/trlgtxts/t53/ham/htm*, p. 2.

[9]Alan Lamborn, "Risk and Foreign Policy Choice," *International Studies Quarterly,* Vol. 29 (1985): 385–410.

# HISTORICAL AND POST–COLD WAR INFLUENCES ON FOREIGN POLICY ROLES

To some extent, congressional-executive relations on foreign policy after the Cold War fit the broader patterns established throughout U.S. history. Major foreign policy crises or threats that call for decisive action usually lead to presidential assertiveness and congressional deference in the foreign policy process, and in such times the public generally rallies behind bold presidential initiatives. Then, once a crisis is resolved or recedes, the public's attention returns to domestic issues, and the Congress reasserts itself in the foreign policy process. Periods of U.S. internationalism or involvement in war thus generally coincide with presidential dominance of the foreign policy process, whereas periods of U.S. isolationism tend to exhibit congressional activism in the making of foreign policy. This tendency was true of the War of 1812, the Mexican-American War, the Civil War, World War One, and the years of foreign policy retrenchment that followed each war, as well as of World War Two and the first few years of rapid U.S. military demobilization immediately following it.[10]

This pattern continued through the Cold War as well. During the recurrent Cold War crises from the late 1940s to the escalation of the Vietnam War in the 1960s, the Congress conceded great authority to the executive branch on war powers, the defense budget, intelligence policies, and other foreign policy issues. The rising opposition to the Vietnam War then led to more divided public and elite opinion on foreign policy, a less assertive U.S. foreign policy, and a more activist congress. It was in this period, extending from the late 1960s to the late 1970s, that the Congress passed the War Powers Act and created oversight committees for the intelligence community. With renewed concern over the Soviet threat in the late 1970s, the pendulum swung partly back toward presidential assertiveness in the policy process and U.S. activism abroad, though the Congress continued to constrain presidential policy initiatives (particularly with regard to Central America).

The current cycle shares much with previous ones: it follows the end of a great power competition, and U.S. political parties have traded the mantle of internationalism as they have captured or lost the White House. The current cycle differs from previous historical cycles, however, in both international context and domestic politics. Internationally, the absence of a single overarching threat has diminished the ability of presidents to use the White House as a bully pulpit to rally public and congressional opinion behind their foreign policies. President Clinton has succeeded in mobilizing public support for air strikes against suspected terrorists, but it has proven more difficult to establish sustained public support for peacekeeping or peace enforcement missions in Bosnia, Haiti, Kosovo, Iraq, and elsewhere. Ethnic conflicts generally pose cumulative and long-term rather than immediate threats to the United States and in the absence of clear or easy solutions, it is difficult to win the kind of deep public support that allowed the United States to prevail in the Cold War.

---

[10]Frank L. Klingberg, *Cyclical Trends in America's Foreign Policy Moods: The Unfolding of America's World Role* (Lanham, MD: University of Maryland Press, 1983)·

A second novel international factor is the globalization of markets, communications, and transportation networks, which presents new dimensions to the issues of terrorism, drug smuggling, international crime, immigration, the global environment, and international trade. Trade, for example, has risen from about one-tenth to one-quarter of U.S. GNP through the decade of the 1990s, creating a much greater stake in the world economy for most Americans. Such "intermestic" issues are precisely the ones that the public now rates as among the most important foreign policy problems, and not coincidentally, they are the issues in which the Congress has taken an active interest.[11] Many of these issues have also been the subject of intense interest group lobbying, as they involve the potential allocation of great costs and benefits to specific actors, creating potential tensions between public goods and private interests. The failure to reach an international agreement in the fall of 2000 on implementation of the Kyoto Protocols on global warming, for example, was brought about in part by an odd coalition of antiregulation economic actors and proregulation environmental groups, both of whom, for very different reasons, rejected moderate regulation.[12] International institutions are consequently needed to prevent collective action problems and "race to the bottom" dynamics on everything from pollution control to labor and safety standards. Yet economic or ideological interest groups, whether acting through the Congress or the executive branch, can prevent the achievement of public goods if an apathetic public fails to act upon its interests and its internationalist preferences.

A set of domestic trends, most of them having little to do with the international changes that ended the Cold War, have also shaped congressional-executive relations on foreign policy and are likely to continue to do so. First, organized interest groups of all kinds—ethnic groups, business groups, single-issue groups, ideological factions—have been increasingly influential as they have found new ways to circumvent campaign finance laws developed in the 1970s. These groups' influence was most visible on matters concerning trade (such as the NAFTA agreement and the extension of Permanent Normalized Trading Relations (PNTR) to China), defense spending (particularly shipbuilding, aircraft procurement, and ballistic missile defenses), and issues of concern to particular ethnic groups (such as U.S. relations with Cuba, Israel, and Armenia).[13]

---

[11]Four of the public's top five foreign policy priorities in a 1999 poll were "intermestic" issues (stopping drug smuggling, protecting U.S. jobs, combating terrorism, and securing energy supplies; the top priority was preventing the spread of nuclear weapons). John Rielly, *American Public Opinion and U.S. Foreign Policy* (New York: Council on Foreign Relations, 1999), p. 16.

[12]Andrew Revkin, "Odd Culprits in Collapse of Climate Talks," *The New York Times*, November 28, 2000, p. F1. On the interest groups that have opposed international environmental regulation, see Robert Paarlberg, "U.S. Environmental Policy Abroad: Explaining Fluctuations in Leadership by an Essential Country," in Lieber, ed., *Eagle Rules?*.

[13]See John T. Tierney, "Interest Group Involvement in Congressional Foreign and Defense Policy," in Randall B. Ripley and James M. Lindsay, eds., *Congress Resurgent: Foreign and Defense Policy on Capitol Hill* (Ann Arbor: University of Michigan Press, 1993), pp. 89–111; see also Ralph Carter, "Congress and Post–Cold War U.S. Foreign Policy," in James M. Scott, ed., *After the End: Making U.S. Foreign Policy in the Post–Cold War World* (Durham, NC: Duke University Press, 1998), p. 118. Carter points out that because of lobbying by Armenian-Americans, Armenians are now the second-highest per capita recipients of U.S. aid, after Israelis.

Second, the predominance of divided governments since the 1970s has made it difficult for presidents to enact their programs, both foreign and domestic, without substantial compromises with the opposition party. The new kind of divided government that emerged in the 2000 elections, with an almost exactly equal split between the parties in both the House and the Senate as well as in the presidential vote, is likely to continue this pattern, though it may also confer greater power to the moderates in both parties.

Third, demographic changes and the creation of an all-volunteer military force in the 1970s have made members of Congress and the executive less likely to have served in the armed forces or to have spent time overseas. According to one estimate, about one-third of the members of Congress do not even have passports.[14] Also, the percentage of House members who are veterans has declined from 75 percent in 1971 to 25 percent in 1999, and a parallel but smaller decline took place in the Senate.[15] On the whole, this trend has probably reduced the congress's expertise in and leverage over military affairs more than that of the executive, which can draw upon the advice of the uniformed military but also vet it through the civilian policy organizations under the secretary of defense.

Fourth, the foreign affairs committees in the House and particularly the Senate have lost some of their ability to build strong congressional majorities. This loss is in part because the diminished importance of foreign policy in the eyes of the public has made membership on these committees less sought-after than it was during the Cold War, when foreign affairs experience was considered important for House members who aspired to run for Senate and senators who hoped to run for president. The electoral defeat of prominent members of the foreign affairs committees, including Senate Foreign Relations Chairs Senators Charles Percy and Frank Church, discouraged some of the more moderate and capable members from seeking these committees.[16] Partly as a result, the Senate committee has most recently been chaired by Senator Claiborne Pell, who was not generally considered an effective chair of the committee, and Senator Jesse Helms, who has exercised the com-

---

[14]Michael Krepon, "That Old Isolationist Feeling," *The Los Angeles Times,* January 18, 1998, p. M2, citing an estimate by the National Security Caucus Foundation, a private group that arranges and funds foreign visits for members of congress. This figure has not been verified, but overseas travel by Congress is nonetheless quite limited by fears of being labeled as taking "junkets" overseas. In 1995, for example, two hundred members of the German parliament visited Washington, but not a single member of Congress made an official trip to Bonn. Tyler Marshall, "As 'Junket' Becomes Dirty Word, Congress Loses Its Overseas Interest," *The Los Angeles Times,* February 10, 1997, p. A22.

[15]William T. Bianco and Jamie Markham, "Vanishing Veterans: The Decline in Military Experience in the U.S. Congress," in Peter D. Feaver and Richard H. Kohn, eds., *Soldiers and Civilians: The Gap Between the Military and American Society and What it Means for National Security* (Cambridge, MA: MIT Press, forthcoming 2001). These authors' statistical analysis shows that the difference in voting patterns between veterans and nonveterans is not great, but they suggest that the more important effect, though hard to measure, may be on the nature of the proposals that get voted upon.

[16]John Spanier and Eric Uslaner, *American Foreign Policy Making and the Democratic Dilemmas* (New York: Holt, Reinhart, and Winston, 1985), pp. 168, 184. See also James M. McCormick, "Decision Making in the Foreign Affairs and Foreign Relations Committees," and Christopher Deering, "Decision Making in the Armed Services Committees," in Ripley and Lindsay, *Congress Resurgent,* pp. 115–153 and 155–182.

mittee's power far more assertively but whose intensely conservative views have put him at odds even with members of his own party (Senator Lugar, a Republican moderate with widely respected views on foreign policy, also chaired the committee briefly in the 1980s, with more success in building coalitions). The Senate Armed Services and House National Security committees, in contrast, have retained their influence and their appeal to capable and moderate members of Congress in view of these committees' control over substantial budgets that affect constituents in every state.

Fifth, political alignments in the Congress have become more partisan and ideological. As David Rohde argues, changes in voter participation and in party loyalties in the South have resulted in greater intraparty homogeneity and interparty disagreement in the congress. This increase in partisanship has been amplified, he notes, by institutional changes in the House that made committee leaders more responsible to party leaders.[17] As Ole Holsti notes in this volume, these changes in Congress have coincided with sharper partisan differences on foreign affairs among the general public.[18] The end of the Cold War has not meant the end of ideology; rather, it has only changed the terms of the ideological and partisan debate on foreign policy.

Sixth, media coverage of foreign affairs has changed dramatically in both quantity and quality. Total foreign coverage on the network television news programs plummeted by about half from 1989 (admittedly a very busy base year in world events) to 1996.[19] In addition, the media have become more willing to publicize revelations on the private behavior of foreign policy officials and advisers, complicating congressional-executive cooperation in the process of nominating and confirming top officials and discouraging many qualified candidates from seeking appointment to public service. The reduced coverage of foreign affairs in traditional media outlets, however, has been accompanied by the increased breadth and immediacy of information available through the internet to all actors in the foreign policy process. At the same time, the fracturing of media coverage from the television networks and leading newspapers to cable and the internet has changed the bully pulpit of the presidency into a "bullied pulpit"; no single news outlet has a great share of the national audience, pundits abound in niche markets, and the television networks no longer automatically cover presidential press conferences or major speeches live.[20]

Finally, the sharp and lasting reductions in the foreign policy and defense budgets are likely to occasion lasting changes in congressional-executive relations

[17]David Rohde, "Partisanship Leadership and Congressional Assertiveness in Foreign and Defense Policy," in David A. Deese, ed., *The New Politics of American Foreign Policy* (New York: St. Martin's Press, 1994), pp. 76–101. See also Carter, "Congress and Post–Cold War U.S. Foreign Policy," pp. 127–128.

[18]Holsti, "Public Opinion."

[19]Garrick Utley, "The Shrinking of Foreign News: From Broadcast to Narrowcast," *Foreign Affairs,* Vol. 76, No. 2 (March–April 1997): 2.

[20]Sebastian Mallaby, "The Bullied Pulpit: A Weak Chief Exectuive Makes Worse Foreign Policy," *Foreign Affairs,* Vol. 79, no. 1 (January–February 2000): 2–8.

on foreign policy.[21] The nondefense foreign affairs budget, in particular, is about 20 percent lower in real dollars than in the 1980s, and it was cut 10 percent by Congress from FY 2000 to FY 2001.[22] The net effect of these budgetary cuts is likely to be a reduction in the relative influence of the executive, which now has not only fewer and smaller programs but also smaller foreign and defense policy staffs.

## THE POST–COLD WAR INTERBRANCH BALANCE ON FOREIGN POLICY

Taken together, the international and domestic trends previously noted have had mixed effects, and there are competing views on whether Congress has been increasingly assertive or deferential in the foreign policy process since the late 1980s.[23] An emergent consensus, consistent with the present chapter, argues that Congress has been increasingly assertive on intermestic issues but relatively deferential on war powers issues, though not as deferential as during the Cold War.[24] The Congress has also emphasized symbolic issues that matter to core political constituencies in each party, including missile defenses, UN funding, the IMF, and issues of concern to particular ethnic groups, such as U.S. relations with Cuba.

Quantitative indicators show that in some sense, Congress has indeed been increasingly assertive: from 1946 to 1949, presidents got what they wanted from their legislative initiatives 66 percent of the time, whereas Congress took its own initiatives only 8 percent of the time. By 1992 to 1995, Congress complied with presidential initiaves only 24 percent of the time and took the initiative itself 28 percent of the time.[25] Quantitative indicators are imperfect, however: a critically important vote such as that on the Gulf War may not be weighted more heavily than a minor issue. Also, there may be strong "selection effects:" presidents may challenge as-

---

[21]Two other developments that changed congressional-executive relations in the 1970s and 1980s, the growth of congressional staffs and the decentralization of power in Congress and within its committees, continued to affect interbranch relations in the 1990s but did not change markedly in that decade (staffs decreased slightly under the direction of the new Congress in 1994).

[22]Richard Gardner, "The One Percent Solution: Shirking the Cost of World Leadership," *Foreign Affairs,* Vol. 79, No. 4 (July–August 2000): 3.

[23]Those arguing that Congress has been more assertive include Randall Ripley and James Lindsay, eds., *Congress Resurgent.* Those emphasizing congressional deference include Louis Fisher, "Without Restraint: Presidential Military Initiatives from Korea to Bosnia," in Eugene R. Wittkopf and James M. McCormick, eds., *The Domestic Sources of American Foreign Policy: Insights and Evidence* (Lanham, MD: Rowman and Littlefield, 1999, 3d ed.), pp. 141–156; Barbara Hinckley, *Less Than Meets the Eye: Foreign Policy Making and the Myth of the Assertive Congress* (Chicago: University of Chicago Press, 1994); and Harold Hongju Koh, *The National Security Constitution* (New Haven, CT: Yale University Press, 1990). Interestingly, the former tends to focus on intermestic issues, and the latter two focus more on war powers.

[24]Ralph Carter, "Congress and Post–Cold War U.S. Foreign Policy," pp. 108–137; James McCormick, *American Foreign Policy and Process* (Itasca, IL: F. E. Peacock, 1998, 3rd ed.), pp. 358–364; Jeremy D. Rosner, *The New Tug-of-War: Congress, the Executive Branch and National Security* (Washington, DC: Carnegie Endowment for International Peace, 1995).

[25]Carter, " Congress and Post–Cold War U.S. Foreign Policy," pp. 109–111.

sertive congresses less frequently or fundamentally, affecting the rate of votes measured a "success." Thus, we need to look at qualitative historical comparisons in specific issue areas where the Constitution mandates that Congress and the president share powers, including trade and finance, the confirmation of appointments, war powers, and the ratification of treaties. These, reviewed in the following sections, undergird the conclusion that Congress has been considerably more assertive in the making of foreign policy on intermestic issues than it was during the Cold War, and somewhat more assertive regarding war powers.

## INTERBRANCH RELATIONS ON TRADE AND FINANCE

Post–Cold War interbranch relations on international trade and finance can be portrayed as either a glass half full or a glass half empty. The high points include congressional approval of the NAFTA trade agreement, the World Trade Organization (WTO), and PNTR with China. Despite numerous tensions and disagreements on these issues within and between Congress and the executive, each of these agreements won consensus in the end. In some instances, most clearly in the case of NAFTA, the Congress served as a "bad cop" that gave the executive greater negotiating leverage with foreign governments.[26]

The overall trend through the Clinton administration, however, was toward a more conflictual and less effective trade policy process. The NAFTA agreement, despite being a great economic success in terms of increased trade with Mexico and Canada, came under such political criticism that the administration avoided using the term "NAFTA" in subsequent trade debates. Moreover, NAFTA and the WTO won approval in part through the fast-track trade process, which partly depoliticized the debate by giving the Congress ninety days to vote on each package without amendments. In both cases, however, the Congress's increasing insistence on side agreements and favorable implementing legislation began to repoliticize the trade process.[27] In addition, the PNTR agreement was delayed for a year when the administration, fearing opposition from labor groups, walked away from a nearly finished agreement with China. It later renegotiated this agreement only with great difficulty and with no substantial new concessions from China. This agreement then won congressional approval only by a modest margin, even though the coalition of business groups supporting PNTR was far more powerful and well-funded than that of human rights and labor groups opposing it. Also, as noted before, the Congress delayed a requested increase in IMF funding for over a year despite the ongoing economic crisis in Asia, and it refused to renew the president's "fast-track" trade negotiating authority. After retreating on trade issues in the face of street demonstrations at the Seattle trade summit, the Clinton administration, which had come

---

[26]Frederick Mayer, *Interpreting NAFTA: The Science and Art of Policy Analysis* (New York: Columbia University Press, 1998).

[27]I. M. Destler, *Renewing Fast-Track Legislation* (Washington, DC: Institute for International Economics, 1997), pp. 10–11.

into office with the NAFTA agreement substantially complete, left its successor with no major new trade agreement in process and no fast-track authority with which to negotiate one.

A number of idiosyncratic factors contributed to the erosion of interbranch cooperation on trade, including the intensification of divided government when the Republican Party took control of the House in 1994, the outburst of partisanship accompanying the Lewinsky scandal, and the Clinton administration's penchant for repeatedly waiting until the last minute to build a legislative coalition behind its trade policies. Several deeper dynamics, however, indicate that the congress's increased assertiveness on trade and finance is a long-term trend that will also give the new Republican administration a difficult time on trade policy. Globalization has made trade more important to a growing number of individuals and groups, increasing the incentives for congressional involvement and complicating the prospects for consensus. It remains to be seen whether it will be the critics of free trade represented in the streets of Seattle or instead the evolving pro-trade coalition of businesses, consumers, and workers who have benefited from globalization that will become more powerful.[28] More problematic is the fact that the Clinton administration had two great advantages on trade policy that its successor may lack: a booming economy and a pro-trade opposition party. Clinton's victories on trade depended on his ability to rely on a solid pro-trade majority among Republicans and to sway enough votes from Democrats to win the day.[29] The importance of labor groups in many close elections in 2000 will make it much harder to win support for free trade from Democratic members of Congress, especially if the economy does not maintain the remarkable growth of the Clinton years. Only about one out of five Democrats in the House voted to renew fast-track authority in 1997, and this proportion is likely to shrink under President George W. Bush.

## FOREIGN POLICY APPOINTMENTS AND THE SENATE CONFIRMATION PROCESS

Complaints about the politicization of the confirmation process are a perennial staple of American political history, and recent confirmation battles should not be compared to some mythical past in which the confirmation process was apolitical and based on merit alone. At the same time, it is clear that the confirmation process has become more partisan, more personal, and generally more frustrating and daunting for nominees. In 1960, top positions were filled on average within ten weeks of

---

[28]See Benjamin Cohen, "Containing Backlash: Foreign Economic Policy in an Age of Globalization," in Lieber, ed., *Eagle Rules?*.

[29]There is evidence that divided government helps the free-trade policies of presidents whose parties are more protectionist, since these presidents can win more support from these same-party protectionists, and limits the success of free-trade presidents from free-trade parties, who have little influence over the protectionist opposition. See David Karol, "Divided Government and U.S. Trade Policy: Much Ado about Nothing?," *International Organization,* Vol. 54, No. 4 (Autumn 2000): 825–844.

President Kennedy's inauguration, but in 1992, it took an average of almost nine months for top officials to take office—more than three-fifths as long as their average tenure in office of just fourteen months.[30] The Clinton administration was partly to blame for its slow vetting of nominees, but the Congress also inhibited the confirmation process through its complex reporting and disclosure requirements for nominees and its increasingly partisan approach.

Many of these dysfunctional aspects of the confirmation process have applied with a vengeance to foreign policy nominees because of the extensive security checks they must undergo, and the Senate Intelligence, Foreign Relations, and Armed Services committees have each produced examples of horrific confirmation struggles. Just as the rejection of Supreme Court Nominee Robert Bork led to a cycle of retaliation by each party of the other party's judicial and domestic policy nominees, the Senate's rejection in 1989 of Senator John Tower as President Bush's first nominee for Secretary of Defense contributed to a cycle of partisan retaliation against foreign policy officials. When Tower's nomination came under fire because of allegations of his excessive drinking, the White House and the Senate agreed on the unusual step of allowing the files from the FBI's background investigation, ordinarily available only to the chair and ranking minority member of the relevant committee, to be reviewed by every member of the Senate. This agreement quickly led to news leaks on the files, and it established a terrible precedent, since such files include raw information gathered by the FBI with no separate check for accuracy and may contain both well-documented facts and outright hearsay. The Senate Intelligence Committee expanded this unfortunate precedent in 1997 by demanding the FBI files on Anthony Lake, Clinton's former National Security Adviser and nominee for Director of Central Intelligence, and later adopting a rule to make the sharing of such files among committee members routine. Lake reluctantly agreed to giving the committee access to his FBI files, but he also quickly found that he could not view the files himself without waiting for several years to procure them through the Freedom of Information Act. In the end, Lake withdrew his nomination and wrote a public letter condemning the vicious politics of the confirmation process.[31]

Another case, the rejection of the nomination of Massachusetts Governor William Weld to be Ambassador to Mexico, further illustrates how factionalized and personalized the confirmation process has become. Although a Republican, Weld was rejected in large part because of the opposition of Senate Foreign Relations Chair Jesse Helms. Helms objected to Weld's support of the medical use of marijuana and needle exchange programs for drug addicts, but Helms may also have been angered by Weld's refusal in his unsuccessful Senate campaign to endorse Helms's continuation as Chair of the Foreign Relations Committee. Despite letters from forty-five Democratic Senators and eight Republican Senators urging

---

[30]Norman Ornstein and Thomas Donilon, "The Confirmation Clog," *Foreign Affairs,* Vol. 79, No. 6 (November–December 2000): 88–89.

[31]Alton Frye, "Nominees and Their FBI Files," *The Washington Post,* May 14, 1997, p. A 21.

that Helms hold a hearing on Weld's confirmation, Helms persisted in the almost unprecedented step of rejecting the wishes of the majority of his committee as well as of the Senate to hold a hearing, and Weld eventually withdrew his nomination. This episode led the committee's former chair, the moderate Republican Senator Richard Lugar of Indiana, to declare that "it seems to me unacceptable for one chairman to say, 'In my committee, I will be a dictator.'"[32]

The media's increasing willingness, even eagerness, to delve into the private lives of public officials even when there is no evident bearing on their public duties has further escalated the increasingly partisan confirmation process. The nomination of Air Force General Joseph W. Ralston to be Chairman of the Joint Chiefs of Staff, for example, was derailed in the summer of 1997 because of highly publicized stories that many years earlier he had a brief extramarital relationship with a civilian at a time when he was separated from his wife. Ralston had the misfortune of facing possible Senate hearings on this issue at the same time that Air Force Lt. Kelly Flynn was facing a court-martial because she had an affair with the husband of an enlisted woman in her military unit, lied to her superiors about the affair, and disobeyed their orders to end the affair. Neither the White House nor the Senate made a strong public argument for distinguishing between the very different circumstances of the two cases, and Ralston's nomination was withdrawn, though he remained the Vice Chairman of the Joint Chiefs. This incident also illustrated the "lemming" effect of the confirmation process: once one nominee comes under fire for some reason, whether nanny taxes or marital conduct, subsequent nominees are quickly held to the same standard. Soon after the Ralston case, special phone hot lines were established in the Defense Department to handle any and all complaints on sexual misconduct, and every officer had to fear that his or her next promotion might be hampered by allegations, whether well-founded or not, on this subject.

Interest groups have also eagerly leapt into the confirmation fray to attack nominees. One particularly egregious example concerns Rose Gottemoeller, a respected expert on arms control and Russia who had been NSC director for Russian affairs early in the Clinton administration. Gottemoeller was offered the top Defense Department position on nuclear weapons policy in April 1997, but she was abruptly told in August 1997, after her resignation from her job at a London think tank and just one week before moving vans were to arrive at her home, that the post had been abolished. Leaks to the media quickly made clear that Secretary of Defense Cohen had decided to pull back from the nomination because of criticism by Frank Gaffney, a conservative Republican activist whose "Center for Security Policy" has frequently opposed Democratic foreign policy nominees. Gaffney had faxed a memo to members of the Senate Armed Services Committee and Defense Department officials criticizing Gottemoeller for her support of the 1972 Anti-Ballistic Missile Treaty and of a National Academy of Sciences report urging

---

[32]Greg McDonald, "Senator Warns Helms to Hold Hearing," *The Houston Chronicle,* August 8, 1997, p. 1. Among other Clinton administration foreign policy nominees blocked by Senator Helms was Robert Pastor, nominated to become Ambassador to Panama.

deeper bilateral cuts in U.S. and Russian nuclear weapons.[33] Although Senate aides indicated that the fax had not produced a groundswell of opposition to Gotte-moeller's appointment, the NSC and the Secretary of Defense decided not to risk a confrontation, prompting one of Gottemoeller's supporters to note that "this is an administration that puts lunch money in the bully's locker even before being threatened."[34]

An even more troubling development in the confirmation process is the in-creasing abuse of the custom in the Senate whereby a single Senator can anony-mously place a "hold" on a nomination, preventing it from being brought to the Senate floor for a vote for an unspecified time period even after it has passed out of committee. This practice has no basis in the U.S. Constitution or the Senate's rules, but as one study noted, "a more individualistic Senate culture has turned the 'hold' from an occasional instrument of modest delay into a lethal weapon used regularly to hold nominees hostage to the whims or unrelated demands of individual sena-tors."[35] The increasing use of such holds finally led the Senate leadership to agree that Senators placing a hold must notify the leadership, the sponsor of the legisla-tion or nomination, and the chair of the relevant committee. Even after this, however, three Senators placed anonymous holds on the nomination of Richard Holbrooke, for reasons unrelated to his qualifications, to be the U.S. representa-tive to the UN. This delay held up for an additional two months the vote on Hol-brooke's confirmation, which finally took place more than a year after his initial nomination.[36]

## WAR POWERS

Since World War Two, Congress has been more deferential to the presidency on war powers than on other foreign policy issues. In all of U.S. history, Congress has declared war only five times (the January 1991 congressional resolution au-thorizing force against Iraq was essentially equivalent to a sixth declaration of war), but the executive branch has used force without such a declaration well over one hundred times, including both minor skirmishes and major conflicts in Korea and Vietnam. As James Lindsay has argued, the Congress is extremely reluctant to take votes authorizing the use of force because such votes have a "use it and lose it" quality. If the Congress rejects an authorization of force, the executive will have less leverage for diplomacy, armed conflict might thereby become more

---

[33]R. Jeffrey Smith, "Aides Question Elimination of Pentagon Job," *The Washington Post,* Sep-tember 23, 1997, p. A1. Ironically, the Bush campaign adopted in the summer of 2000 a more radical po-sition favoring unilateral U.S. nuclear arms reductions, which Gottemoeller criticized for not putting enough emphasis on negotiated Russian reductions. Rose Gottemoeller, "Lopsided Arms Control," *The Washington Post,* December 7, 2000.

[34]Smith, "Aides Question Elimination of Pentagon Job."

[35]Ornstein and Donilon, "The Confirmation Clog," p. 92.

[36]Ibid.

likely, and Congress will be blamed. If the Congress does authorize force, it essentially cedes control over any subsequent military action, and it may share in the responsibility for any escalation. Thus, Congress is usually tempted to sit on the fence as long as possible, largely limiting itself to "sense of the Senate" and "sense of the House" resolutions that neither endorse nor reject the president's policies. This tactic allows the Congress to share the political approval if the engagement ends in victory or to blame the President if it leads to defeat.[37] The 1973 War Powers Act, which prevents the president from placing troops in situations of "imminent hostilities" for more than sixty days without a vote of congressional approval, has not changed this dynamic.[38] With the end of the Cold War, however, the Congress has become incrementally more assertive in exercising its war powers, though it remains less active in this arena than on other foreign policy issues.

It is important to keep in mind that votes are not the only means of congressional influence. Congress can also influence presidential decisions on the use of force through hearings, speeches, media appearances, nonbinding resolutions, and open or private letters to the president. With regard to peacekeeping missions in Haiti, Bosnia, and Somalia, for example, the Congress generally confined itself to "sense of the House/Senate" resolutions expressing generic support for U.S. troops but neither support nor opposition for the president's policies. Although the Congress turned back proposals in several of these cases to require prior congressional authorization for the use of force or to set specific time limits on U.S. deployments, the congress's public statements do appear to have shaped President Clinton's policies.[39] On Haiti, for example, many in Congress were skeptical of using force to restore elected President Jean-Bertrand Aristide to power. This skepticism contributed to President Clinton's reluctance to use force until he felt pressure from a hunger strike by human rights activist Randall Robinson. Clinton ultimately launched an airborne invasion, showing he was willing to use force against armed opposition in Haiti and without prior approval by the Congress. At the same time, Clinton ultimately succeeded in his attempt to forestall armed resistance in Haiti and political opposition in the Congress by concluding an agreement allowing a comfortable exile for the ruling Haitian junta in exchange for its forbearance of armed resistance to the introduction of U.S. troops.[40]

On Bosnia, Clinton waited for several years before acting on his campaign rhetoric calling for a more forceful approach. Once Clinton finally decided to authorize air strikes against the Bosnian Serbs, the Congress chose not to hold any votes

---

[37]James Lindsay, "Congress and the Use of Force in the Post–Cold War Era," in *The United States and the Use of Force in the Post–Cold War Era* (Washington, DC: The Aspen Institute, 1995), pp. 84–88.

[38]An attempt in the House to repeal the War Powers Resolution in the summer of 1995 failed by a vote of 201–217.

[39]Lindsay, "Congress and the Use of Force," pp. 82–83.

[40]See Robert Pastor, "The United States and the Americas: Unfilled Promise at the Century's Turn," in Lieber, ed., *Eagle Rules?*.

that might have challenged this action, but Clinton also sought congressional approval before deploying U.S. ground troops as peacekeepers in Bosnia.[41]

In Somalia, the Congress was moving to establish a time limit on the deployment of U.S. troops after eighteen Americans were killed in a firefight on October 3, 1993, but President Clinton preempted this by setting his own time limit for a withdrawal by March 31 of 1994.

In addition to these presidential efforts to preempt congressional criticism, presidential notifications to Congress on the use of force, consistent with the requirements of the War Powers Act, have often been more extensive than is commonly realized. The 1990–1991 Gulf crisis and War, which included many such notifications, illustrates this trend, as well as many other dimensions of the war powers issue.[42] After Iraq invaded Kuwait in August 1990, President Bush decided, after very little consultation with the Congress, to deploy over 200,000 U.S. troops to Saudi Arabia. Bush later decided in October, with no consultation of the Congress, to double the number of U.S. forces deployed in the region, shifting the U.S. capability and implicitly the mission from defending Saudi Arabia to retaking Kuwait. In this time period, the Congress had several tools at its disposal if it wished to exercise its war powers in ways that limited the use of U.S. forces. It could have cut off any funds for the deployment, for example, or voted to start the war powers "clock" to limit the duration of the deployment. The Congress instead quietly continued to authorize funds for the deployment, and the only substantial action it took was to hold hearings in December, under the auspices of Senator Sam Nunn's Armed Services Committee, on whether continued economic sanctions on Iraq might be preferable to the use of force.[43] In the meantime, President Bush and administration officials insisted they had sufficient authority to use force even without a vote of approval from the congress. It was only after the UN had already voted to authorize force and set a deadline of January 15, 1991, and after opinion polls showed that a solid majority of the U.S. public wanted the Congress to vote on the use of force, that the administration finally requested a vote and that the Congress held one, approving on January 12 the prospective use of force. By that time, if the Congress had voted against the use of force, it would have appeared to undermine U.S. diplomacy, U.S. troops in the field, and the UN. The Congress's deference in this case is consistent with the general pattern since World War Two, whereby the Congress has been likely to take a clear

[41]Ryan Hendrickson, "War Powers, Bosnia, and the 104th Congress," *Political Science Quarterly*, Vol. 113, No. 2 (Summer 1998): 241–258. In the end, Hendrickson notes, both the House and the Senate passed resolutions expressing support for U.S. troops in Bosnia, but not necessarily Clinton's policies there, which Clinton treated as sufficient approval.

[42]On presidential notifications to Congress regarding the use of force in the Gulf War and other conflicts, see Donald Westerfield, *War Powers: The President, the Congress, and the Question of War* (Westport, CT: Praeger Press, 1996).

[43]At the same time, congressional resolutions criticizing U.S. allies for not contributing more to the operations in the Gulf greatly helped the Bush administration in its successful efforts to increase these allies' contributions. See Andrew Bennett, "Sheriff of the Posse: American Leadership in the Desert Storm Coalition," in Andrew Bennett, Joseph Lepgold, and Danny Unger, eds., *Friends in Need: Burden Sharing in the Gulf War* (New York: St. Martin's Press, 1997), pp. 37–68.

stand only when large numbers of troops are involved, the conflict in question is likely to last more than a few weeks, and there is ample time to deliberate.[44]

In contrast, the 1999 conflict that arose from Serbia's repression of Albanians in Kosovo indicates how much more constrained Clinton was in exercising war powers in 1999 than Bush had been in 1990–1991. The House voted by 219–191 on March 11 to authorize a U.S. contribution to a NATO peacekeeping force in Kosovo if an agreement could be reached with Serbia. When the negotiations with Serbia ended without agreement, Clinton engaged in intensive consultations with dozens of members of Congress on the possible use of force. To win support for air strikes, administration spokespersons indicated that U.S. ground troops would not be introduced into Kosovo without a prior peacekeeping agreement with Serbia. With this reassurance, the Senate adopted a resolution on March 23, by a 58–41 vote, supporting the use of air and missile strikes against Serbia. On March 24, the House passed by 424–1 its by now customary resolution expressing support for U.S. troops but neither endorsing nor opposing U.S. policies. On that same day, the U.S. and NATO began air strikes against Serbia. At the same time, U.S. aircraft were ordered not to fly below 15,000 feet over Kosovo, a step that minimized the risk of U.S. casualties and hence of public and congressional opposition, but that also decreased the effectiveness of air strikes against ground targets. For the next several weeks, U.S. air strikes successfully hit stationary Serbian targets and did not incur any U.S. combat casualties, but they did less damage to mobile Serbian forces in Kosovo and produced little indication that Serbia was willing to concede. Meanwhile, the Congress avoided any votes on whether to continue, escalate, limit, or end the use of force.

Up to this point, the Congress's behavior was fairly typical of its previous efforts to avoid a direct confrontation with the president over war powers and to preserve its flexibility to praise or condemn the use of force after the fact. However, the House then took a step that it has traditionally gone to great lengths to avoid: voting directly on the continuation of a military mission at the same time that U.S. troops were engaged in active combat. On April 28, the House defeated a resolution calling for the withdrawal of U.S. troops by a vote of 139–290, but it came to a 213–213 tie on a resolution echoing the Senate's support of the air campaign. Also, although Clinton publicly pledged to seek prior congressional approval of any deployment of ground troops to Kosovo, the House voted by 249–180 to require that he do so. Administration officials warned, with less effect on the Congress than in the past, that such votes during an ongoing operation could undermine the credibility of U.S. policy, and they were quite critical of the results. As White House spokesman Jake Siewert argued, "The House today voted no on going forward, no on going back and they tied on standing still."[45] Within days, however, the House

---

[44]For a similar view, see David Auerswald and Peter Cowhey, "Ballotbox Diplomacy: The War Powers Resolution and the Use of Force," *International Studies Quarterly*, Vol. 41, No. 3 (September 1997): 523.

[45]Charles Babington and Juliet Eilperin, "Clinton Signals Raids May Last 3 More Months; House Votes to Require Assent for Ground Troops," *The Washington Post*, April 29, 1999, p. A1. William

also approved a $13 billion increase in the defense budget, including funds to pay for the military operations in Kosovo.

These votes left the administration's continuing use of force in an ambiguous position. The president was for the first time using force when a vote in Congress to authorize that use of force had failed to pass, in this instance on a tie vote.[46] On the other hand, the Senate had already voted to support the use of air power, and both houses soon approved funds for the military operations. The Senate, however, rejected a resolution in early May that would have gone beyond its previous support of air strikes and approved the use of "all necessary means" to win Serbia's withdrawal from Kosovo. The ambiguity grew when the bombing extended past May 25, which would have been the sixty-day time limit under the war powers clock. This awkward situation was ultimately resolved weeks later, not by further congressional or presidential action, but by Serbia's capitulation to NATO's demand for the withdrawal of Serbian troops from Kosovo. On the whole, then, in order to maintain public and congressional approval of air strikes, Clinton consulted with the Congress prior to using force, tightly controlled U.S. military operations, and avoided the use of ground forces, even at the cost of less immediate or certain success in Kosovo. The result in Kosovo was more successful than most foreign policy experts anticipated, although it came at a high cost to the Albanians in Kosovo. At the same time, both Clinton and the Congress exercised their war powers more aggressively than in the past, setting precedents that might emerge again in future clashes over the use of force.

## THE TREATY RATIFICATION PROCESS

The constitutional requirement that the Senate ratify treaties by a two-thirds majority sets a difficult standard for presidents to meet, making treaties among the most vulnerable of foreign policy instruments in periods of congressional assertiveness. The recent record on treaties is mixed: some, including the START II arms control treaty and the NATO enlargement treaty, were popular with the public and won Senate approval by overwhelming majorities. Others, notably the Chemical Weapons Convention (CWC) and the Comprehensive Test Ban Treaty (CTBT), did not fare as well in the Senate despite substantial public and political support. On these treaties, the Senate Foreign Relations Committee proved very assertive in pushing its reservations or outright opposition.

---

Kristol, the editor of the conservative *Weekly Standard* and a former Bush administration official, also criticized the House votes, saying that the use of the War Powers Resolution, "legislation the Republicans have always despised, in order to cut off a military action that is under way and upon whose success American credibility depends, is really appalling, really irresponsible." Adam Clymer, "Surprise on Capitol Hill: No! And Then Billions," *The New York Times,* April 30, 1999, p. 14.

[46]For a view that emphasizes this fact and argues that President Clinton, rather than the congress, exercised his war powers in Kosovo even more assertively than his predecessors, see David Gray Adler, "The Clinton Theory of the War Power," *Presidential Studies Quarterly,* Vol. 30, No. 1 (March 2000): 155–168.

The CWC was negotiated and signed by the outgoing Bush administration and continued to have the public support of Bush and his top foreign policy officials after they left office. The treaty ran into difficulty, however, when the Clinton administration failed to give it high priority early on when the Democrats held the majority in the Senate. Once the administration finally presented the treaty to the Senate, Senate Foreign Relations Committee chair Jesse Helms refused to move the CWC (or START II or ambassadorial nominations) through his committee until the administration made concessions on his proposals for reorganizing the State Department and related agencies. The treaty, which continued to languish in Helms's committee for over three years, was finally voted upon in April 1997 only after the Republican Senate leadership under Senator Trent Lott took the unusual step of using a unanimous consent agreement to discharge the treaty from Helms's committee. As the price for Lott's and Helms's agreement to this procedure, the Clinton administration and its Senate allies not only agreed to Helms's proposals for restructuring the State Department but also acquiesced to twenty-eight conditions that Helms attached to the treaty. The administration also agreed to having the Senate hold votes on five additional Helms amendments (all eventually rejected by the Senate) that would have constrained the treaty even more severely. After these concessions, the treaty passed by a vote of 74–26 on April 24, 1997.[47]

Similarly, Helms refused for many months to hold hearings on the CTBT, which prohibits signatories from testing nuclear weapons. In contrast to the CWC case, Lott did not raise the prospect that the Senate might circumvent Helms's committee and bring the treaty directly to the floor for a vote, even though opinion polls showed that it had the support of 70 to 80 percent of the public.[48] With growing pressure to address the treaty after nuclear tests by India and Pakistan, Helms finally agreed to hold hearings on the treaty in the fall of 1999. Despite the long delay leading up to the hearings, however, the White House failed to make an early and high-profile effort to win public and congressional support for the treaty in preparation for the hearings. In the hearings, Helms raised concerns over the reliability of the stockpile of U.S. nuclear weapons and the ability to verify whether other states were abstaining from nuclear tests. With conflicting expert testimony on these issues, and a belated and ineffective lobbying effort by the administration, it quickly became apparent that the treaty would not win the 67 votes needed for ratification. The Clinton administration and Senator Lott proved unable to agree on terms for postponing a full Senate vote on the treaty, however, and the treaty went down to defeat by a vote of 51–48 on October 13, 1999. This failure led to international criticism of the United States for reversing forty years of efforts by administrations of both parties to achieve a test ban. It also prompted Clinton to unleash his harshest rhetorical criticism of his entire term of congressional action on foreign policy, calling the Senate vote "partisan politics of the

[47]Erik Leklem, "Senate Gives Advice and Consent: U.S. Becomes Original CWC Party," *Arms Control Today,* Vol. 27, No. 2 (April 1997):32–36.

[48]Daryl Kimball, "Holding the CTBT Hostage in the Senate: The 'Stealth' Strategy of Helms and Lott," *Arms Control Today,* Vol. 28, No. 5 (June–July 1998): 3–9.

worst kind" and accusing the treaty's opponents of exhibiting "signs of a new isolationism."[49]

# CONCLUSIONS

The American public's post–Cold War apathetic internationalism and its focus on domestic and intermestic issues, combined with the differing constituencies of the presidency and the Congress, have led to an increase in congressional involvement in intermestic issues and, to a lesser extent, in decisions on the use of force. This greater congressional role has at times helped win additional concessions from U.S. negotiating partners and international institutions, as in the NAFTA agreement and allied burden-sharing in the Gulf War. The Congress has also readily contributed to successful foreign policies when the goals of the most powerful interest groups have coincided largely with presidential views of the public interest, as in the cases of NATO enlargement and PNTR with China. Yet when partisan purposes or interest group pressures have propelled congressional or presidential action on foreign policies, as in the failure to renew fast-track authority, the delays in IMF and UN funding, the defeat of the CTBT, the collapse of the BRAC process, and the capricious treatment of foreign policy nominees, the result is often detrimental to U.S. interests and to America's reputation and credibility as a world leader. The Congress's structure has made it somewhat more susceptible to interest group pressures, but neither branch has been above partisanship. The resulting process has not taken full advantage of the comparative strengths of either branch of government.

Increased congressional assertiveness on foreign policy has been due only in part to potentially short-lived developments such as the recent prevalence of divided governments. The lack of an overarching threat has reduced the pressure on the two branches to work together. Globalization has given more actors a stake in foreign policy, and interest groups of all kinds are more active than ever before. Demographic changes have reduced the pool of foreign policy experience in the congress, where opinions are partisan and ideologically polarized. The media are more pervasive and uninhibited than ever before, and the foreign affairs budget and the foreign relations committees in Congress are in a prolonged state of disrepair. The new Bush administration will still have to confront all of these difficulties even though the Republican Party holds a majority in the House and can break tie votes in an evenly divided Senate.

In view of these constraints, success in working with U.S. allies and building international institutions will require the new Bush administration to moderate the campaign rhetoric critical of both. For example, Colin Powell's statement accepting the nomination to be Secretary of State was rightly less critical of U.S. allies' peacekeeping efforts in the Balkans than other Bush advisers had been during the

---

[49]Craig Cerniello, "Senate Rejects Comprehensive Test Ban Treaty," *Arms Control Today,* Vol. 29, No. 6 (September–October 1999): 28.

campaign. The new administration will also have to be careful not to create unrealistic expectations about what kind of missile defenses can be achieved, at what expense, and with what international implications. On this and many other issues, including relations with Russia and China, the role of the UN and the IMF, and the defense budget, the Bush administration is likely to have a difficult time squaring international realities with the views of the more conservative members of its own party, the Democrats in Congress, and prominent interest groups. If President Bush sides too closely with the conservative Republican Congress on these issues, not only will he miss an opportunity for building international institutions at a time of American preeminence, but also he will face strong international opposition and perhaps even an electoral setback should an international economic or security crisis awaken the public from its apathetic internationalism.

Whether the Bush administration and the new Congress are more successful at managing their relations on foreign policy depends on process as well as substance. The sine qua non of success, emphasized by both Democratic foreign policy leaders and advisers to George W. Bush, is consultation.[50] The White House should undertake regular and institutionalized consultations on overarching foreign policy and national security issues with congressional leaders of both parties and with the relevant committees, in addition to specific consultations on immediate crises and regional and functional issues. Consultations with the Democratic minority will be particularly important in view of the narrow divide in Congress and the contested nature of the presidential election. New presidents, including George W. Bush, invariably promise to consult broadly and deeply with the Congress and the opposition party, yet none so far has adequately followed through. The White House cannot afford to wait until the last minute or until issues reach a crisis, as the Clinton White House did all too often, in order to build a consensus in the Congress on trade, treaties, appointments, or the use of force. The congressional leadership also needs to work to attract more moderate and effective leaders to its foreign affairs committees, and it must also work to get involved earlier and to share responsibility for decisions on the use of force. Both branches need to renew and expand processes, such as fast-track trade procedures and the BRAC commission, that shield them from factional politics. Finally, the most immediate challenge for George W. Bush and the Congress is to streamline and depoliticize the confirmation process.

The Bush Administration's interactions with Congress in the first few months of 2001 indicated that the two branches were able to manage their relations fairly well on these fronts, but they also highlighted the fault lines for the more difficult interbranch conflicts that may lie ahead. The top foreign policy nominees were quickly confirmed with little controversy. President Bush and Secretary of Defense Donald Rumsfeld also encountered only muted congressional criticism when they announced that there would be no sharp increase in the defense budget until after a thorough review of U.S. defense strategies and forces. Bush was even fairly suc-

[50]Hamilton, remarks to the Trilateral Commission; Robert Zoellick, "Congress and the Making of U.S. Foreign Policy," *Survival,* Vol. 41, No. 4 (Winter 1999–2000): 36.

cessful in restraining the Congress from escalating the confrontation with China in April over the collision of a U.S. EP-3E aircraft and a Chinese F-8 fighter and the subsequent detention of the U.S. aircraft's crew. The Congress's simmering anger over the incident, and its implicit threats to retaliate against trade ties with China and China's bid to host the 2008 Olympics, helped the President play out a "good cop-bad cop" strategy that resulted in the release of the U.S. air crew. On both the defense budget and the crisis with China, the Bush administration benefitted from the fact that the strongest potential opposition in Congress was from conservative Republicans, who muted their criticism of the President in ways that would have been unlikely had a Democratic president held the defense budget steady and skirted close to an apology to China. Similarly, President Bush and Secretary of State Powell stand a good chance of winning their proposed 14 percent increase in the State Department's budget, which would have been difficult for a Democratic administration to achieve.

On these and other foreign and defense policies, however, more controversial issues lie ahead that may strain the limits of interbranch cooperation even in the absence of a divided government. More controversial nominees slated for the second tier foreign policy jobs may not fare as well as the top appointees in the confirmation process. The toughest battles on the defense budget and the hardest lobbying by the service branches, defense contractors, and their allies in Congress will ensue once the defense review is complete and its associated budget goes before the congress. On China, difficult decisions on trade, human rights, and arms sales to Taiwan will be even harder to manage in the wake of the aircraft crisis. Finally, the State Department needs more than just a one-time infusion of resources to bring its technology up to the demands of the information age, and it remains to be seen if the Congress will provide extended support for higher spending. Interbranch cooperation on these and other issues will be crucial to success on longer-term foreign policy concerns. The United States can hardly expect to build international institutions and rules, despite its enormous material power, if it cannot first get its own nest in order.

# 4

# The United States and Europe
## From Primacy to Partnership?

### IVO H. DAALDER
The Brookings Institution

The 1990s demonstrated that the United States remained in Europe—and else-where—the "indispensable power," in Madeleine Albright's infelicitous, though accurate, phrase.[1] In Europe, American power and influence was central in key ways. The United States propagated the central vision guiding U.S. and European policy for the continent in the aftermath of the Cold War—to build a Europe that is "whole and free" (in President George H. W. Bush's words), "peaceful, undivided, and democratic" (as President Bill Clinton would say).[2] It developed the strategy for turning that vision into reality—a strategy that emphasized the need to promote a stronger Europe, transform NATO, engage Russia, and bring peace and stability to the Balkans. And it proved crucial to the successful implementation of the strategy throughout the 1990s. For all these reasons, the United States was the indispensable power in Europe.

The central question confronting U.S.-European relations in the immediate future is whether the United States will remain indispensable in the new century.

Ivo H. Daalder is a senior fellow in Foreign Policy Studies at the Brookings Institution. He served as director for European affairs on President Clinton's National Security Council from 1995–96. He is the author, most recently, of *Getting to Dayton: The Making of the America's Bosnia Policy* (Washington, DC: The Brookings Institution Press, 2000); coauthor with Michael O'Hanlon of *Winning Ugly: NATO's War to Save Kosovo* (Washington, DC: The Brookings Institution Press, 2000); and coeditor with Frances Burwell of *The United States and Europe in the Global Arena* (New York: St. Martin's Press, 1999).

[1]This phrase was first uttered by Madeleine Albright following her appointment as secretary of state in December 1996. See "Remarks by the President in Announcement of New Cabinet Officers" (White House, Office of the Press Secretary, December 5, 1996).

[2]See President George Bush, "Remarks to the Citizens in Mainz, Federal Republic of Germany" (May 31, 1989), available at http://bushlibrary.tamu.edu/papers/1989/89053104.html; and President Bill Clinton, "Statement by the President" (The White House, Office of the Press Secretary, October 31, 1995).

Although an alternative center of power capable of either challenging or supplanting the United States is unlikely to emerge any time soon, a decade of unbridled leadership has produced costs at home and abroad that do call into question the sustainability of this role in the long run.

In Europe, there is growing resentment of American dominance and European dependence thereon, spurring greater efforts to enhance Europe's capacity to control events and take action on its own. Recent efforts to supplant European economic integration and long-standing political coordination with a security and defense dimension are an important indication of that growing resentment. At home, there is growing political resentment (especially on Capitol Hill) at having to bear what many regard as the excessive costs of leadership, particularly when doing so does not garner the degree of support or respect for U.S. policy preferences that many expect. This sentiment is reflected in the sometimes heated rhetoric concerning comparatively minor trade disputes over issues ranging from bananas to airplane hush kits. It is also apparent in the widespread congressional unease, echoed by Texas Governor George W. Bush during the 2000 presidential campaign, about the continued American military role in the Balkans—a role many on the Hill and elsewhere believe to be necessary principally because the European allies are not carrying their fair share of the global security burden.[3]

The growing opposition to the dominant American role in Europe at home and abroad suggests the need to rebalance the U.S.-European strategic relationship—away from U.S. primacy toward a genuine strategic partnership. Achieving such a rebalancing in the relationship will not be easy. It will require major adjustments on the part of Europe and the United States alike. Europe must increase its capacity for joint action—especially in the military field. The decision to add a defense dimension to cooperative efforts in the European Union (EU) is a good start, although much depends on the follow-through. Europeans must also demonstrate a willingness to carry more of the burdens not just in Europe (where they have done a fair amount) but increasingly beyond Europe as well. Doing this will require Europeans to extend their strategic vision beyond the geographic restrictions of Europe to include much of the rest of world—and not simply in terms of economic opportunity and development needs (though these will remain important) but also in terms of overall security and political requirements. Finally, the relationship can be rebalanced only if the United States demonstrates a willingness to accord Europe a greater—if not an equal—voice in their relationship. Too often, still, Washington's approach to European allies is, if not condescending, at the very least paternal rather than brotherly. That attitude will have to change if the relationship with Europe is to be transformed into a partnership of equals.

Together, these three adjustments represent a very tall order, indeed. Success in the effort to rebalance relations will be difficult to achieve. But there may be no real alternative.

[3]For an evaluation, see Ivo H. Daalder and Michael E. O'Hanlon, "The United States and the Balkans: There to Stay," *Washington Quarterly*, Vol. 23, No 4 (Autumn 2000): 157–170.

# THE INDISPENSABLE POWER

During forty-plus years of the Cold War in Europe, the U.S.-led West confronted the Soviet-led East over the question of Europe's future—whether it be Western and democratic, Eastern and communist, or divided along the iron curtain that had risen in the wake of the allied victory over Germany in World War Two. Because the continent's division was both cause and consequence of the Cold War, the conflict could not be ended, in any real sense, until Europe was once again "whole and free." Yet, although this conclusion remained an article of faith of American and, indeed, of European and NATO policy, with each passing decade of Cold War confrontation, the status quo was increasingly viewed not only as an acceptable condition but also as the most natural one.

## The Bush Administration

The perception of Europe's condition—of what was and was not possible—began to change in the 1980s, as a new regime in Moscow, led by Soviet President Mikhail Gorbachev, began to challenge many of the fundamental assumptions of Soviet society and behavior with its policies of perestroika and glasnost. All of a sudden, the European status quo appeared neither natural nor acceptable. But while most Western officials (including, notably, President Ronald Reagan and his Secretary of State, George Shultz) focused on the winds of change emanating from Moscow, the true focal point of action was centered west of the Soviet Union, in the Eastern Europe that Moscow had long dominated.[4] The Bush administration understood this situation almost from the outset of its tenure. A central conclusion emerging out of the "strategic review" undertaken by Bush's National Security Council (NSC) staff in early 1989 was that U.S. and Western efforts ought to focus first and foremost on Eastern Europe—and its liberalization.[5] As Bush declared in April 1989, "the Cold War began in Eastern Europe, and if it is to end, it will end in this crucible of world conflict." [6]

Of course, Bush's was not a new thought. There had been the "roll back" policy championed by John Foster Dulles in the 1950s; the German push for *Wandel durch Annäherung* ("change through rapprochement"), championed by Egon Bahr and ultimately adopted in the form of a new Ostpolitik in the 1960s; and the different types of détente supported by Nixon and Kissinger, and, subsequently, more

---

[4]On Reagan's policy toward Gorbachev's Soviet Union, see especially Don Oberdorfer, *The Turn: From the Cold War to a New Era, 1983–1990: The United States and the Soviet Union* (New York: Poseidon Press, 1991); and George Shultz, *Turmoil and Triumph: My Years in the State Department* (New York: Scribners, 1993), chapter 25ff. On developments in Eastern Europe, see Charles Gati, *The Bloc That Failed: Soviet–East European Relations in Transition* (Bloomington: Indiana University Press, 1990).

[5]See, especially, Robert Hutchings, *American Diplomacy and the End of the Cold War: An Insider's Account of U.S. Policy in Europe, 1989–92* (Baltimore: Johns Hopkins University Press, 1997), pp. 35–40.

[6]See President George Bush, "Remarks to Citizens in Hamtramck, Michigan" (April 17, 1989), available at http://bushlibrary.tamu.edu/papers/1989/89041700.html.

forcefully by America's European allies in the 1970s. But Bush tried to take the focus away from changing the Soviet Union as a means of ending the Cold War (which had been the aim of America's containment policy), to changing Europe—and thereby promoting change within the Soviet Union itself. More ambitiously still, the strategy was, Bush said in May 1989, to move "beyond containment" and, instead, to "seek the integration of the Soviet Union into the community of nations." The goal, in other words, was for "a Europe that is whole and free."[7]

The revolutionary events of the second half of 1989 were to move Bush's pronouncements from the realm of rhetoric to that of reality. With the fall of communist regimes in Hungary, Poland, East Germany, Czechoslovakia, Bulgaria, and Romania, the USSR's erstwhile Warsaw Pact partners were all of a sudden confronted with the possibility that their peoples might be able to determine their own destiny. A Europe whole and free—with a newly united Germany at its core—was no longer the stuff of dreams but had increasingly become a real possibility, one that the peaceful disintegration of the Soviet Union two years later would make still more real.

## The Clinton Administration

The Clinton administration inherited a Europe rich in possibilities but only very marginally prepared to seize any of them. To the contrary, while the overriding danger of the Cold War confrontation had disappeared, Europe faced challenges on multiple fronts. In the West, an economic downturn had left the European Union in a state of "eurosclerosis," marked by high unemployment, exploding budget deficits, and meager (if not negative) economic growth. In the southeast, the multinational federation of Yugoslavia had imploded in a violent chasm brought about by former communist leaders using destructive nationalism as a means to hold onto power. In the center and eastern parts of Europe, the original euphoria brought about by the smell of freedom soon gave way to a realization that the economic, social, and political transitions necessary to join the rest of Europe would involve much hardship and sacrifice. And in the former Soviet Union, including Russia, the years of deception and outright lying and decades of economic mismanagement had left the countries in a state of economic and social disrepair that would take a generation or more to turn around. In other words, Europe in 1993 might have been free (in the sense that most of its people were no longer oppressed politically) and whole (at least in terms of the continent's shared misery), but it was hardly peaceful, undivided, or even very democratic.

The challenge facing the Clinton administration and its European allies was to turn this situation around—and to do so in a holistic rather than a piecemeal fashion. Although the Clinton administration was often accused of lacking an organizing vision for its foreign policy and, instead, conducting policy in an ad hoc and

---

[7]See President George Bush, "Remarks at the Texas A&M University Commencement Ceremony in College Station" (May 12, 1989), available at http://bushlibrary.tamu.edu/papers/1989/89051201.html.

reactive fashion, these charges have little merit, at least as far as Europe is concerned.[8] Not only did the administration lay out a clear vision and strategy for achieving that vision early in its tenure, but it also then, for the most part, pursued that strategy with vigor and energy.[9]

The essence of Clinton's European strategy was to create a Europe that is peaceful, undivided, and democratic. As Clinton put it in first laying out his vision: "We must build a new security for Europe; the old security was based on the defense of our bloc against another bloc. The new security must be found in Europe's integration—an integration of security forces, of market economies, of national democracies."[10] Not only would fulfilling this vision be good for Europe, but it would also serve two key American interests. First, a united Europe that was both democratic and prosperous was unlikely to be the source of the instability, conflict, and war's that had marked much of the twentieth century—wars that had kept the United States engaged at great cost and sacrifice for much of the previous one-hundred years. Second, a strong Europe at peace with itself was more likely to be a faithful and full partner of the United States in addressing the many challenges and opportunities around the world. U.S. engagement in Europe even after the Cold War had ended was not, therefore, a measure of altruism; in fact, a Europe at peace, united, and democratic would serve real American interests.

How was this vision to be achieved? From the outset, the Clinton administration pursued a four-pronged strategy to help create an undivided, peaceful, and democratic Europe: promoting a stronger Europe, transforming NATO, engaging Russia, and bringing peace and stability to the Balkans and other regions in conflict.

• *Promoting a Stronger Europe.* For decades, America's Europe policy has shifted uneasily between supporting European integration as a means to lessen burdens on the United States and fearing that a united Europe would be a competitor of the United States and the Atlantic institutions that it dominated. This tendency changed under the Clinton administration, which unreservedly supported the creation of a stronger Europe. It looked to Europe as a partner for addressing a host of challenges and opportunities within and beyond Europe. And it strongly supported further European integration—including in the defense and security sphere, which had long been seen by Washington as the sole preserve of NATO.

The U.S.-EU relationship that was inaugurated by the Transatlantic Declaration of November 1990 became institutionalized during the 1990s through a series of biennial meetings conducted from the presidential level on down. These meet-

---

[8]For one such indictment, see William G. Hyland, *Clinton's World: Remaking American Foreign Policy* (Westport, CT: Praeger, 1999).

[9]The basic construct of both can be found in two major speeches: Anthony Lake, "From Containment to Enlargement" (Washington, DC: Johns Hopkins University, School of Advanced International Studies, September 21, 1993); and President Bill Clinton, "Remarks by the President to the Multinational Audience of Future Leaders of Europe" (Brussels, Belgium: The White House, Office of the Press Secretary, January 9, 1994).

[10]Clinton, "Remarks by the President to the Multinational Audience of Future Leaders of Europe."

ings proved to be useful for addressing issues of common concern in a cooperative and mutually beneficial manner—issues that ranged from data privacy and the impact of biotechnology to Balkan stability and African debt relief. [11] In addition, the meetings provided a regular forum for managing transatlantic policy differences over trade, economic sanctions, and other issues that, if left untended, could have negatively affected the overall relationship. As one example, at the U.S.-EU summit in Britain in May 1998, a solution was found to the highly contentious issue of unilateral U.S. sanctions and their extraterritorial application. [12]

The United States also endorsed continued European integration, including in the economic and security spheres. As President Clinton said in June 2000, "America must continue to support Europe's most ambitious unification efforts." [13] Although some fretted that economic and monetary union (EMU) and the issuance of a single European currency might pose a threat to the singular position of the American greenback, official Washington welcomed and supported the introduction of the "euro" in 1999. [14] The United States subsequently even intervened in financial markets to buttress the new currency's value following its precipitous slide against the dollar. [15] The administration was initially less enthusiastic about the prospect of the EU taking on a defense and security policy role, fearing that this might undermine the long-standing primacy of NATO. [16] But once the relationship between the budding European defense arm and the Atlantic Alliance was spelled out more clearly—including agreement that the EU would act in the defense field only when

[11]For an overview of these efforts, see Anthony Gardner, *A New Era in US-EU Relations? The Clinton Administration and the New Transatlantic Agenda* (Aldershot, UK: Avebury, 1997). For a summary of cooperative efforts, see "Report of the Senior Level Group," EU-U.S. Summit, Queluz, May 31, 2000, available at http://www.eurunion.org/partner/summit/0005sum.htm.

[12]James Bennet, "To Clear Air with Europe, U.S. Waives Some Sanctions," *New York Times,* May 19, 1998, p. A6.

[13]President Bill Clinton, "Remarks Upon Being Presented the International Charlemagne Prize 2000" (Aachen, Germany: The White House, Office of the Press Secretary, June 2, 2000). See also Strobe Talbott, "The U.S., the EU, and Our Common Challenges," Remarks to the U.S.-EU Conference "Bridging the Atlantic: People-to-People Links" (Washington, DC: May 6, 1997).

[14]See Stuart Eizenstat, "The Euro: Implications for the United States and Transatlantic Relations," Address to Conference on the European Union (Baltimore, Maryland: Johns Hopkins University, May 4, 1998); and Lawrence H. Summers, "Transatlantic Implications of the Euro: Global Financial Stability," Remarks to the Transatlantic Business Dialogue (Charlotte, N.C.: U.S. Treasury, Office of Public Affairs, November 6, 1998). For criticism of the EMU and the euro, see Martin Feldstein, "EMU and International Conflict," *Foreign Affairs,* Vol. 76 (November–December 1997): 60–73; Jeffry Frieden, "The Euro: Who Wins? Who Loses?" *Foreign Policy,* No. 112 (Fall 1998): 24–40; and Charles W. Calomiris, "The Impending Collapse of the European Monetary Union," *Cato Journal,* Vol. 18 (Winter 1999): 445–452.

[15]Edmund L. Andrews and Joseph Kahn, "Central Banks Move to Rescue an Ailing Euro," *New York Times,* September 23, 2000, p. A1.

[16]See, for example, Madeleine K. Albright, "The Right Balance Will Secure Nato's Future," *Financial Times,* December 7, 1998, p. 22; Alexander Vershbow, "ESDI: Berlin, St. Malo and Beyond" (Paris: Western European Union Institute for Security Studies, January 28, 1999); and Strobe Talbott, "A New NATO for a New Century," Address at the Royal United Services Institute (London: March 10, 1999).

NATO "as a whole is not engaged"[17]—Washington fully backed the creation of a European security and defense policy apart from NATO. As Defense Secretary William Cohen told his NATO colleagues in October 2000, "it is right and natural that an increasingly integrated Europe seeks to develop its own security and defense position: we agree with this goal—not grudgingly, not with resignation, but with wholehearted conviction."[18]

• *Transforming NATO.* The Clinton administration labored successfully to transform an alliance originally created as a bulwark for defending a weak and divided Europe against an overwhelming Soviet military and political threat into an institution that could support efforts to make the vision of a peaceful, undivided, and democratic Europe a reality. It did so by promoting NATO as the primary security instrument for extending the stability that its members had long enjoyed to the rest of Europe. As Clinton put it in 1999, "We want all of Europe to have what America helped build in Western Europe—a community that upholds common standards of human rights, where people have the confidence and security to invest in the future, where nations cooperate to make war unthinkable."[19] Two key elements lay at the heart of that effort: encouraging as many of the European countries that were not members to take part in NATO's efforts to promote security throughout Europe (up to and including offering membership in NATO) and changing the alliance's guiding mission from collective defense of its members' territory to providing security for all of Europe.[20]

The single most important element in the Clinton strategy was the effort to use the promise of NATO membership as a positive inducement for countries in Central and Eastern Europe to make the difficult economic, political, and military transitions to becoming open, democratic, and market-based societies. In principle, EU enlargement could have fulfilled this purpose, but its members proved neither willing nor able to take the lead. In contrast, the United States and, over time, the rest of NATO were determined to open the Alliance's doors to new members. The basic U.S. decision in favor of enlargement was made in late 1993, as the Clinton administration made preparations to attend the president's first NATO summit in January 1994.21 There, the allies promulgated the Partnership for Peace, which, as

[17]"Washington Summit Communiqué," issued by the Heads of State and Government participating in the meeting of the North Atlantic Council in Washington, D.C., on 24th April 1999, available at http://www.nato.int/docu/pr/1999/p99–064e.htm.

[18]William S. Cohen, "Remarks at the Informal NATO Defense Ministerial Meeting" (Birmingham, United Kingdom: October 10, 2000), p. 2.

[19]President Bill Clinton, "Remarks on Foreign Policy" (San Francisco: The White House, Office of the Press Secretary, February 26, 1999).

[20]Cf. Ivo H. Daalder, "NATO in the 21st Century: What Purpose? What Missions?" (Washington, DC: The Brookings Institution, April 1999); and Ivo H. Daalder, "NATO At Fifty: The Summit and Beyond," *Brookings Policy Brief,* No. 48 (April 1999).

[21]The U.S. decision on NATO enlargement is brilliantly recounted in James Goldgeier, *Not Whether, But When: The American Decision to Enlarge NATO* (Washington, DC: The Brookings Institution Press, 1999).

Clinton announced, "will advance a process of evolution for NATO's formal enlargement. It looks to the day when NATO will take on new members who assume the Alliance's full responsibilities."[22]

It would take three more years, until the July 1997 NATO summit in Madrid, for the Alliance formally to invite the Czech Republic, Hungary, and Poland to join the organization in March 1999. At the same time, NATO reaffirmed what it had said in Brussels in early 1994—that the door to membership would remain open to any European country that wanted to join and that met the criteria for doing so.[23] The NATO policy of enlargement—which offered the prospect of joining NATO, the EU, and the West more generally—has been a major reason why the countries of Eastern and Central Europe remain willing and able to exhort their peoples to make the sacrifices necessary for a successful transition to functioning market democracies. As President Clinton put it just days before NATO welcomed the first new members, "we must keep NATO's doors open to new democratic members, so that other nations will have an incentive to deepen their democracies."[24]

The second element of NATO's transformation emerged more subtly and slowly. It was only in 1999 that the allies agreed that NATO's primary purpose was not only to defend its members' territory but also increasingly to ensure the security of Europe as a whole. As the new strategic concept, adopted at NATO's fiftieth anniversary summit meeting in Washington, stated: "The Alliance has striven since its inception to secure a just and lasting peaceful order in Europe. It will continue to do so. The achievement of this aim can be put at risk by crisis and conflict affecting the security of the Euro-Atlantic area. The Alliance therefore not only ensures the defence of its members but contributes to peace and stability in this region."[25] This formal commitment codified what had already become a practical reality—NATO's primary focus, if not its main mission, since 1995 had been to stabilize the Balkans. Increasingly, therefore, NATO has come to regard threats to peace and stability anywhere in Europe as issues that are of direct interest to the Alliance and even as possible reasons for intervention, since no other security organization (be it the UN or OSCE) would prove able to do so.

• *Engaging Russia.* Together with its European allies, the Clinton administration made a conscious effort to approach Russia not as a potential future enemy but as a likely partner in the joint enterprise of building a Europe that is undivided, peaceful, and democratic. That effort concentrated on three elements: dealing coop-

---

[22]Clinton, "Remarks to the Multinational Audience of Future Leaders of Europe."

[23]"Madrid Declaration on Euro-Atlantic Security and Cooperation," Issued by the Heads of State and Government, Meeting of the North Atlantic Council, Madrid, Spain, July 8, 1997, para. 8.

[24]Clinton, "Remarks on Foreign Policy."

[25]"The Alliance's Strategic Concept," approved by the Heads of State and Government participating in the meeting of the North Atlantic Council in Washington, D.C., on 23rd and 24th April 1999, para. 6, available at http://www.nato.int/docu/pr/1999/p99–065e.htm.

eratively with the Cold War military residue left over by the Soviet Union, particularly with regard to safeguarding Russia's large WMD programs; promoting democracy and economic development; and keeping Russia engaged in, or at least abreast of, other aspects of U.S. policy toward Europe. In contrast to the other elements of U.S. strategy toward Europe, the jury is still out on whether these efforts have been successful or, as some have claimed, they have largely proven a failure.[26] At the same time, there is little doubt that success in forging a peaceful, undivided, and democratic Europe requires the active engagement of Russia as a partner rather than as an actual or a potential adversary.

The most important element of U.S. policy toward Russia in the 1990s concerned the development of a cooperative effort to reduce the threat posed by the large Soviet arsenal of nuclear, chemical, and biological weapons, including their means of production. From 1991 to 2001, the United States spent about $3.0 billion in an effort to assist Russia with implementing the provisions of the strategic arms treaties, enhancing accounting and control of nuclear weapons and fissile materials, eliminating biological and chemical weapons programs, preventing the proliferation of Russian materials and expertise, and undertaking military reductions and reform.[27] Although much still remains to be done in curtailing the WMD threat in and from Russia—and Moscow's behavior in some instances (notably with regard to assisting Iran) still leaves much to be desired—the totality of the U.S. effort has been significant. Nuclear weapons that were deployed outside Russia by the Soviet Union were transferred back without incident, hundreds of tons of fissile materials have been safeguarded and rendered less dangerous, and thousands of nuclear weapons and delivery systems have been destroyed. Much of this effort, moreover, was the product of cooperative U.S.-Russian endeavors.

The second major effort of U.S. policy toward Russia was to assist Moscow in making the political and economic changes necessary to strengthen democracy and promote the emergence of a market-based economy. Here progress is far from ideal. To be sure, Russians have gone to the polls three times to elect a parliament and twice to vote for president in elections that were both free and fair. Russia still enjoys a free press, vigorous debate, and an open political system. And a market-based system is slowly emerging from the state-controlled command economy that dominated life for decades.[28] Nevertheless, progress in Russia has been slow, and it is by no means certain that the democratic experiment will succeed. Vladimir Putin's rise to power has been disquieting, and so has his conduct since coming to power. In contrast to his predecessor, Putin has ruled as autocratically as possible and as democratically as neces-

---

[26]See Gail Lapidus, "Transforming Russia: American Policy in the 1990s," in this volume.

[27]Amy F. Woolf, *Nunn-Lugar Cooperative Threat Reduction Program: Issues for Congress* (Washington: Congressional Research Service, March 23, 2001), p. 29

[28]Cf. Michael McFaul, "Getting Russia Right," *Foreign Policy*, No. 117 (Winter 1999–2000): 58–73.

sary. He has tried to muzzle important media outlets and has conducted a brutal war in Chechnya that has left hundreds of thousands dead, wounded, and homeless. And much of the economy remains in the hands of a few powerful yet corrupt oligarchs. Although there is no clear alternative to engaging this Russia and encouraging the necessary political, economic, military, and social reforms, engagement alone is not likely to produce the needed change.

Finally, the Clinton administration has tried to make Russia a partner in forging the new Europe, notably in the Balkans but also as part of NATO's transformation. Along with Britain, France, Germany, the United States, and (later) Italy, Russia participates in the Contact Group, which was established in mid-1994 to develop common approaches to ending the war in Bosnia and used later to address the conflicts in Kosovo and the region more broadly. Russia had a seat at the negotiating table prior to and at Dayton, where it had as much influence on the proceedings as the European representatives, which admittedly was not all that much. Russia also fully participated in the design and implementation of the Contact Group strategy for the Kosovo conflict—up to the point of NATO's decision to use force against Serbia. Of course, Russian opposition to the NATO bombing campaign was vociferous and its support for Belgrade unseemly, given what Serb forces were perpetrating in Kosovo against a largely civilian population. Even so, Russia did not intervene militarily (though it tried to do so unsuccessfully once the war ended), and in the end it actually played an important supporting role in helping to bring Belgrade around.[29]

U.S. efforts to engage Russia in NATO's transformation have had more mixed results. Successive U.S. defense secretaries expended considerable effort to secure Russia's military participation in Balkan peace operations, first in Bosnia and then in Kosovo.[30] As a consequence, Russian soldiers have served alongside NATO soldiers, under American command, in both operations. And although Moscow clearly opposed NATO's enlargement, it did agree to formalize its relationship with the Alliance as part of the NATO-Russia Founding Act. Of course, implementation of the act's main provisions has left much to be desired, but the basis for a cooperative Russian-NATO relationship was created by its passage in 1997. The choice is now up to Moscow as to whether it wants to move forward on that basis.

• *Bringing Peace and Stability to the Balkans.* Although the Clinton administration was at first hesitant to get involved in the Balkans, it finally did so believing that the success of its entire European policy hinged on achieving peace in the region. Starting in 1995, the administration expended a major effort to end the brutal Bosnian war (which had left more than 100,000 dead and over two million

---

[29]Ivo H. Daalder and Michael E. O'Hanlon, *Winning Ugly: NATO's War to Save Kosovo* (Washington, DC: The Brookings Institution Press, 2000), pp. 165–176, 219–220.

[30]On the Bosnian effort, see Ashton B. Carter and William J. Perry, *Preventive Defense: A New Security Strategy for America* (Washington, DC: The Brookings Institution Press, 1999), chapter 1.

displaced), to prevent a major catastrophe in Kosovo, and ultimately to help bring about a change of regime in Belgrade.

Clinton came to office pledging a more forceful policy toward the former Yugoslavia, notably in Bosnia, which was witness to the most brutal conflict in Europe since the Second World War. However, the new administration soon discovered that an effective U.S. policy required a degree of military commitment—notably in the form of ground troops—that the new president was unwilling to provide. For two years, strong rhetoric vied with inaction to make a mockery of America's Bosnia policy—and, not incidentally, to poison U.S.-European relations. The failure of Europe and the United Nations to act forcefully without the United States taking equal risks left the Bosnian people with little assistance to ward off the violence that engulfed them. The logic of war—and international failure to act—culminated in the disaster of Srebrenica, when in the short span of ten days, nearly eight-thousand Bosnian men were murdered in cold blood as the world stood by.

The Srebrenica debacle emphasized the complete bankruptcy of UN, European, and U.S. policy toward Bosnia. The collective failure to prevent this crime galvanized a policy reassessment in Washington, which resulted in a decision to take the lead in ending the Bosnian war—through negotiations if possible, but through military intervention if necessary.[31] Not only did this decision set in motion the process that would lead to the peace agreed on at Dayton, but it also finally and completely committed the United States and, with it, the Atlantic Alliance, to bringing peace and stability to the region. NATO's subsequent war against Serbia over Kosovo, though late in coming, emerged out of this very commitment. As U.S. Secretary of State Madeleine Albright stated when the Kosovo conflict first started, "We are not going to stand by and watch Serb authorities do in Kosovo what they can no longer get away with doing in Bosnia."[32]

Although U.S. policy toward Bosnia and Kosovo was originally motivated by an overriding humanitarian impulse, the decision to engage militarily, politically, and economically reflected real strategic interests as well. Of most importance, by 1995 it had become abundantly clear that the Clinton administration's entire European policy—from promoting a stronger Europe and transforming NATO to engaging Russia—was negatively affected by the spiraling violence in the Balkans. Indeed, how could one build a peaceful, undivided, and democratic Europe if its southeast was characterized by the brutality of war, deep-seated division, and the prevalence of virulent nationalism? Bringing peace and stability to the Balkans was,

---

[31]Ivo H. Daalder, *Getting to Dayton: The Making of America's Bosnia Policy* (Washington, DC: The Brookings Institution Press, 2000).

[32]Madeleine K. Albright, "Press Briefing at the Ministry of Foreign Affairs" (Rome: U.S. Department of State, March 7, 1998). For an overview of U.S. policy prior to and during the Kosovo war, see Daalder and O'Hanlon, *Winning Ugly*.

therefore, a core requirement of the Clinton administration's Europe policy—and a test of U.S. credibility and leadership.[33]

# GROWING RESENTMENT OF AMERICAN POWER

There can be little doubt that the United States played a central role in helping to promote a more peaceful, united, democratic, and prosperous Europe to emerge in the wake of the Cold War. Yet, despite its importance, American power and leadership in helping to create a more secure and stable Europe has been somewhat of a mixed blessing. Abroad, many of America's key allies have begun to resent U.S. power—a resentment compounded by the frustration of their own continuing dependence on the United States in fulfilling many of their aspirations for the continent. The sources of the resentment are many—and multiplying—including not only America's military and economic power but also its political and cultural dominance. Throughout Europe there is a growing fear that U.S. power will translate in an ability not only to impose Washington's will when important strategic issues are at stake but also increasingly to force America's values onto a Europe that does not always accept these values as its own—be it American support for the death penalty, its gun-toting culture, or its faith in individual rights over those of the community. As one European sage summed up this sentiment: "The essence of European attitudes toward America as the new millennium opens is a broad resentment that almost no field of human activity is left that is not dominated by the military, economic, cultural, technological, and political hyperpower. American products and services, and American manners have penetrated every aspect of European life, while luring away many of the cleverest and most ambitious of its students to American business and graduate schools."[34]

Resentment of American power has been fueled by—and has itself, in turn, stimulated—a growing U.S. tendency toward the unilateral exercise of that power. As resistance to American power, products, and ideas has increased abroad, so has the temptation at home to exercise, sell, and promulgate them without regard for the perspectives of others. In each specific instance, the cause of American unilateralism may be different, ranging from the natural inclination to use power by those

---

[33]See Anthony Lake, "Our Place in the Balkans," *New York Times,* October 8, 2000, p. 15; and Madeleine K. Albright, "The Balkans Stride Toward Europe; Mainstream," *Washington Post,* April 8, 2001, pp. B1–2.

[34]Martin Walker, "What Europeans Think of America," *World Policy Journal,* (Summer 2000): 36. See also more generally François Heisbourg, "American Hegemony? Perceptions of the U.S. Abroad," *Survival,* Vol. 41 (Winter 1999–2000): 5–19; Peter W. Rodman, "The World's Resentment: Anti-Americanism as a Global Phenomenon," *National Interest,* No. 60 (Summer 2000): 35–39; Suzanne Daley, "Europeans Deplore Executions in the U.S.," *New York Times,* February 26, 2000, p. A8; Suzanne Daley, "Europe's Dim View of U.S. Is Evolving into Frank Hostility," *New York Times,* April 9, 2000, p. 1; and Martin Kettle, "U.S. Bashing: Its All the Rage in Europe," *Washington Post,* January 7, 2001, p. B2.

who have it to the fact that many of the most disquieting U.S. actions have been forced upon the executive by a Congress in which unilateralism, if not isolationism, has become a defining feature of its foreign policy attitude. Any thought that President George W. Bush, who had campaigned on the need to strengthen alliances by engaging in more consultation and providing better leadership, would turn the unilateralist tide was quickly disproved when, on issues from the missile defenses to global warming, the new administation struck a decidedly unilateralist tone.[35] Whatever the reason, however, the consequences for U.S.-European relations are severe.

The catalog of European complaints is both long and familiar:

- *The Helms-Burton and Iran-Libya Sanctions Acts.* In 1996, Congress passed two separate laws mandating the imposition of sanctions on foreign companies if they conducted business involving expropriated U.S. properties in Cuba, or oil and gas investments in Libya and Iran. For European governments, it is one thing for the United States to pursue a policy of isolation toward these three countries that all believe to be fundamentally misplaced. It is quite another to apply U.S. laws extraterritorially, as both laws sought to do. Europe's opposition was vociferous, and the crisis caused by the laws' passage abated only when President Clinton waived the provisions that would have forced the imposition of sanctions against some European and Canadian companies.[36]
- *The Land Mines Ban.* In 1997, the Clinton administration announced that it would not join 120 other countries in signing the treaty banning antipersonnel landmines (APLs), even though President Clinton had called for precisely such a ban three years earlier.[37] The reason for rejecting the APL ban concerned the peculiar geographical requirements of defending South Korea, in which the placement of antitank mines similar to those banned by the treaty was judged to be a military requirement. The Clinton administration did commit to developing alternative technologies to deal with this particular requirement by 2006, at which time the United States could join the APL ban.[38]
- *The International Criminal Court.* In 1998, the United States was one of a handful of countries that refused to sign the international treaty establishing an International Criminal Court (ICC) responsible for prosecuting serious vio-

[35]On this, see Huge Young, "We've Lost that Allied Feeling," *Washington Post,* April 1, 2001, p. B1.

[36]On U.S. and European views of the laws, see Richard N. Haass, ed., *Transatlantic Tensions: The United States, Europe, and Problem Countries* (Washington, DC: The Brookings Institution Press, 1999), pp. 17–22, 37–42, 55–59, 83–87, and 151–155. For the May 1998 U.S.-European compromise on the implementation of the legislation, see Bennet, "To Clear Air with Europe, U.S. Waives Some Sanctions."

[37]Anthony DePalma, "As U.S. Looks On, 120 Nations Sign Treaty Banning Land Mines," *New York Times,* December 4, 1997, p. A1; and President Bill Clinton, "Address at the 49th Session of the U.N. General Assembly" (New York: The White House, Office of the Press Secretary, September 26, 1994).

[38]See "Fact Sheet: U.S. Efforts to Address the Problem of Anti-Personnel Landmines" (The White House, Office of the Press Secretary, September 17, 1997).

lations of humanitarian law, including war crimes like those committed in the former Yugoslavia and Rwanda.[39] The rejection of the ICC was all the more surprising, since the idea of establishing a permanent international court for this purpose had originally been proposed by President Clinton.[40] Although the United States signed the ICC on December 31, 2000, the Clinton Administration did so with the explicit proviso that the treaty could not be ratified until major provisions to which Washington objects—including the right to prosecute nationals of countries that are not party to the ICC—are amended.[41] The Bush administration has reiterated U.S. opposition to the treaty.

- *Failure to Pay UN Dues.* Over the past half dozen years, the U.S. refusal fully to fund its UN regular and peacekeeping dues left a $1.9 billion hole in the United Nation's budget.[42] Failure to pay past and present dues had many causes—not the least was U.S. concern about budgetary mismanagement and congressional antipathy toward much of what the organization is believed to stand for. After years of haggling, Congress finally passed a bill that would repay most, but not all, U.S. arrears over three years, provided that the UN institutions would be substantially reformed and the U.S. share of the organization's annual budget would be reduced from 25 to 22 percent (and the share of the peacekeeping budget from 31 to 25 percent). Although European governments opposed the congressional demand and refused to make up the shortfall, the General Assembly agreed in December 2000 to reduce the U.S. share to 22 percent of the general budget (and to about 27 percent of the peacekeeping budget).[43]

- *The Veto of EU's IMF Candidate.* When in early 2000, Germany let it be known that it wanted to nominate the EU's candidate for the IMF directorship, the United States indicated it would support any qualified candidate the EU put forward. However, Berlin's actual nominee, Germany's deputy finance minister, Caio Koch-Weser, proved unacceptable to the Clinton

[39]Alessandra Stanley, "U.S. Presses Allies to Rein in Proposed War Crimes Court," *New York Times,* July 15, 1998, p. A8; and David J. Scheffer, "Testimony Before the Senate Foreign Relations Committee" (Washington, DC: July 23, 1998), available at http://www.state.gov/www/policy _remarks/1998/980723_scheffer_icc.html. For a balanced assessment, see Sarah Sewall and Carl Kaysen, *The United States and the International Criminal Court: Choices Ahead* (Cambridge, MA: American Academy of Arts and Sciences, 2000).

[40]President Bill Clinton, "Remarks at the Opening of the Commemoration of '50 Years After Nuremberg: Human Rights and the Rule of Law'" (The White House, Office of the Press Secretary, October 15, 1995).

[41]President Bill Clinton, "Statement on the Signature of the International Criminal Court Treaty" (The White House, Office of the Press Secretary, December 31, 2000).

[42]The United States owed $1.9 billion to the United Nations, as of September 2000 for current and prior assessments. This included $430 million for the regular UN budget and just over $1.5 billion for peacekeeping. "Setting the Record Straight," The UN Financial Crisis Fact Sheet, available at http://www.un.org/News/facts/finance.htm.

[43]Colum Lynch, "U.N. Assembly Votes to Reduce U.S. Dues," *Washington Post,* December 24, 2000, p. A16.

administration, and Washington warned that it would veto his candidature even if the EU were to support the choice, which it eventually did.[44] Washington held fast, noting at the IMF that it could not support this candidate. Although Germany accepted the inevitable and withdrew its preferred candidate, the resentment was evident in a subsequent comment by Michael Steiner, the German Chancellor's foreign policy adviser: "The way this case was handled tells us something about how the United States now thinks it can throw its weight around as the world's most powerful nation . . . It really is a demonstration of how the United States lacks sensitivity toward its allies, and the response has been to unite the Europeans more than ever against American bullying."[45]

- *The U.S. Senate's Rejection of the CTBT.* The Senate's rejection of the Comprehensive Test Ban Treaty in October 1999 came as a rude shock not just to the Clinton administration but also to governments in Europe and around the world. The test ban had been pursued by every American administration since Eisenhower. It had been negotiated and completed on Clinton's watch. And the United States had been the first country to sign the treaty when it was opened for signature in 1996. But since then, the treaty had languished in the Senate, and the administration had done little to mount the kind of political drive necessary to secure a favorable vote in what was sure to be a difficult ratification battle. Instead of a serious debate about the role of nuclear weapons in American policy, the treaty vote was transformed into a political football, with a hard core of Republican Senators succeeding in forcing the treaty's actual defeat on the Senate floor.[46] European governments were appalled that so serious a matter as nuclear testing and nonproliferation efforts could fall victim to internal U.S. politics.

- *The Kosovo War.* U.S. diplomacy in the run-up to the Kosovo war, as well as the conduct of the war itself, proved deeply dissatisfying to many European governments. Diplomatic efforts were to a significant extent undercut by Washington's refusal to wield a military stick—either the threat of air strikes or the promise of ground troops to enforce a cease-fire. As for the actual conduct of the war, the U.S. military dominated not only the skies over Serbia but also the scope and pace of the war, including the choice of bombing targets with only limited input from its NATO allies (only France and Britain could veto certain targets) and ruling out the use of ground forces to achieve NATO's objective until the final days of the war.[47]

---

[44]Press reports indicated that London and Paris were also unhappy with the choice but were happy for Washington to exercise its veto. See Roger Cohen, "I.M.F. Issue Divides U.S. and Germany," *New York Times,* March 12, 2000, p. 12; and Joseph Kahn, "Heavy Posturing Seen in I.M.F. Rift," *New York Times,* March 2, 2000, p. A1.

[45]Quoted in William Drozdiak, "Europeans Decry U.S. 'Bullying' on IMF," *Washington Post,* March 2, 2000, p. A1.

[46]On the political machinations surrounding the CTBT vote, see John M. Broder, "Quietly and Dexterously, Senate Republicans Set a Trap," *New York Times,* October 14, 1999, p. A16.

[47]For details, see Daalder and O'Hanlon, *Winning Ugly.*

- *National Missile Defense.* In January 1999, Secretary of Defense William Cohen announced that the United States would move ahead with deploying a limited missile defense to counter the missile threat from North Korea and other so-called "rogue states." Cohen made clear that if Russia refused to negotiate modifications in the Anti-Ballistic Missile Treaty, which bars the deployment of nationwide defenses, the United States would withdraw from the treaty. Although President Clinton announced a deferral of a final deployment decision in September 2000, his successor has made clear that the United States will develop and deploy a defense system as soon as possible. Moreover, while President Bush has assured the Europeans that he will consult with them on the issue, he has also made clear that these consultations will not change his basic decision to go ahead, even though most allies have yet to be convinced that defenses offer the best and most stabilizing response to any perceived threats.[48]

- *Global Warming.* Although the United States signed the Kyoto protocol mandating reductions in carbon dioxide emissions by advanced industrial states, the Clinton administration made clear that ratification by the U.S. Senate would both require modifications in how the protocol's terms were to be implemented and necessitate that developing countries agree to curb their $CO^2$ emissions. Subsequent negotiations on how to implement the agreement's provisions failed to narrow the gap between the United States, the European Union, and developing countries, and when Clinton left office the future of Kyoto was highly uncertain. The Bush administration, which entered office skeptical about the science of global warming and the utility of international regulations, ended the uncertainty by announcing in March 2001 that Kyoto "was dead." However, while it unilaterally declared "dead" a multilateral agreement, the administration offered nothing in return to deal with the global problem of climate change—a problem for which the United States, which produces 28 percent of the globe' greenhouse gasses while possessing just four percent of the world's population, bears much responsibility.[49]

For many Europeans, what is most disquieting about this catalog of complaints is the seeming disconnect between Washington's proactive stance in calling for the establishment of rule-making institutions and regimes (e.g., the United Nations, the International Criminal Court, the Kyoto protocol, and bans on nuclear testing and antipersonnel landmines) and its subsequent failure to accept or to live by the rules and institutions that emerge from the negotiations that follow. Some of this behavior can be dismissed as the inevitable product of America's privileged position in the world—which the French foreign minister has, not

---

[48]Dana Priest "Cohen Says U.S. Will Build Missile Defense," *Washington Post,* January 21, 1999, p. A1; Eric Schmitt, "President Decides to Put Off Work on Missile Shield," *New York Times,* September 2, 2000, p. A1; and President George W. Bush "Remarks to the Students and Faculty at the National Defense University." (The White House, Office of the Press Secretary, May 1, 2001).

[49]See Robert Paarlberg, "U.S. Environmental Policy Abroad: Explaining Fluctuations in Leadership by an Essential County," in this volume.

inaccurately, characterized as one of hyperpuissance.[50] But for others, it reflects the more alarming tendency of the United States to behave as a "rogue super-power"—a power that, like other rogues, refuses to adhere to commonly accepted norms of behavior.[51] It is not surprising, therefore, that some in Europe have deliberately sought to distance themselves from the United States and the policies it pursues, not least by enhancing Europe's own capacity for independent action.

## Europe's Response: Increased Independence

Europe's response to the growing American tendency to exercise power unilaterally has been to try to enhance its capacity for independent action in both the economic and the foreign policy and security realms. Although economic and monetary union and the development of a European security and defense policy (ESDP) had multiple origins, one element common to both was the belief in European capitals that with the end of the Cold War and the growing importance of economic issues more generally, Europe should find ways to reduce its dependence on the United States.

The primary motivating factor for the development of a common European currency—the euro—was to stimulate further European integration, in part to tie a united Germany more firmly into Europe.[52] At the same time, there can be little doubt that monetary union has cemented the economic might of the twelve EU members that joined the EMU—who are known collectively as "Euroland"—into a major economic power. As Fred Bergsten has commented, "Euroland will equal or exceed the U.S. on every key measure of economic strength and will speak increasingly with a single voice on a wide range of economic issues . . . Economic relations between the U.S. and the EU will rest increasingly on a foundation of virtual equality."[53] That assessment may have been premature, given that the euro dropped 25 percent in the first eighteen months following its introduction as a trading currency in January 1999. For some time, moreover, the euro is unlikely to rival the dollar as an investment, an anchor, or a reserve currency.[54] Nevertheless, there is little doubt that the monetary union and the advent of the euro provide Europe with the foundation for becoming an economic power that will be the near-equal of the United States.[55]

[50]See Hubert Védrine, *France in the Age of Globalization,* (Washington, DC: The Brookings Institution Press, 2001).

[51]Cf. the discussion in Heisbourg, "American Hegemony? Perceptions of the U.S. Abroad," pp. 10–13.

[52]See Peter B. Kenen, *Economic and Monetary Union in Europe: Moving Beyond Maastricht* (Cambridge: Cambridge University Press, 1995).

[53]C. Fred Bergsten, "America and Europe: Clash of the Titans?" *Foreign Affairs,* Vol. 78 (March–April 1999): 20–34. See also Steven Everts, *The Impact of the Euro on Transatlantic Relations* (London: Centre for European Reform, 1999).

[54]Cf. Norbert Walter, "The Euro: Second to (N)One," *German Issues 23* (Washington, DC: American Institute for Contemporary German Studies, 2000), pp. 22–25; and John Vinocur, "The Weakening Euro," *International Herald Tribune,* September 8, 2000, p. 1.

[55]Cf. David P. Calleo, "The Strategic Implications of the Euro," *Survival,* Vol. 41 (Spring 1999): 5–19.

A similar evolution is now under way in the security sphere. Although Europe accepted—indeed welcomed—its reliance on the United States for its security throughout the Cold War period, it was the crisis in the former Yugoslavia throughout the 1990s that finally convinced European governments that this dependence was no longer tenable. Notwithstanding the fact that Europe had, with Washington's full support, taken the lead in addressing the crisis as it enveloped southeastern Europe in the early 1990s, American diplomatic and military power proved crucial both in ending the Bosnian war in 1995 and in curtailing a major humanitarian calamity in Kosovo in 1999. Not only did American intervention demonstrate Europe's essential diplomatic and military weakness, but it also underscored that this weakness enabled Washington to dictate the strategy and tactics for resolving an essentially European conflict. It was this latter aspect, fully underscored by the response to the Kosovo crisis, that proved to be most troubling in European capitals.

It is perhaps surprising that, given its historical closeness to Washington and long-standing opposition to strengthening Europe's ability to act without U.S. involvement, it was a Britain led by a Labor government closely aligned with the Clinton administration that made the crucial decision to push for a greater European capacity for independent action. Although the British initiative launched by Prime Minister Tony Blair in October 1998 reflected in part an attempt to prove London's European bona fides at a time when it had decided to opt out of the euro, the timing unquestionably reflected Blair's displeasure with the Clinton administration's handling of the Kosovo crisis in the summer and fall of 1998.[56] As Blair wrote in the *New York Times,* "to speak with authority, the European Union needs to be able to act militarily on its own when the United States is not engaged."[57] In other words, had Europe been able to deploy a sizable and credible ground presence into Kosovo, it would not have been at the mercy of the American decision that no such forces could be deployed there. At the same time, Blair was interested in a larger concept for Europe as well. As he explained in May 1999, "For Europe, the central challenge is no longer simply securing internal peace inside the European Union. It is the challenge posed by the outside world, about how we make Europe strong and influential, how we make full use of the potential Europe has to be a global power for good."[58]

Britain's support for building up Europe's capacity for independent action in the foreign and defense policy arena first became fully apparent in December 1998,

[56]Britain was particularly displeased with Washington's decision to reject the idea, first proposed by London, to deploy NATO ground troops in Kosovo to supervise a cease-fire agreement. It accordingly regarded the agreement worked out between the U.S. special envoy Richard Holbrooke and Yugoslav President Slobodan Milosevic to supervise the cease-fire with unarmed monitors as deeply flawed. For further details, see Daalder and O'Hanlon, *Winning Ugly,* pp. 49–59.

[57]Tony Blair, "It's Time to Repay America," *New York Times,* November 13, 1998, p. A31. See also Tony Blair, "NATO's Role in the Modern World," Remarks to the North Atlantic Assembly (Edinburgh: November 13, 1998); George Robertson, "The Future of European Defence" (Paris: WEU Assembly, December 1, 1998); and Tony Blair, "NATO, Europe, and Our Future Security" (London: Royal United Services Institute, March 9, 1999).

[58]Tony Blair, "Address at Ceremony to Receive the Charlemagne Prize" (Aachen, Germany: May 13, 1999), available at http://www.bccg.de/Publications/Karlspreis99RedeBlair.htm.

when Blair and French President Jacques Chirac issued a statement on European defense following their meeting in St. Malo. There, the two leaders agreed that the European Union "must have the capacity for autonomous action, backed up by credible military forces, the means to decide to use them, and a readiness to do so, in order to respond to international crises."[59] This perspective was endorsed in a succession of bilateral, EU, and NATO statements.[60] In December 1999, the EU committed to a "headline" goal of being able to deploy sixty-thousand troops within two months for a period of up to one year for peacekeeping, peace enforcement, and crisis management purposes. To date, member countries have identified the inventory of troops and equipment that each will contribute to meet that goal by the end of 2003.[61]

Although there remain major obstacles to achieving this headline goal within the time frame set by the EU itself (see later), the intent of the effort is clear: the EU members are committed to developing "an autonomous capacity to take decisions and, where NATO as a whole is not engaged, to launch and conduct EU-led military operations in response to international crises."[62] In so doing, Europe would possess the capacity to act independently in the military field, thus lessening its dependence on the United States in many, if not most, of the contingencies that are likely to emerge.

# REBALANCING THE U.S.-EUROPEAN RELATIONSHIP

The growing European resentment of Europe's continued dependence on the United States and the increased interest in enhancing Europe's capacity for independent action suggest that the old model of U.S.-European relations no longer suffices. Some have argued that the differences between the two sides—differences magnified by the absence of a common threat to unite them, growing disputes over trade and financial matters, and generational and other changes at home—imply the need for disengagement, ultimately leading to an actual divorce.[63] But such a prescription ignores the many ties—economic, military, political, and cultural—that do, in fact, bind the two sides of the Atlantic. And although these ties may no longer be suffi-

---

[59]"Statement on European Defense" (Saint-Malo, France: Franco-British Summit, December 4, 1998), para. 2.

[60]See "Washington Summit Communiqué"; "Presidency Conclusions: Cologne European Council" (Cologne, Germany: June 3–4, 1999), Annex III; "Joint Declaration Launching European Defence Capabilities Initiative" (British-Italian Summit, July 19, 1999); "Presidency Conclusions: Helsinki European Council" (Helsinki, Finland: December 10–11, 1999), paras. 25–29, Annex IV; and "Presidency Conclusions: Santa Maria Da Feira European Council" (Santa Maria Da Feira, Portugal: June 19–20, 2000), Annex I, Appendix 2, para. B.2.

[61]"Declaration of the Military Capabilities Commitment Conference of the European Union" (Brussels: November 20, 2000).

[62]"Presidency Conclusions: Helsinki European Council," para. 27.

[63]See, for example, Stephen Walt, "The Ties That Bind: Why Europe and America Are Drifting Apart," *National Interest,* No. 54 (Fall–Winter 1998–99): 3–11. Peter Rodman shares Walt's analysis, if not his prescription. See Peter W. Rodman, *Drifting Apart? Trend in U.S.-European Relations* (Washington, DC: The Nixon Center, June 1999).

cient in and of themselves to perpetuate the alliance in its current form, they do provide the basis for a new, more up-to-date relationship that conforms more closely to prevailing, as well as to emerging, realities. The need, therefore, is not to abandon but to refashion the alliance by moving away from American dominance toward creating a genuine strategic partnership of equals. As Christoph Bertram has argued,

> It should be America's prime interest to lay the foundations today for a partnership with the Europe of tomorrow. U.S. supremacy may last for a generation but it will not last forever. What better use to make of this temporary advantage than to establish now the institutional framework for a partnership in which a Europe that will be stronger than it is today and America that will be weaker can work together for order, prosperity and democracy in tomorrow's world?[64]

A genuine strategic partnership would serve both sides equally well. More issues unite than divide the United States and Europe—indeed, neither side threatens vital or important interests of the other. Both sides of the Atlantic share a basic commitment to market democracy and the need to uphold and strengthen the underlying values that have given rise to it over the past decades and centuries. As a result, the United States and Europe hold key economic and strategic interests in common (even if there are often differences on how best to protect or advance them). And U.S.-European cooperation is necessary (and in many cases sufficient) to address many of the most important global issues—ranging from defending and promoting human rights and protecting the environment to assuring global economic stability. In other words, whether they like it or not, the United States and Europe need each other, now perhaps more than ever.[65]

Although the need and benefits of a strategic partnership are evident (and generally go undisputed), the transition from the current, unequal relationship to genuine equality will be difficult. Ultimate success will require Europe to acquire the capacity necessary for genuine partnership, the emergence of a European strategic outlook that is global in scope, and a willingness on the part of Washington to grant Europe an equal voice in decision making. None of these requirements is likely to be easy, but a rebalancing of the relationship demands nothing less.

## Europe's Capacity for Partnership

Europe's capacity to become a true strategic partner of the United States hinges on developments in three areas—the nature and extent of political integration in Europe, the future strength of EMU and the euro, and the evolution of European defense policy. Only a Europe that is united politically, strong economically, and robust militarily will be in a position to be a full and an equal U.S. partner.[66]

---

[64]Christoph Bertram, "Comments on Brzezinski," *National Interest,* No. 60 (Summer 2000): 30–31.

[65]This theme is further developed in Frances G. Burwell and Ivo H. Daalder, eds., *The United States and Europe in the Global Arena* (New York: St. Martin's Press, 1999).

[66]For one such vision, see Charles Grant, *EU 2010: An Optimistic Vision of the Future* (London: Centre for European Reform, 2000).

The first challenge for Europe is political. Fifty years after the European experiment commenced with the establishment of the European Coal and Steel Community in 1951, there still is no European consensus about where this experiment will end. Throughout this time, there have been periodic debates about the political form that Europe should take—whether the goal of a Europe embarked on "ever closer union" is a federal or an intergovernmental entity. In 2000, the debate once again surfaced, this time as key EU members contemplated the consequences of the Union's enlargement to twenty-five or more members in the decade ahead. This debate showed major divisions, with some (like German Foreign Minister Joschka Fischer and EU Commission President Romano Prodi) supporting a more integrated federal model, others (including the British government) strongly favoring the looser intergovernmental model, and yet others (including French President Jacques Chirac, Valéry Giscard d'Estaing, and Helmut Schmidt) proposing a hybrid model in which a core, or "pioneer group," would integrate further even while the Union as a whole expands.[67]

History suggests that neither a complete federal state nor a strictly intergovernmental entity will emerge from the competing efforts to further European integration. Instead, although the basic structure of the EU will remain intergovernmental, the scope of activity conducted at the European level is likely to continue to increase over time. Moreover, it is almost certain that some EU members will continue to move forward at a faster pace than the Union as a whole. Indeed, such is already the case in the monetary, defense, and internal policy (Schengen) realms. A similar evolution in other areas, including possibly in political affairs, is bound to continue among some EU member states, especially if and when the Union as a whole brings in new members.

What are the implications of Europe's likely political evolution for partnership with the United States? Clearly, America's partner will not be a United States of Europe—a federal state, headed by a single government with full competence over defense policy and foreign affairs. In that sense, the partnership will not be between equals. But over time, Europe is bound to speak with a single voice on more issues and with increasing frequency. Already today, Europe speaks with one voice on issues ranging from nonproliferation to development assistance. And Europe is represented internationally by a single person, Javier Solana, the High Representative for Europe's Common Foreign and Security Policy, so that on an increasing number of issues (from trade to the Balkans and the Middle East), there now is a single telephone number for American leaders to call. Of course, when circumstances of major importance arise and when the costs and risks associated with a particular action are high, national governments rather than the EU will still have the decisive voice.

[67]Joschka Fischer, "From Confederacy to Federation—Thoughts on the Finality of European Integration" (Berlin: May 12, 2000); Romano Prodi, "Speech before the Plenary Session of the European Parliament" (Strasbourg: October 3, 2000); Hubert Védrine, "Letter to Joschka Fischer" (Paris: June 8, 2000); Robin Cook, "Speech to the Hungarian Ambassadors' Conference" (Budapest: July 25, 2000); Tony Blair, "Speech to the Polish Stock Exchange" (Warsaw: October 6, 2000); Jacques Chirac, "Our Europe: Speech Before the German Bundestag" (Berlin: June 27, 2000); and Valéry Giscard d'Estaing and Helmut Schmidt, "Time to Slow Down and Consolidate Around 'Euro-Europe,'" *International Herald Tribune*, April 11, 2000.

The second challenge for Europe in terms of building sufficient capacity is economic. This issue boils down to a simple question: will Euroland succeed? Despite the precipitous drop in the euro's value after its introduction as a convertible currency in January 1999, the answer to this question is almost certainly yes. The reason is less economic than it is political. Just as the origins of EMU were fundamentally political in nature, so its future success is determined by one overriding political reality: the EMU simply cannot be allowed to fail. If EMU failed and the euro's introduction as legal tender in Euroland were halted or reversed, the political implications for the European Union as a whole would be incalculably grave. The EU's six original members—France, Germany, Italy, and the Benelux—have staked the union's (and their own) future on EMU's success—and the six other Euroland participants have joined them for that very reason. If the euro is allowed to go down, then so would the European experiment writ large. Of course, this does not mean that there will be no setbacks (as the 25 percent drop in the euro's value in relation to the dollar in 2000 has already shown) or that the economic and other policy adjustments necessary for making integration work will not be exceedingly difficult. But it means that these difficulties will not add up to failure. For the Euroland countries, failure is simply not an option.

The final challenge, and the one receiving the most attention within the transatlantic framework, concerns the future of European defense policy. Will the effort launched in 1998–99 be yet another on a long list of failed attempts to enhance Europe's military potential separate from that of the United States, or will this time be different? Although obstacles to success are great, there are at least two reasons to anticipate greater success this time. First, this effort is being launched with the full support of all EU members, including the major powers. This was not the case in the past, when Great Britain (usually supported by smaller allies like Denmark, Portugal, and the Netherlands) viewed most efforts to enhance Europe's capacity in the security sphere as threats to Atlanticism (as, in some cases, they were intended).[68] Now, however, London not only supports but also is, in many ways, the driving force of the European defense effort. Second, the likely challenges that may require the use of military force that may confront Europe over the next decade or so will probably fall on the low end of the conflict spectrum. Europe today faces nothing like the Soviet military threat of the Cold War years—even a Kosovo-type conflict is not all that likely. As a result, the military demands of the common defense effort will for some time be relatively modest—giving the EU countries time to acquire the kind of military capabilities necessary to mount a credible effort.

Of course, achieving even this modest defense effort will prove to be a major task, if not an insurmountable one. At least four obstacles stand out. First, for all the progress in the political realm, Europe remains—and will remain for some time—a collection of fifteen independent countries in the security field whose aggregated

---

[68]For a good overview of these past European efforts, by a sympathetic source, see Willem van Eekelen, *Debating European Security, 1948–1998* (The Hague: Sdu Publisher, 1998).

power is, in important ways, less than the sum of its parts. Efficiencies and joint efforts are both possible and necessary, but the reality of national division will pose an ineluctable limit on the effectiveness of the whole. Second, even if the EU manages to achieve the headline goal—including by identifying the 150,000 to 180,000 troops necessary to sustain a major operation over an extended period of time—that would still fall short of what will be needed for Europe to be able to conduct major military operations autonomously. Indeed, conducting just the current peacekeeping operations in the Balkans would be a stretch for the EU. Third, it does not seem very likely that the EU will achieve the headline goals by 2003. Even if it proves able to deploy the troops and basic equipment, it will not be possible to support them logistically over any significant distance. In other words, by 2003, the EU may be able to take over the operations in the Balkans, given existing lines of communication and the relatively quiescent security environment there, but it would not be able to embark on a similar type mission anywhere else. Finally, given the wide and continuing disparity in defense spending generally and on research and development in particular, the technological gap between the United States and Europe in the military field—already wide—will continue to grow inexorably.

None of this is to suggest that Europe will lack the military (or political or economic) capacity to be a strategic partner of the United States. Clearly, Europe is moving in the right direction, but much more will have to be done, especially in the defense realm. Part of the problem is the time frame; given the state of European militaries following a decade or more of declining defense budgets, it is not realistic to expect fundamental changes in just a few years' time. A more realistic time frame would be the next ten to fifteen years, based on a demonstrated commitment to embark on a major overhaul of European militaries immediately.[69] Even then, the effort will require an uncommon dedication on the part of all the EU countries—to improve existing capabilities, transform military personnel practices (including possibly replacing the draft with a volunteer force), reprioritize defense spending, and commit additional resources.[70] So far, it is clear that Europe is at least committed to a serious, sustained effort to acquire military capabilities necessary to enable the EU to act militarily on its own, and that in itself is a major change from the past.

## Europe's Outlook for Partnership

Larger, perhaps, than attaining the necessary capacity for partnership with the United States, is the challenge Europe faces in acquiring the necessary outlook for such a partnership. For all practical purposes, Europe's predominant outlook remains regional in perspective. The primary strategic concern of European governments (with

---

[69]Cf. Bertelsmann Foundation, ed., *Enhancing the European Union as an International Security Actor: A Strategy for Action* (Güterloh, Germany: Bertelsmann Foundation Publishers, 2000).

[70]For details, see especially François Heisbourg et al., *European Defence: Making It Work*, Chaillot Paper 42 (Paris: Institute for Security Studies of the Western European Union, September 2000).

France and Britain being the only possible exception) is Europe—and Western, Central, and Southeastern Europe at that. Europe's strategic vision very much remains geographically restricted—extending no farther than Northern Africa in the south, the Balkans in the Southeast, and Russia in the East. The Middle East and sub-Saharan Africa are zones of conflict and, therefore, of humanitarian and perhaps economic concern, but not of overriding strategic import. The world beyond—to the Americas in the West and Asia in the East—is important principally for the economic benefits that engagement can bring; for Europe, it is not of political or security concern. As Zbigniew Brzezinski has, not inaccurately, remarked, "on the global scene the emerging Europe is likely to be more similar to a Switzerland writ large than to the United States."[71] Like Switzerland, Europe's global perspective extends to trade and financial matters; its strategic engagement is limited to staying aloof from the threats and other challenges—especially those outside the region—that might affect world order.

Yet, a genuine partnership with the United States will require equality of effort not only in Europe but also outside it, thus requiring Europe to expand its outlook geographically beyond its own region and to encompass much of the rest of the globe. The alternative is not likely to be the status quo but what Condoleezza Rice, President Bush's national security adviser, termed a new division of labor: "The United States is the only power that can handle a showdown in the gulf, mount the kind of force that is needed to protect Saudi Arabia and deter a crisis in the Taiwan Straits. And extended peacekeeping [in Europe] detracts from our readiness for these kinds of global missions."[72] This is not an attractive alternative, however. Rather than encouraging a move toward partnership, a division of labor would more likely widen the gulf between the United States and Europe even further. Not only would a division of this kind do nothing to encourage Europe to acquire a global outlook appropriate to the twenty-first century, it would also deprive the United States of a potential partner in meeting the challenges and threats around the world that affect interests common to both. In short, a genuine strategic partnership cannot be built on an artificial division of labor but must instead encourage the development of a European strategic outlook that is both global in nature and concomitant with its overarching strategic interests to work with the United States in promoting world order.

## Sharing Power and Responsibility

Even if Europe acquires the capacity and outlook necessary for partnership with the United States, a successful rebalancing of the relationship cannot be guaranteed. Genuine partnership must rest not just on the existence of potential partners—which Europe's accretion of power and vision would provide—but on a willingness to

---

[71]Zbigniew Brzezinski, "Living with a New Europe," *National Interest,* No. 60 (Summer 2000): 20.

[72]Quoted in Michael R. Gordon, "Bush Would Stop U.S. Peacekeeping in Balkan Fight, *New York Times,* October 21, 2000, p. A1. See also Kay Bailey Hutchison, "A New Division of Labor for a New World Order," *Washington Post,* January 3, 1999, p. C7. For another view, see Ivo H. Daalder, "Bush Plan Would Weaken Crucial Link to Allies," *Los Angeles Times,* October 30, 2000, p. B7.

engage one another on the basis of equality. And that, in turn, entails a readiness on the part of the United States to give Europe an equal voice not just in implementing decisions but also in making them. The past does not bode well for Washington's ability to match its demand for burden sharing with a willingness to engage in greater decision and responsibility sharing. Yet, a true strategic partnership demands no less.

The initial U.S. reaction to the so-called Blair initiative on European defense demonstrated continued American unease with a possible curtailment of its role as NATO's first-among-not-so-equals. Although many welcomed the possibility that Europe would be able to carry more of the collective burden, many also worried that a stronger Europe would be more likely and able to strike an independent stance on issues of importance. Of particular concern to Clinton administration officials, congressional supporters of NATO, and Atlanticist policy analysts alike was the fear that a stronger EU voice in the defense realm would compete with, and consequently undermine the vitality of, the Atlantic Alliance, which remains America's singular institutional entry into Europe.[73] As Strobe Talbott put it, "We would not want to see an ESDI that comes into being first *within* NATO but then grows *out of* NATO and finally grows *away from* NATO, since that would lead to an ESDI that initially duplicates NATO but that could eventually compete with NATO."[74]

In the end, the European Union proved able to reassure the United States that its search for an autonomous capacity to decide and act in the military realm was designed to supplement rather than supplant NATO. But the initial U.S. reaction to the European proposal demonstrated the continued American resistance to regarding Europe as a potential equal, as would be necessary for the establishment of a genuine partnership. And that resistance is not likely to change any time soon. Not only is Europe not yet ready to act in genuine partnership with the United States, but also Washington will likely continue to hew to the somewhat unilateralist course it has adopted in recent years. Both domestic political pressures and international political realities make it unlikely that, on important issues like the Middle East or weapons proliferation, Washington will soon bow to European views.

Although friction between the United States and Europe is inevitable within the context of any relationship, a genuine partnership between the two is impossible

[73]This concern is the main theme running through otherwise differing perspectives on European defense. See Albright, "The Right Balance Will Secure Nato's Future"; Vershbow, "ESDI: Berlin, St. Malo and Beyond"; Strobe Talbott, "America's Stake in a Strong Europe," Remarks at a Conference on the Future of NATO at the Royal Institute of International Affairs (London: October 7, 1999); *Testimony of John R. Bolton* before the Committee on International Relations, House of Representatives, on the "European Common Foreign, Security and Defense Policies—Implications for the United States and the Atlantic Alliance," 106 Cong. 1 sess., available at http://www.house.gov/internationa_relations/106/full/106first/testimony/bolton.htm; *Senate Resolution 208*, S. Res. 208, 106 Cong. 2 sess. (October 28, 1999); and Philip Gordon, "Their Own Army? Making European Defense Work," *Foreign Affairs,* Vol. 79 (July–August 2000): 12–17. For an assessment of these perspectives, see Charles A. Kupchan, "In Defence of European Defence: An American Perspective," *Survival,* Vol. 42 (Summer 2000): 16–32; and Stanley R. Sloan, *The United States and European Defence,* Chaillot Papers 39 (Paris: Institute for Security Studies of the Western European Union, April 2000).

[74]Talbott, "America's Stake in a Strong Europe," emphasis in original.

unless Washington demonstrates a much greater willingness to give Europe a greater the voice in common decisions than it has in the past. Of course, doing so has specific implications for policy.[75] For example, the United States should whole-heartedly support the development of a European defense policy within the EU, even if doing so could weaken its dominant role over European security questions that its primacy within NATO has long guaranteed. Washington should also cede the lead in the making and implementation of policy toward the Balkans, an area where Europe provides over 80 percent of the troops keeping the peace and nearly 90 percent of the financial assistance. And Washington would do well to engage Europe intensely on the issue of deploying missile defenses, including jointly exploring the role of defenses in strengthening deterrence and managing missile proliferation.

# TOWARDS STRATEGIC PARTNERSHIP

Throughout the first post-Cold War decade, the United States has been, as it was during the preceding decades of the Cold War, Europe's indispensable power. Prior to 1990, America was at once Europe's protector and Europe's pacifier—defending it from the military and political threats posed by the Soviet Union while providing it with the security blanket under which European integration and cooperation could proceed. After 1990, Europe tried to set out on its own, boldly proclaiming that "the hour of Europe" had arrived, only to find that its political division, economic weakness, and military backwardness provided a feeble basis for joint action. Uncomfortably—and reluctantly—Europe turned once again to the United States to help resolve the continent's many problems. Washington eagerly retook the baton, leading the way in transforming NATO, engaging Russia as partner in building the new Europe, and ending the war and violence that had engulfed the former Yugoslavia.

Although America's success in dealing with many of the continent's new challenges confirmed that the United States remained the indispensable power, Europe has nevertheless come to resent American dominance. Part of the reason lies in the shame of continued dependence—and the fact that America succeeded where Europe so clearly failed. But part, too, comes from the overbearing—and unilateralist—behavior that has marked America's indispensability. Washington's hubris, even if well-meant and effective, nevertheless breeds resentment. Whence the effort by all of Europe—by London as well as Paris and Berlin—to enhance its capacity for action across a range of activities independent from Washington.

Europe's search for greater power is often seen on the U.S. side of the Atlantic as an unwelcome attempt to counterbalance American power, as, indeed, it sometimes is (especially as far as some in Paris are concerned). But this view ignores Europe's fundamental interests—as well as America's. Europe's interest is

---

[75]See Ivo H. Daalder and James M. Goldgeier, "Putting Europe First," *Survival,* Vol. 43 (Spring 2001, pp. 71–91).

not to oppose the United States or somehow to balance American power; it is to pursue its own interests without having to rely on Washington. America's interest is not to have a weak, even if thereby obedient, set of allies; it is to have a partner that can pull its own weight. Of course, a more balanced U.S.-European relationship will not guarantee greater comity nor ease resolution of many new disputes that are sure to arise. But a partnership of genuine equality is more likely to foster new forms of cooperation and joint action to defend and advance common interests over a greater range of issues than is possible today. That, at the very least, ought to be the aim of a joint effort to refashion U.S.-European relations in the new century.

# 5

# Transforming Russia
## American Policy in the 1990s

### GAIL W. LAPIDUS
Stanford University

## THE PROMISE AND THE CRITIQUE

The end of the Cold War, the dissolution of the USSR in December 1991, and the emergence of fifteen new states on its former territory radically transformed both the structure of the international system and the geopolitics of Eurasia.* It also created unprecedented opportunities as well as novel challenges for American policy. Not only was American primacy suddenly unchallenged, but also the sweep of democratic revolutions across central and Eastern Europe held out the hope that the community of democratic, market societies would shortly extend across the entire European continent from the Atlantic to the Pacific.

Three features of this transformation constituted a particularly dramatic break with the past: the end of the nuclear confrontation with the USSR, which had long

Gail W. Lapidus is a Senior Fellow at the Institute for International Studies at Stanford University and heads a project on ethnic conflict and regional security at its Center for International Security and Cooperation. A Professor of Political Science at the University of California at Berkeley from 1976 to 1994, where she directed the Center for Slavic and East European Studies as well as the Berkeley-Stanford Program in Soviet and Post-Soviet Studies, she holds a Ph.D. from Harvard University. She is the author of numerous books and articles on Soviet and post-Soviet politics, society, and foreign policy, including recent studies of the war in Chechnya, of center-periphery relations in the Russian Federation, and of the treatment of national minorities in the post-Soviet states. She has served as President of the American Association for the Advancement of Slavic Studies, and as Chair of the Social Science Research Council's Joint Committee on Soviet Studies, and she has also held fellowships from the Kennan Institute, the Center for Advanced Study in the Behavioral Sciences, and the Harriman Institute at Columbia University.

*I would like to express my appreciation to Vadim Rubin and Victoria Levin for their research assistance, and to thank Andrew Bennett, Steven Pifer, Thomas Simons and Elizabeth Sherwood-Randall for their helpful comments on an earlier version of this chapter.

constituted the gravest threat to American security; the beginning of a new chapter in Russia's historical development marked by the emergence of an embryonic nation-state from the ruins of empire, a state whose leaders espoused a novel commitment to liberal democratic values, a market economy, and integration into Europe; and the creation or reemergence of fourteen independent, if fragile, sovereign states around Russia's periphery, proclaiming their commitment to similar goals.

These unexpected developments unleashed a wave of triumphalist rhetoric in the West. But they were not entirely unproblematic. Western political leaders and analysts alike were acutely concerned about the implications of the end of bipolarity for international stability; about the durability and indeed the very viability of the post-Soviet states, as well as their capacity to manage the Soviet nuclear legacy; and about the enormous potential for interstate and intrastate conflict across the region in view of the many ethnonational challenges and territorial claims left unresolved by the sudden and unexpected demise of the USSR.[1] But the wave of euphoria and optimism that greeted the end of communist rule largely submerged these concerns. The public discourse emphasized the promise of democratization, the creation of market economies, and the construction of a new partnership with the West.

A decade later it had become abundantly clear that this vision was utopian and that the expectations of a rapid and comprehensive "transition" were naive and overly simplistic. Even as the first Clinton administration took over the reins of power in Washington in 1993, Russia's reformist Gaidar government had fallen from power; and already by 1994, a leading Western analyst of Russian affairs entitled his essay "Where Have All the Flowers Gone?"[2] Despite the sweeping changes ushered in in 1991, and notwithstanding significant progress across the region in shedding some of the more brutal features of the Soviet legacy, the initial hopes shared by many inside and outside Russia of rapid and successful political and economic reform as well as the development of a close Russian-American partnership have failed to materialize. Russia, along with most of the other states of the region, has been engulfed in a severe economic and social crisis; authoritarian trends are jeopardizing some of the embryonic democratic institutions and practices that had begun to take root; and Russian-American security and foreign policy cooperation has been increasingly strained by differences over a broad range of issues. In a poignant resignation speech delivered on the eve of the new millenium, President Yeltsin expressed his profound personal disappointment at his failure to live up to the expectations and hopes of his people for a better life, and he asked their forgiveness.[3]

---

[1]Indeed, these anxieties underlay the frantic efforts of Western policy-makers to shore up Gorbachev's position in a vain effort to forestall the disintegration of the USSR, and they motivated President Bush's famous speech in Kiev warning against the dangers of "suicidal nationalism" ("Remarks to The Supreme Soviet of the Republic of the Ukraine in Kiev, Soviet Union," August 1, 1991). The violence in Yugoslavia was viewed as the nightmare scenario for the future of the USSR.

[2]Alexander Dallin, in Gail W. Lapidus, ed., *The New Russia: Troubled Transformation* (Boulder, CO: Westview Press, 1995), pp. 245–62; 1994 draft.

[3]"I want to ask you for forgiveness, because many of our hopes have not come true, because what we thought would be easy turned out to be painfully difficult. I ask you to forgive me for not fulfilling some hopes of those people who believed that we would be able to jump from the grey, stagnating, total-

As Yeltsin's remarks underscored, many of the early expectations were unrealistic. This was no simple "transition" replicating the experiences of Latin America or Southern Europe, nor even those of Central and Eastern Europe. Western governments as well as the Yeltsin leadership clearly underestimated the enormous challenge and complexity of coping with the seventy-year long Soviet legacy, of tackling the challenges of state- and nation-building simultaneously with political democratization, economic reform, and the formulation of radically new foreign and security policies in a dramatically changed internal and external environment. They also exaggerated the ease with which new institutions, attitudes, and patterns of behavior modeled on Western templates could be created or transplanted onto Russian soil.[4] Indeed, if the case of Russia was particularly challenging, it was by no means unique. Even the comparatively easier task of German reunification had entailed far greater challenges and costs than the West German government itself anticipated at the time.[5] Under the circumstances, disillusionment and backlash were predictable.

Moreover, the initial strategies pursued by a variety of Western as well as local actors, however well-intentioned, were based on an insufficiently complex appreciation of the effects of the Soviet legacy on the constellation of interests, institutions, attitudes, and behaviors within these countries and among them. Across the entire region, albeit in differing degrees, the effort to undo the effects of the Soviet legacy confronted daunting obstacles, the resources that could be mobilized for the effort were far too limited to produce swift and major results, and the ability of outside actors to have a significant impact on the process—either positive or negative—was marginal.

Above all, the challenge of managing the American-Russian relationship was greatly magnified by the fundamental and growing asymmetry between the two countries as the century drew to an end. At a time of unprecedented and unchallenged American prosperity and power, Russia was confronting a severe economic, social, and demographic crisis; a new array of threats to its power and security; a profound feeling of vulnerability; and a difficult struggle to define a new post-Soviet identity.

As the second term of the Clinton administration drew to a close, a far more sober, if not somber, assessment of the prospects for the transformation of Russia

---

itarian past into a bright, rich and civilized future in one go. I myself believed in this. But it could not be done in one fell swoop. In some respects I was too naïve. Some of the problems were too complex." (Reuters, December 31, 1999).

[4]The somewhat mechanical assumptions underlying these efforts are well captured in the title of a book by political scientist Guiseppe Di Palma, *To Craft Democracies: An Essay on Democratic Transitions* (Berkeley: University of California Press, 1990).

[5]The U.S. government was not alone in underestimating the challenge. Germany's absorption of the GDR entailed costs and obstacles that vastly exceeded the initial estimates: over $500 billion since 1989. The GDR's much-vaunted industrial plant proved noncompetitive and catastrophically unviable in a Western context and required massive infusions of capital, while the psychological and attitudinal division of Germany persisted long after its institutions were formally unified. Charles S. Maier, *Dissolution: The Crisis of Communism and the End of East Germany* (Princeton, NJ: Princeton University Press, 1997), ch. 5; Ullrich Heilemann and Reimut Jochimsen, *Christmas in July? The Political Economy of German Unification Reconsidered* (Washington, DC: Brookings Institution Press, 1993).

(and the region more broadly), and for its integration with the West, had taken hold across the political spectrum. The excessive optimism of the early years gave way to the oppposite extreme. Commentators and analysts vied with one another in denigrating the modest but nonetheless real achievements of the post-communist transformations, portraying Russia's severe political, economic, and social problems in catastrophic terms, and also overstating the contribution of American actions toward them. As the deterioration of Russian-American relations displaced earlier hopes of a "strategic partnership," observers noted that Russian leaders now used that phrase to describe their increasingly close relations with Beijing rather than Washington.

Although controversies over American policy toward Russia had simmered throughout the decade, critics sought, unsuccessfully in the end, to make it a major issue in the presidential election campaign of 2000. While much of the criticism was both superficial and shrill, and made little effort to propose politically feasible alternatives, the Clinton administration's policies became the target both of those who argued that the United States had not done enough to promote political and economic reform in Russia and of those who deplored its excessive and misguided involvement (and even of some who appeared to hold both views at once). [6] In a bitterly partisan attack, Republican critics of the Clinton-Gore administration charged it with squandering the greatest foreign policy opportunity since World War Two, while a prominent academic derided its Russia policy as "the worst American foreign policy disaster since Vietnam." [7]

Broadly speaking, the arguments in the "Who Lost Russia?" debate fell into three general groups:

- The "insufficient assistance" argument asserted that the failure of the United States and the West to deliver on its promise of major economic assistance, as well as the unwillingness to treat Russia as a full partner in creating a new post–Cold War security architecture, was largely responsible for the disillusionment and strains in the current relationship. Its advocates appeared to believe that large infusions of economic assistance in the early 1990s, before even the most rudimentary institutional infrastructure of a market economy was in place, could have been utilized effectively, although all the evidence

---

[6]For several examples among many, see Stephen F. Cohen, *Failed Crusade: America and the Tragedy of Post-Communist Russia* (New York: W. W. Norton & Co., 2000); Janine R. Wedel, *Collision and Collusion: The Strange Case of Western Aid to Eastern Europe, 1989–1998* (St Martin's Press, New York 1998); Wedel, "Tainted Transactions: Harvard: the Chubais Clan and Russia's Ruin," *The National Interest* 59 (Spring 2000): 23–34. A more comprehensive and thoughtful critique is Peter Reddaway and Dimitri Glinski's *The Tragedy of Russia's Reforms* (Washington, DC: United States Institute of Peace, 2000).

[7]The critique was laid out in the superficial, highly partisan, and often contradictory "Cox Report" prepared by a group of House Republicans, the Speaker's Advisory Group on Russia: *Russia's Road to Corruption: How the Clinton Administration Exported Government Instead of Free Enterprise and Failed the Russian People* (Washington, DC: U.S. House of Representatives, 10/23/00). The quote is from Cohen, *Failed Crusade*, p. 9.

suggests that it would simply have exacerbated the patterns of corruption, inequality, and capital flight already evident.

- The "wrongheaded policies" argument asserts that the United States and the West squandered the large reservoir of goodwill that they enjoyed among Russians by pursuing policies inimical to the interests of the Russian people with regard to both domestic transformation and foreign and security policy. These critics accuse the United States government of backing a corrupt and unpopular Russian leadership; of pursuing economic policies that undermined the social and economic well-being of the Russian population; and of seeking to extend its geopolitical influence in the region at Russia's expense. Adherents of this view place much of the blame for the deterioration of Russian-American relations on a series of what they view as misguided American policies—most notably NATO enlargement, Western military intervention in Kosovo, and deepening engagement with the non-Russian states of the former Soviet Union—which they view as threatening to Russian political and security interests.

  Many of these criticisms appeared to assume that the initial widespread enthusiasm for democracy and economic reform in Russia, as well as the hopes and expectations associated with the United States and the West, would prove enduring notwithstanding the inevitable disappointments and hardships of the transition period. Yet even in those countries that have experienced little political and economic reform, and where the American and Western presence has been far more limited, economic dislocation, social alienation, and disenchantment with the West have been widespread. By the same token, in other countries that have experienced equally severe hardship but where nationalism reinforces attempts at reform and at integration with Europe and the West, favorable attitudes toward the United States have actually increased. In short, the increasingly negative attitudes of the Russian population toward reform and toward the United States are, and ought to be, a serious concern, but they are not merely a reaction to badly flawed American policies. They have more deep-seated internal causes and require more nuanced explanation.

- The "Russian threat" argument takes the view that a policy premised on the view of Russia as a potential "strategic partner" of the United States rather than a potential adversary led the Clinton administration to exaggerate Russia's political and economic achievements and to ignore or minimize Russian behavior that threatened American interests. In this view, an excessive and unwarranted preoccupation with Russia's domestic transformation, and excessively close personal involvement with its leaders, diverted attention from the challenges posed by Russia's foreign and security policies, or minimized their importance. Furthermore, arms control agreements such as the thirty-year-old Anti-Ballistic Missile (ABM) Treaty negotiated in a different historical context now unduly constrained America's pursuit of its security interests and should no longer be considered binding. In this view, neocontainment rather than engagement with Russia, possibly combined with stronger support for "geopolitical pluralism" in the former Soviet region more broadly, would constitute a more appropriate response.[8]

These debates have highlighted fundamental differences between the advocates of a sustained and long-term effort at constructive engagement with Russia and those who question its desirability and advocate that Russia be treated at best with "benign neglect" and at worst as a potential adversary. They also raise important questions about the place of Russia in American foreign policy interests more broadly, the U.S. stake in relations with the other states of the region, and the extent to which Russia's domestic arrangements, and not merely its international behavior, are an important interest of the United States and a legitimate objective of American policy-making. At the same time, by focusing on the contradictory features of Russia's development as well as on flawed American policies in the region, these criticisms point to the need for a serious reassessment of Russia's trajectory and future prospects, as well as a corresponding reexamination of the assumptions underlying American policy. As both countries enter a new century with new leaders and priorities, such an effort may be particularly timely, although it is surely too early to provide definitive answers to many of these questions.

This chapter will attempt at least a provisional assessment. It will first lay out the broader assumptions and priorities that shaped the policies of the Clinton administration toward Russia and the other states of the region. It will then examine in more detail the evolution of American policies aimed at promoting democratization, economic reform, and security cooperation, and their interaction with developments in Russia itself. The chapter will conclude by drawing some broader lessons from the experience about the opportunities and constraints that confronted American policy. This analysis of American's Russia policy offers a sobering reminder of the limits of American ability fundamentally to reshape the international environment, or to exert more than a marginal influence over either the internal character or the external behavior of other important international actors.

## THE POLICY FRAMEWORK

The dramatic changes from 1989 to 1991 that culminated in the dissolution of the USSR demanded a fundamental redefinition of American interests abroad. The Soviet threat had provided an overarching rationale for American foreign policy over several decades, as well as the basis for something of a bipartisan domestic consensus. The Clinton administration, even more than its immediate predecessor, faced the formidable challenge of rethinking American interests in a post–Cold War world more broadly, and of forging a new domestic consensus on foreign policy. Moreover, no longer confronted by a single Soviet adversary in a bipolar interna-

---

[8]For a critique of "nation-building," see the Bush-Gore debate, October 11, 2000; on "geopolitical pluralism": Zbigniew Brzezinski, "A Geostrategy for Eurasia," *Foreign Affairs* 76, No. 5 (September–October 1997): 50–64; and *The Grand Chessboard: American Primacy and Its Geostrategic Imperatives* (New York: Basic Books, 1997).

tional system, and faced by a bewildering array of new and often unfamiliar and even unpronounceable new countries, American policy-makers faced the additional challenge of shaping a policy toward post–communist Russia while at the same time creating novel and constructive relationships with the fourteen now independent states—the non-Russian republics of the former Soviet Union—still haunted by what many perceived as the looming threat of imperial revival.

The Clinton administration came to power with a coherent and clearly articulated vision of a Europe that was undivided, peaceful, and democratic,[9] and with a major commitment to support the process of reform in Russia and the other former Soviet states as an overarching foreign policy priority. That vision rested on the underlying premise, best articulated by Anthony Lake in September 1993, that American security interests would best be served by strengthening and enlarging the community of market democracies.[10] With respect to Russia and the other states of the region, the initial strategy had three key components:

- To throw major American and Western support behind both political democratization and economic reform, premised on the view that the internal transformation of Russia was critical to its external behavior and that it constituted a major U.S. national security interest.[11] The emphasis on the centrality of Russian democratization to American security—a view held particularly ardently by Deputy Secretary of State and Russia adviser Strobe Talbott—remained to the end a centerpiece of the Clinton administration's Russia policy.[12] It was also a view that joined the imagery of promise to the hint of menace.[13] In calling for "a strategic alliance with Russian reform," the president warned: "The danger is clear if Russia's reforms turn sour—if it reverts to authoritarianism or disintegrates into chaos. The world cannot afford the strife of the former Yugoslavia replicated in a nation as big as Russia, spanning eleven time zones with an armed arsenal of nuclear weapons . . . "[14]

    Not only was a peaceful and democratic Russia important to the security and integration of the Euro-Atlantic community, but it would also bring

[9]See the chapter by Ivo Daalder, "The United States and Europe: From Primacy to Partnership?"

[10]"From Containment to Enlargement," speech delivered at SAIS, September 21, 1993.

[11]This view was powerfully shaped by the experience of the Gorbachev era, when domestic changes precipitated dramatic shifts in Soviet foreign policy; it also owed much to the influence of the "democratic peace" literature in international relations theory, e.g., Warren Christopher, "America's Leadership, America's Opportunity," *Foreign Policy* 98 (Spring 1995): 6–27.

[12]To what extent the entire region would be viewed through a single prism and to what extent the priority assigned to Russia policy shaped the administration's relations with the other states of the region are beyond the scope of this chapter but comprise a subject that deserves serious treatment in its own right.

[13]Sandy Berger, Assistant to the President for National Security Affairs, reaffirmed this view in an article summing up the Clinton legacy in November 2000. Rejecting the argument that American policy should confine itself to influencing Russia's external behavior, he asserted that "No event in the last half-century has done more to advance our security than Russia's democratic revolution. If both Russia and China become stable, pluralistic, prosperous societies, the world will be safer still." *Foreign Affairs* 79, No. 6 (November–December 2000): 7.

[14]Annapolis Naval Academy speech, April 1, 1993.

considerable domestic benefits in the form of reduced defense spending and increased trade. Seeking to mobilize domestic political support for his Russia policy, President Clinton explicitly linked his foreign policy agenda to American domestic priorities: "Our ability to put people first at home requires that we put Russia and its neighbors first on our agenda abroad."[15]

Although the initial emphasis on "free market democracies" tended to merge political democratization with economic reform, in practice these became two increasingly distinct priorities. They pointed toward different objectives and strategies, involved separate financial appropriations, and were carried out by different institutions and actors. Indeed, the two aims were not necessarily mutually reinforcing. Whereas support for democratization and free markets in theory tended to go hand in hand, in practice the widespread resistance of powerful interests to key aspects of economic reform, as well as the falling living standards of ordinary Russians, made it difficult to win support for key measures from a hostile parliament and an increasingly alienated population. The absence of political consensus on economic reform in turn led toward increasing reliance on executive power to bring it about by fiat.[16] It also led to a growing gap between rhetoric and reality.

- The second priority—and the one to which a major share of resources and attention was utimately devoted—was dealing with the security threat posed by the Soviet nuclear legacy. Although the broader Russian-American strategic relationship remained a central preoccupation throughout the decade, the most immediate challenge was the proliferation risk resulting from the presence of some 25,000 nuclear warheads on the territories of four of the successor states: Russia, Ukraine, Kazakstan, and Belarus. Furthermore, the Soviet nuclear legacy, as well the legacy of massive Soviet weapons of mass destruction (WMD) programs more generally, posed a still broader and more complex set of challenges as the ongoing unraveling of Soviet state structures and capacity raised increasingly grave concerns about the safety and security of the entire Russian nuclear and military infrastructure. Over time, concern over the possible diversion of fissile materials as well as of chemical and biological agents, and of the scientists and engineers who had helped develop them, became an additional focus of American policy and funding priorities.[17]

[15]Ibid.

[16]Although still inconclusive, a growing body of evidence points to a high correlation between political and economic reform. While it has often been argued that strong, indeed authoritarian, executives are essential to implementing economic reform, the experience of Central and Eastern Europe demonstrates that success in implementing economic reform has been greatest where democratic freedoms and civil liberties, as measured by Freedom House, are best protected: Steve Fish, "Democratization's Prerequisites: The Postcommunist Experience," *Post-Soviet Affairs* 14, No. 3 (July–September 1998): 212–47; James Millar, "New Leadership and Direction at the IMF," *Problems of Post-Communism* 47, No. 5 (September–October 2000): 45–46.

[17]Graham T. Allison, Owen R. Cote, Jr., Richard A. Falkenrath, and Steven E. Miller, "Avoiding Nuclear Anarchy," *Washington Quarterly* 20, No. 3 (Summer 1997): 185–198.

The successful pursuit of cooperative denuclearization, however, as well as of a whole range of other arms control initiatives aimed at securing adherence to the Non-Proliferation Treaty (NPT), reducing and securing existing arsenals and preventing nuclear proliferation, could not be confined to Russia alone. Nor could it occur in the absence of broader political relationships. As the early tensions over Ukraine's accession to the NPT demonstrated all too clearly, the success of that pursuit depended in considerable measure on the development of a whole new range of bilateral political, economic, and security ties with these countries to reassure them that their security and political status was not dependent on preserving their nuclear capabilities.[18] American policy gradually shifted over time from its initial focus on Russia, along with the Baltic states, a focus that also reflected the preeminent role of Strobe Talbott as a close friend and key adviser of President Clinton, to a growing recognition that the United States had an important interest in the stability, security, and development of the region as a whole. By 1994, American policy had come to embrace support for the still-fragile sovereignty, stability, and security of the other states of the region from the Ukraine to the Caucasus and Central Asia—states that many in Moscow considered to fall within Russia's zone of vital, if not exclusive, security interests—while simultaneously seeking to develop and sustain a close partnership with Russia.[19]

- The third priority of American policy was to promote the broader integration of Russia and the other states of the region into Europe through cooperation in pursuit of shared goals. The optimistic vision, if not "irrational exuberance" that animated this conception was that of a "strategic partnership" between a democratic and liberal Russia and the United States, cemented and lubricated by close personal ties among their leaders. It was a vision that appeared to be shared by the Yeltsin leadership as well. As then–Foreign Minister Andrei Kozyrev described it, Russia would finally be in a position to regain its status as a "normal country" and to become "a reliable partner in the community of civilized nations."[20] American and other Western assistance for Russian political and economic reform not only would ease the inevitable pain of the economic transition but would also facilitate the cooperation of the Russian leadership, and of President Yeltsin in particular,

---

[18]The underlying rationale is spelled out in Ashton B. Carter and William J. Perry, *Preventive Defense: A New Security Strategy for America* (Washington, DC: Brookings Institution Press, 1999). As Carter and Perry put it, the challenge was to persuade the Ukrainian leadership that Ukraine "would be more secure with friends and no nuclear weapons than with nuclear weapons and no friends" (p. 83).

[19]In February and March 1994, this engagement was highlighted by President Clinton's meetings in Washington with Ukraine's President Kravchuk, Kazakstan's President Nazarbaev, and Georgian President Shevardnadze. The development of the Partnership for Peace Program provided an innovative framework for cooperative security ties and a variety of joint programs with all the countries of the region.

[20]Andrei Kozyrev, "Russia: A Chance for Survival," *Foreign Affairs* 71, No.2 (March–April 1992): 9–10.

in dealing with the whole range of security problems, from nuclear proliferation and arms control to the Yugoslav conflict. Its goal was to encourage
Russia to become an active and cooperative partner in the construction of
new security arrangements in Europe.[21]

Almost from the start, however, these expectations of rapid and successful reforms ran up against a number of obstacles. First and foremost, political developments within Russia revealed the weakness of the democratic reformers who had
emerged as major actors in the late Gorbachev era and demonstrated the continuing
strength of communist and nationalist political forces, whose domination of the legislative branch compelled growing reliance on executive power to push forward a
reform agenda. By the time the Clinton administration came to power in January
1993, leading Russian reformers were already on the defensive; by midsummer, the
strained relationship between President Yeltsin and the Russian parliament had become overtly hostile; in early October, the conflict had escalated to a violent confrontation in which Yeltsin called on military force to dissolve the legislature; and
in new parliamentary elections held in December, voters gave unexpected support
to ultranationalist followers of Vladimir Zhirinovsky. A new post-Soviet constitution approved by referendum in December 1993 strengthened the presidency as an
institution but did little to end the conflict between the legislative and the executive
branches or to encourage consensus-building through the remainder of Yeltsin's
presidency. Not until Vladimir Putin's accession to the position was a new working
relationship established that permitted the passage of long-stalled legislation, from
ratification of the SALT II agreement to tax reform.

Secondly, economic policies intended to unleash market forces had completely unanticipated consequences in the post-Soviet environment. Interacting with
the institutional and behavioral features of the Soviet legacy, as well as with the
economic collapse wrought by Gorbachev's misguided attempts at partial reform,
the sudden opening of a previously closed and heavily militarized economy and the
breakup of a common economic space accelerated a severe collapse of production, a
radical decline in living standards, and a particularly corrupt form of crony capitalism. Moreover, both the ongoing unraveling and fragmentation of state power in
Russia and the continuing power of key industrial managers and regional bosses diminished the ability of the Russian government to implement key measures or to
deliver on international commitments.[22]

In relations with the West as well, the initial emphasis on cooperation and
friendship that characterized the Kozyrev era in Russian-American relations gave
way to growing disagreements over a whole range of foreign and security policy issues, from NATO enlargement to arms control, to nuclear and conventional arms

---

[21]The experiences of the late Gorbachev era played an important role in shaping these expectations. Western political and economic support for Gorbachev, and close personal ties among key leaders,
had smoothed the way for cooperation on a broad range of security issues, including German reunification.

[22]One of the better recent accounts of this process is Thane Gustafson, *Capitalism Russian-Style*
(Cambridge: Cambridge University Press, 1999)·

proliferation, and ultimately to issues of sovereignty and humanitarian intervention raised by Western policy in Yugoslavia. Moreover, as American policy shifted from its initial Russocentric focus to encompass a broader engagement with the other states of the region, American actions were increasingly perceived by growing segments of the Russian elite in alarmist and zero-sum terms, as a geopolitical offensive aimed at reducing and supplanting Russian influence in a region that it considered to be a zone of important, if not exclusive, interests.

Internal struggles over Russia's identity and interests inevitably became entwined with conflicts over Russia's purposes abroad, as critics of the Yeltsin government's domestic policies also attacked what they viewed as its excessively pro-Western and accommodationist stance in foreign affairs. Kozyrev's replacement as Foreign Minister by Yevgeny Primakov in 1996 signaled a shift to a policy that sought to increase both the appearance of Russian autonomy and the substance of leverage in its relations with the United States without altogether jeopardizing economic and security cooperation with the West and Russia's integration into the global economy, all of which were still perceived as essential to Russia's long-term recovery. This strategy of "contingent cooperation"[23] has been pursued with even greater focus and energy under President Putin and Foreign Minister Ivanov. The Russian leadership to date appears to see no realistic alternative to a Western-oriented policy aimed at integration with international institutions if Russia is to attract the trade and the large capital investment essential to building a modern economy. At the same time, the leadership seeks to enhance its political leverage by capitalizing on resentment of American primacy and fears of American hegemony to encourage a countercoalition directed against a "unipolar world." Putin used the first year of his presidency to launch an energetic diplomatic campaign simultaneously to reinvigorate Russian economic and political influence in the neighboring ex-Soviet states while pursuing closer political, economic, and military ties with China, India, Iran, and former Soviet client states—from Iraq to North Korea and Cuba—as a counterweight to American influence. He also sought to rally broader international support for opposing U.S. deployment of a national missile defense and for ending U.S.-supported sanctions against Iraq. If the United States was enjoying an unprecedented international primacy, Russian policy was aimed at constraining it.

These shifts in Russian domestic and foreign policy and the growing strains in Russian-American relations coincided with growing partisanship and fractiousness in Washington, particularly after the Republican victory in the 1994 congressional elections and the attempted impeachment of President Clinton. These events exacerbated existing divisions in the United States over Russia and served to distract and weaken executive leadership in foreign policy. Moreover, the administration's failure to adjust its optimistic rhetoric to changing Russian realities set the stage for greater public disillusionment ahead. At the same time, critics of the administration's Russia policy seized on the brutal war in Chechnya that was launched by

---

[23]The apt term is that of Coit Blacker, "Russia and the West," in Michael Mandelbaum, ed., *The New Russian Foreign Policy* (New York: Council on Foreign Relations, 1998).

Moscow in December 1994 and again in 1999—as well as its failure to live up to other international commitments—as compelling evidence of the policy's failure.

But lying at the heart of all these issues was a more fundamental problem. The Western agenda for Russian transformation underestimated—indeed, virtually ignored—the single greatest challenge that preoccupied Russian elites throughout the decade: defining a new Russian identity and place in the world after the Soviet collapse. At a time of unchallenged and unparalleled American power and prosperity—a decade in which the United States enjoyed rapid economic growth and prosperity, the lowest unemployment in recent history, rapid advances in science and technology, and unprecedented military predominanace—Russia was experiencing a calamitous decline in GNP, a widening gap between rich and poor, increasing breakdowns of its industrial infrastructure, and an inability to sustain even minimal military capabilities. Its vaunted Soviet-era nuclear, chemical, and biological installations were no longer a symbol of power; they were becoming a threat to Russia's own security. In the midst of these alarming developments, the Russian government and people were also attempting to come to grips with a profound and traumatic set of losses: of territories and populations, of allies and client states, of political and economic power, of state coherence, of superpower status, and indeed of its very identity.[24] This loss of power and prestige, moreover, was not the result of military defeat but rather of a process of reform initiated by and consented to by Gorbachev himself in the expectation that his contribution to bringing the Cold War to an end would earn his country a respected place in a new European and global order.

Not only was it difficult for Russian elites and populations to reconcile themselves to the demise of the USSR and to the independence of the former republics, but also the Soviet Union's dissolution created a heightened sense of insecurity over the territorial integrity and security of Russia itself.[25] The United States might enjoy the luxury of focusing on the dangers posed by "states of concern" or terrorist groups based far from its borders. For Russia, security threats increasingly emanated from its immediate neighborhood, internal as well as external.[26] The sudden transformation of a country that had once controlled the fate of millions to a country

[24] The controversies surrounding the choice of a Russian national anthem and other state symbols were emblematic of these unsettled issues; President Putin finally opted for an amalgam that included the Soviet-era anthem (set to a new text); the adoption of the Czarist two-headed eagle and the Russian tricolor as state symbols; and the adoption of the red flag without hammer and sickle as the flag of the army.

[25] A large Russian literature on center-periphery relations focused on the question, "Will Russia follow the path of the USSR?"; and much of the debate over Chechnya was premised on domino theories of Russian disintegration. For one early example among many, see Leokadia Drobizheva, "Povtorit li Rossiia put' Soiuza?" in Lilia Shevtsova, ed., *Rossiiya segodniya: Trudnye poiski svobody* (Moscow: Institut mezhdunarodnykh ekonomicheskykh i politicheskykh issledovanii, 1993). See also Gail Lapidus, "The Dynamics of Secession in the Russian Federation: Why Chechnya?" in Mikhail A. Alexseev, ed., *Center-Periphery Conflict in Post-Soviet Russia: A Federation Imperiled* (New York: St. Martin's Press, 1999).

[26] The national security doctrine signed into law on December 17, 1997 by President Yeltsin's decree #1300 describes a new array of threats to Russia's national security which are primarily internal; *Rossiiskaya gazeta* December 26, 1997. The newest national security doctrine adopted under President Putin January 10, 2000 elaborates further on internal as well as external threats; www.scrp.ru.

that perceived itself to have lost control of its own fate created an unaccustomed and radical sense of vulnerability that deeply influenced the ongoing Russian struggle to define its identity and its place in the post–Cold War international system.[27] How to manage the fundamental asymmetry of power, interests, and priorities had become and would long remain the central challenge of the Russian-American bilateral relationship.

## AMERICAN POLICY AND RUSSIA'S EVOLUTION IN THE 1990s

Having committed itself to assisting the transformation of Russia and the other states of the region, the Clinton administration faced the challenge of devising specific programs to implement it. These choices were not made in a vaccuum; they reflected a variety of pressures and constraints that shaped the way broad intentions would be translated into outcomes.

To begin with, the management of the assistance programs for Russia and the NIS (Newly Independent States) were not created from scratch; the programs that were put in place in 1989 for Eastern and Central Europe provided ready models that were largely replicated and then expanded on for Russia and the NIS. The product of a series of decisions made in the Bush and early Clinton administrations, they were significantly affected from the start by domestic political and budgetary constraints. At a time of considerable pressures to reduce the size of the federal government, it was clearly unfeasible to contemplate creating a large, new bureaucracy to design and manage American programs for the region. Virtually by default, it was decided to channel the bulk of technical assistance through the Agency for International Development (AID), an organization that lacked expertise or prior experience in communist countries. To compensate for its deficiencies while avoiding the problems of large field offices staffed by local employees, the program would be managed and staffed from Washington, with a coordinator's office to supervise its far-flung activities.

Similarly, many of the initial programs in support of political and economic reform in Russia and the NIS were themselves also modeled on or extensions of the technical assistance programs that had been developed for Central and Eastern Europe in 1989. In the case of Eastern Europe, however, the most important element in that strategy was the promise of NATO membership as a positive inducement for change, an inducement that could not be held out, at least in the foreseeable future, to the former Soviet states. And as Ivo Daalder has noted in his own chapter, while EU enlargement could in principle have served this purpose, the unwillingness of its members to contemplate such a step—and the unpreparedness of the NIS for such membership—

---

[27]In the "Who Lost Russia?" debate inside Russia itself, a long legacy of suspicion of the West, still deeply ingrained in older generations and in the military and security services, shaped a simple explanation for Russia's humiliation: hostile Western forces, abetted by their Russian collaborators, were responsible for Russia's collapse and were now plotting its dismemberment.

effectively precluded this option as well. Moreover, there were key features of the transformation of Russia and the NIS that were unique to this region and had no parallel in Central and Eastern Europe. Three features were especially salient for the development of American policy: the urgent need to deal with the Soviet nuclear and WMD legacy; the fact that the very creation of new states, and the development of new ties among them as well as with the United States, made state- and nation-building a central part of the agenda; and the fact that the highly centralized and militarized structure of the Soviet economy was a major obstacle to market reform. And unlike the situation in several Central and Eastern European countries, the absence of a broad and an effective domestic coalition in support of reform deprived the effort of consistent and reliable partners as well as a broader domestic political consensus.

American policy, moreover, was part of a larger international division of labor and developed in loose coordination with other international efforts and institutions. Although the international community was generally in agreement on the broad objectives, it too lacked a comprehensive strategy for developing and implementing assistance; national governments typically set their own priorities in accordance with domestic political requirements and pressures, and they coordinated their efforts through a variety of formal and informal mechanisms. Primary responsibility for macroeconomic stabilization and long-term development assistance fell to multilateral institutions, the IMF, and the World Bank in particular, over which the U.S. government had considerable influence but not full control. The IMF was by far the largest source of financial assistance to the Russian government, here as elsewhere seeking to promote macroeconomic stabilization and structural reforms through loans extended to central banks and tied to the fulfillment of specific conditions negotiated with the relevant governments; through September 1998, IMF had lent Russia over $22.2 billion for these purposes. The World Bank offered project-oriented technical assistance grants and loans particularly focused on energy, agriculture, infrastructure development, and the creation of a social safety net; it disbursed some $7.5 billion in loans over this period.[28]

American government assistance programs initially focused on humanitarian aid, which was relatively uncontroversial and had the added political benefit of disposing of agricultural commodities. It was also especially vulnerable to diversion and corruption. In subsequent years, the emphasis shifted to a virtual alphabet soup of technical assistance programs aimed at privatization and economic reform funded through the Freedom Support Act and channeled primarily through the Agency for International Development; and to other activities carried out most prominently by the Departments of Agriculture, Defense, and Energy.

The cumulative U.S. government expenditures for all NIS assistance programs from 1992 to September 1999 totaled $12.9 billion, of which one third was devoted to food assistance provided through the Department of Agriculture. Of the overall total, roughly half the funds were devoted to Russia. (See Table 1 and Table 2.)

[28]A number of other important actors also played key roles, including the European Bank for Reconstruction and Development and the European Union through its TACIS program.

**Table 1.** Cumulative Expenditures (FY 1992 to Date) for Major NIS Assistance Programs by Country as of 9/30/99

*(millions of dollars, rounded to the nearest $10,000)*

| | TOTAL | NIS-REG | RUS | ARM | AZR | GEO | KAZ | KGZ | TJK | TKM | UZB | BLR | MLD | UKR |
|---|---|---|---|---|---|---|---|---|---|---|---|---|---|---|
| **FREEDOM SUPPORT ACT (FSA) FUNDS** | | | | | | | | | | | | | | |
| **USAID/ENI-BUREAU FOR EUROPE AND THE NIS** | | | | | | | | | | | | | | |
| NIS Special Initiatives (Humanitarian, etc.)[1] | 530.77 | 41.18 | 47.37 | 222.37 | 53.90 | 81.54 | 7.39 | 4.95 | 28.21 | 1.71 | 3.58 | 2.26 | 7.54 | 28.37 |
| Energy Efficiency and Market Reform[1] | 414.49 | 36.73 | 83.89 | 55.37 | 0.08 | 16.71 | 10.41 | 5.97 | | 0.08 | 0.09 | 0.74 | 4.86 | 199.57 |
| Environmental Policy and Technology[1] | 135.26 | 16.42 | 57.48 | 0.53 | | 0.64 | 12.93 | 0.96 | 0.40 | 6.49 | 8.54 | 0.23 | 2.90 | 27.74 |
| Health-Care Improvement[1] | 228.46 | 24.16 | 83.67 | 6.83 | 0.47 | 3.73 | 35.05 | 11.35 | 2.71 | 3.37 | 7.67 | 2.86 | 6.02 | 40.57 |
| Private Sector Initiatives[1] | 977.08 | 16.86 | 533.20 | 29.47 | | 22.94 | 78.09 | 43.65 | 0.23 | 0.10 | 6.23 | 7.00 | 58.31 | 180.99 |
| Food Systems Restructuring | 104.27 | 1.60 | 44.92 | 1.07 | 0.41 | 3.68 | 1.63 | 0.09 | | | | | 7.14 | 43.74 |
| Democratic Reform[1] | 325.82 | 21.08 | 133.82 | 16.09 | 2.30 | 9.13 | 25.17 | 12.59 | 3.67 | 2.24 | 5.52 | 4.83 | 4.61 | 84.78 |
| Housing-Sector Reform | 239.89 | 2.50 | 199.86 | 9.44 | | | 7.17 | 1.70 | | | | | | 19.21 |
| Economic Restructuring and Financial Reform | 321.75 | 23.69 | 81.53 | 22.93 | | 6.60 | 41.05 | 26.13 | 0.47 | 3.09 | 16.33 | 0.12 | 16.42 | 83.39 |
| Eurasia Foundation | 113.46 | 48.90 | 26.21 | 10.48 | 0.60 | 3.69 | 1.01 | 1.10 | 0.32 | 0.22 | 1.28 | 1.04 | 0.71 | 17.90 |
| Enterprise Funds | 411.65 | 54.95 | 221.62 | 2.54 | 2.47 | 2.47 | 14.40 | 11.50 | 1.70 | 7.60 | 16.80 | | 7.56 | 68.04 |
| Exchanges and Training[1] | 173.56 | 2.96 | 88.48 | 10.22 | 2.03 | 3.27 | 10.34 | 6.68 | 4.79 | 5.91 | 8.13 | 2.16 | 1.90 | 26.71 |
| Russia Energy & Environmental Commodity Import Program (CIP) | 59.50 | | 59.50 | | | | | | | | | | | |
| Administrative Expenses | 25.30 | 25.30 | | | | | | | | | | | | |
| **TOTAL USAID/ENI[1]** | **4061.23** | **316.33** | **1661.53** | **387.33** | **62.24** | **154.39** | **244.65** | **126.68** | **42.50** | **30.81** | **74.16** | **21.24** | **118.37** | **821.01** |
| **OTHER USAID PROGRAMS** | | | | | | | | | | | | | | |
| Humanitarian Assistance—Armenia (155-0001) | 10.78 | | | 10.78 | | | | | | | | | | |
| Presidential Medical Initiative (156-0001) | 5.00 | | | 5.00 | | | | | | | | | | |
| USAID Farmer-to-Farmer Program & OFDA | 39.95 | 8.32 | 16.79 | 1.29 | | 0.32 | 3.55 | 1.29 | 0.32 | 0.65 | 0.65 | 1.29 | 0.97 | 4.52 |
| Ukraine Credit Facility | (NOT APPLICABLE—SEE COMMERCIAL FINANCING AND INSURANCE CHART) | | | | | | | | | | | | | |
| Transfers to Other USAID Bureaus[2] | 32.14 | 24.98 | 0.84 | 2.14 | | 0.35 | 1.26 | 0.39 | 0.13 | 0.73 | 0.89 | | 0.02 | 0.42 |
| Parking Fines | | | | | | | | | | | | | | |
| **TOTAL OTHER USAID PROGRAMS[3]** | **87.87** | **33.30** | **17.63** | **19.21** | | **0.67** | **4.81** | **1.68** | **0.45** | **1.37** | **1.54** | **1.29** | **0.98** | **4.94** |
| **TOTAL USAID[3]** | **4149.09** | **349.63** | **1679.16** | **406.54** | **62.24** | **155.06** | **249.46** | **128.36** | **42.95** | **32.18** | **75.69** | **22.53** | **119.53** | **825.94** |
| | TOTAL | NIS-REG | RUS | ARM | AZR | GEO | KAZ | KGZ | TJK | TKM | UZB | BLR | MLD | UKR |
| **TRANSFERS TO OTHER AGENCIES** | | | | | | | | | | | | | | |
| **U.S. DEPARTMENT OF COMMERCE** | | | | | | | | | | | | | | |
| Business Information Service for the NIS (BISNIS) | 10.15 | | 4.98 | 0.26 | 0.21 | 0.26 | 1.13 | 0.27 | 0.12 | 0.17 | 0.39 | 0.23 | 0.26 | 1.87 |
| Business Information Service—Russia (BISTA) | 0.97 | | 0.97 | | | | | | | | | | | |
| American Business Centers (ABCs) | 13.33 | 1.39 | 10.05 | | | | 0.60 | | | | 0.46 | 0.26 | | 0.57 |

*(continued)*

**Table 1.** Cumulative Expenditures (FY 1992 to Date) for Major NIS Assistance Programs by Country as of 9/30/99 (continued)

*(millions of dollars, rounded to the nearest $10,000)*

| FREEDOM SUPPORT ACT (FSA) FUNDS | TOTAL | NIS-REG | RUS | ARM | AZR | GEO | KAZ | KGZ | TJK | TKM | UZB | BLR | MLD | UKR |
|---|---|---|---|---|---|---|---|---|---|---|---|---|---|---|
| **U.S. DEPARTMENT OF COMMERCE** | | | | | | | | | | | | | | |
| SABIT Business Internship Training Program | 15.52 | 0.01 | 8.50 | 0.40 | 0.20 | 0.47 | 0.98 | 0.41 | 0.29 | 0.27 | 0.72 | 0.29 | 0.31 | 2.69 |
| Commercial Law Development Program (CLDP) | 6.57 | 0.25 | 2.45 | | | | | | | | | | 1.00 | 2.87 |
| Business Development Committees (BDCs) | 2.50 | 0.56 | 1.82 | | | | 0.05 | | | | | 0.01 | | 0.07 |
| Consortia of American Businesses in the NIS (CABNIS) | 4.50 | | 4.50 | | | | | | | | | | | |
| **TOTAL DEPARTMENT OF COMMERCE** | **53.53** | **2.21** | **33.26** | **0.65** | **0.41** | **0.72** | **2.77** | **0.67** | **0.41** | **0.43** | **1.57** | **0.79** | **1.57** | **8.07** |
| **USIA FREEDOM SUPPORT ACT EXCHANGES** | **440.61** | **9.29** | **226.04** | **21.57** | **10.86** | **14.17** | **19.66** | **12.42** | **4.95** | **5.42** | **10.84** | **15.19** | **12.60** | **77.59** |
| **U.S. DEPARTMENT OF ENERGY** | | | | | | | | | | | | | | |
| Nuclear Reactor Safety | 179.11 | | 69.40 | 10.13 | | | 0.42 | | | | | | | 99.16 |
| Initiatives for Proliferation Prevention (formerly Industrial Partnering Prog.) | 34.40 | | 30.21 | | | | 0.64 | | | | | 0.37 | | 3.18 |
| Chornobyl Initiative | 109.30 | | | | | | | | | | | | | 109.30 |
| **TOTAL DEPARTMENT OF ENERGY** | **322.81** | | **99.61** | **10.13** | | | **1.06** | | | | | **0.37** | | **211.64** |
| **U.S. DEPT. OF STATE—S/NIS/C HUMANITARIAN ASSISTANCE** | | | | | | | | | | | | | | |
| Transportation Costs and Grants | 279.29 | 3.06 | 59.10 | 56.55 | 14.58 | 50.05 | 16.21 | 10.27 | 5.10 | 3.49 | 7.83 | 8.46 | 12.86 | 31.73 |
| Cargo Value (DoD excess and privately donated)[4] | 2196.18 | | 602.16 | 196.81 | 15.23 | 308.67 | 156.28 | 103.64 | 32.92 | 34.28 | 86.91 | 145.02 | 97.68 | 416.58 |
| **TOTAL S/NIS/C HUMANITARIAN** | **2475.47** | **3.06** | **661.26** | **253.36** | **29.81** | **358.72** | **172.49** | **113.91** | **38.02** | **37.77** | **94.74** | **153.48** | **110.54** | **448.31** |
| **ASSISTANCE** | | | | | | | | | | | | | | |
| **U.S. DEPARTMENT OF STATE** | | | | | | | | | | | | | | |
| INL / Anti-Crime Training & TA | 27.99 | 3.96 | 17.29 | 0.22 | | 0.31 | 0.98 | 0.52 | 0.09 | 0.09 | 0.34 | 0.98 | 0.60 | 2.84 |
| INR / Title VIII Research Program | 20.48 | 7.61 | 9.31 | | 0.21 | 0.27 | 0.42 | 0.25 | 0.21 | 0.24 | 0.47 | 0.14 | 0.10 | 1.02 |
| Science Centers | 67.36 | 0.80 | 37.00 | 4.35 | | 2.27 | 5.80 | 0.75 | | | 1.34 | | | 15.05 |
| **TOTAL DEPARTMENT OF STATE** | **115.83** | **12.37** | **63.60** | **4.57** | **0.21** | **2.85** | **7.20** | **1.52** | **0.30** | **0.33** | **2.14** | **1.12** | **0.70** | **18.91** |
| **U.S. DEPARTMENT OF JUSTICE—Criminal Law Assistance** | **4.78** | **0.81** | **1.64** | **0.68** | | **0.40** | | | | | **0.04** | | **0.13** | **1.08** |
| **OVERSEAS PRIVATE INVESTMENT CORPORATION (OPIC)** | (NOT APPLICABLE—SEE COMMERCIAL FINANCING AND INSURANCE CHART) | | | | | | | | | | | | | |
| **U.S. TRADE & DEVELOPMENT AGENCY (TDA)** | **65.94** | **1.69** | **41.32** | **1.04** | **0.29** | **1.64** | **4.55** | **0.15** | | **3.44** | **2.48** | **2.87** | **0.11** | **6.37** |
| **PEACE CORPS** | **51.26** | | **13.45** | **4.29** | | | **6.82** | **4.38** | | **4.34** | **4.59** | | **4.22** | **9.16** |
| **ENVIRONMENTAL PROTECTION AGENCY** | **18.36** | **0.38** | **14.80** | | | **0.01** | | | | | | | **0.01** | **3.16** |
| **NSF / CIVILIAN RESEARCH & DEVELOPMENT** | **2.85** | **0.90** | **0.24** | **0.70** | | **0.05** | **0.30** | **0.25** | | | **0.11** | | | **0.30** |

| Program | TOTAL | NIS-REG | RUS | ARM | AZR | GEO | KAZ | KGZ | TJK | TKM | UZB | BLR | MLD | UKR |
|---|---|---|---|---|---|---|---|---|---|---|---|---|---|---|
| U.S. CUSTOMS SERVICE / GEORGIA BORDER SECURITY | 8.85 | | | | | 8.85 | | | | | | | | |
| U.S. NUCLEAR REGULATORY COMMISSION (NRC) | 22.33 | | 11.30 | 0.70 | | 0.38 | | | | | | | | 9.95 |
| **U.S. DEPARTMENT OF AGRICULTURE (USDA)** | | | | | | | | | | | | | | |
| Cochran Fellowship Program | 10.75 | 0.17 | 2.77 | 0.59 | 0.44 | 0.47 | 1.07 | 0.85 | 0.53 | 0.60 | 0.94 | 0.24 | 0.74 | 1.34 |
| Faculty Exchange Program | 1.77 | | 0.73 | | | | 0.15 | | | | | | | 0.88 |
| Agricultural Extension Programs | 19.92 | | | 19.92 | | | | | | | | | | |
| Collaborative Biotech Research Program | 1.59 | | 0.96 | | | | 0.07 | | | | | | | 0.56 |
| **TOTAL USDA EXCHANGE PROGRAMS** | **34.02** | **0.17** | **4.46** | **20.51** | **0.44** | **0.47** | **1.29** | **0.85** | **0.53** | **0.60** | **0.94** | **0.24** | **0.74** | **2.78** |
| **U.S. DEPARTMENT OF THE TREASURY** | | | | | | | | | | | | | | |
| G-7 Support Implementation Group | 2.29 | | 2.29 | | | | | | | | | | | |
| Technical Advisors | 30.32 | 6.56 | 9.17 | 2.39 | | 2.21 | 1.87 | 0.99 | 0.11 | | | 1.18 | 1.82 | 4.02 |
| **TOTAL U.S. DEPT. OF THE TREASURY** | **32.61** | **6.56** | **11.46** | **2.39** | | **2.21** | **1.87** | **0.99** | **0.11** | | | **1.18** | **1.82** | **4.02** |
| CONGRESSIONAL RESEARCH SERVICE (CRS) | 4.69 | | 1.92 | | | | | | | | | | | 2.77 |
| **TOTAL TRANSFERS TO OTHER AGENCIES** | **1457.74** | **37.44** | **582.19** | **123.78** | **26.79** | **81.42** | **62.11** | **31.51** | **11.41** | **18.05** | **30.54** | **30.22** | **34.77** | **387.52** |
| | TOTAL | NIS-REG | RUS | ARM | AZR | GEO | KAZ | KGZ | TJK | TKM | UZB | BLR | MLD | UKR |
| **TOTAL CUMULATIVE FSA EXPENDITURES AS OF 9/30/99** | **5606.84** | **387.07** | **2261.34** | **530.32** | **89.04** | **236.48** | **311.57** | **159.87** | **54.36** | **50.23** | **106.23** | **52.75** | **154.12** | **1213.46** |
| NON-FREEDOM SUPPORT ACT FUNDS | TOTAL | NIS-REG | RUS | ARM | AZR | GEO | KAZ | KGZ | TJK | TKM | UZB | BLR | MLD | UKR |
| **U.S. DEPARTMENT OF DEFENSE (DoD) COOPERATIVE THREAT REDUCTION (CTR) PROGRAMS (Nunn-Lugar)** | | | | | | | | | | | | | | |
| Weapons Dismantlement | 763.06 | | 366.18 | | | | 70.13 | | | | | 26.72 | | 300.02 |
| Chain of Custody | 404.11 | | 301.78 | | | 1.21 | 32.95 | | | | | 19.60 | | 48.57 |
| Demilitarization | 324.44 | 60.51 | 93.88 | | | | 33.18 | | | | | 25.68 | 40.00 | 71.19 |
| Other | 80.69 | 52.49 | 28.20 | | | | | | | | 0.01 | | | |
| **Total CTR** | **1572.30** | **113.00** | **790.04** | | | **1.21** | **136.26** | | | | **0.01** | **72.00** | **40.00** | **419.78** |
| DoD Warsaw Initiative | 51.81 | 47.72 | 0.31 | | | 0.37 | 0.79 | 0.04 | | 0.04 | 0.23 | | 0.91 | 1.40 |
| DoD Customs Border Security / Counterproliferation | 10.21 | 9.00 | | 0.12 | 0.16 | 0.35 | | | | 0.01 | 0.22 | | 0.35 | |
| DoD/FBI Counterproliferation | 2.77 | | | 0.03 | | 0.59 | 0.85 | 0.44 | | 0.01 | 0.50 | | 0.36 | |
| **TOTAL DEPARTMENT OF DEFENSE** | **1637.08** | **169.72** | **790.35** | **0.15** | **0.16** | **2.52** | **137.90** | **0.48** | | **0.06** | **0.96** | **72.00** | **41.62** | **421.18** |
| NON-FREEDOM SUPPORT ACT FUNDS | TOTAL | NIS-REG | RUS | ARM | AZR | GEO | KAZ | KGZ | TJK | 0.13 | UZB | BLR | MLD | UKR |
| **U.S. DEPARTMENT OF AGRICULTURE** | | | | | | | | | | | | | | |
| Food Assistance | 4276.22 | | 2418.28 | 361.84 | 57.80 | 354.64 | 42.04 | 236.57 | 181.25 | 101.40 | 17.00 | 218.20 | 126.87 | 160.33 |
| Cochran Fellowship Program | 5.85 | 0.08 | 2.90 | 0.13 | | 0.20 | 0.60 | | 0.20 | 0.20 | 0.14 | 0.20 | 0.10 | 1.10 |
| Agricultural Research Services | 0.34 | | | | | | 0.27 | 0.07 | | | | | | |
| **TOTAL DEPARTMENT OF AGRICULTURE** | **4282.40** | **0.08** | **2421.18** | **361.97** | **57.80** | **354.84** | **42.91** | **236.64** | **181.45** | **101.60** | **17.14** | **218.40** | **126.97** | **161.43** |

*(continued)*

113

**Table 1.** Cumulative Expenditures (FY 1992 to Date) for Major NIS Assistance Programs by Country as of 9/30/99 (continued)

*(millions of dollars, rounded to the nearest $10,000)*

| | TOTAL | NIS-REG | RUS | ARM | AZR | GEO | KAZ | KGZ | TJK | TKM | UZB | BLR | MLD | UKR |
|---|---|---|---|---|---|---|---|---|---|---|---|---|---|---|
| **U.S. DEPARTMENT OF ENERGY** | | | | | | | | | | | | | | |
| Nuclear Reactor Safety | 107.45 | | 69.59 | 0.37 | | | 0.06 | | | | | | | 37.43 |
| Materials Protection, Control and Accounting (MPC&A) | 392.56 | | 374.84 | | | 0.21 | 13.93 | | | | 1.51 | 0.63 | | 1.44 |
| Initiatives for Proliferation Prevention (formerly Industrial Partnering Prog.) | 62.85 | | 53.92 | | | | 2.02 | | | | | 1.64 | | 5.27 |
| Export Control Programs (Nuclear) | 8.81 | 0.99 | 3.57 | | | | 2.16 | | | | | | | 2.09 |
| Uranium Supply Enrichment | 1.00 | | 1.00 | | | | | | | | | | | |
| Arms Control Support | 31.64 | | 30.90 | | | | 0.03 | | | | 0.01 | 0.20 | | 0.50 |
| Research & Development—FSU States | 13.80 | | 13.80 | | | | | | | | | | | |
| Fissile Materials Disposition | 31.60 | | 31.60 | | | | | | | | | | | |
| Nuclear Cities Initiative | 3.78 | | 3.78 | | | | | | | | | | | |
| RERTR / Reduced Enrichment for Research & Test Reactors | 1.00 | | 1.00 | | | | | | | | | | | |
| TOTAL DEPARTMENT OF ENERGY | **654.49** | **0.99** | **584.00** | **0.37** | | **0.21** | **18.20** | | | | **1.52** | **2.47** | | **46.73** |
| **NSF / CIVILIAN R & D FOUNDATION** | 19.03 | 18.13 | 0.90 | | | | | | | | | | | |
| **NSF / COOPERATIVE RESEARCH PROJECTS** | 10.80 | 10.80 | | | | | | | | | | | | |
| **U.S. DEPARTMENT OF COMMERCE—CABNIS** | 1.50 | | 1.14 | | | | 0.36 | | | | | | | |
| **U.S. EXPORT-IMPORT BANK** | 300.00 | 300.00 | | | | | | | | | | | | |
| **U.S. TRADE AND DEVELOPMENT AGENCY (TDA)** | 11.14 | 0.62 | 7.46 | 0.06 | | 0.10 | 0.51 | 0.02 | 0.02 | 0.12 | 1.10 | 0.01 | 0.09 | 1.03 |
| **U.S. INFORMATION AGENCY (USIA)** | 250.65 | 15.95 | 126.23 | 8.45 | 5.94 | 9.80 | 14.24 | 6.19 | 1.99 | 2.28 | 12.41 | 9.33 | 5.82 | 32.03 |
| **U.S. DEPARTMENT OF STATE** | | | | | | | | | | | | | | |
| International Military Exchanges and Training (MET) | 20.89 | | 4.07 | | | 1.57 | 2.10 | 1.32 | | 1.24 | 1.66 | 0.90 | 1.65 | 6.38 |
| NADR / Counterproliferation | 5.24 | 0.39 | 2.72 | 0.12 | 0.34 | 0.11 | 0.43 | 0.02 | 0.02 | 0.06 | 0.02 | | 0.04 | 1.00 |
| Nonproliferation Disarmament Fund | 20.39 | 6.03 | 7.01 | 1.67 | 1.78 | | 1.22 | 0.82 | | 0.11 | 0.82 | | 0.82 | 0.11 |
| Warsaw Initiative | 52.15 | | 4.50 | | | 14.00 | 5.55 | 3.70 | | 1.55 | 4.20 | | 5.50 | 13.15 |
| TOTAL DEPARTMENT OF STATE | **98.67** | **6.42** | **18.30** | **1.79** | **2.12** | **15.68** | **9.29** | **5.85** | **0.02** | **2.96** | **6.69** | **0.90** | **8.01** | **20.64** |
| **PEACE CORPS** | 56.64 | | 14.11 | 5.21 | | | 6.83 | 4.55 | | 4.21 | 5.99 | 5.99 | 5.06 | 10.69 |
| | TOTAL | NIS-REG | RUS | ARM | AZR | GEO | KAZ | KGZ | TJK | TKM | UZB | BLR | MLD | UKR |
| **TOTAL CUMULATIVE NON-FSA EXPENDITURES AS OF 9/30/99** | 7322.41 | 522.71 | 3963.67 | 377.99 | 66.02 | 383.14 | 230.24 | 253.72 | 183.47 | 111.23 | 45.81 | 303.12 | 187.56 | 693.73 |
| | TOTAL | NIS-REG | RUS | ARM | AZR | GEO | KAZ | KGZ | TJK | TKM | UZB | BLR | MLD | UKR |
| **TOTAL CUMULATIVE USG (FSA+ NON-FSA) EXPENDITURES AS OF 9/30/99** | 12929.24 | 909.78 | 6225.01 | 908.32 | 155.05 | 619.62 | 541.80 | 413.59 | 237.83 | 161.46 | 152.04 | 355.86 | 341.68 | 1907.19 |

*Source:* US Government Assistance to and Cooperative Activities with the New Independent States of the Former Soviet Union. FY 1999 Annual Report. Prepared by the Office of the Coordinator of US Assistance to the NIS. January 2000.

**Table 2.** Funding Levels for Major U.S. Programs With Russia Since 1992 (Budgeted and Expended, Respectively)

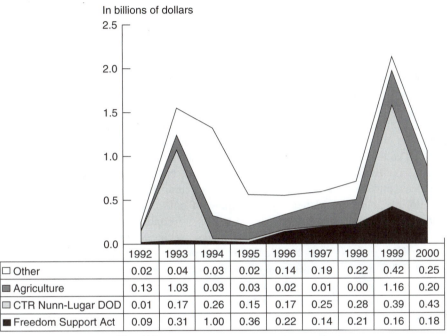

In billions of dollars

|                       | 1992 | 1993 | 1994 | 1995 | 1996 | 1997 | 1998 | 1999 | 2000 |
|-----------------------|------|------|------|------|------|------|------|------|------|
| □ Other               | 0.02 | 0.04 | 0.03 | 0.02 | 0.14 | 0.19 | 0.22 | 0.42 | 0.25 |
| ▨ Agriculture         | 0.13 | 1.03 | 0.03 | 0.03 | 0.02 | 0.01 | 0.00 | 1.16 | 0.20 |
| ▦ CTR Nunn-Lugar DOD  | 0.01 | 0.17 | 0.26 | 0.15 | 0.17 | 0.25 | 0.28 | 0.39 | 0.43 |
| ■ Freedom Support Act | 0.09 | 0.31 | 1.00 | 0.36 | 0.22 | 0.14 | 0.21 | 0.16 | 0.18 |

Fiscal Year

The particular programs selected for support were largely donor-driven rather than a response to host country requests. They were a function of the available American expertise, the efforts of various federal agencies to share a piece of the pie, the pressures from the usual array of domestic constituencies, both ethnic and economic, that were pressing their own agendas, and the desire to placate influential members of congress by awarding lucrative contracts to favored constituents. To speed the distribution of funds and assure the necessary accountability, programs were often turned over to large contractors or consulting groups with prior experience managing U.S. government contracts. A major consequence of these choices was the fact that a very substantial share of the funds went to American corporations, consultants, and NGOs, which helped sustain political support for the program in the United States but was often a source of resentment abroad.

## 1. Supporting Democratization and Civil Society Development

The Freedom Support Act originally approved in October 1992 and funded throughout the Clinton administration was explicitly intended to offer support for the development and consolidation of democracy in Russia and the other NIS states. Translating this broad commitment into concrete policy inititatives, how-ever, proved far more problematic and contentious than its initial supporters antici-pated, and the resources devoted to this effort in fact constituted a relatively small part of the total assistance. Democracy-assistance programs constituted under 3 percent of total U.S. aid programs to Russia and the NIS during the 1990s, with the budget for these activities in 1999–2000 a modest $16 million.[29] Including the wide array of government-funded exchange programs that have brought some 45,000 Russians to the United States would raise that total by $524 million since 1992.[30] Even had the ambition been present, serious attempts at reform of govern-mental institutions in a country the size of Russia, or a comprehensive reform of the judicial system, was hardly feasible with such modest resources; hence the em-phasis on civil society assistance and the focus on NGO support.

The early programs tended to focus on advocacy groups engaged in the de-sign of political and electoral institutions, were based on American models and practices, and emphasized party development, campaign techniques, and electoral monitoring. They relied heavily on American political consultants and activists, often with limited familiarity with the region, to conduct training programs built around American institutional arrangements, technologies, and organizational forms. Over time, support broadened to incorporate a wider range of nonstate ac-tors, NGO activities, and regional or local groups as well as national ones, with in-creasing focus on civic education, educational exchanges, and support for independent media. Even these, however, constituted but a small portion of a Rus-sian associational universe that also included labor unions and other workers' orga-nizations, religious associations, sports clubs, and charitable groups.

Evaluating the impact of these efforts on the actual course of Russia's political development, however, is highly problematic. Clearly, democratization in Russia has proceeded fitfully and incompletely, with serious setbacks and shortcomings, and considerable public disillusionment. The key achievements have been the avoidance of communist restoration, nationalist and neofascist revanchism, or civil war and an-archy, all considered highly likely outcomes in the early-1990s. Competitive elec-tions have come to be accepted across the political spectrum as the only legitimate mechanism for winning political power. Since 1991, Russia has experienced three nationwide parliamentary elections and two presidential elections, including its first peaceful and more-or-less democratic transition of power in its entire thousand-year history. Many of the institutions and techniques associated with Western democracy, from political parties, election campaigns and consultants, NGOs (over 65,000 at last count), and a great variety of media outlets—virtually all of which were absent just ten years ago—now dot the political landscape. But for all their impact on institu-tional forms and technologies, these Western efforts have had considerably less im-pact on the actual functioning of these institutions. With the possible exception of

---

[29]Cited in Sarah Mendelson, *Heritage Lectures,* No. 690, October 20, 2000, p. 7.
[30]See Table 1.

environmental movements, they have relatively weak linkages to Russian society more broadly, and their sustainability absent Western support is questionable.[31] Moreover, political corruption, increasing political and financial constraints on the mass media, and manipulated voting are widespread, while much of the substance associated with democratic governance—rule of law, well-institutionalized political parties linked to established constituencies, social and political activism, effective guarantees of human rights, a strong and independent media—are still lacking. In short, Russia and the other NIS states combine elements of electoralism with authoritarian institutions and values; democratic consolidation remains a distant goal.[32]

Moreover, the sustainability of these achievements remains uncertain. The ascendancy of Vladimir Putin to the presidency has been accompanied by a further and worrisome erosion of democratic norms and procedures. His ascent to power was facilitated by the renewal of a brutal war in Chechnya that again targeted the civilian population and infrastructure of the republic, was accompanied by massive violations of human rights, and has driven over 150,000 refugees from the territory. His preoccupation with restoring state power has been expressed in policies that have curtailed press freedoms and placed the media under ever-greater state supervision. He has drawn heavily from the military and FSB (Federal Security Services), successor to the KGB, in appointments to key positions, and he has encouraged or acquiesced in the arbitrary and selective use of police powers to undermine political opponents and intimidate critics. He has challenged important features of evolving federal relations in an effort to strengthen the vertical structure of power, creating a system of "viceroys" to oversee regional governors and republic presidents, substituting appointed officials for elected ones, and emasculating the Federation Council. And a number of recent trials of Russians accused of betraying state secrets to foreign journalists or NGOs, conducted under exceedingly dubious procedures, but with courts in some cases exonerating the defendants, have not only reflected the traditional FSB suspicion of "outside forces" but also are equally a warning to Russian citizens to be more wary in dealings with foreigners. In many of these cases, NGOs and independent media have played an important role in questioning authoritarian trends and in bringing abuses to public attention, but their activities and influence are increasingly circumscribed.

---

[31]These impressions are reinforced by the conclusions of a recent evaluation of democracy-assistance programs: Sarah Mendelson and John K. Glenn, "Democracy Assistance and NGO Strategies in Post-Communist Countries," *Carnegie Endowment Working Papers*, 2000; see also Marina Ottoway and Thomas Carothers, eds., *Funding Virtue: Civil Society Aid and Democracy Promotion* (Washington, DC: Carnegie Endowment for International Peace, 2000), ch. 7.

[32]For a debate over the emergence of "illiberal democracies," see Fareed Zakaria, "The Rise of Illiberal Democracy," *Foreign Affairs* 76, No.6 (November–December 1997): 22–32; responses in subsequent issues, e.g., Charles A. Kupchan, "Illiberal Illusions: Restoring Democracy's Good Name," *Foreign Affairs* 77, No.3 (May–June 1998): 122–125; John Shattuck, J. Brian Atwood, Marc F. Plattner in *Foreign Affairs* 77, No.2 (March–April 1998); Sarah E. Mendelson, "The Putin Path: Civil Liberties and Human Rights in Retreat," *Problems of Post-Communism*, 47, No.5 (September–October 2000); also Mendelson and Michael McFaul, "Russian Democracy—A U.S. National Security Interest," *Demokratizatsiya* 8, No.3 (Summer 2000).

A recent episode dramatically illustrates the contradictory tendencies of the current Russian political landscape, demonstrating both the continuing vitality of the Russian NGO sector as well as the government's ability to utilize administrative maneuvers to block its efforts. After failing to halt a series of measures reversing a decade of environmental achievements, including the abolition of the very ministry created to protect the environment, environmental groups across the country coalesced around an initiative to block an attempt by the Ministry of Atomic Energy to earn hard currency by providing storage facilities for nuclear wastes on Russian territory. In support of a national referendum on the issue, environmental groups swiftly gathered the necessary 2,500,000 signatures. Reluctant to attack the campaign directly, a government commission proceeded arbitrarily to invalidate enough signatures to nullify the effort.

If current trends in Russia raise concern over the potential erosion of some the gains in political freedom of the past ten years, in several of the other new states—from Belarus to Central Asia—the achievements of the early post-Soviet years are seriously endangered if not largely eradicated.

Much of the criticism of American policy toward Russia has focused on the extent to which support for democratization came to be identified with support for a Yeltsin administration increasingly perceived in Russia to be both ineffective and corrupt. American policy has also been faulted for its excessively strong support of, and close personal involvement with, the Yeltsin leadership, to the exclusion of other political actors and forces and at the expense of consistent and well-funded support for building democratic institutions. And yet, interstate relations are necessarily constrained by the need to work with a country's leaders, and in situations in which institutions are weakly developed and the personal roles and qualities of leaders are especially influential, these personal relationships can play a particularly critical role. Furthermore, notwithstanding Yeltsin's many shortcomings, his presidency was one that sought to distance Russia from its Soviet past and to delegitimate both communist and fascist political alternatives. It tolerated a considerable degree of domestic political pluralism and pursued a comparatively conciliatory policy in relations with neighboring states and with the West. Moreover, support for Yeltsin's leadership was not so unconditional as to compromise an even stronger American commitment to competitive elections. When in the spring of 1996 Yeltsin faced possible defeat in the upcoming presidential elections by the communist candidate, Gennady Zuganov, and was considering canceling the elections at the urging of close advisers, the Clinton administration weighted in strongly against such an action. It clearly signaled to Moscow that its commitment to the electoral process outweighed the risk of an unfavorable outcome and that cancellation of the elections would adversely affect U.S-Russian relations.

Nonetheless, American policy toward Russia suffered from a tendency to view the political landscape through an overly simple prism: as a dichotomous struggle between reformers on the one side and communists and nationalists on the other. Even if this picture was somewhat accurate in the early period, it failed to capture the growing complexity of the political spectrum, especially after the 1996 elections. Washington could also be faulted for failing to reach out to a broader Russian public and to deal with a broader spectrum of political forces. At the same time, there were real limits to how effectively American policy-makers could have worked with leading communists or nationalist opposition figures during this period and to how congress would have reacted to the use of taxpayers' money to fund them.

Serious questions can also be raised about the extent to which American support for democratization and human rights was subordinated to other objectives. The muted American response to the brutal war in Chechnya between 1994 and 1996, and again between 1999 and 2000, poorly served the larger long-term goal of building a democratic law-governed state. Although a number of considerations affected Western deference on the issue, the most central consideration in the minds of Washington policy-makers was the priority of other issues requiring the cooperation of the Yeltsin government—from nuclear dismantlement to START II ratification, and from joint peacekeeping efforts in Bosnia to NATO enlargement— compared with which the war in Chechnya appeared relatively marginal. Moreover, the very emphasis on inclusionary strategies for influencing Russian domestic and foreign policy militated against the use of political or economic sanctions to influence behavior. Only when it became clear that Yeltsin's policy in Chechnya was undermining his own political effectiveness and was jeopardizing his prospects for reelection could criticism of the war be presented as congruent with support for Russian reform.[33]

## 2. Supporting Economic Transformation

Russia's economic transformation has been similarly problematic. Whereas some analysts insist that Russia has taken giant strides toward the creation of a market economy, others have argued that the Russian transformation represents not so much a transition toward the market as the creation of a peculiar and deformed economic system variously characterized as "a virtual economy," "crony capitalism," or "industrial feudalism."[34] The extent to which American and more broadly Western policies have been responsible for the outcome is similarly controversial: some critics insist that Western advice and financial support were central, whereas others emphasize that the key choices were made by Russian policy-makers themselves, often resisting or disregarding Western advice, and that notwithstanding much

[33]For a more extensive treatment of the war in Chechnya and the American and Western responses, see Gail W. Lapidus, "The War in Chechnya: Opportunities Missed, Lessons to Be Learned," in Bruce W. Jentleson, ed., *Opportunities Missed, Opportunities Seized: Preventive Diplomacy in the Post–Cold War World* (Lanham, MD: Rowman and Littlefield, 2000).

[34]The most positive assessment is offered in Anders Aslund's *How Russia Became a Market Economy* (Washington, DC: Brookings 1995); more critical views include Richard Ericson, "Russia at the End of Yeltsin's Presidency," *Post-Soviet Affairs* 16, No.1 (January–March 2000); and Clifford Gaddy and Barry Ickes, "Russia's Virtual Economy," *Foreign Affairs* 77, No.5 (September–October 1998)·

self-advertising by a variety of consultants and would be-advisers, the Western role here too was relatively marginal.[35]

Few question the fact that Russia is in the throes of a severe economic and social crisis. Moreover, its length and severity far exceed anything anticipated by either Russian or Western policy-makers or economic advisers, none of whom had any blueprint for the "great leap backward" from a centralized planned economy to a market system. While the economies of the Baltic states and several Central European countries appear to be entering a period of stabilization and growth after undergoing substantial restructuring (arguably, with more favorable initial conditions and with the added incentive of membership in the European Community), Russia (and other NIS states) has experienced a precipitous economic decline. Industrial output is roughly 40 percent of its prereform level, and Russia's GNP has fallen below that of Mexico, Brazil, and Indonesia; capital investment has declined drastically; a significant share of the population finds itself below the poverty level, and the gap between rich and poor continues to widen. Economic crisis has also brought with it the collapse of the already inadequate Soviet-era health-care system and has exacerbated alarming social and demographic trends: the life expectancy of males has fallen further, and epidemic diseases are spreading. The economy has experienced a substantial recovery since the August 1998 financial crisis, with a revival of domestic production, an increase in currency reserves, an increase in tax revenues, and a decline in reliance on barter. But these improvements have been largely a result of the combined effects of high global energy prices and the ruble's sharp devaluation, and are likely to be short-lived unless the opportunity is seized for further structural changes. Despite the introduction of important elements of a market economy, including substantial privatization of the state sector, key economic activities continue to be controlled by personalized networks of tightly entwined political-economic elites with close ties to mafia structures. A small number of wealthy "oligarchs" control the most lucrative economic activities—above all, the extraction and export of natural resources—while the majority of the population has experienced severe impoverishment. Absent a functioning rule of law, property rights remain tenuous and uncertain and are enforced by private coercive mechanisms; corruption and rent-seeking dominate economic behavior, and profits fuel massive capital flight rather than domestic investment.[36] Meanwhile, the flow of foreign capital into Russia remains miniscule, roughly comparable to investment in Poland.

Much of the blame for this situation has been assigned to the overall strategy of economic reforms pursued by the Gaidar government and some of its successors, with varying degrees of commitment and consistency, with the support and encouragement of key Western financial institutions, most prominently the IMF and World Bank, and the United States government. This approach, largely based

[35]See, for example, Mark Kramer, "The Limits of US Influence on Russian Economic Policy," Policy Memo 173; PONARS Washington Conference, December 8, 2000.

[36]The estimates are necessarily imprecise, but range upward of 100 billion dollars since the mid-1990s.

on the standard repertoires of the so-called "Washington Consensus," had three key features:

1. to assign highest priority to macroeconomic stabilization and ruble convertibility through strict fiscal and monetary policies intended to prevent hyper-inflation and to impose budgetary discipline;

2. to abolish price controls and liberalize domestic and foreign trade to open the Russian market to competititon and to encourage the efficient allocation of resources; and

3. to encourage rapid privatization of state-owned property, premised on the view that rapid destatization was essential to reducing the power of the communist nomenklatura over economic activity, and to putting economic assets into the hands of real property owners who would be motivated to use them productively. It was largely taken for granted that once the state got out of the way, the market would emerge automatically to effectively allocate resources and promote economic growth. The long-term goal was to create an economic environment that would attract the large amounts of private capital investment essential to a fundamental restructuring of the Russian economy.

However laudable the overall goals, the implementation of the strategy was deeply flawed. IMF loans, for example, became a device for financing budgetary deficits rather than extraordinary measures to deal with balance-of-payments crises. At the same time, stringent conditionality was relaxed in the Russian case under pressure from the United States and other Western governments and in deference to political considerations. The argument that Russia was too important to be allowed to fail, however well-intentioned, distorted economic decision-making, weakened transparency and accountability for the use of funds, and contributed to a mounting debt burden until the financial crisis of August 1998 and the devaluation of the ruble compelled a fundamental reassessment of Western lending.

Moreover, elements of the "Washington Consensus" have themselves been called into question in recent years. One of its most prominent critics, noted economist and former Deputy Director of the World Bank Joseph Stiglitz, has argued more broadly that "the set of policies which underlay the Washington Consensus are neither necessary nor sufficient, either for macro-economic stability or longer-term development."[37]

Quite apart from the merits of the overall approach in principle, it had three particular weaknesses when applied to the distinctive conditions of the former Soviet states.[38] First, the assumption of the "automaticity" of market forces associated with orthodox macroeconomic theory largely ignored the political and institutional requisites of functioning markets, and the complex historical develop-

---

[37]Helsinki, January 1998 WIDER conference; Joseph Stiglitz, "Whither Reform: Ten Years of Transition" (paper presented to annual World Bank Conference on Developing Economies, April 28–30, 1999, Washington, DC); see also Oleg T. Bogomolov, "Russia Facing the Challenges of the Twenty-first Century," *International Social Science Journal* 163 (March 2000): 95–107.

[38]See, for example, Marie Lavigne, "The Economics of the Transition Process: What Have We Learned," *Problems of Post-Communism* 47, No.4 (July–August 2000); 2nd ed. (New York: St. Martin's Press, 1999); Stiglitz, "Whither Reform," op cit.

ment of these requisites in the West. It failed to recognize that capitalism is fundamentally a cultural and social system, resting on ingrained habits, norms, expectations, and understandings, and not merely a set of institutional arrangements. Even in the West, the development of market economies owed much to the role of the state in establishing the necessary framework of legal norms and institutions. In the former Soviet states, the most rudimentary legal foundations of a market economy were completely absent.

Second, the lack of familiarity of many of the Western experts and advisers with key features of Soviet economic organization and behavior as well as with Russian history contributed to the failure to anticipate how particular recommendations would play out in the distinctive political and economic setting of post-communist societies, particularly those—unlike the Baltic and Central European states—long incorporated into the USSR.[39] As just one example, the economic and political elites who dominated the Soviet command economy were in a particularly advantageous position during the last years of Soviet power to profit from the new opportunities presented by the opening up of the system to the outside world—and by the disappearance of any real control over their activities. Lacking both awareness of and interest in such arcane issues as transparent governance, the separation of public and private spheres, or conflicts of interest, it was all too easy to use state power for private gain. A system was put in place where incentives encouraged asset-stripping rather than wealth creation.[40] Moreover, globalization both encouraged and facilitated a massive outflow of assets to more secure environments. In short, the economic strategy pursued in Russia was not based on an adequate appreciation of the inhospitable environment that it confronted.

Thirdly, insufficient attention was devoted to devising a social safety net that would cushion the poorer segments of the population from the shocks of the transition. Soviet enterprises typically combined production with welfare functions, providing workers not only with paychecks but also with a variety of social services from subsidized housing and consumer goods to day care and polyclinics. Resistance to closing inefficient and essentially bankrupt enterprises was magnified by the absence of an alternative social safety net as well as of new employment opportunities in small business or the services.

Finally, the public prominence of Western advisers and experts and their close personal ties to Russian counterparts made the United States particularly vul-

---

[39]Ruble convertibility, for example, has had the perverse effect of encouraging rather than restraining fiscal recklessness. Rather than promoting an inflow of foreign capital, it has actually served to drain large amounts of capital out of the country; J. Brada, *PSA*, 2000. Another example is the failure to appreciate the way in which Soviet enterprises fused productive with welfare functions, which resulted in policies divesting enterprises of "inefficient" activities before giving attention to the construction of an alternative social safety net. Similarly, the initial hopes associated with defense conversion reflected an overly optimistic view of how readily and willingly military production facilities could be converted to the manufacture of consumer goods.

[40]Joseph Stiglitz, *Newsweek* supplement. December 1999–February 2000, p. 58. See also Steven Lee Solnick, *Stealing the State: Control and Collapse in Soviet Institutions* (Cambridge, MA: Harvard University Press, 1998).

nerable to charges of complicity in the sell-off of assets, the diversion of funds, the "brain drain" to the West, and the impoverishment of the population.[41] The disillusionment, and indeed the bitterness, at the consequences of these economic policies encouraged a widespread suspicion in Russia that the West was engaged in a deliberate and systematic effort to weaken Russia by undermining its economy. It is no surprise then, that this suspicion was reflected in an increase in anti-American attitudes among the Russian population.[42]

The financial crisis of August 1998, combined with investigations into the diversion of funds from IMF loans and the Bank of New York financial scandal, subjected Russian economic practices to new scrutiny. These events also brought a temporary halt to further IMF and World Bank lending, compelled a reexamination of Western assistance programs more broadly, and forced issues of structural reform and improved governance to center stage.[43] Nonetheless, contrary to expectations that a post-Yeltsin leadership was likely to repudiate this entire strategy of economic reform, some of its features have taken on new impetus under President Putin, who has committed his government to a wide-ranging agenda of tax and regulatory reforms and has won parliamentary backing for several hitherto-controversial measures. Whether they will in fact be implemented in the face of widespread resistance from influential interests will be a key test of his leadership.

## 3. Russian-American Security Relations

The efforts of the Clinton administration to promote the domestic political and economic transformation of Russia and its neighbors was accompanied by an equally ambitious effort to construct a new security partnership. Russian-American cooperation across a broad range of issues was viewed as essential to dealing with common threats and to building on new opportunities, and would well serve the national security interests of both countries. Here too, the record of the past 10 years has been mixed. Unprecedented forms of cooperation on a number of issues stand out

---

[41]Corrupt behavior and conflicts of interest was not limited to Russian actors; the behavior of a number of Western entrepreneurs and even of key American advisers and consultants funded through AID contracts was hardly beyond reproach. See Carla Anne Robbins and Steve Liesman, "Aborted Mission: How an Aid Program Vital to New Economy of Russia Collapsed," *The Wall Street Journal*, August 13, 1997; Janine Wedel, "Tainted Transactions: Harvard, the Chubais Clan and Russia's Ruin," *The National Interest* 59 (Spring 2000).

[42]Opinion surveys conducted in Russia by the U.S. Department of State Office of Research indicate that the percentage of Russians who have a favorable view of the U.S. declined sharply over the past decade, from over 70 percent in 1992–93 to under 40 percent in February 2000, and that some 85 percent of Russians surveyed in early 2000 believed the U.S. seeks world domination and is attempting to reduce Russia to the status of a second-rate power. ("Opinion Research Memorandum: Russians View US and other Western Democracies Favorably," August 10, 1992, p. 5; "Opinion Analysis: Russians' Mistrust of the US at New High," March 14, 2000, p. 2.) Somewhat parallel trends have been reported by the Russian Center for Public Opinion Research in Moscow.)

[43]For a recent evaluation of Western assistance programs by the GAO, see *Foreign Assistance: International Efforts to Aid Russia's Transition Have Had Mixed Results*, GAO Report to the Chairman and to the Ranking Minority Member, Committee on Banking and Financial Services, House of Representatives; November 1, 2000.

as bright spots against the broader background of a steadily deteriorating Russian-American relationship, profound disappointment on both sides, and growing suspicions.

Arguably, the single most innovative and successful of the Clinton administration's policies has been the Cooperative Threat Reduction program (CTR), a novel effort by imaginative DOD leadership to deal with the new security challenges resulting from the dissolution of the USSR.[44]

While the end of the Cold War sharply diminished the threat of nuclear confrontation, the potential loss of control or diversion to hostile actors of the vast stockpiles of nuclear, chemical and biological weapons, materials, and expertise across the territory of the former USSR presented a new and alarming threat to American and Russian security and to global stability. Not only did weakening state capacity and resources threaten Moscow's ability to maintain and control these weapons and materials, but also the economic crisis engulfing the region created temptations as well as opportunities to sell both materials and expertise to a variety of outside bidders. The development of the CTR program, conceived as part of a broader strategy of what former Defense Secretary William Perry labeled "preventive defense," was a novel effort to pursue national security interests by non-traditional means. It provided American financing and technical expertise for measures to destroy nuclear warheads and dismantle delivery systems, to improve the storage and enhance the security of nuclear materials, and to provide research grants and employment to nuclear scientists. Requiring a high level of cooperation between the defense establishments of both countries, it involved the fundamental transformation of a highly adversarial set of military relationships into cooperative ones. It also reflected the emergence of the DOD as an important and innovative policy actor in the region, increasingly engaged in direct contacts with counterparts in the states of the region.

Weapons destruction and dismantlement, including both warheads and delivery systems, were the first and highest priority, beginning with strategic offensive arms. Indeed, among the first major achievements of the effort were the decisions by Belarus, Ukraine, and Kazakhstan to become nonnuclear states, and the withdrawal of some 3,300 strategic warheads from their territories. The program also assisted the dismantlement of Russian strategic offensive arms pursuant to the START I agreement. Facilitating the safe transport and secure storage of fissile materials, and securing the cooperation of Russia's Ministry of Atomic Energy as well as the Ministry of Defense were considerable achievements.[45] However, the conversion of defense industries to civilian production encountered serious obstacles that were not initially anticipated. More recently the CTR program has focused on the

---

[44]From 1992 to 1999, $3.4 billion was allocated for these programs. *U.S. Government Assistance to and Cooperative Activities With the New Independent States of the Former Soviet Union: FY 1999 Annual Report* (Office of the Coordinator of US Assistance to the NIS, January 2000).

[45]Project Sapphire, which transferred a large quantity of highly enriched uranium from Kazakstan to the United States for safekeeping, was a particularly notable success of preventive defense activities; see Carter and Perry, op. cit., pp. 68–69.

dangers posed by the large stockpiles of chemical and biological weapons produced during the Soviet era, as well as by the facilities that developed and manufactured them and the scientists whose livelihood depended on them. In the case of chemical weapons, the prohibitive cost is a major obstacle. Less progress has been achieved with respect to biological weapons, an issue of even greater Russian sensitivity and secrecy. But any effective strategy for addressing these issues requires a substantial investment in commercialization as well as destruction to create new uses for Russian facilities and for their highly skilled scientific and technical personnel.[46]

In addition to dealing with the Soviet WMD legacy, the preventive defense initiative also involved the development of a whole new set of military-to-military relations with Russia and the other states of the region. The Partnership for Peace (PfP) was initially intended to facilitate political and military cooperation between all the states of the region and the West and to help stabilize the potentially volatile region of Central Europe and the former Soviet Union. It provided a framework within which a great variety of joint programs could be pursued, tailored to the particular circumstances of individual states. During the early and the mid 1990s, particular attention was devoted to developing close working relationships with the Russian military leadership and to planning and conducting joint military exercises. When NATO enlargement threatened to jeopardize those ties, intensive diplomatic efforts by the Clinton administration not only succeeded in concluding a Russia-NATO partnership agreement but also secured Russian military participation in the NATO-led Bosnian peacekeeping operation in a unique and an inventive arrangement that placed Russian forces under American rather than direct NATO command.

The PfP, also encouraged and assisted military and political cooperation among other states of the region, including the formation of a Baltic battalion, a Central Asian military grouping, and a joint Polish-Ukrainian unit, and supported a variety of exercises involving emergency operations and peacekeeping. This highly visible role of the the U.S. military in engaging important local actors in the new states was partly the result of successful policy entrepreneurship by key individals within the administration responding to new opportunities and needs. It also reflected, as Robert Lieber notes in his introductory chapter, the dramatic decline in federal funding of traditional "shaping" mechanisms—civilian diplomacy, participation in international organizations, and foreign assistance—and the corresponding diminution of the role of the U.S. State Department. Because the Pentagon had the presence and the resources to engage in productive cooperative activities in this region, it played an innovative and constructive role in developing American ties to local elites and populations. By the same token, the visibility and initiative of the DoD as an important instrument of

---

[46]One important set of initiatives have been aimed at providing grants to individual scientists and research centers in an effort to provide gainful employment while also supporting a redirection of scientific talent from military to civilian purposes. Another initiative has focused on Russia's "nuclear cities," seeking ways to develop commercially viable outlets for segments of the military research infrastructure. For a useful overview, see the report of the Secretary of Energy's Advisory Board, "A Report Card on the Department of Energy's Nonproliferation Programs with Russia," January 10, 2001, Washington, D.C.

American policy in the region exacerbated suspicions and alarm in some circles about American intentions, and was interpreted as an effort to extend American political and military hegemony into a Russian sphere of influence.

Notwithstanding the considerable levels of cooperation that have been achieved in specific areas, the deterioration of Russian-American relations over the course of the past decade in the face of differences over a growing range of issues has been a source of profound disappointment to the many figures in both countries that anticipated that Russian-American partnership would serve as the cornerstone of a new system of international security. The difficulties both countries face in re-defining their relationship has a number of causes. Some are rooted in the legacy of the Soviet-American superpower relationship and the assumptions and expectations associated with it, many elements of which have been undermined by the changed international context. Others are more a product of domestic political competititon. But the underlying source of problems is the fundamental and growing asymmetry of power, wealth, geostrategic interests, and perceptions as a result of the dissolution of the USSR and the severe internal crisis confronting Russia.

Six issues have played an especially important role in the increasing strain in Russian-American relations. First and foremost from the perspective of Moscow has been the West's failure to live up to Russian expectations concerning a central Russian role in a new European security architecture, and indeed the West's willingness to disregard Russian views on key security issues on which Moscow believed it had been promised, and was entitled to, not merely a voice but a veto. The decision to pursue NATO enlargement despite Russian opposition—although skillfully managed by simultaneously creating the NATO-Russia partnership—nonetheless fed already growing suspicions of Western intentions and elicited only grudging acquiescence from the Yeltsin leadership.

NATO's intervention in Kosovo significantly compounded these strains. The suspicion that NATO was not merely a defensive alliance but one that was capable of undertaking offensive political and military actions was suddenly and dramatically confirmed by the campaign against the Milosevic government. The notion that NATO could launch a military attack on a sovereign state and that it could do so without explicit UN authorization, thereby avoiding the Security Council and a Russian veto, both alarmed and infuriated the Russian political elite. It fed into an already heightened sense of Russia's own vulnerability and fueled highly implausible anxieties about Kosovo as a precedent for possible future Western intervention in Russia's internal affairs, particularly in Chechnya. At the same time, ostentatious Russian support for the Milosevic regime, its failure to condemn the brutal campaign of ethnic cleansing against the Albanian Kosovars, and the sudden defiant movement of Russian forces to the Pristina airport further tarnished Russia's reputation in American public and elite opinion. Although the Yeltsin leadership ultimately played a positive role in helping negotiate the conflict, Kosovo helped crystallize Russian opposition to emerging international norms concerning the limits of state sovereignty and both the doctrine and practice of "humanitarian intervention." Indeed, in its actions toward Yugoslavia as well as in a variety of public statements and agreements since (most notably with China), the Russian government has explicitly challenged efforts by the United States and others to weaken or otherwise limit the principles of state sovereignty and nonintervention when issues of human rights or national self-determination are at stake.[47]

The two wars in Chechnya, as well as the condemnation by Western governments and international human rights groups of Russian military atrocities against the civilian population, were yet a third source of friction in Russian-American relations. The Clinton administration's criticism of Russian actions in both cases was, in fact, comparatively mild, indeed, so much so, as to evoke condemnation itself.[48] Not only did the administration try to avoid harsh attacks on the Russian leadership to avoid jeopardizing other interests and priorities in Russian-American relations, but also by late 2000, it was prepared to acquiesce in Moscow's assertion that international terrorism and Islamist extremism posed a sufficient threat to both countries to warrant cooperation on the issue. Nonetheless, the war in Chechnya remains a serious irritant, since Western analysts view Russian policy as counterproductive and vengeful, while many in Moscow remain persuaded that Washington fails to appreciate the serious security threat that Russia faces in the south.

Proliferation issues, particularly involving Russian assistance to potential Iranian nuclear capabilities in the construction of the Bushehr nuclear reactor but also involving overt and covert military ties to several other "states of concern," have constituted yet a fourth source of strain in Russian-American relations. These strains have been exacerbated by an increasingly aggressive effort to expand Russia's role in lucrative international arms sales as a key to the survival and modernization of its languishing defense industries. Moreover, Moscow deliberately aggravated these tensions—and provided additional ammunition to critics of the Clinton administration—by choosing the eve of the U.S. presidential election to repudiate a secret agreement concluded by Gore and Chernomyrdin in 1995 to halt future arms exports to Iran. Expanding Russian military sales to Iran, along with simultaneous Russian campaign to win international backing for curtailing American-supported sanctions against Iraq, has added to the suspicion that Moscow is both willing and even eager to flaunt its independence of Washington in the search for new economic and military partners among states with dubious records and intentions.

---

[47]The official visit to Moscow of Yugoslav Defense Minister Dragoljub Ojdanic, under indictment by the Hague tribunal for war crimes, was a particularly pointed demonstration of defiance. The Russian government has also used a campaign against loosely defined "international terrorism" to link Russian security interests in the North Caucasus with those of China in Sinjiang and of the Central Asian states' concerns with radical Islamic groups. Exaggerated claims about the role of Uigur separatists, Central Asian Islamists, (and even Baltic volunteers) in Chechnya are a transparent effort to promote solidarity and cooperation around this issue, and to oppose Western criticism of Russian behavior and Western efforts to involve the OSCE more actively in conflict resolution in the region.

[48]For a discussion of Western and American responses to the war, see Gail W. Lapidus, "The War in Chechnya: Opportunities Missed, Lessons to be Learned," in Bruce Jentelson, ed., *Opportunities Missed, Opportunities Seized: Preventive Diplomacy in the Post–Cold War World,* (Rowman and Littlefield, New York, 2000). President Clinton was criticized for drawing parallels between the Russia's war in Chechnya and the American Civil War, implicitly comparing Yeltsin to Lincoln, and for referring to the Russian military as "liberating" Grozny.

The Russian-American strategic relationship has also become increasingly strained in the past few years and is likely to become even more so under the new Bush administration. For the Russian government, a strategic relationship with the United States based on mutual deterrence remains central to its security as well as to its status as a great power. On the American side, Russia has become progressively less salient to key security concerns. The Duma's protracted refusal to ratify the SALT II agreement stalled further arms reduction negotiations and deprived them of momentum, at the same time that the progressive deterioration of Russian military capabilities diminished their urgency. At the same time, growing hostility among congressional Republicans to past arms control arrangements, reflected in the rejection by Senate Republicans of the Comprehensive Test Ban Treaty in 1999, as well as concern about emerging new security threats emanating from the so-called "rogue states," prompted increasing pressure on the Clinton administration to develop a national missile defense program, even at the cost of abrogating the 1972 ABM treaty, which the Russian government viewed as the cornerstone of strategic stability. Although the failure of key tests enabled President Clinton to defer a decision on NMD to the incoming Bush administration, Moscow's refusal to relax its opposition in the course of protracted negotiations and President Putin's systematic and relatively successful campaign to win European support for the Russian (and Chinese) position will compel the Bush administration to consider the political and security costs as well as the technological feasibility of its proclaimed intentions to proceed with NMD. Although there may be some areas in which parallel unilateral reductions on both sides could facilitate further arms control progress, the entire process is clearly up for fundamental reassessment.

Finally, the perceived American challenge to Russian interests in what Moscow considers its "near abroad" has been a growing concern of Russian political elites and policy-makers. A timely and complete withdrawal of Russian forces from the Baltic states was one of the early achievements of Russian-American cooperation, along with Ukraine's accession to the NPT. However, American efforts to support regional stability and development, to promote the peaceful resolution of conflicts in the region—from Karabakh to TransDniester and Abkhazia—and to encourage and facilitate the promised withdrawal of Russian military forces and bases, have all been resisted by elements of the military and security communities in Moscow as efforts to eliminate Russia's political and military influence in the neighboring states. These anxieties have recently focused on the Caspian region, where American support for developing the energy resources of the region as a motor for its economic recovery, and support for the construction of multiple pipelines to mitigate the risks in bringing these resources to Western markets, have been portrayed by actors in Moscow in highly alarmist terms. American commercial involvement in the region, in this view, already accompanied by American military penetration, is designed to drive Russia out of the region altogether and to establish it securely under American control. These tensions are likely to increase if President Putin seeks to use Russian control over the energy infrastructure of the region—and the heavy dependence of neighboring states on Russian energy supplies and transport—to extract political concessions, while the West assists these states' efforts to diversify their sources of supply and to increase their energy independence.

Notwithstanding all these serious areas of disagreement, however, and the particularly sharp initial estrangement surrounding Kosovo, the Clinton administration remained committed to a policy of continued engagement with Russia, albeit a policy pursued with greater detachment from the intricacies and conflicts of Russian domestic politics, and with a more cautious and less personalized set of relationships with the Putin leadership.

Although the incoming Bush administration initiated a comprehensive review of Russia policy which has not yet been completed, a variety of statements and writings by key officials during and after the presidential elections already signalled a determination to depart from key features of the Clinton administration's policies. While these statements did not convey a consistent and well-defined approach, the new administration announced its intention to pursue a more selective rather than comprehensive engagement, premised on the view that Russia would no longer occupy so central a place in American priorities and that its international behavior, but not its domestic arrangements, ought to be the central focus of American policy. Moreover, these statements were pervaded by a more sceptical, if not sharply critical, perception of Russia's domestic and foreign policies, focusing with particular sharpness on Russia's role in nuclear and conventional arms proliferation.

The new administration also indicated a willingness to act unilaterally where it considered that core strategic interests were at stake, offering the Russian government an opportunity to negotiate modifications to the ABM Treaty but announcing its determination to pursue NMD with or without Russian agreement and even at the cost of growing estrangement from its European allies.

Finally, the new administration's broader effort to reduce government spending, promote major tax cuts, and transfer more responsibilities to the private sector is likely to result in sharp reductions in funding for programs devoted to Russia's transformation, including not only civil society assistance and economic reform but also programs aimed at WMD proliferation that require substantial cooperation, engagement, and mutual trust. At the same time, the critical role of Russia in Eurasian and global security, as well as the continuing importance of supporting Russia's integration into the international economy, will contribute to a mix of shared as well as conflictual interests in American policy toward Russia, and define a broad agenda requiring Russian-American and multilateral cooperation in the years ahead.

## CONCLUSION: THE LIMITS OF INFLUENCE

The process of transformation under way in Russia and the other states of the region will be a protracted one, and it is far too early to offer a comprehensive and sober assessment of the scope and limits of Western influence. Nonetheless, several broad lessons can be drawn from the experience of the last decade.

The single most decisive determinant of the trajectory of transformation across the region has been the influence of different starting conditions. The earliest success stories in the postcommunist world have taken place in those countries—East Central Europe and the Baltic states—where there was some prior experience of national independence, market economies, and political democracy, and where a clear and an unambiguous commitment to rejoining Europe has bolstered a wider popular consensus favoring reform. Russia in 1991 enjoyed none of these attributes and faced a far less favorable set of circumstances. Long before Yeltsin's ascension to power, the Soviet system was in crisis, and by 1991, Gorbachev's ineffective attempts at reform had produced sharply falling output; high inflation; a state in disarray; widespread asset stripping by enterprise directors; and elite ambivalence, if not strong opposition, to cooperation with the West. The initial conditions facing the new states of the Caucasus and particularly of Central Asia were even less promising, and those states have suffered even more acute economic and social problems, even where Washington's presence and role was relatively limited and no radical political or economic reforms were pursued. Western approaches to Russian reform aggravated some problems, even as they helped mitigate others, but they were not the basic cause.

Secondly, the West approached the challenges of postcommunist transformation with a flawed conceptual framework that resulted in an inadequate framing of the issues. However well-intentioned, the initial strategies pursued by a variety of Western as well as of local actors—and the messianic discourse that accompanied them—were often based on an insufficiently complex appreciation of the effects of the Soviet legacy on the constellation of interests, institutions, and behaviors within these countries. Sweeping adherence to political and economic orthodoxies, coupled with insufficient appreciation of their likely consequences given the actual and diverse conditions of postcommunist societies resulted in a variety of unintended and often counterproductive consequences. A "cookie-cutter" mentality often neglected the importance of the context, and the relevant time frame would be a matter of generations rather than of years. Moreover, the tendency to depict Russian political life in oversimplified terms carried over from the Gorbachev era—as a struggle between reformers and conservatives—long after these labels had ceased to capture a changing reality further distorted understanding of the real array of political and economic interests that has emerged in Russia. Additionally, touting the success of political and economic reforms while ignoring or minimizing the massive looting of resources and impoverishment of the population may have been intended to maintain congressional and public support for engagement with the region but contributed to subsequent public disilllusionment, dwindling credibility, and the erosion of support in both countries.

This lack of fit between framing and reality was manifest in foreign policy as well. American engagement with Russia tended to perpetuate the bipolar imagery and discourse of the Cold War era, long after the growing disparity between American and Russian power had rendered it anachronistic.[49] Although Russia continued

---

[49]This was in some measure an effort to assuage the sensitivities of the Russian leadership by treating it with particular deference, as, for example, by creating a place for President Yeltsin at the G-7 meetings, elevating them to G-8. But they also reflected a certain degree of inertia in adapting to new realities.

to be an important partner of the United States, and a critical one for addressing a whole range of foreign policy and security issues, it was increasingly one important piece of a larger set of relationships and problems rather than their centerpiece. A fresh rationale for the bilateral Russian-American relationship was called for that emphasized the importance of continuing cooperation with Russia and its leadership, but that more forthrightly acknowledged the altered context and diverging interests.

The Clinton administration's Russia policy was also affected by a variety of inherent constraints—economic, political, and bureaucratic—that are all too often overlooked by its critics. The unprecedented wealth and prosperity of the United States, for example, did not automatically translate into congressional willingness to appropriate significant funding for foreign assistance programs or for new institutions to design and implement them. It was therefore necessary to adapt existing institutions and programs for new and largely unfamiliar purposes, with consequences that were not always optimal. Other constraints were imposed by a variety of political constituencies. Whatever the initial vision, the realities of American policy toward the region would inevitably be shaped not by some grand design but by the interplay of bureaucratic politics, and of contending economic and ethnic interests and lobbies. The political influence of the Armenian diaspora, to mention just one example, not only obtained substantial funding for assistance programs for Armenia but also secured the passage of Resolution 907 inhibiting the administration's ability to support a variety of programs in Azerbaijan. Competing priorities and trade-offs among them are at the core of any political process, and the formation of American policy toward Russia and the other states of the region faced constant choices involving the subordination or sacrifice of some objectives for the sake of others. Here, too, policy would inevitably be shaped and distorted by continuous bargaining, compromises, and trade-offs among political actors, in Washington as well as in Moscow.

Critics all too often fault the Clinton administration for a long list of alleged "failures" without recognizing the possible price that had to be paid to achieve the successes, or whether any alternatives were available that would have achieved these objectives at lower cost. Moreover, in Washington's dealings with the Yeltsin government, there is considerable evidence to suggest that the personal relationships helped smooth the way to cooperative political and military solutions, even as they constrained the willingness of Washington to speak out frankly about issues of concern. As others have argued, the same Yeltsin who used force against a recalcitrant parliament in 1993 and launched a brutal war in Chechnya in 1994 also negotiated the withdrawal of Russian troops from the Baltic states; supported joint efforts to destroy nuclear weapons and to enhance control over fissile materials; largely acquiesced in NATO's expansion; and cooperated with the United States in ending the war in Kosovo. The same Putin who launched a second brutal military campaign in Chechnya, brought former FSB officials into leading official positions, curtailed freedom of the press and other rights, and is pursuing a strategic partnership with China to counter U.S. "hegemonism" has also thrown his support to market institutions, expressed the view that Russia's future is inseparable from Europe, and has sought to rebuild ties with NATO and particularly with Western Europe.

Finally, many of the critiques of the Clinton administration exaggerate the influence of American policy on Russian developments. Indeed, the greatest single conclusion that can be drawn from this entire experience is the extraordinarily limited ability of the United States to translate its political primacy and power into effective influence. This is as true of America's relations with Ukraine or with the smaller states of the Caucasus as it is with respect to Russia. It is equally the case for nongovernmental or private actors, whether giant American corporations, small entrepreneurs, or NGOs. All have experienced firsthand their limited ability to translate promising programs into desired outcomes, effectively to deploy and monitor the use of resources in regions where personal ties remain of paramount importance, transparency is largely absent, agreements are subject to continuous renegotiation, and legal recourse is largely unavailable. Clearly, American efforts have played a role at the margins but have been far from a decisive factor. The case of American Russia policy offers a sobering illustration of the limits of American ability to reshape the international environment or to exercise more than a marginal influence over either the internal character or the external behavior of other important international actors. The humility that George W. Bush called for in the election campaign of 2000 would be a useful ingredient of America's Russia policy in the years ahead.

# 6

# The United States and the Americas
## Unfilled Promise at the Century's Turn

## ROBERT A. PASTOR
### Emory University

As Americans look outward toward the world at the end of the Cold War, the sensation of "primacy" may be a new experience, but it's an old one as they look toward Latin America. From the dawn to the dusk of the twentieth century, the United States stood astride the Western Hemisphere as its most formidable power. No combination of countries in the Americas could contest the United States. Coping with dominance has been a permanent condition for the United States in the Americas.

Primacy, however, has not assured unity, clarity of purpose, or effectiveness. Indeed, America has been more ambivalent than strategic in considering its role in the region. Washington has often been divided, both in defining U.S. interests and in choosing the wisest course for pursuing them. The reason for this division is that America's political system puts a premium on debate and on restraining executive power; but a second reason why the United States has often found it difficult to translate its strength into effective influence is Latin American resistance to any action that could later justify intervention in their internal affairs.

Standing back from a century of U.S. policies toward Latin America and the Caribbean, one can see patterns that offer some lessons for America as it enters the twenty-first century as the only superpower. The first pattern has a cyclical quality that ricochets off the three great wars—World Wars One and Two and the Cold War. Just before each war, the United States became acutely sensitive to threats in

Robert A. Pastor is Professor of Political Science at Emory University, and from 1985 to 1998, he was the Founding Director of the Latin American and Caribbean Program and the Democracy and China Elections Projects at the Carter Center. He was the National Security Advisor for Latin America from 1977 to 1981 and is the author or editor of thirteen books, including *Exiting the Whirlpool: U.S. Foreign Policy toward Latin America and the Caribbean* (Westview, 2001) and *A Century's Journey: How the Great Powers Shape the World* (Basic, 1999).

its neighborhood, and it often responded with military force. After each war, the United States turned inward to focus on domestic problems; it tried to shut the world out by erecting barriers to goods, people, and ideas. Foreign policy issues dropped to the bottom of the public's attention in the 1920s and 1990s, and were already declining in 1947 when the Cold War intervened.

The dynamic, however, was not simply one of a pendulum with which U.S. policy swung outward toward intervention during crises and then inward toward isolationism when the crisis passed. There was also a secular dimension. *Over time, and after each war, the United States was less isolationist and more aware of its international responsibilities.* Having learned from America's mistake of rejecting the League of Nations after the First World War, President Franklin Roosevelt built a bipartisan consensus *during* the Second World War that assured continued U.S. leadership in the world after the war. And after the Cold War, both Presidents Bush and Clinton struggled hard to remain engaged globally despite growing disenchantment from many in congress.

Beyond the cyclical and secular rhythms of war, a second characteristic of U.S. policy has been the search for a "special relationship" in the hemisphere—one that was different and nobler than Europe's colonial approach. On the eve of the Spanish-American War, the U.S. Congress declared that it would liberate, not annex, the war's main prize, Cuba. This declaration—the "Teller amendment"—shocked Queen Victoria and her fellow European monarchs. From the establishment of the Pan American Union in 1890, the United States articulated a vision of the Americas based on the sovereign equality of states, and President Franklin Roosevelt's "good neighbor policy" aimed to translate that sentiment into policy. In the Organization of American States, the United States did not seek a voting system that would allow it a veto or greater weight than the others. Of course, U.S. policy did not always conduct itself in accordance with these fine principles. It chose to intervene covertly to overthrow a democratically elected, leftist regime in Guatemala in 1954 and to try to overthrow Fidel Castro in Cuba in 1961. U.S. foreign-policy-makers responded to realistic calculations, but they were also moved by idealism, a quality that rarely inhibited great powers.

The third pattern—perhaps the most important—that has affected U.S. policy has been the oscillation in the character of Latin America's regimes and economic policies. Throughout the twentieth century, democracy in Latin America was rare and lightly rooted. Just since the Second World War, the pendulum has swung three times between dictatorship and democracy, but the swing had a dialectical quality, never returning to the point it had left. In key cases, countries moved from dictators to fragile democracies to authoritarian institutions to broader democracies. Similarly, the countries' economic policies swung from populist and protectionist to those that were more fiscally responsible, outward and market-oriented. Since the mid-1970s, the pendulum swung with majestic force toward democracy and the market. That swing permitted the Americas to envisage the region's historical promise—to be a club of sovereign, democratic partners.

At the same time, changes in the United States and in the inter-American system increased the prospects that the United States would meet the region halfway. In the United States, the 1965 Immigration Law unleashed the second largest influx of immigrants in its history, and half of the total came from Latin America. A disproportionate number landed in the four most populous states—California, Texas, New York, and Florida. By the 1990s, salsa had replaced ketchup as the most frequently used condiment, and in 1998, "Jose" became the most common name of newborn babies in California.[1] The cultural distance between the United States and Latin America narrowed, and the capacity for respectful communication increased. Another major change followed the end of the Cold War: trade became more important for the United States, and Latin America became its fastest growing market.

The inter-American system was transformed by democratization. Whereas the OAS had long resisted any involvement in internal affairs, in 1990, it established a new Unit for the Promotion of Democracy for that express purpose. More accountable governments in Brazil and Argentina ended their long rivalry and established a Common Market. After a century of standing apart, in 1990, Canada joined the OAS, and it soon began to play a leading role. NAFTA and the promise of a Free Trade Area of the Americas opened the door to fundamental changes. All of these changes set the stage for the kind of partnership in the Americas that U.S. presidents had long promised but had never delivered. *And yet the story of the 1990s was not the promise of democratic partnership, but just how difficult it was to fulfill.*

This chapter will explore the post–Cold War rhythms, the stumbling but eventually effective effort by President Clinton to restore Jean-Bertrand Aristide to the presidency of Haiti, to secure the approval of NAFTA, and to convene an unprecedented Summit of the Americas. Having achieved these three goals, the administration put its policy engine in neutral and never quite got it started again. The capture of the U.S. Congress by a resurgent Republican Party and the failure to anticipate the Mexican peso crisis diverted Clinton's attention and undermined his ability to realize the Summit's goals. And so the twenty-first century arrived with a question as to whether the United States will find the imagination and the political will to fulfill the long-standing dream of establishing in the Americas a sturdy collective system for defending democracy and a model for integrating rich and poor countries.

# THE BUSH-CLINTON AGENDA

American applause for President George Bush's triumph in the Persian Gulf ended long before the 1992 election. Candidate Bill Clinton read the changing American mood better, and his focus on the economy and domestic issues helped win him the election. Once elected, however, Clinton could not avoid Bush's unfinished agenda for Latin America—specifically, Haiti, NAFTA, and the Enterprise of the Americas Initiative.

---

[1]Jorge I. Dominguez, ed., *The Future of Inter-American Relations* (NY: Routledge, 2000), p. 7.

The challenge on Haiti was twofold: what should be done to prevent another wave of Haitian refugees, and how much effort should be invested to restore Jean-Bertrand Aristide to the presidency? On the North American Free Trade Agreement, which was signed by President Bush in December 1992, the challenge for Clinton was to try to make it more palatable for his Democratic colleagues and to gain congressional approval. The Enterprise of the Americas Initiative was a mélange of proposals that included debt-for-nature swaps and an investment fund, but the key element was Bush's promise for "a hemispheric free trade zone from Alaska to Argentina." The proposal was brushed aside by the incoming administration, but its message soon returned in another guise.

In December 1990, Haiti conducted the first free and fair election in its history with the substantial assistance of international monitors. Jean-Bertrand Aristide, a young priest, was elected with two-thirds of the vote. His election turned Haiti's traditional power pyramid upside down, putting the champion of the masses on top in the Presidential Palace and pushing down the elite. It was a delicate transition, and it did not last. On September 30, 1991, barely seven months after his inauguration, the military overthrew Aristide.

Three months before, the OAS General Assembly had met in Santiago, Chile, and approved a resolution of solidarity for democracies. In the case of an interruption of constitutional rule, the Foreign Ministers all agreed to convene an emergency meeting of the OAS to consider specific steps to restore the constitution. Haiti, the country in the hemisphere with the least democratic experience, provided the first test. Within days of the coup, the OAS Foreign Ministers met in Washington, quickly condemned the coup, and sent a delegation to Haiti to demand the return of Aristide. They failed, and they returned to Washington and recommended economic sanctions against the regime.

Secretary of State James Baker said the coup would not stand, but it did. In the spring of 1992, to cope with a refugee influx, Bush ordered the U.S. Coast Guard to return to their country any Haitians found at sea. Candidate Clinton criticized the policy as "cruel," but as president-elect, he announced he would continue it, signaling the importance that his administration would attach to stopping flows of refugees.

Clinton also acted on NAFTA before his inauguration. He met with Mexican President Carlos Salinas, reaffirmed his commitment to NAFTA, and promised he would expedite the completion of side agreements on labor and the environment.[2] But on taking office, he decided to give highest priority to reducing the budget deficit, and when Congress approved that, his political advisers suggested a further postponement until after his health plan was approved.[3] But NAFTA's implementation was set for January 1, 1994, and so the Administration could delay no longer. Negotiations were completed on the side agreements, and it was signed at the White

---

[2]Thomas L. Friedman, "Clinton Says U.S. Will Act Fast on Trade Pact If . . . ," *The New York Times*, January 9, 1993, p. 8.

[3]Bob Woodward, *The Agenda: Inside the Clinton White House* (NY: Simon and Schuster, 1994), pp. 55, 314–319.

House with the support of all the former presidents on September 14, 1993. Clinton then launched an intense effort to gain congress's approval. The toughest battle was in the House of Representatives, but on November 17, the president won, 234–200. In the House, 132 Republicans voted with the Democratic president, but only 102 Democrats. Three days later, the Senate approved NAFTA by a vote of 61–38. The president had scored his second victory.

The promise to restore Aristide in Haiti proved far more difficult. The Haitian military could not be moved without a credible threat of force, but Clinton did not want to send American soldiers. The congressional Black caucus would not let him abandon his promise, and Randall Robinson, the Director of TransAfrica, a non-governmental group in Washington, D.C., working on Caribbean and African issues, began a hunger strike that finally compelled the president to act. In July 1994, pressed by the United States, the UN Security Council passed a resolution calling on member states to use force to compel the Haitian military to accept Aristide's return. This was a watershed event in international relations—the first time that the UN Security Council had authorized the use of force to restore democracy to a member state. In August, preparations for an invasion began.

On September 15, in a national address, President Clinton declared that all diplomatic efforts had been exhausted, and he publicly warned the Haitian military leaders to leave power immediately. The next day, he decided to send former President Jimmy Carter, Senator Sam Nunn, and General Colin Powell to try to negotiate the departure of Haiti's military leaders.[4] The three convinced the Haitian military high command that an invasion would occur if the talks failed, and they came close to success when Haitian General Philippe Biamby learned that U.S. forces were already on their way. It would be hard to find a better example of the difference between a credible threat, which was essential to reach an agreement, and the actual movement of troops, which in this case and at this moment, was counterproductive. Because the Carter team had conveyed a threat with credibility but without brandishing it, commanding General Raoul Cédras was ready to sign the agreement. After learning that the attack was under way, he refused to sign or even to negotiate further.

To keep alive the chance for an agreement, Carter changed the venue of the negotiations from the Military Headquarters to the Presidential Palace, and he asked Cedras to accompany him. There, the de facto President Émile Jonnaissant signed the agreement. Carter, Nunn, and Powell returned to Washington, and I remained to brief the U.S. ambassador and senior Pentagon officials and to arrange meetings with the Haitian military. Because of the suspicion of both sides, it proved difficult to arrange such a meeting, but we were able to do so shortly before U.S. forces landed. Twenty thousand U.S. troops disembarked without a single casualty or even

---

[4]The author was an adviser to the Carter team and has described parts of the negotiations in "The Clinton Administration and the Americas: Moving to the Rhythm of the Postwar World," in Robert J. Lieber (ed.), *Eagle Adrift* (NY: Longman, 1997); and "More and Less Than It Seemed: The Carter-Nunn-Powell Mediation in Haiti, 1994," in Chester A. Crocker, Fen O. Hampson, and Pamela Aall, (eds.), *Herding Cats: Multiparty Mediation in a Complex World* (Washington, DC: U.S. Institute of Peace Press, 1999), pp. 507–525.

one civilian being hurt. There was no question that U.S. forces would have prevailed in an invasion, but because of the need to minimize U.S. casualties, the U.S. military planned a ferocious assault that would have meant hundreds, perhaps thousands, of Haitian casualties, and inevitably, some American losses. General Hugh Shelton, the commanding officer, said that such an invasion would have engendered long-term bitterness among some Haitians, making it more difficult for the UN to secure order. General Cedras and the senior Haitian military leadership stepped down from power on October 12, and three days later, Aristide returned.

Like NAFTA, Haiti was transformed from an unwelcome, politically costly problem into a success story: NAFTA passed, and Aristide returned. But the process by which the Administration made that journey was so inept and, at times, so accommodating to demands of pressure groups that the president was denied the credit that he deserved.

## THE SUMMIT AND OTHER PIECES OF THE HEMISPHERIC AGENDA

NAFTA and Haiti were the main issues in inter-American relations during the first years of the Clinton administration, but hardly the only ones. Much of Latin America hoped NAFTA would be the beginning of a hemispheric free trade area, not the last trade agreement. Haiti's was the first democratic government in the Americas overthrown in the 1990s, but fragile democracies in Peru and Venezuela were also threatened.

In December 1993, the administration decided to build on its success on NAFTA. Vice President Al Gore visited Mexico and proposed a summit of all "democratically-elected heads of state" of the Americas. It was a bold idea, but the Administration was slow to follow up. It took four months, and a heavy lobbying campaign by Florida's politicians, before the administration decided to convene the summit in Miami. The administration, however, waited until almost the eve of the Miami Summit in December 1994 before deciding on its goals.[5]

The main domestic issue driving American foreign policy to the region was drugs. The problem sat at the intersection between domestic fears and foreign threats. Democrats and Republicans accused each other of not doing enough to keep drugs from America's children. The result was that government spending to fight drugs soared, and Latin America feared that the drug war had replaced the Cold War as America's principal obsession.[6]

---

[5]For the best analysis of the weakness, delay, and strengths of the Summit process and outcome, see Richard E. Feinberg, *Summitry in the Americas: A Progress Report* (Washington, DC: Institute for International Economics, 1997); and Peter Hakim and Michael Shifter, "U.S.-Latin American Relations: To the Summit and Beyond," *Current History* 94, 589 (February 1995): pp. 49–53.

[6]Bernardo Vega, *The Second Cold War: U.S. and Caribbean Law and Order* (Washington, DC: Center for Strategic and International Studies, Policy Papers on the Americas, Vol. IX, Study 7, September 9, 1998). Vega was the Dominican Republic's ambassador to Washington.

The Clinton administration's strategy contained all of the elements of its predecessors'—eradication, crop substitution, cartel-busting, interdiction and, in the United States, education, treatment, and enforcement to reduce demand. Over time, the strategy placed more stress on the demand side of the equation, but two-thirds of the expanded funding continued to be devoted to interdiction and enforcement.[7] The drug program appropriated an increasing share of a much reduced aid program to Latin America.

By the 1990s, most Latin American governments had come to realize that drug trafficking was a more serious menace to their political and territorial integrity than it was to the United States. However, instead of the shared threat being a stimulus to a cooperative approach to the problem, Congress used the aid to mandate a new paternalism. The State Department was required by law either to certify that individual governments were working diligently on the problem or to suspend aid. This requirement created a demeaning process. Instead of building more mature relationships, the United States was compelled to grade Latin American governments, and they naturally resented it.

The Clinton administration's policy toward Central America was shaped also to a great degree by congress, but by fewer members, most of whom, like Senator Jesse Helms, were still fighting the Cold War. This situation was particularly tragic because the governments in the region were desperate to escape the Cold War demons that had ravaged their countries in the 1980s. In Nicaragua, instead of encouraging national reconciliation, the State Department, under pressure of congress, withheld aid in a manner that exacerbated divisions within the country. In El Salvador and Guatemala, the Clinton State Department downplayed its Republican predecessors' policies. A panel report on atrocities in El Salvador during the Reagan Administration was criticized by *The Miami Herald* as "disturbingly evasive." [8] Administration officials repeatedly denied information to Jennifer Harbury, an American lawyer, about her husband, a Guatemalan guerrilla, who had been captured by the Guatemalan military. In 1995, a Democratic congressman disclosed that a Guatemalan colonel was a paid agent of the Central Intelligence Agency when he was alleged to have been involved in the torture and death of Harbury's husband and in the obstruction of an investigation into the murder of an American citizen in Guatemala in 1990. But the administration stood up to the threat against democracy when Guatemalan President Jorge Diaz Serrano shut down his Congress in May 1993.

Every country in South America made significant democratic progress with positive implications for the region's geopolitics. Brazil and Argentina ended their nuclear weapons programs, reduced their defense expenditures, and joined with Uruguay and Paraguay to establish Mercosur in 1991. On January 1, 1995, Mercosur

---

[7]Abraham F. Lowenthal, "United States–Latin American Relations at the Century's Turn: Managing the "Intermestic" Agenda," in Albert Fishlow and James Jones (eds.), *The United States and the Americas* (New York: W. W. Norton and Company, 1999), p. 120.

[8]*Report of the Secretary of State's Panel on El Salvador*, July 1983, pp. 3, 10. "Half Truths of Whole Cloth: U.S.'s Salvador Report," *The Miami Herald*, July 17, 1993.

made 90 percent of their trade duty-free. On the same date, the Andean Pact countries established common external tariffs, ranging from 5 to 20 percent, and the Group of Three—Mexico, Venezuela, and Colombia—pledged to eliminate all tariffs and quotas within a decade. From 1991 to the Miami Summit, the region reduced its trade barriers by 80 percent.[9] In just four years—from 1990 to 1994—Latin American exports grew 10 percent each year (three times faster than its gross product).[10] Trade within each of the subregions—Mercosur, Andes, Central America, Caribbean Community (CARICOM), NAFTA—grew faster than their world trade, meaning that regional integration was proceeding at a fast pace.

These democratic and economic changes made possible a convergence in values and gave the Miami Summit an historic caste.[11] Of course, NAFTA and the Summit were born in original sin in the sense that a founding member of the democratic community—Mexico—was not then democratic. Some progress in electoral institutions was made in Mexico, but it was grudging and slow.

Nonetheless, the hemisphere was ready to reach for the golden ring, and Clinton guided his colleagues to it—free trade—embedded in a "Declaration of Principles" and "A Plan of Action"—fulsome statements of solidarity on behalf of democracy, prosperity through economic integration and free trade, and sustainable development through environmental protection. Besides the rhetoric and the many committees established to discuss a wide agenda, one goal stood out: the presidents agreed to conclude talks on a "Free Trade Area of the Americas" no later than 2005. That was the single goal that gave the Summit meaning.

## A DIVIDED U.S. GOVERNMENT

For the Clinton administration and much of Latin America, the Miami Summit was a moment of sunshine between two ominous clouds—the Republican takeover of congress, which jeopardized Clinton's domestic and international programs, and the collapse of the Mexican peso, which called into question the purpose of NAFTA and the premise of the Summit, that Latin America was on a high-speed trajectory to the First World.

The Republicans won control of Congress in the November 1994 elections with an aggressive agenda—The Contract with America. They promised less government and reduced taxes, but they were silent as to foreign policy. The victory was so complete and ideological that the Republican leadership began immediately

[9]James Brooke, "On Eve of Miami Summit Talks, U.S. Comes Under Fire," *New York Times*, December 9, 1995, p. A4.

[10]The Inter-American Development Bank, *Economic Integration in the Americas* (Washington, DC, July 1995), p. 2.

[11]For the idea of a convergence of values in the context of a "democratic community," see Robert A. Pastor, *Whirlpool: U.S. Foreign Policy Toward Latin America and the Caribbean* (Princeton, N.J.: Princeton University Press, 1992); Chapter 15: "Crossing the Sovereign Divide: The Path Toward a Hemispheric Community"; and *Convergence and Community: The Americas in 1993*, A Report of the Inter-American Dialogue (Washington, DC: Aspen Institute, 1992).

to press their agenda and prepare for the presidency four years later. By moving to the right on a number of issues, although not as far as the Republicans, Clinton was able to win reelection, but the partisan struggle before and after the election was so intense that it impeded any serious progress on the hemispheric agenda.

The Republican approach to Latin America was hardly coherent or uniform. Although the party supported free trade with labor or environmental provisions, for example, the Republican chairmen of both the Senate Foreign Relations Committee, Jesse Helms, and the House International Relations Committee, Benjamin Gilman, opposed NAFTA, the WTO, and all trade agreements. Nonetheless, most of the Republican congressional leadership wanted to tighten the embargo on Cuba; opposed aid to President Aristide in Haiti; wanted less economic aid to Latin America but more military aid to fight the drug war; and distrusted international treaties and organizations. On Haiti, the differences between the Republicans and the Democrats proved less significant than between the United States and the Haitian government. Neither Aristide nor his successor René Preval accepted minimal economic and electoral reforms, which the international community demanded before giving $500 million in promised development aid.

Clinton's policy toward Cuba was dictated by two considerations: to prevent an exodus of Cubans to the United States and to keep the Cuban-American community reasonably satisfied. During his 1992 campaign at a fund-raiser in Miami, Clinton promised the conservative Cuban-American National Foundation (CANF) to support a bill proposed by Representative Robert Torricelli to tighten the embargo, even though President Bush then opposed it because of its adverse effect on Canada and other trading partners. Bush then reversed his position and signed the law. Torricelli predicted that Castro would fall "within weeks,"[12] but George Bush fell first.

When Cubans began using rafts to flee to the United States, Clinton instructed the U.S. Coast Guard to take the refugees to Guatanamo. The base commander, however, feared riots. The Clinton administration negotiated an agreement that permitted that group to go to the United States; but to prevent a new exodus, the United States would intercept at sea and return to Cuba any future migrants. In other words, Cubans fleeing the island were no longer automatically considered refugees; they would be returned if they failed to prove that they had a well-founded fear of persecution. This secret agreement was announced on May 6, 1995, and the Cuban-American community went wild. The Clinton administration was saved by a public opinion survey published by *The Miami Herald* on May 15 that showed most Florida residents supportive of the president's decision restricting immigration.[13]

---

[12]Cited in Wayne S. Smith, "Shackled to the Past: The United States and Cuba," *Current History* (February 1996): 51.

[13]John Lantigua and Stephen Doig, "Limit Cuban Immigration: Yes, Most in Survey Agree," *Miami Herald*, May 15, 1995, pp. 1, 16. For a good analysis of why Clinton risked a little by alienating the Republican Cuban-American vote but gained a lot by "sending a big message on immigration to other important states such as California," see William Schneider, "Immigration Politics Strikes Again," *National Journal* (May 13, 1995): 1206.

The Cuban-American National Foundation retaliated by getting Helms to introduce a bill with Congressman Dan Burton of Indiana to tighten the embargo even more, discourage foreign investment, and prevent meaningful negotiations until Fidel Castro was removed from power. The bill would permit those Cubans who had become U.S. citizens to sue in U.S. courts anyone who had purchased their property. The administration opposed the bill until the Cuban Air Force shot down two civilian aircraft for violating Cuban airspace. The president signed the bill on March 12, 1996, the day of the Florida presidential primary. Clinton won the state of Florida, and after Pope John Paul II's visit to Cuba in January 1998, the president began to relax some travel restrictions and permit more remittances, which soon exceeded U.S. aid to all of Latin America. The ugly divorce between the Cubans in Miami and those in Havana reached their most emotional apogee over the custody struggle of a young boy, Elian Gonzalez, whose mother drowned while trying to bring him to Florida. His father wanted the boy returned to Cuba, but the boy's Miami relatives used every legal device to delay that from happening. This, too, became a partisan issue, with Clinton trying to return the boy to his father and the Republicans fighting to keep him in Miami.

American farmers wanted to sell their food to Cuba, and they were supported by American business, and also by many in the country who were distressed about the behavior of Cuban Americans on the Elian case. With the support of the farmers, Congress passed a bill lifting the embargo on food and medicines to Cuba, the first time that Congress weakened the embargo. The bill, however, did not permit credits to Cuba, and Castro protested that restriction. By 2000, the only country in the Americas with less democracy than Haiti remained Cuba.

The main setback to the promise implicit in the Miami Summit of the Americas was the collapse of the Mexican peso, soon after President Clinton had expressed confidence in Mexico's economy before and at the Summit.[14] On December 20, 1994, Mexico devalued the peso by about 13 percent and then let it float. It sunk, as capital fled the country. Mexican President Ernesto Zedillo had taken office just three weeks before, and both his team and Clinton's fumbled trying to put together an economic plan to attract confidence and capital. Robert Rubin, Director of the Clinton administration's National Economic Council, had just been named Secretary of the Treasury. His first reaction was "to let the market sort it out."[15] On January 12, the Clinton administration announced its support with an endorsement by the new Speaker Newt Gingrich and the new Majority Leader Bob Dole. When their party rebelled, they deserted the president. On January 31, President Clinton announced a larger, $53 billion package that included $20 billion from the U.S. Exchange Stabilization Fund. Another month would pass before the agreement was signed, and by that time, Mexican reserves had declined so much that the government had to accept an unusually austere economic program. The result was massive unemployment, a catastrophic number of bankrupcies, a 7 percent decline in Mex-

---

[14]Cited in "White House Statement," *Foreign Policy Bulletin* (January–April 1995): 26.

[15]Cited in David Sanger, "The Education of Robert Rubin," *New York Times*, February 5, 1995, p. III, 1, 3.

ico's gross domestic product for 1995 (the worst drop since 1932), a maimed presidency, and a discredited NAFTA.[16]

NAFTA had not failed. The problem was that NAFTA was only a trade agreement; it was inadequate to the challenge of integrating three such divergent economies. NAFTA attracted large movements of short-term capital, but there was no coordinating mechanism to monitor or cope with the fast exit of such capital. Within a couple of years, the Mexican economy began to recover, and it repaid its debt, but the shock of the crisis rippled through all of Latin America and left many people uncertain that the region had escaped its volatile past.

The United States could offer only limited support. In his second inaugural address on January 20, 1997, Clinton spoke of building bridges to the twenty-first century. He spent most of his second term, however, protecting his back, fighting personal battles at home and ancient struggles abroad. An angry Republican majority in Congress transformed a humiliating personal scandal into the nation's first impeachment trial since that of Andrew Johnson. While his domestic energies were focused on his political survival, his foreign policy concentrated on the countries that could not find an easy exit from the Cold War—Yugoslavia, Russia, and China. Latin America was largely shunted aside.

This is not to say that the region went out of business in the last years of the twentieth century, only that the United States did not play the leadership role that it could have on the positive agenda of democracy and free trade. Instead, the United States pursued a transnational police agenda—against drugs, corruption, money-laundering, terrorism—while Latin America grappled with difficult economic and democratic reforms.

The economic reforms that had begun in the aftermath of the debt crises of the early 1980s continued, albeit at a slower pace. As trade barriers declined, inefficient industries began to suffer. This was one reason why there was so little progress on trade talks since the Miami Summit. A second reason was that Brazil, with about half of South America's population and gross product, wanted time to consolidate Mercosur and extend it to the other countries of South America. Brazil hoped to establish a South American Free Trade Agreement (SAFTA) that would be able to negotiate with NAFTA on the basis of greater equality. A third reason was that Mexico and Canada were not eager to share their exclusive access to the world's largest market. *But the fourth reason is pivotal: the U.S. president could not obtain fast-track negotiating authority from Congress, and without that, no government wanted to make costly commitments. So the question is, why, at the peak of its power, would the United States not be able to lead, particularly as the negotiating target was to open Latin America's market to the point that the U.S. market was already opened?*

There are several answers to the question. Tactically, Clinton did not prepare the groundwork as he had on NAFTA, and the business community did not throw its weight behind it. He had a moment at the very beginning of his second term when he could have reached agreement, but he let that pass and did not seek congressional

---

[16]"Poll Records Mixed Results for Zedillo," *Reforma*, republished in *FBIS*, November 21, 1995, pp. 10–12.

approval for negotiating authority until September 1997.[17] Secondly, the two parties had polarized since the 1994 elections. The Republicans had accepted side agreements on labor and the environment in 1993, but they had shifted to the right and rejected these provisions after the election. At the same time, the Democrats had become more dependent on the labor unions, and therefore, more resistant to freer trade. Although Clinton could have brokered an agreement that included provisions on labor and the environment with the Democrats and then could have tried to secure enough Republicans to pass such a bill, he instead chose a "Republican strategy"—to seek a "clean" bill without those provisions. After two months of jockeying, he alienated the Democrats, and the Republicans deserted him. At a third level, the American people were still digesting two huge trade agreements—NAFTA and the Uruguay Round—and were not ready for another. For the first time in a century, an American president failed to obtain authority to negotiate trade agreements, and without U.S. leadership, there was little incentive for Latin America to press ahead.

The thirty-four democratic presidents convened in April 1998 for the second Summit of the Americas. Since both Presidents Bush and Clinton had promised Chile that it would be the first country in line for a free-trade agreement, it was particularly embarrassing that the site was Chile's capital, Santiago. All the leaders understood that serious negotiations on trade were not possible until U.S. negotiators had fast-track authority, because that would have required them to negotiate with the U.S. Congress after completing agreement with the U.S. trade representative. Nonetheless, they decided to launch the FTAA anyway and established eleven groups to begin work on different elements of the agreement. In part to deflect attention from trade, the leaders placed "education" as the premier issue on an agenda that read like a laundry list of every imaginable subject. Although education was of undoubted importance, most governments, including the United States, viewed it as a local—not a national and certainly not a hemispheric—issue.

Between South America and North America were a string of twenty-three vulnerable, smaller economies in the Caribbean and Central America. These could not compete with Mexico because of its preferential access to the U.S. market, although the region was a larger market for U.S. exports than Brazil or France. The Caribbean Basin asked for "NAFTA Parity," but Congress instead chose to advantage the region by relaxing import restrictions on selected products, such as textiles and apparel. On May 18, 2000, after nearly six years of lobbying, President Clinton signed into law these trade provisions for the Caribbean Basin (and also Africa).[18] This was an important step for these countries, but it was so long in getting approved that it was impractical for the president to fit it into a broader geoeconomic strategy toward the region.

---

[17]I worked with former President Jimmy Carter in April 1997 to fashion a potential compromise between John Sweeney, the President of the AFL-CIO, and Speaker of the House Newt Gingrich, but the White House failed to close the deal.

[18]Office of the White House Press Secretary, remarks by the President on the Signing of the "Trade and Development Act of 2000," May 18, 2000.

In the final years of the twentieth century, democracy did not retreat in the Americas, but it was under siege in some countries and transformed in others. The idea of "no reelection" had been Mexico's contribution to political stability in the Americas, and it was based on a simple premise: the best way to ensure a free and fair election is to prevent an incumbent from running. Therefore, when incumbent presidents in Argentina, Brazil, and Peru tried to revise their constitutions to permit reelection, this step caused considerable anxiety. In the end, all three succeeded in winning reelection without serious dispute. Democracy was stronger in Argentina and Brazil, but Alberto Fujimori of Peru tested the boundaries of accountability when he fired the Supreme Court justices who said that the new reform could not tolerate a third term and then ran for president in the spring of 2000. The OAS Electoral Mission criticized the campaign conditions, and when the Election Commission refused to provide sufficient time to review the software for counting, the OAS and the principal opposition candidate, Alejandro Toledo, boycotted the election. Fujimori's victory was a hollow one.

The OAS sent a high-level mission to promote negotiations with the Peruvian opposition but failed to make any progress. Then, a secret videotape was released of Vladimiro Montessinos, the head of intelligence, bribing an opposition legislator to support Fujimori. This event led to a firestorm of protest, so that on September 16, 2000, Fujimori announced that there would be new elections for president and that he would not run.

The pleasant surprise of the 1990s was the progress of democracy in Central America, which had preoccupied the United States for the previous decade. In the October 1996 presidential election in Nicaragua, the Sandinistas were beaten by the conservative Mayor of Managua, Arnoldo Aleman, yet both sides reconciled. In Guatemala, on December 29, 1996, the government signed an agreement with the guerrillas, ending the longest civil war in Central America—a war that had claimed 100,000 lives. The revolutionaries were incorporated into the political system as they had been in El Salvador, where former guerrilla leaders won key municipalities and second place in the national elections behind their formal arch rivals, ARENA. In November 1998, when Hurricane Mitch wreaked havoc throughout Central America, the United States provided nearly $600 million of relief. The democratic governments survived and used the foreign aid effectively.

The four South American countries of Mercosur reinforced each other's democracies by incorporating in their treaty a "democracy clause" to expel any member that reverted to dictatorship. Brazil and Argentina used that clause effectively when Paraguay's government was threatened on two occasions.

In the late 1990s, the Central American disease of political instability seemed to migrate south to the Andean countries. Ecuador was the most unstable. The legislature first dismissed one elected president, Abdala Bucaram, in February 1997, and nearly three years later, they pasted a patina of respectability on a military coup against President Jamil Mahuad by replacing him with the vice president. Nearby in Venezuela, on December 6, 1998, the people elected Col. Hugo Chavez, the leader of the military coup in 1992, as president. His principal priorities were to change the constitution, shut down the old political parties and institutions, and involve the military in political life. A high oil price facilitated the achievement of his goals, but his demagogic appeals to the poor unsettled businesspeople, who reportedly sent their capital north to Miami.

The Andean country with the most serious problems in the 1990s was Colombia, the one with the longest history of democracy. The government faced a three-sided war—against narco-traffickers, who supplied about 80 percent of the cocaine used in the United States; two long-standing guerrilla groups, the FARC and ELN; and a plague of corruption and violence, exacerbated by deadly paramilitary forces. The election of Ernesto Samper in 1994 amid reports that he had received campaign contributions from drug lords caused the United States to freeze relations, and the result was that all three wars grew worse. In 1998, Andres Pastrana was elected president, and the United States was almost as desperate to come to his support as he was to seek help. He developed a $7.3 billion "Plan Colombia," and the United States pledged to provide $1.3 billion, most of it in military aid and equipment. This pledge occasioned a heated debate in Congress as to whether the United States was about to embark on a "new Vietnam," a wholly implausible analogy, but one that still could raise the temperature of a debate. In the end, Congress approved the aid with stringent human rights conditions, and the president signed the law on July 13, 2000.

The democratization of the region permitted some tentative steps toward resolving long-standing territorial disputes. The boundary dispute between Ecuador and Peru had erupted into war in January 1995, but its neighbors and the United States mediated and helped the two sides reach agreement on October 26, 1998. Chile and Argentina resolved all twenty-four territorial disputes between them.[19]

Democracy also encouraged some reduction in the amount of most of Latin America's defense expenditures, but again, the absence of an agreement to restrain arms purchases may mean that this trend could be temporary. On leaving power in 1989, General Augusto Pinochet of Chile compelled the civilian government to accept measures that would assure increased resources for Chile's military. The Chilean Air Force sought bids for supersonic aircraft from France, Sweden, or the United States, and U.S. defense contractors persuaded the U.S. government in August 1997 to revise a twenty-year policy of not selling advanced supersonic aircraft to the region. The civilian presidents in Argentina and Brazil feared that expensive arms purchases by Chile would lead their own armed forces to put pressure on them to follow suit. The arms race was postponed, if not prevented, by an unlikely set of dynamics beginning with the Asian financial crisis, which reduced the price of commodities, including copper, on which Chile's defense purchases relied. The arrest and seventeen-month detention of Pinochet in England in October 1998 for high crimes also undermined the military's position, as did the election of Ricardo Lagos, a Socialist, as president. Nonetheless in December 2000, the Chilean government announced that it would purchase 12 F-16 fighter jets from Lockheed-Martin for $600 million.

[19]David R. Mares, "Securing Peace in the Americas," in Jorge I. Dominguez (ed.), *The Future of Inter-American Relations* (NY: Routledge, 2000), pp. 35–48.

The agenda that preoccupied the United States most in the second term of the Clinton administration was a transnational police agenda that could be considered the dark side of integration. As barriers to the legitimate movement of goods, capital, and people declined, the possibilities for illegitimate traffic—on drugs, money, arms, and people—naturally increased. The American predisposition to addressing these problems in the hemisphere has often been unilateral and insensitive to the sovereign needs of its neighbors. U.S. agents kidnapped a Mexican in his own country in 1990, who was accused of being involved in the torture of a DEA agent, but his case was thrown out of U.S. court for lack of evidence. Having promised not to repeat such an intervention, American customs agents lured scores of midlevel Mexican bankers into the United States through a "sting" operation, which was named Casablanca, in May 1998, and arrested them on money-laundering charges. In the Caribbean, the United States pressured governments to accept "ship-rider agreements" that permitted U.S. ships to enter the territorial waters of these countries without bothering to seek permission in order to pursue alleged drug traffickers.[20]

The annual certification of countries in the region for cooperating, or failing to cooperate, on drug matters was, in many ways, the most difficult for Latin Americans to accept. On the one hand, the U.S. government claimed that it wanted a partnership, and on the other, it acted unilaterally. In response to the protests, the United States agreed to establish a mechanism in the OAS to review the war on drugs on a multilateral basis, but it was not clear that this would replace the annual unilateral judgment by the United States.

Who was winning the drug war? Since 1990, funding for drug programs increased without any reduction in the number of hard-core drug users in the United States.[21] The war reduced coca crops in Bolivia and Peru, but there was a corresponding increase in Columbia. This pattern is an old one: as long as the demand for drugs remains the same, drug production re-locates to wherever it can operate. President Clinton's appointment of General Barry McCaffrey as Director of the White House Office of National Drug Control Policy was a deft political move, and McCaffrey was a very effective leader, but the overall policy message was ironic. At a time when America's principal interest was to consolidate democracy in the area, the two most visible and important Latin American policy-makers in the Clinton administration were McCaffrey and the head of Southern Command—both military leaders.

The Clinton administration's second term was one of missed opportunities. The promise of the FTAA was unfilled. The United States and Latin America defended democracy in several instances but failed to forge a proactive strategy. The U.S. government failed to negotiate an agreement to limit arms purchases in the region, and although it took a few tentative steps toward a multilateral approach on

---

[20]See Tom Farer (ed.), *Transnational Crime in the Americas* (NY: Routledge, 1999).

[21]See Office of National Drug Control Policy, *National Drug Control Strategy, 2001* (Washington, DC: 2001); Mathea Falco, "U.S. Drug Policy: Addicted to Failure," *Foreign Policy* 102 (Spring 1996): 124; Coletta Youngers, "Fueling Failure: U.S. Drug Control Efforts in the Andes," *Issues in International Drug Policy* (Washington, DC: Washington Office on Latin America, April 1995).

drugs, it did not go very far, and in any case, the OAS might not be as effective an institution to assume that task as, say, a nongovernmental organization. The symbol of the administration's diminished interest was the reluctance on the part of the president or the secretary of state to attend the concluding ceremonies transferring authority over the Canal to Panama on the last day of the century. The Mexican President and the King of Spain were on hand with numerous other notables, but U.S. government leaders chose not to be party to an event that symbolized the new partnership between North and South America.

## THE POSTWAR POLITICAL TEMPLATE AND THE CLINTON PARADOX

Bill Clinton was the first U.S. president to take office after the Cold War. The anti-communist landmarks that had guided his predecessors across a treacherous international political landscape were no longer of use. The compass bequeathed to him by the American electorate compelled him to look inward and to address the fiscal deficit, crime, drugs, and health care. Secretary of State Warren Christopher's role was to counsel the president on how to avoid mistakes or foreign commitments. Latin America was among Christopher's lowest priorities. He visited South America only in February 1996 after being criticized for visiting Syria seventeen times and the South American region not once.[22]

Christopher's successor, Madeleine Albright, National Security Advisor Sandy Berger, and Secretary of Defense William Cohen represented the most politically attuned security team ever assembled by a president, and together with the most political of presidents, they groped for ways to make America's international interests resonate for a largely disinterested public. Clinton talked of the connection between trade and jobs, between weapons of mass destruction in Iraq and security in Oklahoma, between drug addiction in our inner cities and the crisis in Colombia. But despite his eloquence, he never found the right notes, nor could he connect them in a way that provided a moving symphony for the country.

In the Western Hemisphere, the Clinton administration had inherited two problems—Haiti and NAFTA. At the end of agonizing journeys, the president made the difficult decisions necessary to restore Aristide and to secure the approval of NAFTA. He followed up both initiatives with a Summit of the Americas, which set a hemispheric goal of free trade by the year 2005. These, together with his rescue package for Mexico, were four achievements on issues that were not politically popular, and he accomplished these in his first two years in office. After that, the administration seemed to tread water—failing to get the authority to negotiate the FTAA, failing to organize a forward-looking coalition of countries to preempt the Democratic challenges and to shore up the weak reeds like Haiti. In September 2000, after spending nearly $100 million over six years to establish a new police

---

[22]Thomas L. Friedman, "Three Little Words," *New York Times*, February 11, 1996, p. E15.

force and judicial system in Haiti, the U.S. government stopped all aid, and the General Accounting Office concluded that the institutions were politicized and could not conduct "its basic law enforcement responsibilities."[23]

As a result, the administration's overall policy to the Americas seemed less, not more, than the sum of these parts. The president made a few politically courageous decisions, but he received little credit for them. Indeed, he was frequently criticized for being excessively responsive to interest groups and captive to public opinion surveys. What accounts for this paradox?

The answer lies not in the president's achievements but in the journey—the process—before and after the decisions. The administration initially treated NAFTA and Haiti as distinct problems rather than as opportunities to grasp a "regionalist option" or construct a democratic community. Similarly, separate midlevel groups in the administration addressed the rest of the hemispheric agenda, namely, drugs, immigration, Central America, and Cuba without relating each issue to one another or to a hemispheric strategy.

Ironically, the mistake-avoidance strategy that typified the State Department's approach may have sapped more of the president's time and capital than would have been the case had he either moved decisively at the beginning or fashioned a longer-term strategy, as Franklin D. Roosevelt had done. Within one year of America's entry into World War Two, Roosevelt began to prepare for the shift in the public mood that he expected when the war would end. He designed international institutions and forged a bipartisan consensus to keep America engaged globally despite the desire to avoid entangling alliances. Instead of formulating a foreign policy to counter the swing in mood in the post–Cold War era, Clinton administration officials argued that "containment" was not discovered in a day but that it was a product of trial and error. That is true, but Roosevelt's vision and strategy locked the United States into the post–World War Two world before the Cold War started.

In the post–Cold War world, Clinton reacted to crises. There was no design or strategy beyond "engagement and enlargement"—two succinct principles for aiming the United States toward the world. The hard questions were about priorities and trade-offs: Should the United States use force, and, if so, where and how? Which crisis should engage the administration? To answer these questions, the administration used a political template—a composite of public opinion, media exposure, and pressure from ethnic or interest groups. If a crisis did not engage the public or attract the media or an interest group, it was ignored. The administration, however, could not ignore intense objections from a core constituency, such as the congressional Black caucus on Haiti. It was wary of antagonizing an ethnic group, like the Cuban Americans, unless a broader interest, for example, on stopping refugees, compelled a recalculation.

What was missing in these political judgments was some picture of what the world should look like and how U.S. policy should try to influence its shape. In the

---

[23]U.S. General Accounting Office, *Foreign Assistance: Lack of Haitian Commitment Limited Success of U.S. Aid to Justice System*, GAO/T-NSIAD-00–257, September 19, 2000, p. 2.

Americas, the United States did not face a problem, but rather an unprecedented opportunity—to create a community of democratic, market-oriented neighbors. This community could have been assembled if Latin leaders, who wanted NAFTA extended but did not much care for Haiti, were persuaded of the need to address the two sides of America's challenge. If Congress saw Latin America as cooperative on Haiti, it might have been more sympathetic to extending NAFTA. Assembling such a package would not have been easy and would not have been possible by sending cautious midlevel officials without plans to the region.

The State Department was on the margins of both negotiations. If one were to believe the rhetoric about the centrality of NAFTA to its policy, then the State Department should have redesigned itself not to preempt Jesse Helms but to ensure that each interest would be woven into a thick fabric representing the entire nation. The administration did not pursue a strategic approach because the post–Cold War motives driving the policy were domestic—interests and interest groups; the fear of refugees, drugs, and terrorism; and the desire to please groups of hyphenated Americans.

There is a second compelling reason why this strategic approach was not pursued. The Republican Congress had other priorities and was battling the president. A divided government could not pursue a hemispheric community. This is a sad state of affairs because the geopolitics were never more propitious. The democratic transformation of Argentina and Brazil permitted the two rivals to become partners, and both sought a cooperative relationship with the United States. But the president and Congress could not agree on a formula for free trade, and the U.S. government gave disproportionate attention to peripheral issues such as intellectual property rights in Argentina and the drug issue in Brazil—both of which drove leaders away from a unifying strategy.

The Summit provided the vehicle to pursue an Americas strategy, but the administration wasted almost all of the year before it began to consult with Latin America. By the time that the Summit was held in December 1994, the attention of the American people had shifted, the Republicans had captured congress, and the regional spillover of the peso crisis was about to spoil the party. The decision to hold the Summit in Miami made political sense given the intensity of the community's interest and commerce in the region, but it invited a public focus on the one head of state who was not there, Fidel Castro, rather than on the thirty-four heads of state who were.

President Clinton recognized the importance of the Summit, and in the course of discovering that his domestic goals were shared by his Latin colleagues, he began to articulate the overarching concept of an Americas policy. But after 1994, he could not deliver, and he seemed almost to lose interest. There passed, then, the opportunity to fill in the outline of a democratic community drawn so graphically by the president. Still, President Clinton's choices on NAFTA, Haiti, the Miami Summit, and the peso crisis were the defining ones of his policy toward the Americas.

As the twenty-first century began, the economy of the United States was three times larger than all of the other economies of the Americas combined. The gap in military capacities was even wider.[24] The question of primacy does not need an answer in the Americas. Moreover, the convergence of values around democracy and freer-trade throughout the Americas frames a formidable set of common goals. The question, then, is how to translate those goals into policies and agreements. The problem is that the United States has been divided as to the relative importance of the region in the panoply of U.S. interests and on the appropriate means—whether unilaterally or collectively—to pursue the two paramount goals—democracy and freer trade—and other interests. Much of Latin America is similarly ambivalent— unsure whether to seek greater autonomy or more interdependence.

U.S. interests in the region have deepened in the last three decades—as half of its burgeoning immigrant population has come from the region and as the region became the fastest growing market for U.S. goods and services. But lacking a compelling security threat, the United States has not seized the opportunity. And Latin America, uncertain of the U.S. commitment and preoccupied by a multitude of problems, has been reluctant to reach out to the United States. Leadership from both directions could make the difference, deepening NAFTA and transforming it into a community dedicated to reducing income disparities among the countries.

The election of George W. Bush as President might offer that opportunity. As Governor of the state of Texas, Bush stresses the importance of relating positively to its neighbor in Mexico. He was the only candidate for President in 2000 who devoted an entire speech to Latin America, and in that address in Miami on August 25, 2000, he promised: "Should I become president, I will look South, not as an afterthought, but as a fundamental commitment of my presidency." His first two meetings as President were with the Prime Minister of Canada and the President of Mexico, and his first foray into multilateral diplomacy came at the Third Summit of the Americas in Quebec City on April 20–22, 2001.

A host of opportunities await the decisions of the region's leaders. The three nations of North America could deepen their relationship into a Common Market, which could serve as the core of a Hemispheric Community of Democracies. The Community could then forge a multilateral approach to counter drug trafficking that would be more effective than a unilateral policy. It could deal with the entire hemispheric agenda while taking steps to strengthen its democratic foundation. The promise of the Americas, in brief, can begin to be fulfilled.

---

[24]Robert A. Pastor, *Exiting the Whirlpool: U.S. Foreign Policy Toward Latin America and the Caribbean* (Boulder, CO: Westview Press, 2001), chapter 14.

# 7

# A Cautionary Tale
## The U.S. and the Arab-Israeli Conflict

❧

**HARVEY SICHERMAN**
Foreign Policy Research Institute

America's victory in the Gulf War, followed not long thereafter by the demise of the Soviet Union, ushered in a decade of U.S. supremacy in the Middle East. This region, so much contested throughout the Cold War, became instead a forum for the exercise of a dominating American diplomacy. Both the Bush and the Clinton administrations made the Arab-Israeli conflict in particular the focus of their efforts and indeed facilitated an unprecedented peace process between Israel and her neighbors. Continuing American interests in the security of Israel, the flow of oil, and the support of other U.S. friends were well served by the resulting reduction in tensions. Overall, the Arab-Israeli conflict itself shrank from a threat to world peace to a regional (or even local) disturbance.

Superior American influence through this period can be attributed to several factors. These include the prestige of U.S. arms following the Gulf War; the lack of a major international rival; leadership of an international coalition ready to facilitate Arab-Israeli reconciliation including such important local allies as Egypt and Saudi Arabia; and a bipartisan domestic consensus behind presidential initiatives. Moreover, the United States (and its allies in Europe and Japan) benefited from a falling oil price throughout the decade, reducing the leverage of oil producers (Arab, Iranian, or Russian) who opposed U.S. policy.

All of these elements reinforced the American mediatory role. This role is understood best not as the neutral between two conflicting parties but rather by Amer-

Dr. Harvey Sicherman is Director of the Foreign Policy Research Institute in Philadelphia. He served as Special Assistant to Secretary of State Alexander M. Haig, Jr., a consultant to Secretary of the Navy John F. Lehman, and as a member of Secretary of State James A. Baker III's Policy Planning Staff. He is the author of *Palestinian Autonomy, Self-Government and Peace* (Westview, 1993).

ica's standing as the single most influential outside power. The Arabs are well aware that Washington is Israel's ally, but they expect that to translate into U.S. pressure on the Israelis should it be in the American interest. The Israelis, for their part, expect U.S. support to reduce their security risks and to persuade the Arabs that Israel cannot be overcome by force. Washington thus acts in multiple roles, ranging from ally to mediator, from facilitator to guarantor, in the course of a negotiation.

Through much of the 1990s, the local powers also had compelling reasons to move forward. The intifada made Israel's rule over two-and-a-half million Palestinians increasingly onerous, sapping military resources just as Iraq's Scud missile attacks during the Gulf War illustrated new threats from afar. Syria needed money and could no longer count on the USSR. The Palestinians could not rely on the Arab states to risk a military clash with Israel on their behalf, and their role in the Gulf War earned them the lasting enmity of their former benefactors. In short, the status quo had become untenable.

The decade following the Gulf War was therefore marked by a fitful but apparently steady progress toward peace. The U.S. purpose in launching the Madrid Conference (1991) following the Gulf War was to reach formal agreements that could end the Arab-Israeli conflict, preferably through direct negotiations that could rely on American assistance when necessary. Both the Oslo Accords (1993) and the Jordanian Peace Treaty (1994), although largely negotiated without U.S. diplomatic help, depended upon Washington's support. But the diplomacy encountered increasing difficulty even before the murder of Israeli Prime Minister Yitzhak Rabin (1995). The United States was forced to intervene ever more frequently thereafter reaching its highest pitch in the spring of 2000, when the United States failed in two successive summits to arrange final agreements between Israel, Syria, and the Palestinian Authority. In the wake of these reverses, the Palestinians began a new intifada, and the ensuing violence vitiated President Clinton's mediation.

By the end of the decade, superpowerdom had met its limits. Some of these limits were self-imposed, the product of maladroit diplomacy and indecisive use of military power. Numerous visits by Secretary of State Christopher to Syria and three summits with President Clinton arguably increased Hafez al-Assad's prestige but lacked any appreciable return for the U.S. effort. The Camp David Summit risked all. Unlike most such encounters, including its famous predecessor in 1978, no minimum agreement had been reached ahead of time that might have cushioned a failure to achieve the maximum. At times, too, Washington's obvious preference for one leader or another in Israel harmed personal and political confidence, notably during the Netanyahu premiership. Nor did the United States seem to have a will or a way to enforce the promises in the agreement that it underwrote, especially the performance of the Palestinian Authority. Finally, American military actions against Iraq in several crises throughout the decade were underwhelming despite the expansive rhetoric of threat that accompanied them. All told, these blunders eroded the Gulf War coalition, making the attainment of U.S. regional objectives even more difficult.

Other problems also appear on the increase. Not only have the local powers retained a considerable measure of independence in resisting the United States, but other states, notably Russia and China, remain quite capable of obstructing American purposes primarily through arms and technical assistance to regional opponents. More recently a sharp rise in oil prices has reminded the United States of continuing economic vulnerabilities. In Washington, the U.S. Congress has also grown restive over the cost of the peacemaking even though others—the Europeans, the Gulf States, and the Japanese—are bearing major portions of the burden. Finally, American leverage in the Arab-Israeli diplomacy is also subject to the outcome of an increasingly problematic U.S. position in the Gulf as Saddam Hussein erodes international containment. Thus, the costs of American commitments and resistance to U.S. policy are rising simultaneously. The United States remains the single most important power, but its domination of the diplomacy is not sufficient, in and of itself, to achieve Washington's objectives.

## GLOBAL CONFLICT TO REGIONAL DISTURBANCE

The seeds of American supremacy in the Arab-Israeli conflict were sown in the October War of 1973, launched by Egypt and Syria to undo the defeat of 1967. In the course of that desperate struggle, both the United States and the Soviet Union went on a nuclear alert, illustrating the potential for a global conflict. Another consequence of the war, the Arab oil embargo, badly damaged economies around the world, again emphasizing the far-ranging ramifications of this violent quarrel.

Paradoxically, the war also began the process of isolating the conflict, turning it from one of global to primarily regional significance. In the words of the journalist Hussain Haikal, Egypt's President Anwar Sadat "took off with the Russians and landed with the Americans." Sadat's desire to free Egypt of dependence on the Soviet Union was grounded in his view that only the United States could regain land lost to Israel and could deliver Egypt from poverty. The resulting shuttle diplomacy conducted by Secretary of State Henry Kissinger began the "step-by-step" process. After a brief attempt to reach a comprehensive settlement through a large international conference, President Carter built on the dramatic Sadat-Begin negotiations to reach the Camp David Accords (1978) and the Egyptian-Israeli peace treaty (1979).[1] The Accords were underwritten by U.S. economic and military assistance to both sides, some $3 billion for Israel and $1.5 billion for Egypt.

These promising achievements petered out in a series of crises and mishaps that marred most of the 1980s. A Rejectionist Front, led by Iraq, Syria, and the PLO and supported by Moscow, isolated Egypt. The Palestinian Autonomy provisions of Camp David remained stillborn despite some progress in the U.S.-Egyptian-Israeli negotiations on the subject.[2] In June 1982, Israel invaded Lebanon as part of its war

---

[1]Kissinger's account can be found in *White House Years* (Boston: Little, Brown, 1979). William Quandt's *Peace Process* (Washington, DC: Brookings and University of California Press, 1993) covers the 1967–93 period, including the Camp David Accords where he was a participant.

[2]See Harvey Sicherman, *Palestinian Autonomy, Independence and Peace* (San Francisco: Westview Press, 1993).

with the PLO. This act led to a clash with Syria and the near-breakdown of the U.S.-Israeli alliance. Then in September, another U.S. initiative, the Reagan Plan, came to naught, as did the U.S.-brokered Israeli-Lebanon peace treaty the next year. Symptomatic of these failures was the destruction of the Marine barracks at Beirut airport in October 1983, at the cost of 247 lives, by a Syrian and Iranian supported suicide bomber.[3]

Nor was American policy more successful in the Gulf. The Shah's overthrow in 1979 turned Iran from ally to adversary overnight, and the damage might have been even more far-reaching if Iraq had not launched a war against Iran. This ten-year struggle turned the most powerful anti-American regimes in the area against each other, leading eventually to the U.S. tilt in Iraqi favor and then the Iran-Contra Scandal. When the war ended, the United States still found two hostile powers in the Gulf.

The Palestinian revolt, or intifada, against Israeli occupation, which began in 1987, offered Washington the occasion to prod both Israel and the PLO in the hopes of reviving the diplomatic process.[4] But initiatives by both the Reagan and the early Bush administrations ran aground, and stalemate might have continued for some time had Iraq not invaded Kuwait in August 1990.

This crisis caught the United States by surprise. The Bush administration, pre-occupied with German reunification and the end of the Cold War, had been reluctant to intervene in what appeared to be an inter-Arab quarrel. When Saddam seized his small neighbor, however, Bush proved quick to organize a coalition of international forces consisting of two rings: the "inner" (Saudi Arabia, the Gulf States, Egypt, Syria, Turkey, with Israel a passive partner) and the "outer" (Western Europe, Japan, the USSR, and China, which contributed its abstention at the UN). Despite considerable domestic political controversy and a barely passing vote of support in the U.S. Senate, Bush was able to go to war within six months. Desert Storm did not topple Saddam, but it did inflict a crippling defeat on Iraq with few American casualties.[5]

At one stroke, the American victory in the Gulf War also broke the deadlock in the Arab-Israeli conflict. The Rejectionist Front of Iraq, Syria, and the PLO had been smashed: Iraq lost its ability to intimidate its neighbors; Syria defected and joined the American-led side; and the PLO cast its lot with Iraq, costing many Palestinians their jobs in the Gulf and Arafat his financial largesse from the region's

---

[3]Surprisingly frank accounts of these events are to be found in George P. Shultz's *Turmoil and Triumph: My Years as Secretary of State* (New York: Scribner's, 1993); and on the military side, John F. Lehman, Jr., *Command of the Seas* (New York: Scribner's, 1988).

[4]See Zeev Schiff and Ehud Yaari's *Intifada* (New York: Simon and Schuster, 1990) for a good account of the impact on Israel. See also Shultz, *Turmoil and Triumph*, pp. 949, 1016–1030.

[5]A huge literature exists on the Gulf War. Diplomatic accounts include James A. Baker III's *The Politics of Diplomacy* (New York: Putnam, 1995) and George Bush and Brent Scowcroft's *A World Transformed* (New York: Knopf, 1998). For the military aspects, see Anthony H. Cordesman and Abraham R. Wagner, *The Lessons of Modern War, Vol. IV: The Gulf War* (Boulder, CO: Westview Press, 1996); Colin Powell with Joseph E. Persico, *My American Journey* (New York: Ballantine Books, 1995); and General H. Norman Schwarzkopf with Petre Petre, *It Doesn't Take a Hero* (New York: Bantam Books, 1992).

rulers. Israel, faced with Iraqi attacks that it could not counter, was newly dependent on U.S. help against the next military threat, long-range rockets loaded with chemical, biological, or nuclear weapons. Thus, neither the Arabs nor Israel could resist Washington's call for a peace conference.

Although the Soviet Union joined the United States as a cochairman of the Madrid peace conference in October 1991, Moscow was clearly fading from the scene. The Soviet Union itself had only two more months to live; its successor, the Russian Federation, consumed by political and economic distress, had neither the means nor the interest to play a major role. Thus, not long after the Gulf War, the end of the Cold War reduced the Arab-Israeli contest from one of potential global conflict to a regional disturbance, from a superpower contest for influence to the domination of the United States.

## MADRID: RATIFYING U.S. SUPREMACY

Following Saddam's defeat, President Bush deliberately chose to move on the Arab-Israeli issue even though the Gulf remained unsettled. This move was due in great part to a mistaken belief that Saddam would soon fall and that a skeleton U.S. force, assisting Syrian and Egyptian troops, would secure Kuwait. But it also reflected Washington's view that fixing the Arab-Israeli problem would help to secure vital U.S. interests, easing the challenges to Israeli survival and to the lines of vital Western energy supplies. America now had unprecedented means, in the form of the successful Gulf War coalition, for achieving an unprecedented end: peace in the Middle East under American auspices.

The Madrid Conference (October 30–November 4, 1991) itself was organized to account for the new facts of American influence.[6] It exemplified several U.S. objectives: (1) direct negotiations between Israel and its Arab neighbors, including for the first time a separate, non-PLO delegation drawn from the West Bank and Gaza, although Arafat's influence over the delegates was understood; (2) the "two-track" system: Israel, Lebanon, Syria, and Jordan to negotiate peace treaties on one track, Israel and the Palestinians to negotiate a transitional autonomy on the other track; (3) a third multilateral "track" giving the Europeans, Gulf States, and Japanese a direct stake in the success of the project;[7] (4) acknowledgment of Washington's role as the "majordomo," offering its diplomatic services to the parties as needed. Thus, unlike Camp David, all of Israel's Arab neighbors were participants; others beside the United States would bear financial responsibility, yet America retained the dominant role.

---

[6]See Baker, *Politics of Diplomacy*, pp. 411–429 and 487–513 for details of the sometimes maddening run-up to the Madrid Conference.

[7]"We want everyone to invest in the process so it's not so easy to walk away from it," wrote Baker to Bush. Baker, *Politics of Diplomacy*, p. 444. The Madrid Conference also combined the Carter comprehensive approach by including all the parties at a single forum with the Kissinger "step-by-step," the separate, essentially bilateral tracks.

Although neither Israel nor the Arab participants were entirely happy with Madrid, these arrangements testified at the very least that both sides wanted peace with the United States—if not with each other. The question was whether this in itself was enough. Could Washington, even with its Gulf War coalition, bring the parties to agree?

The answer between October 1991 and August 1993 was "no." Except for predictable progress on the Israeli-Jordanian front where there was a history of secret cooperation, the other negotiations quickly reached impasses that the United States could not overcome. Nor did Washington attempt to impose its own settlement, which, in the view of U.S. leaders, would be both unwise and beyond American capabilities to guarantee for any length of time. Instead, it was hoped that the local leaders would convince each other of their desire to make a deal and then, in Camp David fashion, the United States would act to reduce their risks. By late 1991, in any event, the presidential election campaign had already distracted Washington. It was thus not until the election of Bill Clinton that the United States could resume its focus on the stalled process.

# THE PARTIES ACT, AND THE U.S. REJOICES

The post-Madrid stalemate was broken in 1992–93 when a new Israeli government, headed by the veteran general and Labor Party leader Yitzhak Rabin, acted to reach an agreement with the PLO outside the Madrid forum. Rabin's initial emphasis on the strategic importance of Syria was counterbalanced by his view that the Palestinian front, still wracked by tension on the ground, held more urgency because both Israel and the Palestinians wanted to move beyond the status quo. An unexpected advance on the Israel-Syria track broke down when the sides could not agree on a common approach. Syria insisted on an Israeli commitment to return to the June 1967 line before negotiating the quality of the peace, whereas Israel sought to know the details of the peace before agreeing to a line of withdrawal.[8] Secret negotiations between Israel and the PLO with Norway's help, however, yielded the breakthrough Oslo agreement in August 1993. American diplomats had been "aware of secret discussions" as Secretary of State Christopher later wrote, but they knew little and expected less.[9]

The Oslo Agreement provided for staged Palestinian autonomy in Gaza and the West Bank, mutual recognition, special security and economic provisions, and a

---

[8]See Itamar Rabinovitch, *On the Brink of Peace: The Israeli-Syrian Negotiations* (Princeton, NJ: Princeton University Press, 1998). Rabinovitch, an academic expert on Syria, was Israeli Ambassador to the U.S. and Rabin's personally picked envoy to head the Israeli team negotiating with the Syrians.

[9]See Warren Christopher, *In the Stream of History: Shaping Foreign Policy For a New Era* (Stanford, CA: Stanford University Press, 1998), p. 77. "I had been aware of secret discussions between Israelis and Palestinians in Oslo and other venues . . . Because of Rabin's open skepticism . . . I had never looked for much to come out of these discussions . . . There was no doubt that we should bless this breakthrough." David Makovsky's *Making Peace With the PLO* (Boulder, CO: Westview Press, 1996) contains a good account of the process and a wealth of supporting documents.

timetable for final status negotiations, all to culminate five years later in an end to the Israeli-Palestinian quarrel. It thus incorporated a set of ideas nurtured under American auspices dating back to Camp David, but without Washington's direct participation. Still, both Rabin and Arafat eagerly sought direct U.S. political and financial endorsement of the deal, and a beaming President Clinton happily obliged at the White House on September 13, 1993. (The United States pledged about 20 percent of $4.1 billion raised to support the autonomy regime.) The self-starting nature of Oslo and the evident willingness of the parties to continue their direct dealings with a minimum of American help left the United States free to concentrate on the Syrian track.

## LIMITS OF INFLUENCE

This was to prove an arduous and disappointing effort. Two meetings between President Clinton and President Assad; twenty trips by Secretary of State Warren Christopher to Damascus; and innumerable interventions by other U.S. diplomats—all failed to achieve agreement. The process was also punctuated by periodic violence in Lebanon that required strenuous American efforts to contain.

On the surface, Assad's policy was an inexplicable defiance of American supremacy. Syria, although heavily armed, was a backward, isolated tyranny at odds with all its neighbors. State controls discouraged international investors, and, as a sponsor of international terrorism, Syria was prohibited from obtaining U.S. aid. The Israeli government had gone very far to assure Assad, through Christopher, that it was prepared to yield strategic positions in the Golan Heights in return for military and political arrangements similar to those obtained with Egypt (the so-called Rabin "deposit").[10] But Syria's President Assad had different calculations. He regarded Oslo as a Palestinian betrayal that weakened his leverage; he also expected it to fail, bringing a chastened Israel and America back his way. Moreover, Assad indignantly refused to make Sadat-like gestures that suggested his readiness to reconcile with Israel. His attention was fixed on Washington; he preferred to negotiate primarily with the United States. And to pressure Israel, Assad supported the Hezbollah militia, whose attacks on Israel's "security zone" in southern Lebanon relied on Iranian arms transferred through Damascus.

Most U.S. (and Israeli) analysts were convinced that Assad did want to make a deal sooner or later, using the process to gain time and Washington's interest. But the process itself was not enough; Syria was never removed from the terror list. From 1993 until 1996, most of the drama concerned the working out of Oslo while Assad bided his time.

---

[10]See Rabinovitch's *On the Brink of Peace* and Christopher's *In the Stream of History* for details of this curious transaction. See also Uri Sagie, *The Israeli-Syrian Dialogue: A One-Way Ticket to Peace?* (Houston, TX: The James A. Baker III Institute for Public Policy of Rice University, October 1993). See Helena Cobban's *The Israeli-Syrian Peace Talks 1991–96 and Beyond* (Washington, DC: U.S. Institute of Peace, 1999) for a good account of the Syrian view.

When Arafat and Rabin signed Oslo II in September 1995, also called the Cairo agreement, the Israeli-Palestinian track was already in considerable trouble. "Autonomy" had become partly a success and partly a failure. Israel retained strategic control of the West Bank and Gaza, while shedding responsibility for the two-plus million Arab inhabitants; the PLO, through the Palestinian Authority, established itself and strengthened its claim for ultimate statehood. Yet terrorism against Israel had increased, and Arafat was in no hurry to court civil strife with the Islamic Hamas party in order to curtail it. The Palestinian economic situation worsened despite international aid. Various zones of control were established ("A" all Palestinian; "B" Palestinian civil administration, Israeli security control; and "C" all Israeli) impeding the flow of trade. Israeli security measures in times of tension disrupted the income of 100,000-plus Arab day workers who lived in Gaza and the West Bank but who were employed in Israel. The Palestinian Authority itself created monopolies and an administration rife with corruption.[11]

The disillusion was mutual. Israeli leaders, including Rabin, campaigned on the theme of "separation" from the Palestinians; despite their economic dependency, the Palestinians stressed independence from Israel. Arafat kept his people mobilized on anti-Israeli themes. The bitter Israeli debate over Oslo threatened civil strife. Thus, although neither Israel nor the Palestinians wished to return to the pre-Oslo situation, the autonomy process had gotten off to a slow and shaky start.

Rabin's murder on November 4, 1995, by a Jewish fanatic opposed to the peace process shocked all of the parties into a renewed effort to make Oslo work. In January 1996, the Palestinians elected both Arafat as head of the Palestinian Authority and a new Legislative Council.[12] Shimon Peres, Rabin's successor and an architect of Oslo, carried out the initial stages of Oslo II and simultaneously gave fresh impetus to the Syrian track. An Israeli-Syrian negotiation at Wye Plantation in January 1996 under U.S. auspices made considerable progress in some of the security arrangements crucial to a deal on the Golan Heights, but it still failed to resolve the earlier differences in approach. Meanwhile, a fresh outburst of Palestinian bombings in Israeli cities highlighted Arafat's deficiencies. When the Syrians applauded the violence, Peres angrily suspended the talks. This step was followed by Hezbollah guerrilla attacks against Israel's northern border towns, whereupon the

---

[11]See Ishac Diwan and Radwan Divza (eds.), *Development Under Adversity: The Palestinian Economy in Transition* (Washington, DC: The World Bank, 1999). See also *The West Bank and Gaza Economic Policy Framework Progress Report*, prepared by the Palestinian Authority in collaboration with the staff of the International Monetary Fund, May 31, 2000 (available on the Palestinian Authority website at *http://www.pna.net/events/economic_ahlc.htm*). After a sharp recession in 1995–96, the Palestinian economy grew rapidly. Still at the end of 1999, per capita income remained 10 percent below 1993; unemployment was nearly double in an area with a highly dependent population—only 19 percent work.

[12]See David Schenker, *Palestinian Democracy and Governance: An Appraisal of the Legislative Council* (Washington, DC: Washington Institute for Near East Policy, 2000). He concludes that despite its parliamentary trappings, the Council had not been able to hold the Executive Branch—Arafat—accountable, or to exercise its powers.

Israelis launched a heavy artillery and air bombardment of southern Lebanon and Beirut's electrical infrastructure.

Stymied on the Syrian front, Peres had decided on an early election. He found himself hard pressed by his opponent, Likud's Benjamin Netanyahu, a fierce critic of Oslo, who drew upon rising Israeli doubts about the peace process. Arafat's actions to control Hamas proved too little, too late. Fearful of the outcome, the Clinton administration made obvious its preference for Peres, organizing an international conference (boycotted by Syria and Lebanon) at Sharm el Sheikh to condemn terrorism and boost Peres's prestige. American intervention into Israeli electoral politics was not new (Bush clearly disliked Shamir, and Carter eventually lost confidence in Begin). The Israelis, too, had been known to favor one American candidate over another (Rabin himself generally liked Republicans, although American Jews favored Democrats). But these tactics got Clinton off to a bad start with Netanyahu when on May 29, 1996, he eked out a small majority over Peres in the first direct Israeli election for prime minister.

## TROUBLE IN THE GULF

The sudden turn of events for the worse in the Arab-Israeli diplomacy was accompanied by an erosion of U.S. influence in the Gulf. "Dual Containment," as the policy was called, committed the United States to restrain both Iraq and Iran until Saddam fell and the Mullahs dropped their anti-American campaign. But Saddam did not fall. In 1994, his threats against Kuwait brought heavy U.S. reinforcements to the region until he withdrew his offensive posture in the south. Then in 1996, he successfully overran the U.S.-supported resistance forces in Irbil, a major Kurdish town, bringing ineffectual U.S. missile barrages in retaliation. Two years after that, Saddam created a crisis over the UN inspection system; once again the U.S. proved unable to prevent its dismantling, despite evidence of continuing Iraqi efforts to conceal, or to develop, chemical and biological weapons. Nor had the United States been notably successful in preventing Iranian progress in building longer-range missiles or a nuclear weapons program.

In all of these cases, Washington found the Gulf War coalition ebbing. At the end of the decade, the United States could not count on Russia, China, and sometimes France, for support in the UN Security Council. Dual containment was on the defensive even as the United States was forced to station a growing military force in the Gulf to deter Iraq. These developments also shadowed the difficulties besetting the Arab-Israeli diplomacy. In at least one instance, it led to direct U.S. pressure on Israel during the winter of 1997–98 to ease tensions with the Palestinians as the United States prepared to take military action against Iraq.[13]

These political and military disturbances had remarkably little effect on the price and supply of oil through much of the decade. A steady price of $18 to $20 per

---

[13]See Harvey Sicherman, "The Containment of America," *Orbis* (Summer 1998).

barrel had been sustained in the early 1990s by the slow growth of industrial Europe and America. Asia's growing consumption took up some of the slack, but then, after 1996, Saddam's agreement to the UN's "oil for food" program gradually brought two million–plus barrels onto the market. When the Asian financial crisis of 1997 suddenly reduced demand, oil prices plummeted to the $10 a barrel range. This decrease in turn threatened to wreck the economics of the Gulf producers, foremost Saudi Arabia, which had been running a serious deficit for years.[14]

In 1999, the Saudis joined the other members of OPEC in a concentrated effort to curtail production. Given the oil companies' propensity to maintain low inventories under conditions of sinking demand, the stage was set for a sudden crunch when the U.S. and European economies surged forward, and Asia began to recover. By the end of the decade, prices were at near record levels, exceeding $35 a barrel, leading to political trouble in Europe and the release of some of the U.S. strategic reserve. Their coffers replenished, the Saudis then acted to increase OPEC supply although without much immediate effect.[15] Throughout this turbulence, the Arab oil producers were careful not to speak of the "oil weapon." The sudden fluctuations of the oil markets in the late 1990s did not seem to make any impact on U.S. policy toward the Arab-Israeli conflict.

## SALVAGING THE PEACE

After 1996, the United States took a much more direct and active role in Israeli-Palestinian talks, largely to salvage them from a complete breakdown. The immediate occasion was a violent Palestinian outburst not long after Netanyahu's election. The Israeli leader began by assuring the United States, Egypt, and the Europeans that he would "fix" Oslo rather than discard it, primarily by insisting on greater Palestinian compliance with earlier agreements such as the revision of clauses in the PLO's Charter calling for Israel's destruction promised by Arafat in 1993. But Netanyahu was slow to engage Arafat, meeting him only briefly in early September, while the Palestinian leader complained about Israeli delays. Then on September 26, 1996, the opening of an archaeological tunnel along the Western Wall of the Temple Mount was exploited by Arafat to stage violent demonstrations, including PA police fire on Israeli troops with weapons given to them by Israel as part of the original Oslo Accords. Fifteen Israelis and seventy Palestinians were killed.

President Clinton personally intervened to bring both Netanyahu and Arafat to Washington, where the two spent considerable time together and shook hands for the cameras. But there was no trust between them. From that point forward, the United States took an increasingly direct role in salvaging the negotiations. The

[14]See F. Gregory Gause III, "Saudi Arabia Over a Barrel," *Foreign Affairs* (May–June 2000); Robert A. Manning, "The Asian Energy Predicament," *Survival* (Spring 2000). For Iraq's role, see Bhusan Bahree, "Iraq Pumps Critical Oil, and Knows It," *Wall Street Journal*, September 19, 2000, p. A21.

[15]During interviews in Saudi Arabia (July 2000), the author was told that that country's national interest dictated a long-term price between $20 and $25 per barrel.

Hebron Accord (1997) and later the Wye Plantation Memorandum (1998), the latter brokered by Clinton himself, were the product of these interventions, which inevitably reoriented the direction of the parties from each other to Washington. Among other provisions, for example, the CIA became a significant "supervisor" of the Israel-PA security cooperation and also the conduit for extensive training of the Palestinian police in counterterror operations.[16]

Netanyahu, facing enormous resistance in his cabinet and from the settlers to further withdrawals, sought to abandon the transition phase and enter final status negotiations. Neither Arafat nor Clinton would accept this move, leaving the Israeli leader in an increasingly difficult domestic political impasse. Arafat appeared to be the clear gainer as slowly but surely he took advantage of U.S.-Israeli tensions to secure increased American patronage. He was to visit the White House thirteen times over the Clinton years—more than any other foreign leader—and his influence reached a high point when, in December 1998, Clinton addressed a Palestinian assembly in Gaza, assuring them of America's support for Palestinian "determination of their own future"—code words for a Palestinian state.

Unknown to the United States, Netanyahu had opened a secret track with the Syrians through an American businessman and sometime diplomat, Ronald Lauder. These exchanges, begun in July 1998 and continued into early fall, remain shrouded in controversy, but it is hard to believe that the Likud leader offered the June 4, 1967, lines.[17] Assad's motives for running such a channel may have been influenced by the new military cooperation between Turkey and Israel. In the fall of 1998, the Turks, disturbed for years by the Kurdistan Workers' Party (PKK) terror tactics, demanded the ouster of the PKK leader Abdullah Ocalan and the end of his base in Syria. Damascus complied. By conceding to the Turks, and negotiating with the Israelis, Assad avoided a two-front conflict.

## CRISIS OF THE END GAME

Israel's shaky right-wing coalition government did not long survive the Wye Memorandum, and new elections were called for May 1999. Once again the Clinton administration conveyed its preference for the Labour candidate, this time the much-decorated General Ehud Barak who had displaced Shimon Peres as Labour Party leader. Casting himself as a smoother version of his mentor, Yitzhak Rabin, Barak decisively defeated Netanyahu (56 percent to 44 percent).[18] But Barak's

---

[16]See the *New York Times*, November 13, 2000, p. A10, for a succinct review of the CIA's unusual—and unwanted—participation in these relationships.

[17]See Danna Harman, "Netanyahu was ready to yield Golan—Ramon," *Jerusalem Post Internet Edition*, December 14, 1999, for a good review. See also Dan Margalit, "On Netanyahu's Path but with a map," *Ha'aretz English Internet Edition*, November 15, 1999; Zeev Schiff, "Three Reckless Steps," *Ha'aretz English Internet Edition*, October 19, 1999; and Aluf Benn, "Shephardstown Began at Wye," *Ha'aretz English Internet Edition*, December 28, 1999.

[18]Both sides made heavy use of American consultants, Barak benefiting from a team used by Clinton himself, and Netanyahu from a firm associated with Republican candidates.

Labour Party, renamed One Israel and portrayed as a kind of "third way" centrist coalition, fared much less well, winning a mere 26 seats in the 120 member Knesset. The new prime minister had a base smaller than that of any of his predecessors.

Both major parties lost ground. Together, One Israel and a shrunken opposition Likud of 19 added up to only 45 of 120 seats, versus 66 in 1996 and 76 under the old system in 1992. The Sephardic religious party Shas went from 10 in 1996 to 17—the third largest in the Knesset—despite the conviction of its leader Arya Deri for bribery. Barak was thus forced to create a broad coalition to govern at all. At the outset it numbered 74, half of which consisted of parties that had served in the previous government, including Shas.

The new Prime Minister's surprising success in this exercise allowed him to accelerate both diplomatic tracks. Barak persuaded Clinton that the Palestinian negotiation would benefit from less direct U.S. involvement, and he sought to establish a relationship of trust with Arafat. He found the Palestinian leader much less interested in final status talks than in acquiring as much territory as possible through interim withdrawals. The Sharm, or Wye II agreement in September 1999, confirmed this approach. Then in December, the Syrian track came suddenly alive, and President Clinton personally brokered the Shephardstown, West Virginia, talks between the Israeli Prime Minister and the Syrian Foreign Minister. Both the Israeli and American leaders expected a major breakthrough and put the talks with Arafat in second place. A high point was reached when the United States drew up a draft Israeli-Syrian treaty, subsequently leaked by both the Syrians and the Israelis.[19]

These promising developments, however, soon crashed on the reality of Israeli-Syrian differences. Assad suspended the talks ostensibly because Barak had been too circumspect in his willingness to withdraw from the Golan. Under some pressure, including renewed fighting in Lebanon, from which Barak had pledged to withdraw, preferably in the framework of an agreement with Syria, the Israeli Prime Minister indicated his willingness to leave Golan. In Geneva on March 8, President Clinton conveyed Barak's "bottom line" to Assad personally. To this would be added a set of American assurances to both sides that included such subjects as intelligence, international forces (similar to those posted in Sinai as part of the Israeli-Egyptian treaty), and the provision of financial and military assistance. But it turned out that Assad, still unwilling to make public gestures of peace toward Israel, also insisted on recovering Syria's pre-1967 position on the Sea of Galilee, Israel's largest freshwater resource. Barak would not meet this demand, and the meeting proved a failure.

The Israeli leader then made good on his promise to withdraw from Lebanon unilaterally, a move the Syrians had criticized earlier as an act of war. Once behind the international border, Israel threatened severe retaliation should its northern communities be attacked. The United States supported the Israeli position, and the UN certified the Israeli withdrawal to the international border, although Lebanon did

---

[19]John Lancaster, "Syria Offers Israel Major Concessions," *Washington Post*, January 14, 2000, p. A1.

not. An early clash between Israel and Syria may have been averted by Assad's sudden death on June 10, 2000. His son Bashar, groomed for the succession, indicated soon thereafter his desire to avoid immediate trouble on the Lebanese border.

## CAMP DAVID II: THE THREE-BLUFF SUMMIT

All attention now focused on the Palestinians. Arafat, clearly Barak's second choice, was in no hurry to talk about final status negotiations, demanding instead the delayed last stage of Israeli withdrawals, the extent of which had not been covered by Wye II. Both Arafat and Barak had agreed on a deadline of September 13, 2000, for the completion of the final status agreement. But the gaps between the parties on borders, refugees, settlers, and Jerusalem remained very wide and the potential for violence was palpable. On May 15 (the anniversary of Israel's founding), PA police participated in selected rioting, alarming the United States and Israel.[20]

After the failure at Geneva with the Syrians, Clinton was not eager to enter another high-stakes negotiation without some assurance of success. Yet the alternative was a crisis in September and even before that, the possible end of the Barak government. The Israeli prime minister had steadily lost ground over coalition squabbles and sharp criticism of his willingness to concede the Golan so quickly. After sacrificing his secular Meretz partner to retain Shas, he persuaded Clinton and a clearly reluctant Arafat to attend a summit, only to lose both Shas and his foreign minister David Levy, on the eve of the meeting. Their suspicions that the prime minister would break some of his self-declared "red lines" on an agreement with the Palestinians proved prescient.

The summit itself, lasting from July 12–26, was intended to repeat the feat performed twenty-two years earlier, thereby capping two decades of American peacemaking. But these negotiations lacked the basis for partial agreement: unlike Sadat and Begin, who knew they could achieve an Egyptian-Israeli peace but were divided over the Palestinian element, Arafat and Barak faced broad gaps on all of the main issues. Clinton sought to "bridge" the gaps by relying on cues from the Palestinians and the Israelis so that they would be seen as conceding to him rather than to each other, and by playing on their fears of appearing to be the obstructionist. He was prepared to sketch the costs of the alternative to agreement, principally the loss of American patronage, vital for both Israel and any future Palestinian state.

It soon developed that all three leaders were running bluffs, and bluffs that were called. Barak argued that his flexibility on the issues made him the best Israeli deal-maker Arafat would encounter; Clinton, obviously seeking a legacy for his presidency and with a federal budget surplus ahead, made the case why now was the time and why he was the best U.S. leader for a deal; and Arafat, sensing the de-

---

[20]A senior PA police official told the author in an interview in July 2000 that the police shootings had been a serious lapse of discipline, noting that six had been killed by Israeli snipers. Given the liaison role then being performed by the CIA between the PA and Israel, he was clearly concerned to disown such actions lest he injure Arafat's relationship with Washington.

sire of his would-be partners to go for broke, held out for even better terms, posing in the background the threat of blowing it all up through a unilateral declaration of independence on September 13, 2000.

When the leaders emerged exhausted from their ordeal on the mountaintop, each of the bluffs had been called. Barak had gone far, but not far enough for Arafat, and Clinton had not been able to bridge the gaps. Although the discussions remain largely secret, there was apparently some movement by both sides: on security, the Palestinians seemed agreeable to an Israeli military (but not civilian) presence in the Jordan Valley, although not on a long-term basis. On territory and settlements, the Israelis seemed agreeable to giving the Palestinians areas near Gaza in exchange for a border that would encompass 80 percent of the existing Israeli settlements that lay beyond the June 4, 1967, line. These details largely preserved the Palestinian insistence on Israel's return to the prewar lines, the Israeli insistence that they would not, and the American position that UN Security Council Resolution 242 allowed for "minor changes" in the interest of a secure peace.

On refugee issues, the parties agreed on a compensation fund. The Israelis rejected the "right of return" to pre-1967 Israel but accepted that a small number might be accepted in the name of family reunification. The Palestinians insisted on the "right of return" but argued that few refugees would do so.

That left Jerusalem. Abdullah, the new King of Jordan (his father Hussein, a Middle East fixture for four decades, died on February 8, 2000), had advised before the summit that the city should not be tackled, in line with the old diplomatic wisdom that all other issues should be decided before this one, because of its volatile mix of politics and religion. But neither Barak nor Arafat would do a deal omitting Jerusalem. For Barak, this would leave the conflict unsettled, defeating his main objective.

As for Arafat, he was determined to press claims that would earn him the broadest Muslim support. Palestinian denials that the Jewish temples had ever been on the Haram es Sharif or Noble Sanctuary, as the Muslims call the Temple Mount, effectively foreclosed any compromise based on religious rights. Arafat would offer the traditional formula: Muslim control of the city, with the Jews allowed their own Quarter and access to the Western Wall, as befitted the Dhimmi, the non-Muslim but protected religious minorities—a position offensive even to a secular Zionist. Barak had thus encountered a Palestinian stance insistent on the two most neuralgic issues: the Palestinian Right of Return, which, if exercised, could end the Jewish majority; and Arab sovereignty over Jerusalem, which was the equivalent of taking Zion out of Zionism.

Arafat left the summit to the acclaim of his people for having resisted both Israel and the United States. His position on Jerusalem had been supported by Egypt and Saudi Arabia, America's most important Arab friends. In contrast, Barak returned to an uproar: he had apparently been willing to breach some of his own self-declared red lines, including a division of authority if not sovereignty in the Old City, but had received no comparable offer from Arafat. Most serious of all, however, was the stark reality that the American president had convened the summit yet failed to broker even a minimal agreement. For a diplomatic process that had always counted on Washington's ability to move the parties forward, this was a signal defeat. If Arafat and Barak could not agree themselves, and could not be brought to agree by Clinton, then the ultimate stalemate had been reached. There was no obvious way out.

## JERUSALEM REDUX

Clearly angry at Arafat, Clinton fingered him as the obstacle, threatening a reassessment of U.S. relations with the Palestinian Authority and the long-delayed movement of the U.S. embassy to Jerusalem. Anger soon became anxiety over the loss of America's mediating role, and the White House retreated into a call for more diplomacy. Clinton tried again with Arafat and Barak at the Millennium UN Summit on September 6, and later that month, low-level negotiating teams talked in Arlington, Virginia. National Security Advisor Samuel Berger was the most inventive: "The good news," he said on September 8, "is that it is no longer just an iceberg, it's a hundred pieces of ice. Can this be reassembled into something like a bridge? I don't know." But Clinton's public blaming of Arafat and the extent of Barak's concessions also called the Palestinian bluff about September 13. A quick globe trot convinced Arafat that he could not get much international support for a unilateral declaration of independence. On September 10, the Palestinian Council voted to delay.

Arafat had been caught in this kind of a bind once before, in the summer of 1996, and had played the Jerusalem issue to escape it. This time, instead of a tunnel, he got the sudden visit of the leader of the opposition, Netanyahu's last foreign minister, General Ariel Sharon, to the Temple Mount on Thursday, September 28, 2000, the very day the Israeli and Palestinian delegations ended their talks in Virginia.

Sharon's motive was to demonstrate Israel's hold on the Mount. His timing was apparently a function of his political rival Netanyahu's release from the threat of legal action on charges of bribery and Barak's acknowledgment the day before that there would be two capitals in Jerusalem. Politically vulnerable, the Israeli leader would not heed Palestinian warnings about the hated Sharon, along with their implied veto on Israeli visitation rights.

Sharon's hour-long tour of the area, under the watchful escort of hundreds of police, was immediately followed by protests, but the most violent episode, including stones hurled at the Jewish worshippers at the Western Wall, occurred on Friday afternoon, September 29, following an incendiary sermon at the Aqsa mosque. Six Palestinians were killed and hundreds injured when the police cleared the plaza. According to the Palestinian version, Sharon's "invasion" of the Haram and then Israel's deadly use of force against the "peaceful protestors" called forth the "Al Aqsa Intifada." According to the Israelis, Arafat used the visit as an "excuse" to launch well-organized violence, the planning for which was "evident" during the summer when a September 13 confrontation over Palestinian independence seemed possible.

The Palestinian protests, although expressing a genuine outrage and pent-up frustration, often reflected careful organization. Large crowds of civilians, many of them young boys, moved toward Israeli army checkpoints or settlements, throwing rocks and firebombs. There were also snipers. These were often members of the Tanzim, a paramilitary under the control of Arafat's own political party, the Fatah, and they were armed in blatant violation of the Oslo Accords. The resulting cross-fires were bound to create civilian casualties, and during one such clash, the Israelis killed twelve-year-old Mohammed Aldura, who became the poster boy for the new intifada. Throughout, Arafat remained remote, often not even in the country, while the PA and the Tanzim clearly encouraged the violence.

On October 2, a new front opened when Israeli Arabs rioted, many adopting the slogans of the PA, and disrupted major highways leading north. Long angry over what they regarded as second-class status within Israel, many in the crowds now shouted for the end of the state and death to the Jews. The police killed eight. This episode shocked the Israeli government and dealt another devastating blow to the political left, many of whom had also seen in the peace process a way to mend relations with the Arab minority.

# FINGERS IN THE DIKE: FROM PARIS TO SHARM

The Aqsa Intifada "sanctified" Arafat's political struggle, magnifying his international support and allowing him to join forces with his rivals, the Islamic Hamas. As part of the new unity, the PA released many jailed Hamas activists, who promptly threatened a wave of terrorism against Israel. Arafat's complicity in the violence was a further blow to Barak, who had hosted him at a private dinner only days before the explosion, as part of a new effort to repair personal relations. Barak looked the fool. Clinton, too, had seen his long cultivation of the Palestinian leader turn into nothing. Initially, however, both the Israeli and the American leaders behaved as if this new test of strength was still within the framework of negotiations, and that if only the violence could be halted, the search for a solution would regain momentum.

It took two weeks of effort to dislodge the notion that a cease-fire could be obtained. On October 4 in Paris, Albright had been forced to run after Arafat when he attempted to leave the meeting; still, she could not obtain his signature to an agreement. Instead, both sides were observed to issue "stand down" orders. Barak followed up two days later when for the first time, the Israelis allowed Palestinian police to control the entrance to the Temple Mount and, on October 7, withdrew from the embattled Joseph's Tomb in Nablus. These moves did not prevent either a riot in the Old City or the sacking of the tomb. Barak was further embarrassed when the United States abstained from a UN resolution condemning Israel for excessive use of force and when Hezbollah abducted three Israeli soldiers from Israel's side of the UN-recognized Lebanese border—despite the presence of UN forces nearby. The embattled prime minister then issued a 48-hour ultimatum—that would culminate in harsher military action and a unity government, including Sharon—but he was put off his deadline by U.S. and UN diplomatic intervention.

On October 12, however, the media had a new horror to take its place alongside Mohammed Aldura's death. Two Israeli reservists, captured by the Palestinian police after taking a wrong turn, were lynched and mutilated by a mob at a Ramallah police station. After due warning, Barak launched missile attacks on selected police targets in Area "A," that part of the West Bank and Gaza entirely under the control of the Palestinian Authority and heretofore untouched.

This escalation seems to have galvanized Egyptian president Hosni Mubarak. He had incurred Clinton's anger for supporting Arafat's position on Jerusalem during the Camp David summit, and had in turn been angered when the Americans went to Paris for their cease-fire effort rather than to Sharm el Sheikh under his auspices. Egyptian demonstrations in Cairo against Israel had turned ugly. Now Mubarak feared that the emergency Arab League meeting scheduled for October 21 might pressure Egypt to take actions against Israel that he did not want to take. He, rather than Arafat, had to get control of the diplomatic tide if Egypt's interests were to be served. Mubarak therefore reversed his opposition to any more summits after the Paris fiasco and on October 16, brought Arafat, Barak, and Clinton to the Sharm el Sheikh resort.

That same day, Marwan Barghouti, the head of the Tanzim and by all accounts Arafat's confidante, told the *New York Times* that the "real reason [for the violence was] the disappointment of the Palestinian public in the peace process and continuation of the occupation." At Sharm, it became clear that a simple cease-fire was only part of a larger tactic: the "Al Aqsa Intifada" and the "independence intifada" were Arafat's way of channeling the violence into attainment of his objective, an independent state with international support but no end to the conflict except on terms Israel could never accept. Clinton, who only two months before had been cajoling the parties to compromise on Jerusalem, was now reduced to announcing that Arafat and Barak would each call for an end to the violence, that he would organize a "fact finding" study into its causes, and that the parties would seek a way back to negotiations.

None of the parties liked the Sharm transaction. Arafat, clearly unhappy with American mediation, had wanted an international commission under UN auspices not only to condemn the Israelis but perhaps, as the UN had done in 1947–48, to reach a "partition" resolution—no doubt under more favorable terms than those offered by Barak or advocated by the United States. Barak, in turn, was persuaded to accept a "study" that included U.S. consultation with Kofi Annan and the European Union and also to agree that negotiations under the old framework might continue. This last provision barred easy entry by the Likud opposition into an "emergency" national unity government because Sharon could not bring his party along unless the Camp David concessions were shelved.

Still, this unsigned barely acknowledged agreement was enough for Mubarak. The harsh, threatening words of the subsequent Arab summit in Cairo (including a call for war crimes trials) were still couched within the framework of peace negotiations and did not require Egypt to take any specific action. Thus, the "firebreak" held. Arafat would get sympathy, some money (or the promise of it), and the breaking of ties between some Arab states (notably Morocco) and Israel, but no guns and no threats of war. Mubarak still affirmed Sadat's decision not to put Egypt into a military confrontation with Israel over the Palestinian cause, at least not yet.

## CLINTON'S LAST HURRAH—AND BARAK'S

On December 23, Bill Clinton tried once more to bridge the Israeli and Palestinian positions. His oral suggestions, called "parameters" took the Camp David formulations a step further putting the U.S. itself in favor of positions painful to both sides. Among the proposals: Palestinian sovereignty over the Temple Mount-Haram; Israeli sovereignty over the Western Wall and Jewish Quarter; an international force within a politically divided Old City of Jerusalem; an international force along the Jordan River; Israeli control over the return of Palestinian refugees; Israeli retention of about 4–6% of the West Bank to accommodate 80% of the settlers; addition of Israeli territory near Gaza to compensate.[31] Barak accepted with major caveats; Arafat, beneficiary of yet one more visit to the White House, waffled. Time had run out for Clinton.

None of this was enough to save Ehud Barak's political future. After Clinton's last hurrah, Barak began intense direct negotiating with the Palestinians in Taba, although Arafat failed to call an end to the violence. There was no agreement. On February 8, 2001, Barak was soundly defeated by Likud leader Sharon. The new prime minister cobbled together a unity government and a broad coalition. Shimon Peres, architect of Oslo became foreign minister. Sharon promptly announced that no negotiation would occur unless Arafat publicly called for an end to the violence. He also repudiated Barak's compromises.

## A CLARIFYING ACT OF VIOLENCE

As both sides settled in for a fundamental test of strength, neither the Madrid formula of American supervised talks nor the Oslo formula of direct (and secret) understandings between Israel and Arafat's PLO seemed applicable to the conflict. Instead, there was a deepening crisis punctuated by rounds of violence that have already cost both sides heavily. (By early April 2001, 360 Palestinians had been killed, and 71 Israelis; hundreds more had been injured on both sides.)

Despite its best efforts, the United States found itself increasingly at odds with its Arab friends. This situation was a direct consequence of Arafat's decisions to "go for broke." Certainly after the Camp David summit but perhaps as long ago as 1997–98 (critics of Oslo would argue even earlier), the Palestinian leader had

---

[31]President Clinton's speech to the Israeli Policy Forum on Jan. 7, 2001 covers many of the particulars and defends his deplomacy. See *New York Times,* January 8, 2001 for reactions. *The Jerusalem Post* International Edition Dec. 29, 2000 carries a comparison of the U.S., Israeli and Palestinian positions. A more detailed account, supposedly the Israeli minutes of Clinton's presentation on Dec. 23, may be found in *Harretz* English International edition, Dec. 31, 2000.

apparently concluded that he would never get his conditions—Israeli withdrawal to the June 4, 1967, lines, Palestinian control of East Jerusalem (and the Old City), and the "right of return" for the refugees—under American-mediated diplomacy. No Israeli prime minister was ready to offer such an outcome. And Arafat himself had certainly been unwilling, even under heavy American pressure, to make the compromise on those points that the United States thought necessary. The violence had clarified Arafat's position: he wanted his state, but he would not end the conflict in order to get it.

Could Arafat achieve his objectives without Israeli consent? The answer may very well depend on the United States, for the violence has also clarified the American role. U.S. mediation depends on leaders who want to deal and who can deliver despite political sacrifices. Barak was prepared to sacrifice, although it was not clear whether he could deliver. Arafat, to judge by comments he made at Camp David, thought additional sacrifice on his part would be fatal. He had always preferred the political benefits of martyrdom without having to undergo the rigors of the actual experience. The "al Aqsa intifada" enabled him once more to reap those benefits. A compromise peace might bring him the actual experience.

The United States thus faced the loss of both the mechanism and the Palestinian partner to conduct the diplomacy that might resolve the conflict. Arafat clearly hoped that he could organize international pressure on Washington through the Arabs, the Europeans, and the UN, although at the time of this writing there was scant evidence of success. A political stalemate accompanied by a ferocious guerrilla war will surely put pressure on the "firebreak"—Egypt's resolve to stay out of a confrontation with Israel's military. It could also make it easier for Saddam to rehabilitate himself by taking the lead in an anti-Israel jihad that might free him of American sanctions. If Cairo (or Amman or Riyadh) decide to take risks with Israel and the United States on behalf of the Palestinians, then the Middle East would be pitched back into the perilous conditions that gave rise to the 1967 war. That is the worst case.

Big trouble could also come from the north. An inexperienced Syrian leader might be drawn by Hezbollah and Iran into a military clash with Israel. Israel, whose unilateral withdrawal from Lebanon is attributed by many Arabs to Hezbollah's guerrilla tactics, cannot afford to put its northern communities under new risks.

A troubling but perhaps more hopeful scenario is that under heavy pressure from all quarters, Israel and the PA negotiate a modified status quo—an extended "interim" agreement—that provides for an incomplete Palestinian state but still a modus vivendi, a sophisticated version of crisis management.

## THE LIMITS OF INFLUENCE

These events offered a sobering caution about the limits of influence even for a power as mighty as the United States. A decade of American peacemaking in the Middle East, derived from Washington's sole superpower status and the defeat of Saddam, had not come to a good end. And to make matters worse, recent months have seen the reappearance of a tight, high-priced oil market and an Iraq loosening previous constraints. The Clinton administration had left its successor a full and unappetizing plate.

President Bush and his secretary of State, former General Colin Powell of Gulf War fame, began logically enough by separating themselves from the obvious failure of Clinton's approach. Using the occasion of the ceremonies for the tenth anniversary of the Gulf War in Kuwait, Powell refocused the U.S. sanctions policy to alleviate Iraqi civilian hardships while strengthening those that hampered Saddam's rearmament. This diplomacy had been preceded on February 16 by a U.S.-UK air strike on the Iraqi air defense network outside of the northern and southern no-fly zones, a sharp departure from the low level sparring that had characterized the situation for more than a year. Whether a new combination of military force and political tactics will revive the anti-Saddam coalition remains to be seen but these initial actions did spoil Iraq's plan to turn the March 28 Arab Summit in Jordan into a coming out party against sanctions altogether.

Simultaneously, Bush and Powell indicated their support for the Israeli view that in the absence of a call by Arafat to renounce violence, little diplomacy could be done and the Palestinian leader would be unwelcome in the White House. The Bush administration also accepted statements by Clinton and Barak that the Camp David proposals and Clinton's December 23 "parameters" were off the table. Then the United States followed it up with a veto in the UN Security Council on March 27 of a Palestinian supported resolution calling for an international "protection" force in the West Bank and Gaza.

These moves suggested at the very least that Washington would (1) reassert the strategic importance of containing (or overthrowing) Saddam and try to renew the international coalition to do it, (2) refuse to risk American mediation or the prestige of the Presidency on a formula for settling the Arab-Israeli conflict unless the parties—especially Arafat—persuaded Washington that they wanted an agreement.

Historians and diplomats will no doubt find explanations for what had happened, during the 1990's and not all of these will point to American ineptitude or misjudgment. Sole superpowerdom does not confer omnipotence. Still, a few points deserve closer attention because they indicate either inherent limits to influence that should be understood at the outset, or those policies that inadvertently increased the limits.

- *U.S. domination of the region may be a necessary condition for negotiations about peace but not a sufficient one to attain agreements.* The strength and judgment of the would-be peacemakers remain crucial. The United States did not and perhaps could not compel leaders such as Arafat, Assad, Rabin, Netanyahu, or Barak to cross their own "red lines."
- *The United States needs enforcement mechanisms to ensure that agreements that it underwrites are actually observed by the parties.* Frustrations with the working of the autonomy agreement built up to dangerous levels on the ground, especially among the Palestinians. This was due partially to Arafat's

often corrupt and arbitrary government, Israel's reluctance to carry out withdrawals that the Palestinians believed were due them, and continued expansions of Israeli settlements. The PA itself also compiled a poor record of fulfilling its promises, especially in the security sphere. Meanwhile, the United States, hoping to avoid friction and stay clear of the "judge" role, left it largely to the parties to enforce the agreement.

- *Playing Israeli politics can be counterproductive.* The U.S. decision to "tilt" toward Peres in the 1996 election following Rabin's murder meant that at a critical moment, Clinton and Netanyahu lacked confidence in each other. Following the tunnel disturbances, Clinton's steady drift toward Arafat possibly inflated the Palestinian leader's expectations. A similar logic may have led Clinton to risk Camp David II rather than see Barak's government fall.
- *Summits should always be prepared to yield the minimum, and if not, they should not be held.* Both in Geneva and Camp David, Clinton's willingness to try was brave but not necessarily wise; it squandered the prestige of the presidency and left no clear way forward leaving the impression afterwards that the situation was hopeless.
- *U.S. prestige (and influence) can be crucially affected by American policy elsewhere in the region.* The Gulf War helped to produce Madrid. Saddam's ability to outlast U.S. containment could hardly have facilitated respect for U.S. power. Similarly, Washington did not contain Iranian sponsored terrorism, an important factor in the Israeli-Lebanon-Syrian triangle. Finally, the crippling of the USS *Cole,* a billion-dollar warship, in the harbor of Aden, Yemen, on October 12, 2000, by a suicide attack was a heavy blow to U.S. military prestige.

This cautionary (and darkening) tale should end nonetheless on a brighter note. The basic strategic facts that emerged in the early 1990s remain intact, as of this writing. Limits notwithstanding, the United States is still the dominant outside power in the Middle East. The Israelis do not want to reoccupy the Palestinian areas ceded by Oslo. The Palestinians cannot organize an Arab coalition to make war on Israel in behalf of their state. So long as these strategic factors hold, the parties will find their way back to each other, possibly under U.S. auspices but surely expecting Washington's support.

# 8

# Iraq and Iran
## From Dual
## to Differentiated Containment

## ROBERT S. LITWAK
### Woodrow Wilson International Center for Scholars

The development of American post–Cold War strategy has been strongly influenced by the fact that the end of the Cold War coincided with a hot war in the Persian Gulf to liberate Kuwait from Iraqi occupation.[1] The stunning military victory of the American-led coalition confirmed the United States' status as the "sole remaining superpower" and the "indispensable nation." Indeed, the conjunction of U.S. military primacy with the technology-driven boom in the U.S. economy during the 1990s prompted some even to refer to the United States as a "hyperpower." Yet, as the United States has discovered in its policies toward Iraq and Iran, power alone does not necessarily confer the ability to dictate outcomes.

The end of the Cold War triggered a continuing debate about American interests and the appropriate U.S. role. Absent the Soviet threat and the foreign policy framework of global containment that derived from it, U.S. policy-makers have been hard-pressed to justify to a skeptical public why the United States should remain engaged in distant regions where there are no major material or strategic interests at stake. But this pattern has not been the case with respect to the Persian Gulf, a region for which a broad consensus exists on the region's vital interest to the West

Robert S. Litwak is Director of the Division of International Studies at the Woodrow Wilson International Center for Scholars of the Smithsonian Institution, and Adjunct Professor at Georgetown University's School of Foreign Service. Dr. Litwak is the author or editor of eight books, including *Detente and the Nixon Doctrine, Nuclear Proliferation after the Cold War,* and the recently published *Rogue States and U.S. Foreign Policy.* He served on the National Security Council staff at the White House as Director for Nonproliferation and Export Controls during President Clinton's first term.

[1]This chapter is derived from the author's book *Rogue States and U.S. Foreign Policy: Containment after the Cold War* (Washington, DC: Woodrow Wilson Center Press/Johns Hopkins University Press, 2000), especially chapters 2,3,4,5.

because of its vast oil reserves. After the liberation of Kuwait, the United States retained a significant military deployment in the Persian Gulf and remained directly involved in security affairs—a significant departure from the post–Nixon Doctrine era in which Washington had sought to play this role indirectly through the use of a regional surrogate. The Bush administration warned that the major threat to international security in the post-Soviet era was posed by an aggressive regional power possessing weapons of mass destruction (WMD) and sponsoring terrorism. Iraq was the archetype of what the Clinton administration would later categorize as a "rogue state." In addition to confronting a defeated but defiant Iraq, the United States also faced a postrevolutionary regime in Iran, implacably hostile to the "Great Satan" and politically at odds with the Persian Gulf region's monarchical regimes. To meet the twin challenges posed by Iraq and Iran—the most populous and dominant regional actors—the Clinton administration adopted a strategy of "dual containment."[2]

U.S. policy toward Iraq and Iran in this era of American primacy has highlighted the dilemmas of strategic management that are the leitmotif of this volume. Perhaps most prominent among them has been the tension between multilateralism (i.e., the utility and political desirability of working in tandem with allies) and unilateralism (i.e., the impulse to act independently when allies prove recalcitrant). In the case of Iraq, political support for economic sanctions to compel compliance with UN Security Council resolutions has waned, while U.S. policy objectives have wavered between comprehensive containment to keep Saddam Hussein "in a box" (in Secretary of State Madeleine Albright's phrase) and "rollback" to oust him from power. With Iran, the issue between the United States and its European and Japanese allies has revolved around the utility of engaging the theocratic regime in Teheran to create incentives for improved Iranian behavior. The election of the reformist President Mohammed Khatami in May 1997 dramatically altered the political context of this debate and created pressures for U.S. policy-makers to shift from a "dual containment" strategy to a differentiated approach toward these pivotal regional powers in the Persian Gulf.

The chapter focuses on the evolution of U.S. strategy from dual to differentiated containment and assesses its implications. The starting point is a brief overview of U.S. regional policy from the Nixon Doctrine through the 1991 Gulf War. This historical background is followed by a discussion of the Clinton administration's "dual containment" strategy, as well as of the broader "rogue state" policy within which it was embedded. This assessment will lead to an analysis of the contrasting dangers and political circumstances in Iraq and Iran, and a conclusion exploring the prospects for "differentiated containment."[3]

---

[2]The "dual containment" doctrine was enunciated by Martin Indyk, Senior Director for Near East and South Asian Affairs, National Security Council in "Challenges to U.S. Interests in the Middle East: Obstacles and Opportunities," *The Soref Symposium*, Washington Institute for Near East Policy, May 18–19, 1993, pp. 1–8.

[3]The strategy of "differentiated containment" toward Iraq and Iran was first advanced by Zbigniew Brzezinski, Brent Scowcroft, and Richard Murphy as an alternative to "dual containment"; see Brzezinski, Scowcroft, and Murphy, "Differentiated Containment," *Foreign Affairs* 76, No. 3 (May–June 1997), pp. 20–30.

# HISTORICAL BACKGROUND

After the withdrawal of British forces from the Gulf in 1971, the United States assumed responsibility as the ultimate security guarantor of the region. In pursuit of this objective, Washington followed a balancing strategy aimed at preventing any local power from achieving regional hegemony. During the Nixon-Kissinger years and continuing into the Carter administration, this strategy entailed a tilt toward the Shah's Iran. Under the Nixon Doctrine, Iran and Saudi Arabia purchased American arms (recycling petrodollars in the process) and became the "twin pillars" of U.S. security policy in the Gulf. With Iran's substantial arsenal, sizable population, and pro-American orientation, successive U.S. administrations during the 1970s viewed Iran as the security manager of the Persian Gulf region. This devolution of responsibility was a reflection of both Iran's rise and the realities of American post-Vietnam retrenchment in the Third World. The principal target of this regional strategy in the Gulf was Iraq, which was politically allied with the Soviet Union through a 1972 Treaty of Friendship. This pattern of regional alignments prevailed until the 1979 Iranian revolution and the advent of a virulently anti-American regime in Teheran. The USSR's invasion of Afghanistan that same year heightened concerns about a direct Soviet military threat to the Persian Gulf region.

In the early 1980s, with the continued deterioration in U.S.-Iranian relations, the Reagan administration initiated its famous "tilt" toward Iraq. It dropped the Baghdad regime from the State Department's terrorist list, a move that made Iraq eligible for American export credits. This development came at a time when Iraq was faring poorly in the war that it had started with Iran in September 1980. U.S. claims of neutrality were belied by covert military assistance (e.g., permitting third-party transfers of American-licensed equipment) and limited intelligence sharing. This tilt toward Iraq was complemented by a concerted American effort under the so-called "Operation Staunch" to deny Iran arms through an international embargo.[4] In mid-1985, however, the Reagan administration contravened its own policy by providing U.S. arms to Iran (via Israel) in return for cash (which was then covertly funneled to the Nicaraguan resistance) and for the Teheran regime's assistance in freeing American hostages in Lebanon. When the Iran-Contra scandal became public in November 1986, the Reagan administration had nothing tangible to show from this initiative, and the fiasco exposed it to charges of hypocrisy from European allies that Washington had strongly pressed to limit their dealings with Iran.[5]

---

[4]See Bruce Jentleson, *With Friends Like These: Reagan, Bush, and Saddam, 1982–1990* (New York: Norton, 1994), pp. 44–47.

[5]In the wake of the Gulf War, the *New York Times* (April 25, 1992, p. A22) criticized American policy that in the 1980s turned a blind eye to (and indeed encouraged) transfers of U.S. equipment to Iran (by Israel) and Iraq (by Saudi Arabia), depending on which regional power Washington was then cultivating political relations: "The list of forbidden recipients of U.S.-made weapons during the Reagan and Bush Administrations reads like a roster of the world's chief troublemakers. U.S. law forbade sending them American arms. Yet for almost a decade, the two Administrations circumvented the law with covert transfers."

In the wake of the Iran-Contra affair, U.S. policy reverted to its previous tilt toward Iraq. This change was reflected in the Reagan administration's 1987 decision to reflag Kuwaiti oil tankers and provide them protection against Iranian naval and air attacks. In Washington, the Iranian threat to shipping in the northern Gulf provoked discussion of military options, including a proposal to mine Iranian harbors. The adoption of a more bellicose U.S. stance toward Iran was accompanied in mid-1987 by a tough diplomatic line in the United Nations to compel Iran to accept a cease-fire or face mandatory sanctions. When Iran subsequently accepted a cease-fire with Iraq under duress (likened by Khomeini to drinking poison), there was a widespread perception in the Gulf region that American support for Iraq had been a significant factor. The eight-year Iran-Iraq War left the Baghdad regime financially strapped and exhausted, but also the dominant military power in the region. This conjunction of financial need, military dominance, and Saddam Hussein's proclivity to strategic miscalculation led to the Iraqi invasion of Kuwait within two years of the cease-fire with Iran.

During the period between the end of the Iran-Iraq War in August 1988 and the Iraqi invasion of Kuwait in August 1990, the Bush administration, even in the face of an increasingly bellicose and provocative stance from Saddam Hussein, remained committed to its engagement policy toward Iraq. This course of events was motivated by the belief that continuing engagement could lead to the moderation of Iraqi behavior and that the Baghdad regime would for the foreseeable future be preoccupied internally with the formidable tasks of postwar reconstruction. The Bush administration's engagement policy came to an abrupt halt with Iraq's invasion of Kuwait in August 1990 and the ensuing Gulf War of January–February 1991. In early 1992, given the profound regional change triggered by these events, the administration reassessed U.S. policy toward post-Khomeini Iran, including the consideration of "constructive engagement" through the lifting of selective sanctions. But the National Security Council review concluded that any gesture that would be meaningful in Teheran (such as lifting the ban on oil sales to America) would be politically impossible in Washington.[6]

# DUAL CONTAINMENT OF TWO "ROGUE STATES"

The Clinton administration's policy of "dual containment" was essentially a continuation of the comprehensive containment policy that the Bush administration had pursued toward Iran and Iraq after the Gulf War. After a decade of frustration (notably the failed engagement policy toward Iraq and the "Irangate" fiasco), U.S. policymakers eschewed the notion that Washington could play off one regional power against the other to maintain balance and stability. The enunciation of the dual containment policy came in a major policy address by Martin Indyk, the National Security Council staff's top Middle East expert, in May 1993. In that speech, Indyk stated:

[6]Elaine Sciolino, "After a Fresh Look, U.S. Decides to Steer Clear of Iran," *New York Times*, June 7, 1992, section 4, p. 5.

The Clinton Administration's policy of "dual containment" of Iraq and Iran derives in the first instance from an assessment that the current Iraqi and Iranian regimes are both hostile to American interests in the region. Accordingly, we do not accept the argument that we should continue the old balance of power game, building up one to balance the other. We reject that approach not only because its bankruptcy was demonstrated in Iraq's invasion of Kuwait. We reject it because of a clear-headed assessment of the antagonism that both regimes harbor towards the United States and its allies in the region. And we reject it because we don't need to rely on one to balance the other.[7]

Although the "dual containment" rubric created a linkage that later became a persistent source of confusion and contention, Indyk noted the significant difference in American objectives between the two cases. In the Iraqi case, he stated, "[o]ur purpose is deliberate: it is to establish clearly and unequivocally that the current regime in Iraq is a criminal regime, beyond the pale of international society and, in our judgment, irredeemable."[8] The speech did not explicitly state that the U.S. objective was a regime change; it repeated an earlier formulation that Washington sought full Iraqi compliance with UN Security Council resolutions on the assumption that Saddam Hussein could not meet those requirements while remaining in power. This constituted an implicit policy of rollback. In the case of Iran, by contrast, the focus of the dual containment speech was on objectionable Iranian *external* behavior—its sponsorship of terrorism and support for radical groups seeking to undermine the Arab-Israeli peace process, its efforts "to subvert friendly governments" in the Gulf region, and its sustained effort to acquire WMD capabilities. Indyk stated that the Clinton Administration was "not opposed to Islamic government in Iran . . . We do not seek a confrontation but we will not normalize with Iran until and unless Iran's policies change, across the board."[9]

The rumor of an NSC-State Department rift over dual containment prompted Indyk to clarify publicly that his previous statements had been cleared by the State Department and constituted the Clinton administration's official policy toward the Gulf region.[10] The new line received an authoritative boost from National Security Adviser Anthony Lake in the Spring 1994 issue of *Foreign Affairs*. Although best known for its elaboration of the policy of "dual containment" toward Iraq and Iran, the article also laid out the administration's general approach for dealing with those regimes (North Korea, Libya, and Cuba were also specifically cited) grouped under the rubric of "backlash" or "rogue" states. Lake asserted that these regimes—with

---

[7]Indyk, "Challenges to U.S. Interests in the Middle East: p. 4. A month before the Indyk speech, Elaine Sciolino, Chief Diplomatic Correspondent of the *New York Times,* wrote, "Past Administrations routinely looked at [Iran and Iraq] as players in a balancing act, historic rivals that could be . . . used against each other to insure that one did not become too strong at the expense of the other . . . Now the Clinton Administration argues that neither regime should be strengthened and that each should be dealt with as a separate problem—a sort of parallel containment." See Elaine Sciolino, "Taking on Iran and Iraq, but Separately," *New York Times,* April 11, 1993, section 4, p. 4.

[8]Indyk, "Challenges to U.S. Interests in the Middle East: p. 5.

[9]*Ibid.*

[10]See Kenneth Katzman, "Iran: U.S. Containment Policy," *CRS Report for Congress,* no. 94-652F (August 11, 1994), pp. 5–6 for a discussion of the development of the dual containment policy.

their authoritarian ruling cliques, their "aggressive and defiant" behavior, their "chronic inability to engage constructively with the outside world," and their pursuit of weapons of mass destruction—made clear "their recalcitrant commitment to remain on the wrong side of history." Lake argued that "[a]s the sole superpower, the United States has a special responsibility for developing a strategy to neutralize, contain, and through selective pressure, perhaps eventually transform these backlash states into constructive members of the international community." Having successfully contained Soviet power during the Cold War, the United States "now faces a less formidable challenge in containing [this] band of outlaws."

The article concluded with an acknowledgment to George Kennan whose 1947 essay in *Foreign Affairs* had "made the case for containment of an outlaw empire."[11] The Lake article, in turn, was an effort by the Clinton administration to articulate a post–Cold War containment doctrine to meet the challenge of "rogue states." Secretary of State Madeleine Albright told the Council on Foreign Relations in September 1997 that "dealing with the rogue states is one of the great challenges of our time . . . because they are there with the sole purpose of destroying the system." She argued that the "rogue states" constituted one of four distinct categories of countries in the post–Cold War international system (the other three being advanced industrial states, emerging democracies, and failed states).[12] The "rogue state" policy assumed a still higher profile in the late 1990s when the threat posed by North Korean and Iranian ballistic missile advances was cited by U.S. officials as the primary rationale for a national missile defense (NMD) system.[13]

For the Clinton administration, the assertion that "rogue states" constituted a distinct category of countries had political utility in mobilizing support both at home and abroad for tough measures against them. The underlying assumption, again reflecting one of the dominant recurring themes of this volume, is that the American public will not meet the challenge posed by these states unless roused to action through strong political rhetoric from the top leadership. This phenomenon, of course, is not new to American diplomacy. The enunciation of the Truman Doctrine is an example of how U.S. policy-makers have used expansive rhetoric for actions they believed the public would not otherwise support if cast more narrowly.

The political utility of the "rogue state" policy, however, was more than offset by significant liabilities. First and foremost, the rubric was an American political pejorative with no standing in international law. Because the term was analytically soft and quintessentially political, the policy was widely criticized, particularly by U.S. allies, for being politically selective. Syria, a state that met the key criteria for "rogue state" status because of its pursuit of weapons of mass destruction and sup-

---

[11]Anthony Lake, "Confronting Backlash States," *Foreign Affairs* 73, No. 2 (March–April 1994), pp. 45–46, 55.

[12]Department of State, Office of the Spokesman, Secretary of State Madeleine K. Albright Address before the Council on Foreign Relations, September 30, 1997 (secretary.state.gov/www/statements/9770930).

[13]For example, Speaker of the House Dennis Hastert likewise highlighted the threat of "the rogue state that aims a deadly missile at one of our cities" in his inaugural speech to the Congress. See Remarks of Speaker Dennis Hastert, House of Representatives, January 6, 1999, at *http://thomas.loc.gov*.

port for terrorism, was excluded from this category because of its importance to the Middle East peace process. By contrast, Cuba, which met none of the criteria, was occasionally included in the rogues' gallery under pressure from the politically influential Cuban émigré community in Florida and New Jersey.

A second liability of the "rogue state" policy was its adverse impact on the United States' relations with its key European, Canadian, and Japanese allies. The logic and political dynamic of the "rogue state" approach pushed U.S. policymakers toward a generic strategy of containment and isolation. Why would one even consider limited engagement of states described as being "beyond the pale"? By contrast, the Europeans emphasized the use of political relations and inducements to moderate the behavior of "rogue states" and, conceivably, to promote their positive development by giving them a tangible stake in international order. The most significant and striking example of this approach was the European Union's policy of "critical dialogue" with Iran. The Clinton administration castigated this policy, with some justification, as all carrot and no stick. The political ante was upped considerably in mid-1996 when the U.S. Congress passed and President Clinton signed into law the Iran-Libya Sanctions Act. A key provision of this legislation threatened to impose so-called secondary (or extraterritorial) sanctions on foreign commercial entities trading with those countries.[14] U.S. allies declared ILSA counterproductive and illegal, and threatened to refer the matter to the World Trade Organization. One administration official acknowledged that ILSA changed the political equation from "the United States and the world versus Iran" to "the world and Iran versus the United States."[15]

The third major problem with the rogue state policy was that it sharply limited strategic flexibility. Because these states were called rogues and outlaws, critics viewed any shift from hard-line containment and isolation as tantamount to appeasement. Once a state was relegated to this demonized category, it became very difficult politically to pursue any strategy other than comprehensive containment and isolation. The North Korean nuclear crisis in 1993–1994 illustrated this policy dilemma. To meet the threat posed by the Pyongyang regime's advanced nuclear program that was moving toward weaponization, the Clinton administration reluctantly adopted a policy of limited engagement through the October 1994 Agreed Framework. The agreement committed North Korea to freeze activity at and eventually to dismantle its nuclear reactors in return for two proliferation-resistant reactors provided by a U.S.-led international consortium. The alternatives to the nuclear accord were air strikes on the North's nuclear facilities or UN sanctions, either of which could have triggered a war on the Korean peninsula and neither of which could have guaranteed North Korea's nuclear disarmament. The administration argued that the acute danger

---

[14]A related piece of U.S. legislation aimed at Cuba was the Cuban Liberty and Solidarity Act, commonly referred to as the Helms-Burton Act, which became law in March 1996.

[15]Daniel Poneman, former Senior Director for Nonproliferation and Export Controls, National Security Council to the author. To mitigate the adverse impact of ILSA on allied relations, the Clinton administration has liberally exercised the act's waiver provision, thereby not invoking its highly contentious secondary sanctions provision.

of North Korea's nuclear program and the absence of a better alternative policy necessitated limited engagement. Congressional Republicans and conservative commentators, however, condemned the agreement as a sellout.

The issue of engaging a "rogue state" has also arisen in the case of Iran following the election of President Khatami. The intensifying power struggle in Iran (in
which Khatami's conservative clerical opponents invoke anti-Americanism as a
source of political mobilization and legitimacy) and continuing Iranian behavior of
concern (e.g., ballistic missile tests) have militated against a shift in American policy.
But the "rogue state" policy, with its lumping and political typecasting of a disparate
group of states, hindered the ability of policy-makers to respond adroitly to a national
security exigency (as in the case of North Korea) or to altered domestic political circumstances in the target country (as in Iran). This strategic inflexibility was a major
motivating factor underlying the Clinton administration's June 2000 decision, further
discussed later, to drop the term "rogue state" from the U.S. diplomatic lexicon.

With the shift from dual to differentiated containment, the U.S. administration
has the opportunity and the challenge of devising targeted strategies toward Iran
and Iraq. In devising such strategies of "differentiated containment," American
policy-makers must take into account the two countries' contrasting dangers and political opportunities, as well as the prospects for gaining international political support. As will be developed later, in the case of Iraq, the issue is one of maintaining a
strategy of comprehensive containment and isolation, while aspiring to a long-term
objective of regime change. By contrast, with Iran, the advent of a reformist president has brought to the fore in the American policy debate the issue of integrating a
limited engagement component into an overall containment strategy.

## IRAQ: CONTAINMENT OR ROLLBACK?

Since the Gulf War, the United States has simultaneously pursued two policy objectives toward Iraq—in the near term, containing Saddam Hussein by keeping "him in
his box," while, in the long term, working for his overthrow. These twin goals were
evident during the December 1998 bombing campaign by U.S. and British aircraft
when Clinton administration officials alternately described the mission as "degrad-
ing" Saddam Hussein's WMD capabilities and attacking key elements of his domestic power base to hasten a regime change in Baghdad. The tension between
these twin objectives—containment versus rollback—is at the core of the U.S. policy debate on Iraq.

The Gulf War fulfilled its United Nations mandate to expel Iraqi forces from
Kuwait. Although the UN did not authorize the overthrow of the Saddam Hussein
regime in Baghdad, it was an implicit U.S. war objective. But removing the Iraqi
dictator was not to be achieved by a "march on Baghdad" by the U.S.-led coalition.
The Bush administration rejected such a move on both political and military
grounds: it would have led to the defection of Arab states from the coalition and
possibly led to the indefinite occupation of Iraq. Nor, in a decision that provoked

much subsequent criticism, did the administration pursue the lesser option of continuing Desert Storm for several additional days further to degrade Iraqi military capabilities, particularly Saddam Hussein's elite Republican Guard divisions.

Instead of continuing the war into Iraq, administration officials hoped that the decisive defeat of Iraqi forces in Kuwait would generate enough political pressure within the Baathist regime in Baghdad to lead to a coup d'etat. But rather than triggering a military coup within the regime, the Gulf War precipitated two popular uprisings—one ethnic, by the Kurds in northern Iraq, and the other sectarian, by the Shiite Muslims in southern Iraq. The simultaneous Kurdish and Shiite uprisings caught the Bush administration by surprise. It also posed a major policy dilemma, for while the Bush administration sought the removal of Saddam Hussein from power, it also wanted to ensure Iraq's continuation as a unitary state. National Security Advisor Brent Scowcroft viewed Iraq as a regional counterweight to a potentially resurgent Iran. In the absence of military support from the allied coalition for the Kurds and Shiites, the Iraqi dictator, defying predictions of his imminent downfall, was able to overcome them. As Saddam Hussein maneuvered to maintain power in Baghdad, the flow of Kurdish refugees into Turkey, a NATO ally, prompted the U.S.-led coalition to create a "safe haven" in northern Iraq. The allies barred Iraqi aircraft and mechanized ground forces from this zone. In the south, the Shiites, who suffered an estimated 50,000 dead, were provided less protection. That region was declared a "no-fly" zone but not a "safe haven," thereby permitting Iraqi ground forces to assert fuller control.

United Nations Security Council Resolution (UNSCR) 687 codified the cease-fire terms of the Gulf War in early April 1991. Among its provisions, the resolution required Iraq formally to recognize its border with Kuwait and to compensate Kuwait for losses. It also created the United Nations Special Commission (UNSCOM) to oversee the destruction of any weapons of mass destruction that survived the Gulf War and to establish a verification system to ensure long-term compliance. Iraq would be permitted to resume unrestricted oil exports once the Baghdad regime had complied with the provisions relating to the destruction of Iraq's WMD capabilities.[16] But the UN Security Council did not impose any specific penalties on the Iraqi regime for its aggression against Kuwait. Saddam Hussein was not charged with war crimes, and no change in the character of the Baghdad regime was mandated by the Security Council, again reflecting that body's reluctance to intervene in a member state's internal politics. In May 1991, when it was evident that the Iraqi military was not going to move against Saddam Hussein, the Bush administration declared that sanctions would remain in place until the Iraqi dictator was removed from power.

In a significant shift in the Clinton administration's declaratory policy toward Iraq during a UN Security Council review of economic sanctions in March 1993, senior U.S. officials purposely omitted the call for Saddam Hussein's removal from power. They said that the administration's aim was to "depersonalize" the question

---

[16]Kenneth Katzman, "Iraq: Current Sanctions, Long Term Threat, and U.S. Policy Options," *CRS Report for Congress*, no. 94-465F, May 25, 1994, p. CRS-2.

of Iraqi behavior by dropping a demand that was not supported by other UN Security Council members (i.e., Russia and France), as well as U.S. allies in the Arab world.

The Clinton administration's new declaratory policy was deliberately ambiguous. To maintain multilateral support for continued sanctions, it shifted the focus in that forum from Saddam Hussein to compliance with UN Security Council resolutions. Yet the White House downplayed the change, arguing that it did not believe that Iraq could come into full compliance with UN Security Council resolutions while Saddam Hussein remained in power. This ambiguity was intended to bridge the gap between the contending objectives of the UN Security Council majority (most notably, France and Russia) and the United States (supported by Britain). Within the Clinton administration, two schools of thought emerged over strategy toward Iraq: one advocating an immediate "rollback" and the other promoting a form of long-term comprehensive containment.

The first, which enjoyed strong congressional support, was to keep the focus on Saddam Hussein and make a concerted effort to oust him from power through covert action and support for Iraqi opposition groups in Turkey and Europe. The primary drawback of this "rollback" approach was that it enjoyed scant support from the other members of the Gulf War coalition. The second approach considered by the Clinton administration was aimed not at ousting Saddam Hussein but at keeping him "in his box." This containment strategy emphasized the deterrence of regional aggression, as well as denying the Iraqi dictator the means to threaten the Gulf region. While keeping Saddam Hussein "in his box" in the near and the intermediate term, the long-term aim of this application of comprehensive containment would be to erode Saddam Hussein's domestic power base and lead to his overthrow. The major liability of this strategy was that it relied on multilateral cooperation during a period when U.S. allies, as well as Iraq's regional neighbors, were suffering from sanctions "fatigue."

Multilateral economic sanctions may have proved insufficient in generating internal dissension to oust Saddam Hussein, but he would never have permitted UNSCOM inspections in Iraq without their coercive influence. To lift sanctions, Saddam Hussein has pursued a political strategy that combines assertions of compliance with brazen acts of defiance. Since the Gulf War cease-fire and the codification of its terms under UNSCR 687, the Iraqi dictator has initiated periodic crises and exercises in brinkmanship to pressure the international community into ending the sanctions regime. These crises have ended only after the exercise of force by the United States and Britain, or the credible threat of force.

In mid-1995, Iraq proclaimed that it had met its disarmament obligations under UNSCR 687 and demanded that UNSCOM declare its mission accomplished. Meanwhile, in the UN Security Council, France and Russia pushed for the lifting of sanctions. This crisis, which was moving toward a military showdown, broke when Saddam Hussein's son-in-law, Hussein Kamel, defected to Jordan with evidence of massive Iraqi noncompliance (including the existence of a covert biological weapons program). Although Hussein Kamel's defection yielded an intelligence windfall for

UNSCOM and forced Baghdad to address the serious charges of noncompliance, Iraqi behavior rapidly reverted to what Secretary Albright characterized as "denial, delay and deceit." The defection and its aftermath only deferred the crisis until autumn 1997, when Saddam Hussein, noting the sharp decline in political support to enforce UN Security Council resolutions, again obstructed UNSCOM inspections.

In precipitating the 1997–1998 crisis, the Iraqi dictator's goal was clear: to gain an UNSCOM certification of compliance while retaining WMD capabilities or the production equipment to rapidly reconstitute them. For Saddam Hussein, the acquisition of WMD capabilities is second only to regime survival as a political objective. A telling indicator of that priority status is the estimated $100 billion that he forfeited in lost oil revenue during the 1990s rather than comply fully with UNSCR 687. In 1996, Saddam Hussein finally had acquiesced to the United Nations' "oil for food" program (UNSCR 986) only because the economic consequences of sanctions and runaway inflation on his core domestic political support groups had forced his hand. His main objection to UNSCR 986 was that it placed funds derived from oil sales into an escrow account, thereby depriving him of direct control over vast sums that could otherwise be spent on his military priorities.

In January 1998, the Clinton administration began publicly to raise the possibility of military action with or without UNSC authorization. But senior officials were hard-pressed to answer questions about its "post-strike strategy." The Joint Chiefs of Staff, painfully recalling the unsuccessful use of airpower as an instrument of coercive diplomacy in Vietnam, cautioned the administration not to oversell what air strikes alone could accomplish politically or militarily.[17] Meanwhile, congressional Republicans and others who favored an explicit "rollback" strategy to overthrow Saddam Hussein criticized the administration for not being bolder in its articulated goals. Columnist Charles Krauthammer argued, "The real objective of any air campaign against Iraq must be to depose Saddam . . . Let's be clear: A return to the status quo would be a defeat. It makes no sense to resume this war aiming so low."[18] The Clinton administration's diplomatic strategy to build a Security Council consensus to meet Iraq's defiance of UNSCR 687 with the threat of force required the White House to mute its own preference for a change in regime. President Clinton indirectly acknowledged the tension between "rollback" and a less ambitious containment strategy: "Would the Iraqi people be better off if there were a change in leadership? I certainly think they would be. But that is not what the United Nations has authorized us to do; that is not what our immediate interest is about . . ."[19]

Airstrikes on Iraq were forestalled in February 1998 when UN Secretary General Kofi Annan went to Baghdad and received assurances of renewed cooperation.

---

[17]Barton Gellman, "Shift on Iraq May Signify Trade-Off," *Washington Post*, August 17, 1998, p. A1.

[18]Charles Krauthammer, "To Bomb Without Serious Intent," *Washington Post*, February 6, 1998, p. A25.

[19]USIA transcript, President Clinton and British Prime Minister Blair in the White House Oval Office, February 5, 1998.

Iraq's failure to abide by those terms triggered a four-day air campaign—Operation Desert Fox—in December 1998. The Clinton administration was again caught politically between domestic critics, who wanted more sustained air attacks aimed at undermining Saddam Hussein, and the UN Security Council, who were reflexively opposed to the use of force and sought only Iraq's compliance with UNSCR 687. Addressing the tension between these twin objectives, National Security Advisor Sandy Berger stated, "The strategy we can and will pursue is to contain Saddam in the short and medium term, by force if necessary, and to work toward a new government over the long term."[20]

After Operation Desert Fox, the U.S. policy debate on Iraq moved in two divergent directions. The first, strongly advocated by the Congress, was the hard-line turn toward an explicit "rollback" approach as manifested in the Iraq Liberation Act of 1998. This policy, which called for U.S. support of the fractured and militarily ineffectual Iraqi opposition, was a post-Cold War analogue to the Reagan Doctrine that supported insurgency movements to overthrow pro-Soviet regimes in the Third World during the 1980s. Whereas the Congress pushed the Clinton administration (including a reluctant Pentagon) to implement an explicit "rollback" strategy, the UN Security Council and Arab states increasingly favored a shift from comprehensive to a more limited containment policy. Declining international support for comprehensive containment was manifested in the erosion of the sanctions regime and the UN Security Council's unwillingness to compel Iraq's cooperation with UNMOVIC (the successor to UNSCOM) through the use of force, if necessary.[21] Since Desert Fox, the United States remains committed to the objective of "containment plus regime change," at least in terms of its declaratory policy.[22] As discussed in the concluding section, the policy tension between these two strategies—rollback and comprehensive containment—persists. But the United States is increasingly isolated internationally even in achieving its minimal objective of keeping Saddam Hussein "in a box."

# IRAN: A REVOLUTIONARY OR AN ORDINARY STATE?

Since the 1979 revolution, American administrations from Carter to Clinton have grappled with the dual nature of political power in postrevolutionary Iran—a duality reflected in its very name, the Islamic Republic of Iran. As a "republic," Iran exists as a sovereign state in an international system of like states. After the revolution, radical elements of the country's new theocratic leadership vowed that

---

[20]James Risen, "U.S. Stands Firm in Calling for U.N. Inspections in Iraq," *New York Times*, December 24, 1998, p. A6.

[21]UNMOVIC (United Nations Monitoring, Verification and Inspection Commission) was established by UNSCR 1284 in December 1999 as a follow-on to UNSCOM. At the time of its creation, many questioned whether UNMOVIC would be as committed and effective as its predecessor. Iraq has continued to call for the immediate lifting of economic sanctions and refused to permit new UN inspections.

[22]John Lancaster, "In Saddam's Future, A Harder U.S. Line," *Washington Post*, June 3, 2000, p. A4.

Iran would "export" its revolution to other Middle East countries to create a transnational Islamic community. For this faction, revolutionary activism abroad remains an integral part of the Islamic Republic's identity and a source of legitimacy at home. Although this rhetoric has moderated over time, the question remains: is Iran an "ordinary" state that accepts the legitimacy of the international system or a revolutionary state that rejects its norms and seeks to radically alter, if not overturn, it? This political duality—the contending visions of Iran as an ordinary versus a revolutionary state—is a major cause of the political schism evident within the Teheran regime and Iranian society at large. In turn, this duality has been reflected in the American policy approach toward Iran.

During the postrevolutionary era, American administrations have periodically sought to engage "moderates" inside the regime who are purportedly desirous of normalizing Iran's relations with the external world. This rationale, in part, underpinned the Reagan administration's covert initiative in 1985–1986 that became the Iran-Contra scandal. A similar debate arose in mid-1989, after the death of Ayatollah Khomeini, when Hashemi Rafsanjani, viewed at that time as a political pragmatist, became Iran's new president. President Rafsanjani took two specific actions that Iranian officials characterized as a concerted effort to respond to President Bush's inaugural address in which he declared that "good will begets good will." First, Rafsanjani expended capital, both political and financial, to win the release of the last American hostages held in Lebanon by groups under Iran's influence. Second, during the 1990–1991 Gulf War, the Rafsanjani government assumed a position of positive neutrality, thereby taking no action to complicate the U.S.-led coalition's campaign to oust Saddam Hussein's forces from Kuwait. Iranian Foreign Ministry officials claimed that both moves were intended to facilitate improved bilateral relations and expressed frustration that the Bush administration had failed to respond.

From the Bush administration's perspective, Iranian words and actions were contradictory. The Teheran regime remained implacably hostile to the Middle East peace process and on the State Department's list of terrorist nations. In addition to these concerns, the Bush and the succeeding Clinton administration became increasingly concerned about Iran's efforts to acquire WMD capabilities. CIA Director Robert Gates told a congressional committee in March 1992 that Iran could develop nuclear weapons by the year 2000. The CIA's 1992 National Intelligence Estimate (NIE) on Iran's nuclear program was consistent with this archetype of what would later be characterized as a "rogue state"—a Third World regime armed with weapons of mass destruction and threatening a region of vital interest to the United States. This predisposition in the wake of the Gulf War affected American perceptions of Iran. The failure of the Bush administration's engagement strategy toward Iraq prior to 1990 reinforced the political rationale against pursuing a "constructive engagement" strategy toward Iran or offering any inducements to the Teheran regime for reformed behavior.

The Clinton administration initiated a policy review vis-à-vis Iran upon assuming office in January 1993. In the ensuing months, the elements of a tougher policy emerged that reversed the Bush administration's "good will begets good will" line. An early sign of the this new approach was Secretary of State Warren Christopher's March 1993 characterization of Iran as "an international outlaw" for its support of international terrorism and its drive to acquire weapons of mass destruction. The Clinton administration did not formally eschew the possibility of dialogue with the Teheran regime but did make clear that its objectionable behavior made normal relations impossible. The Clinton administration's political demonization of Iran was intended diplomatically to isolate the Islamic Republic and mobilize diplomatic support for what Secretary Christopher called a "collective policy of containment." The administration's enunciation of the "dual containment" strategy came in May 1993.[23] As discussed earlier, the linking of U.S. policy toward Iran and Iraq directly led to the administration's broader "rogue state" policy with its central assertion that these countries, as well as Libya and North Korea, constituted a distinct class of states in the post–Cold War international system.

The Clinton administration was unsuccessful in its efforts to win multilateral backing for its tougher line toward Iran. As noted before, the United States strongly opposed the European Union's policy of "critical dialogue" that sought to foster more moderate Iranian behavior through the development of a web of relations. The Clinton administration argued that such an approach, rather than giving Iran a tangible stake in stability, would simply reward behavior that violated international norms and would prop up the clerical regime. And yet, the credibility of U.S. efforts to convince allies to curtail economic relations with Iran was undermined by the fact that the United States remained Iran's largest trading partner through American oil companies. In March 1995, the Clinton administration moved to close this loophole in U.S. sanctions after the news that the American oil conglomerate Conoco was on the verge of concluding a major deal with the National Iranian Oil Company to develop offshore oil. President Clinton issued an executive order prohibiting U.S. companies and their subsidiaries from investing in the Iranian energy sector, thus heading off the Conoco deal. In May 1995, this limited ban was followed by a broader executive order cutting off all U.S. trade and investment with Iran, including purchases of Iranian oil by American companies.[24]

As official U.S. policy toward Iran further hardened with the 1996 enactment of the Iran-Libya Sanctions Act, some prominent commentators and policy experts outside government questioned the efficacy of the American approach. They noted that Iran had not emerged as the expansionist regional threat that some had feared in the wake of the Gulf War and that the Clinton administration had been unable to produce enough hard evidence of Iranian sponsorship of terrorism to win international support for sanctions. Moreover, unilateral U.S. economic sanctions were unlikely to generate sufficient domestic pressures within Iran to force the Teheran regime's acceptance of the Bush and Clinton administrations' proposal for an "au-

[23]Elaine Sciolino, "Christopher Signals a Tougher U.S. Line Toward Iran," *New York Times*, March 31, 1993, p. A3.

[24]Todd S. Purdum, "Clinton to Order a Trade Embargo Against Teheran," *New York Times*, May 1, 1995, p. A1.

thorized" dialogue. Some country specialists argued that the sanctions policy bolstered the position of hard-liners within the Teheran regime who used the image of America as an implacable enemy to justify the country's isolation and strict Islamic controls. Some called for dialogue and a reciprocal arrangement in which specific behavioral changes would lead to an easing of U.S. sanctions.[25] An influential Council on Foreign Relations task force, cochaired by Brzezinski and former Bush National Security Advisor Brent Scowcroft, argued that dual containment had become "more a slogan than a strategy" and advocated "a more nuanced and differentiated approach." Such a strategy, characterized as "differentiated containment," would promote targeted policies geared to the particular circumstances in each country.[26] Despite these calls for dialogue with Iran, the Clinton administration remained committed to its strategy of comprehensive containment.

Because of the Iran-Contra legacy and the political dynamic of its own "rogue state" approach, the Clinton administration had refused publicly to draw any distinctions between contending "moderates" (also called "pragmatists" and "technocrats") and "radicals" inside the Teheran regime. The May 1997 presidential election exposed the sharp cleavage in Iranian domestic politics. This split again reflected the political tension between the Islamic Republic's twin identities as a revolutionary and an ordinary state. This duality was symbolized by the two leadership positions created by the Islamic Republic's constitution—the "Supreme Leader," who is the country's head of state and highest religious authority (Ayatollah Ali Khamenei, who succeeded Khomeini) and the president, who heads the government. This bifurcation of authority is at the heart of the country's ongoing domestic political struggle in which the issue of relations with the United States has been central.

Although Ayatollah Khamenei and others maintained their anti-Western stance, President Khatami espoused a conciliatory approach. In January 1998, in an interview with CNN that received worldwide attention, the Iranian president called for a cultural dialogue between the two countries (e.g., academic exchanges) that he carefully distinguished from "political relations." Six months later, Secretary Albright delivered a major policy address at the Asia Society in New York that was the administration's first comprehensive response to President Khatami's conciliatory statements. She welcomed the change in Iranian declaratory policy, citing President Khatami's denunciation of terrorism, and said that if his words "are translated into a rejection of terrorism as a tool of Iranian statecraft, it would do much to dispel the concerns of the international community . . ." In response to Khatami's call for cultural and academic exchanges and increased people-to-people contact, Secretary Albright stated:

> We are ready to explore further ways to build mutual confidence and avoid misunderstandings. The Islamic Republic should consider parallel steps. If such a process can be initiated and sustained in a way that addresses the concerns of both sides, then we in the United States can see the prospect of a very different relationship. As the wall of

[25]Thomas L. Friedman, "Rethinking Iran Policy," *New York Times*, September 11, 1996, p. A19.

[26]The findings are summarized in Brzezinski, Scowcroft, and Murphy, "Differentiated Containment."

mistrust comes down, we can develop with the Islamic Republic, when it is ready, *a road map leading to normal relations.*

Secretary Albright's pathbreaking speech embraced the differentiated policy that the critics of dual containment had advocated—a process of "parallel steps" that "addresses the concerns of both sides." The speech, with its assertion that "America cannot view every issue or nation through a single prism," also attempted to break with the administration's generic "rogue state" policy. And yet, the very success of that policy in mobilizing political support for a hard-line policy through demonization hindered the ability of the Clinton administration to navigate such a shift in response to changed circumstances in Iran. There was formidable opposition in the Republican-led Congress and beyond to any change from a comprehensive containment policy toward Iran.

The continuing cleavage in American domestic politics over relations with the Islamic Republic has been mirrored on the Iranian side. In January 1999, a senior State Department official stated that Albright's initiative was "basically moribund" because of pervasive hostility toward the United States in Iran's theocratic regime. The official concluded that "We continue to believe that Khatami is the best opportunity for change we have seen since 1979 . . . [He is] preoccupied . . . fighting a very difficult domestic battle."[27] That struggle included an attack by security forces on pro-democracy student demonstrators in July 1999, capping a dramatic week of civil protest in the Iranian capital. Khamenei's hard-line faction has made persistent efforts to stifle reformist publications and, in the February 2000 parliamentary elections, maneuvered to disqualify pro-Khatemi candidates. At the heart of this continuing political cleavage is the core issue of relations with the United States. On the American side, relations with Iran are not such a defining foreign policy issue, but the formidable domestic political impediments to dialogue and limited engagement mirror those on the Iranian side.

## IMPLEMENTING "DIFFERENTIATED CONTAINMENT": PROSPECTS AND DILEMMAS

This chapter traced the close linkage between the dual containment and rogue state policies during the Clinton administration. The 1993 enunciation of the dual containment strategy led within a year to its broadening into a general approach toward so-called "rogue states." This rubric encompassed a disparate group of countries (including North Korea, Libya, and Cuba) that the Clinton administration asserted to be a distinct category of states in the post–Cold War international system. By demonizing and lumping these states as an instrument of political mobilization, the rogue state policy obscured understanding of these countries and distorted policy-making. The political dynamic generated by the policy pushed the administration toward a generic

[27]Thomas W. Lippman and David Ottaway, "Iran Requests $500 Million in Food Items," *Washington Post,* January 19, 1999, p. A13.

strategy of comprehensive containment toward these very different states. The two cases that highlighted the liabilities of the rogue state policy and called into question its utility were North Korea and Iran. With North Korea, the acute threat posed by its advanced nuclear program necessitated dialogue and negotiation by the Clinton administration. In the Iranian case, the Khatemi election fundamentally altered the Iranian political landscape and created the potential for some movement in U.S.-Iranian relations (notwithstanding the substantial domestic political impediments addressed later). Just as the dual containment strategy gave rise to the broader "rogue state" approach, so too did questions about the former precipitate a reevaluation of the latter.

That policy change came in June 2000 when the State Department announced that the term "rogue state" had been dropped from the U.S. foreign policy lexicon in favor of the more diplomatic-sounding "states of concern."[28] This move was sharply criticized by foreign policy hard-liners in the Congress and press who viewed it as a political rationalization for a policy of engaging odious regimes. In actuality, the State Department decision facilitated the move from a constricting generic approach to differentiated strategies geared to the particular circumstances in each country. This move toward targeted strategies has implications for a broader group of states beyond those in the rogues' gallery (such as Sudan, Burma, and Afghanistan). The demise of the "rogue state" policy shifted the focus to state behavior—anywhere—that contravenes international norms, not on a select group of countries unilaterally designated by the United States. Contrary to the critics' claims, the change was not an argument for blanket engagement: Iran's domestic politics in the Khatemi era have created potential conditions for limited engagement, whereas in Iraq, politics simply do not exist beyond Saddam Hussein's brutal cult of personality.

The Clinton administration jettisoned "dual containment" and the "rogue state" approach in order to facilitate its ability to implement differentiated strategies of containment toward these key regional states. But, as on other functional issues and in other regions of the world, American primacy does not necessarily translate into an ability to determine policy outcomes. Indeed, the striking story of U.S. policy in the Gulf region is the extent to which Washington has become isolated politically and has faced an uphill struggle in winning multilateral international support for policies that are increasingly perceived as unilateral. This policy tension between unilateralism and multilateralism has been especially evident since President George W. Bush succeeded Bill Clinton.

## Iraq: Keeping Saddam Hussein "In a Box"

The sanctions regime mandated by the UN to compel Iraqi compliance with Security Council resolutions, particularly with respect to WMD disarmament, has eroded to the point of near collapse. Since the Gulf War, sanctions, international arms inspections, and the enforcement of no-fly zones and the Kurdish northern sanctu-

---

[28]Steven Mufson, "A 'Rogue' Is a 'Rogue' is a 'State of Concern'," *Washington Post*, June 20, 2000, p. A16.

ary have been the centerpiece of U.S. containment strategy, in Secretary of State Albright's words, to keep Saddam Hussein "in a box." A December 2000 *Wall Street Journal* editorial warned that the Iraqi dictator was now "Outside the Box."[29]

Indicators of this erosion in international support for a strategy of comprehensive containment and isolation are evident on several fronts. In August 2000, Venezuelan President Hugo Chavez, a populist leader who has railed against American primacy, visited Baghdad ostensibly to confer about OPEC matters. Russian and French groups flouted the ban on civil air flights into Iraq. During the December 2000 debate about extending the "oil for food" program, the UN Security Council, at French instigation, approved a measure over American objections giving Iraq some direct access to the funds accumulated in that account. A tight international oil market, in which occasional shortfalls have led to price spikes, has given Saddam Hussein considerable influence. In addition, Saddam Hussein continues his political rehabilitation in the Arab world—supporting the Palestinians in their autumn 2000 uprising against Israeli occupation and cultivating diplomatic ties with some Gulf states.

These developments undermining Iraq's containment and isolation have emboldened Saddam Hussein and given him political leverage. The most significant manifestation of this attitude and improved political position is continued intransigence against the resumption of weapons inspections by UNMOVIC. It is testimony to the priority that Saddam Hussein attaches to WMD capabilities that he has foregone an estimated $100 billion in oil revenues since the imposition of sanctions. Iraq has resumed short-range missile tests, and former UNSCOM head Richard Butler believes, notwithstanding arms inspections and episodic Anglo-American airstrikes, that it retains the ability to rapidly reconstitute its WMD capabilities.[30] In the UN Security Council, France and Russia, two of Iraq's largest creditors, have pressed for a rapid conclusion of arms inspections and the end of economic sanctions.

Many have questioned the continued utility of economic sanctions. Saddam Hussein has cynically used the suffering of the Iraqi people to increase international pressure to lift sanctions on Iraqi terms. Meanwhile, the Iraqi dictator has been able to insulate the estimated 1 million people from the military and the key Sunni tribes that constitute his core support group, thereby reducing the chance of a coup. In 1996, intense pressures on this group from sanctions had compelled Saddam Hussein to accept, very reluctantly, the "oil for food" program. Despite these trends, others defend the continuation of economic sanctions as a means of denying Saddam Hussein the access to the funds and technology that would permit him to revive his WMD programs.

Even as international support for comprehensive containment cools, many American policy-makers continue to emphasize the need for an explicit rollback strategy to oust Saddam Hussein. Critics, including several high-level officials in the George W. Bush administration, contend that the Clinton years were a squandered

---

[29]"Outside the Box" (editorial), *Wall Street Journal*, December 5, 2000, p. A26.

[30]See Richard Butler, *The Greatest Threat: Iraq, Weapons of Mass Destruction, and the Crisis of Global Security* (New York: Public Affairs, 2000).

opportunity—that the practical possibilities for a successful rollback of the Saddam Hussein regime remain scant because the administration lacked the political will to implement the strategy. Congress again authorized support for Iraqi opposition groups, but Marine General Anthony Zinni, the former head of U.S. forces in the Gulf region, concluded that they have "no credibility in the region. Containment is hard, but when you don't have popular support or the political will to do anything else, you're stuck with it."[31] Under these conditions, the implementation of a narrower but more realistic containment strategy requires, at minimum, holding Iraq accountable to established international norms and being willing to exercise the U.S. veto in the UN Security Council when necessary. In particular, that treatment means compelling Saddam Hussein to comply with the obligations laid out in UN Security Council Resolution 687 with respect to WMD disarmament. This objective remains an imperative for international security because with Saddam Hussein, a leader who invaded two adjacent countries within a decade, capabilities do imply intention.

## Iran: Continuing Impasse or Limited Engagement?

Iran poses contrasting dangers and opportunities to those of Iraq. Unlike Iraq, Iran does not have a comparable record of direct external aggression, notwithstanding U.S. concerns about Iran's sponsorship of terrorism and efforts to acquire WMD capabilities. The starkest contrast, however, is between Iraq's totalitarian cult of personality revolving around Saddam Hussein and the Islamic Republic of Iran's hotly contested (if circumscribed) domestic politics. Indeed, the domestic political struggle between the contending reformist and hard-line theocratic faction is the key determinant of U.S.-Iranian relations. That is the case because the issue of relations with the United States goes to the heart of the Iranian revolution's continuing legacy.

Attacking the Khatemi faction's domestic agenda and its openness to dialogue with the United States, Ayatollah Khamenei stated, "Those who try to raise the hopes of the enemy for a return to Iran with their talk, their behavior and their political activities, are betraying Iran."[32] President Khatemi has called on the United States to take additional steps toward reviving bilateral relations. Such prospects were set back substantially when an Iranian court convicted ten Iranian Jews of spying for Israel, a move strongly condemned by President Clinton. While improved relations with the United States remain stalled, Iran has launched a diplomatic offensive both with European Union members (Khatemi visited France, Italy, and Germany in 1999–2000) and with the Gulf states. The United States, warning of Iran's continuing threat, has urged these countries to proceed cautiously but has not vigorously tried to halt this diplomatic warming trend as it did in the mid-1990s when the European Union was pursuing "critical dialogue."

---

[31]Elaine Sciolino, "He Knows How to Torment Presidents. Who's Next?" *New York Times*, December 10, 2000, section 4, p. 5.

[32]Agence France Presse, "Ayatollah Khamenei Urges Fight against US Influence," November 17, 2000.

President Khatemi is increasingly caught between the regime's theocratic hard-liners and zealots within his own reformist faction who want him to press for more radical change, and to do so faster. Checkmated by the Islamic Republic's constitution that bestows great power to the country's Supreme Leader, currently Ayatollah Khamenei, Khatemi acknowledged that he lacks "sufficient powers" to implement his program and overcome the opposition of theocratic hard-liners.[33] Iran's severe economic difficulties provide an incentive for the Teheran regime to normalize relations with the United States and gain access to American capital and technology. But hard-liners oppose such a move, fearing that it would undermine their power and leading role in Iranian society. In short, a soft landing for Iranian society into the global economy would mean a hard landing for Khamenei's theocratic faction.

Secretary Albright observed that the two countries were going "through a very interesting kind of pas-de-deux of trying to talk to each other and signal our intentions."[34] In shaping U.S. policy, political scientists Shahram Chubin and Jerrold Green have correctly observed that the American concern, articulated by senior officials, of "whether Khatami can deliver" should be reformulated as "what can the US do to see that Khatami can deliver?"[35] This process of normalization, given the gulf of mutual mistrust, is certain to be lengthy—consider the quarter century that it took after the Vietnam War to normalize relations with the Hanoi government. On the American side, the domestic political impediments to dialogue and limited engagement with Iran are formidable. Iran has been called the third rail of American foreign policy: the hostage crisis brought down the Carter administration, and the Iran-Contra scandal nearly did the same to President Reagan. Iran's unique status in American domestic politics ensures that any measure that could make a real difference in Teheran in terms of supporting Khatami (e.g., lifting economic sanctions) is likely to be politically impossible in Washington. To break the impasse, some analysts have recommended that the U.S. administration be more explicit in articulating what concrete steps it would take with respect to sanctions if Iranian behavior changed in the key spheres of U.S. concern, such as terrorism.

The key issue raised by the shift from dual to differentiated containment is that of dialogue and limited engagement with Iran. In the case of Iraq, political conditions have changed since dual containment was enunciated, but the goal of comprehensively containing and isolating Iraq in the short term, while aiming for regime change in the long term, remains unchanged. The dilemmas and challenges for the United States in implementing this strategy have been addressed in this chapter. The major differentiation in differentiated containment lies in America's policy toward Iran. Iran's domestic politics—specifically the rise of a reformist

[33]Molly Moore and John Ward Anderson, "Iran's Khatami Is Caught in the Middle," *Washington Post*, November 28, 2000, pp. A1,21.

[34]Agence France Press, "Washington Continues to See Opening with Iran: Albright," November 20, 2000.

[35]Shahram Chubin and Jerrold D. Green, "Engaging Iran: A US Strategy," *Survival* 40, No. 3 (Autumn 1998), p. 165.

president—have created an opportunity for American diplomacy. Will Iran remain a revolutionary state, or is it ready to rejoin the "family of nations"? The United States has the ability, if only marginally, to influence this complex, unfolding process.

Running through the shift from dual to differentiated containment is the continuing tension in U.S. foreign policy between the competing pulls of unilateralism and multilateralism. Like the Clinton administration before it, the George W. Bush administration has declared a desire to work multilaterally, but a willingness to act unilaterally when concerted action is not possible and important U.S. interests are at stake. The key question (a generic one for American diplomacy, but of particular salience with respect to strategies toward Iraq and Iran) is the extent to which U.S. policy will be multilateral—and the economic and political price Washington will be prepared to pay to "go it alone" when deemed necessary.

On Iraq, during his February 2001 visit to the Middle East, Secretary of State Colin Powell called for modified or "smart" sanctions, more narrowly focused on preventing the reconstitution of Saddam Hussein's military, in order to bolster waning international support for the sanctions regime. But, in Washington, political support for an overt "rollback" strategy, whatever its realistic prospects, remains substantial. On Iran, the Bush administration is open to a bilateral dialogue along the lines proposed by Secretary Albright. Moreover, Vice President Cheney, before assuming office, declared his general opposition to unilateral sanctions of the kind contained in the Iran-Libya Sanctions Act. But the domestic political impediments to dialogue, let alone the normalization of relations, remain formidable in both Iran and the United States. An additional factor, again reflecting the unilateralist-multilateralist tension in U.S. policy, is the revival of the "rogue state" rubric by the Bush administration in order to mobilize domestic political support for ballistic missile defense. For the same reasons discussed earlier in connection with the Clinton administration policy, the return of the unilateral U.S. "rogue state" policy will hinder the new Bush administration's ability to pursue differentiated policies toward these two pivotal Gulf states.

# 9

# Lone Eagle, Lone Dragon?
## How the Cold War Did Not End for China

## EDWARD FRIEDMAN
### University of Wisconsin, Madison

When Bill Clinton ran for president in 1992, his campaign reflected an American snapshot of China frozen at the moment when its paramount leader, Deng Xiaoping, ordered the June 4 bloody crushing of peaceful demonstrators for democracy in Beijing in 1989.[1] Clinton promised not to coddle "the butchers of Beijing." An image of China as a major violator of human rights pervaded American politics. But when in office, the new president learned, as his campaign had generally stressed, "it's the economy, stupid." To grow the American economy required expanding international trade. Authoritarian China, a brutally corrupt country, also seemed to American business to be the world's largest emerging market.[2] Not to compete in China was not to be a world-class player.

When an increasingly confident and assertive Communist Party (CP) dictatorship would not concede on human rights to American pressures and blandishments in 1993, Clinton had to choose between normal trade with China, despite its authoritarian repression, or sanctioning Beijing and thereby unintentionally wounding America's economic recovery. The president put the economic well-being of America's citizens first. However, the U.S. political priority in dealing with China is neither human rights nor the economy.[3]

Edward Friedman, the Hawkins Chair Professor of Political Science at the University of Wisconsin, Madison, is a specialist in Chinese politics. He served for three years as a China specialist for the U.S. House of Representatives Committee on Foreign Affairs. His most recent book is *What If China Does Not Democratize? Implications for War and Peace* (Routledge).

[1]For overviews of Clinton administration foreign policy from the perspective of America-China relations since Nixon, see both James Mann, *About Face* (NY: Knopf, 1999) and Patrick Tyler, *A Great Wall* (NY: Century Foundation, 1999).

[2]William Overholt, *The Rise of China* (NY: Norton, 1993).

[3]Edward Friedman, "The Challenge of a Rising China," in Robert Lieber (ed.), *Eagle Adrift* (NY: Norton, 1997), pp. 215–245.

President Clinton learned in office that despite all the campaign talk about human rights and despite all the practical focus on expanding the American economy, the priority issue in U.S.-China relations was national security. The CP rulers, seeking to earn foreign exchange and cause problems for America, were major proliferators of destabilizing weapons of mass destruction to regimes from Pakistan to Libya, nations seen in Washington as threats to the peace. Also, China was engaged in a rapid military build-up, especially of its navy, aiming at predominance in Asia.[4] And China's territorial ambitions in the South China Sea on islands and waters that are closer to the Philippines, Indonesia, and Vietnam than to the mainland of China, and in the Taiwan Strait and Western Pacific region of Taiwan, and in the East China Sea and the Senkaku islet area belonging to Japan, threatened friends and allies of the United States and also threatened the peace and prosperity of the entire Asia-Pacific region, and especially threatened the autonomy of the flourishing democracy of 23 million people on the island of Taiwan.[5] National security problems with a rising China consequently would bedevil the Clinton administration at the end of the twentieth century and pose harsh challenges to American foreign policy to the Bush administration early in the twenty-first century. National security had to be priority number one.

## HUMAN RIGHTS

In the United States, the 1989–1991 end of the Cold War, the implosion of the Soviet Union, and the attempted breakthrough to a frail and fledgling democracy in Russia all seemed to signal a triumph for universal standards of human rights and for democracy as the best political system. There was a momentary euphoria that, starting in the 1970s in southern Europe, a wave of democracy was sweeping the world, including Asia, where since the late 1980s, democracies rose in the Philippines, South Korea, Taiwan, Mongolia, Thailand, and Indonesia.[6]

But rulers in Beijing saw these events as traumatic threats to their rulership. Rather than imagining an end to the Cold War, China's CP imagined a new Cold War led by the United States against China, with America out to democratize China. For rulers in authoritarian Beijing, the Cold War continued in their region.

Suddenly, China became the only major surviving Communist dictatorship.[7] Its rulers were threatened by what they understood as an American offensive against the socialist world. The dictators in China felt endangered. They would have to respond to an America that was perceived not only as enemy number one but also as the sole remaining superpower, a nation bearing tremendous clout. For China, it

---

[4]You Ji, *The Armed Forces of China*, (NY: I.B. Tauris, 1999).

[5]June Teufel Dreyer, "China and Its Neighbors," in Edward Friedman and Barrett McCormick (eds.), *What If China Does Not Democratize?* (Armonk, NY: Sharpe, 2000), pp. 163–191.

[6]Larry Diamond and Marc Plattner (ed.), *Democracy in East Asia* (Baltimore: The Johns Hopkins University Press, 1998).

[7]The other CP states are Cuba, North Korea, Vietnam, and Laos.

was a given that America ruled the roost and that China should do all it could to knock America off its high perch.

In the United States, the government did seek ways to use economic aid conditionality to advance good governance, to rein in corruption, and to institutionalize public accountability in developing nations. This weak but real early-1990s trend was later legitimated by a post-NAFTA debate about improving labor standards, meaning the legalization of free labor unions to represent worker interests. In Beijing, meager American efforts to promote democratic forces were seen as a concerted foreign superpower attempt to foster a Chinese equivalent of Poland's Solidarity movement in order to undermine the Communist system. Anti-American chauvinism surged among CP rulers.

But by 1993, anxieties in Beijing were accompanied by swelling self-confidence. China defeated the international sanctions regime imposed after the June 4, 1989, Beijing massacre. Its economy rose rapidly, making it the world's most attractive emerging economy. Foreign investment poured in even from the Republic of China on Taiwan, one hundred miles off the south China coast in the western Pacific.

Taiwan had served as the refuge of a ragtag army led by Chiang Kai-shek, which had fled the mainland of China in 1949 after defeat by Mao Zedong's red armies in a civil war. But by the 1990s, Taiwan, an island home to more people than two-thirds of the member countries of the UN (Taiwan has 23 million people and only one-third of the planet's nations are more populous,) was a prospering economy and a flourishing democracy. In Asia (including Taiwan), which is the source of over 80 percent of China's foreign direct investment (FDI), the human rights situation in China was not a top priority. The government in Beijing understood that in Asia, China was treated as a cheap labor export platform from which to get into the American market. All hoped to benefit from the 1990s resurgent American economy.

Buoyed by their defeat of international sanctions, by the surge of FDI, and by a continuing economic rise, the ever more chauvinistic rulers in Beijing chose to take the offensive against purportedly American-led forces of human rights and democracy.[8] Popular xenophobic passions against America became even nastier than the official nationalism following the International Olympics Committee vote in 1993 to award the year 2000 Olympics to Sydney, Australia, rather than to Beijing, China. The Chinese tended to feel that, as regional neighbors, Japan in the 1960s and South Korea in the 1980s had proved that they had risen to global greatness by hosting the Olympics, so too it would now be with an emerging China. National celebrations were prepared. When Sydney's bribing of IOC voters won out, China ignored Australia and scapegoated America, imagining the U.S. as the cause of China's experienced humiliation. A virulent populist nationalism spread like a forest fire, even attacking the regime for proving to be insufficiently patriotic. Nationalism mattered.

---

[8]For Chinese perspectives, see Yong Deng and Feirling Wang (eds.), *In the Eyes of the Dragon* (Lanham, MD: Rowman and Littlefield, 1999).

China was no longer a totalitarian Leninist system whose legitimacy came from trying to build socialism and to keep out foreign capital. China's government was more like a right-wing populist authoritarianism, a regime similar to those that flourished in Europe and elsewhere in the 1920s and after (e.g., Mussolini's Italy, Peron's Argentina, Hirohito's Japan). To save itself and to prove its nationalistic credentials, Beijing took the offensive against the international human rights movement that was first spearheaded, not by Americans, but by Europeans.[9] Starting in 1993 at the UN human rights conferences in Bangkok and Vienna, representatives from Beijing argued that human rights had to be related to cultural particulars and economic stages of development. Backed by Burma, Iran, and North Korea, Chinese delegates contended that Asian values put the collective good way ahead of liberal individualism and that a developing China had to put growth first in order to end the poverty of its more than one billion people. International human rights activism was dismissed in China as an anti-China plot of ill-willed foreigners.[10]

This rhetoric was very popular in China. People saw human rights criticisms as malicious attempts to smear China's achievements and to block China's return to glory. Ironically, this popular rejection of human rights diplomacy was accompanied in China by an increasing exercise of rights as the people, freer than ever, protested publicly and in groups that included illegally burdened farmers, unpaid teachers, and urban pensioners not receiving their stipends. But even protesters tended to be superpatriots.

The government in Beijing successfully used its economic leverage to get democratic governments in Europe to back off from publicly pressuring China on its repression of Uighur Muslims, Tibetan Buddhists, Falun Gong spiritual movement practitioners, and ethnic Han Christians. China's CP used both carrot and stick with the rich democracies, especially with the Europeans, punishing Denmark for leading a UN human rights effort by canceling a planned Danish trade delegation to China and by rewarding France with billion-dollar contracts for refusing to support UN resolutions to investigate the regime's continuing repression of its own people, including jailing, torture, and death for Chinese who were trying peacefully to open up the authoritarian system. As Robert Lieber points out in Chapter 1, the French and others have used Beijing's opposition to Washington to serve their own commercial interests.

It then seemed that only the American eagle dared challenge the Chinese dragon. That caricature allowed Beijing to depict Washington as unfairly picking on the Chinese people with nefarious ulterior motives, that is, to keep China down, to make it weak, and to reduce it to chaos through separatism.

Actually, the Clinton administration did not stress human rights in dealing with China after 1993. However, it tried to work quietly to get leading prisoners of conscience released from Chinese prisons, and a number of them were. The real

---

[9]Edward Friedman, "Post-Deng China's Right Populist Authoritarian Foreign Policy, in Chen-Wen-chun (ed.), *The PRC and the Asia-Pacific Region* (forthcoming).

[10]Samuel Kim, "Human Rights in China's International Relations," in *What If China Does Not Democratize?*, *loc. cit.*, pp. 129–162.

human rights pressure in America came from nongovernmental organizations and from the U.S. Congress. Included in these efforts were both the left wing of the Democratic Party, which was most tied to labor unions worried about American factories closing down and relocating in China in the new age of globalization, and also the right wing of the Republican Party, which was most tied to the Christian right and was committed to ending abortion. In China, abortion was legal, widespread, and, at times, even coerced at the local level where unaccountable tyranny could be most cruel.

In China, a nation of 1.3 billion people, limiting population growth was experienced as a moral imperative. Consequently the right-wing Republican effort to defund popular international population control aid to China—education, contraceptives, abortion by free choice—discredited the humane attempt to expose monstrous local abuses, places where abortion against a woman's will did in fact regularly occur.

This congressional activism on human rights vis-à-vis China seemed hypocritical to ruling groups in Beijing. They noted that the U.S. Congress has refused to ratify a number of human rights covenants that even China has signed. In addition, Beijing, in rejecting UN Secretary General Kofi Annan's attempt to put universal human rights ahead of national sovereignty, has virtually copied the U.S. Congress's similar rejection of Kofi Annan's position. Presuming American hypocracy, foreign policy specialists in China perceive members of the U.S. Congress as irresponsibly bashing China to strengthen the credentials of American politicians with their home constituencies and funders. Forgetting the national interest, American politicians play to the anti-Beijing sentiments in the United States engendered by the 1989 televising of Beijing's massacre of democracy demonstrators. Narrow U.S. domestic interests can trump America's national interest, as Robert Lieber points out in Chapter 1.

With the Cold War over for the United States, Washington no longer viewed China as a counter to the Soviet Union (now Russia) as it had during the presidencies of Nixon, Ford, Carter, Reagan, and Bush. Consequently, on issues like China's barring of independent unions, its limits on freedom of religion, and its coercion of abortion, the congressional left and right joined together to press American administrations and the rulers in Beijing for action on ending human rights abuses. This trend was insulting to the Chinese, who wanted to be treated with the respect that was, they felt, deserved by one of the world's few great powers. Beijing had veto power on the UN Security Council. It was a nuclear armed nation. Therefore, it wanted to be treated as its power status merited, not as a naughty child to be corrected by parents.

The notion that the United States was the sole superpower, the indispensable nation for facilitating the solution of regional tensions—such as in Kuwait, Kosovo, and Korea—easily hid the real limits on American power from the Balkans and Chechneya to Rwanda and Somalia. In the China region, neighbors sought cooperation with a rising and militarily strong China. They did not wish to further arouse xenophobic Chinese sensitivities. They did not, from democratic India to democratic Japan, wish to prod China on violations of internationally recognized human rights. Should America, the lone eagle, unnecessarily irritate China on human rights matters, thereby strengthening hard-line militarists in China, Asian neighbors would blame America.

Consequently, Washington, however powerful it is while entering the twenty-first century, can not afford to act as a lone eagle. The United States needs its friends and allies, especially if military action became necessary. As a result of these priority security concerns, no American president has been overly forceful on human rights with China. This tendency has led, since the June 4, 1989 massacre in Beijing, to attacks on both the Democratic and the Republican administrations from the right and the left in the United States. Of most significance, China's success in beating back efforts of the international human rights community to investigate, judge, and ameliorate pervasive human rights abuses in China reveals the limits on U.S. power even in a post–Cold War era, when America is often expected to solve all problems everywhere.

In fact, it is precisely because Washington must cooperate with friends and allies in Asia in dealing with China that the American president, Republican or Democrat, cannot readily act as a lone eagle on the human rights agenda of the Republican Party right or the Democratic Party left. It is not clear that this presidential choice hurts the president's standing with the American people, since, as Ole Holsti's chapter shows, the public is not enthusiastic about promoting American values abroad.

## ECONOMICS

Because of a policy of continuing to engage China positively since the end of the Cold War partnership of Washington and Beijing against the Soviet Union, economic mutual benefit has been highlighted as the positive core of the Beijing-Washington relation. Washington applauded Beijing's sense of responsibility in not devaluing its currency further after the Asian financial crisis exploded in July 1997. Beijing and Washington also cooperated in 1998 in urging Japan to allow the yen to strengthen, a change that would help the economies of the rest of Asia in export competitiveness.[11]

Since reform began in China in 1978, the PRC has enjoyed the fastest sustained growth of any nation ever. Yet analysts differ on what the sources of this success are and on how much the still unreformed parts of the economically irrational Leninist command economy remain ultimate obstacles to sustained growth. However, there is no doubt that the keys to China's rise include moving toward a market-regarding economy, first in the countryside, and opening up to the opportunities of the world economy, including tourism (the world's largest industry), FDI (in which China is regularly among the top handful of host countries in the world),

---

[11]Selig Harrison and Clyde Prestowitz (ed.), *Asia after the "Miracle"* (Washington DC: Economic Strategy Institute, 1998).

and technological exchange (including sending many tens of thousands of students abroad to return home with the world's best practices).

Poverty reduction for hundreds of millions of the rural poor in China, villagers who had previously been locked in to stagnant misery by the self-wounding Third Worldist Mao-era policies of self-reliant delinkage from the world's forces of wealth expansion, is a matter of global significance. Recent poverty reduction in China means that the popular belief that the poor cannot rise in the globalized new economy is utterly false. Yet, because China is only partially reformed, rural dwellers suffer from both intensifying polarization and brutal corruption.

Despite rapidly growing U.S.-China economic interactions, China's rise has become increasingly contentious in American politics. Business tends to believe that unless an enterprise succeeds both in selling to China's 1.3 billion people and in using China as an export platform, a firm cannot be world-class in an era that requires global competitiveness.[12] Hence, business in America has lobbied very hard to get the American government to follow policies in regard to China that will permit U.S. firms to be treated normally in China so that competitors from Europe and Asia are not advantaged to the detriment of U.S. business.

American labor, on the other hand, despite a virtual full employment economy at home on entering the twenty-first century, worries about U.S. businesses moving factories to China and thereby costing American workers, especially in the old economy, good jobs, while facilitating a polarizing "race-to-the-bottom" in the United States. Studies suggest, however, that America's changing economic profile is related mainly to technological progress, such as when the auto displaced the horse and buggy. The anxieties of American workers also reflect the negative impact of U.S. policy decisions, such as not providing portable, national health insurance. The speed of change in the high technology economy, combined with growing uncertainty about health care, pensions and decent jobs for the less skilled in the new economy, impels workers in sectors as diverse as apparel and autos to resist technological change and to scapegoat globalization. Anti-immigrant sentiment has also risen in America. China is scapegoated.

China has become a symbol for American anxieties about the pains of the new economy. In fact, China is not the major recipient of U.S. FDI (much more U.S. FDI goes to Europe, Canada, and Latin America). But U.S. FDI to China is politically repugnant to Americans since the June 4, 1989, massacre in Beijing of a couple of thousand of the millions of Chinese peacefully demonstrating for a democratic opening in their country. The AFL-CIO's Denise Mitchell argued that China was "the proxy for all our concerns about globalization."[13] As Ole Holsti's data show, protecting American jobs is a very popular political issue in the United States. America-China relations suffer as a result of blaming China for a problem that it has not caused.

[12]Daniel Rosen, *Behind the Open Door* (Washington DC: Institute for International Economics, 1999).

[13]Quoted in Alexander Cockburn, "Short History of the Twentieth Century," *The Nation*, January 3, 2000, p. 9.

Although certain regions of the American economy, especially in the agricultural Midwest and along the West Coast from Boeing through Silicon Valley to Hollywood, strongly support maximizing mutually beneficial economic exchange with China, old union areas and the general citizenry are skeptical that such benefits are real. As a result, American presidents—Carter, Reagan, Bush, Clinton, and Bush—tend to argue that integrating China into the world economy will both decrease human rights abuses in China and also facilitate a peaceful world in which America is less likely to be drawn into an Asian war. The hope is that by giving China a seat at the table of decision makers in the G-8 (G-9?) or on an Asian currency reserve fund, leaders in Beijing will develop a stake in the rules of the international game, considering themselves as beneficiaries of the economic status quo. The hope is that a China treated with the respect that its actual power merits, a China experiencing itself as a rule-maker and not a rule-taker, a China benefiting from win-win international economic exchanges, will abjure risky war-prone actions.

Presidents invoke such arguments to legitimate comprehensive engagement with China, to win support for economic, cultural, and virtually all other exchanges. Many independent analysts agree that comprehensive economic engagement facilitates growth in China and that rising standards of living in China enhance the prospects for Chinese democratization, which, in turn enhances the likelihood for peace in the region. This is because the rational economic actors running China will be aware that the nation's rise and the regime's legitimacy rest on economic performance that requires good political relations with the United States.

Although much of the argument for comprehensive economic engagement with China is persuasive, the claims about how market-oriented growth creates a virtuous cycle bringing democracy and then peace tend to oversell engagement and to rest on debatable premises. Democracy is supposedly greatly facilitated by a growing, self-interested middle class, by expanding the numbers of property owners who inherently resist arbitrary government impositions, and by a broad experience of gaining from economic liberty, supposedly leading people to create a civil society and engendering a consciousness favoring the blessings of liberty in general. In addition, democracy in the new high tech economy is said to be facilitated by a free flow of knowledge via information technology (IT) that government censors cannot prevent. IT is said to subvert the pro-authoritarian propaganda of the power-holders in Beijing. President George W. Bush's national security adviser argued for "faith in the power of markets and economic freedom to drive political change."[14] Hence, the notion of a virtuous cycle legitimates comprehensive engagement with China.

There is no doubt that many in China fear these developments, seeing what to Americans seems a virtuous cycle, as a vicious cycle that should be halted, if not reversed. China's CP tries to control the internet and has jailed IT users who were described as subverting the regime. Believers in the virtuous cycle theory of IT contend that the only way Beijing's censorship and repression can succeed would be if China opted out of global economic competition in IT. Yet Beijing's desire to

---

[14]Condoleeza Rice, "Promoting the National Interest," *Foreign Affairs* 79, No. 1 (January–February 2000): 56.

be equal to and to compete with the United States precludes such economically self-wounding repression.

China's left conservatives and right populists oppose this democratization/peace tendency as a vicious cycle that shreds Chinese society and makes China dependent on America. This opposition consists of groups tied to prereform notions of state-guaranteed, egalitarian self-reliance. They are entrenched in Soviet style institutions, and they embrace the virtues of Confucian collectivism, seeing it as superior to an alleged Western individualism. The result is an emerging Chinese red-brown alliance similar to that of Milosevic in Serbia, forces that in democracies are described as right populist authoritarian because of their combination of racist xenophobia tied to demagogic appeals to cultural purity. In China, such forces are increasingly popular and ever more vocal.

China's right populists want reform and openness restricted, claiming that they otherwise will produce subordination to a liberal United States, as well as an infusion of individualistic values that would subvert China's egalitarian socialist values. They fear a reliance on jobs in an imagined polarizing private sector that will negate the weight of state-owned enterprises (SOE). The SOE are imagined, not as the black hole of money-losing factories swallowing up the hard-won wealth of the society, as they indeed are, but as the guarantor of socialist egalitarianism.

Many American social scientists doubt whether a cycle of wealth-democracy-peace exists, whether one deems it virtuous or vicious. In fact, democracy is a political struggle that has to be won by political agents in a political arena.[15] Democracy is no automatic reflection of wealth expansion, as numerous experiences from Singapore to Saudi Arabia demonstrate. In addition, since the Asian financial crisis beginning in July 1997, which helped implode Suharto's authoritarian kleptocracy in Indonesia, China's CP has actually intensified political, religious and media repression. The desire for avoiding chaotic change among Chinese citizens makes the authoritarian order quite legitimate, not threatened by IT[16] or by an actually coopted middle class or by an emerging civil society, most of whose members in fact experience this as the freest moment ever in the history of the PRC. Most Chinese oppose anyone trying to sink the unsteady ship-of-state.

On the other hand, even if wealth expansion does not automatically lead to democratization, there is good evidence that China's deepening relations with the world economy foster groups in China that prefer peaceful progress to xenophobic war. Already in 1996, when Beijing launched so-called military exercises, the firing of missiles off the coast of Taiwan's two great container ports, Kaohsiung and Keelung, regional leaders in Chinese provinces lobbied to end the adventurous acts. The people and places doing best in attracting FDI did not want their government to scare away needed FDI, a huge chunk of which, since 1990, actually comes from Taiwan.

In addition, the use of military means to try to persuade (i.e., terrorize) Taiwan into conceding to Beijing's demand that it become part of one authoritarian

---

[15]Giuseppe DiPalma, *To Craft Democracies* (Berkeley: University of California Press, 1990).
[16]James Luh, "The Internet Can't Free China," *New York Times*, July 25, 2000.

China whose dictatorial capital is Beijing, worries rulers in Japan. They do not wish to see all of Japan's ocean routes to West Asian oil, Japan's economic lifeline, dominated by the Chinese military. In Japan, anti-Beijing sentiments have greatly strengthened.[17] Nonetheless, Japan is still committed to comprehensive engagement with China, including large amounts of economic aid to lock China into win-win games in the world economy. China's right populists fear that deepening engagement might indeed facilitate peaceful evolution into democracy.

Reformist Chinese political forces, who had been using the rising chauvinism merely to legitimate the regime, worry about the potential antireform impact of the right populist atmosphere. The tension became clear after angry riots against American property in 1999 were sparked by a NATO bombing of China's embassy in Belgrade. The government-censored media unleashed daily America-bashing, treating America as an evil threat to Chinese values, to China's return to greatness, and to Chinese unity and stability. Those Chinese who understood that China's economic rise depends on openness to tourism, FDI, trade, and technology exchange argued that a violent explosion of nativism had to be constrained to keep China on its upward trajectory. War-prone chauvinism has time and again been limited by the imperatives of growth through world-market openness. The unanswered question is whether ruling reformers can continue to rein in militaristic passions for revenge or whether the new political atmosphere of nativistic xenophobia has become so powerful that it will eventually undermine both reform and peace in the region; that is, reform rulers are uneasy riders on a nativist tiger's back.

These conflicting tendencies were evident in China's entrance into the World Trade Organization (WTO). The U.S. side had negotiated for Taiwan's entrance when Beijing got in, something that democratic Taiwan very much wants. American business was pleased with the deal that President Clinton's special trade representative got China to agree to.

But the repressive CP regime was in such bad odor in America that when China's Premier arrived in the United States in spring 1999 agreeing to America's terms, the U.S. president was politically unprepared. Brushing aside China's concessions created a furor in Beijing where the dominant view was that, given the recent bombing of the Chinese Embassy in Belgrade by an American plane, economic reformers had already paid a high political price in pressing ahead with concessions to America to get entry into the WTO. Once in the WTO, China should be able to expand apparel and light industry exports to the United States and to win new capital to revitalize China's moribund SOEs. In fact, starting in 2000 the mere appearance that China might soon be in the WTO reversed capital flight from China, making far more money available for job creation which is vital to social stability in China.

In order for the United States to enjoy China's concessions made on services, finances, tariffs, sourcing, and much more, all designed to win entry into the WTO,

---

[17]Edward Friedman, "Preventing War Between China and Japan," in *What If China Does Not Democratize?*, *loc. cit.*, pp. 99–128; Wu Xinbo, "The Security Dimension of Sino-Japanese Relations," *Asian Survey* 40, No. 2 (2000): 296–310.

Congress had first to agree that China would have a permanent normal trading relationship (PNTR) with the United States, not one conditioned on adhering to particular standards of good governance, human rights, and democracy. That agreement was not easy because Beijing continued to proliferate weapons of mass destruction to Pakistan and Iran and because many Republicans in Congress believed that Chinese had also stolen U.S. nuclear secrets and bought special favors with President Clinton through illegal campaign donations. Actually, a consensus of independent analysts found little evidence for either of these latter two charges.[18] In any case, the U.S. congressional debate on China's WTO entry via PNTR was prolonged and heated. In 2000, presidential candidates Ralph Nader and Pat Buchanan both appealed to workers anxious over factories leaving America for China. But the final snag blocking Chinese membership in the WTO was agricultural subsidies that could block cheap grain exports to China.

As seen from Beijing, obstructionism and name-calling in America seemed further proof of ulterior motives in dealing with China, a view strengthened by a mid-2000 decision by the World Bank, pressured by the American and Japanese governments, to deny China U.S. $40 million to relocate nearly 60,000 poor, mostly Tibetan Buddhist, farmers. Beijing withdrew its application for the loan, rejecting new terms that would better protect the affected Tibetans. Beijing also raged in summer 2000 when President Clinton successfully pressured Israel to cancel a major sale of weapons technology to China. Leaders in Beijing searched for ways to get even with the United States. Beijing momentarily pressed the WTO to deny Taiwan membership unless Taiwan conceded to Beijing's terms.

The Chinese CP portrays America as a lone eagle trying to hobble the Chinese dragon. The politics of the economic relationship is not experienced as win-win by American unions or by superpatriots in China defending money losing economic sectors entrenched by the prior economically irrational command economy. One can expect the economic relationship to become more contentious even after China's entrance into the WTO because China is self-consciously emulating the rise of other East Asian economies. Beijing therefore will play hardball on opening its market to American products and services while continuing, as a knowledgeable observer notes, "to shield its [China's] infant industries" and maximizing its exports to "become a world-class industrial power." Rather than being involved in economic relations promoting good political relations, Washington will be engaged in "a long, bitter diplomatic struggle to make China live up to its promises and open its markets according to the [WTO] rules."[19]

Washington is well aware of this prickly situation. The American belief is that getting China to play by the rules is far more likely to succeed when China is inside the WTO facing all the member nations than with an effort merely pitting a lone eagle against a lone dragon. Such bitter struggles will not make it easier for American voters to see that comprehensive American engagement with China is indeed an

---

[18]Alistair Iain Johnston et al., *The Cox Committee Report: An Assessment* (Stanford University Center for International Security and Cooperation, December 1999).

[19]William Grieder, "China and Globalisim," *The Nation*, June 5, 2000, p. 5.

enlightened American interest. Still, in the year 2000, both the Republican and Democratic Party presidential candidates agreed on the value of economic engagement. When push came to shove, the America-China relation was so important to war and peace that neither the president nor the Congress played politics with it.

# NATIONAL SECURITY

After the Cold War ended and the Soviet Union imploded, the two hot spots with the highest likelihood of sparking a larger war were both in Asia: the Korean peninsula and the Taiwan Strait region. Both danger spots involved China. But in Korea, China cooperated with the forces of peace and reconciliation, whereas on the cross-Strait relation, rulers in Beijing displayed a war-prone chauvinism.[20]

Since President Nixon's initial overture to China at the start of the 1970s, the security issue has usually dominated U.S.-China relations. By the beginning of the 1980s, the reformist Deng Xiaoping administration abandoned partnership with Washington against Cold War adversary Moscow for an independent policy of wooing the Soviet Union.[21] When the Cold War ended after 1989 and the Soviet Union withdrew from Vietnam, Afghanistan, and Mongolia, the stage was set for what Beijing dubs a China-Russia strategic partnership, a relation that China has used to buy high technology weapons from Russia to deter America from confronting China when Beijing acts on its territorial agenda.[22]

Since the bloody crushing of China's nationwide democracy movement in 1989, China's CP has barraged its people incessantly with vicious anti-American propaganda, so that most politically conscious Chinese became persuaded that the United States intends to keep China down, foster separation for Tibetan Buddhists and Uighur Muslims, and hurt the Chinese economy and spread chaos in China. America is believed to be anti-China despite China's rise being premised on earnings from huge exports to America and cheap capital from the World Bank, in which America is the major player.

As in the pre-reform Cultural Revolution era when Soviet Russia was scapegoated in China, most Chinese believe that their nativistic passions are products of their own personal judgment. They find that the government in Beijing is not doing enough to stand up for the Chinese people. As shown in the chapter by Gail Lapidus, China seeks to use Russia to balance against America as, in the late Mao era, when China asked America to balance against Russia. Since 1991, Beijing has treated Washington as a Cold War adversary. It has been purchasing from Russia weapons systems that will permit China to achieve its ambition of predominance in Asia, which is perceived as a rightful restoration of Chinese greatness.

[20]This chauvinism is spoofed in a satirical novel, Wang Shuo, *Please Don't Call Me Human* (NY: Hyperion East, 2000).

[21]Robert Ross (ed.), *China, The United States, and the Soviet Union* (Armonk, NY: Sharpe, 1993).

[22]Sherman Garnett (ed.), *Rapprochement or Rivalry? Russia-China Relations in a Changing Asia* (Washington DC: Carnegie Endowment for International Peace, 2000).

U.S.-China cooperation in the interest of peace in Korea therefore is an anomaly. As Cindy Williams's chapter shows, U.S. policy has made South Korea quite secure. But the Chinese CP is worried that if the rapidly declining North Korean CP regime does not begin economic reform or if it again militarily provokes the United States and its democratic Asian allies, Japan and South Korea, then foreign intervention in the Korean peninsula could lead to the fall of the useless North Korean CP. That result could lead to a reunification of Korea by a democratic Korean military ally of the United States, leaving U.S. forces on the Korean peninsula free to go right up to China's Yalu River border with Korea.

To prevent unacceptable outcomes, Beijing has facilitated policies of peace and reconciliation on the Korean peninsula, hoping that such developments could even lead the democracy in South Korea to feel secure enough to ask the United States to remove its trip wire of armed forces from the Korean peninsula. Doing that would make China feel more secure. However, Japan, which in 1998 had a North Korean missile aimed over its territories, worries, as described in Michael Nacht's chapter, that the United States has not been tough enough with the dangerously militaristic North Korean regime, which has a history of aggression, terrorism, and international irresponsibility. Nonetheless, Tokyo will join Washington, Seoul, and Beijing in promoting peaceful reconciliation in Korea. The Bush administration is debating backing away from the four party—U.S., South Korea, North Korea, and China—effort at peaceful reconciliation.

In addition to having overlapping interests in maintaining the peace on the Korean peninsula, Beijing and Washington have a joint interest in not seeing a nuclear arms race in South Asia between Pakistan and India. But since the end of the 1950s, China has befriended Pakistan, first to balance an India, which was seen as a military ally of the Soviet Union, and then, since 1991, to balance an India redefined as increasingly dependent on the United States, which China defines as its number one enemy. Consequently, China has provided Pakistan with help in building weapons of mass destruction. Beijing has been a major proliferator also in West Asian hot spots, happy to earn money in weapons sales and delighted to complicate life for the United States. The United States has twice imposed sanctions on China for its provision of weapons of mass destruction because such sales automatically trigger American legal responses. Beijing may back away from Pakistan because of its indirect involvement with Muslim Uighur militants in western China north of Afghanistan.

Entering the twenty-first century, Washington hopes that Beijing will become more responsible and cooperative because of changes in China's security environment. First, China is an ever larger oil importer and needs secure access to the energy resources of a peaceful West Asia. Second, with Pakistan and India now both nuclear weapons states, China does not want a war to occur between them on China's southwest frontier, a war that could potentially drag in foreign powers on the borders of China's regions that are most replete with angry minorities, especially Tibetan Buddhists and Uighur Muslims.

Another potential hot spot involving China is the South China Seas, which the Chinese navy has been gradually incorporating through salami-slicing tactics since

1974, although the territories that China claims are many hundreds of miles from China's mainland and right off the coasts of Indonesia, the Philippines, Vietnam, and other countries. Consequently, Southeast Asian nations want the U.S. military in the South China Sea.

Even though China, seeking to isolate Taiwan and America, may momentarily let up on pressure on Japan and Southeast Asia, China's neighbors view America as the indispensable power as long as it acts in a restrained and responsible manner. Because China is engaged in a major naval buildup and wishes to project its power well out into the ocean, China's Asian neighbors, from Japan to Singapore, want American's Asian military force of 100,000 there as a guarantor of security stability. Still, if it came to war, the United States would likely be alone: it would be lone eagle, lone dragon. Comprehensive engagement with quiet vigilance is the preferred American alternative to dangerously self-fulfilling policies of treating China singularly as an immediate threat to the peace.

Complicating active cooperation with America is the Asian perception of a Chinese bully that will act yet more belligerently if one accurately describes its bullying. Asian friends of the United States therefore oppose treating China as an enemy to be contained, preferring to bet on the long-range force of policies of economic integration and global engagement, much as West Germany treated Eastern Europe after 1969 with so-called "ostpolitik." Were Washington to reject a policy of comprehensive engagement and to choose a policy of containing China, America would be seen in Asia as the cause of China's bullying, and America would be alienating itself from friendly Asian countries. The eagle would be isolated. Asians worry that the ideologues of the Republican Party right and the Democratic Party left, who seem to some to carry increasing weight on U.S. policy toward China, could cause Washington to abandon the China policy established in Nixon's time of comprehensive engagement accompanied with quiet vigilance. As Litwak observes in his chapter, America's policy toward China cannot be defined by either mere engagement or containment.

The result of this complexity is that at home, American presidents who act responsibly toward China can be maliciously portrayed as "soft on China," even though the charge is without merit. The hot spot where all these forces are most sensitive and explosive is the Taiwan Strait region.[23]

# TAIWAN

In the post-Mao era, reformers in China have legitimated their power through super-patriotism. They redefined Taiwan from being an unfinished issue of a prolonged civil war, to being both an imperialist humiliation that must be swiftly ended and also an eternal and integral part of a pure Chinese race that arose in Asia about 5,000 years ago, the loss of which would be race betrayal. By the 1990s, under the

---

[23]Suisheng Zhao (ed.), *Across the Taiwan Strait* (NY: Routledge, 1999).

leadership group headed by President Jiang Zemin, the Chinese have reimagined Taiwan as similar to other lost colonial territories, Hong Kong and Macao. Just as the British colony of Hong Kong was returned to China in 1997, and just as the Portuguese colony of Macao was returned to China in 1999, so, in the early part of the twenty-first century, the former Japanese colony of Taiwan, which was ceded in perpetuity to Japan's Meiji emperor by the Qing dynasty in 1895, must become part of the China whose capital is Beijing. This policy Beijing dubs the "one-China principle."

America's policy to Taiwan since 1943, during the Chinese civil war, was to allow Chiang Kai-shek's Nationalists, who led the Republic of China, to take Taiwan back from a defeated Japan in 1945. But after China and the Soviet Union facilitated North Korea's invasion of South Korea in 1950, President Truman interposed the U.S. Navy to prevent Mao's CP from using force to seize Taiwan, to which Chiang's defeated army had retreated. Consequently, the Republic of China has been located on Taiwan continuously and independently since 1945, totally separate from Mao's People's Republic of China. Taiwan has actually been separated from China since 1895, when it became a Japanese colony.

When President Nixon began to normalize relations with Mao's China in 1971, National Security Advisor Kissinger agreed not to support an independent Taiwan state. At that time, the Chiang Kai-shek dictatorship on Taiwan legitimated itself as a continuation of the Republic of China, the legitimate government of all of China since a 1911 republican revolution overthrew the Qing dynasty emperor. Generalissimo Chiang did not seek legitimacy as an independent Taiwan. In fact, Chiang's regime repressed the Taiwanese, who sought autonomy and democracy. That anti-Chiang alternative had gained in strength since 1947 when Chiang's brutal military, retreating from defeat on the mainland, plundered and slaughtered the people of Taiwan.

By the late 1980s, Taiwan had been transformed into a flourishing democracy. Taiwan's prospering people were proud of what they had accomplished and had no desire to be incorporated into a poor and tyrannical People's Republic of China. They preferred a friendly policy of comprehensive engagement with China, including trade, tourism, and investment. Japan saw an autonomous Taiwan region as guaranteeing Japan's sea-lanes, its economic lifelines. Since 1998, Japanese governments have rejected Chinese pressure to copy America and guarantee, as Henry Kissinger did in 1971, that there would be no support of Taiwan's political autonomy, whatever the rubric.

American policy since the 1979 Taiwan Relations Act has been to sell Taiwan defensive weaponry and to accept any peacefully negotiated resolution of cross-Strait problems that was satisfactory to the people of Taiwan. Rulers in Beijing interpret this well-established American policy as a secret agenda of splitting China and allowing Taiwan to serve a containment policy of Tokyo and Washington that is supposedly surreptitiously aimed at squeezing China and preventing China's rise to greatness. Beijing woos politicians in Taiwan and declares that it will resort to force if Taiwan does not soon agree to a so-called "one China principle" dictated by

Beijing. Chauvinistic Chinese impatience with peace and the status quo in the Taiwan Strait region could intensify in the first decade of the twenty-first century.

The big question is whether war can be prevented. By 2000 the democratically elected president of Taiwan had made generous conciliatory offers to rulers in authoritarian Beijing. But given the racial chauvinism that has increasingly infused Chinese politics, the mere existence of a democratically prospering Taiwan seemed to the Chinese to be a threat to unity, a continuation of unacceptable colonial-era losses, an attack on the "race," and an effort to strangle China. Beijing kept brushing off Taiwan's peace diplomacy as insincere.

In 1996 the Clinton administration had sent aircraft carrier task forces to the Taiwan region when, in March, Beijing tried to terrorize Taiwan, intimidate its voters and destabilize its economy with missile exercises. Beijing then pressed America to stop arms sales to Taiwan, but the United States is committed to continuing such sales as long as peace in the region is not secured. The Bush administration has to decide what American weapons systems can reassure Taiwan without provoking Beijing.

Chauvinists in China have been persuading themselves that once China has the proper weapons and America sees that it will have to pay a heavy price in lives to keep democratic Taiwan free, then an America that backed out of Lebanon and Somalia when American lives were lost, an America that refused to risk ground forces in Kosovo or Rwanda, that "cowardly" America will back down before Chinese willing to lay down their lives for their nation and race. Chinese people believe that Beijing has promised that China will soon be able both to impose its will on Taiwan and to achieve great power predominance in Asia.

Many American analysts think that the Chinese posture of readiness to launch a war against Taiwan is a bluff. They see Beijing as wanting to win the war without fighting a battle and believe that the reformers who run China would not risk good relations with America, which are crucial to China's continuing economic growth. But superpatriots in Beijing see Taiwan as similar to Chechneya, where, despite international condemnation of Russia for its brutal war against an autonomous Chechneya, the United States and the other rich democracies did not even sanction Russia, let alone sever economic relations. Thus, Beijing believes that in today's globalized economy, America would never embargo and isolate China. It is the political struggle in Beijing which is decisive for war or peace.

On a July 2000 visit to Beijing, U.S. Secretary of Defense William Cohen, told an audience at China's National Defense University that he was worried that the political propaganda inside China was making it impossible for China to understand American policy. I believe he is correct. Unless there is a fundamental shift in politics in Beijing, the Cold War confrontation that the lone dragon is imposing on the lone eagle could well produce extraordinary difficulties and potentially explosive challenges in the years ahead. This possibility is apparent on issues of arms sales to Taiwan and on the question of whether or not to include Taiwan in a Theater Missile Defense (TMD) effort that already includes a Japan worried about North Korea. Many in Congress are promoting both expanded arms sales to Taiwan and Taiwan's inclusion in TMD. Aside from issues of TMD cost and feasability, which are discussed elsewhere in this book, Beijing threatens an arms race and a missile buildup across from Taiwan should Washington proceed with TMD or expanded arms sales to Taiwan. The Bush administration faces daunting challenges on this intractable issue.

China already has placed hundreds of missiles across from Taiwan and is committed to increasing that number in order to bully Taiwan to surrender whether or not America further enhances Taiwan's defenses. It is probably best for America, in maintaining cooperation with friends and allies in the region, that weapons sales to Taiwan clearly be limited and defensive so that it is obvious which side of the Taiwan Strait is the war-prone aggressor in the region. But it would be wrong to underestimate the military resolve in Beijing. Since the Taiwan Strait, a Cold War hot spot, could all too easily flare up again, comprehensive engagement must be accompanied by a diplomacy of quiet vigilance and a long-term commitment to continue comprehensive engagement even if it will be interrupted by Beijing-initiated military events. Maintaining a steady hand at the helm through roiling waters will not be easy because of those powerful voices in America shouting that the captain of the ship of state should change course and treat China as an enemy.

## CONCLUSION

The Chinese, like everyone else who saw America's painful stagflation of the 1980s as proof that America had permanently declined, were shocked by the resurgence of the American economy during the Clinton presidency. Beijing strongly dislikes the way American power subsequently set the rules. Although the financial volatility of the post–Bretton Woods era should preclude straight-line extrapolations of economic growth for any country—as both Saudi Arabia, the big winner in the 1970s, and Japan, the big winner in the 1980s, discovered—Beijing does look to the United States for clues to economic success for itself in the age of the new economy. Nonetheless, the 1990s American rise is a two-edged sword: it not only makes America admirable but also makes it the hated obstacle to China's rise to predominance in Asia.

When in the late 1980s, the Moscow-Washington Cold War wound down, and when in the early 1990s, the Soviet Union disintegrated and Russia seemed caught somewhere between a fragile democratic project and cruel social and economic forces, many wise and politically conscious Chinese not only asked, quite naturally, what all this meant for China, but also asked that question in a way that assumed the Chinese dragon was unique. That is, with former U.S. President Reagan and his successor triumphantly declaring victory over an evil Soviet empire, these politically involved Chinese interpreted the question of what the end of the Cold War held for China to mean "what will an arrogant, superpower America be trying to do to China now?"

Patriotic Chinese imagined American foreign policy as global, uniform, malignant, and inevitably aimed peculiarly against China, the world's only remaining major Communist Party dictatorship. Yet the struggle of East versus West was about Europe, west Europe versus east Europe not about Asia, except when allies of the USSR were included. The Cold War East meant the Soviet bloc. But Beijing broke with Moscow by the end of the 1950s. Asia consequently has long been populated by independent states complexly related to the United States and its major Asian ally, Japan. The Chinese notion that a Washington that had triumphed against Moscow was in the process of turning all its might against Beijing was nonsense, but it is what Chinese rulers tend to believe. Those convictions lead China's CP to treat America as enemy number one. Rulers in Beijing act as if UN action in Kuwait in 1991 and NATO action in Kosovo in 1999 were mainly dress rehearsals for American action against China. The fall of Milosevic in Belgrade in 2000 was seen as an American plot, a warm-up for action against Beijing.

Even during the Cold War, it was not the case that every U.S. act to contain a Stalin (and his heirs) incorporating an empire in East Europe was also a behavior to be followed in dealing with China in Asia. As senior U.S. Department of State official George Kennan noted already in 1947 when President Truman acted on behalf of anti-Soviet forces in Athens and Ankara, "If I thought for a moment that the precedent of Greece and Turkey obliged us to try to do the same thing in China, I would . . . say we had better have a whole new approach to the affairs of the world."[24] There was no American quest for uniformity in dealing with Moscow and Beijing, something much commented on by Washington hard-liners toward Beijing who complained, and still complain, about a U.S. double standard that supposedly permits Beijing a free ride on human rights and on sanctions, despite its role in proliferating weapons of mass destruction. But China was not, and is not, a global challenge as was the Soviet Union.

Why, then, would rulers in Beijing imagine America as out to get China? Why has China been pursuing a Cold War against America since the early 1990s? Has the American response been adequate? There is a danger, and a serious one, that the political class in China, imagining the government of the United States as inevitably out to do to China what rulers in Beijing believe rulers in Washington did to those in a "socialist" Moscow and to Milosevic, will misunderstand the United States, will treat Washington as an ultimate enemy and unnecessarily turn inherently complex and difficult China-America relations into a Cold War that could become a hot war. In short, Chinese racialistic and chauvinistic preconceptions may be unintentionally igniting or intensifying a Chinese Cold War with the United States. The outcome of the power struggle in China is what matters most.

Ruling groups in Beijing—economic reformers who are right populists—perceive Washington's military actions elsewhere as if these dramatic American performances were mainly dress rehearsals for the presumed real show, actions against China in Tibet, Taiwan, Xinjiang, or North Korea. A key question then is, can ruling groups in the dragon called China abandon their Cold War attitudes toward the American eagle? American policy toward China should not inhibit Beijing from

---

[24]Cited in Bruce Robbins, *Feeling Global* (NY: New York University Press, 1999), p. 212.

moving in that healthier direction. This may be a matter of war or peace in our time, since the real Cold War between Washington and Moscow all too often, whether over Berlin, Cuba, or the Middle East, threatened to turn into a global conflagration. The danger of a larger war persists, with China tending toward making itself a threat to the peace.

This trend is increasingly obvious in Japan where, by early 2000, 30 percent of the people feared that China would spark a war.[25] Some American security analysts, however, believe that surrendering Taiwan to China would sate Beijing's appetite. Some see Japan and other worried nations in Asia as too divided domestically to respond to the Chinese challenge. These American analysts therefore see Chinese hegemony in Asia as a foregone conclusion, leaving America with no better option than to accept and accommodate Chinese predominance.

Yet others believe that Beijing's economic imperative is sufficient in itself to constrain China from military actions that would upset the economic apple cart and that the virtuous cycle of market, democratization, and peace that was described before will eventually bring friendship and prosperity to U.S.-China relations. These alternative pessimistic and optimistic scenarios, both of which minimize the importance of military assurance for America's Asian friends and allies, would either betray basic American values and interests or keep the United States from committing itself to a long-term policy of comprehensive engagement with quiet vigilance.

Real and important American interests in the Asia-Pacific area are at stake. Too much of the American political debate, however, has focused on whether a particular president—Nixon, Carter, Bush, or Clinton—was too soft on China, an appeaser. If Bush sells less than the maximum in weapons to Taiwan, he too will be tarred. But one must approach China from a long run perspective. It is important to focus both on the realities of a chauvinistic China and the military challenge emanating from its economically rising, militarily ambitious, right populist authoritarianism and also on clashes and alternative prospects within Chinese politics fostered by key groups that do not wish China to lose its opportunity to rise economically as a result of military confrontation with America.

For the immediate future, China is a military challenge. Although the Chinese military cannot compare with America's military globally, Beijing's armed forces have great weight in their region. China is a rising economic power whose new wealth is funding and fueling military chauvinism and ambitions of regional predominance, while rationalizing this expansive militarism as mere defense against a superpower America trying to suffocate an emerging China. The Chinese government and the Chinese people are confident that they are the defender, the aggrieved party, the ones with their backs against the wall. China is imagining itself as in a position from which it has ever less room for maneuver and compromise. Nevertheless, for the United States, the goal of comprehensive engagement should continue to be to create America-China win-win games so that the Chinese see that they have plenty of space in which to grow and rise in a peaceful way.

[25]George Tett, "An Electorate That Does Not Yet Feel The Pain," *Financial Times*, May 29, 2000, p. 15.

Because the Chinese dragon may, in the first decade of the new millennium, confront the American eagle in the Taiwan Strait region or someplace else in the Western Pacific, it is extremely important that the U.S. not act unilaterally as a lone eagle. As detailed throughout this chapter, it is important that America stay in harmony with its friends and allies in the region. Washington therefore should continue a patient and complex policy of comprehensive engagement with China along with quiet vigilance in the region. Only such a complex and nuanced policy can deter war in the medium term and can continue good and mutually beneficial relations in the long run while forces in China arise that can choose win-win internationalist policies in dealing with America and all the peoples of the Asia-Pacific region. Clearly, China policy will prove a trying challenge for America in the twenty-first century.

# 10

# The United States and Africa
## Power with Limited Influence*

## DONALD ROTHCHILD
### University of California, Davis

*For almost half a century, whenever we talked about foreign policy, we did so within a Cold War context . . . But then, our chess rival left the table. The game has changed and the rules to the new one are still being written.*

Madeleine K. Albright[1]

In contrast to experiences in the Balkans and Asia, America's primacy in Africa has been less robust than might be assumed. The end of the Cold War has left the United States with no compelling reason to rally the industrialized states to promote Africa's economic and political transformation. Whereas the Reagan and Bush administrations had narrowed their agendas to a few overriding diplomatic objectives, the Clinton administration voiced concern over a diffuse set of issues—including security, conflict management and transformation, the training of peacekeepers, the enlargement of democracy, human rights, trade, debt relief, health protection (particularly the threat of HIV/AIDS, which has already infected 24.5 million people in sub-Saharan Africa), and the protection of the environment.[2] Clinton's agenda was broad—but deficient in depth and commitment. Encountering intense opposition at times on African-related issues in congress and lacking an effective constituency base to pressure for change, the Clinton administration tended toward activism

Donald Rothchild is Professor of Political Science at the University of California, Davis. He is coauthor of *Sovereignty as Responsibility: Conflict Management in Africa* (Brookings, 1996); author of *Managing Ethnic Conflict in Africa: Pressures and Incentives for Cooperation* (Brookings, 1997); and coeditor of *The International Spread of Ethnic Conflict: Fear, Diffusion, and Escalation* (Princeton, 1998). He is currently collaborating with Phillip A. Roeder on a project on "Power Sharing and Peacemaking."

*I am grateful to Robert Lieber, Ole Holsti, and Timothy Sisk for their thoughtful comments on the first draft of this chapter and to Nikolas Emmanuel and Mark Davis for their research assistance. This chapter is a revised version of a paper first presented at the 20th Annual Conference of the African Studies Program of SAIS-Johns Hopkins, Washington, D.C., April 14, 2000.

[1]"Remarks to the National War College," National Defense University, Fort McNair, September 23, 1993. Mimeo.

[2]Reuters Newswire 2000, "AIDS causes falling population rates in Africa-US," July 10, p. 1.

without a sustained concern for outcomes. It reacted to immediate challenges without an overarching policy framework for coping effectively with the continent's complex challenges. The effect was to create legitimate misgivings over Africa's growing "marginalization."[3]

On balance, the Clinton administration's record on Africa proved to be a mixed one. Although the Clinton team took positive actions to enlarge democracy, increase trade, and offer debt relief, it acted cautiously, after the Somali debacle, to resist obligations arising from UN peacekeeping initiatives and to allow aid levels as a percent of GNP to sink to inappropriately low levels. On the whole, strong rhetoric was not matched by achievement. With the American public mesmerized by the country's prosperity and largely uninformed about complex problems abroad, there was little public pressure to close the gap between global power and influence. Rather than a coherent strategy for coping with African challenges having been developed, the policy problem, as John Clark remarked, "has been left to the foreign policy bureaucracies to work out the priorities, as well as to translate vague presidential concerns into concrete initiatives."[4] There is little reason to anticipate a shift in American priorities in the years immediately ahead.

As Africa's marginalization became an increasingly accepted fact in U.S. and Western policy circles, the push for disengagement spread, and it became more and more difficult for a concerned U.S. administration to overcome the inertia. Paradoxically, increasing trends toward economic globalization were leading to a decreasing U.S. knowledge about and interest in interacting on a sustained basis with Africa. This reflected a growing tendency in the United States to trade with wealthy countries that are fully integrated into the world capitalist system. It also reflected a skepticism about dealing with societies that have weak states and were unable to enforce their laws and regulations throughout their territories. A liberally inclined United States, with a mind-set supportive of democratic values, political stability, and the politics of compromise, has not always been effective in promoting its values in Africa's weakest states or in its intense conflict situations (such as Rwanda, Sudan, Sierra Leone, and the Democratic Republic [DR] of Congo).[5] The consequences of this neglect were sometimes unfortunate. Not only were U.S. and Western influences limited as Africa remained largely beyond their reach, but the resources and technological prowess of the industrialized states were not sufficiently available to meet Africa's legitimate needs.[6] To fail to use Western strengths to push African development forward more rapidly in potentially receptive countries was to forego an opportunity to relate to Africa in a creative way.

[3]Claude Ake, *Democracy and Development in Africa* (Washington, DC: Brookings, 1996), pp. 98–99.

[4]John F. Clark, "The Clinton Administration and Africa: White House Involvement and the Foreign Affairs Bureaucracies," *Issue: A Journal of Opinion* 36, No. 2 (1998): 8.

[5]Donald Rothchild, "The Clinton Administration and Ethnic Conflict Management: Limits of Intervention in a Partially Autonomous Africa," *Issue: A Journal of Opinion* 36, No. 2 (1998): 41–46.

[6]Thomas L. Friedman, *The Lexus and the Olive Tree* (New York: Farrar, Straus, Giroux, 1999), p. 357.

Because of its power and resources, the United States does possess at least a limited capacity to influence African actions, but this applies mainly to policy issues that are in line with the preferences of African leaders and publics. When it comes to more contentious problems such as genocide, dealing with warlords, electoral manipulation, or the abuse of internally displaced persons, however, the partially autonomous African state lies to some extent beyond the reach of the liberal Western regime. American primacy, as outlined in the introductory chapter, is qualified, particularly in those parts of Africa that have weaker links to the global economy. Why has a powerful United States come to appear somewhat irrelevant to many of Africa's most vexing questions in the twenty-first century? In probing this matter, this chapter will start by looking at the nature and extent of U.S. national interests in Africa. It will then examine the tendency toward a low-profile American policy that has been manifest, with some prominent exceptions, over the postcolonial period, and the contribution of this tendency to the distance that exists in American relations with Africa. Then, after examining the gap between the executive branch and both the congress and general public on African-related issues in the Clinton period, the chapter will conclude by discussing the likely approach of the Bush administration toward the region and the impact of weak American constituency support for Africa's needs and aspirations.

## AMERICAN NATIONAL INTERESTS IN AFRICA

The United States has real, albeit limited, national interests with respect to Africa. Most important are such objectives as promoting regional stability and conflict management, accelerating Africa's integration into the global economy, encouraging Africa's economic development and trade, and furthering democracy and human rights. Recent U.S. administrations have developed particularly close ties with governments in Egypt, Nigeria, and South Africa, building trade relations and looking to them for important support in managing conflicts on the continent. Also significant to Clinton administration policy-makers was working in partnership with African governments to deal with transnational security threats such as terrorism and drug trafficking.[7] Although American policy-makers have not sensed a direct military threat to their interests in the post–Cold War period, they nonetheless expressed concerns over regional stability in the Horn of Africa, West Africa (especially Liberia and Sierra Leone), and the DR Congo. Most notably, Assistant Secretary of State for African Affairs Susan Rice, when discussing U.S. national security interests, stated that "Ethiopia's and Eritrea's neighbor, Sudan, has long supported international terrorism, fostered the spread of Islamic extremism beyond its borders, actively worked to destabilize neighboring states, including Ethiopia and

---

[7]See the U.S. International Affairs Strategic Plan (as outlined in the Fiscal Year 2001 budget) on the seven fundamental national interests of the United States, in Office of the Spokesman, U.S. Department of State, *International Affairs Fiscal Year 2001 Budget Request—Summary and Highlights*, February 7, 2000, pp. 1–2 (http://www.state.gov/www/budget/fy2001/).

Eritrea, and perpetuated massive human rights violations against its own citizens."[8] She also noted that the problem of arms proliferation on the continent was high on the Clinton administration policy agenda.[9]

The main U.S. interests in Africa are interrelated: sustained stability depends in part on Africa's economic development, which requires attention to the processes of conflict management and effective governance.[10] As a 1994 Clinton administration strategy statement maintained, "All of America's strategic interests—from promoting prosperity at home to checking global threats abroad before they threaten our territory—are served by enlarging the community of democratic and free market nations."[11] In this regard, democracy was viewed as a conflict management strategy that reconciled a responsive and an effective state with civil society, thereby providing a political foundation upon which human rights and economic development goals could be furthered. Thus, National Security Adviser Anthony Lake, pointing to "the drain of civil war and ethnic conflict" on African countries, stressed the necessary role that the United States played in managing violent conflict as a prerequisite for achieving other critical objectives.[12]

Moreover, in terms of creating new opportunities for promoting American trade and investment in the future, the United States could not expect to gain access for its exports to the region unless it heeded the economic and social development needs of the African continent. The Clinton administration, when pressed by congressional opponents to make the case for trade promotion and continued economic assistance to Africa on the basis of U.S. interests—not on African needs or American humanitarian values—attempted as best it could to be responsive. President Clinton described the Africa Growth and Opportunity Act, which aimed primarily at increasing African-U.S. trade, as a "win-win proposition" for the United States and Africa, and Susan Rice estimated that as many as 100,000 American jobs were linked to U.S. exports to Africa[13] America indeed has political, economic, security, and humanitarian interests in Africa. Because these interests were limited in scope in post–Cold War times, however, various administrations were in a position to

---

[8]U.S. Department of State, USIA Archives, Public Diplomacy Query, *State's Rice on U.S. Policy Options in Horn of Africa War (5/25 testimony to House Africa Subcommittee)*, May 25, 1999, p. 3 (http://pdq.state.gov/scripts/cqcgi.exe/@pdqtest1.env?CQ_SESSION_KEY+XKOYITFFSMCM&CQ_QUERY_HANDLE=124022&cq_CUR_DOCUMENT=3&CQ_PDQ_DOCUMENT_VIEW=1&CQ-SUBMIT=VIEW&CQRETURN=&CQPAGE=1).

[9]U.S. Department of State, *Washington File: U.S. Official Cites Africa Policy as Part of Clinton Legacy*, April 17, 2000, p. 1 (http://www.usinfo.state.gov/cgi-bin/washfile/display.pl?p=/products/washfile/.../newsitem.shtm).

[10]Donald Rothchild and Timothy Sisk, "U.S.-Africa Policy: Promoting Conflict Management in Uncertain Times," in Robert J. Lieber (ed.), *Eagle Adrift: American Foreign Policy at the End of the Century* (New York: Longman, 1997), pp. 272–274.

[11]Clinton, *A National Security Strategy*, p. 19.

[12]Anthony Lake, speeches at OAU Headquarters, Addis Ababa, December 15, 1994, and Lusaka, Zambia, December 19, 1994, as reprinted in "Afro-realism vs. Afro-pessimism," *CSIS Africa Notes*, No. 168 (January 1995): 2, 5.

[13]Susan E. Rice, *U.S. and Africa in the 21st Century* (Seattle: World Affairs Council, November 9, 1999), p. 2.

pursue a "satisficing" (satisfying and sufficing) strategy—adopting a low profile involvement on African-related issues.

## Clinton 1993–1994: From Principled Action to Inaction

The broad continuities in American policy toward Africa were striking. The period from 1946 to 1976 could be described as one of minimal engagement. Although the styles of the various administrations differed, they were roughly similar in adopting low-profile stances toward Africa. American officials, anxious to avoid any disruption of the international state system following decolonization, encouraged African leaders to refrain from violence and retain close ties with the countries of Europe in the post-independence era.[14]

In 1976, the status quo became difficult to maintain, as the conflict among nationalist parties in Angola became internationalized and as South African and Cuban forces became direct interveners in that country. Unable to secure Senate support for American intervention, Secretary of State Henry Kissinger had little choice but to change his strategy of confronting radical influences in Angola and to accommodate African aspirations in the wider region. The Carter administration that followed voiced a more principled commitment to liberal objectives, championing the principle of "African solutions for African problems." The tentativeness that marked American policies in dealing with radical African states and movements was soon discarded. The Reagan administration was elected to office and sought to restore America's sense of purpose by actively identifying with proven friends and opposing perceived enemies. With the repeal of the Clark amendment in 1985 (banning covert American assistance to antigovernment forces in Angola), the Reagan team assumed a more adversarial stance. For the most part, however, the Reagan administration veered toward caution in its dealings with opponents. His successor, President Bush, initially voiced uncertainty over Soviet intentions after assuming office, but as he came to accept the reality of U.S.-Soviet cooperation in dealing with the remaining regional conflicts on the continent, he returned (with the exception of the humanitarian intervention in Somalia) to the conventional low-profile trajectory on African issues.

Although elected on a platform that gave primacy to invigorating the domestic American economy and achieving a more enlightened social program, Clinton nonetheless committed himself to more magnanimous policy guidelines on Africa. From the time he assumed office in 1993 to the Republican victory in the 1994 midterm elections, he laid the groundwork for an activist course of action in Africa. He set out a post–Cold War agenda, emphasizing the promotion of multilateral (especially UN and OAU) peacekeeping, democratization, economic development, and

---

[14]For a fuller discussion of the evolution of U.S. policy during this period and immediately after, see Donald Rothchild and John Ravenhill, "Subordinating African Issues to Global Logic: Reagan Confronts Political Complexity," in Kenneth A. Oye, Robert J. Lieber, and Donald Rothchild (eds.), *Eagle Resurgent? The Reagan Era in American Foreign Policy* (Boston: Little, Brown, and Co., 1983), pp. 396–398.

the reorganization of economic assistance programs.[15] In an effort to respond to calls for more effective U.S. leadership, Clinton invited some 160 politicians, business leaders, academics, and advocates for African-American interests to a White House Conference on Africa in June 1994. The conference was nearly postponed when members of the congressional Black caucus (who were ranking members of many major committees in congress) threatened a boycott to enhance their influence over the proceedings. Nevertheless, the conference did get under way and proved a timely effort to promote new American thinking on African problems. Reports were received from working groups dealing with six critical questions: the challenge of global issues, the promotion of sustainable development, Africa's intrastate conflicts, human rights and democracy, bilateral trade and investment, and the development of an American constituency for Africa.

At the same time that members of the concerned American public were focusing on matters pertaining to a new U.S. leadership after the Cold War, powerful forces were also gathering at home and abroad, pushing the U.S. toward a reduced political-military engagement with Africa. Americans, already uneasy over major new peacekeeping commitments that might prove financially costly and give rise to substantial American casualties, gained some confirmation of their diffuse fears as the UN operation in Somalia II (UNOSOM II), with American operational support, took on the difficult assignment of maintaining a secure environment in Somalia. Armed with an expanded mandate that allowed the UN troops to use force if necessary under Chapter VII of the UN Charter, UNOSOM II set out in earnest to achieve such ambitious objectives as the disarming of the militias. This proved a difficult task, especially as there was no surviving Somali state and weapons were spread throughout the country.

The inability of UN peacekeepers to achieve their mission goals became increasingly evident by June 1993, as Somali National Alliance militiamen assaulted a poorly armed UN patrol, slaying twenty-four Pakistanis and three Americans.[16] The UN Security Council, placing the responsibility for this attack on General Mohamed Farah Aidid, launched a series of raids in an effort to arrest him. At the time, the United States was supportive of the UNOSOM II initiatives, regarding them as "necessary and appropriate response[s]."[17] These forays by reinforced UNOSOM II units culminated in a disastrous battle in central Mogadishu on October 3 that left eighteen American and one Malaysian soldier dead; ninety U.S., Malaysian, and Pakistani soldiers wounded; and many hundreds of Somalis killed or injured. The American contingent was drawn from the highly trained Army

---

[15]Parts of this section draw upon Rothchild and Sisk, "U.S.-Africa Policy," pp. 274–277.

[16]John Drysdale, "Foreign Military Intervention in Somalia: The Root Cause of the Shift from UN Peacekeeping to Peacemaking and Its Consequences," in Walter Clarke and Jeffrey Herbst (eds.), *Learning From Somalia: The Lessons of Armed Humanitarian Intervention* (Boulder, CO Westview, 1997), p. 132.

[17]Michael G. MacKinnon, *The Evolution of US Peacekeeping Policy Under Clinton: A Fairweather Friend?* (London: Frank Cass, 2000), p. 42.

Rangers and Delta Forces; even so, when surrounded by a hostile crowd of Aidid followers in a packed marketplace area, it found itself embattled and under siege, not able to leave the scene of combat until the next morning.

For most Americans, the initial Somali intervention was acceptable as a humanitarian effort; questions arose, however, as the mission's objectives widened. When members of the public were asked on September 23, 1993, whether they thought U.S. troops in Somalia should be responsible for disarming the rival warlords or should be responsible only for making sure that food was delivered to the areas affected by the famine, 22 percent replied they should disarm the warlords, 69 percent said they should only deliver food, and 9 percent indicated they were not sure.[18] On October 5, 1993, when respondents were asked whether the United States should keep troops in Somalia until a functioning civil government was in place, 28 percent agreed, 64 percent disagreed (replying that U.S. troops should be pulled out), and 8 percent had no opinion.[19]

As congress learned about the extent of the troop losses and witnessed television images of Somalis dragging one of the American bodies through the streets of Mogadishu, it prompted opposition on the part of some of its members to a continuation of the Somali peacekeeping initiative. For example, Senator Sam Nunn, an influential and well-informed analyst of American strategy, resisted calls for military support to an enlarged UN mission. Nunn declared, "Our role is too important in areas of the world that are significant to United States military interests, security interests, and economic interests to allow our military effectiveness to be dissipated in places where we have no economic and no security interests."[20] He was not questioning America's international role, only the prudence of a commitment to a humanitarian intervention in Somalia. The October 3 firefight in Mogadishu, and the intense criticism that followed in its wake, clearly represented a critical juncture in U.S. and UN involvement in Somalia. Encountering intense resistance in congress, an embarrassed president, ranking his domestic priorities higher than an expanded peacekeeping effort, avoided a clash with congress. Clinton announced a narrower mission for American troops and an intention to withdraw American forces from Somalia by March 1994.[21] The UN soon followed this lead, with the final withdrawal of UN forces occurring in March 1995.

The calls by the U.S. congress and the American public for a disengagement of U.S. peacekeeping forces in Somalia had broad ramifications for other crisis areas. Even though Presidential Decision Directive (PDD) 25 (which described a limited U.S. role in peacekeeping activities and urged that both U.S. and UN involvement in multilateral peacekeeping operations be more selective and effective)

---

[18]Conducted by Yankelovich Partners Inc., for Time and Cable News Network. Question No. 043. Roper Center for Public Opinion Research. (Miroslav Nincic archives.)

[19]Conducted by ABC News. Question No. 003. Roper Center for Public Opinion Research. (Miroslav Nincic archives.)

[20]*Congressional Record—Senate*, vol. 139, no. 133 (October 5, 1993), p. S13043, and vol. 139, no. 134 (October 6, 1993), p. S13146.

[21]MacKinnon, *The Evolution of US Peacekeeping*, p. 97.

was not finalized until May 1994, U.S. officials were already referring in April 1994 to the guidelines set out by this long-awaited policy statement to argue against peace operations in Rwanda. Then, when the murderous fury ensued in Rwanda in 1994, the U.S. government decided against taking action of a preventative nature, fearing, according to President Clinton, that the risks of strong military action outweighed the potential benefits of intervention.[22] The U.S. government justified its inaction by questioning whether these planned killings in fact constituted a genuine case of genocide. By downplaying the nature and extent of Rwanda's systematic effort to murder its Tutsi and moderate Hutu citizens, the United States was avoiding its obligations under the Genocide Convention. As President Clinton told an audience of genocide survivors during his 1998 trip to Africa, "We in the United States and the world community did not do as much as we could have and should have done to try to limit what occurred in Rwanda in 1994."[23]

The U.S. government, determined to avoid being drawn into multilateral peacekeeping operations, resisted efforts at the United Nations to mount a strong international response. Three days into the crisis, an American delegate at a secret meeting of the UN Security Council reportedly cast serious doubts on whether the small force of UN peacekeepers then in the country should remain on the scene and, on April 12, declared that the peacekeeping mission did not look viable "under current circumstances."[24] On April 21, with full American backing, the UN Security Council voted to withdraw the main body of peacekeepers from Rwanda, leaving behind a token force of 264 troops.[25] Having viewed the crisis in terms of two extreme options— strong military action or withdrawal—policy-makers opted for the least risky course of action. However, as Astri Suhrke and Bruce Jones observe, the failure to recognize the range of choices at hand had fatal consequences in terms of possible reactions to the violence. Because the killings were organized "by a small but determined group of coup makers and carried out by lightly armed thugs and civilians," a relatively small force of professionally trained troops would likely have proved effective in shielding many of the civilians from the violence.[26] Even so, the normal trajectory of minimal engagement held firm and was to haunt U.S. policy-makers for years to come.

This decision became part of a larger administration policy the following month when the long-awaited Presidential Decision Directive on multilateral peace operations was issued. Although PDD 25 recognized that "UN and other multilateral peace operations will at times offer the best way to prevent, contain or resolve

---

[22]Donald Rothchild, "The Impact of U.S. Disengagement on African Intrastate Conflict Resolution," in John W. Harbeson and Donald Rothchild (eds.), *Africa in World Politics: The African State System in Flux* (Boulder: Westview, 2000), p. 179.

[23]Quoted in James Bennet, "Clinton Declares U.S., with World, Failed Rwandans," *New York Times*, March 26, 1998, p. A1.

[24]Correspondent, "How the World Failed to Save Rwanda," *Mail & Guardian* (December 9, 1998).

[25]Ibid.

[26]Astri Suhrke and Bruce Jones, "Preventive Diplomacy in Rwanda: Failure to Act or Failure of Actions," in Bruce W. Jentleson (ed.), *Opportunities Missed, Opportunities Seized: Preventive Diplomacy in the Post–Cold War World* (Lanham: Rowman & Littlefield, 2000), p. 261.

conflicts that could otherwise be more costly and deadly," it emphasized the need to take into consideration such factors as American interests, the existence of a significant threat to international peace and security, the specific objectives of an intervention, and the means to carry out the mission before supporting a UN undertaking.[27] In line with this low-key strategy, some members of congress proposed legislation during the following year to make significant cuts in U.S. contributions to international peacekeeping and to bar U.S. troops from serving under foreign commanders except in specific circumstances. Clearly, Clinton administration policy was shifting from principled multilateral engagement to what Ivo Daalder has described as a "wary endorsement of UN peacekeeping."[28] In line with this shift of emphasis, the U.S. government interpreted its interests narrowly and stood passively on the sidelines in 1994 as intrastate conflicts wreaked havoc not only in Rwanda but also in Sudan, Burundi, and the DR Congo.[29]

## Clinton 1998–2000: The Return to the Normal Trajectory

The period between the formal issuance of PDD 25 and the new millennium was one of mixed signals. Following the U.S. disengagement from Somalia and its passivity in the face of genocide in Rwanda, the Clinton administration seemed lacking in direction on African issues. Only with the president's trip to six African countries in March and April 1998 was some of the lost momentum regained. The Clinton trip coincided with a new effort to develop an American policy that dealt with African issues on security, trade, and democratization. While in Africa, Clinton variously deplored America's treatment of Africa during the Cold War; pledged assistance to deal with the challenges of education, health, and development; and acknowledged the world community's failure to recognize the reality of genocide in Rwanda. Indicating a preparedness to do more in the event that such security emergencies occurred in the future, Clinton told the Rwandans that he had ordered his administration to improve early warning systems, thereby enabling the international community to take preventive action.

In order to gauge the extent of Clinton's reengagement with African affairs after his 1998 trip to the region, it is useful to begin by examining the main areas where he proclaimed and selectively acted upon a liberal internationalist agenda. Four areas stand out in this respect: continuing support for the enlargement of democracy, efforts to increase U.S. trade with Africa, the promise to back a partial write-off of African debts, and sponsorship of the African Crisis Response Initiative (ACRI). It was apparent that the first three objectives were quite in line with domestic American values; moreover, the ACRI training program conformed to the normal trajectory of low-profile American relations with Africa.

---

[27]*The Clinton Administration's Policy on Reforming Multilateral Peace Operations* (May 1994), p. 4. (Typescript copy.)

[28]Ivo H. Daalder, "Knowing When to Say No: The Development of US Policy for Peacekeeping," in William J. Durch (ed.), *UN Peacekeeping, American Politics, and the Uncivil Wars of the 1990s* (New York: St. Martin's Press, 1996), p. 59.

[29]Brian Urquhart, "Foreword" to MacKinnon, *The Evolution of US Peacekeeping*, p. viii.

**Enlarging Democracy.**  Clinton administration support for the principle of enlarging democracy was one of its primary claims to a distinguishable African strategy.[30] Although formulated in the initial years after his coming to power, this principle was referred to intermittently throughout Clinton's time in office.[31] "The successor to a doctrine of containment," declared National Security Adviser Anthony Lake, "must be a strategy of enlargement—enlargement of the world's free community of market democracies."[32] The spread of democratic regimes was seen as being in American interests, because democracies were inclined toward peaceful relations with each other and because the United States could cooperate with them "to counter . . . threats to our mutual security."[33] Certainly, African societies have long been attracted to democratic values and practices. Thus, it came as no surprise when political protesters and leaders, challenging the one-party, authoritarian regimes in the early 1990s, made their appeals for public support in the language of liberal democracy.[34] In attempting to further democratization, the Clinton team championed regular elections and good governance and promoted strong party systems and civil societies. Even so, African governments have all too often eluded the pressures for reform, managing elections and denying oppositions an equal opportunity to organize and compete for political power.

As consistent as the Clinton team was in upholding the principle of democratic enlargement, it found itself constrained in putting its democratic principles into effect. According to the 1999 Freedom House Index, eight African states (15 percent) were classified as free, and twenty-four as partly free (45 percent), a significant increase in electoral democracies as compared with the 1989 data.[35] Nevertheless, as a National Summit on Africa working paper concluded, "for most places on the continent, democratic consolidation is likely to be slow, halting, and uneven—in the short term at least."[36] Such large and important countries as Sudan, (Abacha's) Nigeria, Angola, and DR Congo remained beyond American influences, reflecting both the autonomy of these countries and the cautious engagement of the United States itself. With entrenched elites benefiting from the status quo in these countries, U.S. policy-makers sometimes found it difficult to promote democratic transitions. And in Uganda, Eritrea, Ethiopia, and Rwanda, they prudently backed

[30]Richard Haass, "Fatal Distraction: Bill Clinton's Foreign Policy," *Foreign Policy*, No. 108 (Fall 1997): 113.

[31]Peter J. Schraeder, "Introduction: Trends and Transformation in the Clinton Administration's Foreign Policy Toward Africa (1993–1999)," *Issue: A Journal of Opinion*, 26, No. 2 (1998): 4.

[32]Anthony Lake, "From Containment to Enlargement," School of Advanced International Studies, Johns Hopkins University (September 21, 1993), p. 5.

[33]Susan E. Rice, "The U.S. Stake in a Secure, Prosperous Africa," Washington, D.C., Howard University (November 3, 1999), p. 2.

[34]Michael Bratton and Nicolas van de Walle, *Democratic Experiments in Africa: Regime Transitions in Comparative Perspective* (Cambridge: Cambridge University Press, 1997), pp. 28–29.

[35]Adrian Karatnycky, "The 1999 Freedom House Survey: A Century of Progress," *Journal of Democracy* 11, No. 1 (2000): 193.

[36]Edmond Keller (Chair), National Summit on Africa Expert Group on Democracy and Human Rights, *Democracy and Human Rights* (National Summit on Africa: June 1998), p. 4.

the new men of power, despite their evident tendencies toward authoritarian governance.[37]

The United States itself was not prepared to invest generously in democracy-building. John Harbeson calculated that the United States spent only 8 percent (or $244.24 million) in 1995–96 on development assistance to achieve its democratization objectives, with 90 percent of its support going to thirteen countries in eastern and southern Africa.[38] Subsequent research, using 1997–2000 data, indicated a similar pattern, for the American commitment to democratization in Africa fell to 5.4 percent ($249.477 million) out of a total USAID development assistance allocation of $4,514.3 million. During the 1997–2000 period, moreover, six countries had their democracy assistance suspended for human rights abuses, while other key recipients (such as Angola, Ethiopia, Guinea, Kenya, Zambia, and Zimbabwe) continued to receive democracy assistance despite the undemocratic trends in these states.[39] The call for democratic enlargement remained logical and appealing, but if the United States was not prepared to commit significant resources to the task of promoting democratic institutions, its efforts to nurture political reform were not likely to have a sustained effect.[40]

**Promoting Trade.** In seeking to overcome the widening gap between Africa and the industrialized West, the Clinton administration relied primarily upon trade and market forces (not foreign economic assistance) to stimulate Africa's economic growth. Clinton officials viewed increased trade both as a catalyst to African growth and as a symbol of America's partnership with the continent.[41] Although Africa accounted for a low 1 percent of U.S. total world trade, and 4 percent of U.S. trade with the developing countries, U.S. trade with sub-Saharan Africa has increased positively at a rate of 5 percent a year since 1988 (except for the depressed 1997–98 period). Africa (mainly Nigeria, Angola, and Gabon) accounted for over 16 percent of U.S. petroleum imports, equal to U.S. imports from Venezuela or Mexico. The United States also imported important strategic minerals such as platinum, cobalt, bauxite, and manganese as well as coffee, tea, cocoa, and spices from Africa. On the export side, U.S. trade with Africa was increasing rapidly, including a wide array of industrial machinery, telecommunications equipment, computers, aircraft, and electrical and power generating machinery. These trends point to a potential that can be further tapped into in years to come (see Tables 1 and 2).

[37]Marina Ottaway, *Africa's New Leaders: Democracy or State Reconstruction?* (Washington, DC: Carnegie Endowment for International Peace, 1999).

[38]John W. Harbeson, "The Clinton Administration and the Promotion of Democracy: Practical Imperatives for Theoretical Exploration," *Issue* 26, No. 2 (1998): 39–40.

[39]I am grateful to Nikolas G. Emmanuel, a graduate student in the Department of Political Science at the University of California, Davis, for sharing these research findings with me. Calculated from USAID Fact Sheet, "Assistance to Africa: 1990–2000" (www.info.gov/press/releases/2000/fs000118_3.html); and USAID, FY1997–2000 Congressional Country Reports.

[40]Marina Ottaway and Theresa Chung, "Toward a New Paradigm," *Journal of Democracy* 10, No. 4 (1999): 99–113.

[41]Jim Fisher-Thompson, "Officials Renew U.S. Commitment to Passage of African Trade Bill," February 11, 2000, p. 1 (http://www.eucom.mil/africa/usis/00feb14.htm).

**Table 1:** Major U.S. Imports from African Countries
*(Imports for Consumption, Customs Value, $US Thousands)*

|  | 1988 | 1993 | 1998 |
|---|---|---|---|
| Algeria | 1,805,494 | 1,589,801 | 1,612,294 |
| Angola | 1,217,489 | 2,100,965 | 2,225,141 |
| Cameroon | 217,978 | 101,219 | 53,339 |
| Congo | 375,715 | 500,009 | 314,725 |
| Congo, D.R. | 365,134 | 240,746 | 170,874 |
| Côte d'Ivoire | 297,335 | 178,221 | 423,341 |
| Egypt | 219,118 | 599,660 | 706,908 |
| Ethiopia | 53,800 | 22,063 | 52,278 |
| Gabon | 174,694 | 922,682 | 1,130,273 |
| Ghana | 201,805 | 208,469 | 143,858 |
| Kenya | 63,881 | 92,276 | 99,523 |
| Morocco | 92,375 | 185,045 | 352,197 |
| Namibia | 4,305 | 22,028 | 51,676 |
| Nigeria | 3,284,465 | 5,309,470 | 4,603,620 |
| South Africa | 1,528,429 | 1,851,045 | 3,053,323 |
| Tunisia | 42,484 | 39,717 | 61,134 |
| Zimbabwe | 116,716 | 142,301 | 123,198 |
| **Sub-Saharan Africa** | **8,662,151** | **12,421,815** | **13,359,500** |
| North Africa | 2,159,471 | 2,414,223 | 2,732,533 |
| Total for Africa | 10,821,622 | 14,836,038 | 16,092,033 |

*Source:* USAID, *US Total Imports from Asia and the Near East,* 1999: *http://www.info.usaid.gov/ economic_growth/trdweb/Viewdata/ANE/aneimtot.html;* and USAID, *US Total Imports from Sub- Saharan Africa,* 1999: *http://www.info.usaid.gov/economic_growth/trdweb/Viewdata/ANE/afrimtot.html.*

In helping to create the World Trade Organization in 1995, the Clinton administration highlighted the effort to foster an environment conducive to increasing U.S. trade with the world. Other efforts to construct multilateral arrangements for trade promotion included the North American Free Trade Agreement, the Caribbean Basin Initiative (CBI), and the African Growth and Opportunity Act (AGOA), the latter being combined with the CBI when enacted into law. As President Clinton wrote in a letter to the members of both houses of congress, he regarded AGOA as representing "the legislative cornerstone of our African trade policy."[42] The AGOA Act, originally introduced in 1996, moved slowly through the two houses of congress, being passed by the House in 1998 and then, in amended form the following year, by the Senate. The act, as finally agreed upon by Senate and House leaders in April 2000 (and signed by the president), provided that specific African products, especially textiles and apparel, could enter the American market duty-free, provided that such exports did not exceed 1.5 percent of U.S. textile imports in the initial years, rising to 3.5 percent over an eight-year period. The

[42]"Text: Clinton Reports on Africa Policy to Congress," January 21, 2000 (http://www. eucom.mil/africa/usis/00jan24.htm).

**Table 2:** Major U.S. Exports to African Countries
*(Total Exports, F.A.S. Value, $US Thousands)*

|  | 1988 | 1993 | 1998 |
|---|---|---|---|
| Algeria | 731,229 | 897,977 | 650,168 |
| Angola | 100,981 | 168,660 | 354,303 |
| Cameroon | 31,398 | 48,352 | 75,174 |
| Congo | 20,776 | 27,385 | 92,020 |
| Congo, D.R. | 122,208 | 35,277 | 34,036 |
| Côte d'Ivoire | 75,053 | 88,131 | 151,555 |
| Egypt | 2,095,259 | 2,762,594 | 3,059,794 |
| Ethiopia | 180,635 | 136,621 | 88,379 |
| Gabon | 53,896 | 48,239 | 62,420 |
| Ghana | 117,265 | 214,471 | 223,379 |
| Kenya | 91,287 | 116,476 | 199,029 |
| Morocco | 357,950 | 602,144 | 552,338 |
| Namibia | 2,072 | 19,710 | 51,202 |
| Nigeria | 355,786 | 890,992 | 819,619 |
| South Africa | 1,690,279 | 2,196,766 | 3,626,112 |
| Tunisia | 174,802 | 232,268 | 196,793 |
| Zimbabwe | 34,343 | 83,602 | 93,090 |
| **Sub-Saharan Africa** | **3,700,051** | **4,783,454** | **6,696,917** |
| North Africa | 3,359,240 | 4,494,983 | 4,459,093 |
| Total for Africa | 7,059,291 | 9,278,437 | 11,156,010 |

*Source:* USAID, *US Total Exports to Asia and the Near East*, 1999: *http://www.info.usaid.gov/ economic_growth/trdweb/Viewdata/ANE/aneextot.html*; and USAID, *US Total Exports to Sub-Saharan Africa*, 1999: *http://www.info.usaid.gov/economic_growth/trdweb/Viewdata/ANE/afrextot.html*.

act also included provisions on debt relief (writing off certain loans made to multi-lateral institutions as well as concessional loans made by the government of the United States), access to loans and credits through U.S.-government backed equity funds and insurance schemes, and technical assistance. Although key legislators such as Richard Lugar in the Senate and Ed Royce and Charles Rangel in the House gave the AGOA trade act strong support, a coalition of opponents emerged that included members of congress who feared competition in the sale of textiles and some members of the congressional Black caucus who rejected the conditionalities on African participation built into the legislation.[43] Among the latter group, Representative Jesse L. Jackson, Jr., who criticized the act's insufficient concern for African debt relief and AIDS, dismissed AGOA as "worse than no bill at all."[44]

[43]"USA/Africa: Battle lines in Washington and Africa,"*Africa Confidential* 40, No. 7 (April 2, 1999), pp. 1–2. See also Daniel P. Volman, "The Clinton Administration and Africa: Role of Congress and the Africa Subcommittee," *Issue: A Journal of Opinion* 26, No. 2 (1998), pp. 15–16; and Shelly Leanne, "The Clinton Administration and Africa: Perspective of the Congressional Black Caucus and TransAfrica," *ibid.*, p. 20.

[44]Eric Schmitt, "Deal Reached on Bill to Help African and Caribbean Trade," *New York Times*, April 15, 2000, p. A1.

**A Partial Debt Write-Off.**   The origins of Africa's debt crisis can be traced back to the dramatic rise in oil prices that took place in 1973 and the heavy demand for loans in the developing countries afterwards. In the period that followed, external indebtedness increased steadily as commodity prices fell, exports failed to rise rapidly enough, local currencies became overvalued, governments pursued wasteful policies and mismanaged their investments, and foreign bankers became increasingly cautious in their lending practices. Structural adjustment reforms, intended to unleash new productive forces, also contributed over time to the debt burden. As one Ghanaian social scientist bemoaned, "the ERP [Economic Recovery Program] has not only increased the level of indebtedness but has increased debt servicing to unrealistically high levels."[45] By 1998, Africa's level of external indebtedness was estimated to be $176 billion, primarily "official" debt owed to Western creditor countries, the World Bank, and the International Monetary Fund (see Table 3).[46] Such levels of indebtedness complicated economic reform, because of the lack of available capital for new investments and the "deterrent effect" that such large debt obligations had on potential investors.[47]

Recognizing that debt reduction was essential if sustained economic development was to take place, Clinton policy-makers joined others in proposing measures to give Africa some relief from its debt and debt servicing burdens. The Clinton team resisted an across-the-board cancellation of current debts, arguing that such a move would complicate Africa's ability to secure future credit and would fail to distinguish between governments that managed their economies responsibly and those that did not.[48] Nevertheless, the administration provided various debt relief initiatives. It made a commitment to forgive $250 million in official nonconcessional debt under the Paris Club of creditor countries and forgave more than $1.2 billion in official bilateral debt owed by twenty of Africa's poorest countries.[49] U.S. officials also worked closely with other creditor countries under the Heavily Indebted Poor Countries (HIPC) debt relief initiative. Under this scheme, those countries prepared to enter into and implement the IMF/World Bank reform plans would have debts they owe to the Fund and the Bank reduced or canceled. The HIPC program, which began in 1996, received an important boost in March 1999 when Clinton called for its expansion. He proposed an additional $3 billion in U.S. bilateral debt reduction and the leveraging by the international community of an additional $70 billion in

[45]Kodwo Ewusi, quoted in Donald Rothchild, "Ghana and Structural Adjustment: An Overview," in D. Rothchild (ed.), *Ghana: The Political Economy of Recovery* (Boulder: Lynne Rienner, 1991), pp. 10–11.

[46]Thomas M. Callaghy, "Africa and the World Political Economy: More Caught Between a Rock and a Hard Place," in Harbeson and Rothchild (eds.), *Africa in World Politics*, 3rd ed., p. 63.

[47]Thomas M. Callaghy and John Ravenhill, "How Hemmed In? Lessons and Prospects of Africa's Responses to Decline," in T. Callaghy and J. Ravenhill, *Hemmed In: Responses to Africa's Economic Decline* (New York: Columbia University Press, 1993), pp. 526, 552.

[48]USIS Washington File, "Text: Fact Sheet on U.S.-Africa Partnership Ministerial," March 17, 1999, p. 4 (http://www.eucom.mil/africa/usis/99mar17a.htm).

[49]Bureau of African Affairs, State Department, "U.S. Assistance and Debt Relief in Sub-Saharan Africa," March 27, 1998 (http://www.state.gov/www/regions/africa/fs_debtrelief_971204.html).

**Table 3:** Highly Indebted African States
*(in $US Millions)*

|  | 1980 | 1998 |
|---|---|---|
| Algeria | 19,365 | 30,665 |
| Angola | ? | 12,173 |
| Cameroon | 2,588 | 9,829 |
| Congo, Rep. | 1,526 | 5,119 |
| Congo, D.R. | 4,770 | 12,929 |
| Côte d'Ivoire | 7,462 | 14,852 |
| Egypt | 19,131 | 31,964 |
| Ethiopia | 824 | 10,352 |
| Ghana | 1,398 | 6,884 |
| Kenya | 3,387 | 7,010 |
| Morocco | 9,258 | 20,687 |
| Mozambique | ? | 8,208 |
| Nigeria | 8,921 | 30,315 |
| South Africa | ? | 24,711 |
| Tanzania | 5,322 | 7,603 |
| Tunisia | 3,527 | 11,078 |
| Zambia | 3,244 | 6,865 |
| **Sub-Saharan Africa** | **60,820** | **230,132** |
|  |  | **(65.5% of 1998 GDP)** |
| **North Africa** | **83,836** | **94,394** |
|  |  | **(47.7% of 1998 GDP)** |
| **Total for Africa** | **144,656** | **324,526** |
|  |  | **(59.1% of 1998 GDP)** |

*Source:* World Bank (2000) "External Debt," *World Bank Development Indicators*, Washington, DC: World Bank, 248–250, <http://www.worldbank.org/data/wdi2000/pdfs/tab4_18.pdf>.
*GDP Source:* World Bank, *African Development Indicators*, Washington, DC:World Bank, 1999 <http://www.worldbank.org/data/countrydata/adi/adi2–1.pdf>.

debt. Although the U.S.–Africa Ministerial Conference (that included senior ministers from forty-six sub-Saharan African states), praised the Clinton proposals for debt relief, it raised questions about the conditionalities under the HIPC program as well as its underfunding.[50] Although the level of support that the U.S. government would be able to secure from congress for its debt initiatives remained uncertain, it was encouraging to see that congress did authorize some $445 million for this purpose in late 2000.[51]

**Sponsorship of ACRI.** During his trip to Rwanda in March 1998, President Clinton spoke of the need to take action to prevent future threats of genocide. His call for the development of a deterrent capacity in the event of new emergencies gained substance as plans for some type of rapid reaction force were consid-

[50]U.S. Department of State, "Susan E. Rice et al., Briefing on final day of U.S.-Africa Ministerial Conference," Washington, D.C. March 18, 1999 (http://www.state.gov/www/regions/africa/).
[51]Peter Lewis, Comment, November 4, 2000.

ered. Initial American proposals in 1996 for an African Crisis Response Force (ACRF) encountered opposition from members of the U.S. congress, who voiced concerns over the potential costs of the program and the possibility that it might lead to new American interventions in African conflicts.[52] The ACRF proposal also encountered strong resistance in Africa and Western Europe, where it was regarded as vague on relations with the UN and other international organizations, unclear as to the nature of command and control, and lacking in specifics on external support.[53]

In response to this criticism, the Clinton administration revamped the proposal the following year and gained congressional acceptance for a more modest arrangement with a new name—the African Crisis Response Initiative (ACRI). The new program avoided the standing military force approach and sought instead to enhance the capacity of democratic African partner states to respond to evidences of violence or humanitarian emergencies on the continent. As Ambassador Marshall McCallie, the Special Coordinator of the ACRI Interagency Working Group, noted in 1998, the objective of the Initiative was "to assist in developing rapidly-deployable, interoperable battalions and companies from stable democratic countries that can work together to maintain peace."[54] Proceeding in partnership with Western European countries, ACRI military trainers began offering technical assistance to some 12,000 African troops drawn from battalion-sized units in Senegal, Uganda, Malawi, Mali, Ghana, Benin, and Côte d'Ivoire. Deployment of ACRI-trained units was a decision made by the ACRI states in response to a call from the UN, the OAU, or an African subregional organization. The program had some limited impact in the initial period. Mali and Ghana sent forces to Sierra Leone, Benin dispatched a unit to Guinea-Bissau, and Senegalese troops were engaged under the UN mission in the Central African Republic.[55] In sponsoring ACRI, the United States was edging away from the paralysis in peacekeeping activities that had gripped it after the Somali debacle. Yet its commitments under the scheme were minimal, amounting to some $20 million annually in the 1997–2000 years.[56] Moreover, in training Africans to take on the military tasks that the United States and the international community were not prepared to assume, ACRI could be interpreted as an undertaking that had the long-term effect of enabling the U.S. government to remain on the sidelines as new crises surfaced.

[52]Daniel Volman, "The Development of the African Crisis Response Initiative,"*Africa Policy Report*, April 23, 1998, p. 1 (http://www.africanews.org/usaf/stories/volman0427.htm).

[53]Dan Henk and Steven Metz, *The United States and the Transformation of African Security: The African Crisis Response Initiative and Beyond* (Carlisle, PA: Strategic Studies Institute, U.S. Army War College, 1997), p. 23.

[54]Marshall F. McCallie, "The African Crisis Response Initiative (ACRI): America's Engagement for Peace in Africa," speech delivered at the "Emerald Express" Symposium, Camp Pendleton, CA, April 8, 1998, p. 1.

[55]Jim Fisher-Thompson, "Secretary of State Albright Highlights U.S. Africa Initiative," October 18, 1999, p. 1 (http://www.eucom.mil/programs/acari/usis/99oct18.htm).

[56]Craig M. Brandt, "Legislation and Policy: Fiscal Year 1999 Security Assistance Legislation," *DISAM Journal* (Spring 1999), p. 21. See also International Institute for Strategic Studies, *Strategic Review 1998/99* (London: Oxford University Press, 1999), p. 281.

In sum, in supporting the policies discussed before on liberal democracy, enhanced trade, and partial debt relief, the Clinton administration was pursuing goals that were minimally costly for the United States and were compatible with American values. "Clinton's strategy," writes Stephen Walt, "is hegemony on the cheap, because that is the only strategy the American people are likely to support."[57] However, as the potential costs and risks of the engagement rose and as congress resisted U.S. commitments in Africa, the Clinton reaction in the post-Somali period was generally prudent and circumspect. This caution has been similarly evident in American policy toward foreign economic assistance and UN peacekeeping and peace implementation.

**Foreign Economic Assistance.** The end of the Cold War had a significant impact on American priorities regarding economic assistance to Africa. No longer driven by the perceived need to compete with the Soviet Union strategically and ideologically, feeling less pressured to extend aid as a result of West European and World Bank assistance programs, and disappointed over the ineffectiveness of aid in achieving economic development in the absence of a local reform process, U.S. policy-makers in the 1990s exhibited little sense of urgency about providing direct development assistance to many states in Africa. During the Cold War period, the existence of common security interests with African countries (such as opposition to a Soviet proxy state or access to military facilities) proved an important factor in determining U.S. aid levels—and sometimes quite irrespective of the authoritarian and repressive character of the regime involved (for example, Liberia, Somalia, and Sudan).[58] However, as Cold War competition ceased, U.S. commercial and business activities grew in importance, and trade gained a higher priority than aid as a means of accelerating Africa's growth and development. The doubts of donors increased as foreign assistance sometimes overwhelmed local institutional capacity to implement agreed-upon programs and as incentives for local savings and extractions were at times undermined by external aid.[59] Without the presence of a favorable policy environment (including macroeconomic stability, trade openness, secure property rights, the rule of law, and the absence of corruption), U.S. aid officials were more and more inclined to allow aid levels to drift lower and to become more selective in choosing who should receive aid.[60] In addition, as likely returns on U.S. investments and the pursuit of structural adjustment and democratization objectives became important criteria, governments that resisted political and economic reforms

[57]Stephen M. Walt, "Two Cheers for Clinton's Foreign Policy," *Foreign Affairs* 79, No. 2 (March/April 2000), p. 79.

[58]Peter J. Schraeder, Steven W. Hook, and Bruce Taylor, "Clarifying the Foreign Aid Puzzle: A Comparison of American, Japanese, French and Swedish Aid Flows," *World Politics* 50, No. 2 (January 1998), pp. 310–311.

[59]Deborah Brautigam, "State Capacity and Effective Governance," in Benno Ndulu and Nicolas van de Walle (eds.), *Agenda for Africa's Economic Renewal* (New Brunswick: Transaction Publishers, 1996), p. 98.

[60]Carol Lancaster, "Africa in World Affairs," in Harbeson and Rothchild (eds.), *Africa in World Politics*, p. 219.

(such as Gambia, Zimbabwe, and DR Congo) witnessed sharp declines in assistance.

As Table 4 indicates (and keeping in mind the effects of inflation on the value of this assistance), continuing declines in U.S. economic development allocations to Africa were apparent. Despite a domestic economic boom, the United States devoted a smaller percentage of its GNP to economic assistance to sub-Saharan Africa (0.01 percent of GNP in 1998) than any other industrialized society.[61] This reluctance to commit to foreign aid was more than a partisan matter, but represented, according to Peter Schraeder, "the consensus viewpoint" in both the executive and the legislature.[62] Not only was development assistance reduced from the 1992 level, but also deep cuts were made in the Development Fund for Africa. As budgetary pressures eased in the late 1990s, overall foreign aid levels stabilized, and a request was made for the provision of $533 million for the Development Fund for Africa under

**Table 4:**  U.S. Economic Assistance to Africa
*FY 1987–2000 (in current $US Millions)*

| FY | Development Assistance[a] | Economic Support | Food Aid Funds[b] | Foreign Disaster Assistance and Rehabilitation[c] | Total |
|---|---|---|---|---|---|
| 1987 | 396.2 | 164.8 | 400.3 | 16.6 | 77.9 |
| 1988 | 572.0 | 39.7 | 525.5 | 37.4 | 1,174.6 |
| 1989 | 587.5 | 99.3 | 385.8 | 32.3 | 1,104.9 |
| 1990 | 612.5 | 28.9 | 447.6 | 30.9 | 1,119.9 |
| 1991 | 826.3 | 59.3 | 613.0 | 40.3 | 1,538.9 |
| 1992 | 872.4 | 37.8 | 935.6 | 87.6 | 1,933.4 |
| 1993 | 821.6 | 22.4 | 674.3 | 168.9 | 1,687.2 |
| 1994 | 826.7 | 16.1 | 635.1 | 139.6 | 1,617.5 |
| 1995 | 869.8 | 5.0 | 555.4 | 116.9 | 1,547.1 |
| 1996 | 715.6 | 0.7 | 455.9 | 71.8 | 1,244.0 |
| 1997 | 688.8 | 11.8 | 356.4 | 123.1 | 1,180.1 |
| 1998 | 727.5 | 9.9 | 448.4 | 105.7 | 1,291.5 |
| 1999 | 738.6 | 92.0 | 224.5 | 93.9 | 1,149.0 |
| 2000 | 736.8 | 62.5 | 134.4 | TBD[d] | 933.7 |

[a]Includes DFA, DA, Sahel, other OYB transfers.
[b]Includes Title I, although administered by USDA after 1991. Includes Section 416 and emergency food aid. Includes transport costs for Title II and Section 416, beginning in FY 1985.
[c]FY 93 includes $100 million from the African Disaster Assistance Account.
[d]To be decided.
*Source:* Statistics for Fiscal Years 1995–2000 retrieved on January 10, 2000, from http://www.info.usaid.gov/press/releases/2000/fs000118_3.html.

[61]Calculated from World Bank, ("Total GNP 1998, Atlas Method," World Development Indicators Database, July 1, 1999, p. 1 (www.worldbank.org/data/databytopic/GNP.pdf); and OECD/DAC, "Aid at a Glance:USA," *1999 Development Cooperation Report* (http://www.oecd.org/dac/htm/agusa.htm).
[62]Peter J. Schraeder, "Foreign Assistance in Francophone Africa," *Journal of Modern African Studies* 33, No. 4 (December 1995), pp. 559–560.

the FY2001 budget.[63] Even so, the trend in foreign aid allocations was downward, and the domestic constituency demanding a change in these priorities remained relatively small.

In limiting the extent of foreign aid, the government appeared to be clearly in line with the sentiments of the general public. Thus, the 1998 survey sponsored by the Chicago Council on Foreign Relations found a continuance in the long-term trend of low support for external economic assistance; some 45 percent of the public resisted extending such aid in the 1995 survey, with the percentage of aid opponents rising to 48 percent in 1998. Nevertheless, even though the American public remained cautious about broad, long-term aid commitments, it did rally in the face of drought, floods, and other types of emergency situations in Africa and elsewhere. An indication of public altruism was the support of a substantial majority of Chicago Council on Foreign Relations respondents for combating world hunger, an objective these respondents regarded as an important goal of U.S. foreign policy.[64]

The actions of U.S. government officials were largely in line with these public preferences, as Table 4 indicates. Whereas foreign aid and food assistance declined during the 1990s, the allocations for foreign disaster assistance and rehabilitation increased noticeably in FY1993 and FY1994, the period when the Somalia and Rwanda relief operations reached their peak. This preparedness to act in the face of emergencies has continued. For example, as severe flooding occurred in early 2000 along the low-lying river areas in Maputo Province in Mozambique, the U.S. committed $12.8 million from U.S. Agency for International Development and Department of Defense funds to support disaster relief operations, and the president announced an intention to augment U.S. assistance efforts substantially in the months ahead.[65]

Such a willingness to rise to the challenge of short-term emergency relief was important in terms of alleviating human suffering, but it did not counterbalance the overriding need to attend to long-term policies that result in an environment favorable for economic development. As Nicolas van de Walle and Timothy Johnston have observed on the many important achievements of aid over the past decades, "Individual aid efforts have helped to improve physical infrastructure, improve health and education, and introduce new agricultural technologies across the African landscape."[66] Certainly, past assistance indicates that false optimism about the correlation between aid and development is not warranted. In most cases, a fa-

[63]Carol Lancaster, *Aid to Africa: So Much to Do, So Little Done* (Chicago: University of Chicago Press, 1999), p. 91; and U.S. Agency for International Development, *USAID's FY2001 Budget Request: Summary*, March 15, 2000, p. 1 (http://www.info.usaid.gov/press/releases/2000/budget2001.html) .

[64]John E. Rielly (ed.), *American Public Opinion and U.S. Foreign Policy 1995* (Chicago: Chicago Council on Foreign Relations, 1995), p. 31; and John E. Rielly, "Americans and the World: A Survey at Century's End," *Foreign Policy*, No. 114 (Spring 1999): 105–107.

[65]The White House, Office of the Press Secretary, *Statement by the President*, March 1, 2000 (http://www.usia.gov/regional/af/mozambique/e0030102.htm); and "Relief Pours Into Flood-Ravaged-Parts of Southern Africa," *Foreign Broadcast Information Service*, Daily Report, Sub-Saharan Africa, 2000, No. 0229 (February 29, 2000).

[66]Nicolas van de Walle and Timothy A. Johnston, *Improving Aid to Africa*, Policy Essay No. 21 (Washington, DC: Overseas Development Council, 1996), p. 2.

vorable policy environment must be in place before aid can be expected to lead to growth and development. Nevertheless, unless the United States is prepared to be generous in funding economic assistance when the right circumstances are in place, Africa may remain desperate for critically needed technical, infrastructural, and economic support in the years ahead. The United States cannot afford to appear indifferent in an increasingly desperate situation.

**Peacekeeping and Peace Implementation.**   Another major area of cautious Clinton policy-making in the post-Somali period has been that of conflict management and transformation. As of 1998, fourteen of Africa's fifty-three countries were plagued by armed conflicts, most of which were civil wars.[67] A return to stable relations in the DR Congo, Angola, Sierra Leone, and along the Ethiopian-Eritrean border is critical to the well-being of these countries and their surrounding regions. It was clearly in American national interests to help end Africa's terrible civil wars, for they involved frightful suffering, political instability, and economic retardation.[68] In seeking to enlarge the number of liberal democratic regimes in Africa and elsewhere, the Clinton administration was partly motivated by the goal of encouraging moderate politics, both as a good in itself and as a means of keeping politics manageable. Such moderation sought to avoid winner-takes-all mind-sets, with the latter's potential for group fear and the escalation of violence.

In pursuing its objectives on conflict management and transformation, the Clinton administration followed a number of strategies after the Somali debacle, most of which were low in costs and risks. These approaches could be grouped under the headings of communicating between adversaries, providing them with information, exhortation, mediation, assistance (economic and military), pressures and incentives (including side payments, reassurances, legitimation, diplomatic influences, and sanctions[69]), support for regional organizations and the OAU, and military training (under the ACRI initiative). Although all of these options were potentially important in terms of advancing the peace process, it is necessary here, for reasons of space, to focus on the critical alternatives of mediation and support for regional and continental African organizations.

The Clinton administration was following the example of its predecessors as it pursued the course of direct mediation. Clearly, a powerful global actor such as the United States, with enormous political and economic resources at its disposal, was favorably situated to organize negotiations, offer new options to adversaries, attempt to influence their preferences, and help stabilize the implementation of agreements. In the past, Assistant Secretary of State Chester Crocker's mediation of the international conflicts in Angola and Namibia in the 1980s and his successor,

---

[67]Peter Wallensteen and Margareta Sollenberg, "Armed Conflict 1989–98," *Journal of Peace Research* 36, No. 5 (1999): 596.

[68]Anthony Lake, speech at OAU Headquarters, Addis Ababa, December 15, 1994, as reprinted in "Afro-realism vs. Afro-pessimism," *CSIS Africa Notes*, No. 168 (January 1995): 3.

[69]Donald Rothchild, *Managing Ethnic Conflict in Africa: Pressures and Incentives for Cooperation* (Washington, D.C.: Brookings, 1997), chapters 2, 4, and 9.

Herman Cohen's, coordination of the regime transition in Ethiopia in 1991, represented high points in U.S. efforts to take the lead in African peacemaking.[70]

The Clinton administration has at times attempted to follow these precedents, engaging, for example, in a direct mediation effort in support of an OAU initiative to end the highly destructive Ethiopian-Eritrean war. Although this confrontation flared up over a disputed border area around Badme, it also appears to have had its roots in wider territorial claims, the uses of local currencies across state borders, and Ethiopia's access to Eritrean ports. With troop losses running into the tens of thousands, the Clinton administration soon became involved in efforts to restore peace to the region. Initial efforts by Susan Rice, in conjunction with Rwandan diplomats, to broker a settlement proved unsuccessful. Some headway was achieved in negotiating acceptance of a moratorium on air strikes following President Clinton's phone calls to the leaders of both countries, but the ground war continued, placing heavy human and material burdens on both countries. Subsequently, the U.S.-Rwanda peace proposals provided the basis for the OAU plan on containing the conflict. This plan, which had important backing from U.S. diplomats, provided for the withdrawal of Eritrean troops from the contested area, the reestablishment of Ethiopian administration in Badme, the deployment of a peacekeeping force for six months along the 600-mile border, the demilitarization of the Badme zone, the delineation of the border under UN supervision within a six-month period, and an end to the expulsions of the nationals of the rival country.[71] Anthony Lake, the former U.S. National Security Advisor, shuttled frequently between the capitals of Asmara and Addis Ababa in 1999 and 2000, attempting to build support for the OAU agreement and the modalities and technical provisions for its implementation. As heavy fighting took a terrible toll in the spring of 2000, Lake worked with Algerian mediators to hammer out an agreement on a cease-fire and the deployment of a UN peacekeeping force along the 15-mile buffer zone inside Eritrea until the border is finally demarcated.[72] In late 2000, the UN Mission in Ethiopia and Eritrea (UNMEE) began deploying a 4,200-strong UN peacekeeping force led by the Netherlands to patrol the border and to firm up the cease-fire. The signs are cautiously hopeful, but whether, in light of the prevailing climate of distrust in the region, a final agreement can be negotiated remains to be seen.

Given the difficulties in the way of achieving peace by means of direct mediation, it was not surprising that U.S. policy-makers, with limited leverage in Africa, turned increasingly to indirect types of mediatory activities—that is, working behind the scenes under the auspices of another state, international organization, or private actor. With African sensitivities about Western involvement in the continent's internal affairs continuing in evidence, indirect mediation often proved the

---

[70]See Chester A. Crocker, *High Noon in Southern Africa: Making Peace in a Rough Neighborhood* (New York: Norton, 1992); and Herman J. Cohen, *Intervening in Africa: Superpower Peacemaking in a Troubled Continent* (New York: St. Martin's Press, 2000).

[71]"Ethiopia: AFP Details OAU Peace Plan on Ethiopia, Eritrea," *FBIS*-AFR-98-313 (November 9, 1998).

[72]Reuters Newswire 2000, "Ethiopia, Eritrea Sign Peace Deal to End Border War," June 18.

most prudent route for achieving basic U.S. goals on conflict management and transformation. The effectiveness of this low-profile approach lay in its ability to combine the political legitimacy of the middle power, international organization, or private third-party actor with the economic and political resources of a great power—and at a relatively low cost to the United States.

In the 1980s and early 1990s, U.S. diplomats frequently assumed important supporting roles in the negotiations over Zimbabwe, Mozambique, Angola (1991 and 1994), Namibia, and South Africa. Later, with Clinton determined to play a role in mitigating African conflicts without arousing public ire at home, it was not surprising that his administration often found indirect mediation to be an attractive course of action. Clinton's involvement under the auspices of other lead negotiators assumed various forms, including advancing the OAU and UN initiative in Rwanda, assisting the Economic Community of West African States mediation efforts in Liberia and Sierra Leone, backing the Intergovernmental Authority on Development attempt to develop a framework for peace in the Sudan, and supporting the Carter Center efforts to broker the 1999 Uganda-Sudanese agreement on restoring ties and exchanging prisoners. In Burundi, presidential envoy Howard Wolpe gave key international support to former Tanzanian President Julius Nyerere's efforts and, after Nyerere's death, to former South African President Nelson Mandela's attempts to facilitate the peace process, even meeting on his own with Burundian officials to bring the warring parties to a negotiated settlement.

In the DR Congo's spreading war, which involved not only President Laurent Kabila's government forces and the various insurgent movements but also troops from Angola, Zimbabwe, Namibia, and Chad on the side of Kabila and units from Rwanda, Uganda, Burundi, and UNITA in association with two Congolese rebel movements, peace seemed a possibility as the two sides accepted a cease-fire agreement in Lusaka negotiated in July 1999 under the leadership of Zambian President Frederick Chiluba. However, the cease-fire faltered as fighting broke out intermittently, raising doubts about the durability of the agreement. In an effort to shore up the cease-fire, U.S. Ambassador to the United Nations Richard Holbrooke, acting in his capacity as president of the Security Council, declared January 2000 the month of Africa. Holbrooke, focusing world attention on the destructive conflicts in the DR Congo, invited seven African presidents to New York where, under the spotlight of world attention, they pledged to uphold the cease-fire agreement. "New York," Bizima Karaha, the intelligence director of the rebel Congolese Rally for Democracy declared, "has rescued the Lusaka peace process."[73]

Karaha's statement proved overly optimistic, however. The fighting continued, not only between the government forces and the rebels but between the rebel militia groups and between their external supporters. In this very confused situation, the Kabila government signed a new agreement with a seven-member UN Security Council delegation led by Ambassador Holbrooke in May 2000 allowing UN peacekeepers

[73]"Congo Rebels Take Part in Talks," January 28, 2000 (www.washingtonpost.com/wp-dyn/world/specials/africa/congo/A44131–2000Jan28.html).

access to areas under Congo government control and guaranteeing protection for UN personnel. However, the fighting that erupted around this time between Rwanda and Ugandan troops in the Kisangani area and Kabila's continuing unwillingness to allow UN monitors to visit certain areas raised questions about the seriousness of Kabila's commitment. The tensions eased somewhat when President Laurent Kabila was assassinated in January 2001 and his son, Joseph Kabila, succeeded him in office. In a change of stance regarding the peace process, the new Congolese president accepted the former president of Botswana, Sir Ketumile Masire, as facilitator of the stalled inter-Congolese dialogue. African leaders in the region moved closer to deescalating the conflict by beginning to implement the 2000 disengagement plan and pulling their forces back nine miles from the front lines. The United Nations, heartened by this progress, began deploying a unit of "blue helmets" in late March to monitor the cease-fire and the disengagement of troops.

In supporting multilateral and other types of third-party peacemaking initiatives, the United States assumed only limited risks and costs to further regional stability in Africa. It thereby avoided being targeted as a political intervener in Africa's internal affairs and eluded domestic censure. U.S. hesitation to commit American troops to major peacekeeping operations in part represented a holdover of the PDD 25 mind-set, with its strict standards on the participation of U.S. military personnel in a UN or other peace operation. It also reflected the legitimate concerns of U.S. policy-makers over the ineffectiveness of UN peacekeepers in coping with military challenges in such places as Sierra Leone. In that West African confrontation, rebel Revolutionary United Front forces successfully delayed the process of disarmament and demobilization that had been agreed to under the peace plan, and they kept the UN peacekeeping force from the lucrative diamond-mining areas under insurgent control, killing four Kenyan soldiers and capturing up to five hundred Zambian, Kenyan, Indian, and Nigerian troops. The ineffectiveness of the UN peacekeepers under battle conditions raised serious questions about the credibility of a UN intervention against entrenched local insurgents who secured arms and exported their diamonds to world markets through a neighboring state (Liberia). Ambassador Holbrooke, at a ceremony in the Congo, commented that the poor showing of peacekeepers in Sierra Leone cast a "potential shadow" on UN operations, and he contended that it would make it more difficult to persuade the U.S. congress to finance peacekeeping operations elsewhere.[74]

In addition, the 1998 Chicago Council on Foreign Relations survey illustrated the general public's aversion to the use of U.S. troops in foreign military interventions.[75] Another survey conducted in June 1999 provided some insight into the reasons for this aversion. Thus, 57 percent of respondents stated that they were concerned over the financial cost of sending U.S. troops to Kosovo, and 79 percent of respondents asserted that they were worried that U.S. troops might suffer casual-

[74]Norimitsu Onishi, "A Shadow on Africa," *New York Times*, May 5, 2000, p. A1.

[75]John E. Rielly, "Americans and the World: A Survey at Century's End," *Foreign Policy*, No. 114 (Spring 1999), pp. 106–107.

ties as part of their peacekeeping mission there.[76] Congress, which employed similar arguments to pressure the Clinton administration to oppose American peacekeeping operations in Somalia, made use of such public misgivings "to bolster their demands . . . for the curtailment of [U.S. participation in] UN peace-keeping activities in Africa and other parts of the world."[77] Subsequently, peacekeeping became an issue in the 2000 presidential campaign, with Al Gore arguing for active U.S. participation in preventing conflicts abroad, whereas George W. Bush supported a new division of labor under which the European countries would have increasing responsibility for peacekeeping and the U.S. would concentrate on deterring and combating hostile actions in Asia, the Middle East, and elsewhere.[78]

As a result, the Clinton administration had to tread warily on the issue of committing peacekeepers to critical African conflicts. In the DR Congo conflict, with Ambassador Holbrooke pressing for action, the UN Security Council voted 15 to 0 to authorize a 5,500 member force to monitor the cease-fire. The effectiveness of this response was open to question, for the force was roughly one-third the size of the one approved for much smaller Sierra Leone. It is not surprising that one UN military officer estimated that more than 100,000 troops would be required to enforce a peace between the various belligerents on the Congolese scene.[79] Perhaps as a recognition of this requirement, the Security Council delayed deploying the DR Congo units until the parties to the conflict started pulling back their forces and indicated that they would respect the cease-fire. A senior U.S. administration official underlined the limited American involvement in the undertaking, telling a press briefing just prior to the Security Council vote that the proposed DR Congo operation would be a UN mission and that the administration did not envision any participation by U.S. troops.[80] Thus, the United States was leading the call for an expanded UN Observer Mission in the DR Congo but, true to PDD 25 and congressional and public preferences, was refraining from joining the peacekeeping force.[81] Such reluctance to participate in a peacekeeping mission pushed by a great power inevitably raised questions about the credibility of international commitments. In this regard, it is significant that a growing sentiment within the UN itself, recognizing past failures in intervening in African conflicts as well as the lack of political will on the part of some member states for an overly assertive approach, expressed itself in favor of greater selectivity in

[76]Princeton Survey Research Associates, *New Interest Index Poll*, Accession Numbers 0330405 and 0330406 (Storrs, Connecticut, University of Connecticut: Roper Center, June 15, 1999).

[77]Daniel P. Volman, "The Clinton Administration and Africa: Role of Congress and the Africa Subcommittee," *Issue: A Journal of Opinion* 26, No. 2 (1998), pp. 15–16.

[78]Michael R. Gordon, "Bush Would Stop U.S. Peacekeeping in Balkan Fights," *New York Times*, October 21, 2000, p. A1.

[79]Glen McKenzie, "Congo's Govt. Readies for War," May 5, 2000, p. 1 (A HREF = "mailto: AOL News" >AOL News</A>).

[80]Press Briefing on National Africa Summit, Washington, D.C. (February 17, 2000), p. 4 (http://www.state.gov/www/regions/africa/).

[81]See "Prepared Testimony of Richard C. Holbrooke, United States Ambassador to the United Nations, Before the House International Relations Committee Subcommittee on Africa," *Federal News Service*, February 15, 2000, pp. 1–2 (Lexus-Nexus Academic Universe).

undertaking peacekeeping missions while calling for the commitment of more "robust peacekeeping forces" to the field once the decision to intercede was made.[82]

# CONCLUSION

Regardless of an activist foreign policy orientation, the U.S. trajectory on Africa has, on the whole, tended toward a low-profile involvement.[83] American interests are real but for the most part limited, allowing successive U.S. administrations to adopt "satisficing" (ie, satisfying and sufficing) strategies on African issues. To be sure, there have been notable exceptions (such as the 1986 Comprehensive Anti-Apartheid Act, the 1988 mediation of the Angola-Namibia accords, and the humanitarian intervention in Somalia), but in general, American administrations, Republican and Democratic alike, have been cautious in their engagements with Africa. The Clinton administration, despite its rhetoric on partnership, held firm to the post–World War II trend of limited involvement. Its initiatives on enlarging democracy, promoting trade, backing a partial debt write-off, and sponsoring ACRI represented low-cost and low-risk efforts that were largely in line with American interests and values. Its record on foreign economic assistance and peacekeeping was hardly what one would expect of a great power. In acting pragmatically, the Clinton administration was responding in part to the preferences of members of congress and of the general public and in part to the inherent difficulties of achieving results in the face of severe regional obstacles.

In the initial period, George W. Bush and his new team do not appear to have given much thought to the daunting problem of Africa's marginalization. As Bush candidly remarked during the presidential campaign: "While Africa may be important, it doesn't fit into the national strategic interests."[84] Bush officals are concerned primarily with security challenges to American global interests and with resisting high profile U.S. involvement in the internal affairs of other countries. As was true with the Reagan administration, these officials are again narrowing the foreign policy agenda to what they perceive as essential. Bush II policymakers do not seem likely to be drawn into major conflict prevention efforts or new multidimensional peacekeeping operations. They have cut the number of special envoys back by a third—a sign that the new administration has no yearning to send its diplomats "to fill the empty seats at bargaining tables."[85] And when intense conflict has taken place, they have exhibited no penchant to become an active part of the conflict management process through mediation of the dispute.

[82]Executive Summary, UN General Assembly, *Report of the Panel on United Nations Peace Operations*, 55th Sess., A/55/305 (August 21, 2000), p. xi.

[83]Michael H. Hunt, *Ideology and U.S. Foreign Policy* (New Haven: Yale University Press, 1987), p. 177.

[84]Quotes in Ian Fisher, "Africans Ask if Washington's Sun Will Shine on Them," *New York Times* (February 8, 2001), p. A3.

[85]Alan Sipress, "Bush Retreats From U.S. Role as Peace Broker," *Washington Post,* (March 17, 2001), p. A1.

Within the new Bush administration itself, signs of bureaucratic dissonance are already surfacing. Whereas Donald Rumsfeld, the Secretary of Defense, and Vice President Richard Cheney are reported to be following a largely unilateralist foreign policy approach, Secretary of State Colin Powell appears more inclined toward working closely with American allies to build a consensus on foreign policy issues.[86] Powell has moved slowly to stamp his imprint on American policy toward Africa, but the continuities in alignments and initiatives seem apparent. For example, in West Africa, the United States has supported a UN Security Council proposed embargo on Liberia's exports of diamonds that fuel the war in Sierra Leone and a travel ban on Liberia's senior officials in an effort to raise the costs of trafficking in diamonds coming across the border from Sierra Leone. Moreover, Powell, under heavy pressure from the religious right to support minority religious groups in the Sudan, described that country as possibly the world's greatest contemporary tragedy at a House of Representative hearing. His statement reflects widespread concern that the discovery of significant new deposits of oil in the Sudan will lead to a worsening of the civil war.[87] While these positions are largely in line with enlightened thinking the world over, it remains unclear whether the current Powell pragmatism will result in an American leadership befitting the country's status in the world. If Bush caution combines with bureaucratic inertia, Africa is likely to become more isolated, and therefore more marginalized, than at any time in recent history.

Despite America's enormous economic and military power in much of the world, Africa remained partially autonomous from the effective influence of the United States and other industrialized countries in the post–Cold War years. Because African states and their state system were in flux, their capacities for effective administration were in question, and their economies were only partially integrated into the global capitalist system, they stayed partially insulated and beyond the reach of American policy-makers on critical issues. Particularly when state failure occurred, as in Somalia, U.S. diplomats lacked reliable leaders with whom to negotiate, and consequently their ability to influence events in these countries ebbed accordingly. In intense conflict situations, the effects of Africa's partial autonomy seemed quite evident. Thus, U.S. influences on the treatment of refugees in eastern Congo or on the settlement of intrastate conflicts in Burundi, Sudan, and Sierra Leone, or on the war between Ethiopia and Eritrea, seemed limited. Moreover, globalization has not resulted thus far in an increasing U.S. concern with the transfer of advanced technology or training to Africa. Whereas a dynamic America appeared bent upon increased trade and investment in other prosperous regions of the world, it hesitated over significant commitments to areas in Africa where problems of civil war, authoritarian leaders, corruption, the absence of the rule of law, and the failure of some state elites to protect their proclaimed values on democracy and civil liberties were in evidence.

The result was a mutual restraint that was for the most part tragic. On the one hand, Africa did gain some of the distance it had long sought from external influences;

[86]Jackson Diehl, "Our Champion of Continuity," *Washington Post* (March 19, 2001), p. A16.
[87]Editorial, "Wanted: A Sudan Policy," *Washington Post* (March 16, 2001), p. A20.

on the other hand, however, the gap of relevance that was emerging between Africa and the United States contributed to Africa's marginalization in the world economy. To the extent that American and Western financial and technological resources bypassed Africa's development, the region risked being left with circumscribed opportunities at a time of unprecedented economic and technological change. To bridge this chasm and avoid a backlash, the United States and other industrialized countries must become more relevant to Africa, and Africa must become more relevant to the United States and the industrialized world. The United States, as Thomas Friedman asserted, has "the tools to make a difference"—if only it can muster the political will to rise to the challenge.[88]

Under these circumstances, what could be done to increase America's relevancy to what Secretary of State Albright described at the outset as the new rules of relationship that were being set for its relations with Africa in the twenty-first century? Clearly, one would not want an activist foreign policy that made aid conditional and therefore did not respect Africa's deep-felt desire for political and economic autonomy, but rather a policy that supplemented responsible African decision making to achieve its own goals and purposes. Such a spirit of self-effacing cooperation and enlightened self-interest might prove essential to achieve long-term African and American interests, but it would not be easy to cultivate. To accomplish this goal, the congressional Black caucus has exerted increasing influence on legislation affecting Africa. Even so, political leaders will have to commit greater energies to encourage more public and congressional understanding of Africa's needs and aspirations, and a stronger American constituency will have to emerge that is intent on supporting Africa through the difficult transition toward equal opportunity with other regions of the world.

An encouraging sign of this political and educational effort was the National Summit on Africa, which brought together 2,300 delegates in Washington, D.C. in February 2000, to agree on a draft National Policy Plan of Action that would push important priority issues on trade, debt relief, crisis management, the HIV/AIDS epidemic, education, and the development of Africa's infrastructure. With an eye to wielding the influence of other national and ethnic groups on U.S. foreign policy, Leonard H. Robinson, Jr., the president of the National Summit, described this "power block of voters and activists" as representing "the fundamental cornerstone of political leverage on which the American political system functions."[89] The National Summit certainly was necessary to overcome the trend toward drift and detachment that marked U.S. policy toward Africa, but it remains too early to assess whether it will prove sufficient to meet this challenge.

---

[88]Thomas L. Friedman, *The Lexus and the Olive Tree* (New York: Farrar, Straus, Giroux, 1999), p. 352.

[89]*Address by Mr. Leonard H. Robinson, Jr., President and CEO, The National Summit on Africa Before the African Development Forum, Economic Commission for Africa.* Addis Ababa (October 24, 1999), p. 9 (http://www.africasummit.org/Speeches/ADDIS2.htm).

# 11

# Defense Policy for the Twenty-First Century

## CINDY WILLIAMS

Security Studies Program
Massachusetts Institute of Technology

In the military dimension, the United States holds uncontested primacy today, but there are signs of strain. The array of functions that the military is expected to perform daily has expanded since the late 1980s. Defense leaders complain that overseas deployments and other day-to-day commitments lower readiness to fight the two nearly simultaneous major theater wars (MTWs) that policy holds are the military's first priority. Some of the military services failed to meet their recruiting goals late in the decade. Commanders worry that frequent deployments and overwork are harming morale, making it difficult for the services to retain their best people. Some military units with special skills and equipment have had to deploy repeatedly, whereas others seem increasingly ill-suited for the actual operations the armed forces face. Despite half a decade of ebullient rhetoric about a revolution in military affairs, adherence to Cold War ways of thinking stifles innovation.

Following a decade of post–Cold War reductions in the cost of the military, defense spending is on the rise. Absent changes in policy, force structure, and modernization plans, the military will require tens of billions of dollars more each year as it struggles with weapons cost overruns, increases in pay and benefits for service members and retirees, and the rising costs of operation and maintenance. Embracing

Cindy Williams is a Principal Research Scientist in the Security Studies Program at the Massachusetts Institute of Technology. Previously she has served as Assistant Director for National Security at the Congressional Budget Office, as a director at the MITRE Corporation, as a member of the Senior Executive Service in the Pentagon's Directorate of Program Analysis and Evaluation, and as a mathematician at the Rand Corporation. She is the editor of *Holding the Line: U.S. Defense Alternatives for the Early 21st Century* (Cambridge, MA: MIT Press, 2001). Dr. Williams holds a Ph.D. in mathematics from the University of California, Irvine. She is an elected fellow of the National Academy of Public Administration and a member of the advisory board of Women in International Security.

a more ambitious national security strategy and expanding the military's forces and modernization programs would require substantially larger budgets.

America needs and wants a strong military. But despite substantial downsizing and some reshaping, America's armed forces have not yet adapted to the end of the Cold War. Force structures and modernization programs appear to be misaligned with declared policy priorities; budgets do not match force structures and equipment plans. Senior defense leaders and some policy authors argue that the best way to fix the problems is with dramatic increases in defense spending. This chapter argues that a better choice is to adjust policies, force structures, and modernization programs to the world we actually live in.

The chapter focuses on conventional forces—the land, naval, aviation, and mobility forces that are the backbone of the nation's military might and that consume most of the defense budget. It begins with a brief comparison of broad national security choices, or grand strategies, that the nation could embrace for the future. After a discussion of the extent of American primacy in the military dimension and a look at the reasons why that preeminence may not always translate into effective influence, the chapter continues with a brief review of budgetary concerns. As a departure point for discussing realistic priorities for the future, it examines the military strategy, defense priorities, and conventional force sizing criteria that the Clinton administration espoused. The chapter then proposes setting new priorities that reflect more realistic threats and missions. It ends with suggestions for trimming and reshaping force structure and modernization plans consistent with such priorities.

## AMERICA'S STRATEGIC CHOICES

Policy-makers and independent observers differ in their understanding of the broad goals of national security strategy as well as in their assessments of how the nation should size, shape, and equip the armed forces for the future. Moreover, even in an era of large budgetary surpluses, the costs of maintaining and equipping the armed forces must be weighed against other national priorities—reducing the federal debt, lowering taxes, or investing more in health care, education, and public infrastructure.

At one end of the strategy spectrum, neo-isolationists argue for a policy of restraint that would focus on U.S. interests in North American self-defense and would virtually eliminate our military commitments to European and Asian allies, paving the way to reduce force structure about one-third below 2001 levels.[1] At the other end, proponents of a policy of primacy hold that the United States should consoli-

---

[1]Eugene Gholz, Daryl G. Press, and Harvey M. Sapolsky, "Come Home, America: The Strategy of Restraint in the Face of Temptation," *International Security*, Vol. 21, No. 4 (Spring 1997): 5–48; Earl Ravenal, "The Case for Adjustment," *Foreign Policy*, No. 81 (Winter 1990–1991): 3–19; Eric A. Nordlinger, *Isolationism Reconfigured: American Foreign Policy for a New Century* (Princeton, NJ: Princeton University Press, 1995); Barry R. Posen and Andrew L. Ross, "Competing Visions for U.S. Grand Strategy," *International Security*, Vol. 21, No. 3 (Winter 1996–1997): 5–53.

date the gains of its Cold War victory by working to preserve for generations its status as the world's sole superpower. They argue that the United States needs a military large enough and strong enough that it can not only prevail in warfare against any adversary but also can convince other nations that even attempting to become a global peer competitor would be futile.[2]

But a policy that seeks to extend American primacy in this way would cost vastly more than the United States spends on the military in 2001. Proponents of such a policy argue for expanding the share of gross domestic product that the nation devotes to defense from 3 percent in 2001 to 4 or 4.5 percent. As the economy grows in the future, such expansion would mean an increase of 80 to 100 percent in real (that is, inflation-adjusted) outlays for national defense by the end of the decade and would consume a substantial portion of federal surpluses projected for the future. Combined with proposals for tax reductions and nondefense spending increases, the expansion could lead to the return of large deficits and threaten the nation's economic vitality.

Moreover, a policy of primacy can backfire politically and militarily as other nations seek to balance against the enormous power that one nation wields. Although some authors maintain that the American lead is already so overwhelming that it would take decades for any other country to counterbalance, others see evidence of balancing behavior already.[3]

Between the extremes of neo-isolationism and primacy lie two other broad national security choices: selective engagement and cooperative security. Supporters of a policy of selective engagement call for remaining engaged in the world and maintaining a military that is close in size to the 2001 level, but for limiting American engagement to those places where the risk of sparking a world war among great powers is the highest: Europe, East Asia, and the oil-rich Persian Gulf. Proponents of cooperative security hold that the United States has a far-reaching interest in peace everywhere and should use its military might as well as the power of international institutions to thwart aggression, whether internal or across states, anywhere in the world.[4]

This chapter favors a policy of selective engagement. Rather than retreating from military alliances and engagement, the United States should focus on areas that matter the most. Rather than spending enormous amounts of money in an attempt to prevent the emergence of a global peer competitor for decades to come, the

---

[2]Joshua Muravchik, *The Imperative of American Leadership: A Challenge to Neo-Isolationism* (Washington, DC: AEI Press, 1996); Zalmay M. Khalilzad, "Strategy and Defense Planning for the Coming Century," in Zalmay M. Khalilzad and David A. Ochmanek (eds.), *Strategy and Defense Planning for the 21st Century* (Santa Monica, CA: Rand, 1997); William Kristol and Robert Kagan, "Toward a Neo-Reaganite Foreign Policy," *Foreign Affairs*, Vol. 75, No. 4 (July–August 1996).

[3]In "Contemporary Conflict in Theory and Practice," Kenneth Waltz argues that balancing behavior has already begun. *International Security*, Vol. 25, No. 1 (Summer 2000): 37. For another point of view, see William C. Wohlforth, "The Stability of a Unipolar World," *International Security*, Vol. 24, No. 1 (Summer 1999): 5–41.

[4]In "Competing Visions for U.S. Grand Strategy," Posen and Ross compare these four strategies and their implications for national security, forces, and spending.

nation should adjust its military priorities and measuring sticks to reflect genuine interests and threats and should reduce the military's role in missions that can be handled by civilian institutions. The chapter recognizes, however, that the pressures that drew the United States into cooperative security arrangements in Africa and the Balkans during the 1990s are unlikely to disappear in the new millennium. As a result, the United States should rebalance its policy priorities and reshape the military to be better prepared for such operations.

## THE U.S. MARGIN OF MILITARY SUPERIORITY IS VAST

U.S. primacy in the military dimension is extraordinary. America holds a greater lead over all the other great powers in the world combined than any other leading state in the last two centuries.[5] Although China has a population four times the size of America's and more troops in the military, the United States prevails globally in every other important measure of military potential and might.

U.S. gross domestic product (GDP) is more than twice as large as Japan's and four times as great as Germany's, the next two contenders. It exceeds Russia's by a factor of about eight and China's by a factor of twelve.[6] In addition, the United States controls more than one-third of the manufacturing production of all the great powers combined.[7] In measures of high-technology manufacturing, research and development, and personal computers and internet hosts per capita, the United States also greatly overshadows any other nation—an indication of substantially greater wherewithal to support a military in the information age.[8]

America spends far more on its military (see Figure 1) and has substantially more modern military equipment than any other country in the world. For example, only Russia and China have more main battle tanks than the U.S. Army. But nearly three-quarters of China's 8,300 tanks are based on a 1950s-era Soviet design. Compared with more than 7,600 U.S. M-1 Abrams tanks, only 2,300 Chinese tanks have features characteristic of modern ground forces. Similarly, of Russia's 15,500 tanks, only 5,200 are T-72s or T-80s, the two systems that entered production after 1970.[9]

U.S. inventories of fighter aircraft exceed those of any other country. The United States has about twice as many tactical fighters as Russia, 50 percent more than China, and nearly five times as many as any other nation in the world. But as with tanks, numbers do not tell the full story of U.S. superiority. For although virtually all U.S. and Russian fighter planes have the sophisticated electronics,

[5]Wohlforth, "The Stability of a Unipolar World," p.7. This section draws liberally on Wohlforth's discussion.

[6]Based on 1998 GDP figures in International Institute for Strategic Studies, *The Military Balance, 1999/2000* (London: Oxford University Press).

[7]Wohlforth, "The Stability of a Unipolar World," p. 17.

[8]Wohlforth, "The Stability of a Unipolar World," p. 19.

[9]*The Military Balance, 1999/2000*; Christopher F. Foss, *Jane's Tank Recognition Guide* (Harper Collins: Glasgow, 1996).

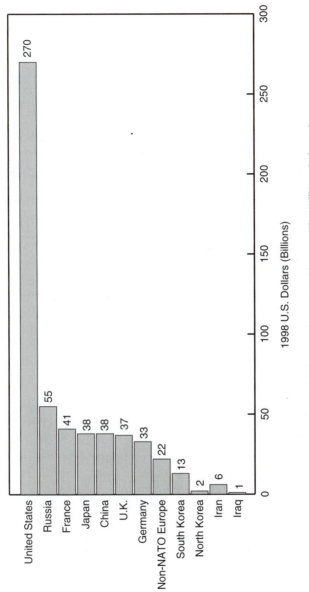

**Figure 1.** 1998 Defense Spending of Selected Countries (*Source: The Military Balance.*)

powerful engines, and capable missiles of so-called "fourth-generation" planes, China has very few fourth-generation tactical aircraft; indeed, about three-quarters of China's planes have the much more limited combat capabilities of first- or second-generation aircraft.[10]

American preeminence in terms of naval equipment is even greater. The United States has 12 aircraft carriers, compared with 1 for Russia, none for China, 1 for France, and 3 for Britain; 130 surface combatant ships, compared with 53 for China, 35 for Russia, 41 for France, and 34 for Britain; and 76 ocean-going submarines, compared with about 70 for Russia, 71 for China, and 15 or fewer for any other country.

The U.S. military also excels in the capabilities of modern conventional warfare. Only the United States has a significant ability to project power globally and to operate and fight in naval battles far from shore. Only the United States has stealth aircraft, a substantial arsenal of precision munitions, and the means for large-scale suppression of enemy air defenses. U.S. logistics, surveillance, reconnaissance, and integrated command and control are second to none. U.S. military training is unsurpassed by any other nation's and is vastly superior to Russia's or China's. For example, U.S. Air Force pilots fly more than 200 training hours a year, compared with 20 in Russia and fewer than 100 in China.[11] U.S. forces repeatedly conduct rigorous and realistic training and exercises at every level of organization, often against highly capable and well-equipped "opposing forces"—U.S. teams using enemy tactics to test and develop the mettle and ingenuity of those being trained. The level and the intensity of such unit training vastly exceed that of any potential enemy and of most U.S. allies.[12]

# MILITARY PRIMACY AND EFFECTIVE INFLUENCE

As Robert Lieber points out in the introductory chapter, however, American power will not always translate into effective influence. Though the United States needs a strong military to defend its vital interests, the overall utility of America's current military preeminence does not necessarily provide comparable political and diplomatic influence. Having the largest, most expensive, best trained, and best equipped military in the world does not mean that the United States will always be able to influence other nations to do as it wishes or even that it will prevail in every military confrontation.

In many potential disputes, our adversaries will care more about the issue than we will. As other chapters of this book describe, public interest in foreign policy appears to have diminished. The absence of any galvanizing threat to American security interests makes it more difficult for policymakers to gain domestic support for

---

[10]Congressional Budget Office, *A Look at Tomorrow's Tactical Air Forces* (CBO: Washington, DC, January 1997), p. 13.

[11]*The Military Balance, 1999/2000.*

[12]U.S. nuclear capabilities also exceed those of any other nation.

foreign policy in general and for wars in particular. Despite the "CNN factor" that brings the humanitarian consequences of local and regional conflicts around the globe into American living rooms, wars halfway around the world are less important to Americans than they are to the local actors.

Unless vital U.S. interests are at stake, the United States may be unwilling to risk significant numbers of American lives in military action. Thus, despite enormous advantages in military power, the United States may choose not to engage militarily. And when it does—especially in conflicts that do not involve vital interests—it will gravitate toward war-fighting concepts and equipment that reduce the risk of U.S. casualties. Operating under these constraints, the United States may not find it easy to influence outcomes through the use of force.[13] For example, during the NATO air war against Yugoslavia, U.S. pilots were largely instructed to maintain altitudes above 15,000 feet to avoid being shot down by Serbian air defenses. As a result, according to independent assessments, they were unable to distinguish decoys from military vehicles on the ground or to have much effect on Serbian ground forces. In the end, the United States and NATO prevailed: Serbian forces withdrew from Kosovo, multinational forces took up peacekeeping posts, refugees were returned to their homes, and bloodshed was halted. But for eleven weeks, the Serbs controlled the fate of Albanian civilians whose welfare was ostensibly the main reason for the air campaign.

A potent military is an important asset, but it is not a panacea. Even when the United States chooses to engage and is willing to risk substantial numbers of lives, the armed forces' vast margin in size and technology may not guarantee a win in every engagement. Cheap enemy equipment can be the undoing of expensive systems: surface-to-air missiles and even antiaircraft artillery can down sophisticated stealth airplanes; underwater mines and torpedoes from the least expensive submarines can sink multi-billion-dollar ships; as the attack on the U.S.S. *Cole* in the autumn of 2000 demonstrated, even the most unsophisticated boat loaded with high explosives can cause grave damage to the most advanced warship.

Finally, even winning wars decisively will not ensure that America's political preferences prevail. A decade after the Persian Gulf War, Saddam Hussein is still in power. And years after the intervention in Bosnia, European and U.S. troops still stand guard.

As other chapters make clear, the world has probably not seen the last of the problems of the past decade: from regional wars to internal conflicts to mass migration, famine, terrorism, and proliferation of weapons of mass destruction. As Robert Lieber points out in the introductory chapter, American leadership may be the necessary catalyst for international efforts to solve such problems.

Not all leadership has to be military. America has a broad range of tools to choose from in exercising leadership: diplomacy, influence through international institutions, financial aid, economic and trade sanctions, and finally military force.

---

[13]For a discussion of asymmetric interests, see Owen Cote, "Buying '. . . From the Sea,'" in Cindy Williams (ed.), *Holding the Line: U.S. Defense Alternatives for the Early 21st Century*" (Cambridge, MA: MIT Press, 2001).

Nevertheless, the history of the post–Cold War period indicates that America will continue to call on the military across a spectrum of operations. America's armed forces need to be configured and equipped to handle such activities. The special capabilities that are required probably do not contribute directly to the maintenance of military primacy—but they are essential to the success of the policies that the United States has embraced since the end of the Cold War.

# PRESSURES ON THE DEFENSE BUDGET

During the 1990s, defense budgets declined as the Cold War ended and the armed forces shed force structure, constrained modernization plans, and trimmed infrastructure. National defense spending fell in real terms from a peak of $400 billion in 1989 to about $280 billion in 1998, and then it grew to a level above $290 billion for 2001. (Although the decline appears to be very steep when compared against the spending peak that occurred in 1989 as a result of the Reagan era defense buildup, 2001 defense outlays actually come to more than 90 percent of the average Cold War dollar level.) Defense outlays in 2001 account for about 3 percent of gross domestic product (GDP) and 16 percent of total federal spending.[14]

The Defense Department's budget plan for 2001 to 2005 assumed that military spending would change very little in real terms over the five-year period. But unplanned overruns in the costs of weapons, growth in spending for operation and maintenance, greater-than-planned increases in pay and benefits for service members and retirees, and unforeseen costs of research and development could add more than $35 billion a year to annual defense budgets by the end of the decade.[15]

## Paying for a Policy of Primacy

Attempting to extend American dominance for a period of generations by precluding the rise of another global superpower, as some authors advocate, would cost even more.[16] Those who espouse a policy of primacy (as opposed to primacy the circumstance) are not always specific and do not all agree about what the large amounts of added funding would buy or about the size, shape, or equipment the armed forces would need to prevent any other country from competing to become a global superpower. But they all seem to agree on one thing, namely that the defense budget has been cut much too far. Joshua Muravchik argues for boosting defense spending from

---

[14]Calculated from *The Budget for Fiscal Year 2001, Historical Tables*, Table 6.1, Composition of Outlays, pp. 103–109. Unless otherwise noted, budget figures in this chapter are in constant 2001 dollars and reflect outlays, the moneys spent in a given year, rather than budget authority, the amounts authorized by congress for that year. The national defense budget category includes defense spending by the Department of Energy and other agencies, as well as the Department of Defense.

[15]Williams (ed.), *Holding the Line,* "Introduction."

[16]For a description and comparison of possible grand strategies, including primacy, see Barry R. Posen and Andrew L. Ross, "Competing Visions for U.S. Grand Strategy," *International Security*, Vol. 21, No. 3 (Winter 1996–1997): 5–53.

about 3 percent of GDP in 2001 to 4 percent.[17] Senior U.S. military leaders have also called on Americans to devote 4 to 4.5 percent of GDP to defense to support the military's global mission and continued U.S. prominence on the world stage.[18] At the lower end of the spectrum of fiscal aspirations, Zalmay Kahlilzad believes that by giving up some unneeded force structure, America might keep the military cost of a policy of primacy at today's share of the economic pie, 3 percent of GDP.

Advocates of tagging defense spending to growth in the economy are arguing implicitly that as the economy grows, the nation can afford to spend more on defense. This argument may be true, but of course the same argument can be applied to all public spending: as the economy expands, the nation can afford to spend more on welfare, education, health care, public infrastructure, and Social Security. Indeed, as GDP grew over the course of the Cold War, federal outlays largely kept pace. But the nation appears to have reached a consensus in favor of reducing the federal debt and building up the Social Security trust fund to ensure pensions for future retirees. Those goals can be met only if total federal outlays decline substantially as a share of GDP during the coming decade.

Advocates also argue that we should devote much more of the economic pie to defense, because we have done so in the past: during the Cold War, we spent an average of 7 percent of GDP on defense each year. But during the Cold War, the composition of federal outlays shifted as the nation embraced policies and priorities that would be virtually impossible to reverse today. For the first half of the Cold War, for example, the United States had no Medicare or Medicaid programs. Today, those programs claim about 3.5 percent of GDP. And when defense's share of the economic pie expanded during the 1980s, the nation paid for that growth by accumulating hundreds of billions of dollars in new debt—a prospect widely opposed in today's policy environment.

Proponents of large defense budget increases argue that America can afford to pay for them out of the huge federal surpluses that economists project for the coming decade. "A nation with a projected $1.9 trillion budget surplus can afford consistently to allocate a minimum of 4 percent of GDP to ensure its security," argues Frank Gaffney.[19] Because both White House and congressional projections of the surplus assume that defense and other appropriated spending will not grow at all in real terms, however, such increases would consume a substantial portion of the projected surpluses. As economic growth outstrips inflation by several percentage points each year, even holding defense outlays to 3 percent of GDP would mean spending $700 billion more for defense in the coming decade than January 2001 surplus projections assume—thereby reducing by $700 billion the $2.7 trillion surplus that the Congressional Budget Office (CBO) projects could accrue outside of the Medicare

[17]Joshua Muravchik, *The Imperative of American Leadership: A Challenge to Neo-Isolationism* (Washington, DC: AEI Press, 1996), p. 138.

[18]See, for example, Hunter Keeter, "Marine Commandant Calls for Defense Spending Increase," *Defense Daily*, August 16, 2000, p. 6.

[19]Frank J. Gaffney, Jr., "The 4% Solution," *Washington Times*, August 8, 2000.

and Social Security trust funds between 2001 and 2010. (The tax reductions enacted in May 2001 will consume $1.3 trillion of that surplus. Coupled with the new non-defense spending initiatives in the May 2001 Congressional Budget Resolution, the tax package will reduce the 10-year projected surplus from $2.7 trillion to $500 billion.) In addition, interest costs that stem from using the surplus for a purpose other than debt reduction would amount to about $100 billion. Thus, holding defense spending at 3 percent of GDP throughout the decade would claim a total of $800 billion—nearly 30 percent of the projected surplus. At 4 percent of GDP, defense increases would consume about twice as much, nearly $1.5 trillion of projected surpluses. Combined with approximately $250 billion in extra interest payments, the added spending for defense would claim about $1.7 trillion—nearly two-thirds of the pre-tax cut surplus that CBO projected in January 2001.[20] Pushing defense spending to 4 percent of GDP would thus leave little federal surplus to pay for tax breaks or for improvements in education, health care, and physical infrastructure—changes that could result in substantially higher long-term payoffs to the nation's well-being.

Advocates of a policy of primacy intimate that an increase in defense spending from 3 percent to 4 percent of GDP would be pretty insignificant: "We have an opportunity to become so strong, so technologically advanced, that no country, not even an emerging China, could challenge us for 100 years. The cost: a slight bump of 2 percent or 3 percent of GDP in defense spending, an increase that would go unnoticed in a healthy economy."[21] Certainly, when viewed as a simple fraction—just 1, 2, or 3 percent of GDP above what we pay today—the increase sounds minimal. But in dollar terms, 1 percent amounts to $104 billion in 2001. And as the economy grows faster than inflation over the decade, the 4 percent share that Muravchik wants would also grow, bringing defense outlays to roughly $530 billion by 2010—80 percent more in real terms than the 2001 level.

In real terms, U.S. defense outlays are already more than 90 percent of their Cold War average and vastly exceed the dollar levels of spending in previous postwar periods. Holding defense outlays at 3 percent of the rapidly growing economy that forecasters project (as Kahlilzad suggests) would mean increasing military budgets by 27 percent in real terms over the coming decade. As Figure 2 illustrates, such increases would push defense spending well above the Cold War average. At 4 percent of GDP, by the end of the decade, defense spending in real dollar terms would exceed even peak Cold War funding levels by about a third.

Ultimately, the question for policy-makers is not just how much money the nation can afford to spend for any public good, but how much it must spend to address the most pressing needs and how to set priorities among the diverse goals and benefits of public activities. In an era of unprecedented military preeminence, when no nation is in any position to take the place of the former Soviet Union as a

---

[20]Much of the projected surplus will probably not be available for spending, in any case. James Horney and Robert Greenstein, "How Much of the Enlarged Surplus Is Available for Tax and Program Initiatives?" (Washington, DC, Center on Budget and Policy Priorities, July 7, 2000), available at http://www.cbpp.org/6-29-00bud.

[21]Walter Boyne, "U.S. Spending Too Little on Defense," *Long Island Newsday*, August 23, 2000, p. 35.

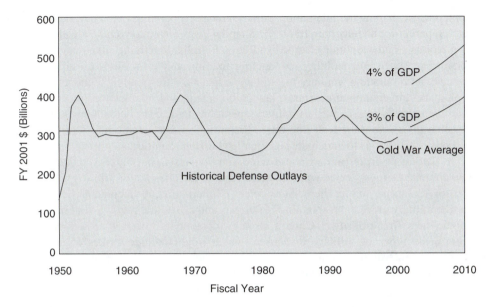

**Figure 2.** Spending More on Defense

threat to the United States, it makes no sense to return defense budgets to their Cold War levels, let alone to raise them dramatically above Cold War peaks.

How can it cost the country vastly more in dollar terms to maintain security than it ever cost to triumph in a five-decade struggle against a rival superpower? The prima facie case for vast increases in defense spending is weak. It seems that the U.S. public is being asked to pick up the bill for the failure of decision makers to set new priorities for defense and to make choices that reflect the new strategic environment.

# SETTING NEW MILITARY PRIORITIES

## The Strategy of the 1990s

The national security strategy articulated by the Clinton administration combined elements of three grand strategies: cooperative security, selective engagement, and, to a lesser extent, primacy.[22] Termed "a strategy of engagement," the policy sought to make Americans secure and prosperous, to thwart regional aggression, and to reshape the world more in America's image by promoting democracy, free markets, respect for human rights, and the rule of law.[23] Beginning with the 1997 Quadrennial Defense Review, the administration described the strategy as consisting of three

---

[22]Posen and Ross, "Competing Visions for U.S. Grand Strategy", Williams (ed.), *Holding the Line*, "Introduction."

[23]The White House, "A National Security Strategy for a New Century," December 1999. Earlier versions espoused a similar view of strategy.

components: shaping the international environment, responding to threats and crises, and preparing for an uncertain future.[24] "Shaping" was meant to include a wide array of diplomatic and economic efforts, in addition to military activities like maintaining forward presence and mobility, conducting training and exercises with allies and friends, and pursuing military-to-military contacts. "Responding" encompassed diplomatic and economic measures, law enforcement, and intelligence and counter-intelligence activities, as well as military operations to deter or defeat a broad list of possible threats to American interests. "Preparing" meant positioning the military and other institutions to anticipate and handle new opportunities and threats.

Setting priorities among these three components is not an easy matter. The Quadrennial Defense Review purported to resolve the question of priorities by calling for "balance" among them. Subsequent Clinton strategy documents held that, for the military at least, "responding" to threats and crises that involve vital interests should take first priority.[25] Clinton strategy documents also set up a hierarchy among the types of military responses, which might include strikes at terrorist bases, drug interdiction, fighting and winning theater wars, and conducting smaller-scale contingencies such as humanitarian assistance, peace operations, or enforcement of embargoes and no-fly zones: "Fighting and winning major theater wars is the ultimate test of our Armed Forces—a test at which they must always succeed. For the foreseeable future, the United States, preferably in concert with allies, must have the capability to deter and, if deterrence fails, defeat large-scale, cross-border aggression in two distant theaters in overlapping time frames." Furthermore, "U.S. forces must also remain prepared to withdraw from [smaller-scale] contingency operations if needed to deploy to a major theater war."[26]

In short, despite expansive rhetoric about shaping the international environment and preparing for the future, President Clinton's declaratory strategy was clear about its priorities: for the military, the primary mission was to deter and, if necessary, fight and win conflicts in which vital interests are threatened. And among these conflicts, fighting and winning two major theater wars in overlapping time frames took priority.

What conventional forces does the United States need in order to fight and win two such wars? Obviously, much depends upon specific circumstances. The Bottom Up Review, conducted in 1993 during the first Clinton term, put forth the concept of a "building block" of U.S. forces that might be required in each of two wars, one against Iraq and one against North Korea. Although the enemies, allies, locations, and geography would differ greatly for the two wars, the review postulated that the "building block" for each war would be about the same as the U.S. contingent sent to Operation Desert Storm in 1991. One "building block" would

[24]William S. Cohen, *Report of the Quadrennial Defense Review* (Washington, DC: Department of Defense, May 1997).

[25]The White House, "A National Security Strategy for a New Century," January 5, 2000, p. 7.

[26]Ibid., p. 25.

amount to about half of America's conventional forces: four to five Army divisions, four to five Marine expeditionary brigades, ten Air Force fighter wings, one hundred heavy bombers, four to five Navy aircraft carrier battle groups, and some number of special operations forces.[27]

## President Clinton's Policy in Practice

But declaratory policy and policy in practice are not always the same thing. In reality, the Clinton administration engaged the military in several smaller-scale contingencies, some of which may last for decades. U.S. forces conducted daily patrols of the no-fly zones established after the Gulf War over northern and southern Iraq; twice during the Clinton years the military action in that region escalated to the level of a small air war. The United States also led two smaller wars in the Balkans, both of which ended with a standing commitment of U.S. military forces for peacekeeping and nation-building. In addition, U.S. forces were called upon to restore democracy in Haiti, to conduct missile strikes on Afghanistan and Sudan, to assist in military operations in East Timor, and to provide humanitarian assistance around the globe. Forces were also committed day-to-day to numerous shaping missions: maintaining presence overseas, supporting military-to-military contacts, exercising diplomacy, and conducting training exercises around the globe.

The discrepancy between declaratory and de facto priorities causes two big problems. First, the declared emphasis on fighting two major wars at about the same time reinforces a preference for the force structure and the equipment plans inherited from the Cold War—a structure and plans in many ways ill-suited for the humanitarian and peace operations that in reality claim much of the military's effort. Second, since the armed services calculate their combat readiness on the basis of their ability to send half of their conventional units to each of two wars, any time that forces are committed to operations other than those wars, the services see their readiness for "the real mission" as reduced.[28]

The Quadrennial Defense Review presumed that the second problem could be solved by withdrawing forces from smaller-scale contingencies if major war erupted. That possibility is clearly not realistic. If two major wars over vital interests had unfolded in rapid succession during the Kosovo operation of 1999, for example, it seems highly unlikely that the United States could have or would have withdrawn forces from Bosnia and halted operations in Yugoslavia in time to fight in the second major war.

Some of these problems could be resolved simply by increasing the size of the military.[29] But given the vast sums we already spend on the military, we should first inquire whether we might be doing something wrong. Perhaps America's armed

---

[27]Les Aspin, *Bottom-Up Review* (Washington, DC: Department of Defense, 1993).

[28]Congressional Budget Office, *Making Peace While Staying Ready for War: The Challenges of U.S. Military Participation in Peace Operations*, December 1999.

[29]Ibid.

forces have not yet adapted to the post–Cold War world. A better choice is to adjust declaratory priorities, force structures, and modernization plans to the world that we actually live in.

## Adjusting Priorities to Reflect the Real World

Many observers are not happy with the uses to which the military has been put since the 1991 Persian Gulf War. They feel that the military's foremost tasks should be to deter hostile activity toward the United States through great visible strength and to prepare for major wars in regions and over stakes of vital interest. They find that participation in peacekeeping operations, humanitarian activities, and other smaller-scale contingencies steals resources from more important tasks and also raises a risk of bloodshed that is disproportionate to the potential gains. They argue, and rightly so, that the United States should be much more selective in its military engagements than it was during the 1990s.

Nevertheless, the history of the past decade demonstrates that America's political leaders will continue to call on the military to engage in operations apart from wars over vital interests. To improve the military's readiness and capability for the genuine activities it faces, the nation needs to align declaratory priorities more closely with likely operations. Therefore, in contrast to the previous policy priorities of the Clinton administration, peace operations and other smaller-scale contingencies should replace the second major theater war on the Pentagon's list of priorities.

# RECALIBRATING THE MTW MEASURING STICK

Another reason for reexamining the "two-MTW standard" is that the so-called "building block" for MTWs seems out of proportion and ill suited to the real threats that the military may face in the future. Iraq and North Korea pose substantially smaller threats to their neighbors today, and U.S. forces are better equipped than they were in the early 1990s, when the two-MTW standard was adopted and the MTW "building block" was sized.

During the late 1990s, another favored scenario emerged in writings outside the Defense Department: U.S. military protection of Taiwan against aggression by mainland China. The U.S. obligation to assist Taiwan militarily is not clear-cut, and Taiwan's military is very well equipped and trained to fight on its own behalf. Nevertheless, some observers believe that war with China over Taiwan should replace the Iraqi or North Korean MTW as a more likely and challenging near-term scenario. As this section outlines, however, such a war would bear very little resemblance to the Pentagon's MTW template.

## War on the Korean Peninsula

According to the 1993 Bottom-Up Review, U.S. and South Korean forces would likely be able to halt and reverse an invasion by North Korea against the South, using one MTW "building block." The Korean scenario could evaporate if North and South come to peaceful terms on reunification. Whether or not that solution occurs, however, the United States no longer needs to devote to the problem the level of forces contained in the 1993 building block.

Since the time of the review, North Korea's economy has virtually collapsed. Widespread hunger has taken a toll on the well-being of the population. Shortages of food and fuel have greatly constrained the military's ability to train. Estimates of the North's gross national product dropped from $21 billion in 1993 to $14 billion in 1998. North Korean defense spending fell from $5.3 billion in 1993 to about $2 billion in 1998. In contrast, rising defense budgets in South Korea totaled $13 billion by 1998.[30] North Korean imports of military equipment have fallen drastically. Although the North is believed to retain large standing forces and substantial levels of equipment, and although training levels improved in 2000 compared with markedly low levels the previous year, the South has significant advantages: a better educated and more technically trained military; geography that favors the defender in many respects; prepared defenses; significant levels of advanced equipment; and access to U.S. intelligence and reconnaissance resources.[31]

Military analysts inside and outside the Defense Department believe that war on the Korean peninsula would be brutal and result in large numbers of casualties on both sides. But recent independent studies find that coming to the South's defense if North Korea attacks would require only half the U.S. forces (fewer according to some) envisioned by the Bottom-Up Review.[32]

Critics of these studies say they assume that North Korea will engage in World War Two–style combat, massing armor and hammering at the South in an old-fashioned attempt to break through the defenses. In reality, they argue, the North will capitalize on long-range artillery, tunnels, special forces, chemical weapons, and ballistic missiles to achieve surprise, sneak through defenses, and terrorize civilians.

[30]*The Military Balance 1995/96*, pp. 183–184; *The Military Balance 1999/2000*, p. 193. Figures are in current dollars.

[31]The Defense Department's "2000 Report to Congress: Military Situation on the Korean Peninsula" states that the North Korean military "continues to grow in both conventional and asymmetric forces with increasing emphasis on the latter." The report focuses on the areas North Korea has traditionally emphasized, however: number of troops, ballistic missiles, artillery pieces, special operations forces, and weapons of mass destruction. In other areas of military capability, South Korea enjoys clear advantages. Moreover, although the report makes much of the North's improvements in its exercise regime during 2000, it admits that the training was needed to "arrest a decline in readiness and improve its military capability." In fact, a 1999 report to congress indicated that the failing North Korean economy had seriously undermined conventional capability. By 1999, North Korea's winter training exercise was less than half the previous year's size—already greatly reduced from the early 1990s. Thus the improvements in 2000 might have been both more needed and less significant than the DoD report would lead one to believe. "Final Report," North Korea Advisory Group, October 29, 1999, http://www.house.gov/international_relations/nkag/report.

[32]Nick Beldecos and Eric Heginbotham, "The Conventional Military Balance in Korea," *Breakthroughs*, Vol. IV, No. 1 (Spring 1995): 1–8; Michael O'Hanlon, "Stopping a North Korean Invasion: Why Defending South Korea Is Easier than the Pentagon Thinks," *International Security*, Vol. 22, No. 4 (Spring 1998): 135–170; Stuart K. Masaki, "The Korean Question: Assessing the Military Balance," *Security Studies*, Vol. 4, No. 2 (Winter 1994–1995): 365–425.

But most U.S. units not already stationed in Asia would not arrive for weeks or months into the war. They would have little effect in averting or countering such North Korean tactics. Rather, such tactics would probably best be countered by ensuring U.S. and South Korean ground forces are well equipped with counterbattery radars and long-range artillery; that air forces have sufficient lethal munitions; that air and ground forces are equipped and trained to work cooperatively; that South Korea has sufficient well-trained security troops behind the forward defenses; and that troops and key infrastructure are provided with chemical protection and decontamination equipment and training.

Another criticism sometimes lodged against these analyses is that they do not fully account for the difficulty of conducting counteroffensive operations with the aim of overthrowing North Korea's government and perhaps occupying the country. In fact, in North Korea's weakened state, a counteroffensive would likely require fewer forces than critics imagine. Occupying the country, however, could pin U.S. ground forces down in another commitment of indefinite duration—a situation that would be better avoided altogether.

## War against Iraq

The Bottom-Up Review held that the U.S. military would likely be able to thwart and counter an attack by a remilitarized Iraq against Kuwait and Saudi Arabia, using the same type of "building block"—about half of U.S. conventional forces—as would be required in the Korean scenario. That building block was predicated on an Iraq rearmed to the levels that it had achieved before the Gulf War. Far from rearming since that war, Iraq has been held in check by international trade sanctions, constant enforcement of two no-fly zones, and occasional concentrated strikes by aircraft and missiles. Although the country retains significant levels of ground units and equipment, its air force is virtually nonexistent. Furthermore, observers believe that all of its units (other than the Republican Guard) are operating at 50 percent combat effectiveness and that 50 percent of all its equipment lacks spares.[33] It seems highly unlikely under the circumstances that Iraq would attempt an invasion of Kuwait or Saudi Arabia. But if it did, repulsing it would require substantially smaller U.S. forces—possibly less than half the force envisioned for that purpose by the U.S. military in its current Desert-Storm-size MTW building block.

## Protecting Taiwan

As Edward Friedman discusses in Chapter 9, tensions between China and Taiwan pose potential military concerns for the United States. Some people view a war with China over Taiwan's continued de facto autonomy to be more likely than either of the two scenarios the Defense Department used during the 1990s as force-sizing templates. America's military obligations toward Taiwan are less than clear, however. Under the "one-China" policy that the United States embraced in the 1970s,

[33]*The Military Balance 1999/2000*, p. 134.

Taiwan is not a nation but is a province of China. Although the Taiwan Relations Act (TRA) of 1979 offers a vague security guarantee to the people on Taiwan, U.S. policy has been one of "strategic ambiguity."[34]

Some observers call for ending that policy in favor of a promise to come to Taiwan's aid militarily in the event that China uses force against the island. But such a policy might embolden Taiwan to declare formal independence or to take other actions certain to cause a war that is otherwise avoidable. A better policy might be to clarify the ambiguity, letting both China and Taiwan know for certain that the United States will not come to Taiwan's aid militarily if the island provokes the mainland's use of force, for example by declaring formal independence; but that conversely, America will not stand by if an unprovoked China uses force against Taiwan.[35]

Can Taiwan fend off China without help from the U.S. military? Chinese armed forces greatly outnumber Taiwan's, but not all of the mainland's military power can be brought to bear against the island. Taiwan enjoys substantial qualitative advantages in equipment and in the education levels and training of troops. Should China attempt to invade and occupy the island, geography and weather would strongly favor the defense.[36]

The Pentagon's reports to congress on the subject indicate that invading would pose great difficulties and bring almost certain damage to China's economy and diplomatic interests. Nevertheless, the reports find that, with a massive commitment of military and civilian assets over a long period of time—and assuming that no third party intervened—PLA success would be possible.[37] Others in the Defense Department hold that China would not be able to invade for at least a decade, however.[38] Outside the department, a comprehensive and credible analysis by Michael O'Hanlon finds that for at least the next decade, China will not have the basic capabilities needed to invade and occupy Taiwan, even if U.S. forces refrain from intervening on Taiwan's behalf.[39]

---

[34]Taiwan Relations Act, Public Law 96–8, April 10, 1979. For a discussion of the vague nature of the security guarantee, see Thomas J. Christensen, "Posing Problems Without Catching Up: China's Rise and Challenges for American Security" (International Security, Vol. 25, No. 4, (Sprint 2001): 5–40).

[35]Thomas J. Christensen, "Clarity on Taiwan," *The Washington Post*, March 20, 2000.

[36]Michael O'Hanlon, "Can China Conquer Taiwan?" *International Security,* Vol. 25, No.2, (Fall 2000); Admiral Dennis C. Blair, Statement before the Senate Armed Services Committee on Fiscal Year 2001 Posture Statement, March 7, 2000, p. 11; "Taiwan's Military: Assessing Strengths and Weaknesses," *Strategic Comments* (London: International Institute for Strategic Studies, Volume 6, Issue 4, May 2000); Christensen, "Posing Problems Without Catching Up: China's Rise and Challenges for American Security."

[37]Department of Defense, "The Security Situation in the Taiwan Strait," Report to Congress Pursuant to the FY99 Appropriations Bill, February 1999; Department of Defense, "Report to Congress Pursuant to the FY2000 National Defense Authorization Act," June 2000.

[38]Admiral Dennis C. Blair, Statement before the Senate Armed Services Committee on Fiscal Year 2001 Posture Statement, March 7, 2000, p. 11; Richard Lardner, "DoD Intelligence Chief Downplays China's Threats Against Taiwan, U.S.," *Inside the Pentagon*, March 2, 2000, p. 2, as quoted in Michael O'Hanlon, "Helping Taiwan Fend Off China."

[39]O'Hanlon, "Can China Conquer Taiwan?"

Some observers concerned about the island's ability to defend itself cite shortfalls in the skill levels of Taiwan's military personnel; problems with logistics, command and control, and force interoperability; a failure to harden or protect critical military and civilian infrastructure; a paucity of minesweepers; and limited capabilities for anti-submarine warfare.[40] Given the relative ambiguity of the U.S. military commitment, it seems prudent for Taiwan itself to take action on its own behalf to plug such holes.[41]

A growing number of Western observers believe that invasion would cost China too much at any time in the coming decade. Rather, they fear that China would turn to missile strikes and blockades to destroy military and civilian infrastructure, terrorize the population, and cause economic hardship, thereby coercing the island to accept terms favorable to the mainland. If faced with these threats, how might Taiwan fare on its own?

By 2010, China might have as many as 700 ballistic missiles facing Taiwan.[42] Because those missiles are extremely inaccurate and carry limited conventional payloads, however, the PRC might have to use hundreds of them just to destroy a single military target.[43] Thus, it seems likely that China would use the missiles as weapons of terror rather than in a strategic role. Such attacks using hundreds of missiles could kill a total of several thousand people and disrupt Taiwan's economy.[44] But the result might be a hardening of resolve on Taiwan rather than the capitulation that the mainland seeks.

China has a large fleet of attack submarines that could block shipping routes into and out of Taiwan. But not all the submarines are fully operational, and even in wartime, not all of the operational ones could be brought to bear at once on the blockade. Using realistic estimates of submarine operational rates, cycle times, and deployment rates, plus estimates of ship-finding and ship-killing probabilities that are very favorable to the Chinese, Michael Glosny finds that over a period of six months, the submarines would destroy less than 4 percent of shipping in the Taiwan Strait—even if Taiwan did not erect antisubmarine barriers or set up convoys for merchant ships. If Taiwan responded to the blockade with antisubmarine barriers and with convoys protected by its frigates and destroyers, the Chinese might destroy at most 2.75 percent of the shipping in the Strait and could lose more than half of

---

[40]Ibid.; "Report to Congress Pursuant to the FY99 Appropriations Bill," p. 16; Christensen, "Posing Problems Without Catching Up."

[41]In areas that require weapons purchases, however, Taiwan's actions are constrained by U.S. willingness to sell arms that pose technology transfer risks or raise China's fears that Taiwan will pursue formal independence. For example, the United States has not yet been willing to sell Aegis TMD-capable destroyers or nuclear attack submarines to Taiwan. Some authors, including Edward Friedman in Chapter 9, recommend that U.S. arms sales to Taiwan be limited and defensive.

[42]China has 150 to 200 such missiles today. See *The Military Balance 1999/2000*, p. 171. The mainland is adding about 50 missiles a year to that stock. See "Adm. Dennis C. Blair Briefs on U.S. Pacific Command," Department of Defense News Briefing, Tuesday, March 7, 2000—2:30 p.m., available at www.defenselink.mil/news/Mar2000/t03072000_t307uspc.html, p. 6 of 10.

[43]O'Hanlon, "Can China Conquer Taiwan?"; Michael A. Glosny, "Strangulation from the Sea: A Chinese Submarine Blockade of Taiwanese Shipping," unpublished paper.

[44]Michael O'Hanlon, "Helping Taiwan Fend Off China," draft, July 2000.

their submarines in the process.[45] For Taiwan, such losses would surely mean a rise in insurance rates, but they would hardly strangle the island's economy.

Nevertheless, it seems possible that the United States might choose to intervene on Taiwan's behalf if the island's losses began to mount. In addition, for purposes of reassuring allies and deterring aggression in the region, the United States might wish to have the military capability to break a blockade. Such an operation would involve naval and possibly air forces; significant U.S. involvement on the ground seems unlikely. Thus, the 1990s MTW building block—requiring half the conventional forces of the Army and the Air Force as well as of the Navy—seems inappropriate. Michael O'Hanlon estimates that it would require forces equivalent to or smaller than the Navy's currently envisioned contribution to an MTW: two to four aircraft carrier battle groups to provide air superiority and to defend against longer-range threats like bombers; ten to fifteen attack submarines and twenty-five to thirty land-based ASW aircraft to set up ASW barriers to protect a corridor for shipping; and twenty-four surface combatant ships to protect convoys of merchant ships.[46]

O'Hanlon's estimates for such an operation seem to overstate the Navy's requirements. For example, given Taiwan's substantial advantages in air power and air defenses, it is hard to see why the U.S. Navy would need more than two carrier battle groups to ensure air superiority and bolster air defenses. Moreover, operating four battle groups in such close waters might not be easy. If additional aircraft are required because significant numbers of Taiwanese aircraft are destroyed, then the United States might prefer to supplement two aircraft carriers with Air Force fighters operating from Taiwan's bases. Thus, the size of the naval force required to break a Chinese blockade might be substantially smaller than the Navy's portion of the 1990s building block. In fact, the number of units the United States can bring to bear may be much less important than making sure a small part of the force has specific improvements, including additional mine-sweeping ships and aircraft, more capability for ASW in shallow water, and better fleet defenses.[47]

## Changing the Yardstick

The uniformed military and the Defense Department understand that the 1990s conventional forces building blocks are much larger than they need to be to check the real threats they might face. In a marked departure from previous documents, the Pentagon's *Annual Report* of February 2000 barely mentioned Iraq and North Korea as the specific aggressors of concern. Moreover, late in the decade, military

[45]Glosny, "Strangulation from the Sea.

[46]O'Hanlon, "Helping Taiwan Fend Off China." O'Hanlon assumes that the carriers would operate without the submarines that often support carrier battle groups.

[47]Christensen, "Posing Problems Without Catching Up." Others argue that the United States should plan to bring additional offensive capabilities to bear as well, for example, medium-range bombers and long-range stand-off weapons like cruise missiles and ballistic missiles that can attack Chinese ports, air and missile bases, and command and control centers. See Khalilzad, *The United States and a Rising China*. But given the ambiguity of the U.S. obligation as well as China's sheer size and its possession of nuclear missiles capable of reaching the United States, it is not clear that the United States should or would respond to a blockade of the Straits or missile attacks on Taiwan with direct attacks on China.

briefings and department documents introduced a concept of "overmatch" to justify the situation: "U.S. forces must continue to overmatch the military power of regional states with interests hostile to the United States."[48]

The Pentagon argues that it needs this overmatch to ensure success in case the enemy turns out to be larger or the circumstances more difficult than expected. Many observers would agree that the United States should have such an insurance policy for one war. But the Pentagon argues that America needs two of them. This "double-overmatch" insurance seems excessive considering the size and shape of actual potential adversaries today and any realistic trends for the future. And maintaining two insurance policies is expensive. Dropping just one of them—adopting a strategy that emphasized a single "building-block"-sized MTW and multiple smaller contingencies—would allow the military to reduce forces and save money, at the same time easing the consequences of deployments on the military's readiness to execute declared strategy.

## FINDING NONMILITARY SOLUTIONS TO INTERNATIONAL PROBLEMS

Decision makers would also do well to take a hard look at the military's role in a growing list of chores that could be handled by civilian institutions. For example, much of what the Defense Department now considers to be its responsibility in "shaping the international environment" is simply a substitute for old-fashioned diplomacy and foreign assistance. Military-to-military engagements, infrastructure construction projects, educational efforts in foreign countries, and a long list of other activities metamorphosed during the 1990s from "things to do if there is time" to "commitments." As Robert Lieber points out in the Introduction, federal resources for traditional "shaping" mechanisms—civilian diplomacy, participation in international institutions, and foreign assistance—declined dramatically during the 1990s. As a result, in some regions of the world, the military is now the only U.S. actor with the presence and the resources to conduct diplomacy and provide assistance. But relying on the military for these services is expensive. It can lead to an unwanted military orientation of U.S. foreign policy, a negative perception of U.S. goals and interests abroad, and a watering down of the military's ability to fight in wars. Substantially reducing the military's role in this component of national security strategy and modestly increasing the resources for the State Department and other civilian institutions would result in more efficient and reliable "shaping" of the international environment.

Similarly, activities such as preparing to manage the aftermath of a nuclear or biological attack on the United States may sound like reasonable responsibilities for a peacetime military. But such missions belong to civilian enforcement and emergency services. Using the military for them costs money, adds to complaints of

---

[48]William S. Cohen, *Annual Report to the President and the Congress*, Department of Defense, February 2000, p. 7.

overwork, draws leadership attention away from other areas, and may raise risk levels. We owe it to ourselves to seek out nonmilitary solutions to international problems and adopt a positive preference for them.

# CONVENTIONAL FORCE STRUCTURE FOR THE NEW CENTURY

## Reducing Forces and Modernization Plans Across-the-Board

Reducing the role of the armed forces in duties that can be handled by civilian institutions and adjusting strategic priorities to emphasize a single MTW (sized like the Defense Department's 1990s building block, with built-in "overmatch" as a sort of insurance policy) and multiple smaller operations would allow the nation to cut back the military's conventional forces. One possibility would be to trim forces across-the-board by 15 percent to 20 percent from 2001 levels. Reducing the Army from 10 active-duty combat divisions to 8, the Navy from 12 aircraft carrier battle groups to 10 and from about 300 battle force ships to 250, and the Air Force from 20 tactical air wings to 16 would leave the military comfortably sized to fight and win a single major theater war in the manner it currently plans, and at the same time to handle peacekeeping operations and smaller-scale contingencies at least as well as during the 1990s.

Alternatively, with some investment in specific areas of weakness, the smaller force could handle peacekeeping and smaller-scale contingencies at about the same time as two smaller major theater wars—wars sized not with the overmatch the military desires, but consistent with the actual threat that Iraq and North Korea pose after a decade of economic and military decline. If the services match these reductions in conventional units with proportional cutbacks in planned procurement levels, the resulting force will be equipped at least as well as it would be under plans that the Defense Department formulated during the Clinton administration. And as the F-22 air-to-air fighter, the Joint Strike Fighter, the V-22 tilt-rotor transport plane, the New Attack Submarine, the DD-21 advanced surface ship, the Comanche scout and attack helicopter, the Longbow version of the Apache attack helicopter, new precision munitions, and other modernized weapon systems enter the force in quantity, the military—though somewhat smaller than today's—should be considerably more capable.

Trimming forces and procurement plans in this way would save the nation billions of dollars a year. In fact, combined with some reductions and consolidations in military infrastructure, the annual savings could offset the upward budgetary pressure described earlier in this chapter. Rather than growing over the decade to a level exceeding $325 billion (in 2001 constant dollars), national defense outlays could be held at $290 billion or below in real terms for a decade or more.[49]

Such across-the-board reductions in conventional forces would be consistent with the force cuts of the 1990s. Since the fall of the Berlin Wall, the Defense Department has continued to apportion budgets across the military departments according to

---

[49]Williams (ed.), *Holding the Line,* "Introduction."

the same formula of "service shares" that it used during the Cold War (see Figure 3). As the overall military budget fell, the budgets of the Army, the Department of the Navy (including the Navy and the Marine Corps), and the Air Force all dropped by the same percentage. Thus, it is no surprise that the basic units of conventional fighting power were reduced by nearly the same proportions across the services: the Army cut 30 percent of active-duty battalions, the Navy 27 percent of battle force ships, and the Air Force 33 percent of active attack and fighter squadrons.[50]

## Reshaping Forces and Equipment to the Needs of the Future

Rather than reshaping forces to the needs of the future, however, across-the-board reductions would perpetuate a basic force design that was meant for the Cold War. Yet much has changed since then: the location and type of likely operations, the size and equipment of potential adversaries, and a world of new technology. It does not seem possible that the relative utility of or preferences for ground, air, and naval forces would be just the same in the future as they were during the Cold War. Moreover, retaining the Cold War structure fosters a business-as-usual attitude, stifling innovation and ingenuity in every aspect of military affairs.

Similarly, simply trimming procurement levels for all the weapon systems in the Clinton procurement plan makes little sense. The 1997 Quadrennial Defense Review justified its modernization plan—inherited with only minor changes from the 1993 Bottom-Up Review—as vital to its third component of national security strategy, preparing for an uncertain future. The 1997 review paid lip service to the

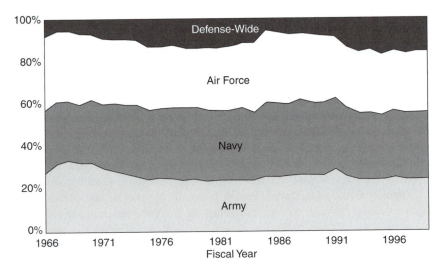

**Figure 3.** Service Shares of Defense Department Spending

[50]"Army Greenbook for Fiscal Year 2001," available at http://www.asafm.army.mil/pubs/greenbook; Appendix D of the Department of Defense *Annual Reports to Congress* for 1995 and 2000, available at http://www.dtic.mil/execsec/adr95/appendix_d and http://www.dtic.mil/execsec/adr00/appendix_d.

concept of a revolution in military affairs—a fundamental transformation in the essential elements of the armed forces, sparked by rapid advances in information technologies, information processing capabilities, precision munitions, and stealth technology that will favor forces with a decisive advantage in future warfare. Yet Clinton administration plans allocated less than 2 percent of the Defense Department's acquisition budget to the experimentation and technology demonstration programs intended to explore new fighting concepts.[51] In contrast, under the same 1997 plan, tens of billions of dollars are earmarked each year for what the plan called "leap-ahead" systems. But most of those systems—including the Air Force's F-22 air-to-air fighter plane, the Army's Comanche helicopter, and even the Navy's new attack submarine—are based largely on designs developed during the 1980s to solve Cold War military problems.

A better plan is to capitalize on technology that offers innovative solutions to military problems and to reshape conventional force structure and modernization programs in light of the genuine missions and threats that the military faces in the future—letting strategy, missions, and innovative solutions drive the apportionment of funding across the services. In some cases, such innovation might require the new technologies or concepts associated with the so-called revolution in military affairs. In other cases, however, all that might be needed is to bring existing technology to bear in quantity, or to adjust force structure and purchase additional equipment for strained units, with a goal of better matching the realities of future operations.

For example, as discussed in the previous section, a regional war with Iraq or North Korea is not likely to require the size of forces previously envisioned for a major theater war. Moreover, both of those wars may become increasingly unlikely as U.S. forces and international sanctions continue to pin Iraq down, and as North and South Korea proceed with diplomatic efforts toward reconciliation. If that is the case, then breaking a Chinese blockade of the Taiwan Strait may become the most likely large-scale military operation for U.S. forces in the future. But ground forces would be of little use in such an operation. Thus, the nation might want to reduce ground forces more deeply than naval ones. Conversely, if the U.S. role in peacekeeping operations is to be expanded or if rooting regional aggressors out of their capitals and occupying their countries takes priority, then ground forces might be retained in preference to some naval ones.[52]

The nation would benefit from a reexamination of force structure choices within the services as well. For example, the services complain that some units have "high demand and low density" (HD/LD) in the force, that is, there are too few of them to handle the frequent requests for them in military operations. In the Army, civil affairs units and military police are called upon repeatedly (a situation exacerbated by the fact that some support capabilities that the Army needs in today's missions are prevalent not in the active forces but in the reserve component). In the Air Force, Joint STARS ground surveillance units and aircraft equipped to suppress

---

[51]Acquisition includes procurement and research, development, test, and evaluation.

[52]For three views of the future and corresponding strategies and forces, see Williams (ed.), *Holding the Line.*

enemy air defenses face frequent deployments. The Navy's E/A-6B electronic jamming aircraft, now a joint resource, were in constant use during the air wars of the 1990s. In the context of the overall defense budget, fixing these problems would not be expensive, but it would require the Defense Department to make fixing them a priority and to accept the trade-offs.

Similarly, the nation and the military would benefit from adjusting modernization plans to match more realistic threats and priorities. As one example, the Navy's vision of the future emphasizes littoral warfare, that is, fighting in and from the waters along coastlines. The sea service devotes billions of dollars a year to developing and building advanced surface ships, nuclear-powered submarines, and complex tactical airplanes. Nations with vastly smaller defense budgets cannot afford such expensive systems. Instead, they buy less advanced diesel electric submarines and plan to lay underwater mines—cheap solutions to exploit potential U.S. weaknesses. Yet the U.S. Navy devotes relatively little attention and limited resources to countermine warfare and antisubmarine warfare in shallow water. Small investments in these areas could make a big difference in the operations the Navy faces.

Likewise—as often urged by advocates of a revolution in military affairs—the Army might purchase unmanned aerial vehicles for reconnaissance at much lower cost than Comanche armed reconnaissance helicopters. If Apache Longbow helicopters could provide most of the attack capability the Army hoped to get from Comanche, it might be able to forego the purchase of some or all of the newer helicopters. Similarly, given the heavy emphasis that potential enemies place on surface-to-air missiles and other ground-based air defenses, the Air Force might find that a relatively small investment in defense suppression aircraft makes much more sense than purchasing hundreds of expensive stealth F-22 air-to-air fighters. Given the future difficulty of operating from fixed bases in many locations, the Air Force might also get more leverage from investing in conventional capabilities on its existing bomber force than from new fighters.

These suggestions are offered not as the single best path to a stronger and more cost-effective military, but as examples of trade-offs that would make the armed forces more capable in likely future missions than it is today—and that would cost far less than current plans. The point is that alternatives exist and that decision makers must set priorities and make choices that reflect the future, rather than the past.

## SUMMARY

The United States enjoys a wide margin of primacy in the military dimension. Yet primacy does not guarantee that the nation will always get its way. It is also not clear that retaining primacy for generations is an achievable or even worthwhile goal of military policy. What is clear is that to prevent the eventual emergence of any global competitor, as advocated by those who adhere to a policy of primacy, could cost substantially more than the United States ever spent during the Cold War to triumph over a global peer with huge economic and military resources. Adopting a policy of primacy could consume the lion's share of the federal budget surplus that economists project could accrue outside the Social Security trust fund during the coming decade.

Despite its preeminence, the U.S. military faces problems. The jobs that the nation asks of it have changed dramatically since the Cold War ended. Yet conventional force structures and modernization plans, though smaller than during the 1980s, still seem better suited to the Cold War demands of high-intensity warfare in Europe than to realistic future threats and missions. Part of the reason is that the Defense Department continues to cling to the two-major-theater war sizing principle as a central element of national security strategy for the military. That principle, adopted during the early 1990s, appears to have outlived its usefulness in the world that the armed forces actually face.

It is time for a serious reassessment of military priorities. This chapter offers one way to adjust priorities and measuring sticks in line with current demands on the military and realistic expectations for the future. Making these adjustments would allow the nation to trim conventional force structure and to hold military spending constant in real terms for another decade, while maintaining a strong and capable military. Simply trimming all the forces equally would leave big problems unaddressed, however. Both the nation and the military would be much better served by reshaping the conventional forces and equipment plans to match real-world needs and to take advantage of innovative solutions to military problems.

The Bush administration seems poised to address the problems outlined in this chapter. During the 2000 election campaign, President Bush promised to keep the military strong and to bolster trust between the White House and American service men and women. At the same time, he vowed to effect change in the military without a large rise in military spending, to reduce the level of military deployments, and to break with the traditional allocation of service budget shares by setting some procurement funds aside for the services that prove most effective in developing new programs.

The review of military strategy, forces, equipment, and budgets that Secretary of Defense Donald Rumsfeld has undertaken as of this writing is reported to address the issues addressed here. Some reports indicate that the administration is likely to abandon, or at least greatly soften, the emphasis that the first Bush administration and the Clinton administration placed on being prepared to fight and win two major theater wars at about the same time, perhaps in favor of scenarios for coming to Taiwan's assistance against a rising China. Changes in force structure and modernization programs to reflect new threats and priorities and to take advantage of modern technologies also appear to be on the table. Time will tell whether the administration will be successful in defining a military strategy that reflects realistic interests, threats, and priorities; developing a plan for reshaping conventional forces and weapons programs that matches the strategy and that capitalizes on technological opportunities to solve military problems; and convincing the military, the American public, and congress of the new plan's efficacy.

# 12

# Use of Force Dilemmas
## Policy and Politics

## BRUCE W. JENTLESON
### Duke University

I began my *Eagle Adrift* article stating that "while much has changed with the end of the Cold War questions regarding the use of military force remain at the core of both U.S. foreign policy strategy and U.S. foreign policy politics."[1] This situation is no less true today, in particular with regard to ethnic and related conflicts. These conflicts have been the crucial military intervention issues for U.S. foreign policy and for the international community more generally over the past decade, and likely will remain so for the coming decade. Also, these conflicts tend to stir the most contentious domestic political debates within the United States and to have problematic collateral effects in U.S. relations with allies and within the United Nations. In these respects, they manifest the problems Robert Lieber raises in his overview chapter of the need for the United States to be more consistent in its leadership and less self-constraining through its domestic politics if it is to have any chance of sustaining its primacy.

Often the arguments are made that little really can be done to prevent such conflicts and that for the United States as a great power, they matter very little and are distractions from the real business of major power geopolitics and balance of

Bruce W. Jentleson is Director of the Terry Sanford Institute of Public Policy and Professor of Public Policy and Political Science at Duke University. He is the author and editor of seven books, most recently *American Foreign Policy: The Dynamics of Choice in the 21st Century* (W. W. Norton, 2000) and *Opportunities Missed, Opportunities Seized: Preventive Diplomacy in the Post–Cold War World* (Rowman and Littlefield, 1999), as well as of numerous articles. In 1993–1994, he served on the State Department Policy Planning Staff as Special Assistant to the Director. In 1999–2000, he served as a senior foreign policy advisor to Vice President Al Gore and the Gore-Lieberman campaign.

[1]Bruce W. Jentleson, "Who, Why, What and How: Debates over Post-Cold War Military Intervention," in Robert J. Lieber (ed.), *Eagle Adrift: American Foreign Policy at the End of the Century* (New York: Longman, 1997), p. 40.

power. This was the approach with which the Bush administration came into office. They largely rejected the "Clinton doctrine" on humanitarian intervention. For key members of the new team, the interests at stake in ethnic and related conflicts tend to be too low, the costs too high, and the options too few. Yet, while many mistakes were made by the Clinton administration in how and when it intervened, there are real questions as to whether the Bush administration is drawing the right lessons.[2] In many of the 1990s cases, the interests at stake proved to be greater than asserted; it was the costs of waiting, more than the costs of acting early, that were so high; and in case after case, far from staying open, the available options narrowed over time. There was nothing inevitable about the ethnic cleansing in Bosnia, or the genocide in Rwanda, or other horrific conflicts of the past decade.[3]

While giving due credit in the Bosnia case to the 1995 Dayton Accords and the follow-on NATO peacekeeping, this success came only *after* three to four years of ethnic cleansing already had been inflicted and only *after* the societies were torn asunder—and even then more as a matter of averting a reversion to mass violence than as having accomplished the postconflict peace-building mission. Similarly, in Kosovo and East Timor in 1999 and since then, whatever has been achieved has been only *after* mass killings, only *after* scores of villages were ravaged, only *after* hundreds of thousands were left as refugees. Yes, these conflicts were stopped from getting worse—but they already were humanitarian tragedies.

The United States is not the only international actor on which these lessons bear. But given its leadership if not primacy, it is the most crucial one. For whether it is through U.S. unilateral policies, its leadership of NATO, its role in the United Nations, or its other multilateral and bilateral roles and relationships, it will continue to play key roles.

Although the focus herein is principally on use of force issues, it is of course true that the optimal overall strategy also must have political, economic, diplomatic, and other dimensions. Yet these elements more often get addressed than does the use of force. This omission or at least analytic imbalance mirror images the critique of Cold War–era deterrence strategy made by Alexander George and Richard Smoke, that one of its fundamental flaws was its "preoccupation with threats of punishment" to the exclusion of a broader approach "that encompasses the utility of positive inducements as well as, or in lieu of, threats of negative sanctions."[4]

---

[2]This article draws heavily on my previous work, particularly Bruce W. Jentleson (ed.), *Opportunities Missed, Opportunities Seized: Preventive Diplomacy in the Post–Cold War World* (Lanham, MD: Rowman and Littlefield, 2000), and Bruce W. Jentleson, *Coercive Prevention: Normative, Political and Policy Dilemmas, Peaceworks 35* (Washington, DC: U.S. Institute of Peace, 2000).

[3]This argument is strongly supported in my *Opportunities Missed* book as well as by many other studies that have called into question the conventional wisdom of these conflicts largely being the "primordialist" playing out of history, and showing instead their more "purposive" dynamics of being historically shaped but not historically determined and the result of deliberate and conscious calculations made by leaders and groups of the purposes to be served by political violence. See, for example, David A. Lake and Donald Rothchild (eds.), *The International Spread of Ethnic Conflict: Fear, Diffusion, and Escalation* (Princeton: Princeton University Press, 1998).

[4]Alexander George and Richard Smoke, *Deterrence in American Foreign Policy: Theory and Practice* (New York: Columbia University Press, 1974).

We thus must address the key policy and political dilemmas involving the use of force as they played out in the Clinton years and as they will continue to be posed for the new Bush administration.

## THE NATIONAL INTEREST DEBATE REDUX

I want to cite again as context my *Eagle Adrift* article, here for the discussion of the difficulties of formulaic approaches to criteria for intervention. Rhetorical invocations notwithstanding, it is exceedingly difficult to set a definition of the national interest that consistently provides genuinely operational policy guidance on when to intervene. Take, for example, the definition offered at the end of the last Bush administration by President George H. W. Bush: "where the stakes warrant, where and when force can be effective, where no other policies are likely to prove effective, where its application can be limited in scope and time, and where the potential benefits justify the potential costs and sacrifice." Anything more specific than that, the outgoing president stated, just was not possible. "There can be no single or simple set of fixed rules for using force . . . Each and every case is unique." The then Chairman of the Joint Chiefs of Staff Colin Powell was no more specific or operational in his 1993 *Foreign Affairs* article, that "the use of force should be restricted to occasions where it can do some good and where the good will outweigh the loss of lives and other costs," and acknowledging that there can be "no fixed set of rules."[5] This is not to say that it should just be left ad hoc. A framework is possible, a formula is not.

It is in this regard that distinctions can be made in the basic orientation that an administration takes to this question, in the framework that it holds and from which it assesses particular cases. Does an administration see such interventions as largely "social work," as Michael Mandelbaum coined the term, a values-based humanitarianism inconsistent with a more classically realist view of the national interest and that thus should be minimized if not avoided? Or does it see the very distinction between interests and values as "largely fallacious," as Stanley Hoffmann responded in their *Foreign Affairs* colloquy, such that "a great power has an 'interest' that goes beyond strict national security concerns and its definition of world order is largely shaped by its values"?[6]

My approach tends to the latter view, for reasons that are borne out by the lessons of the 1990s as noted before. Indeed, in the Bosnia case, it was the Bush-Clinton 1992–1995 efforts to opt out that did the damage to American prestige and that shook NATO. There were real power and interest bases, as well as a values basis, to the calls for a firmer and more robust Bosnia strategy. As for those who

---

[5]Jentleson, "Who, Why, What and How," pp. 51–52.

[6]Michael Mandelbaum, "Foreign Policy as Social Work," *Foreign Affairs* 75 (January/February 1996): 16–32; Stanley Hoffmann, "In Defense of Mother Theresa: Morality in Foreign Policy," *Foreign Affairs* 75 (March/April 1994): 172; see also Hoffmann, "The Politics and Ethics of Military Intervention," *Survival* (Winter 1995–96): 29–51.

then raise the question of values inconsistency and who ask why intervention strategies are attempted here but not there, the answer is that to bring values in is not to knock interests out, that relative assessments still need to be made so as to strike a balance and avoid omni-interventionism. The choice cannot get defined as having to intervene everywhere if we intervene somewhere, or otherwise intervene nowhere. Each situation requires its strategic assessment—but this is an assessment to be made, not an assumption to be set in either direction.

## POLICY CHALLENGES: ETHNIC CONFLICT DETERRENCE AND HUMANITARIAN INTERVENTION STRATEGIES

During the Cold War, we relied on particular versions of deterrence strategy to help keep the peace. One of our major challenges today across the board is how to adapt deterrence strategy to meet the altered geopolitics and threat landscape of the post–Cold War era. A crucial part of this challenge is how to adapt deterrence to convey sufficiently credible threats to help prevent ethnic and related wars from occurring, or at least to limit and contain the levels of mass violence they reach. This question is posed knowing that even during the Cold War, deterrence worked less well at the "subconventional" limited war level than at the strategic or conventional levels.[7] Yet we also know how limited the options are once the Rubicon of mass violence gets crossed, how much of a misnomer "peacekeeping" is in those raging contexts, how demanding it is to undertake even a semi-war-fighting "peace operation," and how endless and protracted postconflict peace-building can be.

The central axiom of all deterrence strategies is that they must be credible, and that credibility is a function of both will and capabilities, the belief that threats will be acted on and the assessment that substantial costs can be imposed. The target of the threat must be convinced that he cannot prevail militarily at acceptable cost. There also is the reassurance function aimed at parties that might be driven to military action less out of aggression than the uncertainties of their security dilemma. Only if they believe that international actors are prepared to respond to aggression by the other side can these parties feel at least somewhat secure in watchful restraint.

The Kosovo case raises important questions in this regard. One of the key debates in this case has been whether more credible threats could have prevented the war from occurring. This argument traces back long before March 1999 or even the October 1998 Rambouillet negotiations. It goes all the way back to the original threat made in December 1992 by President Bush, warning Yugoslav President Slobodan Milosevic that if he started doing in Kosovo what he already was doing in Bosnia, this time the United States and NATO would respond more quickly and

---

[7]George and Smoke, *Deterrence in American Foreign Policy.*

more firmly. However, although restated a number of times during the Clinton administration, this warning was not effectively reinforced in practice. First to close the deal with Milosevic on the Dayton Accords and then as part of the bargaining with him at various stages of their implementation, pressure about Kosovo continued to be sacrificed to other designated higher priorities. There was some validity to this course of action, but only some. To have taken this approach as far as was done was to have reversed the leverage in Milosevic's favor, in effect letting him know that he could repeatedly play the Dayton-Bosnia card to protect himself on Kosovo. There is a basic tenet of proportionality that must be adhered to in seeking accommodation with aggressors, namely, to keep the terms of the deal balanced and not to be so fixated on the issue at hand that too much ground on other associated issues would be ceded to them. That tenet was severely violated in this case.

Moreover, we should not strictly accept the argument that Milosevic was inherently undeterrable on Kosovo because of its cultural-historical symbolism, ideological utility, and different territorial status as part of Serbia proper. Again, it is one thing to acknowledge constraints and pressures, quite another to impute immutability to them. It was not that credible threats were tried but failed to budge Milosevic on Kosovo: it was that they were not genuinely tried.[8] The threats that were made simply were neither consistent nor forceful enough to be credible. Again, this situation was true well before Rambouillet. Milosevic had been stepping up his aggression and repression throughout 1998. The United States and Europe had made tough demands on him in March of that year, only to water these down and stretch them out in the ensuing weeks and months. NATO did undertake some shows of force in its June air exercises over Albania and Macedonia and in its August air-ground-sea exercises in Albania. But getting firm statements through the North Atlantic Council and getting NATO started on planning and mobilization proved difficult and drawn out, undercutting the credibility of NATO's overall posture. As to the United Nations, when a resolution finally passed the UN Security Council in October, it stated only that "action may be needed," and it lacked the now-customary "all necessary steps" clause—even the milder "all appropriate steps" phrasing that had been in the draft resolution eventually was deleted.

It thus should be little wonder that it took the actual initiation of air strikes—of war—for Milosevic to begin even to believe that the United States and NATO were serious. Too little had been done to create credible coercive threats in the months and years leading up to March 24, 1999.

When deterrence fails and humanitarian interventions must be undertaken, we should strive to do better than "winning late" as in Bosnia and "winning ugly" as in Kosovo.[9] Humanitarian intervention operations must be conducted so as to succeed more quickly and more fully, both to limit and end the ethnic violence at hand and, in turn, to strengthen deterrence in regard to the next potential conflict. The Kosovo case is relevant here also with regard to the critique of the U.S.-NATO strategy as too

---

[8]See also Ivo H. Daalder and Michael E. O'Hanlon, *Winning Ugly: NATO's War to Save Kosovo* (Washington, DC: Brookings Institution, 2000), chapters 1 and 2.

[9]"Winning ugly" is Daalder and O'Hanlon's term.

limited a use of force. One element of the critique is that the air strikes moved too slowly to include certain strategic targets; another concerns ground troops having been so explicitly taken off the table at the outset. The shift in late May and early June 1999 to finally threatening to use ground troops is widely considered to have been a crucial factor in forcing Milosevic to concede. While there were other crucial factors such as the shift in Russian diplomacy, not having to face this threat sooner both reduced the actual destructive threat that Milosevic and his army faced on the ground and diluted the credibility of the message of resolve that was being sent to him.

By drawing lessons from Kosovo as well as other cases, we can identify six key parameters for more credible ethnic conflict deterrence and more effective humanitarian intervention strategies.

## 1. Willingness to Use Force Early

The conventional assumption of using force as a last resort needs to be questioned. Force rarely, if ever, should be a first resort, but at times it should be more of an early resort. Last resort amounts to "a lockstep sequencing . . . that is unduly inflexible and relegates the use of force to *in extremis* efforts to salvage a faltering foreign policy."[10] The message "I'll do this only if I absolutely have to" does not convey much credibility. It also cedes the initiative to the target, thus allowing the target to try out all sorts of strategies to see what will work and what advantage can be gained, knowing that there is time available before facing a decision point at which noncompliance may have major consequences.

This situation also poses the problem that strategies that may have worked at one time may have less chance of working at a later time when the conflict has intensified and/or spread, thus illustrating the classic problem in statecraft that the more extensive the objectives, the greater and usually more coercive are the strategies needed to achieve them. Based on the distinction between deterrence and compellence as developed by Thomas Schelling, we know that preventing a conflict from escalating to violence is a more limited objective than ending violence once it has begun.[11] Another aspect is that the capacity of domestic leaders to build "conflict constituencies" is much greater when they have retribution and revenge to invoke.[12]

## 2. Using Force Decisively

As traditionally constructed as the Powell Doctrine, when Secretary of State Colin Powell was Chairman of the Joint Chiefs of Staff, "decisive force" was taken to posit the Gulf War strategy as the model and standard for most, if not all, military

[10]Jane E. Holl, "We the People Here Don't Want No War: Executive Branch Perspectives on the Use of Force," in Aspen Strategy Group, *U.S. and the Use of Force* (Queenstown, MD.: Aspen Institute, 1995), p. 124 and passim.

[11]Thomas C. Schelling, *Arms and Influence* (New Haven: Yale University Press, 1966), pp. 69–74; Alexander L. George and William E. Simms (eds.), The Limits of Coercive Diplomacy (Boulder, Colo.: Westview Press, 1994); Alexander L. George, *Forceful Persuasion* (Washington, D.C.: U.S. Institute of Peace Press, 1992).

[12]Ken Menkhaus and Louis Ortmayer, "Somalia: Misread Crises and Missed Opportunities," in Jentleson, *Opportunities Missed, Opportunities Seized.*

interventions. Forces should be massed in overwhelming numbers and with the central objective of defeating the adversary's military forces as quickly and fully as possible. Moreover, this was not just a strategy but was also a standard, which if it could not be met, would mean that the United States would not undertake military action. The problem was that this concept was a misgeneralization from the Gulf War and did not fit conflicts like that in Bosnia, where the nature of the warfare was less conventional and where the strategy had to be more of a political-military one linked more closely to diplomacy and negotiations.

On the other hand, the Clinton administration's use of force often honed too closely to minimalist tactics of "not too much" or "just enough." The result was that the military capabilities provided were not sufficient in a material sense and that the message conveyed at times undermined rather than enhanced credibility. The accompanying statements may be tough, but if the actual military commitments made are minimalist, the perception is likely to be of a commitment made reluctantly and therefore with questionable will to see it through.

The new Bush administration's challenge is to continue to think in terms of decisiveness but to adapt the strategy to fit better with ethnic and related conflicts. Different balances may need to be struck in air power doctrine on how restrictive to be consistent with political and humanitarian concerns, while on the other hand enhancing the credibility of threats and achieving decisiveness as quickly as possible when force is used. The ground troops question also needs to be addressed, so as to better assess whether the last resort approach may end up making the use of ground troops all the more likely.

## 3. Preventive Deployments

A U.S. Army study defines preventive deployments as "the deployment of military forces to deter violence at the interface or zone of potential conflict where tension is rising among parties."[13] The Macedonia 1993 case is an important example of success. First, as a division of UNPROFOR (United Nations Protection Force, as already deployed in Croatia and Bosnia) and then with its own mandate and moniker as UNPREDEP (UN Preventive Deployment Force), these troops were on the ground at a very early stage in the conflict cycle. Their size and mission were limited, but their presence was felt. The Nordic countries and Canada assumed the bulk of the burden for this operation, but the U.S. troops, despite being small in number and confined to low-risk duties, were disproportionately important as "a signal to all those who want to destabilize the region," as stressed by Macedonian President Gligorov.[14]

In the case of East Timor a strong argument can be made that a preventive deployment force sent prior to the referendum on independence for Indonesia might

---

[13]U.S. Army, Peacekeeping Institute (Carlisle Barracks), *Fundamentals of Peace Operations*, chapter 1, p. 1, http://carlisle-www.army.mil/usacs.../pki/doctrine/fm 100–23/fm 100_3.htm.

[14]Michael G. Roskin, "Macedonia and Albania: The Missing Alliance," *Parameters* (Winter 1993–94): 98; Carnegie Commission, *Final Report*, p. 64.

have made a huge difference, since there was plenty of early warning. In April 1999, during negotiations between the UN and the Indonesian government, local militias backed by the Indonesian army killed more than forty-five refugees seeking shelter in a church compound. Then, even once the referendum agreement was signed, the anti-independence militias intensified their violence and other intimidation. By the eve of the August 30 vote, about ten thousand militia, including two thousand heavily armed irregulars, had "flooded" East Timor.[15]

Can we be certain that a preventive deployment force would have ensured that the mass violence did not occur? Of course not. But a case can be made for the likelihood that it would have been effective. Had it been deployed early enough (e.g., as part of the May 5 agreement on the referendum) and with a firm mandate, it would have carried substantial credibility and there would have been sufficient time to put a strong presence in place on the ground. This action might have had a deterrent effect on the militias and army forces that were planning the violence. And if it did not, the force would have been prepositioned to respond quickly to the first outbreaks of violence. No doubt there would have been some violence, but not likely violence on the scale that transpired while the international community dithered. And although in this case, the United States still would not have needed to take the lead, in other cases of preventive deployments, it might need to do so.

## 4. Adapting Conceptions of Impartiality

There is also a need to adapt traditional notions of "impartiality." Impartiality is relatively straightforward in genuinely humanitarian situations, as in responding to crises caused by natural disasters (e.g., the 1999 Central American earthquake or the 1991 Bangladesh cyclone) or in participating in genuine peacekeeping situations, that is, those in which the parties have reached agreement such that there is a peace to be kept and all parties need to be reassured that they will not be disadvantaged if they abide by the peace. But when the parties are still in conflict, what does it mean to be impartial? Does it mean to apply the same strictures to both sides, even if these leave one side with major military advantages over the other? Or not to coerce either side, irrespective of which one is doing more killing, seizing more territory, or committing more war crimes? In such situations, it is a "delusion," as Richard Betts puts it, to think that absolute impartiality should be the standard.[16] "In some cases," according to Adam Roberts, "impartiality may mean not impartiality between the belligerents, but impartiality in carrying out UN Security Council decisions . . . the UN may, and perhaps should, be tougher with one party than another or give more aid to one side than another."[17]

---

[15]Steven Mufson and Colum Lynch, "East Timor Failure Puts UN on Spot," *Washington Post* (September 26, 1999), p. A1.

[16]Richard R. Betts, "The Delusion of Impartial Intervention," *Foreign Affairs*, 73 (November/December 1994).

[17]Adam Roberts, "The Crisis in UN Peacekeeping," in Chester A. Crocker and Fen Osler Hampson (eds.), *Managing Global Chaos* (Washington, DC: U.S. Institute of Peace, 1996), p. 315. Justice Richard Goldstone, prosecutor for the war crimes tribunal for the former Yugoslavia, felt the same

The guiding requisites for seeking this balance should be along the lines of a "fair-but-firm strategy." On the one hand, the parties to the conflict must have confidence in the fairness of international third parties, with fairness defined as a fundamental commitment to just resolution of the conflict rather than partisanship for or sponsorship of one or the other party to the conflict. But fairness is not necessarily to be equated with impartiality if the latter is defined as a refusal to act even if one side engages in gross and wanton acts of violence or other violations of efforts to prevent the intensification or spread of the conflict. The parties to the conflict must know that cooperation has its benefits and that those benefits will be fully equitable, and also that noncooperation has its consequences and that the international parties are prepared to enforce those consequences differentially as warranted by who does and does not do what. In this regard, fairness and firmness go together quite symmetrically.

## 5. Robust Mission, Rules of Engagement, and Mission-Appropriate Capabilities

Humanitarian intervention forces must be given a robust mission and appropriate training, equipment, and organization to carry out such a mission. Their mandate should include the authority to use force if necessary not just for their own self-protection but for meeting the objectives being pursued. The number of troops must be large enough to make this mandate credible and possible. The troops must be adequately armed. There must be a unified command and effective coordination with other diplomatic and political actors and initiatives, including with NGOs.

This is one of the major challenges the new Bush administration faces in its military and defense strategy. A crucial part of conveying credibility is that the deterring state should have the military capabilities effectively to carry out whatever threats are made. The Pentagon's 1997 Quadrennial Defense Review (QDR) included "smaller-scale contingency operations" (SSC) in its "full spectrum of crises." SSC were defined as "operations [that] encompass the full range of joint military operations beyond peacetime engagement but short of major theater warfare, and include: show-of-force operations, interventions, limited strikes, noncombatant evacuation operations, no-fly zone enforcement, peace enforcement, maritime sanctions enforcement, counterterrorism operations, peacekeeping, humanitarian assistance and disaster relief."[18] Follow-on Pentagon reports have built somewhat on this, but still not nearly to the extent that doctrine and strategy have been developed at the conventional and strategic levels. As Cindy Williams observes in her chapter for the volume, part of the overall defense policy debate concerns whether or how to adapt the classical conventional force-based two major theater wars (MTWs) strategy. Although there are other aspects to this, whether and

---

approach applied to war crimes prosecutions. "Being evenhanded in my opinion doesn't mean one for you and one for you and one for you. Being evenhanded means treating similar atrocities in a similar way." See Tom Gjelten, *Professionalism in War Reporting: A Correspondent's View* (New York: Carnegie Corporation, 1998), p. 13.

[18] U.S. Department of Defense, *Quadrennial Defense Review*, 1997, www.defenselink.mil:80/pubs/qdr/sec3.html, p. 6.

how to give greater centrality to ethnic and related conflicts in force structure planning and the setting of overall strategy are a key part of the debate.

As to the UN, its capabilities tend to be better suited for genuine situations of peacekeeping—that is, when the parties have come to agreement and mostly require a third party to secure the peace that they have made—than for "peace operations" when there still is peace to be made. It was successes of the former type that garnered the 1988 Nobel Peace prize for the UN peacekeeping forces (e.g., Afghanistan, Iran-Iraq war). However, it was failures of the latter type (e.g., the former Yugoslavia) that so decimated the UN peacekeeping reputation. The UN definitely can enhance its peace operations capabilities, and Secretary-General Kofi Annan has made this a high priority. The mid-2000 Report of the Panel on UN Peace Operations (the "Brahimi Report") makes a number of proposals in this regard.[19] Although the proposals have been well received, there are persistent doubts as to whether they will be implemented.

## 6. Political Will of the International Community

Whatever the doctrinal and military capabilities requisites, deterrence also requires credible political will. At the level of the international community this means establishing that there is international political will to intervene even when the conflict is largely an intra-state one. The key issue here is the tension between the norm of sovereignty as the *rights* of states and the norm of sovereignty as also carrying *responsibilities* for states. Article 2(7) of the UN Charter is often pointed to as the embodiment of sovereignty as rights: "Nothing contained in the present Charter shall authorize the United Nations to intervene in matters which are essentially within the domestic jurisdiction of any state." However, numerous other portions of the UN Charter as well as other sources provide normative legitimacy and legal basis for the competing conception of sovereignty as responsibility.[20] The Charter, as Secretary-General Kofi Annan has put it, it "was issued in the name of 'the peoples,' not the governments of the United Nations . . . The Charter protects the sovereignty of peoples. It was never meant as a license for governments to trample on human rights and human dignity. Sovereignty implies responsibility, not just power."[21] Even Article 2(7) needs to be qualified, according to Secretary-General Annan, with "the important rider that this principle shall not prejudice the application of enforcement measures under Chapter VII. In other words, even national sovereignty can be set aside if it stands in the way of the Security Council's overriding duty to preserve international peace and security."[22] Further affirmations of the responsibilities of

---

[19]United Nations, *Report of the Panel on United Nations Peace Operations*, August 2000, http:www.un.org/peace/reports/peace_operations/docs/recommend.htm.

[20]For development of this concept see Francis M. Deng, Sadikei Kimaro, Terence Lyons, Donald Rothchild and I. William Zartman, *Sovereignty as Responsibility: Conflict Management in Africa* (Washington, DC: Brookings Institution, 1996).

[21]Kofi Annan, "Intervention," Ditchley Foundation Lecture XXXV, 1998, p. 2. See also Annan, "Report of the Secretary-General," September 1999.

[22]Idem.

sovereignty are manifested in the Genocide Convention, the Universal Declaration of Human Rights and other international covenants that make no distinction as to whether the offender is a foreign invader or one's own government.

Further complicating this is the debate over whether only the UN Security Council can claim legitimacy in intrastate interventions. Secretary-General Annan has been careful to link his support for the sovereignty-as-responsibility norm to the role of the UN as the principal if not exclusive legitimate international intervener. In criticizing the U.S.-NATO action in Kosovo he strongly asserted his view that the UN Security Council is "the sole source of legitimacy on the use of force." Yet he also acknowledged the failings of the Security Council to act as it should in this crisis, noting that it failed to "unite around the aim of confronting massive human rights violations and crimes against humanity on the scale of Kosovo" and as such was risking "betray[ing] the very ideals that inspired the founding of the United Nations."[23] The two aspects of this statement bring out both the strength and the weakness of the UN as the sole source of legitimacy for such matters.

When major powers claim intervention legitimacy as the United States and NATO did in Kosovo, the concern is raised that normative claims are being used as guises for power politics. To be sure, one cannot go so far as to convey or imply open-ended, or even overly elastic, normative justification for unilateral or mini-multilateral interventions by the United States, NATO, or any other major power or powers. But the consequences of limiting normative legitimacy only to the UN also must be confronted. The concerns about precedent and order are serious, but they can leave the international community unable to uphold the very norms of peace, justice, and human rights that it claims to value.

## U.S. DOMESTIC POLITICAL CONSTRAINTS: HOW FIXED, HOW FLEXIBLE?

Almost every study of U.S. intervention concludes that when all is said and done, the main obstacle is the lack of political will. As an explanatory statement, this assertion is largely true. American administrations have often not acted either at all or soon enough, or with a robust strategy, because there has not been the political will to do so. If the domestic constraints that make this situation so are unchangeable and fixed, then that would be the end of the story. Prevention would continue to be sporadic and mostly too little, too late. There is reason to argue, though, that the domestic political constraints are not necessarily all that fixed, that they have greater potential malleability than typically is presumed.

This point is aptly illustrated by the flaws in the "casualty aversion" view of American public opinion. It is conventional wisdom that the American public will not support virtually any commitments that risk casualties and that even if there is

---

[23]"Secretary-General Says Renewal of Effectiveness and Relevance of Security Council Must Be Cornerstone of Efforts to Promote International Peace in Next Century," United Nations Press Release SG/SM/6997, May 18, 1999.

initial support, it will collapse under the weight of the first casualties incurred. This reaction is attributed to the continuing hangover of the "Vietnam trauma" that was reinforced by the "Somalia trauma," as discussed by Ole Holsti in his chapter. Key decisions made in numerous 1990s cases (e.g., Bosnia, Rwanda, Kosovo, East Timor) as to whether or not to use military force, and if so to do what strategy that action should follow, took the American public's casualty aversion as a hard and fast premise. Although there is no belief that is more ingrained these days, it is a highly simplistic and quite an inaccurate one.

Opinion poll data show the beginning of a "post post-Vietnam" period in the 1980s and the emergence of the "pretty prudent public," a pattern in public opinion that supports some uses of force but opposes others, neither as trigger-happy as some would have liked nor as gun-shy as some have feared. The pattern was based on a distinction between two types of principal policy objectives for which force was being used: restraining aggression and remaking governments. To the extent that the public perceived the principal objective as one of coercing restraint on aggressors threatening the United States, its interests, or its allies, the public was more likely to support the use of force than when the principal objective was to engineer internal political change as in many Third World Cold War interventions.[24] The underlying, albeit usually unarticulated, logic was that the antiaggression objective both had a greater sense of international legitimacy and also was one for which military force was more likely to be efficacious. It was not the case that casualties ever were taken lightly but that the willingness to accept casualties varied with the principal objective for which force was being used. A follow-on study that I did of 1990s cases, now including humanitarian interventions cases as well, showed the public to be "still pretty prudent."[25] Humanitarian interventions actually started with extraordinarily high levels of support, as seen in the early stages of the Somalia case. Although those levels fell precipitously because of the Somalia debacle, as with Vietnam, there was nothing irrational or unstably reactive about not supporting a policy when it appears that the nation's leaders lack a strategy.

The data from Kosovo are especially interesting in this regard. Even though not being overwhelmingly supportive, the public was much more inclined to favor the use of force, *including ground troops and despite possible casualties*, than the Clinton administration kept assuming that it was. As cited in my USIP *Peaceworks* paper, three sets of data are key.[26] First, polls measuring general support for air strike averaged about 57 percent and stayed pretty steady despite the ups and downs and uncertainties of daily news on the war effort. Second, support for ground troops as averaged over twelve polls spanning the course of the Kosovo war showed a slight plurality in support (48 percent/47 percent). Although not an impressive margin in itself, the support is noteworthy in light of President Clinton's telling the

---

[24]Bruce W. Jentleson, "The Pretty Prudent Public: Post Post-Vietnam American Opinion on the Use of Military Force," *International Studies Quarterly* 36 (March 1992): 49–74.

[25]Bruce W. Jentleson and Rebecca L. Britton, "Still Pretty Prudent: Post–Cold War American Public Opinion on the Use of Military Force," *Journal of Conflict Resolution* 42 (August 1998): 395–417.

[26]Jentleson, *Coercive Prevention*, see tables 1, 2, and 3.

American people that ground troops were not necessary and indeed not even "on the table." The numbers thus lack the usual 5 to 10 percent increase in public support that usually comes from a presidential cue. Third, of the five polls directly asking about casualties, four showed majorities agreeing that this war was worth the risk. Here, too, the relative significance of these numbers is greater than their absolute levels. They are surely not as high as the Gulf War numbers, but this tendency is to be expected, since even the strongest supporters of the Kosovo war would not compare its stakes to those of the Gulf War. And again, it was in the context of the president's virtually assuring a zero casualties expedition.

These data show how, despite Kosovo being an intrastate conflict and thus formally fitting the internal policy change objective, Milosevic's track record led the public to perceive the conflict as being about restraining aggression and thus consistent with the type of objective for which support for the use of force tends to be greater. The irony is that separate from any criticism of the administration for giving too much weight to domestic political considerations, the administration was misreading the public and seeing constraints as more fixed than they had to be. There may have been other reasons for not threatening the use of military force earlier than was done and for not considering ground troops earlier, but the presumption of a casualty-phobic public's being unwilling to provide support was fundamentally flawed. This was also the case with the particular type of air strategy chosen, with its priority emphasis on force protection, often to the detriment of achieving the mission.

This is not to say that the American public will ever be eager to use force and to risk casualties, but it is to say that there is no enduring Somalia syndrome among the public.[27] The public may not have the levels of information or pay attention as much as we would like; however, it is less reactive and more deliberative than often portrayed. In its judgment about when, where, and why to use military force, the public fairly consistently takes into account the interests, values, and viability of missions in ways that continue to reinforce my characterization of the "pretty prudent public."

## The "CNN Effect": Overrated

A related misconception is the attribution of exaggerated power over public opinion and political context to the news media, as most often represented by the Cable News Network (CNN) and its real-time, all-the-time global capacity to put breaking events on television. Reference is often made to the "CNN effect" and its two steep opinion curves. On the front end, television coverage initially raises public awareness of a crisis so as to generate great pressure for immediate military intervention and with too little concern for strategy. On the back end, negative coverage of casualties or other major policy disasters fuels a steep drop in public support, thus creating

---

[27]See also the findings in the study by the Triangle Institute for Security Studies (Duke-UNC Chapel Hill), as discussed in Peter D. Feaver and Christopher Gelpi, "A Look at Casualty Aversion," *Washington Post* (November 7, 1999), p. B3.

political pressure for a withdrawal or a major shift in policy even if unwise as a matter of strategy. However, although the effect of CNN and other new telecommunications technologies is not to be denied, it is also not to be exaggerated.

One of the most insightful analyses of this dynamic was done by journalist Warren Strobel. Strobel's main point is that the power of the media is inversely related to how well grounded the policy itself is:

> It is true that U.S. government policies and actions regarding international conflict are subject to more open public review than previously in history. But policymakers retain great power to frame events and solicit public support—indeed, CNN at times increases this power. Put another way, if officials do not have a firm and well-considered policy or have failed to communicate their views in such a way as to garner the support of the American people, the news media will fill this vacuum (often by giving greater time and attention to the criticisms or policy preferences of its opponents).[28]

Strobel bases his argument on two of the cases so often cited as prima facie evidence for the CNN effect: Somalia and Bosnia. His research included over one hundred interviews with senior policy-makers from both the Bush and the Clinton administrations, military officers and spokespersons, journalists, and others. He acknowledges that "CNN and its brethren have made leadership more difficult" and that it is television's inherent nature as a visual medium to "feed on conflict, whether political or physical, emphasizing the challenge to policy." But his emphasis is both clear and well supported: "When policy is well grounded, it is less likely that the media will be able to shift officials' focus. When policy is clear, reasonably constant, and well communicated, the news media follow officials rather than lead them . . ."[29]

## Congress: Formidable, but Not Fixed, Constraints

There can be no doubt about the formidability of the constraints imposed by Congress regarding most uses of force. But these constraints should not be taken, as they so often are, to be so fixed as to be prohibitive of strategies such as coercive prevention. There are three points that are key in this regard.

The first point is that on issues of the use of force, Congress often stops short of going so far as explicitly to block the president from acting. It often criticizes the action, seeks to condition and limit it, and condemns it rhetorically—but rarely does Congress go so far as to try to prohibit the president from using force when a decision has been made to do so. Regarding Bosnia, for example, in December 1995 following the signing of the Dayton Accords, Congress imposed conditions and made extensive criticisms but stopped short of blocking U.S. troops from being part of the NATO deployment. Likewise, regarding Kosovo, Congress has threatened to impose a withdrawal of U.S. troops but has not actually done so. This is not to say

---

[28]Warren P. Strobel, "The Media and U.S. Policies Toward Intervention: A Closer Look at the 'CNN Effect,'" in Chester A. Crocker and Fen Osler Hampson with Pamela Aall (eds.), *Managing Global Chaos* (Washington, DC: U.S. Institute of Peace Press, 1996), pp. 357–376 at 358.

[29]Ibid., pp. 373–374.

that such actions are insignificant, only that they are not prohibitive. Political capital is required to manage such politics, but the politics can be managed if a president is sufficiently determined.

Second, consistent with the preceding analysis of public opinion and the CNN effect, the underlying politics also has some play in them. Public opinion is not so automatically opposed to uses of force, and the CNN effect is less driving and determinative, than is so often assumed. This finding is consistent with the study by Steven Kull and I. M. Destler on how Congress, in many respects, has been "misreading" the public on foreign policy since the end of the Cold War.[30] Some of this also bears on the problem of congressional resistance to the use of force. Indeed, it is not just in the casualty aversion assumption that the public is being misread on Capitol Hill. Other data show the public to be much more internationalist than is typically presumed, as Ole Holsti's chapter indicates. The public essentially understands that the United States has come to be so interconnected in so many ways with the rest of the world, that isolationism is not just undesirable—it simply is not possible.

Moreover, two types of groups that often are pro-intervention have become more assertive players in pressure group politics. One type comprises the NGOs, which at minimum are forces against inaction and inattention to humanitarian concerns. The other type comprises ethnic, religious, and racial groups that, as manifestations of the increasing diversity of the American people, trace their roots to parts of the world in which many of these conflicts are occurring.

Third, strong presidential leadership can have a continuing impact. For all that has transpired in U.S. foreign policy over the last three decades, it remains the case that Americans look to their presidents first and foremost for leadership on international affairs. Congress has its role, politically and constitutionally, and indeed is often looked to for leadership when presidents fail or otherwise fall short. But determined presidents often can make the difference between domestic constraints that are fixed and unyielding, and those that although formidable, can be made somewhat less constraining.

## CONCLUSION: DIFFICULT, BUT DOABLE

Use-of-force questions concerning ethnic and related conflicts are likely to be one of the Bush administration's most difficult foreign policy challenges. The orientation with which the new president and many of his team came into office was to seek to de-emphasize these issues as much as possible. It is more likely that the Bush administration will have to deal with these issues, just as the Clinton and the previous Bush administrations had to and for which they paid the price when they did not.

---

[30]Steven Kull and I. M. Destler, *Misreading the Public: The Myth of a New Isolationism* (Washington, DC: Brookings Institution Press 1999).

The dilemmas posed in this chapter must be dealt with. There can be no doubt about the difficulties of resolving or even managing them. The policy strategies have formidable requisites. The domestic constraints ring of political risks.

But what are the alternatives? Having another decade with a death toll, destructiveness, and inhumanity like the last one? Trying to keep claiming to be the world's "city on the hill" while sticking to a narrow conception of the national interest? Keep trying to put societies back together after they have been devastated? Where is the strategic wisdom in continually doing so little for so long that the "realistic" choices end up being between a bad option and a worse one?

These questions do not bear only on the United States, but they do bear especially on us. A more committed and more robust ethnic conflict deterrence posture and a more effective humanitarian intervention strategy may well be akin to what Winston Churchill said about democracy—the worst alternative except for all the others.

# 13

# Weapons Proliferation and Missile Defense
## New Patterns, Tough Choices

## MICHAEL NACHT
### University of California, Berkeley

Concern about the spread, and eventual use, of nuclear weapons has been evident since the dawn of the nuclear age. The eminent physicist Leo Szilard, for example, recognized before the first nuclear test at Alamagordo, New Mexico, July 16, 1945, what was at stake:

> The development of atomic power will provide the nations with new means of destruction. The atomic bombs at our disposal represent only the first step in this direction, and there is almost no limit to the destructive power which will become available in the course of their future development. Thus a nation which sets the precedent of using these newly liberated forces of nature for purposes of destruction may have to bear the responsibility of opening the door to an era of devastation on an unimaginable scale.[1]

How to stop the acquisition of these weapons, to deter their use, and to protect the American homeland from being destroyed by them has drawn the attention of political leaders, diplomats, defense planners, military officers, legislators, arms control advocates, and scholars from the Acheson-Lillienthal Report of 1946 to the signing of the Nuclear Non-Proliferation Treaty in 1968 to the heated debates at the dawn of this new century. This paper argues, however, that the essence of the weapons proliferation challenge and of the appropriate responses to it is now changing in fundamental ways that will require new thinking and difficult policy choices in the years ahead. Moreover, the challenge typifies the central theme of this volume: namely, that

Michael Nacht is Professor of Public Policy and Dean of the Goldman School of Public Policy at the University of California, Berkeley. From 1994 to 1997, he served as Assistant Director for Strategic and Eurasian Affairs of the U.S. Arms Control and Disarmament Agency.

[1]Richard Rhodes, *The Making of the Atomic Bomb* (New York: Simon and Schuster, 1986), p. 749.

American power has never been greater than today; that without U.S. leadership, ineffective policies result; but that the supremacy of American military power does not translate easily into U.S. influence in shaping the international response to this challenge.

The main adjustments to the policy agenda are these:

**1. From Nuclear Weapons to Weapons of Mass Destruction (WMD).** For decades the focus of weapons proliferation was almost solely on nuclear devices, both fission weapons of the basic types detonated at Hiroshima and Nagasaki in August 1945 and the much more powerful thermonuclear weapons first deployed by the United States in the 1950s. Now the threat concerns the combination of nuclear, chemical and biological weapons and the means for their delivery (both ballistic missiles that are boosted into the atmosphere and then return to earth following gravitational forces, and cruise missiles that are aerodynamically powered throughout their flight path). This collection of weapons and delivery systems is labeled "weapons of mass destruction" (WMD). An emerging issue is whether to use the threat of nuclear retaliation to deter first use of chemical or biological weapons against U.S. forces or allies.

**2. From "Non-proliferation" to "Managing Proliferation" to "Counter Proliferation."** Through much of the Cold War, the proliferation debate was divided into two parts: "vertical proliferation"—the enhancement of the arsenals of the nuclear weapons states, principally the United States and the Soviet Union; and "horizontal proliferation"—the spread of these weapons to states other than those that had acquired them by the mid-1960s (the United States, the Soviet Union, the United Kingdom, France, and China). "Capping" vertical proliferation and stopping horizontal proliferation were dual objectives. By the mid to the late 1970s, with the linkage established between nuclear energy facilities and nuclear weapons programs, a distinct goal of "managing" the process emerged, acknowledging that spread would occur while trying to limit its pace and scope. By the 1990s, an additional element of U.S. policy emphasized "counter-proliferation." Use of this term acknowledged that in some circumstances, the spread of WMD would be a fait accompli. While trying to slow it down—utilizing international agreements, informal understandings, security guarantees, and economic incentives and sanctions—increasing attention turned to military and other means of confronting and, if necessary, destroying, the threat. This shift in turn opened the United States to criticism that it was shifting from a multilateral to a unilateral approach to the WMD challenge. Charges of "unilateralism" intensified after September 1999 when the U.S. Senate refused its consent to ratification of the Comprehensive Nuclear Test Ban Treaty (CTBT).

**3. From "Bilateral Nuclear Deterrence" and "Extended Deterrence" to a Focus on the threat from "Rogue States."** The Cold War was dominated by the U.S.-Soviet nuclear arms competition. The arsenals controlled by Washington and Moscow dwarfed those of the other nuclear powers. While American and Soviet experts refined the details of mutual deterrence and counterforce strategies, the other three nations adopted policies of minimum deterrence, believing that a small, secure retaliatory nuclear force would be sufficient to deter an initial attack. The U.S. also emphasized the requirements to maintain the security of its allies in Western Europe and East Asia. With the collapse of the Cold War, attention has shifted to smaller states, adversarial to the United States, that currently or could soon possess WMD and threaten their use against the American homeland. North Korea, Iran, and Iraq were most often cited, first as "rogue states," then by the late 1990s, as "states of concern, and again as "rogue states" by the George W. Bush administration. A focus on "non-state actors"—groups not directly controlled by any national govern-ment—also developed after the use of chemical weapons in the Tokyo subway in 1993 by the Aum Shinrikyo, a Japanese terrorist organization.

**4. Resurgence of Serious Attention to Missile Defense.** Defense against bal-listic missiles has been a major issue throughout the nuclear age. In the United States, early Nike-Zeus systems gave way to planning for the anti-Soviet Sentinel system during the Johnson administration (the Soviets had already deployed an antiballistic missile [ABM] system around Moscow) and then to a more limited anti-Chinese Safe-guard system approved by President Nixon. With the signing of the U.S.-Soviet ABM Treaty in 1972, missile defenses were placed on the strategic back burner until Presi-dent Reagan unveiled the Strategic Defense Initiative (SDI) in 1983. Reagan's elabo-rate space-based concept was intended to provide an "astrodome" shield over the U.S., but it proved to be beyond technological reach. Instead, especially after the 1991 Gulf War, attention shifted to theater missile defenses (TMD) to protect U.S. forward-deployed forces and allies. But the rogue state threat to U.S. territory generated sub-stantial bipartisan support in congress for a national missile defense (NMD) to protect the American homeland against limited attack. The prospect of NMD deployment, en-thusiastically endorsed by President George W. Bush, has in turn generated tensions in U.S.-NATO, U.S.-Russia, and U.S.-China relations.

Consider first the chief political, military, and technological issues that shaped the historical evolution of weapons proliferation in world politics. Then we will be better positioned to flesh out these emerging patterns and the tough policy choices they raise.

# A BRIEF HISTORICAL REVIEW

## A. The First Two Decades: 1945–1965

The first question to ask is why: why do states acquire these terribly destructive weapons? A substantial scholarly literature plus numerous memoirs of senior gov-ernment officials and archival material from several capitals suggests that there is no single answer. The main elements that shape the decision include the following: response to a perceived security threat; the decision to boost the regime's domestic political stature; an outcome of governmental bargaining; technical momentum; an effort to enhance the state's international prestige; and an expression of nationalism or political ideology.[2]

The five declared nuclear powers proceeded to acquire these weapons for a mixture of motivations. The United States initiated the Manhattan Project out of fear of losing out to Nazi Germany in the first nuclear arms race. Then, after Germany surrendered prior to full-scale bomb development, two weapons were used in anger against Japan to terminate World War Two in the Pacific and to avoid the huge estimated casualties of a land invasion of the Japanese home islands. Despite a notable "revisionist" literature to the contrary, the first nuclear proliferator was motivated by perceived security threats.[3]

The Soviet Union followed suit by detonating its first nuclear device in 1949, much to the surprise of the U.S. national security community. Stalin never wrote his memoirs, but some prominent scholars have pointed to the core reasons: Stalin's desire to compete with the United States for influence after World War Two; his judgment that nuclear weapons acquisition was necessary to deter U.S. blackmail or, even worse, a U.S. attack on his country; and a view that possession of nuclear weapons would be associated with the most modern industrial states. The Soviets were engaged in their own weapons development program prior to the end of World War Two. They planned to be a great power after the war, and this program was part of the "cost of doing business."[4]

The British, who had participated fully in the Manhattan Project, had no such post–World War Two aspirations. Their overseas empire began to crumble. Their economic condition was ruinous. Britain had two needs: a minimum deterrent to protect itself from Soviet intimidation or attack; and a nuclear weapon capability to claim some vestige of great power status. With American assistance, this was more than enough to motivate the first British test in 1952.[5]

The French swayed back and forth on the nuclear decision in the 1950s. But the Suez crisis of 1956 convinced General De Gaulle and many other French leaders that the United States could never be a trusted ally. Once De Gaulle became president of the Republic in 1958, he moved with dispatch toward nuclear weapon acquisition. Security threats, and domestic and international prestige, all played a role.[6]

[2]See, for example, David Holloway, *Stalin and the Bomb: The Soviet Union and Atomic Energy, 1939–1956* (New Haven, CT: Yale University Press, 1994); Margaret Gowing, *Independence and Deterrence: Britain and Atomic Energy, 1945–52*; Wolf Mendl, *Deterrence and Persuasion: French Nuclear Armament in the Context of National Policy, 1945–69*; John Lewis, *China Builds the Bomb* (Stanford: Stanford University Press, 1988); Avner Cohen, *Israel and the Bomb* (New York: Columbia University Press, 1998); George Perkovitch, *India's Nuclear Bomb: The Impact on Global Proliferation* (Berkeley: University of California Press, 1999).

[3]See Harry S. Truman, *1945: Year of Decisions*; and David McCullough, *Truman*. Among the most prominent revisionist accounts is Gar Alperovitz, *The Decision to Use the Atomic Bomb* (New York: Vintage Books, 1996).

[4]See Holloway, *Stalin and the Bomb*.

[5]See Gowing, *Independence and Deterrence*.

[6]See Mendl, *Deterrence and Persuasion*.

China had sought assistance from the Soviet Union to develop its own nuclear arsenal. By the late 1950s, the relationship between Mao Tse-tung and Khrushchev was strained. The competition for leadership of the socialist camp was intense. The Soviets held back in providing state-of-the-art technological assistance. After the Sino-Soviet rift escalated to a formal break, China moved rapidly to acquire its own minimum nuclear force. The Chinese detonation in 1964 also demonstrated that a "developing country" could be a member of this elite club.[7]

In all five cases, the nuclear proliferator was well served by a highly talented and prestigious scientific and technological elite who were given all the resources that the state could provide to make the nuclear aspiration a reality. Selected senior military officers were deeply involved in each case, and they too were treated with the greatest reverence within their respective societies.

After the French acquisition, some believed there might be twenty or thirty nuclear weapon states by the end of the 1960s.[8] This was a plausible prediction at the time, but it was not to be. Students of proliferation perhaps underestimated the role of security guarantees offered by the United States to its NATO and East Asian allies. Probably these guarantees, U.S. political pressure, and the overall international political damage of crossing the nuclear threshold dissuaded Italy, Germany, Japan, and South Korea, among others. Sweden and Switzerland, we now know, also seriously considered the option. In each case, the answer was no.[9] Later we learned that South Africa had fabricated several nuclear devices, allegedly to deter attack from neighboring Black African states, but then scuttled its program rather than handing it over to Nelson Mandela and his associates.[10]

During the 1950s and 1960s, the only other state that tangibly entered the nuclear weapons club was Israel. Under Premier Ben Gurion, the decision to move ahead on nuclear weapons acquisition, with French assistance, was made as early as 1953, five years after the country was established. The program has remained wrapped in secrecy to this day. From what we know of the decision-making process, security concerns were the central motivation.[11] Some claim that Egyptian President Anwar Sadat's strategic decision to go to Jerusalem to make peace with Israel was powerfully influenced by the realization that a nuclear-armed Israel could not be defeated on the battlefield. Israel remains an ambiguous member of the nuclear club because it is not a declared nuclear state and has not openly tested a nuclear device.

## B. Initial Responses to Nuclear Proliferation

With concern growing in Washington and London about the spread of nuclear weapons, diplomatic initiatives were mounted to dissuade further acquisition. Building on the Limited Test Ban Treaty that was completed during the Kennedy

---

[7]See Lewis, *China Builds the Bomb.*

[8]See C. P. Snow, *Science and Government* (1962).

[9]Mitchell Reiss, *Bridled Ambition: Why Countries Constrain Their Nuclear Capabilities* (Washington, DC: Woodrow Wilson International Center for Scholars, 1995).

[10]*Ibid.*

[11]See Cohen, *Israel and the Bomb.*

administration and signed initially by the United States, the United Kingdom, and the Soviet Union, the Johnson administration authorized a full-scale effort to establish an umbrella agreement that would halt proliferation. This effort led eventually to the completion of the Nuclear Non-proliferation Treaty (NPT) that was signed in 1968 and entered into force in 1970. The NPT became and still remains the landmark agreement symbolizing that the vast majority of nations oppose nuclear weapons acquisition. France and China stayed outside this regime for many years, but they ultimately joined. India, Pakistan, and Israel were notable nonparticipants. The Treaty called for the five nuclear states to remain the only nuclear powers and prohibits them from assisting others to acquire these weapons. It allows all nonnuclear states that are party to the Treaty to receive assistance in development of peaceful uses of nuclear energy through the International Atomic Energy Agency as long as they adhere to their nonnuclear weapons pledge. It also calls for the eventual elimination of all nuclear weapons by the nuclear weapons states, without a given timetable. (The Treaty was extended "permanently" in 1995, instead of requiring review at five-year intervals, widely considered to be an important nonproliferation measure).

India then and now has always made the strongest argument against the NPT—namely, that it is inherently discriminatory. Why should the five nuclear powers remain nuclear, with all the others outside the "club"? This situation smacked of "colonialism," the rich exploitation of the poor, that India had long stood against.[12] Counterarguments that it was better to have fewer hands on the nuclear trigger than many hands were totally unpersuasive to the Indians and to several other developing countries.

In the 1970s, however, a growing appreciation developed of the linkage between peaceful nuclear activities and nuclear weapons development. In 1974, India exploded a "peaceful nuclear explosion" near the Pakistan border, utilizing fissile material it had obtained from power reactors purchased by New Delhi from Canada. Also, Germany concluded a major nuclear energy deal with Brazil that suggested a possible Brazilian nuclear weapons program. Subsequent agreements were implemented to control the supply of nuclear materials and to limit the "reprocessing" of spent nuclear fuel in which weapons-grade material could be extracted. The proliferation strategy of nonproliferation was being augmented by a "management" approach, given the large number of peaceful nuclear energy programs.

Also during the 1970s, both Taiwan and South Korea evidenced signs of nuclear weapons development. In both cases, the United States issued sharp warnings and threatened to withdraw its security guarantees (explicit with South Korea, implicit with Taiwan) unless all such activity ceased. The warnings were heeded in both cases.

In the early 1980s it appeared that Iraq was exploiting its peaceful nuclear energy facilities supplied by France to build nuclear weapons. Israel, in a preemptive strike in 1981, destroyed the Iraqi reactor. This was among the first tangible examples of "counter proliferation."

[12]See Perkovitch, *India's Nuclear Bomb.*

## C. Complicating an Already Challenging Situation

In the past fifteen years, although no nuclear weapons were used in anger, several new developments applied added stress to the nuclear proliferation challenge. First, it became apparent that a number of countries—more than twenty—had acquired or were seeking to acquire chemical (CW) or biological weapons (BW) or both. These weapons are far easier to manufacture than nuclear weapons. Agreements to prohibit their spread—the Chemical Weapons Convention and the Biological Weapons Convention—are difficult to verify because of the multiplicity of "dual use" technologies in which peaceful chemical or biological activities could in some instances be a "cover" for weapons development. By the late 1980s, after the Iraqi use of chemical weapons against Iranian forces, it began to be appreciated that CBWs were seen by some as the "poor man's nuclear weapon." It also was recognized that CBWs could be mounted on ballistic missiles and used as terror weapons. That these missiles themselves were sold all over the world led to the establishment of the Missile Technology Control Regime (MTCR), a voluntary arrangement among more than twenty missile-manufacturing states that was signed in 1987 and that was intended to constrain the sale of these weapons.

Second, the Gulf War experience in which Iraq fired Scud-B missiles at U.S. and allied forces in Saudi Arabia and against Israeli civilian targets dramatized the need for theater missile defenses (TMD). Senator Sam Nunn and Congressman Les Aspin, two congressional leaders in defense policy at the time, initiated the Missile Defense Act of 1991 calling for development of TMD systems. An advanced Patriot system has begun to be deployed, and five other land-, sea-, and air-based systems are under development.

Third, the collapse of the Soviet Union produced instantaneous nuclear proliferation when it was understood that not only Russia but also Ukraine, Kazhakstan, and Belarus all controlled Soviet nuclear weapons. After intensive efforts by the Clinton administration from 1993 to 1996, the latter three states relinquished their weapons—a rare happy example of "denuclearization." What remains, however, is the control of weapons grade material in the Russian Federation generated from Russian military, power, and research nuclear facilities.

Fourth, the analytical community expressed concern about the interest of non-governmental groups—either totally independent or state-sponsored—in acquiring weapons of mass destruction. This concern was vividly realized in 1993 when Aum Shinrikyo unleashed sarin gas in a crowded Tokyo subway at rush hour, killing twelve people and injuring several thousand. This was the first, and so far only, known recorded instance of a subnational group using WMD, but it greatly highlighted that civilian populations anywhere are potentially vulnerable to such attack.[13]

---

[13]A number of steps have resulted from this growing concern of CBW use. The Department of Defense is training "first responders" in scores of American cities nationwide to deal with BW use in their communities. The widely published inoculation of American servicemen against anthrax is especially noteworthy.

Fifth, North Korea, until recently the most isolated country in the world, set about to manufacture its own nuclear weapons, producing a full-fledged international crisis in 1994. The Clinton administration, faced with war or a less-than-fully-satisfactory agreement, completed the Nuclear Framework Agreement that called for the cessation of activities at the key North Korean nuclear facility in return for substantial economic and energy assistance.

The collective impact of these developments was the realization that: (1) the "nuclear proliferation" problem had become a WMD problem; (2) substate actors as well as nation states were involved; (3) in the wake of the end of the Cold War, it was "rogue states" that presented a primary threat; (4) the collection of diplomatic instruments, security guarantees, and economic assistance and sanctions was insufficient to provide the necessary security; and (5) more attention needed to be given to means to "counter" proliferation, acknowledging that it could not be stopped. These counterproliferation measures were intended to deter the use of WMD and/or to destroy these capabilities prior to their use.

# FURTHER CHALLENGES AT THE CENTURY'S END

Some prominent members of the scholarly community have long argued that mutual nuclear deterrence is stabilizing, just as it was between the United States and the Soviet Union.[14] But this has never been the accepted view of any U.S. administration from Truman through Clinton. Rather, the official logic has always been that the spread of these weapons, even and especially among regional rivals, would greatly exacerbate the likelihood of nuclear weapon use. The "tradition of non-use" that has amazingly characterized the last half century would be broken, with disastrous consequences for the future of global society.[15]

Given this prevalent view, the end of the century presented three further challenges. First, in May 1998, both India and Pakistan detonated several nuclear weapons and formally declared themselves as nuclear weapons states, the first such declarations since China in 1964. These acts graphically shattered the illusion that there were only five nuclear powers and was demonstrable evidence, the first in three decades, that the aspiration of nonproliferation was unattainable. That India and Pakistan should both ascend to nuclear-weapon-state status is particularly alarming because together they possess all the characteristics thought to make nuclear weapon use most likely: two contiguous states; deep religious and territorial disputes; vulnerable nuclear delivery systems; underdeveloped command and control systems; and volatile domestic political systems. Immediate efforts by the international community and the Clinton administration to "roll back" these programs failed. This realization will have highly significant and yet-to-be-understood implications for the NPT, for security relations in South Asia, and for U.S. bilateral rela-

[14]Kenneth Waltz (University of California, Berkeley, emeritus) and John Mearsheimer (University of Chicago) are the most prominent examples.

[15]The term was coined by Thomas Schelling.

tions with each state. It is a highly "complexifying" development, not at all welcome for those concerned with WMD proliferation.

Second, North Korea tested in the summer of 1998 an intermediate range ballistic missile that traversed Japanese territory. This was a graphic demonstration of North Korean technological capability, which traumatized the Japanese public. And it generated enormous new political support in Washington for a U.S. national missile defense to be coupled with the TMD programs under development. At almost the same time, former Secretary of Defense Donald Rumsfeld issued the findings of a study group he chaired, officially endorsed by the White House, that claimed that one or more rogue states—particularly North Korea or Iran—could develop within five years a capability to launch missiles from their own homelands, armed with WMD that could reach U.S. territory. These two events stimulated the Clinton administration to accelerate its plans for NMD deployment, a decision that was deferred in September 2000 following several tests that experienced technical difficulties. The potential of an NMD deployment decision has greatly stressed U.S. strategic relations with Russia over the status of the ABM Treaty and offensive nuclear weapons cuts. It has also strained relations with China, which sees the mix of NMD/TMD systems ultimately aimed at its forces. And it elevated the issue briefly to one of national public debate during the 2000 presidential election campaign.

Third, the problem of Iraqi weapons of mass destruction has, alas, not been resolved. On the eve of the Gulf War, U.S. intelligence estimates were that Iraq had a tangible but modest nuclear weapons development program that would take five to ten years to reach fruition. Yet, after the War, the laborious work of the United Nations Special Commission (UNSCOM) and the writings of a chief nuclear weapons adviser to Saddam Hussein indicate that the Iraqi leader hoped to have a deliverable nuclear device by April 1991, less than two months after the Iraqis were forced to surrender. Although UNSCOM made enormous progress in identifying and then destroying Iraqi nuclear and chemical weapons development facilities, the pressure of international sanctions against Iraq eased throughout the decade. By late 1998, Hussein was able to evict the UNSCOM inspectors with impunity. Since no international inspectors have since conducted their work on Iraqi territory, only Hussein and a small number of his senior military officers know the actual status of Iraq's nuclear, chemical, and biological weapons program. Given the Iraqi leader's unabashed warrior mentality, it is virtually certain that he will pose a serious military threat to his neighbors and perhaps to Western European and American targets as long as he remains in power.

Finally, the U.S. Senate in September 1999, in an almost unprecedented display of lack of support for a major international agreement signed by a U.S. president, failed to provide its consent to ratification of the Comprehensive Test Ban Treaty.[16] Key senators argued that the treaty could not be adequately verified and/or that it would inhibit the ability of the United States to maintain a secure, safe, and

---

[16]The previous defeat of a major treaty was Senate failure to consent to ratification of the Versailles Treaty after World War One in 1920 that is widely thought to have encouraged developments that led to World War Two.

reliable stockpile of nuclear weapons. The defeat of this treaty has raised serious credibility problems with European states about the willingness of the United States to reduce its reliance on nuclear weapons and to fulfill its international obligations. Moreover, it has caused deep concern whether this rejection will ultimately be seen as a significant proliferatory act, encouraging other states that were "on the fence" about nuclear weapon testing and development now to proceed. As the Clinton administration drew to a close, it had initiated a dialogue with key senators, led by former Chairman of the Joint Chiefs of Staff General (ret.) John Shalikashvili, to determine the conditions under which Senate approval could be realized.

## TOUGH POLICY CHOICES AHEAD

For more than five decades, the United States has been the global leader in both the development of nuclear weapons and in the international means for their control, reduction, and elimination. At the start of the new millennium, the U.S. nuclear force of land-based and sea-based systems including both ballistic and cruise missiles remains unmatched in terms of lethality, survivability, and reliability. At the same time, the history of efforts at nuclear nonproliferation and more recent constraints on WMD development and deployment are dominated by American initiatives: the NPT, the Strategic Arms Limitation (SALT) and Strategic Arms Reduction (START) accords, the MTCR, and the nuclear suppliers agreements, among others. The Chemical Weapons Convention (CWC), the Biological Weapons Convention (BWC), and the Comprehensive Test Ban Treaty (CTBT) are of limited international significance in the absence of U.S. accession.

As in other aspects of international security affairs, American leadership and active and sustained participation have been necessary conditions for the implementation of effective measures of threat control. But, as indicated by the litany of challenges facing the community of nations at the start of the new century, U.S. leadership has not been sufficient to eliminate these threats. Indeed, five decades of nonproliferation policy augmented by efforts at proliferation management and counterproliferation have failed to alleviate the WMD threat facing the American homeland, U.S. forces abroad, and America's key allies in Europe, East Asia, and the Middle East.

There are several tough policy choices facing Washington decision makers in light of these challenges.

**Missile Defense and Possible ABM Treaty Withdrawal.**  Except for the status of American military readiness, the only defense issue that was raised during the 2000 presidential campaign concerned the candidate's positions about the deployment of a national missile defense (NMD). Neither of the major candidates opposed deployment: the Bush campaign proposed a vigorous effort to deploy as soon as possible a major NMD system that would protect the U.S. homeland as well as major allies in Europe and Asia from missile attack; the Gore campaign offered a more cautious approach in which it supported the development of technology for a limited NMD system and would decide on deployment subject to the technological feasibility of the systems under development, the cost of deployment and maintenance, the nature of the threat from states of concern, and the effect of deployment on relations with NATO allies as well as with Russia and China.

Reactions from major European capitals as well as Moscow and Beijing have been largely negative toward the prospect of such deployments. European reservations center on two issues: first, the impact of deployments on the future of the ABM Treaty; and second, the question of whether U.S. NMD deployments would create an asymmetry between the United States and the Europeans in which the American homeland is insulated from ballistic missile attack while the European continent is not. In Europe the ABM Treaty is widely seen by attentive elites as playing an important stabilizing role in strategic relations between the U.S. and Russia, denying each side any prospect of defending against a nuclear attack and therefore reducing to negligible levels any incentive for either side to strike first. European governments have voiced concerns that movement toward U.S. NMD deployments would trigger major tensions in U.S.-Russian relations that would not be in anyone's interests. Moreover, many Europeans seem to question that such systems are necessary, arguing instead that the threat of U.S. nuclear retaliation should be more than enough to deter North Korea, Iran, or Iraq from attacking the American homeland.[17] In addition, Europeans claim that the NATO alliance has been bound together by shared commitments and also by shared risks. If the United States is seen as less vulnerable to missile attack than its European partners, some believe that it will drive an edge within the Alliance, perhaps leading to European defense initiatives that could fundamentally alter the nature of the American commitment to European defense.

The Russians and Chinese have been adamantly opposed to U.S. NMD deployments. Despite American assurances to the contrary, Moscow and Beijing claim that the NMD systems coupled with land-based and sea-based TMD systems will provide the United States with "layered defenses" that would permit the United States to negate the Russian and Chinese nuclear deterrent forces. Both Russia and China suggest that their only plausible response would be to increase the quantity and penetrability of their offensive forces to ensure the continued credibility of their nuclear weapons systems. The great casualty in this process would be the ABM Treaty, and with its demise would be a renewed three-way nuclear arms competition and a deep strain in relations between Washington and Moscow and between Washington and Beijing. It would also complicate Sino-Russian relations. Each would have an incentive to work with the other to thwart the effectiveness of U.S. systems. But a U.S. NMD system could also stimulate a Sino-Russian nuclear arms competition.

The Clinton administration spent four years negotiating with Russia to reach a "demarcation" agreement that would permit TMD deployments without causing injury to the ABM accord (an agreement that was not ratified by the U.S. Senate).

---

[17]See, for example, François Heisbourg, "Brussel's Burden," *The Washington Quarterly* (Summer 2000): 127–133.

Although the American side professes a willingness to revise the Treaty in a manner that would accommodate NMD deployments, there is no indication that Russia is willing to move in this direction. At this writing, a feasible compromise appears to be one in which the United States shares most of its missile defense technology with Russia and perhaps even agrees to joint operation of a system by the two sides. But the Bush administration has not yet shown much interest in this approach.[18]

There may be some time before a final decision on the future of the ABM Treaty needs to be faced. That is the case because the technological maturity of the proposed NMD systems—either a land-based system based on early warning radar's in Alaska and missile interceptors in North Dakota and/or sea-based systems that would focus on intercepting attacking missiles in the early stages of their flight (so called "boost phase intercept")—is still in doubt. The major technical challenge is "hitting a bullet with a bullet," which is an extraordinarily difficult task in its own right and is made more difficult by decoys that would be used by the attacker to fool the defense. It was these uncertainties that led President Clinton in September 2000 to delay an NMD deployment decision until the new administration could revisit the issue. It seems unlikely that the new American administration would move ahead to exercise the supreme national interest clause of the ABM Treaty and remove the United States from being a party to this treaty without having in hand proven technology that could enhance the defense of the United States. It may take one or two or more years, at a minimum, before sufficient component and system testing is completed to determine that the NMD systems are worthy of deployment.

An additional consideration that could delay the face-off on the ABM Treaty concerns evolving judgments of the threat. When the Rumsfeld report was filed in the summer of 1998, North Korea was considered the most likely short-term threat. But in 2000, we witnessed important diplomatic and political developments on the Korean peninsula—the summit meeting between North Korean President Kim Jong-il and South Korean President Kim Dae-jung, the reuniting of selected families in the North and the South, and the visit by Secretary of State Madeleine Albright to Pyongyang that evidently confirmed the North Korean decision to suspend its ballistic missile testing program. Questions also abound concerning the status of the Iranian and Iraqi ballistic missile programs and the likelihood that either could mount credible threats to the U.S. homeland within the next five years. In sum, the constellation of doubts about technological feasibility, NATO reservations, and potentially revised judgments about the nature of the threat may well produce a deferral of the decision about the future of the ABM Treaty.

**U.S. and Russian Nuclear Weapons Reductions, the Future of the Nunn-Lugar-Dominici Program, and Chinese Weapons Increases.** There are numerous cross-pressures facing the major nuclear weapons states in the immediate period ahead. For the United States, the aim has been to implement fully the START I Treaty reductions that, by the end of 2001, would reduce both Russian and American

---

[18]Sharing of U.S. missile defense technology with Russia will someday be opposed by senior American military and some civilian leaders.

deployed strategic nuclear weapons to 6,000 on each side. The second step is to implement the START II Treaty reductions that, by the end of 2007, would reduce the respective arsenals to 3,000 to 3,500 on each side. This process has been held up because the Russian Duma, in ratifying the START II Treaty in the spring of 2000, added conditions that have not yet been ratified by the U.S. Senate. Beyond this, the Joint Chiefs have endorsed reducing to the 2,000 to 2,500 level but have refused to go below this benchmark, in part because it would cause them to make tough trade-offs between retention of U.S. ICBMs and long-range bombers, a decision they would just as well not have to make. The Chiefs also argue that they cannot guarantee that they can meet their targeting requirements if the number of deployed U.S. strategic nuclear delivery vehicles falls below 2000. The Russian side, according to President Putin, wishes to move quickly beyond the START I and START II levels and reduce to a level of 1,500 deployed strategic warheads on each side. This is the case because it is unlikely that Russia could sustain a force above this level in the next five to ten years due to its severe budgetary constraints.

At the same time, however, it would be increasingly difficult to reduce to these levels if the United States continued to move ahead with an NMD system. This is the situation because an asymmetry of defensive capabilities would make each deployed strategic warhead more valuable: the Russians, using standard models of defense planning, would be hard pressed to reduce to levels of 1,500 warheads or less if they sized their forces on the basis of surviving an initial U.S. strike (no matter how far-fetched this might seem in political terms) and then using their retaliatory force to penetrate U.S. defenses and ensure a credible response capability.

Two further considerations complicate matters. First, the United States has spent on the average of $350–400 million per year to support efforts to decommission and destroy excess Russian delivery vehicles and warheads. Initiated by Senators Sam Nunn and Richard Lugar, and continued under the sponsorship of Senator Pete Dominici after the retirement of Senator Nunn, the Nunn-Lugar-Dominici program remains the signature American effort to ensure that excess Russian nuclear materials are safeguarded and that the prospects of diversion or theft of such material are minimized. Would this program continue if the United States and Russia hit a snag over strategic arms reductions generated by planned NMD deployments? Unlikely. In such circumstances, the United States would run the risk of loosening the constraints on and accountability of fissile materials, as well as a suspension in strategic arms reductions, by moving forward with an NMD system that might or might not be effective against an uncertain ballistic missile threat from states of concern. Alternatively, the new administration may judge that NMD deployment is worth the risk and that it will all work out in the end. Note that some comparable arguments were raised against the Reagan administration's decision to move ahead with NATO deployment of intermediate range missiles in 1983 to counter Soviet SS-20s. There was indeed a two-year period of frosty relations that followed this deployment, but eventually the Soviets and Americans returned to the negotiating table with the result reached in 1987 to remove all intermediate nuclear forces from European soil. Depending on technological feasibility and threat assessment,

Washington may simply decide that it is necessary to deploy NMD despite the "costs" of such deployment. It is possible that, over time, this could lead to the fashioning of a U.S.-Russia agreement that included limits on offensive and defensive forces, with some freedom to mix by each party, that satisfies the strategic needs of both parties. But whether such an agreement could actually be completed is very difficult to determine.

The other complication for U.S.-Russian strategic arms reduction is the anticipated growth in Chinese nuclear arsenals in the coming decade. Although Chinese nuclear force planning is far from transparent, there is every expectation that the leadership in Beijing decided some time ago to enhance the quantity and quality of its nuclear forces, in part as a testimony to its emerging great power status and in part to respond to anticipated U.S. NMD deployments. The Chinese logic appears to be that at some point in the perhaps not-too-distant future, China might seek to regain Taiwan by force. In initiating such action, Beijing would seek to deter U.S. intervention. This objective could arguably be achieved by threatening to strike the U.S. homeland if American forces struck China in response to Chinese actions against Taiwan. For Chinese specialists and some Americans as well, the U.S. NMD system is designed ultimately to deny China that option utilizing a mix of TMD, sea-based boost phase and land-based NMD systems. To maintain a credible Chinese option under these circumstances will require China to deploy larger numbers of strategic warheads as well as decoys and other means of defeating American defenses. As China shifts upward from perhaps several hundred to well over a thousand deployed strategic nuclear warheads, Beijing reaches levels on the way up that the U.S. and Russia are considering on the way down. Would the United States and Russia really be willing to reduce forces to levels that would produce a triple parity? There is no indication that decision makers in either Washington or Moscow would feel comfortable with such actions. Therefore, Chinese defense decisions will have an important bearing on the future of U.S. and Russian strategic arms reductions.

**The Future of the International Nonproliferation Regime Structure.** The final and perhaps thorniest policy problem facing the new administration in Washington concerns how to modify the international nonproliferation regime in light of the major new developments of the past several years. Most notably, there are now officially two declared new nuclear weapons states: India and Pakistan. Given the deep, long-standing animosity between these two states that is based on religious, territorial, political, and geostrategic considerations, it would be foolhardy to believe that either side will willingly surrender their nuclear arsenals in the coming decade. What does this reality do to the NPT that recognizes only five nuclear states? The United States recently opened up to India economically and politically, symbolized by President Clinton's five-day visit to India and five-hour visit to Pakistan in the summer of 2000. The United States seems to be willing to accept India, the world's largest democracy, as a potential new partner in South Asia, despite its new nuclear status. American reaction to Pakistan is much more wary, in part because of the collapse of Pakistani democracy, the receipt by Pakistan of nuclear technological support from China, and Pakistan's links with rogue states in the Middle East, notably Iran and Libya. If it is indeed the case that the U.S. is developing a strategic approach to South Asia with little effort at rolling back nuclear weapons in the region, how legitimate is the continuing effort to thwart WMD proliferation elsewhere? Indeed, if India and Pakistan remain in a stalemated situation for many years to come without nuclear weapon use by either party, would this experience validate the views of scholar Kenneth Waltz and others that nuclear proliferation between arch rivals can be stabilizing, therefore leading other regional opponents to follow suit? What are the implications for strengthening the NPT, for modifying the nuclear suppliers agreements, and for U.S. ratification of the Comprehensive Test Ban Treaty? For the first time since 1964, the United States will have to fashion a policy that continues to pursue global nonproliferation norms while conducting bilateral relations with India and Pakistan that take their new nuclear status into account.

The other new dimension of nonproliferation policy is how to incorporate chemical and biological weapons in the international regime. The United States has long perpetuated an ambiguous policy with respect to whether it would use nuclear weapons in response to an attack by chemical or biological weapons. The argument has been that it is best to leave this option open, hoping to deter first use of such weapons. Critics argue that this posture moves away from the delegitimization of nuclear weapon use and makes them a central part of governmental decision-making at a time when many think we should be setting the groundwork for the total elimination of these weapons.[19]

The greatest test case for much of this analysis will be if and when chemical, biological, or even nuclear weapons are used in anger. It seems plausible that witnessing the horror of such use would likely stimulate further WMD acquisition by other states as well as accelerated missile defense deployments. Absent such use and the extreme sense of crisis it would produce, there is reason to expect that American policy will continue to struggle with all the issues outlined above.

# INITIAL PERSPECTIVES ON THE BUSH ADMINISTRATION

As the Bush administration fills out its high-level appointments and begins to grapple with key national security issues, it is exhibiting an orientation to issues of weapons proliferation and missile defense that are already reasonably clear.

---

[19]Among the noted members of the "abolitionist" group that seeks the quick and total elimination of nuclear weapons are former Commander in Chief of the U.S. Strategic Command Lee Butler, author Jonathan Schell, and former U.S. Secretary of Defense Robert McNamara. Others counter that such an approach is fanciful given the security calculations of each of the nuclear states and the inability to verify with high confidence that all parties are in compliance with such an agreement.

The basic philosophical difference between George W. Bush and Clinton is that the former is more concerned with the explicit furtherance of American national interests that are encouraging more of a unilateralist approach than was the case with his predecessor. This approach has already manifested itself in a number of respects:

**1. With respect to Russia, there appears to be a deliberate effort to downgrade the importance of the U.S.-Russian relationship.** In his first international speech as Secretary of Defense in Munich in February 2001, Donald Rumsfeld addressed the need for a U.S. national missile defense system without even citing Russian concerns. He also left the forum before the Russian Defense Minister spoke. In more substantive terms, the Bush administration has requested a reduction in funding for the cooperative threat reduction program, suggesting it is less interested in working with the Russians to control their fissile material and reducing their nuclear arsenals. The administration seems to want to decouple more of its national security policies from consultations or at least formal negotiations with Russia.

**2. There is broad and deep support within the administration to move as rapidly as possible to deploy a robust national missile defense.** This is predicated on several points. First, they judge the rogue state threat to be very real. They also are deeply concerned about having a capability to avoid being blackmailed by China in the event of a confrontation over Taiwan. In this context the ABM Treaty is truly seen as the vestige of a Cold War that is long since over. Removal of the United States from the Treaty is seen as a needed and logical progression toward the development of a realistic national security policy for the new century. Second, there is a moral argument that we have every responsibility to protect our citizens if we are able to do so. This may not have been feasible against massive Soviet nuclear arsenal, but it is against rogue states. The Bush administration has clearly convinced governments around the world, for better or worse, that the U.S. will be moving ahead rapidly on missile defense.

**3. The administration plans to emphasize sophisticated conventional weapons as part of its counter-proliferation strategy to meet the WMD threat.** At least in its initial phase it has shown little interest in reviving the Comprehensive Test Ban Treaty, in resuming talks with North Korea to halt its missile production, or in other formal bilateral or multilateral initiatives at the outset of the administration.

**4. With respect to other WMD proliferators, the Bush team also has a different perspective from their predecessors.** With respect to Iraq, there is a clear preference to rebuild an international consensus to overthrow Saddam Hussein's regime, rather than to tinker with trying to reestablish UN inspections of Iraqi facilities. With respect to South Asia, there is likely to be a clear tilt toward India, as a counterweight to China. In this regard, the U.S. will no linger press for a cessation of Indian nuclear activities. And with regard to China, there is a prevalent view, reinforced by the detention of the downed U.S. air crew on Hainan Island in April 2001, that Beijing is a potential adversary that is building its nuclear arsenal independent of U.S. policy. While we will continue to encourage trade and investment in China., we must deploy military systems and structure defense policies that see China more in adversarial terms.

**5. It is viewed by senior officials in Washington that our NATO allies will ultimately support U.S. policies because they have few options and also because these will be seen to be in their own best interests.** As long as the U.S. does not take steps that endanger the credibility of the British and French nuclear deterrent forces, Washington calculates that NATO will endorse the Bush approach to WMD proliferation.

Should these policy orientations be sustained, the Bush administration will reduce its reliance generally on international organizations, multilateral negotiations, and the general structure of the non-proliferation regime. Instead, a more unilateral approach predicated on American military power will be the hallmark of U.S. policy.

The early twenty-first century is a complex time with one dominant power, many regional powers, WMD proliferation, and an information technology revolution that is greatly enhancing military capabilities. Whether the Bush approach will prove to be successful is difficult to assess. Its implementation may indeed underscore the basic thesis of this volume: namely, that while the U.S. enjoys a preponderance of power and must lead for salutary developments to materialize, it in fact cannot dominate and control developments in a fashion commensurate with its material capabilities. We will all be witnesses to the implications of this ironic state of international affairs.

# 14

# Containing Backlash
## Foreign Economic Policy in an Age of Globalization

BENJAMIN J. COHEN
University of California at Santa Barbara

In international economic affairs, America's primacy at the dawn of the twenty-first century is undoubted. At a time of rapidly growing commercial and financial interdependence among nations—conventionally described by the popular term "globalization"—the United States stands out as a remarkable, if not unique, success story. During the 1990s, Americans enjoyed the longest expansion in the history of the republic, avoiding the high unemployment that plagued Europe, the stagnation that dragged down Japan, and the financial crises that disrupted emerging markets from East Asia to Russia to Latin America. If not once again a "Gulliver among the Lilliputians," as the United States at the end of World War Two could accurately be described (Keohane 1979), America has nonetheless clearly reclaimed its lead among the economies of the world. The aging hegemon has gained a new lease on life.

But this status does not mean that America's primacy has been or will go unquestioned. Quite the contrary, in fact. Around the world, threats of backlash are intensifying, reflecting spreading discontent with what has come to be known as the "Washington consensus"—a newly triumphant "neoliberal" economics emphasizing the virtues of privatization, deregulation, and liberalization wherever possible, which has been widely promoted by the American government together with the Washington-based International Monetary Fund (IMF) and the World Bank. The material benefits of globalization are obvious. Growth of output, in the aggregate,

Benjamin J. Cohen is Louis G. Lancaster Professor of International Political Economy at the University of California, Santa Barbara. Educated at Columbia University, he previously taught at Princeton University and the Fletcher School of Law and Diplomacy, Tufts University. He is the author of nine books, including *In Whose Interest? International Banking and American Foreign Policy* (1996) and *The Geography of Money* (1998).

has been promoted as economies have opened up to the opportunities of international trade and investment. Millions of people around the world have experienced substantial increases in living standards. But what about the costs of globalization? ask a growing number of critics. What about the losers from economic change, the growing inequality of incomes, the alleged environmental decay or cultural degradation? Increasingly, globalization is seen by many as not benevolent but malign—not a friend to be welcomed but an enemy to be resisted. And since America is identified with globalization as its patron and principal beneficiary, that view means that America is the enemy, too. The Washington consensus appears to privilege, above all, U.S. interests and values. As a result, the United States has become a kind of handy scapegoat for all the diverse social groups hurt by globalization.

Can a backlash against globalization be contained? Can today's open, multilateral system be defended against the forces of protectionism and economic nationalism? Therein lies the central challenge for U.S. foreign economic policy today. The costs of globalization cannot be denied. Indeed, there are plainly losers as well as winners from market liberalization; and this situation is true not only in America's overseas relations but inside the United States as well. Backlash against globalization is growing among Americans, too. As one source puts it, globalization "is becoming a four-letter word in American politics" (Ullman 1998: 41). But the benefits of globalization cannot be denied, either. Uncontained backlash, clearly, would put world prosperity at risk, in effect throwing out the baby with the bathwater. The challenge for U.S. policy-makers is to preserve the gains of a system that has so obviously worked to America's advantage, as well as to the advantage of millions elsewhere, while at the same time responding constructively to the system's many critics at home and abroad. Needless to say, the task will not be an easy one.

The purpose of this chapter is to explore that task in some detail: to ask what, in reality, the American government can do to contain the threatened backlash against globalization. A fundamental premise of the chapter is that if the world economy's strengths are to be preserved, it will require determined leadership from the United States. One does not have to be a fanatical devotee of the familiar theory of hegemonic stability to acknowledge the centrality of this country's global role. In economic affairs, even more than in most other dimensions of foreign policy, as Robert Lieber contends in his opening chapter (Lieber 2001), America really is the "indispensable nation"—the only country with the clout needed to organize timely and effective remedies for systemic weaknesses. Primacy generates not only privilege but also responsibility. The world watches the United States carefully; and if the biggest economy of all is inclined to behave irresponsibly, pursuing its own interests unilaterally at the expense of others, governments elsewhere cannot be blamed for succumbing to the forces of protectionism or economic nationalism, too. Responsibility means taking the lead in response to legitimate criticisms in circumstances in which the only alternative might be inaction or decay. America may not always be able to impose its will on economic issues. But as I argued in the previous volume in this series, the United States still enjoys disproportionate influence in relation to other states:

Across a broad range of issues, the initiative clearly remains with the United States. Few governments are willing to pursue programs for long that openly contravene key U.S. interests or preferences. Even fewer feel that they can safely ignore pressures or demands from Washington. (Cohen 1997: 80–81)

Some would argue—somewhat optimistically—that no special initiatives are needed. The threat of backlash, it is alleged, is really more smoke than fire. Both globalization and U.S. primacy are supposedly here to stay, whatever their critics say; and in any event, American policy-makers, ever conscious of their leadership responsibilities, can always be counted upon to resist any significant erosion of past gains. So why worry? Such optimism, however, is misplaced. The threat, I contend, is real and could indeed be highly damaging to American interests unless countered by effective responses in the spheres of both trade and finance. Pride in our good fortune to date is no excuse for either triumphalism or passivity in the future.

# IS GLOBALIZATION IRREVERSIBLE?

In economic discourse, the term "globalization" is used as a shorthand expression for the increasing integration of national economies around the world—a process of commercial and financial interpenetration driven by the forces of market competition and technological innovation, as well as by governmental policies of deregulation and liberalization. In trade, globalization can be seen in the growing openness of markets for goods and services: greater and greater dependence on foreign commerce as a source of domestic prosperity. In finance, it is manifest in a rising level of capital mobility: ever higher volumes of private lending and investment across national frontiers.

True, we are still far from anything that might be described as a fully globalized world economy. Numerous national markets, particularly in developing areas, remain well insulated from outside influence; and even in more developed regions, the industrial centers of North America, Europe, and Japan—the so-called Triad countries—as well as in the emerging markets of East Asia and Latin America, significant divergences persist. Cross-border integration is limited not only by formal restrictions imposed by governments (tariffs and other trade or capital controls) but by all kinds of informal barriers as well, including exchange-rate uncertainties, informational asymmetries, and linguistic and cultural differences. As economist Dani Rodrik, a leading expert on globalization, has written, "international markets for goods, services, and capital are not nearly as 'thick' as they would be under complete integration" (Rodrik 2000: 179). Still, the direction of change is unmistakable. Even if not yet completely integrated, markets clearly are growing ever "thicker" in terms of both the range of transactions encompassed and the number of people affected.

For some, the trend is also inexorable, akin to letting the genie out of the bottle. Once unleashed, it is suggested, the forces of competition are too powerful to be reversed. Governments cannot resist the tides of international trade and finance.

Rather, the best they can do is adapt to the new world economy that is emerging, competing for the benefits of globalization by accommodating themselves as much as possible to the preferences of market agents. In trade, doing this means opening the economy to foreign competition through both commercial exchange and direct investment. In finance, it means creating an environment of "sound" monetary and fiscal policies that will sustain the confidence of creditors and portfolio managers. That is what political scientist Philip Cerny intends by the notion of the "competition state." "The very concept of the national interest," he contends, "is expanding to embrace the transnational dimension in new ways: the so-called competition state is obliged by the imperatives of global competition to expand transnationalization" (Cerny 1994: 225). The competition state, from this perspective, is simply an acceptance of reality—an acknowledgment that the genie cannot be put back in the bottle.

But is that, in fact, reality? History suggests otherwise, despite the evident power of market forces. The present era, after all, is not the first time that a seemingly inexorable process of transnational integration has taken hold. A century ago the world economy also seemed to be well on its way toward something approximating globalization. Indeed, by some measures national markets were even more closely tied together prior to World War One than they are now. Investment funds moved freely between countries, tariffs were comparatively low, and nontariff barriers and capital controls had still not even been invented. Yet when circumstances seemed to warrant, governments felt little inhibition in sacrificing the presumed benefits of trade and finance for the sake of other policy objectives. During the interwar period and beyond, the seemingly irresistible momentum of economic integration was decisively reversed, before the start of what some are now calling the second age of globalization. If the genie could be put back into the bottle once, it does not seem implausible to assume that it be done again, as economic historians have frequently noted (James 1999).

The reason lies in the logic of politics—specifically, in the logic of national sovereignty, which remains the core organizing principle of world politics. However challenged they may feel by the forces of global competition, states remain, in the most fundamental sense, masters of their own destiny—still capable, when motivated, of exercising their legal authority to limit the openness and vulnerability of their economies. In the pithy phrase of political scientist Louis Pauly, "states can still defy markets" if they wish (Pauly 1995: 373). Governments are not condemned simply to accommodate the preferences of multinational corporations. The competition state is not the only choice. Other policy options exist, including overt limitations on trade or capital flows. Globalization will never be irreversible so long as sovereignty continues to reside at the national level.

The argument for the presumed irreversibility of globalization rests implicitly on an assumption that governments value the material benefits of economic integration above all else. Typical is Rodrik's sanguine remark that "short of global wars or natural disasters of major proportions, it is hard to envisage that a substantial part of the world's population will want to give up the goodies that an increasingly integrated (hence efficient) world market can deliver" (Rodrik 2000: 184). In fact, it is not so hard to envisage at all, since the "goodies" are not the only things that matter to much of the world's population. Numerous other core goals and values also figure prominently in the calculations of rational policy-makers. Economic nationalism, therefore, could easily come to take precedence over international integration. Time and again, governments have demonstrated their willingness to limit market openness, sacrificing the benefits of globalization, when deemed necessary for the sake of national security, cultural preservation, or environmental protection. Mercantilism lives.

Most important, policy-makers could feel driven to limit openness abroad by popular discontent at home. Workers and companies may lobby for protection against lost income or jobs. Public-interest groups may protest risks to the environment, human rights, or a traditional way of life. A prime example is provided by France where, in early 1999, an obscure farmer named José Bové bulldozed a McDonald's restaurant to protest the perceived invasion of foreign (particularly American) corporations—and became a national hero. The event unleashed a torrent of antiglobalization sentiment across the country to which politicians felt compelled to respond. Never particularly loath to criticize the United States, which French leaders have taken to calling the world's "hyperpower" (*hyperpuissance*), France now has happily accepted the mantle of leadership in the opposition to globalization. "France feels that nothing short of its identity is at stake," writes one observer. "The debate has been recast as 'Anglo-Saxon globalization' versus the preservation of France's national and cultural values" (Meunier 2000: 105). In turn, French opposition to "Anglo-Saxon globalization" has resonated with other countries, such as Canada and Japan, which are also known to be sensitive to the cultural consequences of what they see as the McDonaldization of the world.[1]

Another example came later in 1999 in the notorious Battle of Seattle, where a coalition of nongovernmental organizations successfully disrupted a meeting of the World Trade Organization (WTO) intended to launch a new round of trade liberalization. Grievances ranged from targeted complaints about labor conditions and pollution to more inchoate concerns about social justice and alleged capitalist exploitation. Similar demonstrations also erupted a few months later in Washington at a joint meeting of the IMF and World Bank, where again many grievances were aired. Among the aims of the self-styled Mobilization for Global Justice was international debt relief. The enemy, in the words of the *New York Times*, was a system seen as "hooking lower-income nations on cheap debt and then insisting that they

---

[1]The cultural concerns of Canada are well illustrated by its repeated efforts to limit the circulation of American magazines like *People* or *Sports Illustrated*, which outsell Canada's own magazine industry. The governments's purpose, in the words of the prime minister, is to protect "part of our national identity" (as quoted in *The Economist*, 6 February 1999: 36). Japanese concerns are well illustrated by the country's determination to continue a long tradition of whale hunting despite U.S. opposition to the destruction of endangered species. Whale meat is considered a delicacy in Japanese cuisine. "Americans are a bunch of culinary imperialists," one Japanese restaurant owner has said. "Telling the Japanese not to hunt whales is like telling the British to stop having their afternoon tea" (as quoted in *New York Times*, August 10, 2000: A8). How different is this from José Bové's denunciation of McDonald's as *la malbouffe* ("lousy food"). Echoed the respected newspaper *Le Monde*, "resistance to the hegemonic pretenses of hamburgers is, above all, a cultural imperative" (as quoted by Meunier 2000: 107).

adopt free markets, unlimited investment, privatization and restrained government spending, or risk a cutoff in new aid."[2] Such is the stuff of the backlash against globalization. "Globalism is the new 'ism' that everyone loves to hate," said the former director general of the WTO.[3] Demonstrations also occurred at the IMF-World Bank annual meeting in Prague, capital of the Czech Republic, in October 2000.

Admittedly, fears for the future can be overdone. Ever since the Cold War ended more than a decade ago, specialists have bewailed the risk of renewed protectionism around the world. With the waning of the Soviet threat, we have repeatedly been told, the major industrial powers could fall to squabbling among themselves, no longer willing to restrain their mercantilist impulses for the sake of the Western alliance. That dour theme has been developed most recently by Robert Gilpin in his jeremiad, *The Challenge of Global Capitalism* (Gilpin 2000), which worries that the clock could soon be turned back to the interwar period when economic rivalries similarly raged unchecked. Faith in the irreversibility of globalization, Gilpin writes, "may turn out to be valid, but it is important to recall that world has passed this way before" (Gilpin 2000: 12).

In fact, however, as I suggested in an earlier *Eagle* volume (Cohen 1992), much has changed in the last half century to lessen the risk of systemic disintegration or breakdown. Most important are the many international regime structures that have been constructed to help promote intergovernmental cooperation and collective management, in most instances formally institutionalized in multilateral organizations like the IMF, World Bank, and WTO, or in regularized procedures such as those of the well-known Group of Seven (G-7). In any event, globalization continues to move forward, seemingly inexorably, despite its diverse critics. "So far," as one informed observer comments, "the manifestations of a backlash are more likely to be found in speeches than in legislative or executive actions" (Naím 2000: 12). Columnist Bruce Stokes speaks of the protectionist myth. "Free trade is not in retreat," he insists. "Crying wolf about false chimeras of protectionism impugns credibility" (Stokes 1999–2000: 89).

Nonetheless, there are valid grounds for concern. As *The Economist* writes, "it would be a great mistake to dismiss this global militant tendency as nothing more than a public nuisance."[4] That the clock has not yet been turned back is no guarantee that popular protests will not be more successful in the future, as more McDonald's restaurants get bulldozed and more Seattles hit the TV screens. Globalization may be powerful, but neither history nor the logic of politics gives comfort to the view that a liberal world economy is truly irreversible. Even Stokes acknowledges that "if these problems are not dealt with, protectionism could return with a vengeance in the first years of the new millennium, with devastating consequences" (Stokes 1999–2000: 101–102). The threat of backlash, it is clear, cannot be ignored.

[2]Joseph Kahn, "Seattle Protesters Are Back, With a New Target," *New York Times*, April 9, 2000: 4.

[3]Michael Moore, as quoted in *New York Times*, January 29, 2000: B2.

[4]"Anti-Capitalist Protests: Angry and Effective," *The Economist*, September 23, 2000: 86.

# WILL U.S. PRIMACY ENDURE?

Even if the threat of backlash is real, however, are American interests at risk? The United States is universally recognized today as the world's dominant national economy—a born-again hegemon, propelled by productivity gains made possible by the flexibility of domestic labor and capital markets, by the stimulus of intense competition, and above all by the epochal revolution in information technologies. Once again, America has demonstrated its remarkable capacity for self-renewal. Moreover, with no serious rival on the horizon, the country's primacy would seem set to endure indefinitely. For some, this is more than enough reason to believe that U.S. prosperity will persist whatever other governments do. In the words of Lloyd Cutler, an influential Washington figure: "Our technological leadership and the size of our economy give us every chance to maintain our position,"[5] boding well for the future.

Certainly it is true that America faces no serious rival to its economic leadership at present. That is a big change from just a few years back, when both East Asia and Europe appeared poised to challenge U.S. hegemony in the world economy. Across the Pacific, Japan was being widely touted as the next "Number One," an emerging China was seen as not far behind, and the smaller "tiger" economies of Korea and Southeast Asia were developing at double-digit rates of expansion. But then Japan's "bubble economy" burst in 1989, leading to a decade of bankruptcies and stagnation. China's prospects were clouded by inefficient state-owned industries, persistent rural poverty, and an insolvent banking sector. And in 1997–98, the tigers were hit by major financial crisis, causing severe recession and soaring unemployment. Much less is heard today about the imminence of a possible new Asian Century.

Nor does Europe now seem quite the same threat it did following the Single Europe Act of 1986, which removed most remaining barriers to free trade on the continent, and then the Maastricht Treaty of 1991 laying the foundation for a new common currency, the euro, for the renamed European Union (EU). At long last, Europeans seemed set to put aside past antagonisms to create an economic powerhouse in the same league as the United States. "Future historians," economist Lester Thurow predicted, "will record that the twenty-first century belonged to the House of Europe" (Thurow 1992: 258). But ensuing years of slow growth and high unemployment sapped European self-confidence and eroded the social and political cohesion needed to make Thurow's prediction a reality. Much less is heard today of the imminence of a European Century, either.

None of this, however, guarantees that America's born-again hegemony will endure indefinitely. Arguably, as Paul Krugman (2000) has suggested, the recent turn of events may be attributed as much to the failures of others as to the success of the United States. The Japanese economy, still the second largest in the world, has demonstrated great resilience in the past and could once again bounce back from

[5]As quoted in *New York Times*, January 1, 2000: C1.

domestic travails. China and the other East Asian tigers have already, in many respects, put the 1997–98 financial crisis behind them. And Europe, impelled by the unifying effect of the euro, could still succeed in overcoming its own internal divisions. Over the longer term, challenges to U.S. leadership in economic affairs will persist and no doubt even intensify.

Moreover, the U.S. economy is not without frailties of its own, which in time could take their toll. The revolution in information technologies, for instance, may be a source of sustained productivity growth, but it is also contributing to a significant widening of income gaps—the so-called digital divide between more fortunate "knowledge workers" and the computer illiterate. Likewise, American financial markets may be among the most efficient anywhere, but they have also encouraged a dangerously high rate of leveraging on the part of both individuals and business enterprise, the risks of which were already evident during the stock-market slump that began in the first year of the new millennium. In 2000 the long expansion of the 1990s came to an abrupt halt. Many observers worry that a prolonged decline of U.S. stock prices could, via a negative "wealth effect," greatly dampen future growth prospects. The wealth effect refers to the relationship between consumption and investment expenditures, on the one hand, and changes of asset prices on the other. With a high level of leveraging, even a mild stock-market setback can lead debtors to cut spending sharply in order to service or reduce liabilities.

Most critical of all, from an international point of view, is the deficit in the U.S. balance of payments. America may still be the world's largest exporting nation, but it also has by far the biggest negative balance in foreign trade, requiring ever greater dependence on financing from abroad. Over the course of the 1990s, the excess of imports over exports of goods and services (technically, the current-account deficit) more than tripled, to a level well above $300 billion a year, equivalent to a record 4 percent of gross domestic product (GDP). America's net external debt, already greater than that of any other nation, swelled in the same period from under $250 billion to more than $1.5 trillion, almost 16 percent of GDP. For many, the foreign deficit is the Achilles heel of the U.S. economy, reflecting an extraordinarily low (at times, even negative) personal savings rate among Americans. In effect, America is living beyond its means, ignoring the future costs of servicing its accumulating liabilities. For others, by contrast, it is more a mark of America's success, reflecting the strength of our growth in recent years relative to that of most other countries.[6] Rising income at home naturally increased demand for imports, even as exports were constrained by stagnation and crisis abroad. Indeed, from this perspective, the U.S. deficit can be said even to have served as a sort of international public good, insofar as employment and production elsewhere have been sustained by sales in the U.S. market. America has functioned, in effect, as a "buyer of last resort" for troubled foreign economies.

---

[6]To sample the two sides of the debate, see, e.g., Lovett (1999) and Griswold (2000). In Lovett's view, the deficit "cannot continue much longer" (Lovett 1999: 138). Griswold, by contrast, contends that the deficit "poses no threat" (Griswold 2000: 68). For a comprehensive and balanced analysis, see Mann (1999).

Can the deficit be sustained? In a very real sense, an excess of imports over exports can be understood as merely the accounting counterpart of a massive inflow of capital, reflecting both the superior attractiveness of investment opportunities in the United States and the worldwide appeal of the dollar as an international currency. Much rests, therefore, on the continued willingness of foreign investors to acquire U.S. assets, which is a weak reed at best. In reality, it is easy to envisage a substantial reallocation of investment portfolios that might be triggered by any number of reasonably plausible developments—a sustained renewal of growth in Asia or Europe, for instance, or the gradual emergence of a strong euro as a global rival to the greenback. Economist Catherine Mann is not alone in predicting that "at some point . . . global investors will decide that U.S. assets account for a big enough share of their portfolios and so will stop acquiring more of them. . . The United States cannot live beyond its long-term means forever" (Mann 2000: 43).[7] Should such predictions prove accurate, Americans will find that they can no longer ignore the burden of external debt service or the vulnerabilities that come with the need to cultivate and sustain the goodwill of international financial markets.

Prudence suggests, therefore, that America's born-again hegemony might not in fact endure—and if it does not, neither can U.S. prosperity be guaranteed in the face of a serious backlash against globalization. Like it or not, U.S. interests are seriously at risk.

# CAN U.S. POLICY-MAKERS BE COUNTED ON?

What, then, can be expected of U.S. policy-makers as globalization increasingly becomes a four-letter word? The United States has long been committed to maintaining an open world economy, and America's leaders generally understand the responsibilities that go with economic primacy. Many observers thus believe that Washington can always be counted on to resist any erosion of past gains even if other governments succumb to the temptations of protectionism and economic nationalism. U.S. policy-makers, it seems logical to assume, will fight to preserve a system from which the United States appears to benefit disproportionately.

There is much evidence for this point of view. Survey results, as Ole Holsti reports in this volume (Holsti 2001), consistently demonstrate that the top ranks of both major political parties remain committed to the Washington consensus. Republican and Democrat leaders alike continue to oppose broad new trade barriers; and when in control of the executive branch, each party has tended to pursue the same kind of agenda of commercial and financial liberalization. The Tokyo Round of trade negotiations, begun in 1973 under the Nixon Administration, was concluded when Jimmy Carter was president. Likewise, the subsequent Uruguay Round as well as the North American Free Trade Agreement (NAFTA), both initiatives of Republican presidents,

[7]This is also the view of a prominent congressional commission appointed to study the deficit, which concluded in late 2000 that the imbalance had become unsustainably large and dangerous for the U.S. economy, though disagreeing on what to do about it (*New York Times*, November 15, 2000: C2).

were pushed through to completion by a Democrat, Bill Clinton. During the presidential campaign of 2000, little substantive difference could be found between candidates Al Gore and George W. Bush on issues of foreign economic policy.[8]

But all this discounts the role of domestic politics, which can significantly alter the cost-benefit calculus of even the most fervently promarket politician. In the United States today, domestic politics are becoming increasingly hostile to Washington's traditional commitment to globalization. The survey results reviewed by Holsti (2001) show that far more Americans support trade barriers than oppose them, and for the general public, "protecting the jobs of American workers" continues to rank among the highest of all foreign-policy priorities. Below the level of party leaderships, there is growing activism in opposition to globalization's perceived costs.

Most prominent is the U.S. labor movement, led by the AFL-CIO, which has undergone a tidal shift over the last generation in its stance on protectionism. Unions were once avid backers of free trade. Today, however, blue-collar workers find themselves among the most threatened by an increasingly open world economy. America's comparative advantage, driven by the technology revolution, is rapidly shifting away from low-skill labor-intensive manufactures, which can now be produced at much lower cost elsewhere. Thus, in spite of record employment growth throughout the 1990s, labor has become ever more vocal in its opposition to market liberalization. The free flow of goods and capital is seen as biased against workers, favoring instead corporations that are able to shift output to areas abroad where labor costs are cheaper—Ross Perot's notorious "giant sucking sound." Globalization, asserts one union leader, "works only for multinationals, not for workers."[9] For blue-collar Americans, the result seems nothing more than lost jobs, increasing insecurity, and a widening gap between rich and poor. The unions see themselves as fighting for social justice—for some consideration for the losers from economic change. Their hope, in the words of the president of the AFL-CIO, is "to make the global economy work for working families."[10]

Joining the labor movement is a growing assortment of other increasingly well-organized lobbyists, each highlighting its own catalog of grievances against spreading globalization. Environmental groups lament degradation of the world's forests, rivers, oceans, and atmosphere, which they see as the direct consequence of an economic system that places profit above all else. Likewise, human-rights organizations protest abhorrent social practices, such as child or prison labor, while cultural activists deplore the adverse impact of increasing economic integration on

---

[8]In fact, during the campaign only one significant point of contention emerged concerning foreign economic policy, prompted by a free-trade pact signed with Jordan in October 2000 (see below). This involved whether, or to what extent, trade agreements should be linked to labor and environmental issues. Both candidates favored trade liberalization. But whereas Al Gore promised not to expand trade in the future without first establishing firm labor and environmental standards, George W. Bush opposed any such linkage.

[9]The union leader was George Becker, president of the United Steelworkers of America, as quoted in *New York Times*, April 12, 2000: A12.

[10]John J. Sweeney, as quoted in *New York Times*, April 13, 2000: A1. For a particularly articulate presentation of the case for social justice for workers in a globalizing world economy, see Kapstein (1999).

cherished local traditions. Leftists attack what they perceive as an illegitimate transfer of decision making from elected governments to impersonal market forces. Conservatives take up arms against the alleged surrender of national sovereignty to anonymous bureaucrats in distant institutions like the IMF or WTO. Not all these complaints are necessarily on target; many, in fact, are exaggerated or misleading, blaming globalization for ills that really stem from other causes. But that tendency does nothing to deter the enthusiasm of the groups that espouse them.

Such groups are not new, of course. What is different today is their growing success in making their voices heard, symbolized most vividly by the Battle for Seattle and Mobilization for Global Justice. Both protests were carefully planned by increasingly professional activists such as Lori Wallach of Public Citizen, a consumer-interest group; as TV spectacles, they and later demonstrations have been highly effective in heightening public consciousness of the issues involved in globalization. For the first time, a broad-based coalition of like-minded movements has been brought together around a common set of themes—all committed, in Wallach's words, to "looking at the public interest, and trying to balance that against the corporate interests."[11] Though doubts have been raised whether the momentum generated by such demonstrations can be sustained, protest leaders express confidence that this is only the beginning of a grand new mobilization of opposition forces.

In the face of such mounting hostility, can U.S. policy-makers really be counted on to defend globalization at all costs? Complacency would not appear to be justified, as Gilpin (2000) and others have rightly warned. At a minimum, America's leaders might feel obliged to offer marginal concessions in order to avoid yet more noisy street demonstrations. At a maximum, if they sense their own electoral prospects at risk, they might abandon the liberal world economy altogether, however much that action might contradict their personal beliefs. Lieber, in his opening chapter (Lieber 2001), suggests that in the twenty-first century, the domestic consensus needed for a coherent foreign policy is becoming ever more elusive. In no dimension of policy is that more true than in economic affairs. Policy-makers will find it increasingly difficult to preserve the gains of the past in the face of the backlash against globalization. The threat, to repeat, is real. Effective responses are called for in the spheres of both trade and finance.

# INTERNATIONAL TRADE

The threat is certainly evident in the trade sphere, where mercantilist impulses are never very far from the surface. Over the last decade, the scale of import liberalization around the world has been impressive—but so too has been the scale of resistance to further opening of markets, both in the United States and elsewhere. Not all the growing pressures for protectionism can be dismissed as mere self-interested

---

[11]As quoted in an extensive interview published under the title "Lori's War," *Foreign Policy* 118 (Spring 2000): 49.

parochialism or narrow economic nationalism. Broader issues are implicated, involving inter alia legitimate questions of income distribution, cultural diversity, the global environment, and national sovereignty. Finding effective responses to the diverse concerns of trade's many critics while preserving the benefits of closer international integration will not be easy.

## Past Achievements

Trade liberalization was high on America's diplomatic agenda throughout the 1990s, with many noteworthy results. For the Clinton administration, coming into office in January 1993, it was "the economy, stupid." Nothing was more vital to the preservation of America's primacy, officials reasoned, than economic expansion; and nothing was more likely to sustain expansion than an opening of foreign markets to U.S. exports. Dismantling trade barriers, an essential element of the Washington consensus, became one of the core themes of U.S. foreign policy. Previous administrations too had placed emphasis on trade liberalization, combining elements of multilateralism, regionalism, and unilateralism (Cohen 1997). But few had placed such a high priority on market expansion as a sine qua non for national success. Consistent with past practice, the assault on import barriers was broad-based, carried out in regional fora and bilaterally as well as in global negotiations.

At the global level, the administration acted decisively to push completion in late 1993 of the Uruguay Round, which had begun when Ronald Reagan was still president, and then to gain ratification from a reluctant congress a year later. Easily the broadest and most comprehensive trade agreement in history, incorporating no fewer than twenty-nine separate accords in a document running to over 22,000 pages, the Uruguay Round represented a new high in the globalization of the world economy. In the industrialized Triad economies, numerous import quotas were liberalized or eliminated, while tariffs on most manufactured goods were reduced to not much more than nuisance levels. On a broader scale, traditional rules previously embodied in the General Agreement on Tariffs and Trade (GATT) were extended to whole new economic sectors such as agriculture, services, intellectual property rights, and foreign investment. And perhaps of most importance, the old GATT was folded into the newly created WTO, an agency endowed with much wider powers to govern the multilateral trading system. Subsequent negotiations produced further opening in several key sectors, including information technology products in 1996 and financial services and telecommunications in 1997. U.S. Trade Representative Charlene Barshefsky was particularly pleased with the telecommunications agreement, which she said would "save billions of dollars for American consumers."[12]

At the regional level, liberalization was promoted on several fronts. In North America, NAFTA's negotiation and ratification were completed in 1993, creating a major new free-trade zone between the United States and neighbors Canada and Mexico. And soon after, in newer initiatives, the administration won agreement

---

[12]As quoted in *New York Times*, February 16, 1997: 1.

with two other groups of states to start building even wider regional accords. In November 1994, the United States and seventeen other countries of the Asia-Pacific region, under the auspices of the recently established Asia-Pacific Economic Cooperation (APEC), declared their intention to achieve full mutual free trade within twenty-five years. Then, a month later at a Summit of the Americas in Miami, thirty-four Western Hemisphere governments agreed to negotiate a Free Trade Area of the Americas (FTAA), aiming for a full and open market within ten years to stretch from Alaska to Tierra del Fuego. For a brief moment there was even talk of a Transatlantic Free Trade Agreement (TAFTA), combining the U.S. and European Union (EU), though the idea never gained much political momentum. Instead, at a 1995 summit meeting in Madrid, Washington and the EU settled for a vaguer new Transatlantic Marketplace, rephrased in 1998 as a Transatlantic Economic Partnership, involving few commitments on either side (Frost 1997, 1998).

Finally, in diverse bilateral negotiations, the Clinton administration brought new vigor to continuing efforts to pry open foreign markets long closed to U.S. goods and services. The major instrument of policy remained the feared Section 301, first enacted in the Trade Act of 1974, which authorizes U.S. negotiators to seek remedy of allegedly "unfair" trade practices abroad—and, of more importance, empowers the executive branch to impose sanctions against foreign governments that refuse to change their ways. Described by its critics as a tool of "aggressive unilateralism," Section 301 is defended by its supporters as unavoidably necessary to assure "comparable access"—a level playing field for American producers. Policy-makers made no secret of their determination to act tough in defense of U.S. commercial interests. Said one top official, "We're convinced that you've got to be willing to show the sword to get results."[13] Of importance, in late 1999, the WTO backed the United States legislation, ruling that Section 301 does not violate existing international trade agreements.[14]

Washington's targets included all the usual suspects, such as the EU and Japan as well as many of the newly industrializing nations. Over the course of the decade, Europe was repeatedly pressed to remove discriminatory barriers to a variety of U.S. exports, both agricultural and industrial, albeit not always with success. More was achieved with the Japanese, who over time were prevailed upon to liberalize market access in a wide range of sensitive areas, including public-sector construction, rice, telecommunications, medical equipment, automobiles, insurance, photograph film, air freight, and shipping. "Economic acupuncture," an observer once called it— a "speak-loudly-and-carry-a-small-needle strategy [that] seems to be producing results."[15] In late 1999, a sweeping new pact was signed with China offering greatly liberalized access for American producers in return for normalization of trade relations; and a few months later, a similar accord was reached with Vietnam, not long

---

[13]The official was Stuart Eizenstat, Under Secretary of Commerce, as quoted in *New York Times*, January 5, 1996: A1.

[14]*New York Times*, December 23, 1999: C2.

[15]Thomas L. Friedman, "U.S. Approach to Japan: 'Economic Acupuncture,'" *New York Times*, March 18, 1994: C1.

ago a country at war with the United States. Successful or not, the Clinton administration's assault on import barriers spared few of our trading partners.

## Present Problems

Yet for all the administration's efforts, many problems remain for the next generation of policy-makers. America's hegemony may be born again but, as Lieber (2001) notes, unchallenged primacy by no means translates into unlimited influence. Resistance to liberalization has grown too, at home as well as abroad—all part of the broader backlash against globalization. The result is a long agenda of unfinished business at all three levels of policy: global, regional, and bilateral.

At the global level, there were great hopes for a new Millennium Round to begin shortly after the start of the new century—only to be dashed by the Battle of Seattle. Numerous issues had been left unresolved by the Uruguay Round, to be addressed in subsequent negotiations. Some were included in a so-called "built-in" agenda for the new WTO. These were items formally mandated for further sectoral bargaining, involving most prominently agriculture and services. In agriculture, the main achievement of the Uruguay Round was agreement to convert existing non-tariff barriers, like import quotas, into more transparent—hence more negotiable—tariffs. Protection levels, however, remain high, limiting market access in most countries. In services, the main achievement was a new General Agreement on Trade in Services (GATS) providing a basic legal framework for future liberalization. The pioneering accords on information technology products, financial services, and telecommunications that followed in 1996–97, impressive as they were, only began the task of converting principle into practice.

Other issues, which many call the "New Trade Agenda," were to be taken up in the aborted Millennium Round. These include such highly charged matters as labor standards, environmental protection, and cultural policy—all sensitive regulatory questions reaching deep into domestic political and social affairs. Should trade agreements incorporate such issues as workers' rights, "fair" labor practices, and prohibition of child or prison labor? Should governments be permitted to use import barriers to promote environmental or cultural objectives? Global trade rules have traditionally limited the role of factors like these on the grounds that they could become an excuse for hidden protectionism—a subterfuge used arbitrarily by powerful constituencies to promote their own particularist interests. But as the Battle for Seattle made clear, they are questions that cannot be ignored if the backlash against globalization is to be contained.

At the regional level, the Clinton administration did have one late triumph when it gained passage of the Trade and Development Act of 2000, unilaterally granting expanded duty-free access in the American market to more than seventy African and Caribbean nations. Little visible progress, however, was made in turning the earlier visions of FTAA and APEC into reality. In part, this was the case because of the Clinton administration's inability to persuade congress, despite repeated appeals, to renew the executive's fast-track authority for trade negotiations—now relabeled "trade promotion authority." Fast-track, which had been part of U.S. legislation since the Trade Act of 1974, meant that once a trade deal was negotiated, congress was given a deadline for ratification under rules prohibiting amendments of any kind. Following the hard-fought battles for NAFTA and the Uruguay Round, however, the Republican-dominated congress was reluctant to give any new powers to an unloved Democratic president. Yet without such authority, as Robert Pastor (2001) suggests, potential partners lacked much incentive to press ahead. Chile, for instance, which had been expected to become the next member of NAFTA, decided instead to establish an affiliate relationship with Mercosur, the Common Market of the South joining Argentina, Brazil, Paraguay, and Uruguay.[16] Progress has also been stalled by geopolitical rivalries. In the Western Hemisphere, Washington's regional aspirations have been resisted by Brazil, Latin America's leading economy, which has its own ambitions to expand Mercosur into a South America Free Trade Area (SAFTA) as a counterweight to NAFTA. Brazil, the *New York Times* warns, is "posing the first serious challenge to undisputed American leadership in the hemisphere."[17] In East Asia, the attractions of freer trade have been overshadowed by emerging great-power struggles involving the United States, China, and Japan.

The Clinton administration also had one late triumph at the bilateral level, when in October 2000 it signed a free-trade pact with Jordan that was notable for including, for the first time in any U.S. trade agreement, explicit commitments to enforce agreed labor and environmental standards.[18] Elsewhere, however, many contentious questions remain outstanding in relations with virtually all of America's trading partners. Typical is a series of festering disputes with the European Union, still unresolved after years of effort to limit EU discrimination against U.S. exports. At issue is a wide range of products, from bananas and other foodstuffs to audio-visual products and aircraft engines. In the case of bananas, the EU has refused to change its long-standing restraints on imports from Central America, where U.S. companies account for most output, despite repeated rulings by the WTO and even in the face of retaliatory U.S. duties. The WTO has also authorized U.S. sanctions in response to European limitations on shipments of hormone-treated beef and genetically modified (GM) foods from the United States, which the EU claims may be a threat to public health. Europe has also sought to control imports of American films and recorded music, largely on cultural grounds, as well as to restrict

---

[16]An affiliate relationship was meant to lead eventually to full membership in Mercosur. But in late 2000, under a new president, Chile reversed itself a second time, announcing its intention to forego the Mercosur option in order to pursue once again a free-trade agreement with the United States. See *New York Times*, December 3, 2000: 9.

[17]Diana Jean Schemo, "As Washington's Attention Wanders, Brazil Plays a Quiet Catch-Up Game," *New York Times*, October 14, 1997: A6.

[18]*New York Times*, October 20, 2000: A14. As indicated above (note 8), this pact generated the one significant difference that emerged during the 2000 presidential contest between Al Gore and George W. Bush. Jordan is only the fourth country to sign a full free-trade agreement with the United States, joining Canada, Mexico, and Israel.

landing rights for U.S. airlines using older aircraft engines that the EU claims are too loud or polluting.

In fact, resistance to further market opening remains strong in most parts of the world. Nor is the United States itself immune from the virus of protectionism, as the EU and many other trading partners regularly point out. Despite a broad commitment to liberalization, Washington frequently acts unilaterally to limit external access to the domestic market. An ample arsenal of weapons is available, including quotas, antidumping measures, restrictive technical norms, and diverse health and safety regulations. From a foreign perspective, U.S. policy often appears contradictory and even unfair. How can America preach free trade to others and simultaneously restrain imports from abroad? "Reciprocity," Brazil's ambassador pointedly remarked not long ago, "is the name of the game."[19] Writes a German commentator, bitterly:

> Many abroad see the United States as a nation divided against itself. It dominates the world economy with its strong economic performance, but at the same time feels deeply insecure about participating in the global economic system . . . Some analysts have begun to compare the trade policy of the United States to its conduct of the Kosovo conflict, with losses to be avoided at any cost. (Walter: 1999, A37)

At home, however, such a seemingly schizophrenic approach to trade—what *The Economist* labels America's "no-body-bags policy"[20]—is easily understood as a byproduct of domestic politics. With opposition to globalization becoming increasingly well organized, compromises become unavoidable as the executive branch seeks to curry favor with legislators or key domestic interests. A good illustration came in 1994, when Washington unilaterally imposed sanctions on Taiwan for refusing to halt sales of tiger bones and rhinoceros horns—the first time ever that the U.S. government had deployed sanctions to protect endangered wildlife. "I am delighted," said the head of a prominent environmental lobby. "It is as if the governor has issued a last-minute stay of execution for those magnificent creatures on the edge of extinction."[21] Another example came in early 2000, when Clinton officials imposed punitive duties on purchases of steel products from Germany, Japan, Korea, and a number of other foreign producers. Ostensibly this action was taken because the U.S. was being "flooded" with cheap imports. But few observers doubted that the main reason was to mollify the United Steelworkers of America and other labor unions, whose support was considered critical to then–Vice President Gore in the upcoming presidential election. If the United States is to preserve the benefits of open markets, it will first have to find ways other than outright protection to satisfy the legitimate demands of aggrieved constituencies like these.

---

[19]Ambassador Rubens Antonio Barbosa, as quoted in *New York Times*, August 7 2000: C4. The remark was made in a hearing before the Subcommittee on the Western Hemisphere of the U.S. House Committee on International Relations.

[20]"After Seattle," *The Economist*, December 11 1999: 19.

[21]Diana E. McKeekin, head of the African Wildlife Foundation, as quoted in *New York Times*, April 12 1994: C1.

# Future Strategy

Trade is manifestly one area where continued U.S. leadership is vital. Can Washington successfully reconcile the responsibilities of primacy with pressures from the system's critics? Though difficult, the task is not impossible. What is needed is a strategy that explicitly addresses the costs of liberalization as well as the benefits—an approach that formally recognizes that trade-offs are required to reconcile trade promotion with other legitimate goals of policy. Market opening matters, but so too do such matters as income inequality, the environment, culture, and national sovereignty.

On the one hand, such a strategy means a refusal to retreat from the long agenda of business left unfinished at the outset of the twenty-first century. Washington should publicly commit itself anew to persevering on past initiatives—global liberalization in the areas of agriculture, services, and other New Trade Agenda items; regional efforts to complete FTAA and APEC; and bilateral bargaining to resolve outstanding disputes such as those with the EU. At the global level, the traditional approach of huge multilateral rounds would best be abandoned, given the increased number and complexity of issues and the rapid growth of WTO membership. As one source observes, "the low-hanging fruit in multilateral trade negotiations has already been picked . . . The 'global-round' approach to trade talks . . . [has] outlived its usefulness" (Cutter et al. 2000: 91). More efficient would be the more narrowly targeted type of bargaining that produced the later accords on information technology products, financial services, and telecommunications. Regional and bilateral talks should continue to emphasize the importance of enhanced market access. Nothing would symbolize Washington's revitalized commitment more than a quick renewal of fast-track negotiating authority.

On the other hand, policy-makers must explicitly couple liberalization with the concerns of its domestic opponents. No longer is it possible to separate trade negotiations from their consequences, as bargaining reaches ever deeper into traditionally domestic issues. If the backlash against globalization is to be contained, critics must be persuaded that policy-makers have not abandoned their social responsibilities. The trading system cannot become identified with limiting the broader authority of governments to promote the public weal. This does not mean giving mercantilists a free rein, but it does mean recognizing the legitimacy of other core social values. Three groups have been at the forefront of the assault on the trade regime: labor unions, social activists, and economic nationalists. Highest priority, therefore, should be given to the issues of most salience to each.

For the U.S. labor movement, obviously, the main issues are job security and income. Unions deny that they have simply become old-fashioned protectionists. But the sad fact is that labor has opposed virtually every initiative to open the U.S. market, from NAFTA and the Uruguay Round to normalization of trade relations with China and the Trade and Development Act of 2000. Ostensibly, unions favor trade agreements so long as they include provisions to protect the rights of foreign workers, such as minimum wages and a ban on child labor—all obviously valid concerns. "We believe in fair trade," says James Hoffa of the Teamsters.[22] In reality, however, it would be disingenuous to believe that America's labor movement has suddenly been seized by a fit of international high-mindedness. Union leaders may be genuinely distressed by labor abuses abroad. Their underlying motive, however, is undoubtedly more self-serving: to slow down the continuing shift of jobs to locations abroad where labor-intensive goods can be produced more cheaply. Adds Hoffa: "American workers should not be asked to compete with foreigners who are not paid a living wage."[23] Foreign governments certainly recognize the cynical element of such demands, which "take away our comparative advantage," as an Indian cabinet minister puts it—"a pernicious maneuver to force our wages up, to undermine our competitiveness."[24]

Can unions be turned away from protectionism? Manifestly a new domestic consensus is needed, more in line with the general public's priority for protecting American jobs as reported by Holsti (2001). The most direct approach would be one that formally ties liberalization to parallel aid measures for those whose incomes and jobs are likely to be most threatened—blue-collar workers. In effect, this approach would mean reviving adjustment assistance as an integral part of our foreign-trade policy. First included in John F. Kennedy's Trade Expansion Act of 1962, adjustment assistance for those hurt by rising imports was allowed to atrophy during the ascendancy of Reaganomics in the1980s. The political reality today, however, is clear. Union hostility to open markets will not be eased without an emphasis on major new programs designed to compensate workers for their losses—enhanced unemployment insurance, moving allowances, retraining programs, and the like. Mobilizing congressional support for such interventionist measures in today's political climate will certainly not be easy. But turning labor away from protectionism without offering an improved safety net will be even more difficult.

For social activists, the main issues are, above all, the New Trade Agenda questions of labor standards, environmental protection, and cultural policy. Workers' rights around the world cannot be ignored simply because the problem has been co-opted by U.S. labor unions for their own purposes. Neither can concerns about pollution or cultural degradation be dismissed as materially irrelevant to international trade negotiations. The likes of José Bové and Lori Wallach have made such issues relevant. The challenge is to design rules that explicitly balance the oft competing goals of economic efficiency and social welfare in the broadest sense—guidelines that carefully define when governments may legally sacrifice gains of trade in order to limit the ancillary costs of open markets. A possible model was provided by the free-trade pact with Jordan signed in late 2000, which explicitly linked market opening to formal compliance with international labor and environmental norms. Opportunistic

---

[22]As quoted in *New York Times*, April 24, 2000: A9. Labor did support the Jordan trade pact signed in October 2000 precisely because the agreement did include explicit commitments on labor standards.

[23]As quoted in *New York Times*, May 21, 2000: WK17.

[24]Commerce and Industry Minister Murasoli Maran, as quoted in *New York Times*, December 17, 1999: C4.

use of such linkage as a rationale for hidden protectionism is always a risk, of course. But that possibility would seem a small price to pay if the alternative is more protests on the model of the Battle of Seattle.

Finally, for economic nationalists, the main issue is the threat that WTO supposedly poses to the historical principle of state sovereignty. Most at issue is the WTO's mechanism for dispute resolution, which was greatly strengthened by the Uruguay Round as compared with the earlier GATT system (Jackson 1996). Critics argue that adverse rulings by WTO panels of experts, which are convened whenever a country is formally accused of a trading violation, could compel a nation even as powerful as the United States to change its standards or regulations against its will. In fact, that argument is an exaggeration. It is true that governments can no longer single-handedly forestall an adverse ruling, as in the past. But it is also true that the WTO lacks enforcement powers of any kind, other than a right to authorize retaliatory sanctions of the sort that Washington has used in its disputes with the EU. As Bill Clinton's Council of Economic Advisers observed, the WTO cannot "preclude the United States or other countries from establishing, maintaining and effectively enforcing their own laws" (Council of Economic Advisers 2000: 219). Nonetheless, there is ample room for improvements that might ease concerns of this sort. Even its supporters admit that the WTO's dispute-settlement process is opaque and slow. Procedures could certainly provide for much greater public access and participation to enhance transparency and accountability.

# INTERNATIONAL FINANCE

Threat of backlash is equally evident in the finance sphere, where market integration has proceeded even more rapidly than in the trade sphere. As the global mobility of capital has risen, so also has the frequency and amplitude of financial crises, generating mounting discontent and denunciation. Here too, broad issues are implicated—most important, the question of what globalization of finance means for the ability of sovereign states to manage their own economic affairs. And here too, finding effective responses to critics while preserving the benefits of closer integration will not be easy.

## Phoenix Risen

Of all the many changes of the world economy in recent decades, few have been nearly so dramatic as the resurrection of global finance. A half century ago, after the ravages of the Great Depression and World War Two, financial markets everywhere—with the notable exception of the United States—were generally weak, insular, and strictly controlled, reduced from their previously central role in international economic relations to offer little more than a negligible amount of trade financing. Starting in the late 1950s, however, private lending and investment once again began to gather momentum, generating a phenomenal growth of cross-border capital flows and an increasingly close integration of national financial markets. Like a phoenix risen from the ashes, global finance took flight and soared to new heights of power and influence in the affairs of nations (Cohen 1996).

Like trade liberalization, financial liberalization ranked high on America's diplomatic agenda throughout the 1990s—another essential element of the Washington consensus. America could expect to gain in two ways. First, open capital markets would make it easier to finance the country's persistent trade deficit, deflecting pressures to restrict imports instead. And second, new market opportunities would be created for U.S. financial institutions, universally acknowledged to be among the world's most competitive suppliers of banking and investment services. An assault on barriers to capital mobility seemed a natural complement to a policy of export promotion. Both promised to help revitalize America's economic primacy.

Here too, as with trade, policy was consistent with past practice. Previous administrations, going as far back as Presidents Ford and Carter, had also placed emphasis on financial liberalization. America itself helped lead the way in the mid-1970s by removing capital controls that had been introduced in the 1960s; and encouragement was later given to other Triad countries as well, all of which followed suit by the time President Clinton took office. But here too, the new administration added fresh vigor to policy, targeting in particular the emerging East Asian and Latin American economies. All were urged to phase out existing capital controls as quickly as possible. Open financial markets, governments were told, were essential to attaining healthy, self-sustaining growth. Like trade based on comparative advantage, capital mobility could lead to a more productive employment of investment resources; it also offered increased opportunities for effective risk management and potentially higher returns for savers. Free capital mobility, therefore, no less than free trade, should be enshrined as a universal norm. The high point came in early 1997 when, at the urging of the United States, the IMF began to prepare a new amendment to the organization's charter to make promotion of financial liberalization a specific Fund objective and responsibility.[25]

But then came the Asian financial crisis of 1997–98, with reverberations that were still being felt at century's end. Crises in global capital markets were nothing new, of course. During the 1980s, there was the prolonged problem of Latin American debt, triggered by Mexico's near-default on its foreign bank loans in 1982. In 1992–93, there was the collapse of the European Union's so-called Exchange Rate Mechanism—a pegged-rate precursor to today's euro—under the pressure of massive currency speculation. And in late 1994, there was yet another near-default in Mexico, which quickly spread to a number of other countries in what came to be known as the "tequila effect." Later dubbed by Michel Camdessus, then managing director of the IMF, "the first financial crisis of the twenty-first century," Mexico's new emergency was distinguished by the fact that unlike during the 1980s, the debts

---

[25]Under the plan, two articles of the Fund charter were to be amended—Article I, where "orderly liberalization of capital" would be added to the list of the Fund's formal purposes; and Article VIII, which would give the Fund the same jurisdiction over the capital account of its members as it already enjoys over the current account. The language would also *require* countries to commit themselves to capital liberalization as a goal. For more detail, see *IMF Survey*, May 12, 1997.

involved were not bank loans but securities—in particular, government bonds—which could be sold quickly by foreign investors. This situation greatly accelerated the pace of events and complicated the task of negotiating a satisfactory solution. Default was avoided only with the help of the U.S. Treasury. A line of credit of some $20 billion from the Treasury's Exchange Stabilization Fund (ESF) was made available to the Mexican authorities to help stem the gathering tide of capital flight. Though criticized at the time in the congress as a deceitful circumvention of legislative authority, the administration's use of the ESF, which was in fact quite legal, proved to be a great success. Financial stability was quickly restored, and Mexico's drawings, which peaked at $11.5 billion, were all repaid by January 1997, with a profit to the Treasury of nearly a half billion dollars (Henning 1999).

None of these prior episodes, however, had prepared policy-makers for the ferocity of the storm that hit East Asia, beginning with an attack on Thailand's currency, the bhat, in mid-1997. Though a rescue package of some $25 billion was quickly assembled for Bangkok, the crisis soon proved contagious—"bhatulism," some called it—spreading first to regional neighbors like Malaysia, Indonesia, and Korea; and then later as far afield as Russia in mid-1998, Brazil in early 1999, and Argentina in 2000. Governments across the developing world were forced to turn for assistance to the IMF, which prescribed tough policy conditions. Monetary and fiscal policies were tightened sharply in hopes of sustaining the confidence of foreign investors, even at the risk of prolonged recession and higher unemployment. Economic development stalled, and living standards tumbled.

It is not surprising that criticisms soon followed. Why, many asked, should sovereign states be forced to tailor their policies to the preferences of private interests? Why should freedom of capital movements be given absolute priority over other considerations of public welfare? In the words of Paul Krugman, it was all a cruel "confidence game":

> The need to win market confidence can actually prevent a country from following otherwise sensible policies and force it to follow policies that would normally seem perverse ... Policy ends up having very little to do with economics. It becomes an exercise in amateur psychology ... It sounds pretty crazy, and it is. (Krugman 1998)

Across the developing world, accordingly, resistance to financial liberalization has rapidly increased—also part of the broader backlash against globalization. The phoenix of global finance is now seen as more rapacious than benign. Many in East Asia took encouragement from the example of Malaysia, which, in September 1998, reintroduced strict controls on capital outflows in order to provide room for more expansionary domestic policies. Capital controls had long been dismissed as a relic of an earlier, more interventionist era. But now, as one source commented, they seemed to become "an idea whose time, in the minds of many Asian government officials, has come back" (Wade and Veneroso 1998: 23). Authorities elsewhere are also known to be reconsidering the virtues of capital mobility, as discomfort with the confidence game grows. Here too, the core issue is clear: can the benefits of open markets be reconciled with the legitimate grievances of critics? And here too, it is evident that continued U.S. leadership is vital.

## Taming the Phoenix?

Can the phoenix be tamed? Once again, what is needed is a strategy that explicitly addresses the costs of liberalization as well as the benefits. Since the Asian crisis broke, there has been much talk of reform of the "international financial architecture"—the rules and institutions governing monetary relations among states. The challenge of reform is to find some way to reconcile capital mobility with the demands of national sovereignty. In this sphere too, critics must be persuaded that policy-makers are not being compelled to sacrifice social responsibilities on the altar of open markets. Improvements are called for in three areas: crisis prevention, crisis management, and currency cooperation.

First, reforms are needed to reduce the probability of more Asian-style financial storms in the future. Consensus already exists on the need for strengthening domestic banking and capital markets, to avoid the kind of fragilities—for example, currency mismatches and excessive short-term borrowing—that are known to have contributed to East Asia's difficulties. Indeed, many governments have already been persuaded to upgrade the supervision and regulation of their financial markets, emphasizing in particular better risk-management practices and disclosure requirements in order to enhance market discipline. But that is only a beginning, as I have suggested elsewhere (Cohen 2001). In addition, the case for capital controls must be reconsidered—particularly the case for curbs on liquid inflows of the sort that Chile maintained, with considerable success, for many years to minimize the risk of massive outflows. Controls are indeed an idea whose time has—or should—come back. The IMF, for instance, has dramatically changed its tune since the Asian crisis, dropping active discussion of a new amendment on liberalization and talking instead of the possible efficacy of selective financial restraints.[26] Most desirable would be a set of rules similar to those proposed for core New Trade Agenda issues—guidelines that, in parallel fashion, would carefully define when and how governments may legally sacrifice the benefits of capital mobility in order to limit the ancillary costs of open markets. Though this approach, too, runs the risk of abuse by opportunistic governments, it would again seem a small price to pay if the alternative is arbitrary market closure.

Reforms are also needed to cope more effectively with crises when they do occur, to reduce their severity and minimize the threat of contagion. At one level, this imperative means creating more orderly market procedures for restructuring problem debts, along lines suggested by economist Barry Eichengreen (1999)—for example, majority voting, sharing clauses, and provisions for collective representation that would make it easier for foreign creditors to negotiate acceptable settlements with their debtors. At a second level, it means taking another look at the role of the IMF, which until now has acted mainly as guardian and enforcer of the Wash-

---

[26]See e.g., Ariyoshi *et al.* (2000).

ington consensus. Conservatives have criticized the Fund for creating a serious moral hazard: a risk that countries will deliberately take on higher levels of debt in the knowledge that the IMF is there to rescue them if they get into trouble. Their solution would be to limit the Fund's activities strictly to the provision of emergency liquidity—in effect, aiding just the most solvent borrowers—as a congressional commission recently recommended.[27] In fact, however, it is hard to see how such a narrow mandate could really reduce the spread of panic in financial markets, once a crisis begins. More to the point would be a streamlining of the IMF's lending programs, as advocated by former Treasury Secretary Lawrence Summers,[28] to enable it to move more quickly and effectively to stem market unruliness. Progress in this direction was achieved in late 2000 when the Fund approved a plan to discourage repeat borrowers, who look to the IMF as a routine source of aid, and instead to make more money available for emergency situations.[29] Over time, the practical implementation of Fund policy conditionality will also have to be reassessed, to put less single-minded emphasis on domestic austerity, particularly fiscal austerity, when governments are forced to play the confidence game with international investors.

Finally, a renewed effort is needed to cultivate cooperation on currency issues, particularly among the Triad countries. Exchange rates among the major currencies—the dollar, euro, and yen—cannot be left solely to the tender mercies of speculators, given the central importance of these currencies to the stability of monetary relations in general. The United States, especially, has an interest in avoiding extreme exchange-rate uncertainties because of its continued dependence on financing from abroad. One reason why America has been able to live beyond its means for so long is that, until now, the greenback had no serious rival as an international currency. With the emergence of the euro, however, that is no longer the case. Europe's new money is widely expected to offer an attractive alternative to global investors, as is the yen once the Japanese economy recovers its stride. Worse, both the EU and Japan may well be tempted to compete vigorously to promote international use of their currencies, in order to enhance their own ability to finance payments deficits, even at the risk of provoking a run on the dollar. Washington thus has a strong incentive to do all it can to improve mechanisms for the collective management of exchange rates. Closer and more effective collaboration should be pursued through both the IMF and G-7.

## CONCLUSION

The agenda for U.S. foreign economic policy is long. At the outset of the twenty-first century, America's primacy in the world economy is undoubted—but insecure. Both at home and abroad, a backlash against globalization is intensifying, threaten-

---

[27]This was the International Financial Institutions Advisory Commission (2000)—otherwise known as the Meltzer Commission after its chair, Allen Meltzer, a prominent academic economist. The Commission was comprised of some eleven private-sector specialists appointed by the Congress. Its report was issued in March 2000.

[28]See e.g., *New York Times*, December 15, 1999: C4.

[29]See e.g., *New York Times*, September 16, 2000: B1.

ing global prosperity. If the material benefits of open markets are to be preserved, the legitimate concerns of globalization's critics must be directly addressed. In trade, this undertaking means doing more to compensate for the effects of open markets on income inequality, the environment, culture, and national sovereignty. In finance, it means doing more to limit the impact of capital mobility on the ability of states to manage their own economic affairs. The irreversibility of globalization cannot be taken for granted, and there is no substitute for U.S. leadership.

Is the administration of George W. Bush up to the challenge? Early indications were not reassuring. Though no less committed than his predecessors to maintaining an open world economy, the new president has indicated little sympathy for criticisms of the Washington consensus. Administration officials, mostly conservative and business-oriented, seem inclined to emphasize gains from market liberalization to the exclusion of other considerations, discounting potential costs; and no encouragement is given to advocates of enhanced adjustment assistance, environmental and cultural protections, or limitations on capital mobility. At a minimum, such a policy stance will make containment of the backlash against globalization more difficult. At worst, it could trigger a wholesale revival of protectionism and economic nationalism around the world. Global prosperity hangs in the balance.

# REFERENCES

Ariyoshi, Akira, Karl Habermeier, Bernard Laurens, Inci Otker-Robe, Jorge Iván Canales-Kriljenko, and Andrei Kirilenko (2000), *Country Experiences with the Use and Liberalization of Capital Controls*, Occasional Paper (Washington: International Monetary Fund).

Cerny, Philip G. (1994), "The Infrastructure of the Infrastructure? Toward 'Embedded Financial Orthodoxy' in the International Political Economy," in Ronan P. Palan and Barry Gills (eds.), *Transcending the State-Global Divide: A Neostructuralist Agenda in International Relations* (Boulder, CO: Lynne Reinner), chapter 12.

Cohen, Benjamin J. (1992), "Toward a Mosaic Economy: Relations with Other Advanced Industrial Nations," in Kenneth A. Oye, Robert J. Lieber, and Donald Rothchild (eds.), *Eagle in a New World: American Grand Strategy in the Post–Cold War Era* (New York: HarperCollins), chapter 5.

—— (1996), "Phoenix Risen: The Resurrection of Global Finance," *World Politics* 48: 2 (January): 268–296.

—— (1997), "'Return to Normalcy'? Global Economic Policy at the End of the Century," in Robert J. Lieber (ed.), *Eagle Adrift: American Foreign Policy at the End of the Century* (New York: Longman), chapter 4.

—— (2001), "Taming the Phoenix: Monetary Governance after the Crisis," in Gregory W. Noble and John Ravenhill (eds.), *The Asian Financial Crisis and the Structure of Global Finance* (Cambridge: Cambridge University Press), 192–212.

Council of Economic Advisers (2000), *Annual Report, 2000* (Washington, DC: U.S. Government Printing Office).

Cutter, W. Bowman, Joan Spero, and Laura D'Andrea Tyson (2000), "New World, New Deal: A Democratic Approach to Globalization," *Foreign Affairs* 79: 2 (March–April): 80–98.

Eichengreen, Barry (1999), *Toward a New International Financial Architecture: A Practical Post-Asia Agenda* (Washington, DC: Institute for International Economics).

Frost, Ellen L. (1997), *Transatlantic Trade: A Strategic Agenda* (Washington, DC: Institute for International Economics).

――― (1998), "The Transatlantic Economic Partnership," International Economic Policy Brief 98-6 (Washington, DC: Institute for International Economics).

Gilpin, Robert (2000), *The Challenge of Global Capitalism: The World Economy in the 21st Century* (Princeton, NJ: Princeton University Press).

Griswold, Daniel T. (2000), "Stop Worrying about the U.S. Trade Deficit," *Georgetown Journal of International Affairs* 1: 1 (Winter–Spring): 67–72.

Henning, C. Randall (1999), *The Exchange Stabilization Fund: Slush Money or War Chest?* (Washington, DC: Institute for International Economics).

Holsti, Ole R. (2001), "Public Opinion and Foreign Policy," this volume.

International Financial Institutions Advisory Commission (2000), *Report to the U.S. Congress* (Washington, DC).

Jackson, John H. (1996), "The WTO Dispute Settlement Procedures: A Preliminary Appraisal," in Jeffrey H. Schott (ed.), *The World Trading System: Challenges Ahead* (Washington, DC: Institute for International Economics), chapter 9.

James, Harold (1999), "Is Liberalization Reversible?," *Finance and Development* (December): 11–14.

Kapstein, Ethan B. (1999), *Sharing the Wealth: Workers and the World Economy* (New York: Norton).

Keohane, Robert O. (1979), "U.S. Foreign Economic Policy Toward Other Advanced Capitalist States: The Struggle to Make Others Adjust," in Kenneth A. Oye, Donald Rothchild, and Robert J. Lieber (eds.), *Eagle Entangled: U.S. Foreign Policy in a Complex World* (New York: Longman), chapter 3.

Krugman, Paul (1998), "The Confidence Game," *The New Republic* (October 5): 23–25.

――― (2000), "Can America Stay on Top?," *Journal of Economic Perspectives* 14: 1 (Winter): 169–175.

Lieber, Robert J. (2001), "Foreign Policy and American Primacy," this volume.

Lovett, William A. (1999), "Rebalancing U.S. Trade," in William A. Lovett, Alfred E. Eckes, Jr., and Richard L. Brinkman (eds.), *U.S. Trade Policy: History, Theory, and the WTO* (Armonk, NY: M.E. Sharpe), chapter 5.

Mann, Catherine (1999), *Is the U.S. Trade Deficit Sustainable?* (Washington, DC: Institute for International Economics).

――― (2000), "Is the U.S. Current Account Deficit Sustainable?," *Finance and Development* (March): 42–45.

Meunier, Sophie (2000), "The French Exception," *Foreign Affairs* 79: 4 (July–August): 104–116.

Naím, Moisés (2000), "Editor's Note," *Foreign Policy* 118 (Spring): 11–12.

Pastor, Robert (2001), "The United States and the Americas: Unfilled Promise at the Century's Turn," this volume.

Pauly, Louis W. (1995), "Capital Mobility, State Autonomy and Political Legitimacy," *Journal of International Affairs* 48: 2 (Winter): 369–388.

Rodrik, Dani (2000), "How Far Will International Economic Integration Go?," *Journal of Economic Perspectives* 14: 1 (Winter): 177–186.

Stokes, Bruce (1999–2000), "The Protectionist Myth," *Foreign Policy* 117 (Winter), 88–102.

Thurow, Lester (1992), *Head to Head: The Coming Economic Battle Among Japan, Europe, and America* (New York: William Morrow and Company).

Ullman, Owen (1998), "America's New Four-Letter Word," *The International Economy* (July–August): 40–41, 62.

Wade, Robert and Frank Veneroso (1998), "The Gathering Support for Capital Controls," *Challenge* 41: 6 (November–December): 14–26.

Walter, Nobert (1999), "Caught in a U.S. Civil War," *New York Times,* 13 December: A37.

# 15

# The Eagle
# and the Global Environment
## The Burden of Being Essential

## ROBERT PAARLBERG
### Wellesley College

In international environmental policy, as in other areas, the United States is the essential country. Leadership opportunities in this area emerge not only from the large relative size of the United States economy or from U.S. military and diplomatic preponderance. The United States is also well positioned to lead internationally in this area because its domestic environmental standards generally exceed international standards; this status implies, in many cases, a convenient option to press for policy changes abroad that the United States has already undertaken at home.[1] If the United States decides to take a lead under such circumstances and if it leads wisely, the strengthening of international environmental policies becomes probable. Yet by the same token, if the United States fails to lead or leads unwisely, progress can be blocked.

In recent years, the United States has not always carried this burden well. In the 1980s on the issue of stratospheric ozone protection, the United States did take an effective lead in promoting the 1987 Montreal Protocol to limit CFC production. Yet during the decade of the 1990s, U.S. leadership faltered badly in two comparably important areas: climate change and biodiversity protection. This faltering of leadership compromised global environmental interests in the area of climate change, and

Robert Paarlberg is Professor of Political Science at Wellesley College and Associate at the Weatherhead Center for International Affairs at Harvard University. His recent books include *Policy Reform in American Agriculture: Analysis and Prognosis* (with David Orden and Terry Roe, Chicago, 1999), *Leadership Abroad Begins at Home: U.S. Foreign Economic Policy After the Cold War* (Brookings, 1995), and *Countrysides at Risk: The Political Geography of Sustainable Agriculture* (Overseas Development Council, 1994). His current research is on international policies toward genetically modified foods.

[1]Elizabeth R. DeSombre, *Domestic Sources of International Environmental Policy* (Cambridge, MA: MIT Press, 2000).

it may have compromised some U.S. economic interests as well in the area of biodiversity protection. In this chapter, we seek to understand some underlying reasons for these fluctuating leadership performances and divergent policy outcomes.

Why does the United States lead effectively on some environmental issues but not on others? If we compare only U.S. ozone policy leadership in the 1980s (successful) with U.S. climate change policy leadership in the 1990s (unsuccessful), we might guess that what made the climate change case difficult was opposition from domestic industry, opposition from organized labor, a significant projected cost to the general economy, a lack of scientific consensus regarding the threat, and weak prospects for international cooperation. In the easier ozone case, all five of these critical blocking factors were missing, so U.S. leadership could go forward. Yet when we turn to the biodiversity case, all five of these blocking factors are again mostly missing, yet U.S. leadership has nonetheless faltered, so the answers are not simple.

In the analysis that follows, we use a comparison of these three separate cases to learn lessons about how ready the United States is to play a leadership role in the area of international environmental policy and what the consequences might be if that leadership falters. We learn that there are limits to the view of the United States as an essential or unavoidable country. In the case of biodiversity policy, when the United States declined to lead policy in a direction congenial to U.S. interests, other states stepped in and took global policy in another direction, compromising some U.S. economic interests in the process.

# A MODEL FOR SUCCESS: THE 1987 MONTREAL PROTOCOL

The United States government is fully capable of highly effective international environmental policy leadership, as evidenced in the case of the 1987 Montreal Protocol limiting CFC production so as to protect the stratospheric ozone layer. Prior to 1986, the Reagan administration had avoided leadership on ozone protection and on most other international environmental policy matters, just as it had avoided strong domestic policy actions against pollution and environmental degradation. Then, thanks in part to pressures from environmental advocates in congress (including then Democratic Senator Al Gore) and from a 1984 lawsuit against the Environmental Protection Agency (EPA) for its failure to regulate CFC production, the Reagan administration changed its posture and began working hard for an international agreement to cut CFC production throughout the industrial world.[2] Once the United States took the diplomatic lead, results came quickly. In September 1987 in Montreal, an international agreement was reached to cut CFC production by 50 percent from the 1986 level. Three years later, this protocol was amended at a meeting in London to require a 100 percent elimination of CFC production.

---

[2]Richard E. Benedick, *Ozone Diplomacy: New Direction in Safeguarding the Planet* (Cambridge, MA: Harvard University Press, 1991).

A rare and important combination of circumstances made effective U.S. leadership possible in this case. U.S. industry resistance was not a blocking factor, ever since a prominent business-based group, the Alliance for Responsible CFC Policy, had formally endorsed international controls on CFCs in September 1986. In fact, the leading U.S. producer, DuPont, had switched from blocking to backing an international agreement limiting CFC production. DuPont was motivated to make this switch partly by successful investments it had been making in CFC substitutes, where it knew it might have an advantage over its competitors in Europe in the event of a global agreement limiting CFC use.[3] Organized labor opposition was not a factor in the case of Ozone, since so few jobs of any kind—let alone union jobs—were linked in the United States to CFC production. CFCs did not loom large either for workers or for industry. Even for DuPont, revenues from CFC production were only about 2 percent of total corporate revenues, and the looming availability of affordable CFC substitutes ensured that the U.S. economy overall would not have to be adversely affected by an international protocol limiting CFC production.

U.S. leadership was also facilitated in the stratospheric ozone case by the presence of a clear scientific consensus on the source and magnitude of the environmental threat. By 1987, massive ozone loss had been measured by NASA-sponsored high-altitude aircraft examining the stratosphere over the Antarctic, and the link between ozone loss and CFCs had become impossible to deny. In addition, atmospheric and medical scientists were able to draw direct quantifiable links between ozone loss, increases in surface UV radiation, and increased skin cancer. The total cost to the U.S. economy of reducing CFC production emerged from these calculations as tiny compared with the projected human health gains.[4]

Finally, U.S. leadership was forthcoming in this case because prospects for effective international cooperation were high from the start. Only a relatively small number of wealthy industrial countries produced CFCs (the United States by itself produced half of all the world's CFCs in the 1970s). U.S. environmental policy diplomats knew that if only the European Union and Japan could be induced to join the United States in limiting CFC production, the problem of international cooperation would largely be solved. It was under U.S. leadership that the original Montreal Protocol agreement cutting CFC production by 50 percent was negotiated in 1987, and it was under still more U.S. leadership that the Montreal Protocol was amended in London in 1990 to require a full phaseout of CFC production. So determined was U.S. diplomacy in this case that a number of European participants claimed that they were being bullied into the agreement (though many welcomed the bullying, as it gave them a way to persuade their own domestic CFC producers of the need for global limits). Moving toward a full phaseout called for commitments from developing countries as well, but this cooperation was easily attainable, partly through

[3]Edward A. Parson, "Protecting the Ozone Layer," in Peter M. Haas, Robert O. Keohane, and Marc A. Levy, (eds.) *Institutions for the Earth,* (Cambridge, MA: MIT Press, 1993).

[4]Total cost as estimated by EPA in 1988 was $27 billion; total benefit in terms of avoided cancer deaths in the U.S. population born before 2075 was estimated at more than 200 times as great—$6.4 trillion.

the promise of a $240 million international fund to help pay incremental costs of compliance in those countries.

# A MODEL FOR PARALYSIS: THE STILLBORN KYOTO CLIMATE CHANGE AGREEMENT

Whereas strong U.S. leadership was available in the case of stratospheric ozone protection, it has not yet been available in the area of climate change, despite occasional high-profile efforts by the Clinton administration (1993–2000) to provide leadership.

During the 1992 presidential campaign, candidate Bill Clinton had strongly criticized his predecessor President Bush for failing to embrace the climate change policy goals proposed at the Rio Earth Summit by the European Union (EU): a limiting of carbon dioxide emissions to 1990 levels by 2000. Clinton promised to embrace this goal as a national priority if elected, and in his first months as president in 1993, Clinton did formally adopt the emissions limit goal. In so doing, he briefly won praise for having restored the United States to a position of international leadership on climate change policy. Yet almost immediately Clinton began to encounter difficulties, more at home than abroad. He failed almost immediately to secure from congress the energy tax needed to meet his new emissions commitment, and he was thus forced to rely on less effective voluntary measures. By the time of a 1995 Berlin climate change conference, U.S. officials had to admit that their domestic greenhouse gas emissions were still going up and that the president's 1993 pledge would not be fulfilled.

Undaunted, Clinton's international negotiators nonetheless went on to embrace a technically ambitious goal of putting a fixed cap on international greenhouse gas emissions. Congress was not comfortable with this approach, and under domestic criticism for the next year and a half, the president equivocated both on how tight the cap should be and on when it should come into effect. In the summer of 1997, the Senate passed a 95–0 resolution warning the Clinton administration not to enter into any binding international agreement on climate change without a provision disciplining the emissions of developing countries.

The Clinton administration's performance at the December 1997 Kyoto summit conference on climate change deepened congressional resistance. Clinton's negotiators sought to lure developing countries into a binding limits agreement by offering a cut in U.S. greenhouse gas emissions larger than anything previously discussed. The United States offered a cut to 7 percent *below* 1990 emissions levels by the years 2008–2012. This tactic failed when the developing countries, led by China, still refused to accept any emissions reduction obligations. The result was the worst of both worlds for U.S. negotiators: a promised cut larger than congress had anticipated and without any guarantee of the developing country participation Congress had warned would be necessary.

In March 2001, the new administration of President George W. Bush decided formally to abandon the Kyoto accord, which was still being supported officially by the E.U. but had been ratified at that point by only one country, Romania. Bush rejected the Kyoto approach on grounds that it would impose an unjust and inequitable burden on the U.S. economy. He said, "We will not do anything that harms our economy, because first things first are the people who live in America."[5] Bush's new EPA administrator, Christie Whitman, explained that in place of Kyoto the new administration would favor a "market-based incentives" approach, although no details were offered. Even before Bush abandoned the Kyoto approach, it had become clear that the U.S. was in no easy position to comply. Total U.S. greenhouse gas emissions had yet to begin falling toward the 1990 level, let alone 7 percent below the 1990 level; instead, these emissions had continued to rise. At the time the Kyoto agreement was negotiated, U.S. greenhouse gas emissions were 10 percent above 1990 levels and rising on a trend that would leave them 30 percent above the U.S. Kyoto pledge level by 2008–2012.[6] Sadly, it had been the policy of the Clinton administration to do nothing to halt this rise in U.S. greenhouse gas emissions at home (no higher fuel taxes, no new auto efficiency regulations, no rationing) even while promoting an international agreement in Kyoto that promised large cuts in the future. The continued refusal of Congress to ratify Kyoto brought the emptiness of this U.S. leadership approach out in the open for all to see.

Why was the United States such a capable leader on ozone protection policy in Montreal in 1987, but then such a weak leader (peddling promises it could not keep) on climate change policy in Kyoto in 1997? If we consider the five key variables noted before, a clear answer seems to emerge.

## Industry Opposition

Although private industry in the United States supported an international agreement limiting CFC production, industry has strongly opposed any firm U.S. commitment to limit greenhouse gas emissions. In 1993, when President Clinton proposed a BTU tax that would have constrained the burning of fossil fuels (although its main purpose was to raise revenue, to help remedy the federal budget deficit), he was opposed by a strong coalition of coal, petroleum, and public utilities interests, and had to abandon the idea. When Clinton's negotiators then began moving in 1996 toward a new international agreement to put a national cap on emissions, domestic industry counterattacked. Prior to the 1997 Kyoto conference, private energy-linked companies spent $13 million on advertisements designed to strengthen congressional resistance to a binding limits agreement. The leading corporate voice against a strong U.S. climate change policy was the Global Climate Change Coalition, a consortium of coal, oil, and automobile companies and utilities (originally spun out of the National Association of Manufacturers in 1989) that

[5]Edmund L. Andrews, "Bush Angers Europe by Eroding Pact on Warming," *New York Times,* April 1, 2001, p. A3.

[6]John H. Cushman, Jr., "Whether It Creates Jobs or Joblessness, the Agreement Will Affect Everyone," *New York Times,* December 12, 1997, p. A16.

fought hard against binding treaty limits. Parallel to this umbrella lobby effort was a more narrow Coalition for Vehicle Choice, a Washington-based group financed by the U.S. auto industry, which spent the two years prior to Kyoto convincing small business, labor, and local civic groups throughout the country that a treaty limiting emissions would be "bad for America." This coalition persuaded 1,300 such groups to sign an ad to that effect in 1997, and just before Kyoto, published the list of signatories in the *Washington Post.*

Corporate money was also used effectively to generate studies that frightened voters and members of congress about the costs of tighter greenhouse gas emissions limits. The Global Climate Change Coalition released a study late in 1997 purporting to show that cumulative losses to the U.S. economy from a climate change treaty could amount to $30,000 for each American household in the years 2000–2020. The Center for Energy and Economic Development, a group with a $4 million annual budget sponsored by the coal industry, targeted business and civic groups in eleven states with a similar message.

Some smaller segments of U.S. industry support greenhouse gas emissions limits, most notably the U.S. Business Council for Sustainable Industry, a group that includes the natural gas industry, which would see its share of the fossil fuel market grow under a tighter emissions regime. The insurance industry is also favorably inclined toward tighter emissions controls, hoping for protection against the larger settlement claims that might accompany sea level rise or violent weather patterns from further global warming. On balance, however, private industry in the United States has been a consistent opponent of more stringent climate change policies.

## Labor Opposition

As a second contrast to the stratospheric ozone case, organized labor in the United States is also actively opposed to tighter U.S. climate change policies. The potentially vulnerable United Mine Workers spent $1.5 million in 1996 and 1997 hoping to block a strong treaty. Although they failed to stop the Clinton-Gore administration from negotiating a strong U.S. treaty commitment in Kyoto, they did not fail in communicating their views to the members of congress who would have had to ratify the Treaty, and will have to vote the policies needed to implement any tough U.S. policy on climate change.

## Public Opposition Due to Economic Burdens

Immediately following the Kyoto summit, Yale economist William Nordhaus estimated that reaching the Kyoto goal in the United States might require a doubling of the wholesale price of crude oil, coal, and natural gas, which would work through the economy to produce the equivalent of a $2,000 per year increase, per American household, in outlays for gasoline and heat. Even official U.S. Department of Energy estimates alluded to additional costs for middle-class Americans in the form of significant job cuts in a number of energy-sensitive U.S. industries, including aluminum, cement, chemicals, oil, paper, and steel.[7] Fuel and fertilizer users in agriculture would also be hurt. Although the American people tend to support stronger climate change policies in the abstract, they have been less enthusiastic when reminded of the short-term domestic employment and welfare impacts of such policies.

## Lack of Scientific Consensus

In the case of the Montreal Protocol, the costs of taking action were relatively low, and the certainty of benefit from those actions was high. In the case of climate change policy, not only are the costs of honoring a Kyoto-like pledge potentially high, but also the benefit in terms of slower human-induced climate change is substantially less certain. A strong scientific consensus does exist regarding a recent increase in atmospheric concentrations of greenhouse gasses, and a consensus also exists that the earth has recently been getting warmer, yet a consensus does not yet exist on an exact quantified connection between these two measurable phenomena.

Atmospheric concentrations of greenhouse gasses can be measured with some confidence, as can changes in the earth's average temperature, yet the extent to which higher greenhouse gas concentrations have caused the recent warming trend has remained elusive to science. This is a relationship that cannot be measured directly; it can only be "modeled" using elaborate computerized calculations that rest partly on a host of sensitive climate system assumptions—regarding such things as the Earth's rotation, surface friction at sea level, the movement of carbon between the atmosphere and the ocean, patterns of rainfall and cloud formation (since naturally occurring water vapor is a greenhouse gas), and solar radiation cycles. Until recently, the modeling techniques used to generate estimates of greenhouse gas–induced temperature rise were not even capable of depicting the present global climate accurately without a great deal of fudging. Moreover, as these techniques have gradually improved, some of the projections of future warming and sea level rise have at times grown more modest rather than more severe.[8]

---

[7]Christina Duff, "Accord May Cool U.S. Economy, Experts Warn," *Wall Street Journal*, December 11, 1997, p. A2.

[8]In its December 1995 Second Assessment Report, the Intergovernmental Panel on Climate Change (IPCC) actually scaled back its projections of global warming significantly, compared with an earlier 1990 report. Instead of a 3.5–8 degree Celsius warming by 2050, the new report estimated only a 1.8–6.3 degree warming by 2100. This report included a strong statement that "the balance of evidence suggests that there is a discernible human influence on the climate," but the IPCC was subsequently criticized by a former president of the National Academy of Sciences for strengthening this statement without formal approval from the panel's scientific board of advisers. One scientist-approved statement deleted from the final report said, "None of the studies cited above has shown clear evidence that we can attribute the observed changes to the specific cause of increased greenhouse gasses." For a critical discussion of these alterations, see Christopher Douglass and Murray Weidenbaum, "The Quiet Reversal of U.S. Global Climate Change Policy," *Contemporary Issues Series* 83 (St. Louis: Center for the Study of American Business, Washington University, 1996), p. 6.

## Uncertainty of International Cooperation

A final contrast between the Montreal Protocol case and climate change lies in the problematic area of international cooperation. In the case of stratospheric ozone protection, it was sufficient to secure cooperation from just a handful of major industrial country CFC producers. In the case of greenhouse gas emissions, securing cooperation from developing countries is far more important and has emerged as far more difficult.

A number of European countries, led by Germany and Britain, have been willing to cooperate in restricting greenhouse gas emissions. Germany can afford to make stringent reductions from a 1990 baseline because of a massive shutdown of dirty industries in the eastern half of the country undertaken for other reasons, and Britain because of a switch already made since 1990 from burning dirty coal to cleaner North Sea natural gas. Yet among most developing countries other than the small island states threatened by sea level rise, willingness to sacrifice to reduce greenhouse gas emissions is close to nonexistent.

Greenhouse gas emissions in the developing countries are growing rapidly enough to constitute a significant problem, but they will not surpass industrial country emissions overall for another twenty-five or thirty years, so at least until then most developing-country leaders will have little reason to feel responsible for the problem. Their attitude was summed up at the Kyoto meetings by Mark Mwandosya of Tanzania, chair of the developing country caucus: "Very many of us are struggling to attain a decent standard of living for our peoples, and yet we are constantly told that we must share in the effort to reduce emissions so that industrial countries can continue to enjoy the benefits of their wasteful life style."[9] On a per capita basis, human activity in the United States today still puts into the atmosphere roughly ten times as much carbon dioxide as human activity in China. Persuading the governments of China, Brazil, India, or Mexico to compromise their hopes for rapid industrial development in order to help the already wealthy countries reduce global greenhouse gas emissions is a problem in international cooperation that has yet to be solved.

Negotiating a cap on developing country emissions is so unlikely that other policy options should be considered, so as to soften the difficult trade-off between reduced fossil fuel use and income growth in today's poor countries. Investments are needed badly in new energy technologies for the developing world that will be less fossil fuel dependent, and one of the best ways to trigger such investments could be through a tax that would increase fuel prices. Rather than waiting to act on climate change until an enforceable international agreement has been negotiated, the United States should begin immediately creating market incentives for technology innovation by taxing fossil fuel use, or at least by not blocking a market increase in fuel prices. A gradually increasing domestic tax on fossil fuel use, with some compensations provided to the industries or workers most burdened by such a tax, would be the most convincing form of international climate change policy leadership that the

---

[9]William K. Stevens, "Greenhouse Gas Issue: Haggling Over Fairness," *New York Times*, November 30, 1997, p. 6.

United States could possibly provide. Particularly in the area of environmental policy, it is often the case that effective leadership abroad must begin at home.[10] Among the industrial powers, the United States should feel a special international obligation to act first in this area since it releases twice as much carbon dioxide per capita as Germany, Japan, or Russia, and almost three times as much as Italy.

A domestic tax on fossil fuels would almost certainly be rejected by congress if presented as part of a larger tax increase plan as it was in 1993. Yet in the current environment of an overall budget surplus in the United States, a new tax on fossil fuels could more easily be paired with highly attractive personal income and capital gains tax cuts. In today's altered budget environment, it would also be easier to offer generous cash compensation to those—such as coal miners—most adversely affected by a fossil fuels tax. A unilateral, revenue-neutral tax reform of this kind would be the most efficient way to generate through energy price incentives in the marketplace the investments needed to innovate more efficient fossil fuel burning technologies, plus renewable forms of energy such as wind, geothermal, and solar, plus safer forms of nuclear power. The long-term international payoff from these investments would be a pipeline of new energy technologies ready for sale or transfer to countries such as China, India, or Mexico. Perhaps only by taking a timely unilateral domestic-tax-policy action of this kind at home can the United States make it possible for poorer nations abroad to reach their industrial development goals within acceptable limits of greenhouse gas emissions. It was a loss for U.S. environmental leadership abroad that the Bush Administration, while abandoning the flawed Kyoto approach in 2001, and while talking about incentives-based approaches, offered a tax cut plan that had no positive climate change incentive component.

More effective international agreements on climate change policy might be the final payoff from a unilateral fossil fuel tax at home. If the United States went first, other states might agree to follow by phasing in comparable domestic taxes of their own, revenue-neutral or otherwise, to build stronger market price incentives for a gradual shift away from fossil fuel dependence. An agreement with other governments to tax fossil fuel use at home (and to keep the revenue at home) would in any case be easier to negotiate and enforce than the binding emissions limits pushed by U.S. negotiators at Kyoto.[11] The unrealistic binding emissions approach, as Thomas Schelling has noted, assumes that all the world's governments will "calmly sit down and divide up rights in perpetuity worth more than a trillion dollars."[12] By embracing this unlikely approach, rather than a fossil fuel tax treaty approach, the Clinton administration made an already difficult task of global cooperation on climate change that much more difficult. And by proposing a massive tax cut without any fossil fuel tax increase, the Bush Administration missed a chance to repair the damage.

[10]Robert Paarlberg, *Leadership Abroad Begins at Home: U.S. Foreign Economic Policy After the Cold War* (Washington, DC: Brookings, 1995).

[11]For a brief discussion of this option, see Richard N. Cooper, "Toward a Real Global Warming Treaty," *Foreign Affairs* (November–December 1997): 8–14.

[12]Thomas C. Schelling, "The Cost of Combating Global Warming," *Foreign Affairs* (November–December 1997): 8–14.

**Table 1.** Points of Resistance to U.S. International Environmental Policy Leadership: Ozone Protection and Climate Change

| | Domestic Industry Opposition | Organized Labor Opposition | Large Burden on National Economy | Lack of Scientific Consensus | Uncertain International Cooperation |
|---|---|---|---|---|---|
| Ozone Protection Policy | No | No | No | No | No |
| Climate Change Policy | Yes | Yes | Yes | Yes | Yes |

Nonetheless, as summarized in Table 1, the climate change leadership challenge was, in every respect, more difficult for the United States than the earlier ozone protection challenge.

# BIODIVERSITY PROTECTION POLICY: FAILING TO RATIFY THE CBD

To test the power of this analytic approach, consider now the policy area of international biodiversity protection. Since most terrestrial ecosystems are not international, biodiversity protection is first of all a local or national-level issue, yet there are also significant international dimensions to the problem. These motivated in 1992 the negotiation of a new international agreement, the Convention on Biological Diversity (CBD), concluded at the Earth Summit in Rio de Janeiro. U.S. leadership in the negotiation and support of this convention has been conspicuously and consistently weak. The elder President George Bush refused to sign the CBD in Rio in 1992; and although President Clinton did sign the CBD in June 1993, when he submitted it to the Senate for approval in November 1993, the Senate refused to ratify. As of 2000, no fewer than 175 other nations had ratified and had become Parties to the CBD, but the United States still had not. Can we explain this U.S. reticence by employing the same five key variables employed earlier for ozone protection and climate change policy?

The refusal of the U.S. Senate to ratify the CBD in 1993–94 cannot so clearly be blamed on industry or labor opposition, or on an inadequate scientific consensus regarding the importance of biodiversity protection, or on any lack of certainty regarding international cooperation. The particularities of this case cloud the simple analysis presented so far.

By the time Clinton submitted the CBD to the Senate in November 1993, the Convention was officially supported by a broad coalition of private companies, environmental and developmental NGOs, scientific groups, and academic institutions. U.S. biotechnology and pharmaceutical companies had been opposed to the CBD when it was first presented in Rio in 1992, and this opposition had contributed to President Bush's refusal to sign. Yet by the time President Clinton submitted the

CBD to the Senate in 1993, the companies had received sufficient assurances from the U.S. government (in the form of unilateral U.S. "interpretations" to the Convention) to endorse ratification. This ultimate willingness of the U.S. private sector to support international cooperation in the area of biodiversity was not surprising, since biotechnology and pharmaceutical companies in the United States are global industry leaders and know that they have large stakes in the shaping of global trade, investment, and bioprospecting policies in this area.[13] Such companies tend to be far more internationalist in outlook than the typical U.S senator. Organized labor likewise had no objections to CBD ratification in view of the tiny number of union jobs involved one way or another. A national lobby group representing large commercial farmers, the American Farm Bureau Federation, was nominally opposed to CBD ratification in 1993–94, despite the Clinton administration's new "interpretations," but the Farm Bureau never made this issue a central part of its lobbying efforts in Washington.

Nor was lack of scientific consensus a central problem in the CBD ratification case. The senators who blocked CBD approval did not base their dissent on lack of a scientific consensus regarding rates of species loss or doubts regarding the potential value of genetic resource protection. It would have been difficult for them to raise such doubts, because by 1993, the CBD was strongly endorsed by most scientific groups and academic institutions.[14] Scientists may disagree on the magnitude of the biodiversity protection problem, but they do not disagree about its human causes or its potential irreversibility. Nor was lack of international support an issue, since more than 150 other governments abroad had already signed and ratified the CBD by 1993, the year the Senate first balked.

The Senate Foreign Relations Committee actually endorsed the CBD with a bipartisan 16–3 vote soon after Clinton submitted the measure in 1993, but a floor vote was postponed later that year, and then again in 1994, when Majority Leader Senator George Mitchell (D-Maine) concluded that the two-thirds vote needed for treaty ratification was not yet available. A group of 35 senators (all Republicans, and one more than needed to block ratification) had made it clear by late 1993 that they opposed the CBD.

These senators claimed various reasons for their opposition. Some said the text of the Convention was too binding on congressional prerogatives; for example it might constrain future options to amend the U.S. Endangered Species Act. Others said the text was too vague and ambiguous, a bit like the original 1973 Convention on International Trade in Endangered Species (CITES). The CBD was initially just a framework convention that encouraged governments to take certain actions without requiring them to achieve particular goals or funding levels. Other senators

---

[13]When President Bush had refused to sign the CBD, some foreign governments (such as Venezuela) had pulled back from cooperative arrangements with U.S. scientific institutions interested in gathering biological materials abroad. Kal Raustiala and David G. Victor, "The Future of the Convention on Biological Diversity," *Environment* 4 (May 1996): 42.

[14]"Congress Fails to Ratify Treaty to Protect the World's Biological Diversity," *International Environment Reporter,* October 19, 1994, p. 845.

stated that the CBD was not needed because CITES was doing fine. Some based their opposition on worries about possible constraints on U.S. business and agriculture, dismissing Clinton's unilateral "interpretations" as not binding on the Convention's other signatories. Some were opposed on principle to any treaty that would strengthen the role of any multilateral decision making forum, since this was purportedly a threat to U.S. sovereignty. Some were even opposed because of popular anxieties that had been generated through an underground campaign against the CBD that was launched by fringe groups (including supporters of gadfly Lyndon LaRouche) depicting the Convention as inspired by paganism and nature worship, and as possibly the first step toward an authoritarian world government.[15]

Some senators also feared the financial obligations that might be incurred if the CBD were approved, since the CBD's Article 20 stated that the developed country parties "shall provide new and additional financial resources to enable developing country Parties to meet the agreed full incremental costs to them of implementing measures which fulfill the obligations of this Convention." What exactly would constitute an incremental cost was not defined in the CBD text. Article 21 seemed to leave the construction of a financial mechanism and specific financial obligations to the Conference of Parties (COP), but at the insistence of the developed countries, the Global Environment Facility (GEF), a mechanism more securely controlled by the donors, was designated as an interim venue for handling project funding. Still, in 1993, at a time of tight U.S. federal budget constraints and collapsing congressional interest in foreign aid programs, the uncertain financial arrangements of the CBD were a major concern. Pure partisanship was also clearly at work in 1993–94, since this was a period when the Republican minority in the House and Senate was trying to block Clinton's legislative initiatives across the board (not a single House Republican had voted for the president's 1993 budget plan). In this partisan atmosphere, it proved relatively easy for Senate Minority Leader Bob Dole (R-Kansas) to find the minimum of thirty-four Republican senators needed to block the CBD. Once these Republicans in the Senate gained a controlling majority following the 1994 midterm election, President Clinton himself put the issue of CBD ratification indefinitely on the shelf.

In this case of biodiversity protection policy, the formula previously developed for predicting when the United States will provide international leadership on global environmental policy issues therefore breaks down. The factors seemingly most important in the CBD case are partisanship, congressional resistance to executive initiative, and the two-thirds Senate treaty ratification rule. This is analytically inconvenient, because these are factors that did not seem to be at work in the earlier climate change and ozone protection cases.

The partisanship explanation does not work well for either climate change or ozone despite a clear wariness by most Republicans toward environmental policy

---

[15]Tim Wirth, "Address to the National Conference of the Ecological Society of America," Salt Lake City, Utah, August 1, 1995.

leadership compared with most Democrats.[16] Recall that it was the administration of Republican President Ronald Reagan that engineered the 1987 Montreal Protocol success, and Democrats as well as Republicans in congress blocked Clinton's pre-Kyoto climate change policy approach (the Senate resolution warning against exclusion of developing countries passed 95–0). Some of the fiercest policy debates prior to Kyoto actually took place entirely among Democrats, both in Congress and within the president's own administration. Top Clinton appointees responsible for the performance of the U.S. economy, such as Treasury Secretary Robert Rubin and Undersecretary Lawrence Summers, argued tirelessly from the inside against tight binding limits on greenhouse gas emissions, and the climate change issue divided Vice President Gore as much from some fellow Democrats (such as House Minority Leader Richard Gephardt) as from Republicans.

Congressional resistance to executive initiative was also a weak factor in both ozone and climate change. In the case of ozone protection, it was congress that was pushing the executive, not the other way around. Nor is the two-thirds ratification requirement in the Senate an insurmountable obstacle. In March 1988, only a few months after completion of the international negotiations on the Montreal Protocol, the Senate ratified the agreement by a vote of 83–0.

A full explanation for the failure of the U.S. Senate to ratify the CBD certainly includes partisanship and the constitutional two-thirds vote requirement, but it must also include less tangible factors. One reason it was more difficult to rally domestic political support in the United States Senate for CBD ratification in 1993–94 was the issue at stake. The goal of protecting *nonhuman* species was laudable on environmental terms, but most Americans cared far more about human health or welfare, the issue at stake in both Montreal and Kyoto. The nonhuman species that Americans care most about were, in any case, already protected by other measures, including a strong domestic endangered species act and CITES. Most of the additional species that the CBD might protect would be plants or insects living in settings far removed from the shores of the United States and unfamiliar to most U.S. voters.

The gains to human health and survival that might come from preserving biodiversity abroad will be undeniable in the long run, but they are not as compelling in the short run as, for example, preserving stratospheric ozone. For every 1 percent loss of ozone, UV radiation at the Earth's surface increases by about 2 percent, and the incidence of skin cancers increases by more than 2 percent. The argument for biodiversity protection in tropical countries is a noble one, in part because it goes beyond the short-term welfare of our own species, but this nobility did not help the issue gain a critical mass of domestic political support in the United States.

---

[16]In the 104th congress (1995–96) Republican committee chairs in the House received on average only a 12.4 rating (on a scale from 0–100) from the League of Conservation Voters. By contrast, Democratic committee chairs in the previous 103rd congress (1993–94) had received a 73.3 rating from the LCV. These LCV ratings are based on percentage of key votes considered "pro-environmental action" rather than "anti-environmental action" and are compiled here from the LCV's published National Environmental Scorecard.

# THE PRICE OF DISENGAGEMENT: NATIONAL INTERESTS COMPROMISED IN THE 2000 BIOSAFETY PROTOCOL

When the U.S. Senate failed to ratify the CBD in 1993–94, the other 175 nations that did ratify went ahead on their own to elaborate various specific international obligations under the new Convention, including obligations in the area of international trade in genetically modified organisms (or "living modified organisms," to use the terminology favored by the Convention). Article 19.3 of the original CBD had called on the Parties to consider the need for an international protocol governing threats to biodiversity from living organisims modified through new techniques of genetic engineering; and after lengthy negotiations between 1994 and 2000, the COP did produce such a Biosafety Protocol (BP), designed to regulate transboundary movements of LMOs. The BP that emerged in 2000 was not in the economic interest of the United States. Arguably, it was not even in any clear global environmental interest.

Regulating international trade in LMOs did not seem to be an urgent issue for the United States in 1994 when the BP negotiations began, because at that time, no plants or animals altered through direct transfers of DNA (rather than through conventional breeding or hybridization) had yet been released for widespread commercial use. Beginning in 1995, however, a number of genetically modified (GM) crop varieties were released for commercial use in the United States and elsewhere, and quickly became popular with U.S. farmers. By 1999, roughly half of the U.S. soybean crop was planted with GM seeds, and one third of the U.S. corn crop was GM. As U.S. agriculture moved toward use of GM seeds, the possibility that a new BP might place limits on transboundary movements of GM plants, seeds, or commodities became commercially worrying, since U.S. farmers export more than 25 percent of the corn, soybean, and cotton they produce, and more than 50 percent of their wheat and rice.

The United States had more reason to worry when it learned that those inside the international Conference of Parties (COP) drafting the new BP had decided to use, as their model for the protocol, the Basel Convention on the Control of Transboundary Movements of Hazardous Wastes, implying that U.S. GM crops entering world commerce might soon come to be treated as comparable to toxic industrial wastes.[17] The Basel Convention had obliged exporting countries to secure the "prior informed consent" of importers before shipping hazardous wastes abroad, and some developing country leaders within the COP now wanted the new BP to place comparable restrictions on LMOs. They sought export restrictions not just on GM seeds and plants intended for release into the environment, but also on normal commodity shipments, such as GM corn or soybeans designed for processing or consumption rather than environmental release. The leading spokesman for the so-called "Like

---

[17]Aarti Gupta, "Creating a Global Biosafety Regime," *International Journal of Biotechnology,* Vol 2, Nos. 1/2/3 (2000): 205–230.

Minded Group" of developing countries within the COP, Behren Gebre Egzhiaber Tewolde of Ethiopia, called for strict regulations on transboundary movements of all LMOs, presumably to protect the developing world from "biological pollution."

The COP negotiators had no scientific evidence that the GM crops approved for use so far in countries such as the United States represented a new threat to biodiversity in the developing world. Most of these GM crops were arguably safer for the environment, since they were designed to be grown with fewer insecticide or herbicide sprays than conventional crops required. Also, if these new crops could boost agricultural productivity on lands already cleared in the developing world, they might help reduce the necessity for farmers to cut down more forest and to plow up new lands. In this sense, they were a means to protect wildlife habitat and biodiversity. Yet a number of leading developing country negotiators were motivated by a general mistrust of the private multinational corporations (such as the U.S.-based Monsanto Company) that were selling the new GM seeds, and this mistrust was reinforced by the advice they received from European-based environmental NGOs such as Greenpeace, which had launched a global campaign against GM crops and against Monsanto in particular. The nations of the European Union went along with this opposition to GM crops inside the COP, since Monsanto was a United States company and since European farmers were not yet producing GM crops and thus had little to lose from a restrictive protocol.

Since the United States was not a Party to the Convention, it had a difficult time countering these tendencies within the COP. Officials from the Department of State were permitted to participate in meetings of the COP only as observers, and it was from this disadvantaged posture that the United States did its best to organize within the COP its own alliance of states called the Miami Group, to block negotiation of an excessively restrictive BP. Eventually five other countries were recruited to this cause, all agricultural exporting countries with interest in GM crops: Argentina, Canada, Australia, Chile, and Uruguay. Argentina and Canada in particular were highly motivated to join in blocking a restrictive BP, since their farmers also had gone ahead quickly after 1995 with the planting of GM seeds.

Opposition from the U.S.-led Miami Group did slow down the pace of the BP negotiations. The negotiation was supposed to conclude at a conference in Cartagena, Colombia, in February 1999, but this meeting ended without agreement, in part because the U.S.-led Miami Group firmly rejected a portion of the draft BP that placed an onerous prior informed consent restriction on exported GM commodities intended for processing or consumption.[18] The Miami Group insisted that such GM commodities did not present even a hypothetical threat to biodiversity, since they would not be released as LMOs into the environment. For such GM commodities, the Miami Group called for merely an information-sharing agreement between exporters and importers rather than a transaction-based prior notification and consent agreement.[19]

---

[18]In the terminology of the BP, these were known as living modified organisms intended for food, feed, and processing, or LMO-FFP.

[19]Gupta, "Creating a Global Biosafety Regime."

This U.S.-led blocking strategy met its limits when the BP negotiations resumed one year later in Montreal, in January 2000. The Like Minded Group was willing to make some compromise at this meeting and gave up on its effort to place a prior informed consent obligation on exporters of GM commodities not intended for environmental release.[20] In return, the United States and its Miami Group had to make compromises as well. The United States agreed to a labeling requirement for commodity shipments that might contain GM crops, and yielded to a provision in the Protocol permitting importers to keep GM commodities out of their market on a "precautionary" basis even where the scientific evidence of an actual risk to biosafety remains uncertain.[21]

This final concession may eventually come back to haunt United States commodity exporters because it gives importers greater leeway to discriminate against U.S. crops than previously permitted under the rules of the World Trade Organization (WTO). Within the WTO, it is permissible under the sanitary and phytosanitary (SPS) agreement to impose import restrictions on GM crops and materials, or on other imports, but only if those restrictions are based on a scientific assessment of the risks.[22] Under conditions of scientific uncertainty, the SPS agreement does allow governments to restrict imports, but only on a *provisional* basis while they seek additional information about the risks that are posed. The WTO does not permit open-ended import restrictions on a precautionary basis, without any time limit and with no effort to seek additional information to resolve the uncertainty.

By allowing "precautionary principle" language into the BP, the United States and its Miami Group allies thus allowed a fundamental WTO provision for nondiscrimination in international commodity trade to be undercut. In Montreal, the United States fought to insert language into the operational part of the BP that would have recognized the privileged position of established WTO and SPS agreement rules on commodity trade, but it was blocked from doing so by the Like Minded Group and the EU.[23]

It might be reasonable to weaken the norm of nondiscriminatory trade if a genuine increase in biodiversity protection in poor countries would be the guaranteed

[20]Rather than insisting on a transaction-based prior notification and agreement procedure, the Like Minded Group and the EU accepted a procedure under which producer countries would promptly notify a Biosafety Clearing House of all domestic approvals of new LMOs to be planted by farmers. Potential importing countries would then have enough timely information to consider whether they wanted to continue importing the commodity in question from that producer country.

[21]In its preamble, the BP explicitly endorses this "precautionary approach," and the body of the agreement states in two places (Articles 10 and 11) that "lack of scientific certainty due to insufficient relevant scientific information and knowledge" should not prevent states from taking precautionary import actions. See Conference of Parties to the Convention on Biological Diversity (CBD), "Draft Cartagena Protocol on Biosafety," final draft text submitted by the Legal Drafting Group, Montreal, January 24–28, 2000.

[22]Nations can use import policy to pursue any level of health or environmental protection they wish, but these import policies must be appropriate to that standard, they must be based on sound science, and they must be consistent with internal policies so as not to discriminate against trade. Donna Roberts, "Preliminary Assessment of the Effects of the WTO Agreement on Sanitary and Phytosanitary Trade Regulations," *Journal of International Economic Law* (1998): 377–405.

[23]*Inside U.S. Trade,* Vol. 18, No. 5 (February 4, 2000): 25.

result, yet there is not any scientific evidence that GM commodities (especially when intended for processing or consumption) present a biohazard greater than non-GM commodities. The hypothetical biohazards involved might include harmful competition with or direct damage to desirable species, unwanted flow of trans-genes into close relative species, or increased resistance within pest populations; yet these same hazards can be encountered with non-GM crop varieties or with conventional pest control technologies (like insecticide sprays), and the biosafety policy procedures currently employed in the countries that have originated GM crops (especially the United States) have already screened for such risks.[24]

Serious threats to biosafety and biodiversity exist in the developing world, but they have little or nothing to do with GM crops. The greatest biohazards tend to come not from crops at all but from exotic wild species that have been introduced either intentionally or accidentally into rural ecosystems from distant regions. By some estimates, such wild exotic species movements, which have nothing to do with LMOs, currently generate tens of billions of dollars in losses to agriculture annually in the developing world.[25] The new BP will do nothing to counter such clear and present biosafety threats to poor countries, because it was written to counter a mostly imagined danger from GM crops.

The United States has little room to complain about these disappointing features of the BP, however, because it gave away its own option for shaping the negotiations when it failed to ratify the CBD and hence disqualified itself from becoming a formal member of the COP. By isolating itself from a CBD negotiation process to which 175 other nations were formal Parties, the United States lost an opportunity to shape the result more to the advantage of the global environment, and more to its own advantage as well.

## CONCLUSION

We have seen from this review that without wise U.S. leadership, the making of sound international environmental policy becomes far more difficult. In this sense, the United States is indeed an "essential" country in global environmental affairs. But we have also seen how difficult it is for the United States government to provide wise leadership. In the exceptional case of stratospheric ozone protection, after a period of hesitation prior to 1986, the United States did take a lead and helped to produce a sound international agreement in Montreal. But this was an exceptional

---

[24]In the United States, most new varieties of crops (GM and non-GM) are subjected to 50 or more site years of testing (number of sites times number of years) for various performance and biosafety characteristics before being selected for seed production and farm use. See "Seeds of Opportunity: An Assessment of the Benefits, Safety, and Oversight of Plant Genomics and Agricultural Biotechnology," Report prepared by Chairman Nick Smith, Subcommittee on Basic Research, Committee on Science, U.S. Congress, 106th Congress, Second Session, April 13, 2000. See also "Genetically Modified Crops: The Ethical and Social Issues," Nuffield Council on Bioethics, London, May 1999.

[25]Examples include losses from virus-carrying whiteflies in South and Central America, and from the exotic cattail weeds now strangling rice in the wetlands of northern Nigeria.

case; it was the one case most likely to produce a U.S. leadership success because U.S. industry and union opposition was nil, the economic costs were low, the scientific consensus was high, and the barriers to international cooperation were not insurmountable. In the far more difficult area of climate change policy where both industry and labor opposition are high, where economic costs are high, where scientific consensus is low, and where international cooperation is difficult to arrange, the occasional efforts of the United States to lead have thus far been embarrassingly ineffective.

Yet we have also seen how risky it can be for the United States to abdicate leadership entirely. In the area of biological diversity protection, the U.S. Senate's failure to ratify the CBD in 1993–94 ensured that the opinions of the United States would be marginalized in subsequent negotiations toward a Biosafety Protocol governing transboundary movements of LMOs. Consequently, a draft BP emerged from these negotiations that was threatening to U.S. trade interests while doing little to address some clear and present biohazards in developing countries. U.S. efforts to modify this draft BP at the last minute were only partly successful.

We thus conclude that in environmental policy, the United States should take little comfort from knowing that it is an "essential" country. Holding this status is anything but a guarantee of policy success. The United States can find it hard to bring domestic groups into line on global environmental policy issues, and being the essential nation abroad does not always help to solve this political problem at home. Nor does being essential mean the same thing as being unavoidable. We learn from the biodiversity case that other countries do not always have to come to the United States to secure prior approval for their own designs. If U.S. disengagement gives them the opportunity to go ahead on their own, they may well do so, perhaps compromising important U.S. interests in the process.

# 16

# The United States and International Organizations

## STANLEY HOFFMANN
### Harvard University

All states, in the pursuit of their interests, either try to enlist the support of the international organizations of which they are members or attempt to prevent these organizations from serving as obstacles on the road to their goals. Membership in several organizations with overlapping scope or purposes allows them to maneuver so as to take advantage of those agencies that are likely to be most favorable to them. There is therefore nothing new or shocking in finding that the United States is often very adept at playing this game—which might be called the search for the most advantageous, or least disadvantageous, use of multilateralism. In this chapter, the brand of multilateralism that I will examine is that which international and regional institutions embody; the range of these institutions goes from organizations with formal charters, complex rules, and numerous components, to informal bodies with limited powers, scope, or membership, such as the G8. Multilateralism is also a defining characteristic of international law, that is, of treaties and customs that assign rights and obligations to states, often depend on international or regional agencies for their enforcement, but do not necessarily set up collective agencies for their purposes. A study of the United States versus both international law and international organizations is beyond the scope of this chapter.

States, in theory, always have a choice between resorting to multilateral action in defense or pursuit of their interests, and unilateral action, when it promises to

Stanley Hoffmann is the Paul and Catherine Buttenwieser University Professor at Harvard University, where he has taught since 1955. He was the Chairman of the Center for European Studies at Harvard from its inception in 1969 until 1995. The author of numerous books on French and international affairs, he is also an essayist for the *New York Review of Books* and the Western Europe review editor for *Foreign Affairs*.

be more effective and less cumbersome. In reality, this freedom of choice is often limited. All states are legally obligated to act multilaterally when international law or the charter of an international organization prescribes such a course, and many states act accordingly, either out of a concern for world order, or a sense of ethical duty, or a worry about their reputation, or a calculation of costs. But unilateral action remains the corollary of sovereignty, and in many areas of foreign policy, there are no obligations to act in concert with others. Even among the members of the European Union, there exists no legal restriction on their right to recognize states and governments as they see fit. Even when obligations exist (such as the ban on the use of force by article 2, paragraph 4 of the UN Charter), states, large and small, sometimes violate them blatantly, as Iraq did when it invaded Kuwait.

For a hegemonic power such as the United States, there is a perpetual tug of war between the desire to push its vision of world order through the intricate mechanisms of regional and international organizations, so as to have it shared by others and to be seen, and accepted, as the leader of the flock, and the itch to act unilaterally whenever these mechanisms are deemed to be hindrances or inefficient. Much depends on the outcome of this calculation, because American statesmen have not only to try to figure out, case by case, whether a resort to multilateral action would enhance or constrain, serve or reduce America's power, but also to deal with the fact that most international and many regional bodies need American leadership or cooperation in order to succeed. They must therefore include in their calculation the short- and long-term effects of weakening, through unilateral action, agencies that may well be, on the whole, important levers for American influence. This is a special concern that few other countries share (although Britain and France know the same tug-of-war with respect to the European Union).

## THE USES OF MULTILATERALISM

In the Clinton years, the United States has behaved in a multiplicity of ways toward the UN system and regional organizations. There has been a fundamental inconsistency, between the faith in multilateralism proclaimed by the members of the president's foreign policy team in the early months of the new administration, and a course that turned out to be anything but straight. In the beginning, the word from Washington (particularly from Anthony Lake) was about the need for the United States, despite its status as the only superpower, to cooperate with the rest of world society in order to resolve common problems. As Ivo Daalder has shown,[1] the Clinton administration began with a review of U.S. peacekeeping policy inspired by Lake's "pragmatic neo-Wilsoniamism" and Mrs. Albright's "assertive multilateralism"—assertive, because of the evident need for U.S. leadership both to steer the UN toward common goals and to prevent multilateralism from harming U.S. interests:

---

[1]"Knowing when to Say No: The Development of US Policy for Peace-keeping," in William J. Durch (ed.), *UN Peacekeeping, American Policy, and the Uncivil Wars of the 1990s* (1996).

hence, a promise to strengthen the UN capacity to manage peace operations. But the policy review, begun in early 1993, resulted in a directive—PDD 25—in May 1994 only, and although it reaffirmed American support for UN operations, it qualified this support heavily. There would have to be "realistic criteria" for ending the operation, it would be undertaken only if inaction's consequences were clearly unacceptable, and if the risks to U.S. troops were acceptable, U.S. forces would remain under U.S. command, and no support was given to the idea of a standing UN army or of earmarking U.S. forces for UN operations. Indeed, where earlier versions had mentioned the need for "rapid expansion" of UN peacekeeping, it was now presented as a limited task, "more selective and more effective" than before. What had happened between February 1993 and May 1994 was the fiasco in Somalia.

This retreat does not mean that "assertive multilateralism" withered away. In the case of Bosnia (1992–95), American diplomacy was anything but assertive at first, because of a protracted disagreement with the European effort at reaching a peaceful settlement, which reflected Britain's and France's reluctance to switch from peacekeeping (although there was no peace to keep) to peace-making (which would have required the use of force). But by 1995, Washington did become assertive—using the so-called Contact Group rather than the Security Council, yet succeeding thereby in putting some force behind the previously empty warnings that the Security Council had addressed to Milosevic. In East Timor in 1999, the United States provided the diplomatic pressure that was necessary to get Indonesia to consent to the peacekeeping force led by Australia. Clinton's leadership of the OAS and of the Security Council resulted, again after many delays, in the return of President Aristide in Haiti, with an international as well as a regional mandate for the restoration of democracy.[2] Nowhere was assertive multilateralism more successfully displayed than in the establishment of the World Trade Organization.[3] In these cases, U.S. leadership served as the catalyst of a consensus that was more than a simple recognition by others of America's superior might.

However, next to this practice of "superpower multilateralism," we find two series of cases that can hardly be described as examples of a multilateralist disposition. First, there are instances of what one might call the unilateralism of dictation: these are exercises of American power *in* international bodies, but they go beyond leadership. What distinguishes them from the cases listed before is not the pursuit of American objectives—this was evidently also the case in Bosnia in 1995, or with respect to free trade—but the way in which the United States used its dominant position in order to obtain outcomes about which it would be hard to prove that a general consensus existed. Preponderance facilitates leadership but does not necessarily amount to dictation. Dictation there was, in the IMF. As Joseph Stiglitz elsewhere[4] and Benjamin Cohen in this volume have shown, it was the United States that pushed the IMF into making imprudent loans and into pressing for financial

[2]See the chapter by Robert Pastor in this volume.

[3]See the chapter by Benjamin Cohen in this volume.

[4]See "What I Saw at the Devaluation," *New Republic* (April 17–24, 2000): 56–61.

liberalization resulting in the Asian crisis of 1997–98. And when that crisis hit a number of countries' currencies and financial institutions, it was the United States that insisted on the imposition by the IMF of familiar, intrusive, and highly unpopular austerity measures.

In several African conflicts, the United States decisively limited the effectiveness of Security Council attempts to cope with disintegrating countries. It was U.S. opposition to a timely intervention in Rwanda—an opposition based on the constricted principles of PDD 25—that led to the Security Council's decision to withdraw its peacekeeping mission.[5] It was U.S. reluctance to commit forces to UN-sponsored peacekeeping operations that obliged the Security Council to keep them limited, and largely ineffectual, in Sierra Leone and in the Democratic Republic of the Congo. The way in which the United States blocked the appointment as head of the IMF of the candidate of the German government, despite previous understandings, and even more the way in which Mrs. Albright demanded and obtained the nonrenewal of Boutros Boutros-Ghali's mandate as Secretary General of the UN are other, rather egregious examples of "bossism." Both Boutros-Ghali and his successor had to accept American demands for administrative reform of the UN, and so did the IMF in 1998–99.

There has been another, even more spectacular kind of unilateralism: that which, in effect, dismisses international institutions whenever this treatment seems more convenient for the United States. Here, the list is long. One might begin, if only in order to give a qualified verdict, with the U.S. decision to bypass the Security Council and to rely exclusively on NATO in order to intervene in Kosovo, in March 1999. On the one hand, action by NATO was an exercise in multilateralism, for even though U.S. predominance in NATO is a political, technological, and military reality, there was no American diktat in this instance: the NATO allies had been preparing a collective operation against Milosevic for some time, and the only unilateral American move was Richard Holbrooke's surprise agreement with the Serbian leader in October 1998—which Milosevic quickly violated.[6] Rambouillet, for all its peculiar flaws, was a collective exercise by the United States and its key allies. But on the other hand, resorting to NATO rather than to the Security Council was more than just choosing a smoother path instead of the rocky road of an agency in which the Russians and Chinese had a right of veto. The Charter of the UN gives to the Security Council only the authority to launch military operations and to empower regional bodies to do so. We all know that the Security Council would have been paralyzed, that such paralysis was unacceptable, and that it was less humiliating for the Council, for Secretary General Annan, and for the Russians and Chinese, to be pushed aside than to be deliberately ignored after a veto. Nevertheless, the precedent that has been set by not following the procedures of the Charter in a case in which there

---

[5]See the chapter by Donald Rothchild in this volume.

[6]See the forthcoming volume edited by Pierre Martin and Mark R. Brawley, *Allied Force or Forced Allies?*

existed an international alternative is dangerous insofar as it could be used in cases in which there is neither a NATO nor a regional organization capable of filling the void—and in which the United States might want to act alone without having first proved that the UN could not act.

Far more clear-cut are a whole series of unilateral American decisions with respect to the UN. There is, of course, the continuing failure to pay America's dues. There was the decision to pull out of Somalia after the casualties of October 1993. There was, once the genocide in Rwanda began, Washington's refusal to support UN and African countries' attempts at preventing it from worsening and to provide logistical aid to efforts by Rwanda's neighbors to organize an intervention. Washington, in its policies toward "rogue states," has gone pretty far in using force (against Iraq) on a slender legal basis—including just at the moment when the Security Council was examining the Butler report—and in using extraterritorial measures and secondary boycotts against states designated by the Helms-Burton and d'Amato-Kennedy bills. The use of force against the Sudan and Afghanistan, aimed at targets assumed to be terrorist bases of Ben Laden, certainly stretched the notion of self-defense.

One must also mention the refusal by the United States to join 121 other countries that, at a conference in Geneva in 1996, had agreed to ban antipersonnel land mines, and the nonratification of the comprehensive test ban treaty, rejected by the Senate.

In several other important areas, unilateralism has been particularly pugnacious. One example is the failure of the United States to sign the treaty setting up the International Criminal Court, even though it was Washington that, in 1997, had asked the General Assembly of the UN to establish such a tribunal. The final vote on its statute was 120 to 7, the United States' only allies being Iraq, Libya, Katar, Yemen, China, and Israel. Many of the concerns expressed by the United States and France in the course of the negotiations were addressed in the statute, but the United States, unlike France, remained unsatisfied: opposed to a prosecutor capable of initiating investigations and to an excessively vague reference to the "crime of aggression." Even the clear principle of "complementarity" under which the court can assume jurisdiction only if national courts fail to investigate or, if necessary, to prosecute, the fact that the prosecutor needs the approval of two panels of judges, and the accountability of the judges to the governments that accept the ICC's jurisdiction, did not appease the critics of the court (see later).

The other triumphs of unilateralism in the UN system concern the environment, and they are more fully described in Robert Paarlberg's chapter. The Kyoto agreement of 1997, concluded by the administration despite a unanimous resolution of the Senate two years earlier against any binding treaty that did not apply to the developing countries, has not been ratified. And the 1992 convention on biodiversity never received the necessary support of two-thirds of the members of the Senate. Finally, despite the creation of the WTO, which was supposed to limit America's resort to unilateral reprisals based on the section 301 of the Trade Act of 1974 and on the "super 301" provision of that of 1988, the American Trade Representative has kept the capacity to resort to such measures.

In the case of non-UN organizations, several U.S. exercises of unilateral power have been in evidence. In Latin America, we are told by Robert Pastor that "the American predisposition to addressing" the problems of illegitimate traffics "has often been unilateral and insensitive to the sovereign needs of its neighbors," and the same tendency has determined recent policy moves aimed at helping the embattled and far from democratic regime in Colombia in its fight against guerrilla groups that are suspected to rely for funds on the drug traffic. In NATO, the decision of the Clinton administration in 1996 to move from its "partnership for peace" policy, open to Eastern European countries and to states of the former USSR, to the admission of three former Soviet satellites into the Alliance was made with practically no consultation of Washington's partners, and indeed with minimal participation by the Pentagon, a divided NSC, and the State Department. This is a story in which the initial unilateralism in decision making led to dictation in enforcement.[7]

## THE CLINTON YEARS

Thus, despite the original intentions and statements of the key members of the Clinton administration, behaving as a responsible "multilateralist" power that seeks the support of international organizations has not been the norm. What are the reasons for these inconsistencies and these lapses from multilateralism? One is the difficulty that the Clinton administration has had in defining a coherent and workable strategy for the post–Cold War world (except insofar as the world economy is concerned: there, the United States has been the champion of globalization—with, however, a very mixed record on environmental issues). The administration has focused on relations with Russia and China and on a number of trouble spots of great strategic importance for the United States (North Korea, Iraq, and the Arab-Israeli conflict). But it has not provided convincing guidelines about when to intervene in domestic breakdowns, even though the disintegration of states has become a far more ominous feature of world politics than interstate conflicts. When does a murderous civil war or a murderous regime constitute a threat to America's national interest? (In the case of Bosnia, before the spring of 1995, the president oscillated from treating it as a kind of atavistic tragedy that required a quarantine to proclaiming that vital American interests were at stake). In shaping the world economy, the United States has frequently resorted to what I have called bossism—not merely using international agencies as instruments of U.S. policy but as if they were agencies of the U.S. government. In coping with a world in which Washington had to keep its eyes on former or potential superpowers, on an epidemic of internal disasters, and on traditional conflicts between neighbors, ad hocism has prevailed. For instance, not all "rogue states" have been treated in the same way (compare the policy toward Cuba or Iraq with the approach to North

---

[7]See James Goldgeier, *Not Whether But When: The US Decision to Enlarge NATO* (1999).

Korea). In the cases of internal breakdowns, the most bloody, Rwanda, has been the most blatant example of U.S. failure to act. One might argue that the common characteristic of those interventions accompanied by force that did occur is that they were triggered by a combination of massive violations of human rights and American "realistic" interests—stopping a flow of refugees from Haiti, preserving overall security in the Balkans. But in the case of the Balkans, the hesitations were as noticeable as the subsequent interventions.

The second and third reasons for America's behavior are provided by the peculiarities of the American political system. First, within the Executive, it can be said that the Pentagon, on issues that involve the use of force and the composition of forces, has behaved increasingly as a sovereign agency, animated by a deep distrust of limitations imposed by foreigners and by an equally deep dislike of casualties and high risks. In the list of unilateral acts provided before, many resulted from Pentagon vetoes. The elaboration of PDD 25 reflected not only the Somalian experience but also the "reluctant military" whose views were expressed in September 1993 by General Colin Powell: the mission of the U.S. armed forces is "to fight and win the nation's wars" (a "warrior culture" that clearly subordinates humanitarian interventions to the need for preserving the ability to fight the "big wars"—and, not so incidentally, distinguishes the U.S. Army from the armies of many of its allies, less reluctant to embrace "social work" activities, in some cases—the Scandinavians, for instance—for traditional reasons of self-image, and in other cases—Britain, France—because of the legacy of an imperial past).[8] General Powell opposed successfully the idea of a rapid reaction force that he saw as a commitment to send Americans "to an unknown war, in an unknown land, for an unknown cause, under an unknown commander, for an unknown duration."[9] The guidelines that led to the final text of PDD 25 reflected the Pentagon's requirement that interventions do not have unacceptable effects on military readiness, and its reluctance to place U.S. forces under UN operational control unreservedly. It was the Pentagon's concern for its forces in Korea that led it to oppose the ban on landmines. It also weighed heavily against the comprehensive test ban treaty and the International Criminal Court—in the latter case, the Pentagon feared that the treaty did not go far enough in protecting the military from charges that the operations they conducted violated the laws of war. For reasons that have more to do with his past than with his philosophy, Clinton has been eager not to overrule the defense establishment (compare the move toward a limited antiballistic defense system, at the expense of the ABM treaty, which the president left for his successor to decide). For very different reasons, a George W. Bush administration might be even more "Pentagonistic," as statements by him and by his adviser Condolezza Rice, and as the influence of General Powell on him suggest.

Secondly (this is the third reason), since 1994 the United States has provided the world with a stark display of the weakness of a presidential system with a sharp

---

[8]Ivo Daalder, in Durch (ed.), *UN Peace Keeping,* pp. 41–42.
[9]*Ibid.*, p. 43.

separation of powers. The old (and often much exaggerated) bipartisan tradition in foreign affairs has vanished, along with deference to the experts on foreign policy in the key committees of the House and the Senate; many of these leaders have actually disappeared from congress. Indeed, congress has, at times, been dominated by a coalition of neo-isolationists, anti-internationalists, and Clinton haters: hence, not only the failure of the administration to get Senate approval for many of its appointments but also the administration's defeat in the case of the test ban treaty, the rejection by congress of the "fast track" for trade deals, the repeated attempts by congress to dictate reforms to the UN, the difficulty that the administration has had in prolonging the presence of U.S. forces in Kosovo. The case of the International Criminal Court is particularly interesting; at this occasion, both the Pentagon's horror at the idea of American soldiers being charged with crimes by foreign states and Republican contempt for such states' hypothetical pretenses of judging American war behavior converged. The most egregious example of congressional foreign policy was Senator Helms's appearance before and speech at the Security Council of the UN—lecturing the UN about its flaws, treating it as, at best, an occasional instrument of U.S. foreign policy—and pretending to speak in the name of the American people.

# THE CAUSES OF U.S. BEHAVIOR

The deeper reasons for what might be called a drift away from Wilsonianism, or from the internationalism that was the spirit of America's foreign policy after World War Two, deserve some analysis. One factor, hard to evaluate with precision, is undoubtedly the hubris of being the only superpower, the "indispensable nation," in a world in which the main rivals are still (China) or currently (Russia) weak and in need of American goods or money. In this world, the United States alone can project technologically superior forces all over the globe. In the days of the Cold War, the existence of Soviet power, especially in Europe, obliged the United States—even before it lost its nuclear monopoly—to behave—even in its relations with dependent allies—in a way that distinguished it from the brutal methods of Soviet domination (with rather frequent glitches in Central America). The one American disaster of that period—Vietnam—fueled the Pentagon's distaste for open-ended interventions, the high costs of ground warfare, and casualties.

A second factor is a gradual disillusionment with political internationalism. In the realm of trade, a United States that had repudiated protectionism and understood that world-wide free trade was a royal road both to prosperity at home and to economic growth abroad obviously had a vital interest in institutions such as the IMF and the World Bank—which it dominates—or the WTO—which can be most helpful in dismantling barriers to U.S. goods and services. But in the strategic-diplomatic arena, a cost-benefit analysis gives less favorable results. Acting with others sometimes means being stopped by them (as when Mr. Christopher suggested to Britain and France, in 1993–94, a "lift and strike" policy in Bosnia) or pressured by them in undesired ways (as when Mr. Blair advocated forcefully a ground war in Kosovo). It is not by coincidence that the United States has kept the General Assembly, and also its European allies, at arms length, and has often used its veto in the Security Council, in order to protect Israel from the wrath of Arab and other Third World countries and to keep control of the peace process (even after it had been temporarily lost by Washington in Oslo). Being the "lone eagle" does not make one more popular, and even though American hegemony has been sufficiently "benevolent" or "benign" to prevent efforts at balancing American power from taking off, many non-American statesmen have been annoyed by America's championing of what they see as Western liberal values (remember the debate about "Asian values") or peculiarly American conceptions of democracy. The fact that most countries seek the advantages of economic globalization does not prevent them from resenting the "Americanization" of their cultures and daily lives and the way in which political globalization—the agendas of NGOs and of international institutions—also wears, more often than not, an American face. All this means that the United States, for all its indispensability, often finds arduous the marshaling of support and consensus.

One may add, to this difficulty in translating power directly into results, American disillusionment with the UN. It has, at times, been a scapegoat (as in Somalia); but often, its bureaucratic heaviness and inefficiency, as well as its inexperience in running military operations or civilian activities of "nation-building," have frustrated Americans who were raised on "can-doism," and who are impatient with delays, overlapping jurisdictions, and poor preparation. It wasn't only congress that has kept pressing for reform.

A final factor, itself resulting from what precedes, has been a backlash against internationalism and multilateralism. Within the Democratic Party, the voices for it have become less audible—in the Clinton years, Lake has dropped out, Holbrooke been more imperious and proconsular than multilateralist, and Mrs. Albright, in whom the old faith is still burning, often more shrill than adept. Al Gore's campaign has been startlingly unfocused on foreign affairs. Among Republicans, unilateralism has gained ever more ground, either in the form of "bossism"—when we have leaders who lead, others follow—and in the form of a rejection of external constraints. The latter is also characteristic of such backlashes against the traditional mainstream as the two antiglobalization movements of the right and the left, Mr. Buchanan's nativism and Mr. Nader's populism.

Indeed, there are many ways of championing a multilateralism à la carte, that is, of justifying a policy of picking and choosing from the menu offered by international organizations only those items that enhance America's power, and of rejecting as indigestible all those that might constrain it. The most candid and nationalistic is the stance of those whom the French, who have their share of them on the left and on the right, call *souverainistes*—the self-righteous protectors of national sovereignty against foreign encroachments. These are the "realists" who explain that world order is based on might, that the network of international law and organizations is a frail scaffolding that holds only as long as there is a structure of power behind it. They also argue that "under our Constitution, any Congress may, by law, amend an earlier act of Congress, including treaties, thus freeing the U.S. unilaterally of any obligation." They "proclaim unequivocally the superior status of our Constitution over the claims of international law." In their view, for instance, the prosecutor of the ICC usurps "a powerful and necessary element of executive power, the power of law enforcement"; his real "potential targets" are America's "top civilian and military leaders." International bodies, such as the ICC, are politically unaccountable and therefore dangerous.[10] The counterargument, about the United States giving up its ability to shape international institutions by withdrawing from them (as in the case of the biodiversity protocol), does not impress those "realists," who are convinced that our absence would doom such agencies.[11]

Another defense of unilateralism is more sophisticated. Whereas the previous one assumes that the only thing that matters is what is good for the United States, the rest of the world be damned, this one posits that what is good for the United States *is* good for the world. If there is such a thing as internationalist unilateralism, here it is: a kind of deformation of Wilsonianism, a curious mélange of international messianism and national self-righteousness (to which Wilson himself was often prone). It explains that the United States plays "a prophetic and reformist role," because its "sense of mission has led it to conceive and support the establishment of international institutions." And the United States also plays a "custodial role as guardian and actor of last resort" for world order.[12] The reformist role may require that the United States withdraws or withholds funds from, so to speak, incorrect institutions (the ILO, UNESCO, etc.)—often for purely unselfish reasons. The custodial role may clash with "the formally prescribed procedures of multilateral institutions," when the way these work is "unlikely to produce the decisons that are called for" (as defined, presumably, by the United States) and to reach "the ultimate goals" at stake: hence, American opposition to the ICC, "viewed as likely to obstruct the custodial role the US could expect to be called upon to perform militarily," and also to the Land Mines treaty seen by some in the Executive as depriving the United States of weapons "indispensable to the performance of certain international security functions that would remain a U.S. responsibility for several decades."

Thus, whether in realist uniform or in Wilsonian disguise, the case for unilateralism has progressed in a country where battle fatigue with external entanglements, proud awareness of America's power (hard and soft), and a desire to show the way to others, produce neither consistency nor coherence in foreign policy. Between an American government sure of America's power but unsure about the best

---

[10]These quotations come from John Bolton in Council on Foreign Relations, *Toward an International Criminal Court?* (New York, 1999), pp. 42–43.

[11]For a sharp critique of this point of view, see Peter J. Spiro, "The New Sovereigntists," *Foreign Affairs* (November–December 2000): 9–15.

[12]See W. Michael Reisman, "The United States and International Institutions," *Survival* (Winter 1999–2000): 62–80, at pp. 63, 66–71, and 75 especially.

uses of it, and international organizations that are increasingly important as sources of legitimacy and stabilizing forces, but often mismanaged and devoid of adequate means, there can be no easy fit. The public seems more "internationalist" than much of the U.S. political class or elite, but the public's willingness to incur high costs or losses is in doubt, and its interest in the world outside is limited.[13]

---

[13]This chapter owes a great deal to Justin Vaïsse's study of the United States and international law, incorporated in: Pierre Mélandoi et Justin Vaïsse, *L'Empire du Milieu* (Paris, 2001).

# Index